SOCIO-ECONOMICS: AN INTERDISCIPLINARY APPROACH

SOCIO-ECONOMICS: AN INTERDISCIPLINARY APPROACH

Ethics, Institutions, and Markets

Beat Bürgenmeier
University of Geneva

Translated by Kevin Cook

SPRINGER SCIENCE+BUSINESS MEDIA, LLC

Library of Congress Cataloging-in-Publication Data

Bürgenmeier, Beat.
[Plaidoyer puor une économie sociale. English]
Socio-economics : an interdisciplinary approach : ethics, institutions, and markets / Beat Bürgenmeier ; translated by Kevin Cook.
p. cm.
Translation of: Plaidoyer pour une économie sociale.
Includes bibliographical references and index.
ISBN 978-94-010-5317-4 ISBN 978-94-011-2966-4 (eBook)
DOI 10.1007/978-94-011-2966-4
1. Economics. I. Title. II. Title: Socioeconomics.
HB71.B8713 1992
330—dc20 91–40613
CIP

Printed on acid-free paper.

Translation and adaption of the original version published in French under the title "Playdoyer pour une économie sociale" © Economica, Paris.

CONTENTS

Foreword

This book is intended as a warning against the kind of hard-core liberalism which blames state intervention for the disappointing results achieved in matters of macroeconomic, competition and social welfare policy. In calling attention to the social dimension of economics, the book stresses the need for an ethical yardstick which can only be provided by an interdisciplinary approach to the economy.

One current school of thought claims to have bridged the gap by portraying economics as both positive and normative. However, this interpretation is inadequate.

The positive aspect of economics, reflecting an approach common in the natural sciences, is based on observable facts. It highlights causal relationships and seeks to analyse economic mechanisms on the basis of available information. This has led to an emphasis on purely deductive methods, which form the basis for many of the conclusions in mainstream economics. This current of thought is typified by the neoclassical school, which takes as its main premise the much-disputed hypothesis of economic rationality. Human behaviour is deemed to be rational when consumers maximize their satisfaction and producers their profits, subject to the constraints of income and production costs respectively. Optimal strategies for both consumers and producers can best be determined by the mechanism of market forces. This leads to the important conclusion that maximum economic welfare is the result of individual strategies, and that society does not exist as a separate entity but is merely the sum total of individuals behaving rationally. The key here is efficiency.

The normative aspect of economics involves value judgements. It is therefore based on a subjective portrayal of the facts and considers the economy as it should be, using criteria which can only be identified by the collective decision-making mechanism of political choice. Economic theory acknowledges that each economic agent is perfectly free to express value judgements, and thus there may conceivably be as many different points of view as there are agents. If one point of view is to prevail, it can only be the majority view, identified as such by a democratic process. Here the key is equity, embodied in laws and regulations which represent an institutional codification of society's moral and ethical judgements.

This rough outline of the positive and normative aspects of economics provides a conceptual link between efficiency and economics on the one hand, and equity and politics on the other. From this point of view, the market economy is indissociable from democracy — neither is conceivable without the other. Accordingly, strict application of the principles of the market economy and political democracy should eliminate the need for a separate ethical approach to economics; ethical issues can be taken into account simply by sustaining both of these collective decision-making mechanisms.

Despite this essential conclusion, which is central to the functioning of Western industrial society, recent years have seen a rapidly growing need to introduce ethical considerations into economics. This is because both the boundary between the normative and positive aspects of economics and the distinction between efficiency and equity are unclear, for the following reasons:

1. The distinction between the normative and positive aspects of economics and their linking with politics and economics respectively are, of course, gross oversimplifications. Political logic displays certain rational traits, and value judgements play an undoubted part in economic behaviour. A great deal of rhetoric — some would say ideological bias — has gone into presenting positivism as the only rational standard for human economic behaviour. Not only is the definition of economic rationality a tautology, but human behaviour and institutions quite definitely influence one another.
   The definition of economic behaviour is tautological in that a deductive approach is used to obtain results compatible with the economic rationality on which much of economic policy is based. This is not to say that the hypothesis of rational economic behaviour is wrong, or to deny that it has profoundly influenced our understanding of how society functions. However, it does mean that economic models based on this hypothesis are bound to treat social issues as mere problems of constrained optimization. Not only is this likely to

result in circular reasoning, but inherent in the market model are value judgements that are not separate from the economic sphere but specific to it. We can then no longer relegate the normative aspects of economics to the political sphere and treat economics as a scientific discipline in the pure positivist tradition. Were ethics nothing more than the expression of value judgements, there would still be a place for it in economics.

As for the influence of economic behaviour on institutions and vice versa, it must be acknowledged that institutional critics of the market model have not succeeded in diverting the mainstream of economic thought. Mainstream economics is eager to prove the existence of economic laws that are independent of place and time. In contrast, an apparent common thread in institutional criticism, and the basis for socio-political approaches to the economy, is the idea that economics is culturally determined and cannot be viewed in isolation from Western cultural history. Once again, were ethics nothing more than a cultural phenomenon, there would still be a place for it in economics.

2. The notion of the market as an efficient allocator of factors of production is tending to be extended to areas other than economics. Ceaseless intellectual effort has gone into attempts to apply economic reasoning to such fields as law, politics, sociology and medicine, on the principle that efficiency must be achieved before there can be any question of equity. Such attempts indicate a wish to see production constraints take priority over all other social, or even ethical, considerations.

Clearly, however, the market is merely one of a number of collective decision-making mechanisms. Others include the democratic process and the civil service. Comparing these mechanisms, one can observe a tendency for decisions to be reached not by market forces or by the democratic process, but by private or public bureaucracies. This shift towards a more administrative form of collective decision-making has caused a change of attitude. Not only are there new groups of voters, but society's image of the economy has changed, transferring the emphasis from efficiency to equity. The market mechanism has begun to make way for more political decision-making mechanisms in which problems of organization have supplanted problems of trade. This development is made easier by the neoclassical misapprehension of the role of the state, and by the problems of redistribution of income and wealth that are inherent in the functioning of any market economy.

Neoclassical theory sees growth as the answer to problems of equity, and suggests that optimal growth will achieved by the operation of individualism in a harshly competitive market. Politics, on the other hand, proposes to deal with problems of equity by creating conditions conducive to the development of solidarity. In a society characterized by numerous market failures and a lack of solidarity, the emergence of bureaucratic mechanisms and the need for an ethical yardstick are thus inevitable.

There is thus a place in economics for an ethical component which reflects particular value judgements or a particular culture and is backed up by the various collective decision-making mechanisms society has established. All that is necessary is to acknowledge that economic theory is essentially normative and that it is merely one part of the social whole. Should ethics then be assigned a universal value and also be approached in positivist terms? An example of such an approach is the demonstration of the universal nature of human rights. If ethics is indeed an inherent feature of human nature, then the hypothesis of rational behaviour needs to be supplemented by an extra dimension. Failing this, a positivist approach to values will exclude them from the scope of economics, relegating ethical standards to the field of theology or political philosophy. This must be avoided at all costs.

In order to ensure ethics a lasting place in economic reasoning, the hypothesis of economic rationality should not be rejected (since the strategies consumers and producers use to maximize their utility and profits respectively reflect essential motives in human behaviour), but it should be developed further. Economic agents act emotionally as well as rationally. Emotional intensity thus adds a moral dimension to economic and social actions and is at variance with scientific interpretations based on the principle of causality, which reduce emotionality to the level of what has been termed "hallucinatory reality". To quote Claude Olievenstein (1988, p. 191):

"What is unspoken, particularly with regard to morality or ethics, cannot be written off as hallucinatory — human memory is too powerful for that. We thus have the astonishing situation in which part of reality is kept, as it were, under cover. Things which exist but cannot be fitted into a logical interpretation are either censored or, at best, contemptuously relegated to the nether world of the social sciences...". Attempting to rethink contemporary economic theory along these lines doubtless involves an unprecedented intellectual challenge; yet such an approach may well be the only way to help economics out of the positivist impasse it is in.

The methodological obstacles are enormous. Economics has only managed to bypass the normative issues by adopting an abstract conceptual approach to society, based on deductive reasoning. For a complete view of social reality, economics must open itself up to other disciplines — yet such an interdisciplinary approach is inevitably more inductive.

Despite the fact that all problems are essentially interdisciplinary, knowledge has hitherto progressed through specialization. Our education system can scarcely be said to have encouraged diversity, but it is worth recalling Plato's story (Blumenberg, 1987) in which the philosopher Thales fell down a well while gazing at the heavens. A Thracian servant girl made fun of him for having his head in the clouds and failing to see things that were right under his nose (and feet). Although nowadays Thales is famous and the servant girl is not, both of them had a point. A socio-economic approach to contemporary problems necessitates an inductive review of contemporary economic theory in the light of knowledge acquired in other disciplines.

* *
*

At the time when this book was first written (in French), the Society for the Advancement of Socio-economics had not yet been founded and I was not aware of the socio-economic groundswell in the United States or of some of the writings that had led up to it. Such blissful ignorance spared me any disheartening sense of going over old ground, allowing me to write this book as a personal account of my own malaise after years as a teacher of mainstream economics.

Many people helped me with their criticism and suggestions, but my special thanks are due to: Claude Raffestin, Charles Roig and Peter Tschopp of the University of Geneva; Pascal Bridel of the University of Lausanne; Xavier Greffe of the University of Paris I, Panthéon-Sorbonne and the Ecole Nationale de l'Administration; Jacques Silber of the University of Bar-Ilan; and, last but not least, Amitai Etzioni of George Washington University, who encouraged me to have the book published in English (with the help of the Hans Wilsdorf Foundation). Finally, this project would not have seen the light of day without Zachary Rolnik's efficient editing, Kevin Cook's competent translation, and the untiring secretarial assistance of Huong Nguyen.

Introduction

Economic research can in some ways be likened to a vast building site; yet the increasingly fragmented and specialized nature of such research suggests that we may simply be building a latterday Tower of Babel. While greater specialization is a logical consequence of progress in economics, it is also prompted by academic self-justification. It does not necessarily lead to a clearer understanding of how the economy works.

One of the problems with specialization is that it tends to produce new diagnoses rather than new remedies. Accordingly, economic policy continues to treat traditional problems with one of two equally traditional — and diametrically opposed — remedies, namely intervention and non-intervention.

Admittedly, specialization and progress in economics have produced more sophisticated justifications for both remedies. Advocates of non-intervention no longer invoke Adam Smith's invisible hand. Instead, the theory of rational expectations provides a neat argument in favour of this remedy whenever the aims of economic policy are frustrated by economic agents. Interventionists, on the other hand, no longer rely purely on Keynesian business cycle theory, but point instead to the existence of public goods and, in particular, the external costs generated by environmental pollution.

However, this clash of remedies inevitably creates a sense of unease, for behind the scientific terminology of economics lie ideological differences which, despite recent progress, refuse to go away. At the same time, both remedies are open to a number of criticisms, two of the most serious of which are as follows. Non-interventionists are accused of failing to recognize the degree of social consensus needed to absorb the adjustments produced by price flexibility. Interventionists, on the other hand, are charged with failing to appreciate fully the selfperpetuating nature of bureaucracy.

In short, economics fails to come up to society's expectations. This is nothing new. What *is* new is society's sense that something must be done about it. A possible explanation is the present-day role of universities, their high cost in comparison with other public services, and the growing challenge to traditional ways of generating and transmitting knowledge.

However, besides such profound and unidentifiable factors, there are others more directly linked with the science of economics itself. Economic theory is at a loss to explain the current increase in macroeconomic disequilibrium, which can only be understood in a wider context extending beyond the purely economic dimension.

The only way out of this quandary is economic research based on a combination of theory and empirical verification and geared to practical application and the needs of economic policy. Such research will reveal the limits to economic policies by identifying cases where their effects are at variance with stated intentions (such as the inequalities created by certain measures designed to promote social justice). Such an approach will also make it clear that private interests must ultimately defer to the common interest. However, this can only be done by borrowing from the other social sciences (and by emphasizing that economics is also a social science). This ideal approach will be difficult to achieve, for the following reasons:

1. An interdisciplinary approach is not merely a matter of opening the door to other disciplines, but also depends upon the the various social sciences being organized and formally linked, something which the universities, beguiled as they are by the mirage of specialized research, have failed to do.
2. In emphasizing purely formal models, economists have turned their back on social issues and retreated into abstraction. Fascination with pragmatic approaches is another kind of retreat, only in the opposite direction.
3. By "exporting" economic patterns of thinking into other social science fields such as sociology, law or political science, economic models encourage a blinkered view rather than open-mindedness.

In economic theory, the myth of the perfect market is currently going through a revival. This magic wand has been waved on various occasions to usher in a supposed age of plenty. If market equilibrium is achieved through price flexibility and markets are exposed to (ideally perfect) competition, society will — it is claimed — be economically organized in such a way as to ensure the maximum possible welfare.

It is worth examining the reasons for this revival, since developments in economic thinking have always occurred in response to major social problems. Economists have tried all kinds of policies ranging from total non-intervention by the state to total state control. However, they can apparently only agree on one point, namely that current economic policy is increasingly unable to explain the links between economic theory and practice (Bell, 1984).

There are those to whom the revival of the perfect market is a return to the straight and narrow after years of Keynesian aberration. Others see it as an illusion which merely proves how isolated from other disciplines economics has become, particularly when it comes to the environment.

The purpose of this book is to clarify this debate by establishing economic policy as the main concern of theoretical analysis. The book is divided into three parts, covering three distinct aspects of the problem: 1. the over-specialization of economic research; 2. economists' misapprehension of the role of the state; and 3. the need for collaboration between economics and the other social sciences.

Part 1 will attempt to show that the increasingly instrumental nature of economic theory is likely to make it more and more remote from applied economic policy. Far from providing a link with economic practice, theory has tended to become an end in itself. Yet it should not be forgotten that economics only explains one aspect of society, and is merely one of a number of social sciences. Such a reminder is necessary because increasing specialization in economics has led to fragmentation, leaving analytical tools as the only common denominator. Skills in mathematics, statistics and data processing are nowadays vital qualifications for professional economists, but they must not be acquired for their own sake.

With the severance of the links between economic theory and practice and the fragmentation of economic research into myriad specialities, the increasingly instrumental nature of economics has revived such issues as the interaction between the economy and its institutional framework, as well as various hypotheses regarding human behaviour.

This debate has been accompanied by renewed controversy over the choice of analytical methods. The methodological requirement that economic theory be systematically tested against observed reality has been challenged by both theoretical and practical researchers, though both groups claim their own approach is superior. However, since a purely deductive approach ultimately does no more than reproduce the initial hypotheses, it can be used to obtain any result whatsoever. A purely inductive approach is no better, since empirical observations can likewise be linked up in any order. Economic research based on a combination of theoretical models and empirical verification must inevitably take account of research data from other disciplines. Such data suggest that human behaviour is more complicated than the hypothesis of economic rationality would suggest.

Part 2 retraces the history of economic theory from the last century to the present day, against the background of the social problems that have arisen over the same period. The conclusion — already touched on earlier — is that economic theory is found wanting in almost every area of contemporary economic policy:

1. in the field of competition policy, concentration of businesses has continued unabated despite the existence of antitrust legislation, and protectionism is increasing in spite of repeated government statements in favour of free trade.
2. in the field of stabilization policy, none of the various strategies proposed by economic theory has succeeded in dealing with the current macroeconomic disequilibrium, reflected domestically in high levels of both unemployment and government deficit and externally in increasing international debt.
3. finally, in the structural field, problems of environmental pollution are being tackled by *ad hoc* responses rather than by approaches based on the existing economic order.

Should we then conclude that state intervention has failed and return to the nineteenth-century liberal doctrine of the perfect market? The fact that the state is nowadays involved in virtually every economic decision does not mean it is powerful. In fact, the state appears to do little more than reflect the balance of power among various organized pressure groups which are holding it to ransom. A consequence of this is a weakening of traditional decision-making mechanisms and the development of private and public bureaucracies. This tendency is indicative of the high degree of organization of society, which can be seen as a network of relationships rather than a trading system. This applies not only to government, but also to private companies. A return to a self-regulating market mechanism will not remedy the institutional paralysis caused by an all-pervasive but powerless state. Economic theory, based as it is on the premise of rational individual behaviour, favours non-interventionist ideologies; yet the simplistic reasoning behind such ideologies is a threat to the internal cohesion of society. It stems from a liberal tradition which treats the state as exogenous to the economic sphere, whereas nowadays the state is quite clearly an endogenous factor. It is a product of the high degree of organization attained in developed societies, in which the role of the state is instrumental rather than political.

In order to take account of these changes, economic theory must draw upon new sources. More than ever, it must become politically relevant; only thus can it rediscover its social dimension and escape from the dead-end of over-abstraction.

Part 3 discusses the conditions under which such a reorientation can take place. Strict application of economic theory in areas other than economics will not do. Wherever economic theory has been "exported" in this way, the results have been disappointing. This will be demonstrated with reference to the family, which is where the social changes set in motion by the shift from an industrial to a service economy are likely to be most noticeable. Policy recommendations in this area mostly reflect economic models based on the rationality of human behaviour. Since they ignore socio-cultural factors, such recommendations are bound to be irrelevant.

What is needed is an analysis that takes account of more subtle human motives than those assumed by the hypothesis of economic rationality. Such motives are a determining factor in productivity, a concept which, though highly disputed, continues to be used as an indicator of economic performance. The concept of productivity has thus profoundly influenced our way of thinking. The symbols society has chosen to express its goals leave little room for value systems other than that dictated by productivity.

Such a blinkered view can only be damaging in the context of the *environmental debate* — a classic example of the kind of dead-end a purely economic approach can lead to. The ingredients of this debate are ones which will recur throughout this book: the severance of the links between theoretical models and a concrete perception of social issues; economic reasoning based solely on the hypothesis of rational individual behaviour; pseudoscientific demonstrations of the superiority of the market over other collective decision-making mechanisms; the apparent institutional paralysis of such mechanisms; the absence of ethical values from economic models; and, finally, obsessive preoccupation with increased productivity. The above factors conceal a real danger, which is that the limitations the environment will increasingly impose on human activity are a threat to individual freedom. Prohibition will take the place of deliberate policy. By retarding the decision-making process and raising consensus costs, the institutional paralysis of collective decision-making mechanisms will pave the way for such developments. In attempting to defend individual freedom, economic theory has ended up making things worse. Its portrayal of the market economy and the state as implacable enemies has deeply influenced our perception of social issues. A change of attitude is clearly overdue. The state is merely one of many components in the vast organizational fabric of society. The myth of economic rationality must make way for a new awareness of the ways in which our institutions evolve, ways which are ultimately determined by the collective decision-making process. All that is needed is the individual will to see things clearly.

This brings us back to the old issue of the role of ideology in economics (somewhat simplistically portrayed as both positive and normative). While every step forward in economic theory can be seen as an advance in the positive at the expense of the normative aspect, it is equally true that "freedom from ideology" is itself an extremely ideological standpoint.

Instead of hiding its ideological face, economics needs to open the door to other disciplines. Indeed, such is the challenge posed by environmental pollution that there is really no other choice.

PART I

Economic theory — Going round in circles?

The theme of Part 1 of this book is a simple one. There is no universally accepted paradigm of economics. Instead, the field has become fragmented. The over-abstract portrayals of the economy which have resulted in specialization at the expense of the interdisciplinary, comprehensive approach so frequently called for by the scientific community are now the subject of growing criticism.

An economic model that takes account of social interaction is certainly too complex to be handled by existing instruments. So why has mainstream economics avoided a path that has proved so useful in helping us to understand other aspects of society?

First of all, the social sciences only blossomed after they split up into various disciplines, each clearly marked off from philosophy, the exact sciences and law. The separate historical development of each discipline created a problem of terminology which is nowadays a barrier between economics and the social sciences. In order to break down this barrier, the lone specialist — a product of the prevailing academic system — needs to be replaced by research teams. Research into social issues requires a number of different talents: intuition, knowledge of institutions, analytical skill, and mastery of instruments.

Intuition allows the conceptual expression of social issues, which may also occur through the medium of art. Thorough knowledge of the institutional framework enables relevant hypotheses to be formulated.

Analytical skill gives ideas and hypotheses a logical foundation. Lastly, mastery of technical instruments makes it possible to falsify the proposed theory.

In economics, great emphasis is laid on the last two of the above four aspects. Besides the serious problems of methodology this raises, the result is increasing fragmentation, since economics originates in universities battling with the dilemma of achieving research goals while at the same time satisfying the needs of the labour market. Economics therefore tends to classify society according to analytical and technical criteria rather than intuitive or cultural ones.

Secondly, and more essentially, it can be broadly stated that the purpose of all models of social functioning is to construct a theory. Though admittedly an over-simplification, this illustrates more clearly the essential causal relationships between the variables concerned. A more comprehensive, multidisciplinary approach would be descriptive, undermining this analysis of causal relationships.

Part 1 is divided into three chapters:

Chapter 1 will attempt to show that the links between theory and practice are extremely vague and lend themselves to conflicting interpretations. Not only is economic theory fragmented, but an empirical approach is hampered by the lack of suitable observations of economic reality.

Chapter 2 discusses methodology, and shows that the fragmentation of economics originated in the dispute as to the methodological foundation of the social sciences. Both deductive and inductive methods are subjected to criteria of falsification and prediction.

This confusion in matters of methodology prepares the ground for a discussion of human economic behaviour. The individual's ability to act rationally is, of course, a key issue.

Chapter 3 deals with the increasingly instrumental nature of economics, which is one more symptom of its fragmentation. Rather than make the social impact of economic policies its main theoretical concern, economics has concentrated on the development of analytical techniques. Mathematics, statistics and data processing could in fact provide a link with the social sciences, since they use the same kind of formalized terminology; as it is, however, they merely help to keep the various disciplines sealed off from one another.

CHAPTER 1

THE LINKS BETWEEN ECONOMIC THEORY AND PRACTICE

The links between economic theory and practice are based on two opposing theoretical approaches — classical theory and Keynesian theory. There are those who would claim that the clash between the two has long since made way for a synthesis which is supported by most economists. In practice, however, Western economic policy continues to reflect a tug-of-war between interventionists and non-interventionists.

State intervention: a theoretical debate

Even though most economists refuse to be labelled as either classicists or Keynesians, and claim to have put this conflict behind them, they continue to refer to one or other of these two basic models.

The classical model sets out from the hypothesis of full employment and stresses the factors that determine a country's long-term production. These factors are the working population and the available production apparatus on the one hand, and constantly evolving technological knowledge on the other. This model is a self-regulating one in which the state plays no active part. Market equilibrium is achieved by exposing economic agents to price flexibility and competition. This is an essentially microeconomic model based on an assessment of the behaviour of economic agents. This behaviour is supposedly rational, in the sense that consumers seek to maximize their satisfaction and producers their profits. The strategies of both are subject to the same constraint: the budget constraint in the case of consumers, and the constraint of production costs in the case of producers. The latter mostly consist of wages, which in turn represent most of the consumers' income. Production and consumption are thus determined by maximizing behaviour which is common to all economic agents. As changes in behaviour are subject to a certain amount of inertia, the classical model is based on the long term; state intervention is limited to providing appropriate market conditions, and economy policy remains passive.

This vision is challenged by the Keynesian model, which not only offers an explanation for unemployment, but suggests that markets can be adjusted by means of quantities. Fluctuations in economic activity then no longer depend on factors that determine production, but on overall demand, including state expenditure.

This is a macroeconomic approach essentially based on an assessment of overall demand. As the general price level remains constant — a phenomenon which is only observable for short periods, when production capacity is not fully utilized — this is basically a cyclical theory, explaining fluctuations in economic activity in terms of a trend dictated by essential economic data. By varying its expenditure, the state can influence the business cycle and thus pursue an active economic policy.

From the Second World War up to the early 1970s, there was fairly general agreement as to how these two schools of thought were to be interpreted. However, in the 1970s two supposedly brand-new approaches came to the forefront of the theoretical debate, namely monetarism and the theory of rational expectations. Both were an attempt to return to the liberal philosophy at the root of classical theory.

However, if we accept that the main thrust of monetarism (Brunner, 1968) can be summed up in the following three statements:

1. money is neutral, and varying the money supply has no long-term effects on production, employment or prices;
2. changes in the money supply are a reliable indicator of the impact of money on the economy; and
3. monetary policy determines variations in the money supply and has led to the practice of announcing monetary growth targets, supposedly determined on the basis of expected real economic growth.

We will see that what monetarism calls for is *more consistent* state intervention rather than an end to it.

Even though the last of the three items leaves room for state intervention, the monetarist approach is clearly in the non-interventionist camp, since it assumes that the economy will regulate itself. Such disequilibrium as occurs can thus only be due to active state intervention. In other words, economic policy must make way for market forces.

A similar conclusion is reached by the theory of rational expectations, which attempts to redefine the behaviour of economic agents by taking account of the time dimension in economic decisions. Choices are made not only between the production and consumption of various goods and services, but over time. Whenever economic agents receive new information that puts market behaviour in a different light, they adjust their expectations. A market that is subject to changes in the expectations of economic agents is then by definition efficient.

The idea is a simple one. When an agent in a market is mistaken in his forecasts, he attempts to discover the reasons for his mistake and change his future behaviour accordingly. Economists have summed up this idea as follows: some people may be wrong all of the time and everybody may be wrong some of the time, but it is most unlikely that everybody will be wrong all of the time. In other words, behavioural parameters cannot be considered constant in economics, and theories do not remain equally applicable all of the time. Each period requires a separate explanation. However, although this approach opens up a huge field of research into the behaviour of economic agents when faced with risk and uncertainty, it remains in the non-interventionist camp. In this sense, the notion of an efficient market is another theoretical attempt to revive a classical view of the economy.

According to this theory, economic agents rapidly learn to anticipate the intended effect of any measure by the government. This process is subject to the hypothesis of rational expectations, which has three main elements, all of them disputed:

1. Economic agents are assumed to use all the available information. The hypothesis ignores the possibility that, for example, inconvenient information may be disregarded, greatly varying significance may be attached to a given piece of information, or access to information may differ from one individual to another.

2. All the available information is used efficiently. This assumes that, taken as a whole, theories on the running of the economy are capable of predicting future macroeconomic behaviour. Such theories are assumed to be well-known and their principal results universally acknowledged.

3. Any discrepancy between forecasts and future results is random. Economic agents learn to avoid systematic errors. Even if briefly tempted to believe that an increase in budget deficit will lead to an increase in real income, they will finally learn that such deficits must be financed and that printing money is not the answer.

Assuming perfectly rational expectations, the real effect of state policy will be nil, as agents can use their knowledge of economic mechanisms to thwart economic policy. In order to have any effect, economic measures would have to take the public by surprise.

This phenomenon can be illustrated with reference to monetary policy. The public discovers that an increase in the money supply announced by the central bank in order to counteract unemployment will ultimately prove inflationary, and correctly predicts the resulting increase in the general price level. In real terms, the economy will not undergo any change; the only changes will be nominal, monetary ones. However, such a conclusion may be drawn about any economic policy. As the state rarely takes measures singly — given that practically all economic decisions involve the state — calculating theoretical results is an extremely complex matter. Mathematical models designed to ensure a better analysis of the dynamic process within such economies often yield indeterminate results — a fact which seriously limits the scope of the theory of rational expectations.

However, perfectly rational expectations are an exceptional case. The more common situations in which imperfect expectations or asymmetrical information prevail can only have a temporary real effect. In the long run, rational use of the available information will make it possible to thwart government measures.

The theory of rational expectations is thus an argument for nonintervention by the state, and for self-regulation of the economy. To put it more plainly, it represents an ideological view in which the state's economic role is merely passive. Not only does this theory take a deterministic view of society, in which the interests of the leaders are defended by those they lead, but it also sees the economy in highly technical terms. Mathematical models are used to demonstrate the existence of general equilibrium even when rational expectations are taken into account — as though ideology could be eliminated by extensive recourse to scientific techniques. In fact, however, an investigation of efficient market models raises questions regarding human behaviour when faced with risk and uncertainty, and should therefore favour research which provides a link with behavioural sciences such as psychology and sociology. By shedding light on the role of the myths that encapsulate society's fears and uncertainties with regard to the future, such disciplines may well provide a more accurate picture of human behaviour than do statements of ideology, even those couched in positivist terms. Ultimately, the formulation of scientific hypotheses is an ideology in disguise; the revival of the myth of the market as a self-regulating social mechanism is an essentially conservative dogma, and may well be a barrier to real progress in our understanding of the economy.

Empirical observation of economic reality

Whenever theories on the running of the economy are compared with empirical observations, the results are ambiguous and our empirical perception becomes less clear.

Below, we will first of all review observations regarding the conclusions drawn from the neoclassical model in an international context, with reference to changes in relative prices (i.e. in the terms of trade) and how competition is perceived in practice. Secondly, we will see how the quantitative theory of money links neoclassical theory to nominal phenomena. Thirdly, the variation in the general price level following a change in the money supply will be compared with the price rigidity of Keynesian theory. Fourthly, we will discuss the Phillips curve, which provides a clear interpretation of both classical and Keynesian models.

Finally, to round off our discussion of the link between economic theory and practice, we will briefly examine the Laffer curve, which appears to have been responsible for the shift towards supply-side economics. This shift again represents an attempt to revive the classical model.

Changes in terms of trade

One of the main conclusions to be drawn from the neoclassical view of the economy is that equilibrium can only be achieved by a change in relative prices caused by real forces. Terms of trade the relative prices generated by international trade in goods and services — thus reflect a confrontation between the real forces prevailing in the trading countries. Obviously, these are not identical to the domestic relative prices which would have prevailed in each country before the advent of international trade. In order for a country with a relative advantage in watchmaking to be tempted to export, the world price of watches must exceed the cost of producing them. For an importing country, on the other hand, the world price of watches must be less than it would cost the importing country to produce them. In other words, terms of trade are an indicator of the gains from trade that a country achieves through international specialization. If, for example, the world price of watches rises in comparison with that of other goods that are the subject of international trade goods, the gains from trade achieved by importing countries will be less.

This mechanism has a powerful influence on the standard of living-within the various economies and is amply demonstrated by the spectacular variation in the price of oil over the last couple of decades. The first oil shock — the doubling of the world price of oil in 1973 — led oil-importing countries into their first real recession since the Second World War. More recently, and especially in 1985, sharp falls in the price of oil have reduced the real incomes of oil-exporting countries.

What happens when these observations are converted into a single indicator which reflects changes in the ratio between the export and import prices of all goods and services that are the subject of international trade? Table 1 suggests that terms of trade have improved for developed countries and deteriorated for developing ones.

Table 1

Terms of trade* change since 1980 (index 1980 = 100)								
	1980	1981	1982	1983	1984	1985	1986	1987
developed countries	100,0	98,6	100,7	102,4	102,5	103,2	113,2	113,2
developing countries	100,0	102,4	102,8	97,9	99,8	99,2	86,1	75,9

* Terms of trade defined as the ratio between the unit price indexes for exports and imports respectively.

Source: International Monetary Fund, "*International Financial Statistics*", various issues.

Various statistical concepts have been devised to measure changes in gains from trade. This raises a number of problems which are identified by index theory. Table 1 shows the net terms of trade defined as the ratio between an export price index and an import price index. These indexes are determined on the basis of nominal prices. However, neoclassical theory clearly refers to real relative prices which are, conceptually speaking, exchange rates. These cannot be measured empirically.

Observations of the main adjustment mechanism of neoclassical theory are thus distorted by the available statistics.

Two other serious problems may be mentioned at this point:

1. As terms of trade reflect relative changes, no account is taken of absolute changes in quantities traded, which determine gains from international trade. Nor is allowance made for international trade in services, which are by their very nature intangible and difficult to quantify.

2. An improvement in the terms of trade is not reflected in real income as measured by the national product at constant prices. For instance, an increase in export prices increases a country's receipts without the amount exported necessarily changing. If import prices simultaneously remain stable, the increase in receipts from exports enables the country to import more. The terms of trade improve,

expressing the fact that more imports can be obtained for the same productive effort in the form of exports. As the larger volume of imports is a component of domestic expenditure, the latter also increases. However, the real national product does not change, since imports are deducted from overall demand when defining it.

More generally, the statistical concepts embodied in the terms of trade do not allow gains from trade to be measured. To begin with, most theoretical analyses rely on models which implicitly assume that marginal utility per unit of income remains identical for all economic agents. Thus the problem of transfers of income from one group of economic agents to another is eliminated. In practice, however, such transfers may entail gains or losses which need to be taken into account. Here we are confronted with the impossibility of measuring the satisfaction obtained by groups of economic agents or by countries. This is one reason why, in practice, we are unable to ascertain gains from foreign trade. Nor, since trade involves an infinite number of heterogeneous goods, are we able in practice to solve the problem of how to compare quantities traded (Bürgenmeier, 1977).

The ambiguous nature of statistical expressions of variations in the terms of trade raises fundamental doubts as to the relevance of the neoclassical model. Nor does it enable the development debate to become more objective. The well-known theory that third-world countries will never be able to develop because their terms of trade are constantly deteriorating cannot be verified empirically. The more price series for manufactured products and raw materials are used in an effort to prove such deterioration, the more intricate the initial problem of expressing gains from trade within a neoclassical model becomes. The North-South debate has turned into a confrontation on development issues and is thus an ideal arena for political science.

Imperfect competition

The notion of perfect competition has often been the subject of misunderstanding. In the real world, of course, there is no such thing as perfect competition. Attempting to criticize the neoclassical model by taking issue with one of its underlying hypotheses is therefore rather naïve.

The idea that every firm is out to maximize its profits subject to the constraint of production costs is hard to reconcile with the frequent occurrence of imperfect competition in actual business practice. Such doubts are particularly common in economic literature. For example, Williamson (1986) proposes the minimization of transaction costs as a more plausible approach to the firm than pure neoclassical theory. However, the models produced by such attempts to bring economic theory closer to reality are no more coherent than those proposed by the neoclassical school. Thus the gulf between theory and practice remains. Nevertheless, theoretical models of imperfect competition have been prominent in attempts to explain monopolies, returns to scale, product cycles, and industrial organization.

The origin of such efforts to bring theory closer to business practice can be found in Edward Chamberlin's writings on monopolistic competition (1933). According to Chamberlin, a firm's power is not expressed by its ability to influence prices — under conditions of perfect competition such influence is nil, while under monopoly conditions it is total — but by its ability to differentiate its products. If products are not homogeneous and differ from company to company, a firm can use marketing techniques to influence demand for its products, either by fragmenting demand — making it harder for the consumer to obtain information — or by making it less responsive to price changes. Firms thus seek to control demand, a notion that runs counter tothe idea of consumer sovereignty, on which the operation of market forces depends. Moreover, information is imperfect, and generates increasing costs owing to the lack of transparency of the market.

The producer must accept lower profits than can be achieved in a pure monopoly situation. At the same time, access to the market becomes more difficult. Potential competitors are discouraged by the cost of advertising.

All this is a long way from the classical self-regulating mechanism of price flexibility or the relative prices of the neoclassical school. Price changes do not signal disequilibrium between supply and demand. Nevertheless, competition by means of product differentiation has found approval among economists. The theory of monopolistic competition has given rise to a field of microeconomics known as industrial organization (Scherer, 1980), which attempts to determine the criteria whereby competition is still possible. This approach is known as "structure, conduct, performance". Structural criteria include the presence in the market of a minimum number of economic agents. An example of a criterion of conduct is the absence of unfair competition, while a typical criterion of performance is the efficient use of factors of production. In short, this approach takes the notion of competition and attempts to make it workable in the context of business practice.

The result has been a torrent of case studies on specific industries and firms, a torrent further swollen by the current craze for business studies, supposedly more concrete and relevant than theoretical economics. The cry has gone up that economic theory is incorrect. Observation of reality will, it is claimed, at last reveal the truth about how the economy actually works. However, this has raised at least two new problems, one methodological, the other theoretical.

The methodological problem is that case studies proceed by induction. They attempt to establish a market theory on the basis of the experience of a single industry. Yet, based as they are on widely differing observations, they are unable to provide a comprehensive theory. In contrast, neoclassical theory (a deductive approach if ever there was one) *is* comprehensive.

As regards theory, case studies have had one important effect. They have conclusively demonstrated that business practice leads to solutions that are always less ideal than those suggested by theory. This obvious fact is summed up by the "second-best" theory, which proves that certainty can never be achieved. This theory is based on the fact that one or more of the conditions necessary for the best solution are bound to be lacking. In the case of the best solution known as perfect competition, one or more of the following conditions will not be satisfied: a large number of producers and consumers, immediate access to information by all market agents, a homogeneous good, and unrestricted access to the market. The absence of any of these conditions introduces an additional constraint on the maximization of consumers' satisfaction and producers' profits. If such additional constraints are taken into account, the market decision-making process becomes so complex that one can no longer tell which measures will come closest to the best solution. One of the most important conclusions of the second-best theory is that if one of the conditions for the best solution is lacking, there is no point in trying to achieve the others (Lipsey and Lancaster, 1956). If, for example, the good in question is not homogeneous, we cannot be sure that having a large number of producers will necessarily bring perfect competition nearer.

While perfect competition may be utopian, it is associated with a production function in which there are constant returns to scale. It is thus no accident that neoclassical theory relies on such production models. A homogeneous production function of degree one expresses a process in which there are constant returns to scale. Allowance for increasing returns to scale presupposes imperfect competition and is thus, in essence, a second-best solution.

However, case studies tell us nothing about the duration of such solutions. Neoclassical theory proposes an optimal solution in the long term. Perfect competition only exerts its beneficial influence on the allocation of resources when all firms are producing at minimum average cost, which implies an extremely long time span. A vision of long-term imperfect competition fails to reckon with real market dynamics; even the most firmly established monopolies will eventually be threatened unless they are regularly reinforced.

Clearly, this attempt to restore relevance to competition mechanisms does not satisfy those who believe that the behaviour of a firm is based on strategies other than mere maximization of profits. Other attempts have been made to bridge the gap between theory and practice. The following are two examples:

1. In practice, non-maximizing behaviour is assumed to be the rule, and must be differentiated from case to case. This is an extension of the "structure, conduct, performance" approach, only this time applied to a firm rather than an industry — as in Leibenstein's famous appeal (1981) for a new micro-microeconomics.
2. Firms are considered in terms of their organization, and approaches such as game theory are used to examine the way in which they operate. In my view, this is a case of "much ado about nothing", or, to quote Radner (1986, p. 19):

   "This state of affairs is probably not a comfortable one for contemporary economic theory, which tends to try to explain observed economic states as locally stable equilibria in a system with a finite set of equilibria. On the other hand, a theory that leads to a continuum of equilibria is open to completion by adding considerations of history and chance to explain the particular equilibrium that is currently observed. This could lead the economic theory of organization back towards the older institutional and historical approaches from which it rebelled not so many decades ago."

This conclusion has given rise to a new field known as "the New Industrial Organization", which revives "the eternal debate between those who see in our industrial economies an efficient adaptation to external technological conditions and those who see complex games of power and economic domination in them" (Jacquemin, 1987, p. 5).

This debate makes it clear that the neoclassical view of competition cannot be the only one. Yet it continues to be used as the main yardstick for market studies. This suggests that the foundations of mainstream economic theory are mythical rather than scientific — which does not, however, reduce its influence in any way, but merely goes to show the power of theory.

The role of money

The neoclassical model is supplemented by the quantitative theory of money which, of course, translates real values into nominal ones and has no effect on relative prices (which remain subject to real forces). Thus this quantitative theory simply recalls the classical economists' distinction between the real economy and the nominal economy.

This theory, which accords so well with the neoclassical view of money, has since been reformulated (Friedman, 1956). It has thus become a causal explanation, demonstrating that the general price level is influenced by changes in the money supply.

Not only does this explanation raise the problem of how to define the money supply, but it also assumes a stable relationship between the money supply and production flows. The problem of definition has given rise to various statistical concepts of the money supply, expressing the varying degrees of liquidity of bank deposits. The idea here is to find a statistical series stable enough to provide a satisfactory indicator for monetary policy, which will accordingly consist of announcing a monetary growth target at the beginning of each year and then achieving it. Graph 1 illustrates the monetary policy pursued by four different central banks:

Graph 1: Comparative growth rates of monetary aggregates in four selected countries: targets and achievements

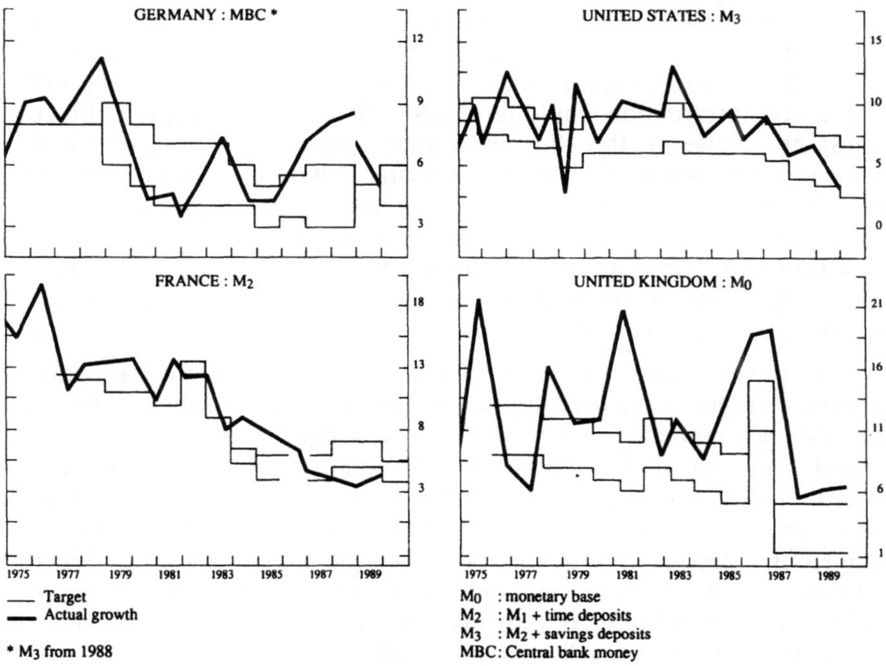

— Targets — Achievements

Source: Annual reports, Bank of International Settlement.

This graph shows that each central bank bases its policy on a different definition of the money supply, though each regularly claims to be pursuing essentially monetarist goals. In some cases, it may be suspected that the targets set are simply a reflection of observed changes in the money supply. Such doubts are certainly justified in the case of the United Kingdom and also the United States, which has set itself a relatively high growth target. There is no definite empirical evidence of a deliberately restrictive monetary policy. Only France appears to have adopted a more restrictive monetary policy during the period concerned.

However, the main problem of monetary policy does not lie in sticking as closely as possible to monetary growth targets, but in maintaining a stable relationship between the money supply and production flows. This means knowing how demand for money is behaving, and in particular the rate at which money iscirculating. This problem is aggravated by the link between the exchange rate and the money supply.

Graph 1 clearly illustrates this constraint in the case of the Federal Republic of Germany. In 1978 there was an excess of dollars on the foreign exchange market. If the Bundesbank had not intervened, the German mark would have appreciated. This would have been a major problem for exporters, since their prices expressed in other currencies would have risen, reducing their potential sales abroad. On the other hand, non-intervention would have allowed the money supply to be kept constant. However, this did not happen. The sharp fluctuation in the monetary base shows that the Bundesbank bought up the excess dollars, creating money but at the same time controlling the appreciation of the mark. This increase in the amount of domestic currency fed German inflation and thus counteracted the intended effect of the government's monetary policy. As the graph shows, the Bundesbank attempted to avert the danger by reducing its monetary growth targets in subsequent years.

However, since oil prices fluctuated sharply in the subsequent period, changes in the overall price level cannot necessarily be attributed to deliberate monetary policy. The more a country is involved in international trade, the more trouble it will have in controlling the money supply, which depends to some extent on individual economic and political behaviour. One may therefore doubt the ability of central banks to control the money supply, especially given the uncertainty created by the spread of new electronic methods of payment. There are those who believe this uncertainty is only temporary, and will cease when such methods have become fully accepted; others believe it will increasingly raise questions as to the part played in the economy by financial intermediaries — a discussion which may well spill over into areas beyond monetary policy.

Price rigidity

Both neoclassical theory and the quantitative theory of money conflict with the observation that markets are not necessarily adjusted by variations in prices. This observation merely repeats the conclusion of the theory of monopolistic competition, which involves an adjustment of the nature of trade. However, the same conclusion is found in the Keynesian model. The Great Depression of the 1930s made it all too clear that price flexibility does not automatically restore full employment. In the Keynesian view, a change in overall demand merely leads to a change in the quantity traded. As long as unemployment prevails, there will be no change in the general price level.

The empirical observation clashes with the fact that, during a recession, there may be a greater tendency to form trusts.

The interpretation of general equilibrium at constant prices is thus both structural and cyclical. It is structural in the sense that the presence of imperfect competition leads to price rigidity. It is cyclical in the sense that changes in supply while underemployment prevails do not necessarily affect prices. Both interpretations theoretically justify intervention. In practice, however, it is difficult to separate the two. Such a distinction can only be maintained at the theoretical level. Structurally, competition policy is compatible with the idea of an efficient market. The role of the state is confined to guaranteeing the conditions that allow such a market to operate. An active state policy is accordingly *dirigiste* and conflicts with the liberal ideal. Cyclically, an active state policy, in the form of increased state expenditure, is only compatible with Keynesian theory. However, such a policy remains strictly limited to temporary intervention. Under no circumstances can it be used to justify permanent state involvement in the economy.

In practice, however, markets are often inefficient. They display cyclical fluctuations whose rates and amplitudes vary over time. State involvement has thus become permanent even though neither of the two theoretical justifications can really be discerned. The main reasons for this are as follows:

1. Firstly, the classical flexible-price model includes the cost involved in seeking an equilibrium price, which is often considered too high. Many markets therefore operate at a publicly displayed price. Changes in supply and demand are brought about by changes in quantities, which has led the state to examine the conditions under which such transactions occur.
2. Secondly, many markets operate at negotiated prices which do not reflect supply and demand so much as the influence of special interest groups or society's ethical goals. A typical example is the

labour market, which is governed by a system of institutionalized negotiations. It should be noted that this does not necessarily lead to less flexibility in wage rates, but it does ultimately reduce the information cost involved in any particular transaction. Since the labour market is governed by negotiations between employers and workers, we are a long way from the efficient market of theory. Ultimately, negotiations are what enable the market to operate, rather than automatic flexibility in wage rates. Yet such a negotiating process is inconceivable without state regulation.

If we examine households' expenditure, as registered in connection with consumer price indexes, we cannot escape the conclusion that the prices they pay are seldom set by efficient markets. For example, expenditure on food also covers the costs of domestic agricultural production; these, however, are not only made up of economic components, but also political and cultural factors which justify state intervention. Once again, comparison with efficient markets is a fiction which merely emphasizes the power of the symbols that govern social relationships.

Housing is a complex network of relationships involving a large number of different state controls and based on a hierarchy of experiences which have at no point been exposed to market forces. The few exceptions to this rule are no more than that.

Expenditure on social insurance is another area which is not subject to competition. The need to redistribute income for purposes of social cohesion has resulted in a dual system of oldage pensions, responsibility for which is divided between the state and private companies. Moreover, the increasing cost of health care is causing the state to intervene more and more in this area. Some health insurance companies only survive byvirtue of state subsidies.

These examples are evidence of the permanent involvement of the state in economic dealings. Highly abstract models based on a discussion of two theoretical outlines which respectively justify and reject state intervention are dogmatic, and must be considered as examples of special pleading rather than rigorous analysis.

The Phillips curve

Opposing theoretical references — classical and Keynesian — are also used in interpreting the Phillips curve, which links inflation and the unemployment rate. Professor Phillips studied the link between variations in unemployment and nominal wages in the United Kingdom from 1861 to 1931. By splitting up nominal wages into real wages and the rate of inflation, and assuming a constant rate of increase in real wages over the whole period, he identified both a monetary and a real phenomenon.

The Phillips curve, which is entirely based on economic observations of the past, suggests an optimum combination of inflation and unemployment which reflects social preferences. This optimum can be achieved by means of an appropriate monetary policy. If the money supply expands, inflation will be high and unemployment low, and vice versa if the money supply contracts.

At first the Phillips curve caused considerable excitement. Policy-makers believed it would enable them to quantify the various alternative targets between the extremes of full employment and price stability. However, when plotted with recent data, the Phillips curve proves to be unstable. This is one of the most intriguing phenomena in contemporary macroeconomics. Attempts to explain it have caused frequent controversies which once more boil down to the traditional clash between the Keynesian and the classical view. The effectiveness of government intervention is thus once again the key issue.

Graph 2 illustrates both theoretical interpretations and compares them with recent Phillips curve data for the United States.

Graph 2

2.1 Traditional Phillips curve: *the Keynesian interpretation*

2.2 Theoretical Phillips curve: *the classical interpretation*

2.3 Recent Phillips curve data for the United States

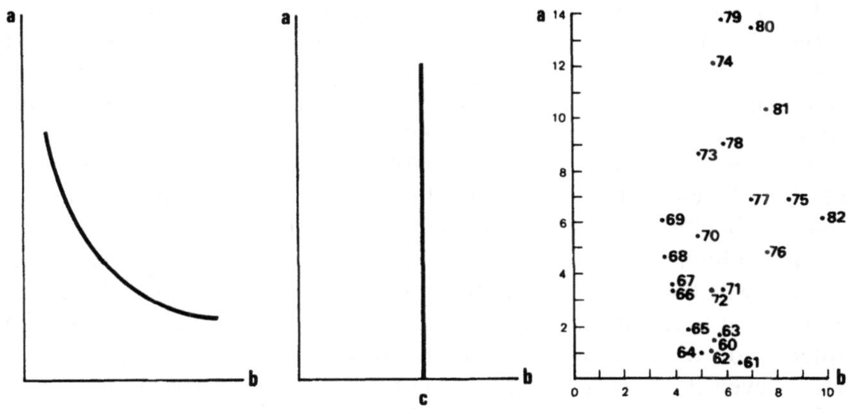

(a) rate of inflation
(b) rate of unemployment
(c) natural rate of unemployment

The relationship illustrated in Graph 2.1 gives the government an empirical tool, based on observations of the past, with which to determine how the inflation rate will be affected by an expansionary monetary policy designed to reduce the rate of unemployment. This link thus depends solely on the shape of the curve. For example, an expansionary policy aimed at reducing unemployment will lead to a higher rate of inflation. This traditional version of the Phillips curve reflects the Keynesian view: in order to combat unemployment, the state decides to stimulate overall demand by increasing public spending. The resulting increase in domestic production reduces unemployment. Assuming diminishing returns, the additional production will generate increasing marginal costs which can only be covered if the overall price level simultaneously rises.

However, experience has shown that either this traditional curve will shift — in which case it is more appropriate to refer to a family of curves — or else its slope will change.

Monetarists maintain that, in the long term, the curve becomes a vertical line located at the so-called "natural" rate of unemployment, as illustrated in Graph 2.2.

According to this interpretation, expansionary monetary policies cause inflation and have no real long-term effects. Unemployment remains at its natural level, i.e. the level structurally inherent in the running of the economy. This level may be relatively high, owing to such factors as failure to integrate a major part of the black population (in the United States), the closing-down of coal mines (in Britain) or the decline of shipyards (in Germany). Expansionary monetary policies can do nothing to eliminate unemployment of this kind.

The theory of rational expectations leads to the same conclusion, but this time in the short term. On the labour market, employees and employers may have differing expectations as to future price and wage trends, either because information is imperfect or because it is used asymmetrically. Employers tend to be guided by production prices, and employees by consumption prices. Accordingly, changes in nominal wages may be either behind or ahead of changes in the expected rate of inflation. If employers expect a higher price rise than employees, the level of employment will increase with the overall price level. The Phillips curve will then maintain its traditional downward slope. If, on the other hand, it is employees who expect a higher price rise (as they will be tempted to do when negotiating to indexlink wages), unemployment will increase, even producing an Phillips curve with an upward slope.

However, more recent empirical Phillips curve observations (Graph 2.3) cannot readily be explained. The effectiveness of economic policies — or of state intervention in the economy — remains a matter of dispute. Other explanations go back to the original Phillips curve which, as we have seen, links nominal wages and employment. In order to link nominal wages and the rate of inflation, the rate of increase in real wages must be assumed to remain constant. However, in neoclassical theory, changes in real wages are determined by changes in labour productivity. An assumption that the latter remains constant is tantamount to dismissing the possibility of any real change in the economy. A vertical Phillips curve can be explained by monetary theory in the long term and by the theory of rational expectations in the short term, but it may again simply reflect a fall in labour productivity. However, this cannot really be verified empirically, since no straightforward observations are available regarding productivity. This point will be discussed further in Chapter 8, which is entirely devoted to theoretical and practical interpretations of the notion of productivity.

It should, however, be stressed that the instability of the Phillips curve may in fact be due to changes in technical knowledge and in ways of organizing production. This brings us to the subject of supply-side economics.

The Laffer curve

The revival of supply-side economics can be traced back to the Laffer curve, which is simply a graph that compares any two variables according to certain mathematical criteria. We could dismiss it altogether, were it not for the fact that from 1981 onwards it led to a complete reorientation of American economic policy under the Reagan administration. In this case the curve was used to compare two economic variables that are politically very sensitive, namely government tax revenues and the rate of taxation. The latter can theoretically lie anywhere between zero and 100%. At either of these extremes, tax revenues will be nil, since zero taxation will produce zero tax and 100% taxation will do the same by stifling all business activity. Somewhere between these two extremes, there must be an optimum rate which will ensure maximum revenues. According to whether the actual rate of taxation is higher or lower than this theoretical optimum, a decrease in the actual rate will cause either a rise or a fall in tax revenues. The prevailing opinion among the general public is that taxes are too high and that a cut in taxation is bound to stimulate business activity by unshackling the spirit of enterprise. The resulting increase in overall supply will increase tax revenues. The state's policy is thus rewarded: by reducing its influence on business, it gets more back in tax. This theory of non-intervention has been the creed of American administrations ever since 1981. Repeated complaints from the business community that taxes were too high have been turned into a political creed without anyone taking the trouble to check whether the complaints are justified. A theory has thus been used to justify a reduction in taxes. Indeed, in the case of the Laffer curve the word "theory" is a misnomer, since it is impossible to tell where the actual rate of taxation lies in relation to the optimum rate. The Laffer curve has simply been used to confirm a preconceived idea. Far from being scientific, it reflects a value system. What evidence there is suggests that the same is true of a good deal of economic theory:

1. Instead of identifying gains from trade, examination of terms of trade leads to a confrontation between developed and developing countries.
2. Observations of competition do not confirm the existence of a self-regulating market mechanism, but instead suggest a highly organized economic system.
3. Reference to money fails to explain its role in the economy and merely reinforces the normative assumption that the state should refrain from pursuing an active monetary policy.
4. Rather than confirm Keynesian theory, price rigidity suggests a consensus among trading partners.
5. The Phillips curve, which is plotted from simple observations of historical data concerning nominal wages and employment, can be used to prove anything.
6. Finally, the Laffer curve, like other attempts to link theory and practice, can really only be interpreted in terms of the normative aspect of economics.

CHAPTER 2

THE FRAGMENTATION OF ECONOMICS

Towards the end of the nineteenth century, mainstream economic thought was based on a model which attempted to explain how prices were determined in the market. Price was interpreted as an indicator of value which reflected both conditions of production and consumption needs — an interpretation which was to be harshly criticized by both Marxist thinkers and the institutional school.

Marxist economists maintained that the value of a good must be closely linked to labour. They distinguished between labour value — defined as the minimum wage that would ensure the working population a living — and value in exchange, which was higher than labour value. The difference between these two expressions of value, known as surplus value, was seized by producers. To classical economists, on the other hand, only value in exchange mattered, since it reflected supply and demand. Rejecting this thesis, most Marxist economists turned to planning, which was supposed to prevent private producers from unilaterally accumulating surplus value. The role of the state was then to protect workers and dictate the production of socially useful goods. A definition of what was socially useful was provided not by the market, but by the planning authorities. Planning was therefore an attempt to put theoretical notions of fairness into practice. In practice, however, it was simply a technique for allocating factors of production which is also used in contemporary market economies in areas such as physical planning, energy and transport.

The ideology behind planning only becomes apparent in its legal handling of ownership of the factors of production. Although factors of production tend to belong to the public sector in planned economies and to the private sector in market economies, combinations of the two are in practice found in virtually every country.

In the first section of this chapter, we will only refer to institutionalist criticisms, which are based on an evolutionary view of the economy; unlike Marxist theories, this approach is compatible with the liberal model.

This evolutionary approach may well stand up better than neoclassical theory to criticisms regarding methodology, which will be discussed in the second section. In any case, it allows more scope for inductive thinking, without which the full subtlety of human economic behaviour cannot be taken into account.

In the third section, an attempt will be made to show that obsession with economic rationality is preventing economics from making progress. Institutionalist criticisms, the controversy over methodology and the behavioural debate are each in their own way evidence of the fragmentation of economics, which nonetheless continues to be dominated by the monolith of neoclassical thinking.

Institutionalist criticisms

Nineteenth-century liberal thought concentrated on studying the operation of economic mechanisms and cut economics off from its socio-political context. It was concerned to identify and explain the supposed essential causal relationships between prices and quantities traded. Classical theory therefore proceeded by deduction, and thus grew increasingly abstract.

This development in economic thought produced a vigorous reaction, which can be divided into three distinct streams: the German historical school, the sociological school, and the institutional school.

The German historical school

This school is perhaps typified by the work of Werner Sombart (4th edition, 1919-1921), who attempted to lend economic models a historical and, more particularly, an institutional dimension by setting out in meticulous detail the basic conditions for economic activity. This approach linked economic mechanisms to social structures. In sharp contrast to this was the marginalist school which, as a logical extension of liberal thought, saw such mechanisms as the outcome of individual behaviour.

The contrast between these two schools was immense, particularly as it led to a political controversy over the importance and role of the state in the economy. If economic mechanisms were linked to social structures, then responsibility for changing the latter lay with the state. Institutional change thus justified giving the state a more active economic role. If, on the other hand, economic mechanisms were determined by individual behaviour — a natural factor, as it were, and one which was exogenous to economic activity — then the state was confined to a watchdog role.

The German historical school also attacked the idea of fatality implicit in classical economic theory. If the state had only a passive role in the economy, economic changes would depend on human behaviour, which always seeks to maximize individual utility. Assuming such one-way causality, society must be seen as a reflection individual maximizing strategies, and social behaviour is merely the sum total of individual behaviour. However, as the German historical school rightly pointed out, social behaviour — as manifested in institutions, cultural practices and collective memory — itself has a considerable impact on individual behaviour, and shapes it according to the rules, symbols and myths used by society to justify its existence to the individuals within it.

The sociological school

Founded by Emile Durkheim (7th edition, 1960), this school called attention to the social dimension of economic phenomena. It first of all criticized the classical model on methodological grounds, proposing case studies in place of abstract models and investigative techniques instead of theoretical constructions. Once again, the purpose was to take account, through detailed description, of the social fabric behind economic mechanisms.

However, the budding late-nineteenth-century science of sociology did not merely propose new methods, but a way of studying social organization which was an actual alternative to economic theory. Instead of adopting the reductionist techniques used by economists, it acknowledged the independent existence of the social field, while relying for its evidence on observable facts. In pursuing its own field of investigation, this school permitted the study of the "vehicular" role of ideology, defined as the means whereby leaders can induce society to accept their way of thinking. It also opened the door to the spiritual aspects of social organization.

The sociological school thus bolstered the criticism levelled at the classical model's assumption that individual economic behaviour was rational. If the latter in fact turned out to be irrational or manipulated, economic analysis would be little more than an academic exercise, and economists would be exposed as puppets of the Establishment, perpetuating values which, far from being universal, were simply those of the prevailing system.

The institutional school

The third group to react vigorously against nineteenth-century economic thought was the institutional school which, especially in the United States, criticized abstract methods of economic research. This school was dominated by the towering figure of Thorstein Veblen (1925).

As an alternative to theoretical models, the institutional school proposed the study of institutions as manifested in social behaviour, customs and laws. This approach condemned the "mechanistic" nature of economic models, and stressed the importance of social structures, the soil without which abstract economic thought could never have blossomed. In this sense, the institutionalists were echoing the criticisms expressed by the previous two schools, but their rejection of liberal thinking extended to its use of purely economic models as a basis for its observations of social issues. Unlike in the exact sciences, such observations were unique and historical. Constructing a theory to explain them necessarily meant turning to the past to show causal relationships. The institutionalists, on the other hand, pointed out that economic activity was evolutionary and liable to change, if only because laws changed. In fashioning the legal framework, the state thus played a much more active part in the economy than the classical model allowed.

What the three schools had in common was that they rejected the classical model of the economy in favour of a comprehensive description of social interactions, on the grounds that the economy was merely a sub-set of the social whole.

Instead of acknowledging the extent to which their own and the classical approach complemented one another, the institutionalists claimed that theirs was an alternative way of studying the economy. Later, however, abstract models took over once more, and became more and more complex. The classical model evolved into a neoclassical synthesis which not really challenged until the advent of Keynesian theory. Today, with the revival of the classical model, this challenge appears to have faded.

Thus these institutionalist criticisms did not have any lasting influence on mainstream economics. They did, however, give rise to a whole new socio-political literature of economics, exemplified by the writings of Lewis (1963), Olson (1983) and Tullock (1986). This literature had its roots not only in institutionalist criticisms but also in the work of, for example, Max Weber (2nd edition, 1967), who saw Protestantism as one of the principal factors in the emergence of capitalism.

One feature which such socio-political approaches would appear to share is the idea that economics is a culturally determined science which cannot be seen in isolation from Western cultural history. On no account, therefore, can its methods or models be generalized, nor can it lay claim to the universality conferred on it by the neoclassical model. An interventionist state seen as an instrument for changing economic structures thus becomes the normative criterion for all economic research which follows the institutionalist path.

Western economic thinking remains alien to cultures such as those of the Islamic world and Africa, in which the notions of production, consumption and maximization of utility are mostly irrelevant. Accordingly, the whole idea of "economics of underdevelopment" may be quite meaningless.

In a societies where the main or indeed only source of wealth is children (who ensure both descendants and the continuity of the prevailing religion), can birth control, for all that it is "economically necessary", be considered relevant? Neoclassical theory patently fails to take account of the diversity of family systems, and no socio-economic theory appears capable of explaining global issues. We will return to this in our discussion of family economics in Chapter 7.

Values are not only geographically but also historically relative. This is well illustrated by the difficulty trade unions have had in responding to current changes in Western values (Roig *et al.*, 1986).

Here we run into a semantic problem, namely that terms such as "rationality", "utility", "market" and "liberalism", though taken for granted by mainstream economic theory, are in fact biased, dated borrowings from terminological systems which wrongly claim to be "scientific".

The same claim lies behind the increasing specialization of contemporary economic theory, which has attempted to answer the criticism levelled at it by resorting to ever more sophisticated models. The main criticisms of the neoclassical approach may be divided into three groups, according to whether they assume the existence of (a) imperfect competition and concentration of businesses, (b) externalities such as public goods or the various kinds of environmental pollution, or (c) inequalities in the distribution of income and wealth.

The criticism directed at neoclassical assumptions regarding competition has been countered by the development of microeconomic theory.

The criticism based on the existence of externalities has given rise to the concept of public goods, as set out in the theory of public choice (Atkinson, 1980), as well as the principle of internalization of external effects (Baumol, 1975). Finally, the criticism based on the clash between equity and efficiency has led to research into distribution of income and wealth (Wolfelsperger, 1980).

In each of these areas, state intervention is no longer questioned, and is justified by specific theoretical reasoning. Such criticism has thus led to economy policy-making which is essentially theoretical and limited in nature, in contrast to the neoclassical notion of general equilibrium achieved by excluding the state from the economy.

Thus, while it is naïve to compare only neoclassical and Keynesian theory without referring to differences in the development of the main branches of economics, it is nonetheless true that the fragmentation of economic research into specialist fields has left theoretical models increasingly divorced from the needs of economic policy.

To put it another way, if economists' view of society is correct, why is it not adopted by economic policy-makers? If, as I believe, there is a malaise in economic research, it is undoubtedly due to this widening gulf between theory and practice.

There is an even more fundamental reason for the renewed interest in institutional economics. This is connected with the growing economic problems facing the developing countries. Economics has been seen as a means of giving such countries the tools they need in order to develop, despite the fact that development implies not only economic growth but also social and cultural change.

Economic theory reduces all of this to a problem of constrained optimization. It sees ability to invest as a particularly serious constraint. Since domestic savings are mostly exhausted very soon, there is an additional constraint on transfers of foreign savings to developing countries.

Such transfers are increasingly threatened by growing external disequilibria (see Table 2). The developed countries, whose financing ability was traditionally high, have since 1977 become net importers of foreign savings, breaking the customary symmetry between the industrialized countries with domestic savings in excess of their needs and the developing countries with domestic savings that cannot cover their demand for investment. The need to finance external deficits has increasingly stood in the way of development projects.

International aid programmes, which are based on neoclassical economic theory, attempt to stimulate external adjustment mechanisms and to strengthen the link between savings and investment. However, such an approach fails to take account of the obvious fact that poor countries have financing needs and rich countries have financing ability.

Table 2

Net current balance (in billions of US$)									
		1977	**1979**	**1981**	**1983**	**1985**	**1987**	**1988***	**1989***
North	United States	− 14	+ 1	+ 5	− 46	−116	−161	−132	−116
	Other developed countries	− 12	− 31	− 37	+ 18	+ 67	+113	+ 71	+ 66
	Total	− 26	− 32	− 32	− 28	− 49	− 48	− 61	− 50
South	Oil exporting countries	+ 26	+ 61	+ 51	− 12	+ 3	− 1	− 21	− 18
	Other developing countries	− 11	− 37	− 82	− 43	− 27	+ 2	+ 8	− 3
	Total	+ 15	+ 24	− 31	− 55	− 24	+ 1	− 13	− 21

* Estimates

Source: Bank for International Settlements, *Annual Report*, various issues.

The real problem of development is not the inadequacy of international transfers of savings, but the culture shock that accompanies them. The essence of this culture shock was first pointed out by the institutionalists, which largely explains the renewed interest in this approach (Myrdal, 1957). However, the formidable problems of methodology it raises have revived the conflict between the neoclassical approach and the comprehensive approach of institutional economics.

In order to study how the economy works, the neoclassical approach resorts to simplification, which enables it to marshal its observations of social reality and so produce a clearer analysis. A more comprehensive approach is necessarily more descriptive. In any case, both analysis and description raise problems of methodology.

The controversy over methodology

Economic theory has often been called unrealistic. Yet the question of what is realistic can only be answered if we have criteria that are universally accepted by economists. Unfortunately, we do not. There are those who say that the answer lies in observing reality — since a theory is simply an attempt to portray reality — whereas others insist on previously defined scientific criteria.

This lack of consensus accounts for the growing malaise among economists, who are not always able to influence economic policy decisions. Currently, this feeling of helplessness is reflected in increasing challenges to the prevailing methodology.

There is no doubt that economic theory has long been dominated by a purely deductive approach which concentrates on the analysis of essential causal relationships. However, such relationships cannot be generalized. It is in fact impossible to talk of economic laws, since theory, by its very nature, is a simplified portrayal of reality and therefore omits elements which may be important in specific situations. In other words, economic theory has mostly refrained from verifying empirically the results obtained by simple deduction from hypotheses.

An economic model can only be compared with an alternative model. If one can be preferred to the other on the basis of their respective results, such a preference can only determined by comparing both models with the results of empirical verification.

This view is still rather ambiguously maintained by many economists who see economics as both an inexact science (owing to the numerous random data it must take into account and the fact that relevant causal relationships must be determined on the basis of hypotheses) and an exact science (since it is based on logical deduction of the causal links between the variables considered, and does not therefore require empirical verification in order to be called exact). The important thing is that theory enables us to alter our perception of how the economy works.

This reassuring view of economic models has been undermined by at least three different methodological approaches which have contributed to the fragmentation of economic theory (Hausmann, 1984).

The sharpest criticism has come from Karl Popper, ably championed by Mark Blaug (1980). These critics claim that, in order to qualify as truly scientific, a theory must be capable of being falsified. This criterion introduces the rule that a theory must be judged by comparing it not with another theory, but with observable reality.

Neoclassical theory quite clearly fails this test, which means that it cannot be considered scientific. Indeed, the same would appear to be true of all deductive approaches, based as they are on "all other things being equal" — a rule which precludes verification.

Obviously, such censure was bound to provoke an indignant reaction, and Popper's methodology is now under attack from a coalition of two special interest groups which are themselves at odds with one another. However, before turning to this, we must digress.

Another tempting criterion was proposed by Friedman (1953), who claimed that a theory should not explain, but *predict*. Regardless of whether or not it could be falsified, a "good" theory would produce reliable predictions. By the same token, the hypotheses on which it was based did not need to be realistic, as long as they provided accurate forecasts. What mattered was the qualitative aspect (the direction of change) rather than the quantitative aspect (the magnitude of change). However, this method can be invalidated simply by asking what happens if a prediction based on such a theory turns out to be wrong — as is frequently the case. The underlying hypotheses must then be examined after all, and the claim that they need not be realistic cannot be maintained. Furthermore, enthusiastic attempts to achieve the status of a true science have led to a profusion of spectacular but at the same time theoretically unsound forecasting models which the public is ill-equipped to understand. Such over-eagerness on the part of economists may well have done their image irreparable harm.

Nowadays, they more prudently state that forecasting models are designed to help us understand the macroeconomic workings of society and are only useful as an aid to further research.

This leaves the deductive method exposed once more to Popper's positivist criticism.

This approach may well prove to be the only one capable of getting economics out of its current predicament, unless of course it is finally accepted that economics is not an exact science but a social science and, as such, needs to develop a methodology of its own. So far, however, attempts to move in this direction remain in their infancy and are hampered by the lack of contact between the various social sciences.

Objections to the criterion of falsification are twofold. On the one hand, orthodox economists who have invested in the development of pure theory reject the criterion as excessively strict. They point out that on this basis, even in the exact sciences, few theories would qualify as scientific. Above all, however, they seek to defend a way of thinking which has had a huge impact on society's perception of its own economic organization. This objection is, I would suggest, ideologically biased. If a market economy in which perfect competition prevails is indeed the best form of economic organization, it may be enough to have faith in it and acknowledge its mystical power. Like any faith, however, it prevents us from advancing our understanding of how highly organized societies work.

The second objection comes from the wide range of theoretical schools based on inductive methods, including institutional economics. Other examples are provided by the host of case studies and above all the countless econometric studies on the subject of industrial organization.

Often, a number of different analytical models of the causal links between the observed variables are proposed. It is therefore tempting to accept a result only if it is confirmed by several different models. However, this approach raises a number of objections, chief among which are the following:

1. Econometric studies often take an aggregate as the endogenous variable. In aggregating, they ignore the possible differentiated effect of the exogenous variable on the endogenous variable.
2. It is often difficult to separate the effect of one variable from that of other variables. The "pure" effect is all too frequently obscured.
3. Lucas (1976) has shown that the coefficients of an estimated equation remain dependent on the economic policy pursued during the period of the estimate. This casts serious doubt on policy conclusions drawn from econometric studies.
4. All econometric models are based on hypotheses that are questionable in one way or another (for example, hypotheses regarding the degree of competition in markets for goods and factors of production, the type of production function, the function to be optimized, and the constraint to be taken into account). Consequently, each model tends to concentrate on a specific aspect. Those models which do attempt to cover several aspects at once must accept more complicated methods of estimation and a considerably reduced degree of freedom.

The above objections suggest the need for a different methodology. An example is the opinion-poll technique, based on questionnaires and interviews, which gets to the heart of the particular problem by talking to the main economic agents involved. Although the opinion poll is an essential tool for the analysis of economic policy, it is insufficient, since it cannot be used to quantify the effect of an exogenous variable; the respondents are mostly unable to distinguish the effect of such a variable from that of other factors involved in their economic decision. Furthermore, opinion-poll results can be skewed by such factors as the representativity of the sample, the response rate, and the phrasing of particular questions.A third method, known as the simulation method, may therefore be helpful. Simulation involves imaginary projects that are subject to variable influences. This approach provides economists with "laboratory conditions" for their empirical research.

In short, no single empirical approach is sufficient to provide a satisfactory picture of the causal links between empirical observations.

There is thus a clear split in methodology. Despite the broad consensus regarding the deductive method, it is challenged by advocates of the criterion of falsification. The latter is in turn attacked by those who wish to see theory replaced by various methods of empirical observation. The criterion of prediction has failed to make things any clearer. A less absolute, more pragmatic approach to economic methodology may possibly succeed, not in achieving a consensus, but in establishing the fact that economics can no longer depend on a single theoretical criterion.

However, it is clear from our discussion that the opening-up of economics to other disciplines will increase the need for a more inductive methodology.

An approach combining several complementary methods is needed in order to provide a useful response to problems of economic policy. At the same time, the range of references must be extended, and it must be recognized that other, non-economic sources can make a worthwhile contribution to the methodological debate.

Basic assumptions

The famous concept of Economic Man has also given rise to a mass of literature on human behaviour. Mainstream economic theory assumes rational behaviour, which serves as the basis for the panacea of economic growth. This basic assumption can be summed up in the following four statements (Kristol, 1984):

1. Most people have a natural and ineradicable desire to improve their material living conditions.
2. Attempts to repress this desire lead to dictatorship and poverty.
3. This desire can only flourish through free trade.
4. It is economic growth that brings about improvements in material conditions, irrespective of the degree of inequality and its variation over time. Put simply, more is better than less.

The synthesis of the above assumptions is the market, where trade between producers and consumers takes place and each agent is induced to maximize his interest. The consumer is out to achieve the greatest possible satisfaction, while the producer seeks the greatest possible profit. Analytically speaking, the consumer maximizes a utility function and the producer a production function. These strategies are subject to the same constraint. For the former, the constraint is income; for the latter, production costs. Thus the microeconomic problem of determining a single price boils down to a problem of optimization. When the optimizing strategies of consumers and producers coincide, the market is said to be in equilibrium.

This view of human behaviour uses an entirely deductive approach, and therefore does not satisfy the criterion of falsification. This is not to say that it is wrong, or that it has not been a decisive factor in our understanding of economic activity; but the assumption of rational behaviour means that economic models can only analyse social issues by reducing them to mathematical problems of constrained optimization. In other words, the market model implies value judgements regarding human behaviour. Not surprisingly, therefore, this approach has been criticized on the grounds that the results of all market models are determined by the initial assumption.

Four such criticisms are set out below. Each in its way is evidence of the fragmentation of basic economic hypotheses.

1. The first concerns the notion of bounded rationality — the principle that, while people may believe themselves rational in their intentions and sometimes in their decisions, such rationality is not always reflected in their behaviour.
2. The second, in the institutionalist tradition, points to the highly organized nature of society, in which transaction costs have become key factors in trade.
3. The third is based on experimental evidence from the field of psychology, suggesting that human behaviour tends to be irrational.
4. The fourth, which is philosophical in origin, proposes a theory of justice centring on the idea of the social contract.

Bounded rationality

Here, the assumption of rational human economic behaviour is presented in less absolute terms. The hypothesis of bounded rationality introduced by Simon (1949) states that, although people want to be rational, they are only imperfectly so — an interpretation which is rejected both by a number of orthodox economists and by certain sociologists who are keen to defend their own theory of organization based on the idea of group strategy. If this hypothesis is accepted, however, the market ceases to be the only way of expressing strategies that seek to achieve the greatest possible utility and profit. Individual market agents whose capabilities are limited will attempt to organize themselves more effectively. The problem of trade will then no longer be confined to the operation of the market, but will include the establishment of alternative organizational structures.

This modification of the assumption of perfect rationality is certainly helpful, since it allows the economic problem of trade to be considered as a problem of organization, of which market theory is only a part. Studies have thus been carried out concerning the decision-making process within firms, which are no longer treated as production functions but as decision-making structures. It then becomes apparent that the decision-making process involves costs which do not confirm the hypothesis of profit maximization. The reasons for this are not only the uncertainty that attends any economic decision, but also organizational complexity and infighting.

With regard to uncertainty, there is no way of telling which specific economic decision will guarantee maximum profits. For one thing, information is never perfect — indeed, the flimsy basis on which decisions are sometimes taken is truly astonishing — and for another, uncertainty increases with the time span over which the decision is taken. Some investment projects only become profitable if the company mobilizes all its resources.

The following argument may be used to sustain the hypothesis of rationality: uncertainty will induce the firm's managers to develop a "collective intuition" which is often based on past experience, and to adopt a strategy which, while it may not always stick to the principle of profit maximization (e.g. by ensuring that marginal costs equal marginal receipts), does pursue the same objective. In other words, whatever means are used to reach a decision, the actual goal is determined by economic models. It should be emphasized that such an argument provides no additional evidence for the profit-maximizing strategy.

In order for company management to reach a decision, there must be a perfect flow of information between the various decision making centres. The scene is thus set for infighting as the various units not only withhold information they need in order to devise their own strategies, but also seek to maintain a high degree of autonomy within the firm. Anyone who has worked in a complex organization will be familiar with the inter-departmental warfare that goes on there. Even if the management succeeds in creating a harmonious atmosphere, it will never have a complete picture of the information held by the various departments.

Organizational problems have, of course, given rise to a considerable number of models, essentially of two kinds. The first, based on systems analysis and game theory, is deductive; the second, more institutional in nature, derives from the sociological theory of group behaviour. If these approaches are subjected to the criterion of falsification, the sociological approach appears to be more promising than purely theoretical models, whose results are determined by the initial hypotheses and can thus be used to support any conclusion whatsoever.

In any case, neither approach answers the following crucial questions:

1. To what extent does organizational complexity force a firm to deviate from its objective of maximizing profits?
2. Is the resulting deviation so great as to justify a theory of organization which contradicts conventional microeconomic theory?

These questions cannot be answered merely by describing all the personal conflicts and real constraints which interfere with profit-maximizing strategies. While the hypothesis of limited rationality brings economic theory and practice closer together, it does not provide clear criteria which with to assess a firm's objectives. Yet, by drawing attention to the power and organizational aspects of economic decisions, it does broaden the analysis — something only made possible by exposing economic theory to the influence of other social sciences.

The transaction costs approach

While the notion of limited rationality leads to the formulation of organizational models, the transaction costs approach (Williamson, 1985) goes much further. In recognizing the existence of not only limited rationality but also opportunism in human behaviour, this approach revives the study of social organizations in the institutionalist tradition.

It thus succeeds in bringing economic theory closer to reality, since it is not restricted to the market but also takes account of kinds of transactions that occur outside the market, such as public and private bureaucracies. The traditional economic problem of trade is thus examined from a broader angle. The analysis concentrates on transaction costs in relation to the various ways of organizing trade developed by society. It usefully points out that every transaction is accompanied by a certain amount of friction; the optimal system of resource allocation proposed by neoclassical theory must therefore be adjusted to take account of the costs of running the system, other than production costs.

Contracts, with their various legal and economic ramifications, are central to a transaction costs approach, which opens the door to an analysis of competition policy.

It explicitly sets out from broader hypotheses of human behaviour than economic rationality, it compares the various ways of organizing trade, and it treats firms as decision-making centres. The decision-making process within a firm is intended to reduce transaction costs. It is subject not only to market forces but also to influences from politicians, special interest groups and the civil service. Contracts therefore reflect intended strategies or decision-making processes within a firm rather than market forces, and vary according to the item traded. Ultimately, the form they take depends on criteria of limited economic rationality and the opportunism of the trading partners. This choice may lead to vertical or horizontal concentration of firms in order to minimize transaction costs, not to exploit a monopoly position.

Clearly, then, the firm is not simply a place where factors of production are combined — as neoclassical theory would claim — but a decision-making structure seeking a mode of organization with which to tackle its many contractual problems.

In the end, although the transaction costs approach does advance microeconomic research, it still reduces economic problems to problems of optimization. The pursuit of profit constrained by production costs is simply extended to include the costs generated by the actual transaction. This approach thus adds relatively little to our discussion of basic assumptions, and provides further evidence of a challenge to the significance of economic rationality.

The psychological approach

The basic assumption of economic theory has, understandably, attracted the attention of psychologists (Lea *et al.*, 1987), who use experimental analysis of human behaviour to develop theories which study the unconscious motives for human behaviour, investigate the stages of cognitive development (which vary from individual to individual), and examine social context. The latter not only shapes individual behaviour, but also creates an entire range of symbols expressing the way in which individuals see themselves and are influenced by preconceived ideas.

Research carried out in this vast experimental field has seriously undermined the hypothesis that individuals behave rationally when taking economic decisions. Empirical verification of the hypothesis has been attempted in three separate areas which, unlike the transaction costs approach, are located on the demand side. These concern (a) consumers' purchasing behaviour, (b) their economic decisions when faced with risk and uncertainty, and (c) their intertemporal choices.

At the experimental level, purchasing behaviour reflects a choice between a number of goods. According to economic theory, this choice is governed by an order of preference, defined by the transitivity rule. However, studies show that this is not the case. When humans are faced with a number of goods, their choice is almost always stochastic. Moreover, when purchasers are questioned as to their intentions, their choice of shops and the quantities they wish to buy, their answers reveal extremely stable average behaviour which suggests that habit plays a major part in their decisions.

As for choices made when faced with risk and uncertainty, there is no empirical evidence that human behaviour is rational. The main difficulty is that subjective probability is not identical to objective probability (as represented, for example, by actuarial statistics). The perception of risk and uncertainty varies so greatly from individual to individual that no obvious conclusions can be drawn.

Intertemporal choice, such an important guide to immediate or — through savings — future consumption, involves a number of factors which are difficult to evaluate. Psychological tests show that individuals have a marked preference for immediate consumption, even if future consumption is substantially greater.

It follows that the hypothesis of economic rationality is mostly unhelpful and sometimes wrong. How then are we to interpret the notion of rationality? Cannot all human behaviour be called rational, since it is consistent with at least some rules? Being rational may simply mean behaving intelligently and coherently and making use of the available information. If that is so, then there is no psychological evidence for rejecting rationality. Furthermore, it is not clear what the alternatives are to the hypothesis of economic rationality. Is human behaviour random? That would imply that human behaviour is too complex for us to understand. Is economic behaviour determined by habit? Habit may conceivably have a perfectly rational basis in a social consensus of which the individual is not necessarily aware. Does irrationality exist, but depend on the importance attached to the economic decision? The objection here is that the degree of irrationality then depends on each individual's intelligence or education.

These questions alone show the potential value of collaboration between psychologists and economists. However, a sterile face-off can only be avoided if both sides admit the lack of precision of their experimental results and set aside their conflicting views as to the rationality or irrationality of human behaviour. Such collaboration is essential if one accepts that economic theory must explain social reality rather than merely prove itself consistent with its own logic. The crucial question is a multidisciplinary one: to what extent does the individual influence the economy, and vice versa? This question concerns the issue of motivation — an area in which only collaboration between psychologists and economists can bring progress.

The philosophical approach

The theory of justice (Rawls, 1972) criticizes economic rationality and follows a philosophical tradition going back to Rousseau and Kant. In an attempt to identify the purpose of justice, Rawls proposes the notion of a social contract underlying the functioning of every society.

The purpose of justice essentially concerns the basic structure of society, the distribution of fundamental rights and duties among individuals, and the benefits they obtain from social cooperation.

According to this theory, individuals do not each pursue a utility-maximizing strategy, but are bound by a social contract which determines the terms under which rights and duties are distributed. The fairer this contract is considered to be, the greater the social consensus and thus the greater the economic cohesion of society. In order for such distribution to be fair, three conditions must be satisfied:

1. The first is compliance with the principle of equal freedom. This principle is reflected in the theory of democracy, and has given rise to an economic order based on freedom of trade and industry and private ownership of the factors of production. The more this principle is violated, the greater the resulting economic conflicts and the higher the running costs. Freedom of trade and industry is restricted by increasing trust-forming and concentration of businesses, while the fact that ownership of land or housing is beyond the reach of large segments of the population makes the notion of private ownership largely meaningless. At the same time, the growing divergence between capital and labour as regards occupational and geographical mobility means that the fiscal burden is largely borne by labour. The result is increasing tension in areas such as competition, housing, physical planning and taxation.
2. The second is compliance with the principle of difference: given the existence of inequality, whether natural (for example, differing physical aptitude) or social (differing standards of wealth), there must be no discrimination. The distribution of social and economic inequality must therefore be organized in such a way that there is no discrimination against individuals.

   This principle is important, since it acknowledges that each individual is different, whereas the utilitarian approach assumes that all individuals behave identically. According to the theory of justice, human behaviour must be recognized as having differing degrees of rationality — which seems consistent with the empirical verifications attempted by psychologists.
3. The third is equal opportunity for all, i.e. unrestricted access to education. This represents an non-elitist view of the transmission of knowledge and culture.

Perfect equality depends on total compliance with all three principles, producing a society with minimum transaction costs. This has implications for economic policy, which can no longer be based on a purely rational approach. It will be recalled that, according to the latter, society is the sum total of the actions of individuals who the state assures can maximize their total utility. This reflects a liberal view of society in which the state is confined to a watchdog role. The theory of justice does not challenge this liberal view, but it does assign the state a more active role. Strengthening of democratic laws, explicit and non-discriminatory recognition of individual differences, and strengthening of equal opportunities are the three pillars of such action. To take an economic example, the almost total absence of unemployment in Switzerland reflects — according to the theory — a social consensus which minimizes the confrontation between labour supply and demand, rather than a well-functioning market; the higher rate of unemployment in other countries can likewise be attributed to their greater deviation from the above mentioned principles rather than a poorly functioning labour market.

I have attempted to show how the fragmentation of the hypothesis of rational human economic behaviour has brought theory and practice closer together (see also Etzioni, 1988). It has also led to the beginnings of multidisciplinary research based on the idea that an economic theory must be systematically compared with observable reality if it is not to become dogmatic. If reality does not confirm the theory, the theory should be challenged. Too many present-day economists pursue research as an academic exercise, pushing economic theory to ever more abstract and complex extremes. Yet, if the initial hypothesis remains unchanged, such an approach cannot really be called scientific. Instead, it is ideological; and ideology, however legitimate, can only prevent economics from making further progress. While tools of analysis proliferate, true debate is extinguished — leaving other supposedly less scientific or less qualified souls to tackle the very real problems that face society.

CHAPTER 3

THE INSTRUMENTALIZATION OF ECONOMICS

It has become a commonplace to say that economics borrowed its analytical tools from nineteenth-century physics. Having opted for a deductive approach, it used mathematical language to build models. The years following the Second World War saw the spread of national accounting, an increasing use of statistics and, in particular, the massive development of computer science. All of this undoubtedly helped to widen the gulf between economic theory and practice.

It is therefore worth taking a closer look at this increasing use of mathematics and quantitative methods.

Mathematics and economic theory

The increasing use of mathematics in economics since it was first introduced by Cournot in 1858 can be attributed to the following main factors.

The extreme formality of mathematical language allows us to describe highly complex situations, and compels us to be consistent. In a causal relationship, the results remain derived from initial hypotheses. It is therefore impossible to surreptitiously introduce an additional hypothesis into the argument, as so often happens when using literary language. Finally, since mathematics requires logical deduction, it is particularly suitable for expressing rational behaviour.

Nevertheless, the use of mathematics is frequently criticized. Such criticism is sometimes dismissed as being due to insufficient mastery of mathematical language: people all too readily reject the unfamiliar. The complacency of this explanation, which is often heard from by mathematical economists, reflects its superficiality.

The formal language of mathematics has been described as the antithesis of literary language (Granger, 1960). In my view, such an interpretation is unfortunate. In fact, the two are complementary, although both have at various times been especially fashionable and have been seized on by particular groups of economists to express their own interests. The ascendancy of either may thus simply reflect an opportunistic wish to gain society's temporary favours.

A whole generation of economists received an essentially classical education, in which selection occurred on the basis of proficiency in ancient languages. Economic reasoning, couched as it was in mainly literary language, came to appear increasingly unscientific and to be regarded as an obstacle to serious progress. Its arguments often seemed muddled: value judgements and personal opinions were mixed in with more rigorous definitions and causal relationships. In short, such approaches were dismissed as "normative" — as though there were something unsound about expressing an opinion of any kind. To make matters worse, they made use of rhetoric, which was increasingly suspect.

This led to the emergence of a form of communication based not-only on pictorial matter and symbols, but also the learning and general use of data processing languages.

In economics, the first step in this process was an infatuation with graphs. A mere glance at writings on the pure theory of international trade published in the 1950s provides dazzling evidence of the heights this reached. Graphs began to compete with literary language as a means of describing hypotheses and deducing causal relationships from them. Since graphs are simply illustrations of mathematical functions, they can be seen as having heralded the fashion for mathematics.

Mathematics had long been used as an instrument of analysis, but at first rather peripherally. Only in the positivist climate of the 1950s and 1960s did mathematical language come into its own as one of the main means of expression in the field of economics. At the same time, a more pragmatic approach was developing. Based on business practice, this application-oriented approach at first left little room for analytical inquiry, and instead encouraged examination of a firm's institutional framework and commercial techniques which, particularly in the field of organization, were transformed into abstract theories. As a result, the use of mathematics became widespread in business studies as well. In the fields of imperfect competition and financial markets, for example, business studies and economics linked up.

The spread of mathematics is well illustrated by the extent of its use in economic journals. In 1950, literary language accounted for a full 86% of the *American Economic Review*; by 1981, this had fallen to 36%. Since then, however, the percentage of text has started to rise again (Grubel, Boland, 1986).

We must therefore ask ourselves why it is that mathematics became so important in economics, and whether the revival of literary language since 1981 is a temporary phenomenon or evidence of a new trend.

Mathematicians: a new pressure group

An explanation for the increased use of mathematics can be found in the nature of the academic world, which — in economics and elsewhere — is organized into clans whose main aim is to attain secure positions and then defend them against all comers. The endless infighting that results is a burden on the running of universities. Scientific journals, an ideal medium for the dissemination of knowledge, become the scene of fierce battles of influence, for articles published in such journals are what determine an economist's university career, and are written mainly to pad out the writer's curriculum vitae. The inevitable result is a flood of formal articles of less than obvious relevance to economic policy.

As Grubel and Boland (1986) point out, the same process occurs among non-mathematical economists but is less obvious, since this group is less homogeneous. The rise of mathematics in economics therefore requires a more subtle explanation, supported by the following arguments:

1. There are few options open to mathematical economists apart from an academic career, since most positions in public and private enterprises do not require a qualification in mathematics. Consequently, mathematicians are a stronger pressure group within universities than nonmathematicians.
2. Proficiency in mathematics appears to lend itself to objective assessment, making it an impartial instrument of selection. It will continue to be used as long as universities see their role in transmitting knowledge in terms of selection, which necessarily implies hierarchization of knowledge.

3. The economic writings of mathematicians are addressed to other mathematicians, thereby generating a need for more of the same. Not only are the results of mathematical models accessible to a limited number of economists, but they become an end in themselves, justifying potentially unlimited expansion in the use of mathematics.
4. Since mathematical language is widely used in the natural scences, there is a tendency to associate its use with a scientific approach and to believe that no serious research is possible without it.

Non-mathematical economists must defend their interests in a different way. Either they turn their backs on a university career — since they have plenty of lucrative alternatives — or else they stress the features that tend to guarantee them a secure academic position. In order to justify the orientation of their research towards concrete applications of economic theory, they may be tempted to devote more effort to outside assignments than to their university responsibilities. There are two reasons for this, one internal and the other external to the university. Internally, battles of influence absorb energy which can be more profitably devoted to paid activities outside the university. Indeed, one of the main problems currently facing universities is how to take advantage of the results of such practical research. Externally, the lack of theoretical knowledge among the general public means that economists who express themselves in readily comprehensible language are more popular than those who do not.

A second strategy is to export economic reasoning to other social sciences which are theoretically and instrumentally less well structured. Economists who deal with political, social or legal issues may thus acquire a privileged position which is envied by mathematical economists. However, common though such situations are, they are not in my view the main explanation for why mathematics has come to dominate economics as it has.

Mathematics for its own sake

Current teaching trends present mathematics as something to be learned for its own sake. Here it is worth stressing the instrumental nature of mathematics, which remains a very useful instrument; it is a precise tool for developing hypotheses and drawing theoretical conclusions from them. Contrary to what certain critics claim, mathematics can perfectly well be used to build models of major aspects of individual economic activity. It provides us not so much with a better understanding as with a better *representation* of human behaviour. It is often alleged that literary language is more appropriate than mathematical language for conveying the complexity of human behaviour; in fact, the opposite may well be true.

When it comes to methodology, however, the limitations of mathematics become apparent, since it can be used to build any model whatsoever. The results depend on the initial hypotheses and often conceal ideological bias. What has essentially happened is that our particular value system has been translated into scientific terminology (von Hayek, 1953). As the highly abstract nature of the results prevents their comparison with observable reality, they are often useless for purposes of economic policy.

Since mathematical models express hypotheses based on normative points of view, they can be used to support either intervention or non-intervention. They are only an effective instrument if they lead to the formulation of theories which are capable of being falsified, of being tested empirically. Otherwise, they merely represent a retreat into abstraction whereby the content of economic research grows increasingly scholastic.

The development of quantitative methods

Quantitative methods grew popular in the 1950s as the use of national accounting became widespread. First established by the UN Statistical Commission in 1952, national accounting creates a data bank on the economy by providing a comprehensive framework for the systematic recording of flows and stocks. It is also the origin of input-output and financial transaction tables. Economic analyses, previously mainly qualitative and descriptive, have been enriched by quantitative techniques which encouraged economic and forecasting studies. The growth of computer science has made it possible to handle more complex models, facilitating empirical investigation of theoretical models. At first sight, this would appear to be a positive development. However, at the macroeconomic level it raises new problems, since aggregates are used in the empirical verification of theories. At the microeconomic level, the result has been a good number of strange applications which have spilled over into other social sciences.

The economic analysis of marriage (in sociology) and strategic studies (in political science) are just two examples of such applications. Other examples can be found in the fields of law, medicine and education. First and foremost they represent attempts to give formal expression to problems which, until recently, were held to be too complex for formal model-making. Deductive reasoning will probably develop at the expense of the inductive methods which are still so common in the social sciences, and the common language of computer science will make it easier to envisage new interdisciplinary approaches.

However, if this development is to be fruitful, we need to make sure — as with mathematics — that the tool of computer science is not merely used for its own sake. Once our fascination with this tool fades and we acknowledge the existence of problems whose solution is a pressing social need, it will become clear that the mere formal expression of problems is meaningless. Though it may seem a formidable intellectual challenge — and eminently interdisciplinary — to use the same kind of mathematical function to express the problems that arise in a relationship between two people and between two nations, such an approach may in fact be completely irrelevant. It does not provide a better understanding of either divorce or the arms race.

It is, of course, tempting to build only models for which data are available. However, there is then the risk that the pursuit of truth will be replaced by what we may term token research, and that scientific terminology will serve to disguise ideologies whose symbolism has become an integral part of our lives and has influenced our reasoning to such an extent that we actually believe we have accepted it of our own free will.

Awareness of this trap may have helped to reduce the percentage of formalized language in recent economic journals. Yet it is still too early to tell whether this is a genuine reversal of the trend, or merely the swan-song of literary language before the final triumph of quantitative methods — an unlikely scenario, however, since quantitative methods have proved disappointing. Far from deciding the outcome of theoretical debates in an empirical context, they have increased the confusion already reigning at the theoretical level and failed to produce models that are more workable for the purposes of economic policy. The tendency for academic feuding to take the place of political debate is sufficient evidence of the limitations of such methods. Morever, their economic predictions have proved reliable only in the short term and in the absence of unexpected shocks. In the long term, their main value is an investigatory one. While the scenario approach has provided a clearer picture of the various economic policy options, it has not necessarily made it easier to reach decisions, and initial hopes have given way to a certain disenchantment. In my view, two factors have been neglected from the outset. The first concerns the quantification of variables, and the second the shifting nature of behavioural parameters.

Problems with data

There are two evident problems. One concerns the content of available statistical data, the other the question of how to interpret them.

As regards content, computer techniques make it possible to store any kind of data that provide an empirical observation of economic phenomena. The selection of data then becomes crucial. Information does not just exist; it is determined by the method of selection, which successively filters out (a) non-quantifiable data and (b) data beyond the range of what is expected. In other words, instead of making research more objective, computer techniques disguise its subjective content, which is linked to the manner in which data banks are compiled. Supposedly objective computerized data may again simply be a reflection of our value system, which we had hoped to cast off by resorting to scientific methods.

Partial awareness of this trap has led to a reorientation of quantitative research towards simulation methods in which the data are no longer assumed to be either relevant or objective. Such analyses make it possible to investigate the response of an economic system over time and thus to reconstruct, in simplified form, the economic interactions which data drawn from empirical observations fail to clarify. However, such exercises remain limited to quantifiable phenomena which, in the social sciences, are merely the tip of the iceberg.

As far as interpretations of statistical data are concerned, they are often incorrect, as we have already shown with reference to prices.

The general price level and relative prices are important indicators of both the overall performance of an economy and economic relationships between countries. The former is usually measured by means of a consumer price index, whose compilation regularly gives rise to technical and political controversy. The latter is measured in terms of trade which, as we saw in the previous chapter, are a bone of contention between developed and developing countries. Although statistical and economic theories have shown the insurmountable conceptual difficulties inherent in both indicators, they continue — for lack of an alternative — to be used in empirical research, which fails to provide any objective criteria for settling the resulting disputes.

Here we may add a reference to the so-called marginalist school, which has provided the basis for contemporary economic theory. The strategies of economic agents appear to be guided not so much by total values as by variations in them. For example, the additional cost generated by an increase in production capacity is assumed to be more important to the firm than its total production costs. Yet industrial accounting is unable to express such marginal costs in figures. For the purposes of empirical research, marginal values must be replaced by average ones. Such "good" results as are then obtained are chiefly attributable to the choice of estimating technique. Moreover, while these results may be interesting from a methodological point of view, they cannot be used to verify a theory.

Measurement of behaviour

Investigation of the learning process undergone by economic agents capable of expressing an intertemporal choice has resulted in the theory of rational expectations which was discussed in Chapter 1. This theory stresses the forecasting character of economic decisions, a feature neglected by traditional empirical studies. This introduces the concept of unceasing change in behavioural parameters. Not only are behavioural parameters not considered constant in economics, but theories cannot be verified outside their own particular period. Each moment therefore requires a different explanation and a different forecast.

This criticism is currently a matter of concern in both theoretical and empirical economics. Particularly in the fields of risk and uncertainty and of behavioural science, it has given rise to new research and techniques made workable by data processing. The impetus has not come from data processing, but from a confrontation between theory and practice which requires collaboration between economics and other social sciences if it is to bear fruit.

PART II

Economic policy in crisis

No coherent policy capable of dealing with the economic problems that face society has yet been devised. Economists have conventionally blamed this distressing failure on politicians, but the roots of the problem go far deeper. Most theoretical economists appear unconcerned by this state of affairs, and continue to turn out a numbing stream of economic policy recommendations. Politicians, on the other hand, continue to pursue short-sighted policies whose main aim is to avoid upsetting potential voters.

Despite conflicting opinions, economics has come up with something of a consensus as to what should be done. Yet, ensconced in its ivory tower, it has failed to ensure that its proposals are acceptable to society, which is faced with the task of satisfying the myriad needs of an ever-changing majority. The difficulties encountered in applying economic policies based purely on theory have encouraged the retreat into abstraction that characterizes so much economic writing. Instead of allowing their theoretical results to be compared with practical evidence from society, economists have continued to pile up models which supposedly clarify the basic issues.

Despite the attractive terms the resulting conclusions are couched in, they are frequently of no practical use. The liberal doctrine is often proposed as a panacea, despite the fact that — to a greater or lesser extent — all Western economies have long since gone over to a combined system in which the state plays an essential part.

Part 2 of this book is subdivided into Chapters 4, 5 and 6. In outlining the history of economic policy, Chapter 4 will indicate the role assigned to the state in liberal theory, and will compare this theoretical view with the facts of economic history. Chapter 5 will show that the state has come to be involved in all economic decisions. Yet, despite this, society seems increasingly incapable of taking action to deal with what are readily identifiable problems. An inventory of economic problems and of the action taken by society to deal with them will reveal how utterly inadequate theoretical solutions have been.

The absence of any strategy to deal with today's persistent macroeconomic disequilibrium is evident from the following:

1. In the field of stabilization policy, the system of floating exchange rates is accompanied by repeated promises of greater international coordination. Inflation is reviving despite continuing high unemployment, which survives all efforts to dismiss it as voluntary or to redefine it for purely statistical purposes.

2. In the structural field, there is no will to develop a technological innovation policy. In clinging to non-interventionism, society can only watch helplessly as industry becomes increasingly multinational (as though concentration of businesses automatically led to innovation).

   Nor is there any evidence of a strategy for the training of human resources, in the interests of solidarity. On the contrary, in countries such as the United States, Britain and France the inadequacies of the educational system are worsening, intensifying the social disintegration which has persisted despite policies aimed at redistributing income and wealth. Such policies will increasingly run into the problem of aging populations and will thus be less available for transfers other than between generations.

3. In the field of infrastructure, energy policy faces the problems posed by nuclear energy, while transport policy is failing to resolve the clash of interests between public and private transport. The dogma of private property thwarts efforts to implement a proper land use policy. Finally, the problems of environmental pollution are dealt with by *ad hoc* measures rather than deliberate policy.

This lack of long-term strategy may point to an institutional malaise. In discussing and comparing the main collective decision-making mechanisms, Chapter 6 will directly confront the issue of institutional paralysis resulting from an all-pervasive but powerless state.

CHAPTER 4

THE ROLE OF THE STATE IN ECONOMIC THEORY

In this chapter we will discuss the origins of liberal thinking, and compare liberal economic theory with actual economic policy. The principal economic thinkers often expressed views on policy even though they disregarded it in their theoretical writings. The main reason for this may be that, in the nineteenth century, the leading states were not sufficiently organized to concern themselves with economic matters. By all accounts, the resources available to governments in those days were modest. Taxation did, of course, require an administrative apparatus, but one that bore no comparison to what we know today. Moreover, since the main burden of expenditure was military, the role of the state was largely supervisory, as a result of which it came to be seen as exogenous to the economy. Yet why did economic theory continue to take so little account of government?

Our discussion of the various controversies that have arisen over the issue of state intervention will attempt to show that the principle of non-intervention has regularly been abandoned as a result of shortcomings in liberal doctrine. Nowhere does liberalism appear to have been restricted by growing state influence. The causal relationship cannot be reversed.

The origins of liberalism

Despite its temporary eclipse by Keynes' General Theory, liberal thinking has survived all the criticisms levelled at it. Today's economists are once again seeking salvation in classical theory. This is convincing evidence — if such be needed — of the mythical power of thought. Society may change, but liberal doctrine remains. The secret of its survival may lie in its transformation into an ideology which expresses the interests of the ruling classes so well that they have succeeded in getting it accepted by those they rule. This refers to the process whereby the whole of society has become subjected to the laws of production. As long as a hierarchical structure has prevailed in the organization of production, society has adopted a similar structure in other areas, placing various minorities at a disadvantage.

No attempt will be made here to explain this transformation of liberal doctrine into an ideology. Instead, the purpose will be to show that, in practice, liberal thinking has not been reflected in economic policy. The thesis of this book is a simple one, namely that present-day society would be better served by more pragmatic concepts. Instead, we should think in terms not of pure liberalism, but of highly organized societies which protect individuals by means of special interest groups. References to perfect competition and efficient markets should be replaced by references to workable competition, and trusts and mergers should be considered as part and parcel of our economic system. Unfortunately, wherever this has been attempted, there has been no serious debate; instead, old theories have simply been revived.

Today's dogmatic interpretations were not part of original liberal thinking. They cannot be found in the writings of JohnLocke, Adam Smith and John Stuart Mill, the founders of modern liberalism.

In the seventeenth century, John Locke's concern with the individual and the protection of individual life, freedom and possessions did not lead him to advocate a weak, passive state (Roll, 1973). On the contrary, he considered that supremacy of the state was necessary in order for each individual to be able to fulfil himself. However, in concluding that man's principal concern was not to be dispossessed, he reduced the political content of society to a purely economic dimension. It is therefore not surprising that social struggles have revolved around the redistribution of income and wealth, an issue which is disregarded in this liberal vision of society. At the same time, it should be noted that the England of John Locke (and later of Adam Smith) went through a liberalization process which was to lead to an affirmation of at least the principles of human rights.

Accordingly, as prosperity grew in the eighteenth century, Adam Smith identified the acquisition of wealth as the individual's primary motive. All the state had to do was keep out of the way. Liberalism thus considered the individual as being separate from the state, and required the state to give priority to the accumulation of wealth, particularly by facilitating trade (hence the importance of fairs), maintaining law and order, and protecting property — especially landed property — both at home and, if necessary, abroad.

As the history of British colonialism was to show, wars between states were thus determined by economic goals. At the same time, social issues were left almost entirely to charity, under the institutional responsibility of the Church (Everett and Burtt, 1972).

Not until the nineteenth century was the social dimension introduced into liberal doctrine, by John Stuart Mill, who can thus be described as the most humanistic of the classical economists. However, while attracted by this alternative approach, he never succeeded in reconciling liberalism and socialism. The collectivistic outlook of socialism soon drove him back into the liberal fold, which in fact he had never really left. He saw society as the sum total of subjective individuals under the authority of the state. One of his most noteworthy statements was that it was up to each individual to look after himself, while taking on a certain proportion of public duties. Society thus consisted of individuals pursuing their own interests, and was accordingly organized in such a way that only individual interests were expressed by the state. The idea of a social contract was rejected, since society did not exist as a separate entity. The role of the state was purely representative. In order that such a society should not be destroyed by allpervading selfishness, Mill relied on education to develop nonutilitarian behaviour.

In practice, this liberal view has gradually adjusted to the needs of a society which has grown more and more complex in the wake of increasing industrialization; essentially, however, it is derived from the political arrangements that prevailed in England in the seventeenth and eighteenth centuries, in which the role of the state was rudimentary. Successive adjustments to the growing needs of a highly organized society — specifically including the need for state intervention in social affairs — have led further and further away from the original views expressed by Locke, Smith and Mill. In fact, a truly liberal society has never existed; economic organization has always had to strike a balance between individual subjectivity and social objectivity. The state has always existed in its own right and, as such, has influenced individual behaviour. It has never simply been the sum total of individuals single-mindedly pursuing their own interests.

The survival of liberalism despite this historically manifest contradiction can, I believe, be attributed to two factors: the history of economic policy in capitalist countries, and the rise of the socialist countries.

As society grew more and more specialized, it was also exposed to social criticism based on both Christian morality and Marxist philosophy. The pragmatic adjustment of liberalism to these social changes resulted in a reorganization of the state which failed to eliminate the inequalities that existed. On the contrary, large-scale intervention by the state created new inequalities. The civil service, for example, developed a selfpreserving strategy of its own. The effectiveness of social policies was often curtailed by bureaucracy, which in turn gave rise to pernicious new kinds of behaviour: instead of helping the underprivileged to become independent by freeing them from material constraints, such policies very often created what was to be known as a welfare-state mentality and led voters to regroup accordingly.

The alternative path proposed by Marxist thinkers had its origins in the Russian revolution, whose call for social objectivity to prevail over individual subjectivity culminated in totalitarianism. Here it may be objected that, historically speaking, no revolutionary process has ever been able to bring about an immediate new social order based on a widespread consensus. According to this point of view, the 1917 revolution is still going on. In socialist countries with planned economies, responsibility for planning is assigned to bureaucracies, which in turn have developed their own selfpreserving strategies and have thus acquired discretionary political power.

Liberalism has now been put forward as a means of reversing both trends (the partial socialization of the Western democracies and the advent of collectivism in the socialist countries). Neoliberalism has accordingly turned its back on more than a century of economic history and attempted to erase all memory of the struggles for social justice that have played such an important part in the development of Western society. Such an approach is possible only if society is viewed in purely theoretical terms. One of the most notable advocates of this return to classical theory is Friedrich von Hayek who, together with Milton Friedman, was a major source of inspiration for the Chicago school, which is behind the current theoretical revival.

Von Hayek distrusted state control of society, preferring selfregulating forces which could only operate in totally unrestricted markets. He therefore called for a social order which trusted individuals and did not restrict their freedom of manoeuvre, since each individual was the best judge of his own interests. As with the classical liberals, the common interest was simply the sum total of individual interests. The notion of society as a community was utopian, and had already led John Stuart Mill to reject the idea of a social contract. Since the state was not an entity in its own right, democracy was the only available mechanism for settling clashes between individual interests. The hierarchical nature of this democratic mechanism and the frequent absence of competition in economic transactions did not strike von Hayek as sufficient reason to seek a middle way. Mankind was faced with a simple choice between collectivism and liberalism (von Hayek, 1944). In my view, however, the choice is by no means so clear-cut. Indeed, the liberal view that only market forces can solve society's problems leads to a new form of alienation — an individualistic society which denies all notion of community and exposes the individual to a sense of solitude and existential *angst.*

Given that the market is only one of a number of social decision-making mechanisms and the economy is only one component of the social whole, economic theory needs to take account of social organization. The evidence is all around us that there *is* a middle way.

Liberal theory and economic reality

Classical theory is clearly dictated by the problem of allocation of factors of production, two of which are taken into account: one, which by definition is constant, is land; the other, considered as variable, is labour. How do these factors influence the rate of growth of the economy?

This question concerns changes in rent for land and the wage rate. The relative reward to factors of production and the variation therein were to be key elements in the economic mechanisms of the neoclassical model. According to classical economists, then, the division of national income into wages and rent was responsible for the process of capital accumulation and ultimately for the economic growth of private companies. Competition was needed in order, through division of labour, to increase specialization and thus real income. It was specialization that made the problem of trade central to the debate and defined the market as the place where such trade occurred. The setting of prices in such a market subsequently raised the issue of how the value of goods involved in a transaction was to be determined.

In this theoretical interpretation, the state clearly had a watchdog function. Its role in the economy was a passive one, guaranteeing the institutional conditions in which markets could operate. However, this theoretical interpretation is not as unchallengeable as it may appear.

The education debate

For centuries, education was in the hands of the Church. Though not exactly private, it was certainly not considered a matter for the community. According to liberal theory, education must be subjected to competition and the price of educating a child must be determined in a private market. In mid-nineteenth century debate, state intervention was a key issue. The identification of human capital as a new factor of production led to a vigorous controversy which reflected the education system then prevailing in countries such as Scotland and England. In Scotland there was no regulation of any kind; teachers were paid directly by the child's parents. In England, on the other hand, the teaching profession was governed by legislation (West, 1964). Not surprisingly, the liberal views of Adam Smith — himself a Scot — were preferred to Mill's arguments in favour of public education. At this stage, it is worth reviewing the main arguments concerning the possibilities of state intervention.

According to Adam Smith, only the payment of a certain income directly to the teacher could guarantee good teaching, which in turn would attract more pupils. Teachers whom parents considered better would thus earn more money. This view, though widely shared, came under criticism in the case of medical training.

In order to protect patients, the state regulated the admission criteria for medical schools as well as the conditions of medical training. Adam Smith objected to this on grounds which have become a cornerstone of liberal thinking. He maintained that regulation of any kind merely strengthened the monopoly position of the medical schools and raised the price of medical care. Instead, medical training must remain in private hands and consumer sovereignty be allowed to prevail.

In the specific case of medicine, Smith's views were not adopted, but Victorian England preferred his arguments to Mill's when it came to private education. In questioning whether the purchaser was always competent to assess a good properly, Mill was the first to envisage the possibility of market failure; if the purchaser was not competent to make the necessary assessment, competition and market forces could not operate, and state intervention was justified. In the case of schools, the quality of education could not be properly assessed by the uneducated, so education must be public. This kind of argument was adopted and put into practice in countries which succeeded in creating a system of public services. Application of the principle of nondenominational, public, free education thus gave the state a more important and more active role than classical liberalism had allowed for. The state, as an entity in its own right, was required not only to protect the weaker members of society, but also to express the notion of community solidarity.

The introduction of public education was a clear example of economic policy. State intervention influenced the qualifications of the working population, and for the first time the state acted as an investor, using human capital to influence the process of economic growth. At the same time, by guaranteeing universal access to knowledge, it brought about a major redistribution of income which was later to reduce the impact of social confrontation and thus the costs of running the economy. The current difficulties facing the education system are only incidentally due to the fact that it is public. What has really happened is that the recent proliferation in methods of communication has destroyed the education system's monopoly on the transmission of knowledge. The resulting loss of prestige has created a problem of motivation among both teachers and pupils. Asimilar crisis of motivation can be found in countries with a private education system. Countries that have opted for public education would gain nothing by reviving classical liberalism.

Imperfect competition

Liberal theory assumes competition as a pre-condition for the operation of market forces. Naturally, this did not escape the attention of economic theorists; as early as 1838, Cournot had built theoretical models of monopoly and duopoly (Blaug, 1985). Soon afterwards, the economic assessment of public works was discussed by Jules Dupuit of the *Ecole des Ponts et Chaussées* in Paris (Dupuit, new edition, 1933). Not only was this the first analysis of public works, but it also raised the issue of how to set the price of a good in which the state has a natural monopoly.

Monopoly is less than optimal in terms of resource allocation and forces consumers to pay a higher price than they would under conditions of competition. It also generates economic rent which the monopolist strives to protect. Why does this lead to alliances between producers and politicians rather than constant efforts by society to eliminate monopolies? Adam Smith condemned monopolistic practices — in line with liberal thinking — but said nothing about how to deal with them. Nevertheless, the liberal condemnation of monopoly has led the capitalist countries to adopt competition policies.

In both cases, the policing role of the state is reinforced. In their radical efforts to combat monopolies, some societies have gone ahead and nationalized the firms concerned. This touches on the legal issues surrounding ownership of the factors of production, since nationalization clearly involves public ownership.

However, even under a liberal system, there is no longer any real dispute as to the need for public ownership in the case of products whose nature and associated technology make them the subject of a natural monopoly (examples being water and electricity). This has produced a middle way between the regulation and nationalization of monopolies.

This middle way was discussed by Alfred Marshall in *Principles of Economics* (1890), who first raised the idea of a public good, whose price must be set outside the market. In order to "confiscate" monopolistic profit, the state may resort to taxation. This increases the importance of the state, which thus obtains additional financial resources. The dilemma is how to pursue an active competition policy while keeping state influence to an absolute minimum.

Given the importance attached by classical economists to competition, it is rather surprising that the regulation of imperfect competition is not more keenly discussed. The tendency towards mergers was a recognized phenomenon as early as the nineteenth century (certain companies were set up as multinationals from the very beginning in order to restrict competition). Previously, mercantilism had had the same purpose. It can, of course, be argued that conditions of imperfect competition are constantly changing, if only because new products are constantly being introduced. Technical progress thus automatically restores a certain degree of competition.Internationally this phenomenon is even more noticeable, and agreements between producers are often undermined by international competition. The current trend among liberal economists is therefore to shift the emphasis away from the number of competitors towards barriers to market entry. However, experience in the period since the Second World War — in which international markets have become more open — points to an increase in international mergers. Instead of restoring competition, technological development has led to new forms of organization which traditional models fail to recognize.

Mechanization

No other economic issue has stirred up passions quite as much as mechanization. The roots of violent social confrontation can undoubtedly be found in the profound industrial changes that occurred in the nineteenth century. The history of mechanization provides the most eloquent evidence so far of the social dimension of economics. Mechanization resulted in structural underemployment which was particularly apparent in the short term. As politicians are only too aware, such abrupt events often have a striking effect on public opinion. Not surprisingly, it has been argued (Berg, 1982) that the unemployment caused by mechanization was what led to the long-term Marxist view of an impoverished working class.

Classical economists are divided in their opinions on this matter. While Ricardo pointed to the benefits of industrialization, John Stuart Mill called for direct state intervention to control the technological changes caused by mechanization. Such a view is surprising, especially from a writer who contributed so much to liberal theory.

Ricardo's demonstration was based on the model of a closed economy with limited land. The rate of capital growth associated with mechanization and the rate of land growth reflected in the growth of the working population were therefore comparable. Growth in such an economy thus left real wages unchanged. However, the growth of capital and population led to the cultivation of less fertile pasture, causing a fall in marginal rates of profit owing to the higher costs of production on the less fertile land. In other words, the constraint of limited land together with capital accumulation and population increase led to diminishing returns. The increasing population also created greater demand for food, driving its price up and thus making it possible to cultivate less fertile land. Conversely, a fall in demand led to a fall in the price of cultivated land, which therefore returned to pasture. Ricardo made a distinction between fixed capital and working capital. Fixed capital was associated with land, and working capital with labour. If mechanization raised the ratio of fixed to working capital, the worker could keep his job by accepting a fall in his real wages.

This interpretation was attacked by John Stuart Mill. Not only did he challenge the idea that the transformation of fertile land into pasture was simply a matter of substituting capital for labour, but he dismissed Ricardo's view that mechanization would lead to the reabsorption of redundant manpower when demand rose following a fall in the price of goods. A fall in prices did not automatically lead to higher investment. In other words, increased demand for goods did not necessarily stimulate employment (Blaug, 1985).

The advantage of increased demand for goods needed to be set against the disadvantage of a fall in the purchasing power of workers made redundant by mechanization. Even though in the long term mechanization led to a fall in prices, stimulating production and thus absorbing the unemployment, in the short term the workers clearly suffered. Moreover, prices would fall only if there were perfect competition. If mechanization occurred under monopoly conditions, prices could remain unchanged and monopolistic profit would increase. This increase in profit had two effects: it led to an even more unequal distribution of income, and it stimulated demand through the spending of the extra profit, without any need for a fall in prices. Production increased to meet the additional demand, and ultimately the redundant worker was taken on again. Mill's liberal position led to the realization that a problem of short-term adjustment might arise. It therefore assumed a need for policies to adjust production structures, the payment of unemployment benefit during the transitional period, and the retraining of redundant workers. In each of these areas, greater state intervention in the economy was unavoidable.

This initial argument regarding mechanization is still regularly used in support of technical progress, most recently with regard to electronics and computer science. The unemployment rate in the OECD countries, averaging some 11% in 1987, needs to be seen in this light. The resulting social unrest is less serious than it would have been in the nineteenth century, thanks to the state's role in providing unemployment insurance and (re)training — a role currently challenged only by neo-liberals who have not read their classics properly.

Factory legislation

In the nineteenth century, the social friction caused by increasing industrialization and the advent of mechanization was aggravated by appalling working conditions. The privately-owned factories failed to guarantee the most basic standards of health and safety. Child labour was widespread and, to take one example, the life expectancy of Swiss metalworkers in the mid-nineteenth century was just 35 years (Bergier, 1983).

However, classical economists were not by any means agreed that the state should intervene, and a consensus only began to appear towards the middle of the nineteenth century. Britain's first Factory Act, which dates from 1833, was mainly intended to regulate child labour, though not on economic or humanitarian grounds — instead, the central argument was that children did not have the necessary discernment to make decisions about how they were employed.

As far as other aspects of factory working conditions were concerned, there was considerable opposition to state intervention. This was based on the liberal doctrine that an individual with responsibility for his or her own choices was the best judge of economic conditions. There were those who felt that a reduction in working hours without a corresponding reduction in wages would simply put firms out of business. Others were afraid that the working class would become work-shy. Few economists saw such measures as a means of increasing productivity; the majority thought that wages would fall and that emigration would increase.

Oddly enough, John Stuart Mill, who favoured state intervention in order to prevent over-rapid mechanization, was this time hostile to such intervention. He was afraid that the brunt of any reduction in working hours would be borne by the weakest categories of workers and that unemployment would increase, especially among women. Ultimately, state intervention in the running of firms would only add to the difficulties of those it was intended to protect. However, Mill did acknowledge the need to protect individuals, not so much to supplant their judgement as to enable them to use it.

Essentially, then, classical economists criticized state intervention on two grounds. The first was that a decrease in working hours would lead to economic ruin unless accompanied by a decrease in nominal wages. The second concerned the freedom of contract of individuals capable of discernment. However, one cannot help being struck by the fact that the age of discernment varied considerably, and increased not in accordance with the immutable principles of liberal theory, but in response to social pressure which grew as economic performance improved.

Moreover, classical theories eventually — albeit reluctantly — reflected the spirit of the age by acknowledging a link between wages and working hours. However, no distinction was made between short-term and long-term effects. There was as yet no theory of the firm seen as a decision-making centre rather than a production function, and the theory of growth remained too abstract to produce workable economic policy recommendations.

This is still the case today. Faced with the need for more flexible organization of the labour market — particularly with regard to part-time work, job-sharing and other kinds of active involvement — economic theory continues to insist that the reward to labour must be based on marginal productivity. This is the reason why one whole chapter of this book (Chapter 8) is devoted to a discussion of the notion of productivity, which likewise conflicts with the idea of a minimum wage.

It is interesting to compare the arguments put forward by economists with those of psychologists, who consider group membership and the resulting social integration more important motives than pay in the decision to work. Recent feminist demands thus coincide with Mill's concerns regarding female unemployment, though the feminist movement does not share his opposition to state intervention in the running of firms.

Railway nationalization

The discrepancy between liberal theory and economic practice is particularly well illustrated by the advent of the railways. The example of France (Doukas, 1945) shows that the development of the railway system was never the exclusive preserve of private enterprise. Up to 1887, private initiatives in this area received massive state subsidies. Even during the period of vigorous growth that preceded the outbreak of the First World War, the *réseau de l'Ouest* (Western Railways), though entirely in private hands, applied for state aid. The state's military concerns made it all the more willing to comply. This was the beginning of two phenomena which have continued to influence economic arrangements to this day.

The first concerns the enormous financial resources which were required by the railways, and which were a contributing factor in the expansion of the banking system. Industrialization and the establishment of an appropriate infrastructure also led to the creation of central banks, another aspect of increasing state influence.

The second concerns state regulation in the field of economic infrastructure, which does not clash with liberal theory as long as it is limited to coordination. However, it parts company with liberal thinking as soon as it introduces the principle of public goods. Both paths have been explored, ranging from concessions for private operations to full-blown nationalization. However, it is impossible to tell which country has benefited most in terms of prosperity. The classical debate on railway nationalization has nevertheless encouraged a view of the state as responsible, through its increasing role in land use planning, for new channels of communication resulting in conditions of trade that extend beyond those recognized by traditional market theory.

The consequence of the above two phenomena has been the emergence of an alliance between the state and private enterprise, in which competition is less and less evident. A striking example is provided by the arms industry. While acknowledging the role of the state in military affairs, liberals do not define it in economic terms. Industrialization and the mass production it allows have altogether changed the nature of weaponry and led to increasing links between the state and the economy. Overriding state interests conflict with liberal thinking, which assumes that each individual has a rational awareness of where his interests lie. The arms industry is totally at variance with the notion of society as the sum total of private interests expressed through competitive markets.

Issuing rights

The history of monetary intervention has been a long one, culminating in total state control justified on the grounds that currency is not just an ordinary good. Non-market control of currency is justified by its role as a universal means of payment which depends on public confidence.

If currency is considered different from goods and services that are bought and sold in a competitive market, exceptional arrangements must also be made for the international exchange of domestic currencies. This function was originally performed by the gold standard, which was the international monetary system up to the outbreak of the First World War.

At that point a number of countries, fearing depletion of their gold reserves, declared that their currencies were no longer freely convertible into gold. The widespread exchange controls which followed were simply a protectionist measure which made international trade subject to quotas. Such measures clashed with liberal theory and could only be justified by the exceptional nature of the war economy.

After the First World War, a system of flexible exchange rates was adopted. This system was theoretically more liberal, since it depended entirely on market forces. However, in practice it did not work, since the scale of exchange rate variations made the nominal evaluation of trade flows extremely difficult. Governments therefore sought a return to a kind of gold standard which would reconcile the shortage of gold with the trade flow advantages of the pre-1914 system. Two similar standards were then adopted: the gold exchange standard in the sterling area, and elsewhere the gold bullion standard, in which domestic currencies were defined in relation to another currency which remained convertible into gold. In both case, convertibility of banknotes into gold was limited.

Both systems were wrecked by the Great Depression in the 1930s, and were replaced by two tried and tested formulas, one of them highly liberal, the other highly interventionist. On the eve of the Second World War, Britain adopted a system of flexible exchange rates, while Germany and Italy resorted to exchange controls. The latter system became widespread during the Second World War, since it allowed international trade flows to be subjected to quotas and other controls in accordance with the needs of a war economy. In 1944, the gold exchange standard was revived by international agreement. The dollar replaced sterling and effectively became the universal standard, while itself being defined in terms of gold. American political hegemony and economic power thus automatically became the basis for the new international monetary system. Self-regulation of money markets made way for considerations of power.

Growing worldwide disequilibrium, and in particular the American external debt after the Vietnam war, led to the abolition of this system, which was felt to be too restrictive. This was because countries which had failed to take effective measures to reduce their external deficit were required to transfer gold to creditor nations. For that to happen, creditor nations had to insist on the debts being converted into gold instead of being held in dollars. The United States responded to such demands by unilaterally abolishing the convertibility of the dollar, leading in 1971 to a new period of flexible exchange rates with the same disadvantages as before.

The foregoing demonstrates both the economic and the political role of the state in monetary affairs. These growing links between economics and politics are, however, the result rather than the cause of classical liberalism's decline.

Income redistribution policy

The debate concerning equity introduces a distinction between the positive and normative aspects of economic theory. The competitive market system, inspired by liberal thinking, generates the greatest possible economic welfare. It stresses the criterion of efficiency in the allocation of productive resources. This is simply a technical problem modelled as a production function which must be maximized and is constrained by the costs of resource acquisition by a firm. This illustrates the positive aspect of economic theory.

Unfortunately, distribution cannot be subjected to the same criterion. Economic theory then becomes normative, and resorts to value judgements. Equitable distribution remains an ideological issue.

This conflict is apparent from the literature. John Stuart Mill, who was perturbed by social inequality (Mill, 1940), made a distinction between a law of production dictated by technical conditions and a law of distribution dictated by institutional conditions. Whereas the first responded to self-regulating mechanisms, the second could be changed by human decisions, even under a system of private ownership of the factors of production. Mill's approach was thus an attempt to combine the positive and normative aspects of economic theory into a single liberal viewpoint.

Although the causal link between the fields of production and distribution cannot be denied, there is no doubt that this approach to the problem greatly influenced classical thinking with regard to social inequality and made it receptive to reforms in this area. If efficiency and equity could be separated, the discipline of economics could become a true science with laws of its own and would after all be able to apply positive criteria to the problem of distribution.

Clearly, however, efficiency and equity cannot be separated. Economics will always be to some extent normative. This reassertion of the link between efficiency and equity indicates the need for an arbiter to lay down rules of equity. This confirms the economic role of the state, and has led to the development of social-democratic systems which combine features of both liberalism and collectivism.

Recognition of the role of the state in reducing inequality has created a particularly heavy burden in the form of social policy. Inequalities in education and training have — in countries which have adopted the principle of public education — led to policies which ensure broad access to education. Inequalities due to differing natural aptitude have led to protective legislation designed to ensure that such differences do not result in discrimination. Here it must be acknowledged that we do not know to what extent natural differences influence individuals' material success. Yet the fact that legislative backing is needed for something so self-evident as the principle of equal pay for equal work shows the extent to which institutionalized inequalities persist within our society. These include inequality not only between men and women, but also between generations and between the healthy and the sick (despite substantial social insurance schemes). Inequality due to inherited wealth is countered by progressive taxation and estate duty. This huge area of social policy is thus largely characterized by treatment of symptoms, while the underlying causes remain untouched by the resulting public debate. Taking the example of inequality due to inherited wealth, investigation of the causes forces us to challenge what is perhaps the one surviving element of liberal thinking, namely private ownership of the factors of production, and especially land. One of the causes of such inequality is undoubtedly land rent, which is a major contributing factor in the inequality found in most developing countries.

In maintaining private ownership of the factors of production, Western society has clung to the liberal view that equity cannot be achieved without efficiency. This view, it should be noted, acknowledges that there are limits to what redistribution policies can achieve. To prove this, let us imagine that all incomes are taxed at 100% and are then redistributed in equal shares to each individual. It is a fair bet that individual initiative — and thus the total income to be distributed — will diminish. However, the scale of state intervention in this area remains a normative issue. There is no economic technique which will enable us to determine its actual extent. For this reason, theories about optimal rates of taxation must surely be regarded as meaningless. At best, they express value judgements; what they do not do is provide objective criteria for fiscal policy.

Historically speaking, it must be stressed that the introduction and spread of social policies were decided by majority votes following confrontations between conflicting special interest groups. The growing importance of the state is thus the result of a normative process rather than economic model-making.

Stabilization policy

Although economic theory has gradually moved away from the liberal ideal and created more scope for state intervention, the principle of a self-regulating competitive market economy has not been essentially challenged. The only such challenge came from Keynesian theory during the Great Depression of the 1930s. In his *General Theory of Employment, Interest and Money* (1936, p. 380), John Maynard Keynes wrote:

"Whilst ... the enlargement of the functions of government ... would seem to a nineteenth-century publicist or to a contemporary American financier to be a terrific encroachment on individualism, I defend it, on the contrary, both as the only practicable means of avoiding the destruction of existing economic forms in their entirety and as the condition of the successful functioning of individual initiative."

In other words, safeguarding the principles of liberalism requires active state involvement to combat cyclical fluctuations. However, it is important to note that Keynesian theory never advocated permanent state intervention. Permanent intervention remains a normative issue. In any case, economists who are now doing everything in their power to revive the classical model dismiss all Keynesian theory as heresy, regardless of the time frame.

Any modern textbook of economics tells us that the classical model is essentially summed up in Say's law. According to this "law", producers will immediately spend the receipts from the sale of their products, thereby stimulating demand for other products. Supply thus creates its own demand. If supply uses up all available productive resources, demand will simply absorb it at prices determined by the self-regulating mechanism of the competitive market. If, however, producers hold on to their receipts and wait for better circumstances in which to spend them, the result — according to Keynes — may be insufficient demand and thus disequilibrium in the market for goods and services, which will no longer be able to ensure full employment. This provides a theoretical explanation for the massive unemployment that occurred in the 1930s. Only if the state intervenes by substituting its own demand for inadequate private demand can such unemployment be reversed.

Although it required a number of exponents, the eventual impact of Keynesian theory was enormous. Such theoretical activity contrasted sharply with relative apathy in practical terms. Apart from a certain amount of public spending which the Roosevelt administration rather belatedly approved in order to combat unemployment, the United States did little to put Keynesian theory into practice. In Germany, unemployment was absorbed by motorway building, but the chief motive here was martial rather than cyclical. The Keynesian revolution mainly took place in the minds of economists, and allowed governments to justify their involvement in the running of the economy. This led to much mechanistic talk of cyclical fluctuations being "fine-tuned", not so much in order to keep the economy close to full employment as to justify growing government budgets.

The above comparison of classical theory with various main points of economic history forces us to conclude that classical theory is an increasingly unsuitable tool for the economic and social organization of a modern state. Classical theory is derived from the notion of a rudimentary state which belongs to the institutional context of an earlier age. Furthermore, its presentation in the form of abstract models has hardly helped it to take explicit account of economic policy. Instead of being a central factor in economic models, more active state involvement has been accepted only with great reluctance, and government is still often treated as an exogenous variable. At the same time, the desire to make economics a true science, in keeping with the positivist spirit of the nineteenth century, has widened the gulf between the positive and normative aspects of economic theory. This may explain why the growing importance of the state has been treated as a normative phenomenon which is subject to the political balance of power. In other words, if policy recommendations based on economic models have not always been implemented, this must have been due to political value judgements. Yet the political dimension is now almost universally acknowledged to be an integral part of economics.

However, the definition of this dimension poses formidable problems in the social sciences, since the notion of the state is basically extremely vague.

The state is an entity made up of numerous objects and phenomena which have economic implications. There is little point in considering it as something existing in its own right. Instead, it makes more sense to concentrate on more limited targets and build limited models accordingly.

There are, moreover, various schools of thought which attempt to take account of the fact that the state, seen as a public entity, is becoming more complex and differentiated. Examples of this are provided by decision theory in the field of business studies and by organization theory in sociology. The theory of bureaucracy, which will be discussed in Chapter 6, is merely one rather ideological aspect of this. Political science has contributed pressure group theory which, in its most abstract form, defines equilibrium in terms not of market mechanisms but of the power struggle between conflicting groups (Bentley, 1908). Coalition theory, which has grown out of game theory, and the theory of industrial conglomerates in the international sphere (arms) and the domestic sphere (agriculture) are further examples of such limited models of the state.

The state thus controls all kinds of constraints which lead it to intervene in the economy; it does so by guiding individual and collective choices and by selecting and/or excluding particular agents or choices (if only by penal legislation). It supposedly "accepts" certain externalities such as pollution or deterioration of the environment, and "regulates" (if necessary by repression) certain social costs such as unemployment, immigration and education.

It should also be emphasized that the state intervenes differently at different periods. This is illustrated by the shift from a peacetime economy to a war economy. War has probably been the decisive factor in events this century, particularly in the field of economics (Keynesian theory being no exception). The way in which economists nowadays disguise military or arms expenditure or treat it as "normal" is quite striking, and contrasts sharply with the position taken by liberals such as Adam Smith.

Even Keynesian theory, which assigns the state a more active role in regulating the business cycle, does not clearly define the interaction between economics and politics. Maintenance of a given level of consumption may be a political or cultural imperative and a democratic requirement as much as an aspect of full-employment policy. This interdependence is well illustrated by the riots that have followed price increases in various North African countries.

Finally, historical interruptions in the functioning of the state must also be stressed. Attention will be drawn in subsequent chapters to the institutional paralysis which seems to threaten present-day government. Such paralysis is only acceptable if the cost of change is considered politically or culturally excessive when compared with the status quo — and this applies to all kinds of societies, even those where there is no such thing as a state. On the other hand, there are times when the state or its components are spurred to action by certain symptomatic phenomena. The only general rule here is that the status quo is usually felt to be safer and therefore less costly.

In my opinion, we have now reached a crossroads. While the idea of an all-pervading state may reassure the electorate, it also contains the threat of institutional paralysis, which we cannot afford to ignore much longer.

CHAPTER 5

THE ALL-PERVADING STATE

It is no exaggeration to say that, by the end of the Second World War, the state was involved in almost all economic decisions. However, behind the scenes, preparations were already under way for a return to the ideal of classical theory. These preparations can be explained in the context of the cold war between the two superpowers in the 1950s. In the United States, theories of individual freedom were widely supported, even though individual freedom was not in any way threatened by the state. It is, however, threatened by an impersonal working environment; hence the adoption of a huge range of economic policies which, instead of resulting in coherent action, have caused increasing confusion as to their effectiveness and goals.

Instruments of economic policy

There is practically no area of state intervention which has not been the subject of recommendations derived from economic models. A common feature of such models is their stress on incentives designed to change the behavioural parameters of economic agents. State intervention, on the other hand, frequently takes the form of regulations or bans.

Below, we will be reviewing (a) measures designed to ensure the basic conditions for the operation of a market economy, (b) structural and cyclical measures, and (c) income redistribution and social insurance measures. We will thus be examining the entire range of state intervention, including the kinds of intervention justified by both classical and Keynesian theory, as well as others totally ignored by economic theory.

Competition policy

Competition policy has borrowed the following main principles from economic theory:

1. the maintenance of competition in domestic markets by means of legislation on restrictive trade practices;
2. the maintenance of international free trade by means of trade policy.

In order to maintain free competition, the state seeks to combat imperfect competition in all its forms. The need for appropriate legislation has caused economists to yield responsibility in this area to specialized lawyers.

The various kinds of legislation illustrate the contradictory nature of views concerning the role of the state in a market economy. If the operation of market forces can only be ensured by increasing state intervention, not even the most liberal of thinkers can continue to confine the state to a passive role.

As regards trade policy, standard neoclassical theory holds that free trade will provide the highest possible real income. Here economic theory clearly reflects the extent to which our value system relies on international trade. Yet practical reality hasled to a whole range of protectionist measures designed to inhibit the free international movement of goods and services. The main aims of protectionism are to limit the amount of external trade and to protect domestic industry. Interestingly, however, trade policy also illustrates the links between economic reasoning and political interests. Simple microeconomic models show that gains from trade will accrue to producers in exporting countries and to consumers in importing countries. Therefore, given that producers have more political "clout" than consumers, it is easier to advocate a free-trade policy in a country with a trade surplus than in one with a deficit. Governments will thus tend to follow the advice of producers when deciding what protectionist measures to take against imports that are competing with domestic industry (something which would in fact merely transfer the gains from trade from producers to consumers).

Both anti-trust policy and trade policy are evidence that the state has had to intervene by means of legislation in the operation of the market economy. There is thus a precedent for state intervention in the business cycle. However, such active intervention has set off an ideological controversy which remains highly relevant to the current theoretical debate, in which analysis in terms of "welfare loss" must make way for analysis which takes account of the influence of special interest groups.

Stabilization policy

State intervention to regulate cyclical fluctuations at first concentrated on measures to combat recession and the associated unemployment. The remedy that emerged from the theoretical debate was an attempt to control overall demand, which comprises domestic components such as consumption and public and private investment, plus an external component in the form of exports of goods and services. Since the latter are largely beyond domestic jurisdiction, they are not usually the subject of direct economic policy. The four types of policy that exist — fiscal policy, monetary policy, exchange rate policy and income policy — overlap and indirectly influence one another.

1. *Fiscal policy*

The aim of fiscal policy is to achieve a level of economic activity at which full employment prevails, essentially by varying public spending.

This instrument originally led economic policymakers to believe that cyclical fluctuations could be completely controlled. It was all too readily forgotten that fiscal policy was only designed for situations of underemployment and that the following wellknown obstacles are likely to arise:

(i) Fiscal policy must be timely, which necessitates advance knowledge of how the business cycle will develop. This raises the thorny problem of forecasting. It is by no means unknown for the business cycle to change direction following exceptional events such as the abrupt and unexpected increase in oil prices in 1973. Furthermore, public decision-making mechanisms are sluggish, and both information and implementation suffer from a time-lag. Experience shows that the effects of fiscal policy tend to come too late: overall expenditure does not start to rise until after the recession is over. All this does is stimulate demand which is already rising anyway.

(ii) Public spending cannot be varied simply to suit the business cycle, since it is itself partly dependent on economic trends. Not only is it the result of a lengthy political decision-making process, but it remains subject to state budget constraints, since increased budget deficits lead to increasing debt service and represent expenditure which is non-productive from the point of view of acquiring public goods.

(iii) The multiplier effect may be counteracted either by a change in consumer behaviour or by a crowding-out effect whereby an increase in public spending leads to a fall in private demand. This may occur when increased public spending and the accompanying need for finance cause the interest rate to rise, discouraging private investment. However, the interest rate is affected not only by public and private behaviour, but also by conditions prevailing on the money market.

2. *Monetary policy*

The purpose of monetary policy is first of all to regulate the business cycle — which means adjusting the money supply according to potential output — but also to stabilize the general price level and stimulate economic growth. Attempts to achieve all three at once are likely to prove self-defeating, but for the purposes of cyclical regulation the standard procedure is to reduce the money supply when there is inflation and expand it when there is deflation.

However, monetary policy also runs into a number of obstacles:

(i) The first is the difficulty encountered by the central bank in controlling the money supply. Evidence of this difficulty can be seen in efforts to find an appropriate monetary aggregate in the form of a statistical series which will serve as an indicator.

(ii) The second concerns the link between the money supply and the real economy. This has given rise to a mass of literature on the nature of money. To cut a long story short, monetary policy can only be effective if demand for money responds to the interest rate and if money circulates at a relatively steady rate.

(iii) The third concerns the degree to which the central bank is free to adjust the money supply in response to purely cyclical requirements. Recent experience shows that, in the case of small economies which are relatively open to international trade, adjustment of the money supply to cyclical requirements will be prevented by the interaction between the money market and the foreign exchange market.

3. *Exchange rate policy*

This involves intervention of the central bank in the foreign exchange market, and creates a dilemma of monetary policy in which governments are torn between maintaining a stable general price level and maintaining a stable exchange rate. This dilemma recurs throughout the discussion of current macroeconomic disequilibrium. If a way out of the dilemma is not found, the result may well be further protectionism and, in the long run, a greater risk of recession.

4. *Income policy*

Income policy may well have originated in the difficulties encountered in implementing budgetary and monetary policy. It consists of control of the prices of goods and services, together with a wage freeze.

Since inflation involves a rise in the general price level, all that is necessary is to prevent such a rise, unless it is due to a change in production. Since wages are the main production cost, they must likewise be prevented from rising. However, the experience of France in 1982 shows that such policies are unlikely to work, since they do not eliminate the underlying causes of an excess of demand over total supply, but merely attack the symptoms. Thus, while income policies may temporarily relieve inflationary pressure, they do not have any real economic effect.

The above four instruments of stabilization policy show the theoretical complexity of state intervention in this area. Not surprisingly, the usefulness of stabilization policy continues to be disputed by both economic and political theorists.

Structural policy

The plethora of laws and regulations in this area suggests the influence of special interest groups rather than the application of economic reasoning, whether classical or Keynesian. Neoclassical models presuppose instant adjustments, on the assumption that there is perfect occupational and geographical mobility of the factors of production; this being so, state intervention can only interfere with the mechanisms of adjustment. Keynesian theory, on the other hand, concentrates on cyclical fluctuations, but has nothing to say about structural matters. It is therefore not surprising that these have been the subject of research in other areas such as law, in order to identify criteria that will serve as a basis for legislation.

There are four types of structural policy:

1. *Agricultural policy*. This is the area in which state intervention in the economy has been most dominated by private interests. Here economic reasoning has seldom led to policies that are in accordance with the objectives. One reason for this is the often contradictory nature of the various goals which agricultural policy is supposed to achieve. How, for instance, can mechanization (which requires large farms) be reconciled with the maintenance of small-scale family farming? How can consumers be ensured a cheap food supply if farmers are to be guaranteed incomes comparable with those paid in industry? How can the government protect agriculture against international competition and at the same time pursue a free-trade policy? And, finally, how can the environment be protected against the ravages of increasingly intensive farming?
   Countless attempts have been made to square these various circles, including protectionism, income policies and measures to improve soil and product quality, not to mention investment financing and

land consolidation measures. In short, since virtually every aspect of agriculture is now subject to state control, it has become absurd to talk of "markets" for agricultural produce.

2. *Industrial policy*. This area is effectively ignored by neoclassical theory, but the state has nevertheless attempted to respond to the various special interest groups that have emerged from the competitive market. In the previous chapter we saw that classical economists were not necessarily hostile to temporary state aid in order to cushion the social impact of sudden technological change, particularly in the labour market. The history of mechanization in the nineteenth century provides plenty of suitable examples. The numerous measures adopted in this area by a country such as Switzerland represent nothing less than permanent state intervention (Bürgenmeier, 1985).
   However, despite this abundance of legislation, one area has been neglected, namely technological innovation. Here, state influence is limited to the funding of university and polytechnic education. However, in areas such as data processing, international research projects and the establishment of bodies to improve links between theoretical and applied research, the state is certain to play a more active part.

3. *Regional policy*. This is merely one facet of spatial economics, which also covers location theory and urban economics. However, these increasingly important areas have been largely left to geographers, and economic theory again remains curiously silent on the issue. Although systems analysis has been applied to the problems of transport and location of businesses, no comprehensive theoretical basis for a real land use policy has as yet been devised. It may be that economists have been overpreoccupied with models in which labour and capital are the only factors of production, or again that they have too readily accepted Ricardo's theory of land rent. In any event, the measures taken by the state in this area are once more evidence of a muddled approach to specific problems. Admittedly, a certain amount of planning legislation has been promulgated in an effort to ensure functional land use, but the piecemeal policies designed to help regions and individuals hit by changes in the economic environment are disconcertingly inadequate to achieve such ambitious goals.

4. *Policy on infrastructure*, in other words communications and utilities. Some countries have left this area partly to private initiative while attempting to supervise it through a system of concessions, while others, considering infrastructure as a public good, have resorted to

nationalization. A highly topical and controversial example is provided by the debate on nuclear energy, which raises the question of how public and private economic decisions can be democratically supervised, and puts the issue of individual freedom in a very different light from classical theory. Efforts by the state to meet demand for energy leave it increasingly exposed to charges of complicity with private interests.

The above discussion of structural measures again shows the allpervading nature of the state. The abundance of laws and regulations clearly illustrates just how differently the state functions in theory and in practice.

Social policy

The instruments of social policy are based on (a) mechanisms for the redistribution of income and wealth, and (b) the insurance principle. Social insurance accumulates sizeable contributions which affect consumption and savings, and absorbs large subsidies which produce indirect macroeconomic effects.

The levying of contributions as a percentage of wages poses an economic problem. Some see it as tantamount to income tax, while others consider it part of the reward to labour.

An increasing portion of wages goes towards social insurance (the remainder being paid by the employer). Under the first interpretation, employers consider such contributions as production costs, while employees see them as reducing their available income. Companies claim that such costs reduce their profits and thus, owing to consecutive price rises, restrict production. Employees compensate for the fall in their income by reducing their voluntary savings. The fully-funded pension system entails the accumulation of contributions in social insurance institutions, which profoundly influences the financing of investments. Voluntary private savings decrease and involuntary institutional savings increase. This effect on the financing of businesses is only one of the consequences of social insurance; others concern economic behaviour in a broader sense, in the form of changing attitudes to risk and uncertainty (examples being provided by the phenomena of gambling and stock-market speculation).

The second interpretation considers the real aspect of rewards to labour, and links wages to productivity (a concept which will be discussed in Chapter 8). Thus the increase in labour productivity resulting from increasingly capital-intensive production, particularly in the tertiary sector, has made it possible for social insurance to be introduced.

Having taken advantage of returns to scale after the Second World War and subsequent rationalization, the tertiary sector has now used the growth of data processing to tap enormous reserves of productivity. In the absence of a social policy, wages would have followed the same trend and would have risen more rapidly. The financing of social policy has thus to some extent absorbed increases in productivity. Discussions about how contributions are to be divided between employers and employees have distracted attention from this key phenomenon and reflect a whole range of social symbols: class antagonism, sham solidarity, and the treatment of social issues in terms of economic cost. In fact, an active social policy remains, in my view, one of the most important ways of maintaining the cohesion of industrial societies. In any case, although social policy measures may be strictly speaking less numerous than structural policy measures, the impact of each such measure in terms of income transfer is considerable. Unemployment insurance, which is a direct subsidy to the unemployed, redistributes income in two ways: firstly between wage-earners (who are forced to pay unemployment contributions) and the unemployed, and secondly between the various income brackets (assuming that there is a ceiling on the amounts paid out). State pension schemes work on the same principle, except that they are now supplemented by private pension schemes based on contributions from wages. Here there is no redistribution of income, since there is no ceiling on the amounts paid out.

In the health sector one finds all kinds of complex arrangements ranging from totally private insurance to a full national health service. In every case the state provides subsidies of various kinds, either directly to patients or indirectly to the medical infrastructure.

Despite the successive increases in compulsory contributions to pay for such services, public spending has continued to rise. The immense sums involved have raised the question of efficiency and have given rise to a new branch of economics known as social economics, itself subdivided into branches such as health economics and insurance economics. Neoclassical theory has come up with proposals based on the notion of negative taxation. The basic idea is a simple one. Instead of a complicated and inefficient system of welfare subsidies and taxes which ultimately only encourages bureaucracy, there would be a single tax system in which the individual would be either a debtor or a creditor of the state. Under the present system, the individual is both at once, and is thus in the curious position of using social insurance benefits to help pay his taxes. This system has led to numerous compensatory arrangements, while not always providing the intended protection.

Under the negative-taxation system, on the other hand, individuals with low incomes would be clearly identified as creditors. Above a certain income level — which society would determine according to its perception of social justice — the individual would become a debtor. Such a system would reduce the size of the social insurance apparatus and thus the role of the state. This would be in keeping with the liberal ideals of "rolling back the state" and establishing consumer sovereignty in the field of social policy; negative taxation would allow a transfer of income which the beneficiary could use as he saw fit (old-age pension, health care, immediate consumption or investment in further education). This would eliminate the paternalism inherent in certain kinds of welfare schemes. In short, this neoclassical proposal for negative taxation once again reproduces the value system on which neoclassical theory is based. In practice, cash transfers that were not earmarked for specific uses would very likely serve to reinforce existing inequalities and moreover create a sense of complacency in those required to pay a positive tax. Problems of social inequality can only be tackled by examining their causes, something which no amount of theoretical model-making can replace. There is also the problem of how collective decision-making mechanisms are to be supervised. How can society's financial efforts to combat inequality be prevented from degenerating into bureaucratic waste? The problem is not merely a technical one. Even such an apparently simple instrument as negative taxation conceals various theoretical problems, such as the substitution effects it could trigger off between wages and working hours or between community solidarity and individual responsibility.

This list of economic policy instruments is by no means exhaustive. It is intended to illustrate the involvement of the state in almost every economic decision, despite which no vision of community policy has emerged. However, the state's efforts to respond to expectations and pressures from various quarters have created the network of interlocking relationships that make up present-day society. Discussion of the importance of the state must therefore make way for a discussion of how collective decisions are to be supervised. Models which attempt to play down the importance of the state ultimately render a disservice to economists themselves, who thereby become increasingly remote from social reality and less sensitive to economic policy issues.

Admission of failure

A good many economic policy instruments have had conflicting results; still others have either failed to solve the problem concerned or have actually made it worse. All of them suffer from two main defects:

their theoretical inconsistency, and their inapplicability. The former defect is illustrated by the huge number of recommendations based on a variety of economic models, each with a particular specification which varies according to the underlying techniques and hypotheses. The latter defect, on the other hand, has seldom been verified and has caused a growing rift among economists. On the one hand, there are those who advocate rigorous models based on deductive reasoning; on the other, there are proponents of *ad hoc* specifications which concentrate on the available data and the causal relationships which such data make it possible to test.

In any case, regardless of their performance, what economic policy instruments share is a tendency to make most economic problems more complex. Some examples are given below.

1. *Competition under threat*

Mergers have become more common over the last two decades, and particularly so in the last few years. However, instead of being recognized as a threat to our economic system, they have been welcomed as a positive development. This response is curious when compared with earlier attitudes to mergers, resulting in an entire legislative process designed to make them illegal. In Britain, to take just one example, the turnover of merged companies in 1985 was five times as high, in real terms, as in 1975 (Sawyer, 1987). These figures only relate to industrial companies, but the trend in the financial sector is similar. The alleged advantages of mergers are as follows:

(a) they allow economies of scale which cannot be achieved under conditions of competition;

(b) they strengthen international competition (however, if foreign businesses also benefit from economies of scale and accordingly obey the same technological laws, this argument falls by the wayside);

(c) mergers make it possible to exploit each firm's specific strengths, either by putting an innovation into practice or by rationalizing pooled resources.

The above arguments fail to explain why such companies do not attempt to achieve the same advantages by means of an independent growth strategy — in other words, why they are prepared to sacrifice their autonomy. Indeed, there are cases where mergers have not improved either profits or production structures. The gains achieved are often cancelled out by organizational costs. All that is then left is the "technological" argument that a merger gives the companies involved an industrial shot-in-thearm. Yet this argument merely disguises a more fundamental problem, which is that modern economies are no longer as dynamic or successful as in the days of the industrial revolution. It is my opinion that companies are using this argument to avoid a crucial issue which will one day have to be faced: the problem of falling productivity. We will be turning to this in Part III.

Internationally, increasing mergers and the spread of imperfect competition have meant that multinational companies are now an integral part of trade flows. Despite much talk of free trade, most present-day trade is subject to protectionist regulations. The pure theory of international trade based on the neoclassical model is thus based on an exceptional situation. It is a moot point whether the spread of multinationals is the cause or the effect of the growing barriers to free international movement of goods and services. Whatever the answer, it is a fact that neither competition policy nor trade policy have prevented what appears to be an irreversible trend. Economies are increasingly controlled and regulated, not so much by the state as by the constraints imposed by multinationals and state-managed firms.

2. *Mismanagement of the business cycle*

At first sight, everything looks fine. Growth rates are encouraging; in 1986 they averaged 2.5% for the Group of Ten industrialized countries (BIS, 1987). The world economy has coped with both the major recession in 1975 and the smaller one in 1982, both due to oil shocks. Oil now sells for the same price as ten years ago, and is thus once more helping to stimulate economic growth.

In 1986 the average rate of inflation was the same as in 1961. Despite a recent increase, it is now around 4%, having peaked at 14% in late 1974. As a result, the disposable income of the ten industrialized countries has increased. However, these figures disguise growing macroeconomic disequilibrium, both domestic and international.

Domestically, the two most striking phenomena are unemployment and national debt. Over the last 20 years, average unemployment in the OECD countries has increased from 3% to 8% (see Graph 3). Within the European Community, this figure is even higher. The national debt in the Group of Ten rose from 37% of national product in 1973 to 62% in 1986, and debt-servicing expenditure accordingly rose to some 13% of national product in the same year.

Internationally, similar phenomena can be observed, such as the growing disequilibrium in balance-of-payments current accounts and the huge international debt incurred by the developing countries.

Graph 3: Unemployment rates since 1970

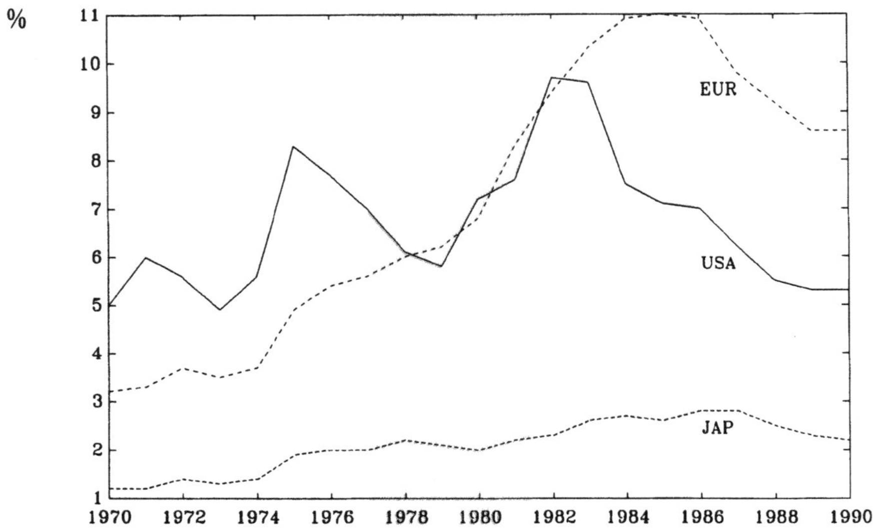

Source: Economic perspectives, OECD.

The principle of developed countries with financing ability and developing countries with financing needs no longer holds true. In 1986, the United States had a deficit of $140 billion — almost three times the *total* debt of the developing countries ($49 billion). This situation is causing an increase in the external debt of the developing countries, which cannot attract foreign investment or finance their deficit by expanding the money supply as the United States has done (see also Table 2).

The macroeconomic coordination agreements reached by the industrialized countries (known as the Louvre and Plaza agreements, after the places where they were drawn up) are in fact tantamount to a beggar-my-neighbour policy.

The diversity of theoretical views on the subject, both interventionist and non-interventionist, serves to disguise the problem of political hegemony which lies at the heart of the current macroeconomic disequilibrium. The situation is reminiscent of the inability of classical economists to account for the Great Depression in the 1930s. But whereas on that occasion they were rescued from their predicament by Keynesian theory, today there is no saviour in sight. Opinions range from ebullient optimism to utter pessimism, from declarations of satisfaction on the basis of positive indicators to dire predictions of recession. Each of these arguments is backed up by sophisticated, highly formalized models.

Such a wealth of differing views ought to produce a vigorous debate. Instead, theorists have chosen to avoid all discussion and bury their heads in their own research. The only exchange of views that occurs is within each school of thought; confrontation is discredited, and polemics is no longer a valid means of expression. Yet only a serious debate can expose the lack of new thinking in current business cycle models.

3. *The aimless drift of structural policy*

The abundance of instruments in this area is evidence of the growing difficulties involved in implementing a structural policy.

(a) *Agricultural policy* has reached a dead-end. Overproduction by Western countries and stagnating exports from developing countries have meant that farmers can no longer rely on an adequate income. The existing arrangements must be supplemented by income subsidies; the political goal of protecting farmers cannot be achieved by manipulating prices and quantities. Everywhere the result has been to encourage concentration, at the expense of small-scale family farming.
Economists are obviously tempted to put the blame on politicians. However, it is now clear that a purely theoretical approach in the competitive-market tradition is no answer either. Ultimately, a new policy can only emerge from economic research which takes account of the views of both agricultural engineers and sociologists. The question of how to make agricultural production less intensive must be answered by agricultural engineers, and the effects of income subsidies on society's attitude to farmers must be assessed by sociologists. Both extensive production and income subsidies are instruments of economic policy.

(b) *Industrial policy* has probably only had localized effects. All too often, it has catered to the interests of influential pressure groups. Although it has seldom been properly evaluated, its overall effect appears to have been minimal. State intervention has not succeeded in either channelling or controlling industrial change. Wherever the state has attempted to maintain manufacturing structures whose comparative advantage was already irretrievably lost, such intervention has merely delayed the adjustment process and made the resulting unemployment worse. Innovation policy has, for its part, been dictated by military considerations.

(c) *Regional policy* has run into the obstacle of large-scale migration both at home and abroad. The poles of attraction are shifting, while at the same time the growth of conurbations is making urban life increasingly unbearable. The badly-needed interdisciplinary approach is not forthcoming. The same conclusion applies to the problem of communications and non-nuclear energy sources.

In response to these problems, economists persist in emphasizing the virtues of market forces. They fail to see that being right about principles is no excuse for refusing to think about how to apply them.

The increasing cost of social policy

The advent of the welfare state has led to growing disillusionment. Redistribution schemes are more and more expensive (see Graph 4) and appear less and less capable of eliminating social injustice. In fact, they have ended up creating new kinds of unequality. Reactions have been varied, from tax revolts to the total abandonment of any sense of solidarity. The much-vaunted neoclassical relationship between efficiency and equity does not appear to obtain (OECD, 1981). A highly efficient economy such as Japan turns out to have the most equitable income distribution, while the reverse seems to be true of countries such as France and the United States. The central issue is thus the way in which tax is collected, rather than of the redistribution technique applied.

Graph 4: Social insurance contributions in selected countries as a percentage of gross wages

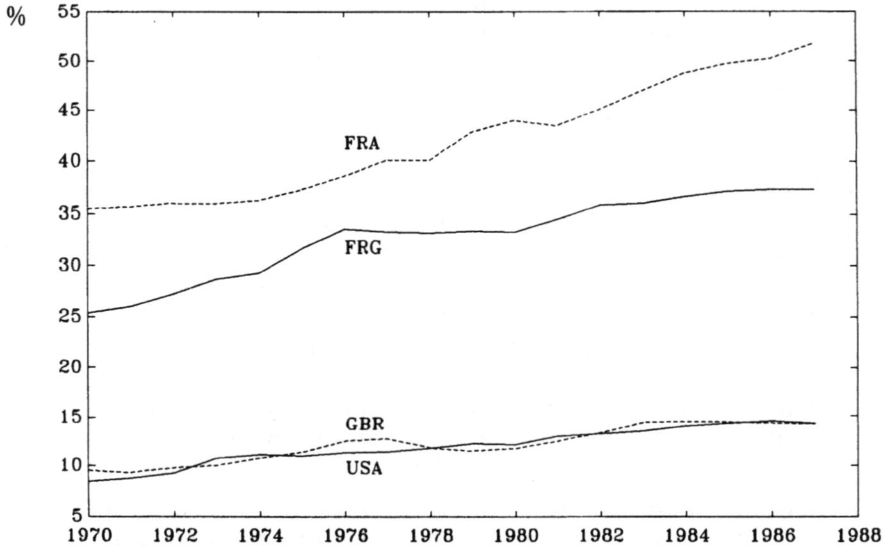

Source: OECD national accounts.

Although there are still those who are unhappy with the scale of state pension schemes, this is certainly one area in which redistribution has worked well. However, what is worrying is that the choice of instruments has become a major factor in the social security debate. The state and its social policy therefore tend to become scapegoats, and bickering among experts takes the place of any serious discussion of goals. Solidarity has become a less important issue than the extent of social insurance coverage.

It is, of course, tempting to attribute this state of affairs to sluggish economic performance. A steadily growing cake is easier to divide up than one whose size remains essentially unchanged.

However, income redistribution policy cannot be held responsible for the explosion in health care costs, the spectacular increase in unemployment, or the aging of the population. All three phenomena are now a threat to social policy, for each is helping in its own way to swell income transfers. The implications for traditional social policy are as follows:

1. Study of the explosion in health care costs depends on collaboration between economists and physicians.
2. An analysis of unemployment requires economists to collaborate with psychologists, who can provide information on people's motives for working and society's current perception of what work means.
3. The problem of aging calls for collaboration between the social sciences and the health professions.

Social policy is thus the area which best illustrates the degree to which economic theory has become isolated. Such isolation — such imprisonment within abstract models — may prove especially disastrous in areas where new needs are emerging. Instead of viewing every social policy issue in terms of redistribution mechanisms of varying degrees of sophistication, it would be better to aim for a more satisfactory distribution of income. Convention economic models do not fit in with the requirement of equal pay for equal work, nor with the need to adjust the working environment to changes in social behaviour, particularly in the family sphere.

While economic theory cannot, of course, be expected to take account of every single feature of social existence, there is no doubt that its high degree of specialization and abstraction have cut it off from social reality and made it increasingly irrelevant.

The search for a miracle cure

Despite the difficulty of applying the numerous instruments referred to above, there is a consensus among economists regarding certain major principles of economic policy.

1. The first is reinforcement of the pre-conditions for the operation of market forces. There is no point in pursuing an economic policy based on competitive-market models if the necessary conditions do not obtain in practice — in other words, if the accuracy of the initial hypotheses has not been verified.
2. The second is explicit acknowledgement of the economic role of the state, which, instead of varying constantly in response to cyclical fluctuations or pressure from various groups, should strive for greater consistency.
3. The third is deregulation and greater use of incentives. In other words, subsidies and taxes are preferable to manipulation of prices and quantities. Structural measures should never be long-term, but should be seen as temporary aids to adjustment. They should not be used to cause a lasting distortion in relative prices.
4. The fourth is that efficiency should take precedence over equity in matters of social policy, while a hierarchy should be established in intervention instruments according to "second-best solution" criteria.

For clarity, let us take the example of stabilization policy. Most economists refuse to revive the old battle between classical and Keynesian theory. Certain points are now generally acknowledged (McCallum, 1987):

1. A discretionary economic policy leads to situations which are less than optimal for society.
2. The development of dynamic models in which individuals buy "what they want, when they want" represents progress, even though the microeconomic approach of seeing the individual as typical of the whole economy is still disputed.
3. The widely accepted hypothesis of a natural rate of unemployment implies that monetary policy can never succeed in maintaining a high level of production in the long term. This proposition is derived from monetarist theory, whose hypothesis of a natural rate of unemployment and approach to monetary policy are still disputed. Monetarists prefer to control the money supply, while Keynesians opt for control of the national product in nominal terms (Gordon, 1987). However, the recent tendency for the natural rate of unemployment to increase remains a mystery.

Since observed economic reality is not in accordance with theory, it is theory which must adapt. The same is true of market adjustment mechanisms, which are generally assumed to achieve equilibrium. What is disputed is the manner in which the adjustments are carried out and their duration.

This consensus among economists with regard to economic policy merely highlights the gulf between theory and practice. Economists can thus be accused of indulging in wishful thinking. This search for a miracle cure at a time of growing economic problems is dangerous for a number of reasons:

1. The clash between classical and Keynesian models, despite efforts to reconcile them, has resulted in the "theory" of supply-side economics.
2. There is a tendency to respond to persistent macroeconomic disequilibrium with authoritarian measures.
3. Endless wrangling among experts may well bring the whole of economic theory into disrepute.

Supply-side economics

In essence, all this approach does is revive the classical view of the economy, emphasizing the factors which determine the supply of available resources within the domestic economy, the efficient use of such resources, and technological progress. Any change in these factors can thus be used to account for a change in overall supply. Policies based on supply-side economics therefore involve state intervention to modify these factors and thereby influence economic growth. However, changes in these factors display by a certain degree of inertia which active state policy can only overcome on a piecemeal, short-term basis. Moreover, its causes lie beyond the range of such policy. After the Keynesian revolution, it was hoped that economic disequilibrium could be remedied by varying the quantities of goods and services demanded by the state. However, a succession of "short-term" state interventions soon culminated in permanent intervention. In most industrialized countries, this led to increasing budget deficits which no amount of taxation appeared capable of reducing. Keynesian optimism as to the effectiveness of government intervention made way for bureaucratic cynicism, enhanced by the fact that servicing of the national debt was becoming an ever greater feature of public spending. At the same time, the inflationary climate allowed a hidden but very real increase in taxation to take place without the need for any change in tax legislation. Unfortunately, inflation got out of control, and only slowed down after 1975 under the joint effects of the oil crisis and a more disciplined monetary policy. While the ensuing recession succeeded in controlling fiscal drag, it also seriously reduced the tax base. The resulting increase in government deficits left very little scope for reflationary policies in the pure Keynesian tradition. Nor was monetary policy — tied as it was to monetary growth objectives held responsible for the previous bursts of inflation — considered suitable as a reflationary instrument.

By the end of the 1970s, economic policy had reached a dead-end which led to a new, short-term interpretation of supply-side economics, namely that calculated tax relief would have a stimulating effect on business activity. The Keynesian causality of an autonomous increase in overall demand and thus in business activity was reversed. By directly reducing production costs, tax relief was supposed to lead to an increase in overall supply.

The results of this policy are now apparent. Macroeconomic disequilibrium has grown considerably worse. Quite simply, supply-side economics has failed. The miracle cure is in fact no more than a placebo, and the idea that our economic problems were solved has been exposed as a temporary illusion.

Enforced solutions

Continuing macroeconomic disequilibrium is likely to result in increasingly authoritarian policies.

Internationally, the world is being forced to accept adjustments that suit the interests of the most powerful nation. Without this necessarily triggering off a trade war, the result may be an even greater wave of protectionism. International debt may cease to be a purely technical matter of debt rescheduling, and instead become a political excuse for countries to extend their influence.

Domestically, disequilibrium is raising social consensus costs and leading to institutional paralysis which in turn is resulting in increasingly radical opinions. A revealing indicator is the high rate of unemployment among young people. Policies that serve the interests of specific groups may then become inevitable, with institutional paralysis being used as an excuse for bypassing democratic procedures. If social consensus costs are felt to be excessive, greater social disintegration will result. An ominous sign is the increasingly discriminatory effect of macroeconomic disequilibrium in certain developed countries. If the economy becomes a self-regulating mechanism watched over by a passive state, any sense of community is likely to vanish, and the unemployed will be left to fend for themselves.

Economics in disrepute

The persistence of economic disequilibrium and the failure of economic policy to deal with it do nothing to improve the increasingly discredited state of economic theory, which can be attributed to three main factors:

1. A comprehensive approach to economic policy has been sacrificed to over-specialization, which is frequently only seen as progress by economists themselves. Yet it is no secret that only economists capable of placing their thinking in a historical, institutional and political context end up being involved in government decisions (Nelson, 1987).
2. Economic policy recommendations based on purely economic models do not take sufficient account of other dimensions. Either they reproduce the existing value system, or else they attempt to justify whatever decisions are taken. Since they are deductive, they remain a useful means of conceptualizing issues and disseminating ideas, but they are of little use to policymakers as a basis for concrete action.
3. Innumerable econometric studies, whose *ad hoc* specifications can establish any causal relationship whatsoever, have abused public confidence in quantifiable data, and their inaccurate economic forecasts have left economic theory in greater disrepute.

Economic policy is thus becoming increasingly a matter for lawyers, politicians and the business community. Economists'obsessive fear of an all-pervading state has led them to advocate policies which are not only biased, but irrelevant. Meanwhile, the world's economic problems grow worse.

CHAPTER 6

THE THREAT OF INSTITUTIONAL PARALYSIS

Is state involvement in virtually all economic decisions a threat to the market economy? The answer, I believe, is no: the wide variety of economic policy instruments and problems of implementation have left the state with very little power. Though all-pervading, the state is weak.

It is therefore no real threat to individual freedom in the West. The real danger lies in the prospect of institutional paralysis, as evidenced by increasing transaction and consensus costs. At the same time, people are no longer motivated by the instrumentalized, impersonal working environment, which has failed to take account of the social changes accompanying the transformation of workers into employees (Raffestin, Bresso, 1979). The prominence of office jobs, which are physically less onerous and more abstract in content, shows that the most pressing economic problems currently concern organization rather than competition. This raises the issue of how such organizational matters are to be managed and supervised.

Below, an attempt will be made to show that market forces are merely one of a number of collective decision-making mechanisms, and also that creeping bureaucracy is everywhere.

Collective decision-making mechanisms

The highly complex manner in which the state is organized reflects its historical development rather than society's current perception of its role. It is not, therefore, a monolithic entity, and allows for a number of different decision-making processes which may collide or be complete independent of one another. Essentially, these may be reduced to two overlapping mechanisms, one of them political, the other administrative. As a result of efforts by special interest groups to influence collective decisions within both mechanisms, the state has come to be largely dominated by the private economic sphere. Far from being controlled by the state, the economy is holding the state to ransom.

The democratic mechanism

This mechanism operates by a simple majority. Under this arrangement, decisions are delegated to the legislature, which legislates so as not to harm the economic interests of the majority. Even if the democratic principle of "one man, one vote" is strictly applied, in practice votes are weighted according to the importance of the various special interest groups involved. Decisions reached by such a process thus show the state to be not so much an entity that is exogenous to economic mechanisms as a reflection of the network of economic relationships. Each member of the legislature attempts to obtain the maximum possible benefit for the particular special interest group that elected him. Since everyone is pursuing the same strategy, the democratic process is necessarily subjected to the subtle pressure of coalitions and indirect influence via extra-parliamentary committees. The result is not only greater public spending, but a weakening of the state. The economic view that the importance of the state can be measured in terms of public spending thus appears increasingly inaccurate.

At the same time, the political decision-making process is decentralized and partly delegated to the executive.

The degree of centralization varies from country to country. In countries with a highly federal structure, the decision-making mechanism has split into three levels. The most transparent of these is the local level. Influence by particular individuals or special interest groups is often recognized and accepted as a community institution. Since in most cases decisions by the authorities at this level are intended to benefit the community, there is no sense of opposition between the state and the local economy. Such conflicts as do arise merely reflect those that already exist within the economy.

At the regional level, the larger scale means that things are less clear-cut, and there is greater scope for indirect influence. Finally, at the national level there is an additional international dimension, and private economic interests coalesce with political decisions on matters of national defence. At each level, implementation of decisions is delegated. In addition to implementing decisions, the executive enjoys a certain amount of discretionary freedom to make decisions of its own. However, there are clearly defined limits to this freedom: initiatives by the executive are subject to parliamentary approval, and decisions are never taken in isolation, but are based on prior consultation with those directly affected. This means that the state is a tool of the existing economic order rather than an independent entity.

The drawbacks of this institutional set-up are particularly apparent when it comes to expressing preferences. Economic theory dodges this problem by assuming that preferences are expressed by society as a whole rather than being the mere sum total of individual preferences, yet the problem of interpersonal comparison remains. In the case of the majority-vote system, the same difficulty presents itself in three distinct forms:

1. The majority-vote system presents the voter with a simple yes/no choice. No provision is made for weighting of any kind. This reflects the very nature of politics, involving the pursuit of decision-making power. The fact that the relative strength of particular preferences is not reflected in the majority-vote system necessarily leads to alliance-forming. For example, let us assume that a subsidy has been proposed for the production of some agricultural good. The members of parliament who represent the producers are obviously most in favour of the subsidy, but they happen to be in a minority. They will therefore seek support by offering to vote for proposals in which other groups have a particular interest. Their preferences are thus expressed on the basis of a tacit vote-swapping agreement. As a result of this practice, some proposals have no chance of getting through, while prior agreements may prevent the majority from rejecting a proposal that only benefits a minority.

2. Economic theory assumes that all market agents are aware of what all the others are doing. In order for the market to function properly, it must be transparent. A similar condition applies in the field of politics, but it cannot be fulfilled, since there is no real obligation on individual voters to make sure they are properly informed. If they think their votes will make no difference anyway, they are quite likely to vote at random — which can hardly be said to further the expression of collective preferences. The main beneficiaries are those who seek to exploit the lack of information, either by suggesting that individual votes count for nothing, or by deliberately circulating distorted information. If there is no incentive to verify the available information, the final result may well be affected.

3. The majority-vote system may distort the result according to how the vote is organized. The result is then not determined by the expression of individual preferences, but by the order in which the two alternatives are submitted to the vote. This inherent weakness in the democratic decisionmaking mechanism is well known from Condorcet's paradox, which conclusively demonstrates how a result can be obtained which does not reflect the preferences expressed.

What are the effects of the democratic mechanism on economic policy? The various kinds of policy have one thing in common: the need for alliances means that all policies must lead to an increase in the state budget. If public spending were kept constant, consensus costs would rapidly increase.

1. ***Competition policy*** scarcely lends itself to application of the majority-vote system. Various special interest groups exploit their dominant position, using employment or the need for cultural diversity as reasons for maintaining trusts. Other pressure groups possess information which they are only prepared to release in return for certain benefits. Transparency itself thus becomes a bargaining counter. As a result, competition policy in most countries is relatively lax.
2. ***Stabilization policy***, which is by definition short-term, may clash with a political cycle whose existence, while hard to prove empirically, very probably influences the economic cycle. This political cycle, which is determined by election dates, requires stabilization policy to be expansive when elections are imminent and restrictive after they are over.
3. ***Structural policy*** may well be determined by the need to form alliances, and is particularly prone to influence by special interest groups. In the labour market, for example, producers can rely on achieving an alliance with workers to ease the adjustment to structural changes in a given sector. In other areas, particularly where infrastructure is concerned, the diverging interests of producers and consumers have caused such alliances to fail; this is again reflected in increasing consensus costs, as illustrated by the debate on public and private transport.
4. ***Social policy*** is particularly dependent on the democratic decisionmaking mechanism, since more than any other kind of policy it represents the normative domain in which everyone can express views as to what is fair and equitable. Moreover, the income-transfer mechanisms of social policy closely affect voters, who display a high degree of mobility in this respect. Although the arguments put forward by economic theory in this area are dominated by moral issues such as the desirable degree of solidarity, they are often

revealed to be self-serving arguments against social income transfers. Regardless of whether such opposition is directed at the scale or the very principle of such transfers, social policy recommendations derived from purely economic models are often viewed with suspicion by the majority of the public. Such suspicion is frequently exploited by governments to encourage populist thinking on social policy.

Thus the democratic decision-making mechanism frequently obeys a different logic than the mechanism of price flexibility. Their normative element makes political arrangements more open to attempts at manipulation than market mechanisms. However, there is no point in trying to determine the relative importance of the two mechanisms. The question is not whether the mechanism of price flexibility should prevail over the democratic decisionmaking mechanism or vice versa, but how economic policies are to be implemented in both areas. Only economists who take explicit account of both aspects can produce workable policy recommendations. However, there can be no doubt that the democratic decision-making mechanism is increasingly used in the purely economic domain (Poole, 1986), indicating an increasingly normative approach to economic issues. This development partly reflects new technological needs and partly new motives in the labour market. For example, the abandonment by a growing number of firms of purely hierarchical systems of organization is dictated by technologies that require new kinds of worker collaboration, participation and responsibility. At the same time, such technological change is affecting every area of activity both within businesses and in their external relations, and this is leading to social change. In political terms, it can be said that the traditional worker is vanishing, and a new, as yet undefined body of voters, probably more diversified and individualistic than before, is starting to emerge.

The consequences of this still largely imperceptible change are twofold: attempts to achieve consensus are more and more costly, and governments tend to gratify established special interest groups. However, established alliances in matters of economic policy must increasingly acknowledge the presence of new special interest groups which as yet have no institutional basis. The established alliances have traditionally acted as a channel for public opinion (which governments do not always perceive correctly) and have thereby helped the latter in determining their policy. At the same time, governments have relied on such alliances to spread information, especially in order to popularize economic policies. The emergence of new and often short-lived pressure groups has therefore proved most disconcerting. As long as such groups are without an institutional basis, governments lack a policy guide, and are therefore tempted to surround their decisions with extra precautions. As a result, expert reports proliferate and the influence of the civil service increases.

Collective decision-making and the civil service

The democratic collective decision-making mechanism reveals the state to be dependent on the balance of power underlying the existing economic order. Within the civil service, however, things are different. By virtue of its complexity, the political decision-making process leaves sufficient scope for interpretation and adjustment, with each government department attempting to turn flaws in the system to its own advantage and thereby increase its decision-making powers. Not only can the civil service prescribe procedures which increase transaction costs, but its influence on people's behaviour in turn affects political decisions. The result is costly bureaucratic expansion — a phenomenon which is by no means limited to the public sector, but affects private bureaucracies equally.

However, it is clear that government departments each have their own specific characteristics, if only because they are subject to differing controls. Maximizing their budgets and increasing their decision-making powers are not the only failings they are charged with. The most serious criticism concerns their lack of productivity compared with the private sector. This aspect will be discussed in more detail in Part III. In this chapter, the civil service will only concern us insofar as it is involved in the decision-making process leading up to economic policy. In general, it seeks to avoid conflict with the public, politicians and established special interest groups.

1. ***The civil service and the public***

   The civil service is a frequent scapegoat. It is responsible for implementing economic policy and therefore bears the brunt of any difficulties that arise in doing so. It accordingly shows a preference for measures which will avoid potential conflict with the public. In particular, it insists on economic policy instruments being practicable. It also insists on economic policy having an unambiguous legal basis, since it is concerned to carry out regulations to the letter and so avoid blame in the event of conflict. All of this encourages a pettifogging approach which slows down the collective decision-making process.

2. ***The civil service and politicians***

   The legislature seeks to remain on good terms with the civil service in order to obtain the information and support it needs for economic policy measures. Many are the proposals torpedoed by civil service doubts as to their feasibility, doubts based on criteria whose complexity mirrors that of the necessary political consensus. Officially the civil service is controlled by the executive, but the latter's authority is temporary and therefore often purely nominal. Accordingly, the executive tries to induce the civil service to cooperate with its proposals, often by means of stimuli such as internal promotion, use of outside experts, and political appointments to senior civil service posts.

3. ***The civil service and special interest groups***

Special interest groups often attempt to arrange for the appointment of civil servants who are especially responsive to specific grievances. Producers' associations can undoubtedly bring more influence to bear in this area than consumer organizations. However, most special interest groups possess information of their own which allows them to maintain a degree of independence from government authority.

In short, relations between the civil service and other groups are not subject to strict controls. This does not necessarily mean that the influence of the civil service on collective decision-making is increasing. However, simply by its involvement in the decision-making process, it slows it down and increases consensus costs. It also tends to exaggerate the theoretical difficulties involved in implementing decisions, thus providing additional factors that encourage institutional paralysis. What are the implications of all this for economic policy?

1. In matters of *competition policy*, the civil service has no vision of its own, but simply complains about the inadequate resources it has been given to carry out its task. This complaint recurs in most areas of economic policy. However, the civil service has a monopoly on the production of all kinds of public goods and seeks to join forces with private economic pressure groups that are similarly unencumbered by market mechanisms. In this way, the civil service works hand-in-glove with various trusts. The latter, which are frequently well organized, provide the civil service with a clear negotiating partner and at the same time allow targeted dissemination of information to groups affected by particular regulations.

   When it comes to international implementation of competition policy, the civil service often acts as a spokesman for producers. In particular, when the latter appeal for protectionist measures, the civil service rarely objects. However, the main purpose of such opportunistic behaviour is to promote solutions which are likely to increase civil service influence. In the case of "trust-busting", for instance, the civil service will press for registration of restrictive trade practices in order to disclose intercompany agreements, since this will justify taking on extra staff. Similarly, in matters of trade policy, national civil services ally themselves with the international agencies in charge of international economic cooperation. The proliferation of international organizations is evidence not only of greater cooperation but also of creeping bureaucracy, which tends to inhibit free trade. Coordinating agencies are then set up to counter this tendency, thereby helping to extend the influence of the international civil service. Here again, it is clear that current economic problems are a matter of organization rather than competition.

2. With regard to *stabilization policy*, Keynesian theory has been a boon to civil services, since it justifies their intervention in the economy. Intervention in the business cycle, originally only meant as a short-term solution, has become more permanent, largely owing to the delay inimplementing decisions caused by the democratic mechanism. Not surprisingly, the civil service uses this to justify its own expansion and advances cyclical arguments even for such things as increases in military spending.
Here, the civil service can count on support from otherwise hostile quarters. Measures which increase the importance of the civil service will be supported by trade unions provided that they help to protect jobs. Businesses, for their part, will always be appreciative of government orders designed to boost the economy. The collective decisionmaking mechanism operated by the civil service thus mirrors that of an economy in which conditions of imperfect competition prevail. However, the above remarks only apply to fiscal policy. Monetary policy is conducted by a branch of the civil service which in most countries enjoys a special status, namely the central bank, which is usually fairly independent of the democratic mechanism. The discretionary margin thus available to central banks makes them keen to ensure that monetary policy remains a major instrument of stabilization policy. This discretionary margin happens to be increased under monetarist theories.

3. In the field of *structural policy*, theoretical justifications are less evident. Here, the civil service attempts to use conflicting interests as an excuse for strengthening its position as a mediator and generally justifying its own involvement. In any case, the same alliance of interests can be observed as in the field of stabilization policy. Concern to maintain full employment results in an extremely dense web of regulations reflected in extensive subsidies to businesses and a mushrooming of economic development agencies. The intention here is clear: the civil service is out to curry favour with business circles which are only too quick to criticize its influence in other areas. If — liberal policies notwithstanding — state intervention cannot be avoided, then all concerned must be seen to benefit.

4. In the field of *social policy*, the same tendency is even more apparent. Transfers between generations, from the healthy to the sick and from one income (or wealth) bracket to another are increasingly common. This is a perfect instance of the normative aspect of economic theory, and all kinds of influence can be and are brought to bear. The resulting clash of interests gives the civil service an ideal opportunity to mediate and to supervise the legislative framework. Such mediation has seldom clarified the balance of power between the various special interest groups; on the contrary, the situation has been further obscured by government-imposed codes of behaviour. The results are only too obvious. Serious debate has given way to expert feuds in which the civil service is the obvious mediator, particularly given the ever-increasing consensus costs of the democratic decision-making process.

Comparison between collective decision-making mechanisms

We have now examined two collective decision-making mechanisms associated with the functioning of the state, and have compared them with the market mechanism. Attention has been drawn to the fact that all three are profoundly influenced by the behaviour of pressure groups. Irrespective of whether these pressure groups have a collective decision-making mechanism of their own (Frey, 1981) or one linked to other mechanisms, their role can only be interpreted if there is close collaboration between the social sciences. Attempts to explain their role from a purely economic viewpoint, on the basis of the utilitarian hypothesis, can only leave economic theory more isolated as the Western democracies find themselves more and more exposed to growing consensus and transaction costs.

Comparison between the various collective decision-making mechanisms inevitably leads to the conclusion that they are interdependent. A society's institutions adapt to a shifting balance of power expressed through political mechanisms, whereas economic theory insists on the immutable nature of human behaviour. Such institutional change gives the economy an evolutionary dimension and shifts the collective decision-making mechanism away from the market and towards administrative procedures. New mentalities have emerged: society's symbols of the economy have changed, with a shift from efficiency to equity. This change is reflected in a more complex civil service, whose very existence is denied by orthodox neoclassical theory.

The collective decision-making mechanism operated by the market has thus yielded in importance to the other two mechanisms, both of which are more political in nature. So far we have indicated two basic reasons for this change: the neoclassical misapprehension of the role of the state, and the problems of redistribution inherent in the operation of market forces. Both reasons are closely connected, and take us back to the discussion of basic assumptions. For a given distribution of income and wealth, economic theory solves the problem of equity by means of growth. The interplay of individualism and selfishness in a harshly competitive market will, it is claimed, produce optimal growth. Another way of solving the problem of equity is to create conditions conducive to the development of solidarity. In either of these utopian situations, state influence can be kept to a minimum. However, given the market failures and lack of solidarity that characterize contemporary society, political mechanisms have become inevitable.

This tendency will certainly increase with the advent of environmental problems, which neoclassical theory considers, like the state, exogenous to the market. Here the same logic is used as with regard to the civil service. Economic theory thus helps to shore up the myth that only a return to market forces can guarantee individual freedom. The fact that this message is expressed in a political context simply emphasizes its ideological content, which neoclassical theory has never managed to erase.

The drawbacks of each collective decision-making mechanism are now apparent. In attempting to correct the failings of the market mechanism, capitalist societies have developed a variety of combined approaches which — to a greater or lesser extent — assign the state an increasingly important role in running the economy. The drawbacks of political collective decision-making mechanisms raise the problem of how to supervise public and private bureaucracies.

Economic theory and bureaucracy

In conceptual terms, public and private bureaucracies can be more effectively supervised by increasing the relative influence of either the democratic or the market mechanism. However, the opposition between efficiency and equity, which has played a major part in increasing the influence of the civil service, may be reduced by the emergence of new motives.

Given the drawbacks of the democratic mechanism when it comes to expressing collective preferences, it is hardly an ideal means of supervising bureaucratic decisions. First of all, it is hampered by the influence of organized pressure groups, and secondly, its operating costs tend to increase as interests diverge. Moreover, it is clear that democratic procedures have played very little part in organization of production. Measures intended to increase worker participation are all based on the instrumental aspect of labour, which continues to be seen as a factor of production.

However, rather than by a direct democratic mechanism, supervision can conceivably be carried by the legislature or the executive. We have already mentioned the absence of political motivation to supervise the civil service more closely. Indeed, it must be admitted that creeping bureaucracy is a direct result of the democratic system, which requires the establishment of administrative bodies at every stage (elections, representation, delegation of decision-making powers, etc.).

It is therefore no surprise to learn that civil services grow increasingly complex as consensus costs rise. They have become organizations in the sense that they represent a system made up of various interdependent components that require coordination. Thus the issue of how to supervise them essentially boils down to identifying their coordinating mechanisms (Bössmann, 1967). Here the key issues are information and communication. Decentralization would be a first step in the direction of greater transparency. However, the additional transaction costs involved are only justified if decentralization actually results in more effective supervision of bureaucracies, either because they are geographically closer to the local or regional communities concerned, or because the civil service becomes structured so as to allow the various departments greater autonomy. The latter solution reflects the current tendency of large companies to split up into separate profit centers, in order to help motivate those in charge of the various units. In this approach, based on the hypothesis of bounded rationality, the problem of bureaucracy is transferred to the field of organization theory, which has developed in both sociology and business studies (Pugh, 1980). The hypothesis of limited rationality, which has more to offer than that of economic rationality, has certainly contributed to the unprecedented expansion of business studies. There can be no doubt that this expansion has put economic theory on the defensive, although none of the resulting organization theories has yielded tangible results which could be used in checking the growth of the civil service (Zand, 1981).

Public choice theory

Public choice theory is an attempt to revive the neoclassical model (Brown, Jackson, 1986). Not surprisingly, its analysis leads to recommendations that the various public services should compete among themselves or even be privatized. The same logic has helped to strengthen the position of the state. Obviously, then, such an analysis cannot divest itself of its ideological content, and fails to answer the question of how the huge public and private bureaucracies are to be supervised.

Public choice theory attempts to analyse the link between individual preferences and collective choices made by government, and assesses public bureaucracies in terms of optimal allocation of resources which is distorted by state intervention. This theory clearly takes us back to the hypothesis of absolute rationality, based on individualistic behaviour, and turns its back on collaboration with other social sciences. Political science, for example, sets out from the hypotheses discussed in Part I with reference to the social contract. This does not get us very far when it comes to the problem of public choice. If we make economic rationality the minimum condition for an acceptable public choice (Arrow, 1977), we can only deduce the superiority of market forces and recommend a reduction in state influence by transferring its administrative duties to the private sphere. Such a recommendation, however, totally ignores the history of state intervention as outlined at the beginning of this chapter. In applying the instruments of neoclassical economic theory to politics, public choice theory simply uses a circular argument in which the results of the model reproduce the initial hypothesis or, to quote Greffe (1981, p. 16):

"Economic analysis of bureaucracy thus leads to a dramatic reduction in the role of the state in favour of market forces. This result, remarkable in itself, is reinforced by an additional element — a barely veiled attack on the whole notion of the welfare state. In challenging the way in which heavily-staffed government departments are run, economic analysis of bureaucracy effectively calls all redistribution schemes into question...".

This approach, already discussed under the heading "The search for a miracle cure", concerns supply-side economics. In pragmatic terms, public choice theory can be seen as an attempt to correct common bureaucratic excesses without at the same time challenging the redistributive role of the state. There is then no need to resort to formal neoclassical theories; the electorate can carry out the necessary corrections itself, for example by voting to limit the number of civil servants or by rebelling against what it considers to be excessive taxes. However, a more fundamental point is, I believe, that public choice theory is just one more attempt to revive the neoclassical model of market forces — despite its failures which have left us with an allpervading but powerless state.

Alternative approaches

If we accept the hypothesis that market failures and considerations of social justice have increased the relative importance of political decision-making mechanisms at the expense of the market mechanism, we are faced with two separate problems:

1. how to compare market failures with the disadvantages of regulation by the state; and
2. how to redistribute income and wealth by means other than state intervention.

Both problems take us back to the discussion of basic assumptions in Chapter 2, which raised the issues of economic rationality, limited rationality, and psychological and philosophical approaches to human behaviour.

Market failures and bureaucratic failures are compared in the context of public choice theory. The underlying hypothesis is that economic rationality introduces an ideological bias, since the disadvantages of state intervention are weighted more heavily than the market failures which led to such intervention in the first place. The predictable result is a recommendation to privatize as many public services as possible.

If both kinds of failure are compared using the hypothesis of limited rationality, the result is more complex, since government departments are then examined in the light of organization theory, which also applies to private bureaucracies. According to this hypothesis, private and public bureaucracies do not necessarily maximize overall profits, but instead pursue other strategies aimed in particular at increasing their discretionary decision-making margins. In the case of a government department, this may entail slackening the political supervision provided either directly or on a delegated basis through the democratic mechanism, or again expansion of a department if a majority of voters acknowledges the existence of a new social problem. The problem of supervising bureaucracies more effectively then requires a more subtle approach. The main aim is then to influence factors responsible for increasing discretionary decision-making margins, for example by increasing transparency through improved information channels or other forms of supervision such as reports on how staff spend their work time. Decentralization may in some cases be an appropriate response. There are thus a number of different answers, not just one as suggested by public choice theory.

Psychological and philosophical approaches to human behaviour revolve around the issues of motivation and social solidarity and thus of state intervention to ensure fair redistribution of income and wealth.

The psychological approach questions the relevance of the hypothesis of economic rationality, on which economic analysis of bureaucracy is based. The psychological approach sees in the spread of bureaucracy such motives as self-affirmation, the pursuit of social status, and social integration of the individual through the kinds of cooperation and association that are possible in administrative organizations as opposed to a competitive working environment. The implications are then that economic theory should be confined to the industrialization process — whose primary achievement has been to satisfy material needs — and that a psychological approach should be used to take account of the increasingly tertiary nature of the economy (and of the civil service).

Finally, the philosophical approach takes us back to the notion of a social contract. Without going so far as to label this a Rousseauist approach, it can be understood as an agreement between social partners. The state is an entity in its own right, expressing the community will that is negated in a society defined simply as the sum total of individual interests. It will be recalled that a social contract results in an institutional framework designed to guarantee three fundamental principles of social justice (Rawls, 1971):

1. the principle of distribution of rights and responsibilities among individuals irrespective of their social position;
2. the principle of each individual's right to be different;
3. the principle of equal opportunity in education and training.

In the long term, strict application of these three principles leads to a reduction in social inequality. A social contract can therefore reduce the need for state intervention to redistribute income and wealth, and create a deeper sense of solidarity which eliminates the need for huge bureaucracies, particularly in the field of social policy.

Meanwhile, however, institutional obstacles to political decision-making mechanisms are increasing. Individual freedom will not be protected by promoting market forces at the expense of state intervention, but by ensuring that public and private bureaucracies are subject to democratic supervision. All developed economies, irrespective of their ideological background, are thus confronted to a greater or lesser extent with the same kind of problem. The state's authority as the arbiter and representative of community interests has been weakened by the influence of private organizations and the expansion of the civil service. The democratic decision-making mechanism has seized up. The failure of economic policy is a failure not only of state intervention but of economic and political decision-making mechanisms in general; it cannot therefore be used to justify a return to liberal doctrine. Economic theory based solely on this doctrine has proved unable to come up with workable answers and, in the absence of a latterday Keynes, has taken refuge in abstraction.

Can an all-pervading but powerless state be said to express a rational choice by its citizens? And is the present economic system conducive to individual freedom? Both domestically and internationally, the spirit of solidarity — surely the very essence of any state — is on the wane. The great debates of twenty years ago, which reflected a collective will to tackle contemporary problems, have become bogged down in matters of procedure and have all come to nothing. The developed countries are no longer able to make decisions based on a vision of the future; instead, they seem to have resigned themselves to the status quo.

PART III

A new approach

So far I have attempted to show how economic theory fails to take account of economic reality. By assuming the existence of a selfregulating market economy, theory has cut itself off from the reality of a society in which economic policy plays an increasingly vital part. Obsession with liberal doctrine has prevented economic theory from progressing.

However, one potential misunderstanding needs to be cleared up. What I am criticizing is not the liberal view of the individual, but its claim to be scientific. Since it reproduces a value system, economic theory remains subjective. This does not, however, mean that it is worthless. It is a powerful tool for conceptualizing economic problems, and it expresses an idea very effectively.

The body of theoretical work continues to grow. There is a multitude of purely theoretical models in all kinds of fields, all based on the assumption of economic rationality and all claiming accuracy. However, such profusion does not necessarily lead to a better understanding of how the economy works. With reasoning based on non-linear relationships and stochastic processes, the result is at best a display of technical virtuosity. Theoretical solutions are often indeterminate (cf. Evans, 1987); and, even where this can be remedied by means of additional hypotheses, the result is of no practical relevance, since it is not subjected to the criterion of falsification.

Such an abundance of theoretical activity reveals a numbingly deterministic vision of society which can ultimately only result in widespread cynicism. Intervention of any kind may then appear pointless, since in any case our lives are governed by forces that seem entirely beyond our control. Economic policy seldom yields the desired results; in most cases it simply distorts the market, introducing additional factors which encourage imperfect competition. The problem-solving approach which should emerge from economic policy is stifled by the fatalism which complex theoretical studies have generated.

Let us recall the two remedies proposed in response to such a pessimistic interpretation. The first is economic research in which theoretical models are systematically compared with concrete observations. The second is the breaking-down of the barriers between economic theory and other social sciences.

In principle, it is universally agreed that only research based on both theory and practice can advance our understanding of the economy. However, practical application of this principle is another matter altogether. Comparison of theory and practice is hampered by a lack of data. In Part I we pointed out the formidable statistical problems associated with empirical observations. In fact, the problems of quantification are so disheartening that some economists have taken refuge in abstract theoretical models or laborious case studies. Yet there are alternatives. To explore them, we must accept that many economically relevant facts are not quantifiable. They are, however, described by institutional research. There is thus a huge potential field of collaboration. This does not mean adopting a purely institutional approach to the economy, but applying knowledge acquired in other fields to economic models. The result may be a social-science methodology which acknowledges the inseparability of theory and practice, if only by bringing together all the instruments developed in the various disciplines in order to tackle a particular social problem. Such a methodology must be pragmatic and requires a clear research goal.

In order for goals to be formulated, society must display a definite political will to deal with a specific problem. This requires collaboration between research institutions and policymakers. Yet such collaboration will remain impossible as long as so much of the research undertaken by universities merely serves to justify decisions already taken by companies, umbrella organizations, government departments or similar bodies. The status quo of fragmented research is appreciated because it is so innocuous. Over-specialization makes it impossible to come up with workable analytical solutions to social problems. In a highly organized society which is divided up into multiple spheres of influence, economic research tends to be used to disguise such influence. In accepting such a role, economic research is failing to fulfil its task. Opportunism is taking over, and helping to extinguish one of the few remaining areas of academic freedom which society has maintained at such great expense. Value judgements by many economists are so greatly influenced by the prevailing ideology that they can truly be said to have lost all sense of criticism. The fact that the results of theoretical models merely reproduce the initial hypotheses is starting to rub off on people's attitudes. How, then, are we to overcome the resulting inertia and repair the damage that overspecialization has caused?

It is just as universally agreed that research teams need to be set up in the social sciences as they have been in the natural sciences. Once again, however, practical application of this principle is another matter altogether. The methods of selection applied by universities encourage specialization. As a result, the lone researcher no longer has all the necessary skills to carry out useful research. There is clearly an urgent need for the social sciences to be re-organized along interdisciplinary lines.

However, if one is not careful, such an approach can become sterile. One cannot help viewing the proliferation of expert reports and the resulting divergence of opinions as a consequence of the lack of clear political options. The absence of a political majority encourages a search for arguments which will provide established special interest groups with the justifications they need. Such a pessimistic view of the inability of economics to deal with policy issues is well expressed by Meehan (1982) when he states that economics is basically a spectator sport. This issue will be discussed in the final part of this book (Chapters 7, 8 and 9).

Chapter 7 outlines how economic theory can be integrated into the social sciences, allowing economic theory to become relevant to economic policy once more. The argument is based on the observation that economic thinking is gradually invading other fields without necessarily adding anything useful to them.

Chapter 8 concerns the notion of productivity. It emphasizes that the purpose of collaboration between the various social sciences must be to improve our understanding of specific social problems. Evidence that this condition can be satisfied is provided by empirical expressions of the concept of productivity. However, if such expressions remain couched in purely economic terms, they may well distract attention from problems such as the increasing consensus and transaction costs caused by state intervention and the costs of environmental protection caused by our way of life.

Finally, Chapter 9 turns to the theme of the environment and shows how fallacious purely economic reasoning can be. In particular, it draws attention to the fact that most measures adopted in this area have taken the form of controls or outright bans, rather than incentives as recommended by economic theory. While showing that this is a particularly suitable field for collaboration between the various disciplines, Chapter 9 also suggests that the problem of the environment is the direct result of a way of thinking based entirely on the hypothesis of economic rationality. If economic theory could open its eyes to other aspects of human behaviour, an analytical solution to the problems of environmental pollution might be within our reach.

CHAPTER 7

ECONOMICS AND THE SOCIAL SCIENCES

Although its theories do not satisfy the criterion of falsification, most economists consider economics to be the most scientific of the social sciences, since it is based on a series of "laws" which have deeply influenced contemporary economic reasoning. At the same time, its history, which is longer than that of most other social sciences, gives it pride of place: it can take advantage of both the current revival of positivism and the inferiority complex that afflicts the social sciences (Machlup, 1978).

It is difficult to make an instrumental comparison between exact sciences and social sciences and draw the conclusion that economics lies halfway between them. In adopting the comparison suggested by Machlup, I want to show that the distinctions, classifications and boundaries separating the natural sciences from the social sciences have become extremely blurred. Of Machlup's nine criteria, the most relevant are the following:

1. *Repetition*

Observations in the field of economics and social sciences are often unique and do not recur unvaryingly throughout history. Each event therefore requires a separate explanation.

2. ***Objectivity***

There can be no doubt that normative elements predominate in the social sciences (although they are also to be found in the exact sciences). It is vital to realize that all analysis has an ideological content, and to avoid the illusion that subjective criteria do not apply to economic theory because of its high level of abstraction.

3. ***Verification***

There is a speculative element in the hypotheses underlying any approach, and not all approaches are susceptible to empirical verification. The same problem arises in economics and in the social sciences. The various conflicting hypotheses cannot be eliminated simply by referring to available observations, since the latter are either based on a theoretical framework — indexes being a case in point — or else cannot be quantified. However, closer collaboration between economics and other social sciences would enable greater account to be taken of qualitative elements. At the very least, a more thorough understanding of institutions would make it easier to model theoretical analysis on perceived reality. The gulf that is beginning to develop has been caused by a tendency to "export" economic thinking into other fields.

The export of economic thinking

More and more disciplines are attracting economists' attention. One conventional explanation for this phenomenon is that fierce competition in American academic circles has led to everincreasing specialization, as illustrated by the development of such specialist areas as law economics, health economics, education economics and family economics. This could, in theory, have a stimulating effect. However, all that is happening is that economic thinking is being applied to more and more fields in an effort to demonstrate the superiority of an economic approach to social issues. Such a demonstration may well turn out to be counter-productive, since it puts real interdisciplinary collaboration even further out of reach. Essentially derived from neoclassical theory, it offers an analysis based entirely on economic rationality. Such an approach ends up going round in the usual theoretical circles and stops our understanding of social phenomena from progressing.

Below, I will refer to Becker's economic analysis of the family (Becker, 1981), and will show that the conclusions he reaches are over-optimistic. When applied to other fields, economic theory may give food for thought and yield interesting results — but the results may be wrong.

An economic approach to the family

Becker's purpose is not to examine the economic aspects of a household, but (as he states in his preface) to use instruments and concepts devised for the study of material behaviour to analyse non-material behaviour in response to events such as birth, marriage and divorce. In other words, Becker is using the apparatus of economic theory in an attempt to prove that economic theory is universally applicable and that economic thinking is involved in all human behaviour — no mean undertaking.

Here the discussion of basic assumptions is used not to qualify the hypothesis of economic rationality, but to reinforce it. Not surprisingly, the entire range of neoclassical hypotheses is brought out to explain how the family works. The family is thus made up of individuals who are out to maximize either their utility function or their production function, subject as usual to either income or cost constraints; transactions between spouses, between generations and between parents and children are governed by markets (which may be implicit), and equilibrium is maintained by the competition mechanism. Here economists are on familiar ground. What is new is the application of these hypotheses to demographic phenomena. If neoclassical theory could successfully demonstrate that changes in the family institution (especially since the spread of contraception in industrialized societies) are merely the sum total of marginal adjustments by individuals, then institutions, cultural acquirements, the historical dimension, and irrational behaviour by individuals would all become irrelevant: we would then have proof that economic theory is the most fruitful method of analysing social reality, and that there is therefore no need for interdisciplinary collaboration between sociologists, psychologists, demographers and economists. In practice, however, things are not so simple.

What are the main themes and conclusions of this approach to the family? Do the results merely reproduce the initial hypotheses? Are we able not only to test the hypotheses empirically, but also to compare the results with other available data on the family?

Not only are these vital questions from the point of view of methodology, but they prepare the ground for further enquiry into human motives for changing one's behaviour, and ultimately for a challenge to the concept of productivity.

Becker begins by describing a household consisting of one person, defined as any economic agent operating in any market. This person maximizes a utility function subject to a budget constraint, justifying the hypothesis that variation in demand for a good is inversely proportional to variation in its price. To make the utility function more realistic, a time constraint is introduced. Time may be allocated to various activities, including work, which generates income. The budget constraint is no longer exogenous, for it depends on the amount of time the individual decides to allocate to working; this allows us to define conditions of equilibrium for the typical individual encountered earlier in our discussion of the efficient market model.

At this point we can introduce a household production function, representing the household's consumption of goods and services which cannot be purchased by a market transaction. Household production includes such diverse "goods" as children, status, health, altruism, selfishness and pleasure. Each of these "goods" has a notional price, but also entails real production costs which again introduce a time constraint.

As thus defined, the household's utility function covers both consumption and production. The model can be completed by adding an education investment function. However, since savings invested in human capital increase over time, the more skilled labour that results can command a higher wage. This reduces the budget constraint and allows either greater consumption of goods produced by external markets, or production of such goods within the household.

If we now introduce the couple, we can see how division of labour operates within a household. The important factor here is the formation of human capital, which introduces the notion of differences in comparative advantages among individuals. The partner with a comparative advantage in the market outside the household will specialize completely in that market, while the one with more relative aptitude for household tasks will likewise devote himself — or herself — entirely to this area. Clearly, however, comparative advantages are determined not only by investment in human capital, but also by factors such as biological differences, differences in personal preference, or the employment situation.

The basic issue here is whether economic behaviour reinforces biological differences. If women are assigned to the implicit household market with its relatively low or indeed non-existent money income, this is bound to encourage men's specialization in the explicit external market. However, economic behaviour may manifest itself differently. If women's wages on the external market increase, time will be allocated differently: women will devote less time to household chores, the elements that make up their stock of human capital will also change, the division of labour within the household will be affected, and the birthrate will fall. Sex roles are thus affected by market forces. Accordingly, it is not clear whether biological differences reinforced by rational economic behaviour are what determine economic sex roles — clearly reflected in lower wages for women or whether such roles are determined by wage structures and are only incidentally influenced by biological differences.

Applied to the household and its external relations, the market concept can also be used to define relations within the marriage market. Here, economic analysis tends to echo the old adage that birds of a feather flock together. An efficient marriage market brings together men and women who satisfy the same economic criteria: the pricing system, which is linked to other qualitative criteria, means that men who fetch a low price will marry similarly low-priced women. However, this market ceases to be efficient if, for example, gains from marriage cannot be shared or powers are unequally distributed. Dowries and legal provisions governing inheritance and divorce are then seen as ways of reducing such inequalities. According to this interpretation, divorce is simply the result of imperfect market information.

It should be remembered that the marriage market can only function efficiently if the following conditions are met: (a) there must be a large number of demanders and suppliers, (b) the good on offer (i.e. marriage) must be homogeneous, and (c) there must be perfect information. If the information available during the marriage is the complete opposite of what was available before the marriage, the logical consequence is divorce. This frankly rather superficial result becomes more complex if there are children involved, as their demand must also be reflected in the model.

If divorce is foreseen, there will be fewer children and hence, supposedly, fewer obstacles to divorce. However, divorce only indirectly affects the number of children, which is chiefly determined in terms of substitution for other goods and services. This in turn depends on both the price of a child and disposable real income, which explains why the birthrate in agricultural communities was traditionally higher than in towns, why increases in the wages of women employed in explicit markets lead to a fall in the number of children born, and why the birthrate has been significantly affected by such things as government schemes to assist unmarried mothers. Such explanations all derive from purely theoretical models of family economic behaviour, and lead to one of the most important features of the entire analysis. In distinguishing between the desired number and the desired qualifications of children, such models give useful pointers for an understanding of how human capital is formed and the problems of inequal distribution of income in our society. One definite consequence is that higher incomes mean more children. At the same time, however, higher incomes also mean greater demands regarding education. Cost constraints then reduce the number of children while at the same time increasing their qualifications. According to this argument, higher incomes rather than improved contraceptive techniques are the reason for the lower birthrate in industrialized countries. In that case, however, higher incomes should lead to a higher birthrate in countries with free public education, since the cost of education there is a far less serious constraint than in countries where education is private yet this is a factor which theory must disregard, since it takes no account of institutional differences. In any case, the highly abstract reasoning used in this demonstration is merely intended to identify a general type of behaviour which can be used to analyse the family context and its impact on children's opportunities for development. The influence of the family environment on children's future income can thus be analysed within the logical framework of economic thinking. A simple initial model establishes a positive relationship between children's income and that of their parents, including such random elements as differing ability and opportunities. The family income is then defined by the parents' income, discounted investment in the children's education, and chance. This family income is shared between the parents and the children. Using the criterion of optimality that is so frequently applied in economic analysis, such sharing can only result in an increasing share for the children as the parents' income level rises. This demonstration raises the issue of inequality and how it is passed on to subsequent generations.

This approach to the family combines aspects of inequality with aspects of inter-generational mobility. Human capital theory is important because it shows that inequality may simply arise from a family's behaviour in maximizing a constrained utility function. Chance or ability play no part here. Investment choices take place between the human and non-human capital of the children and perhaps other members of the family. This theoretical framework thus provides two essential factors which supposedly explain how inequality is passed on from generation to generation. Firstly, parental advantages may be passed on to the children through inheritance; secondly, parents prefer investing in their children's future to using their income for personal consumption.

While these factors do explain income distribution within each generation and between generations, they also raise the problem of altruistic behaviour, which cannot easily be reconciled with the rational behaviour of Economic Man. A standard way of getting round this is to claim that altruism is merely selfishness in disguise. However, this is a circular argument. If all individuals are by definition rational, then altruism must indeed be a form of selfishness. If, on the other hand, all individuals are assumed to be altruists, even apparently selfish behaviour will in fact turn out to be altruistic (Lutz and Lux, 1979).

The importance of altruism within families must therefore be acknowledged. Becker defines it rather oddly in terms of interaction between the various interdependent utility functions. If an increase in the wife's utility causes the husband's to increase also, this does not necessarily mean that the husband is altruistic. Likewise, if an increase in her utility causes his to diminish, this does not necessarily mean he is selfish. The notion of interdependence leads to a theorem which states that even a selfish member of the family will refrain from acting against the interests of the family as a whole. In other words, even selfish individuals learn that acts which damage their own group are not in their own interests.

However, it may be wondered why selfishness should prevail in market transactions and altruism in family ones. Becker's answer is that altruism is not lacking in market transactions, but that the income it provides is psychological rather than monetary. However, altruism is an inefficient way of obtaining such income. On the other hand, altruism is important in family life because the altruistic individual's utility, which depends on consumption by the other individual, gives him a higher income.

To complete his treatise on the family, Becker uses the behaviour of family groups in the animal kingdom to provide additional proof that economic analysis is a powerful and potentially universal instrument. He concludes that the contemporary family is going through a radical transformation: reduced fertility, more frequent divorce, and greater employment of women. All these factors depend on the increase in women's wages, which can thus be seen as an exogenous explanatory factor in this dramatic change.

The comparative advantages of both sexes have thus changed in such a way as to increase the cost of having children and reduce the gains from marriage. Divorce is on the increase, and the greater likelihood of its occurring is reducing the birthrate. The increasingly elaborate social security system is enhancing this tendency and reducing altruism within the family. This trend can only be reversed by slower growth in the developed countries, which would necessitate greater interaction within the family. It should be noted that this explanation scarcely refers to either the spread of contraception or the feminist movement.

A controversial approach

Not surprisingly, this analysis of the family using tools borrowed from economic theory has proved controversial. What *is* surprising is the diversity of the arguments advanced. Indeed, Part I of this book could be entirely re-written in these terms, since much of the criticism levelled at

Becker's treatise on the family applies equally to economic theory pursued as an end in itself. The controversy concerns both methodology and basic assumptions, and raises the issue of whether it is appropriate to use mathematical language in the social sciences.

However, the criticism centres on neoclassical theory's claim to be universally applicable (not in the sense that it can be empirically verified, but in the sense that its analytical framework can be applied to research topics such as the family).

Let us begin by noting that the criticism is occasioned by certain flaws in the theoretical framework. Amazingly, if the initial hypotheses are accepted, every strategy should logically lead to marriage. In the marriage market, the individual is assumed to maximize his utility, and economic rationality makes it clear that his utility will be greater if he marries than if he remains single. Thus the theory merely reproduces the liberal doctrine that the individual knows better than anyone else what is good for him. Divorce — which has become far more common in most Western countries since the 1950s — should then simply be seen as a case of market failure. However, this brings us back to John Stuart Mill's argument regarding education: if the individual does *not* know what is good for him, how can the market operate? The notion that divorce is merely a case of market failure caused by lack of information suggests an astonishing inability to understand this increasingly widespread social phenomenon.

A second conceptual difficulty concerns the distinction between rational and altruistic behaviour.

Economic rationality is the basis for microeconomic trade and results in a market maintained in equilibrium by variation in an explicit price. Within the family, on the other hand, the interdependence of each member's utility functions results in altruistic behaviour reinforced by individual learning. Such selfishness as does occur is thus in the family interest. Let us take the example of two altruists who exchange gifts. Their altruistic behaviour thus leads to trade. The gifts in question may be equal in value and conceptually indistinguishable. Ultimately, then, there is nothing to distinguish the selfish behaviour of the economic agent in the market from the altruistic behaviour of the family member.

However, those who apply neoclassical theory to social issues are so imbued with the normative content of the underlying hypotheses that they fail to see the circularity of their argument. The results of the analysis confirm the initial normative hypotheses, *ergo* economic theory is universal. One can only be amazed at the naïvety of those who use the frequency with which Becker is quoted to conclude that he has made a vital contribution to our understanding of the family (Ben-Porath, 1981).

The main argument in favour of Becker's approach is that it provides a solid analytical framework for family studies, which is bound to help all those who are analysing the family in their various fields. As a reference tool, it certainly helps to clarify the debate. The analytical framework is flexible, and can accommodate anything from data collection to the introduction of new hypotheses. It analyses human behaviour in such varied areas as marriage, reproduction, education, allocation of time, and income distribution. It therefore represents a substantial breakthrough in the social sciences, facilitating research into the causal relationships that form the basis of human society.

The main difficulty with this approach is that it reduces institutional aspects to the sum total of individual marginal adjustments. Institutions are not seen as independent entities. Accordingly, in addition to attacking neoclassical hypotheses, the main criticisms of Becker's approach emphasize the role of institutions.

Neoclassical economists in general, and those concerned with the family in particular, have failed to grasp the role of culture and institutions (Hannan, 1981). They both underestimate it by disputing the interdependence of institutions and human behaviour, and overestimate it by viewing social structures as immutable. According to Hannan, market mechanisms simply reflect institutional rules in terms of preference distribution. However, in assuming that all individuals display utilitarian behaviour, they deny not only the differences between individuals and groups but also their right to such differences. Here we come back to one of the basic criticisms levelled at liberal doctrine by advocates of the social contract, which is that the individualism of "rational" economic behaviour is curbed by expressions of wider solidarity.

If we look at the field studies carried out by sociologists over a long period, an extremely differentiated picture of marriage emerges (Kellerhals, 1982). If we take a representative sample of marriages occurring in a particular year and monitor them over a number of years by means of surveys and interviews, the picture of marriage as a uniform reference institution begins to fade. What we find instead is a variety of ways of living together, each shaped by numerous socio-cultural factors. Such studies remind us that a purely deductive theory cannot be subjected to the criterion of falsification. It needs to be made quite clear that the empirical observations proposed by Becker in support of his own theories will not serve to verify the underlying neoclassical hypotheses or the results of purely deductive reasoning. In order to produce models in which the close link between institutional change and human behaviour is acknowledged, there is no alternative to horizontal, interdisciplinary collaboration.

Economics: a social science

The case for considering economics as a social science goes back a long way. It has a well-established place in the history of economic thought, and comes to the fore whenever authors turn their attention more closely to social issues.

What is striking is that the need for such an approach has never been in dispute. Evidence of this can be found throughout the literature, which nevertheless merely scratches at the surface. On the one hand we have a comprehensive theoretical framework which provides tools for analysis but remains abstract; on the other hand we have strings of data and innumerable case studies which provide an excellent description of social reality but fail to give a comprehensive picture of how society functions. It must be borne in mind that the strength of economic theory lies not only in its ideological content, but also in its ability to conceptualize social issues and provide a comprehensive picture. Its main weakness, however, is its isolation from social reality — hence the abundance of worthless economic policy recommendations that are left to gather dust. The models on which they are based have quite simply overlooked an essential factor which often lies beyond the scope of economing thinking, but within the domain of one of the other social sciences.

At the same time, socio-economics rejects the assumption of economic rationality, relying instead on either the hypothesis of limited rationality or else the social contract and other kinds of behaviour such as altruism or the pursuit of power. In any case, as soon as economists start to collaborate with practitioners of the other social sciences, the notion of utilitarianism is bound to be challenged.

The history of economic thought: a social perspective

Oddly enough, the authors we will refer to in this connection include some of the originators of liberal thinking. Here their views will be presented in a new and somewhat more utopian light. The writings of Adam Smith — often considered to be the founding father of economics — reveal definite traces of a socioeconomic approach. He saw economics as a science for politicians and legislators. It should not be forgotten that the state on which his thinking was based was still rudimentary compared with the kind of state we know today. Smith's assumption of a selfregulating economy governed by individual rationality was a way of making the public interest a central issue, in contrast to the absolute power of the king.

Liberal insistence that this theory should apply equally to any kind of state is, I believe, the cause of the fatal confusion which has isolated economic theory from social reality. This explains the liberal refusal to take account of the institutional framework, which could only be ignored by making economic theory increasingly abstract. This was bound to undermine the credibility of economic policy, whose very origins lie in social institutions.

In explicitly acknowledging the institutional framework, economic policy found an appropriate analytical framework. Adam Smith's "invisible hand", so often quoted as typifying the operation of a market economy, was in fact intended as a means of distributing goods equitably in order to cover each individual's basic material needs (Bridel, 1988). This was not so much a natural law of self-regulation as the expression of moral demands by the people in response to what was an arbitrary feudal regime.

This brings us back to the issue of efficiency versus equity. Liberal economic thinking has clearly established an order of priority: efficiency must come before equity. However, this order can be reversed if a political majority so wishes. As soon as minimum material conditions (in terms of consumption and education) are met, the individual can express his preferences in an economy that operates on the market principle. We need only recall the social conditions prevailing at the time to realize that, from the outset, economics included a moral dimension which was sometimes ignored as industrialization proceeded. Sixteen hour working days, the suffering of children treated as mere factors of production, and economic theories inspired by the writings of Ricardo and Malthus — who saw subsistence-level living standards as the result of some inevitable natural mechanism — can scarcely be reconciled with the moral foundation which Adam Smith provided for the budding science of economics.

Such a contradiction could hardly go unnoticed. The counterattack came from one of Adam Smith's disciples. In 1819, Sismondi published his "New principles of economics" as an alternative to the self-regulating natural laws that were said to govern the economy. Today, the only remaining traces of these principles are those found in Marxist economies. Sismondi's approach is more or less ignored by current mainstream economic theory, which considers his views over-humanistic. Sismondi maintained that the purpose of economic activity was not the accumulation of wealth but man himself. Wealth was merely a tool which should serve the entire community so as to ensure that at least basic needs were satisfied. The economy clearly had an egalitarian basis which could only be maintained by legislation laid down by a government representing the public interest. Not surprisingly, Sismondi began by advocating measures to improve the material circumstances of the working class, including legislation to reduce working hours and outlaw child labour. He also recommended progressive taxation as a means of correcting the inequalities created by the accumulation of wealth. Such views clearly anticipated the role of the modern state. However, this eminent nineteenth-century economist, who recommended that the state should have an active role and that the economy should be run in accordance with moral goals, did not succeed in diverting the future course of neoclassical economic theory.

Sismondi's themes are concrete, and all have a quite definitely normative content. They are specifically based on a broader perception of social issues than economic theory can provide from inside its ivory tower. However, modern social arrangements have done greater justice to Sismondi's recommendations than to classical thinking, since they have resulted in a major institutional change which is still going on. This will be clear if we compare today's environmental requirements with Sismondi's warnings against blind faith in industrialization, or set the growing lack of motivation now found among certain groups of employees against Sismondi's call for measures to help small rural businesses survive in the face of industrialization.

In discussing the origins of liberal doctrine we have referred to John Stuart Mill who, although a member of the classical school, shared Sismondi's concerns in one particular respect: he did not see the accumulation of wealth as the primary aim of human activity. Distressed by the poverty he saw around him, he was an advocate of intervention in social affairs. Foreseeing that the competitive mainspring of the market mechanism might well degenerate into battles between individuals, he proposed that education be used to foster the development of altruism, a necessary condition if culture was to blossom and become the true goal of human activity. This vision of society humanized by an effort of individual and collective education is akin to modern concerns reflected in the growing importance of humanistic approaches to psychology, approaches which are increasingly recognized as a separate discipline (Lutz and Lux, 1979). According to this approach, a hierarchy of human needs can be established in ascending order from basic necessities to the need for self-realization.

Basically, of course, man has physiological needs, and related material needs such as safety and protection. This is clearly economic territory. However, in the hierarchy of needs social motives are added to economic ones. Finally, at the top of the hierarchy we find needs such as the pursuit of truth or existential meaning or the ethical expression of human activity (Maslow, 1970). Such needs, which reflect Mill's concerns, clearly indicate that the value system underlying neoclassical economic theory must be reviewed.

Such a review, attempted in revolutionary fashion by Karl Marx, has created an unbridgeable gulf between economists. As a result, the development of economic theory has suffered from a pernicious dialectic between a liberal philosophy which has become the basis for mainstream economic theory, and a collectivist philosophy culminating in the planned economy. Very probably this confrontation has resulted in polarization which has ultimately prevented economic theory from concerning itself with humanistic goals. The fascination of certain economists with Marx has failed to create the interdisciplinary platform for the analysis of contemporary social issues that has been advocated so emphatically in this book. The economy is subject to a process of evolution which can be traced in institutional change and in the degree of organization of society. Social intervention has become more and more extensive and has led to successive social reforms. This book does not criticize neoclassical economic theory as opposed to a Marxist economy, but rather for its claim to be scientific. It fails to take account of institutional change, particularly with regard to the role of the state. This is therefore essentially a criticism of methodology, a point of view shared by John Ruskin (1970), whose writings — first published in 1862 — were a milestone in the history of socioeconomic thought.

Once again, over-abstraction was the point at issue. Ruskin went onto the attack by declaring that he did not doubt the conclusions reached by economics — he simply considered them irrelevant. He compared them with the conclusions of a supposed "science" of gymnastics which assumed that man did not have a skeleton and then attempted to re-create his bone structure on the basis of its own conclusions (Ruskin, 1970, p. 27).

This is exactly what happens when economic theory attempts to deal with "institutional" phenomena without reference to human behaviour. The criticism thus clearly concerns the pure hypothesis of economic rationality, which cannot produce a workable social science. Instead of the value of a good being defined in terms of market trade, it needs to be assessed according to its ability to satisfy elementary needs, including the need for aesthetic and creative appeal. The basic problem of allocation of scarce resources, as proposed by economic theory, is thus turned on its head. Instead of man being considered as a factor of production to be used as rationally as possible in a production process, it is production that must satisfy man's needs in the hierarchy of needs described by Maslow.

The value of a good is then defined by the degree of creativity released by its production. Not only does this new interpretation bypass the utilitarian approach, it also challenges the concept of mass production due to industrialization. The division of labour inherent in such systems demoralizes the individual, a feeling which the economy must then compensate for by producing more consumer and above all leisure goods. Yet the division of labour is merely one aspect of industrialization, the other being the problem of the environment — another example of what happens when economic models fail to give priority to man and the human social fabric.

Ruskin's arguments were placed in a more analytical context by his pupil John Hobson, whose criticism of classical theory was essentially the same: by defining the field of economics in purely utilitarian terms, it failed either to analyse social issues or to come up with workable solutions.

In drawing attention to the problem of motivation, Hobson's work may be seen as pointing the way to later participation and profit-sharing models. This, at least, is the view taken by Gide and Rist (6th ed., 1944). Ruskin and Hobson may in fact be the originators of new ways of organizing production. Particular examples can be found in the car industry, where the productionline system has made way for production teams or for robot controlled production which allows employees to devote themselves to more responsible supervisory tasks.

Two conclusions can be drawn from this:

1. As Hobson's work on the development of modern capitalism (1926) shows, economic theory must have an institutional basis.
2. Economic activity must be guided by ethical considerations. This requirement has recently become more popular, perhaps because new doubts as to the capabilities of science — particularly in the fields of nuclear energy and genetic engineering — have raised questions which apply equally to economics (Sen, 1973).

Indeed, the growing scepticism about purely positivist explanations has not spared economics. The now evident link between economics and ethics necessarily means abandoning overabstract explanatory models. Once again, an obsession with maximization of material wealth has prevented economics from acknowledging the normative dimension which is so essential to the solution of economic problems.

The further history of economic thought is well known. The fragmentary attempts by Sismondi, Mill, Ruskin and Hobson to introduce humanistic concepts into economic theory were all swept aside by the advocates of marginal utility, the true founders of neoclassical theory. In successfully demonstrating that utility can be measured in comparative terms, they laid the foundations of what they thought was a true science.

Instead of reasoning from total values, neoclassical economists referred to additional values. Finally, they introduced what appeared to be an objective criterion to express the primary purpose of the economy. Constrained utility maximization was thus held to obey mathematical laws, and human economic behaviour was reduced once and for all to a utilitarian dimension. Economic theory could at last specialize and stay aloof from the other social sciences.

The rift between the apparently ever more scientific approach of economics and the value judgements of the social sciences was thus total. However, among the co-founders of marginal utility theory, a lone voice stressed the need to develop the social dimension of economic theory. The voice was that of Léon Walras (1896). Nowadays he is chiefly known as the founder of mathematical economics and theoretical constructions of general equilibrium, and as the person who finally provided neoclassical theory with a utilitarian basis. He is therefore associated with liberal thinking — a posthumous assessment which, judging by the three courses he gave in Lausanne between 1870 and 1892, would surely have disappointed him. These courses were nothing less than a treatise on economics and socio-economics. Of the three volumes he wrote (dealing with pure economics, applied economics and socio-economics respectively), only the one on pure economics was published in its entirety, establishing a reputation which Walras enjoys to this day. The fragments published under the title *Etudes d'èconomie sociale* (Socio-economic studies) (Walras, 1896) are therefore disconcerting. The kind of intervention proposed by Walras flagrantly contradicts the neoclassical label history has placed on his work. His main proposal, the nationalization of land property, was rejected and indeed brought him into discredit. He was accused of being a socialist. Yet his thinking was in fact much more subtle: it was a reflection on the role and the function of the state. If taxes were abolished, the state budget would be entirely derived from land rent. As land is by definition a fixed factor of production, any pressure, whether demographic or economic, will result in an increase in state receipts, enabling the state to increase its expenditure in accordance with the burden placed on the economy by the environment. This is how Walras's writings can be interpreted in today's context. However, there can be no doubt that he was concerned to identify the boundary between the relative spheres of influence of the state and of the individual. Such detailed thinking, nowadays reduced to the theory of general equilibrium, deserves more attention. On the link between theory and practice, he writes:

"As far as theory and practice are concerned, it is accepted that:

1. *perfection, or the absolute, is the essential principle of theory and of science;*

2. *imperfection, or the relative, is the essential principle of practice and of art."*

Accordingly:

1. *"the idea of social perfectibility, which implies that of a theoretical and scientific social ideal emerging from an understanding of social reality as provided by experience, thereby implies the idea of perfection;"*
2. *"the idea of social perfectibility, which implies that of social reality to which theoretical and scientific social principles are applied, thereby implies the idea of imperfection."* (Walras, 1896, p. 11).

In basing its approach on the first of these propositions, neoclassical theory was bound to remain abstract and isolated from social reality. This gives a clue to the possibility of interdisciplinary research which could strike an admittedly difficult balance between the pursuit of perfection and the acceptance of imperfection.

In subtitling his socio-economic studies *Théorie de la répartition de la richesse sociale* (Theory of the distribution of social wealth), Walras clearly identified the clash between the normative and positive aspects of economics. As this book has tried to show, income distribution remains a normative issue, all attempts to introduce an objective criterion in this area having failed.

As Dumez (1986) mentions, Walras dreamed of a multidisciplinary-institution which would abolish the distinction between literary and scientific training, so harmful to economic analysis.

At the same time, Walras's vision concerned both materialism and spiritualism: "Materialism reduces man's destiny to the satisfaction of physical needs and considers human destinies mutually hostile, whereas spiritualism, while it sees human destiny in the triumph of freedom, considers human destinies independent of one another". However, "will is not exercised under conditions of total individual freedom, but partly under the influence of social necessities. Human destinies are not absolutely independent, but to some extent dependent on one another. There is a social morality which is distinct from individual morality" (Walras, 1896, p. 74).

Between these extremes there is an intermediate position which socio-economics can usefully fill. Its criterion for intervention would be the satisfaction of elementary physiological needs rather than the maximization of a utility function or the kind of retreat into spiritual experience currently advocated by an growing number of sects.

After Walras, only the institutional schools were to repeat this appeal for a social dimension to economics. However, my purpose in this book is not so much to revive institutional thinking as to try and create a basis for a more thorough integration of economic theory into the social sciences.

The conditions for socio-economics

Collaboration between economics and the social sciences can be pursued once the idea of an all-embracing theory has been abandoned. Such a theory must be necessarily be too abstract to provide a concrete basis for economic policy. It does not even provide a comprehensive view of the world, since it fails to take account of its cultural symbols.

In socio-economics, on the other hand, intervention — that is to say economic policy — is the central issue. Socio-economics sets out from the premise that economic and social organization can be changed, and that man is capable of controlling it. In order to do this, it is not necessary to comprehend the whole of society. All that is needed is to forge tools that indicate a will to act. Fatalistic acceptance of the constraints imposed by social organization results in a mystifying view of the individual as dependent on a hierarchical social system. Economics and the social sciences can only progress if the workings of the state and of public and private bureaucracies are explicitly acknowledged, a process which is not yet completed. In exalting individual freedom, neoclassical theory has helped reduce man to his selfish dimension. Social history, however, has shown that that this dimension is merely one aspect of community life. Society has grown up through by institutional change which has always been caused by human intervention. At the same time, the nature of human intervention has always been determined by institutions.

Such interdependence is explicitly acknowledged in socioeconomics. At the same time, socio-economics can gradually rid the social sciences of an excessive ideological bias. However,if this approach is to be reflected in research, a number of conditions must be satisfied:

1. Economists must acknowledge that most of their theories are based on circular reasoning, and the social sciences must provide more coherent indicators of institutional change. In this way our understanding of collective decision-making mechanisms can shift away from a purely economic interpretation. The market is, after all, merely one of a number of collective decision-making mechanisms.
2. Having diagnosed the problems, society must of course demonstrate its willingness to tackle them squarely. Only then will it be possible to set out clear goals for interdisciplinary research. The universities,

for their part, must reorganize the field of social sciences so as to create research strategies capable of responding to specific social requirements, and their training and selection criteria need to be reviewed accordingly.

In fact, however, everyone may be perfectly happy with the status quo. Society prefers economics to embrace its role as a provider of training for the needs of the present-day working environment. Research is thus either used to further academic careers — its impact on the organization of society then being minimal — or else serves as an excuse for avoiding collective decisions. The resulting malaise may well culminate in an institutional crisis which will leave neither the universities nor society unscathed. Meanwhile, the problems are there for all to see. The aging population, land use planning, the environment, and development are all matters crying out for interdisciplinary solutions. In each case, purely utilitarian approaches must make way for a proper enquiry into the purpose of what we are doing.

CHAPTER 8

THE MEANING OF PRODUCTIVITY

Optimal allocation of resources is the stated aim of economics, and requires productivity to be measured statistically. In everyday usage the terms "profitability", "performance" and "efficiency" — which are embodied in the concept of productivity — are often treated as synonyms, indicating that even the definition of productivity is unclear. It is no exaggeration to state that society has built up a veritable myth around this concept, showing once again that economic terminology is full of symbolism (strength, power, ability to adapt, competitiveness, motivation, and faith in material goals) which reflects the interaction between institutions and human behaviour. In short, the concept of productivity is a source of controversy.

This chapter will attempt to highlight the various aspects of the controversy. After defining productivity in purely theoretical terms, it will point out the close links between growth and variation in factors of production which economic theory commonly considers as productive resources. Finally, attention will be drawn to the statistical difficulties involved in obtaining empirical observations of theoretical concepts.

The results of psychological research into work motivation will then be examined, and an attempt will be made to show the social changes that have accompanied the structural shift from an industrial to a service economy, as reflected not only at the technological and sectoral levels of the economy but also in the emergence of new attitudes and aspirations. There is evidence of changes in the value system prevailing in certain social strata. While economic theory does not succeed in taking account of such changes in motivation, the concept of productivity does.

I believe the concept of productivity is a useful way of achieving a synthesis between purely economic approaches and approaches derived from other social sciences. It will also prepare the ground for the demonstration in the final chapter that the organization of production aggravates the environmental problems resulting from a purely utilitarian analysis. The issues raised by environmental pollution are thus very much in line with the approach adopted throughout this book, and suggest the need to review the excessively economic content of the concept of productivity.

Economic interpretations of productivity

The fact that economics has provided so many definitions of productivity is due not only to the various origins of this concept in the history of economic thought, but also to the lack of a unanimous interpretation in the field of production. Productivity may be defined as the share of production which can be attributed to a given factor of production, i.e. the relationship between the productive resources used and the resulting production.

A distinction can also be made between productivity of labour and productivity of capital, although it is still perfectly possible to talk of the productivity of a given sector or even of an entire country. The idea is to express productive effort and its results, if possible in quantifiable terms. The concept of productivity undoubtedly includes a value judgement expressed in terms of the equity and fairness of income distribution within an economy. However, the most relevant theoretical interpretation links the concept of productivity to firms' demand for resources.

The ratio between a country's total production and its working population is expressed as an average, indicating each worker's average contribution to value added over a given period. However, according to neoclassical economists, a firm's economic calculus is dictated not by average but by marginal values — in other words, what will be the increase in production if one extra worker is hired? This question defines productivity in terms of variations in both the factor of production and the product.

In order for physical production to be conveyed in terms of value, it is assessed according to the price at which it can be sold. This not only allows an empirical observation of productivity — since most statistics are expressed in nominal terms — but also shows that productivity is influenced by market conditions (supply *and* demand). Neoclassical theory has responded to these difficulties with a neat definition of the concept of productivity.

Marginal productivity theory

This theory demonstrates that the reward to each factor of production is determined by its marginal productivity, provided that the economy is in equilibrium and that conditions of perfect competition prevail. Equilibrium is defined according to Pareto's criteria of optimality: the optimum is reached when the production of a good cannot be increased without harming the production of another good.

This interpretation immediately defines the reward to factors of production in terms of general equilibrium, and can also be applied to a firm. Here it need only be remembered that a company is assumed to maximize its total profits. For example, as long as a unit of labour costs the company less than it brings in, the firm will continue to hire workers and so increase its profits. If, on the other hand, a unit of labour costs more than it brings in, the firm will dismiss workers until the last unit hired brings in exactly the same amount as it costs. The nominal marginal productivity of this last unit is equal to its cost, i.e. the wage rate as determined by the labour market. Under conditions of perfect competition, the firm cannot affect the price of the good it produces by varying its supply. The price can therefore be considered as a constant. If this constant is reduced to unity, nominal marginal productivity will be identical to physical marginal productivity. In other words, nominal measurement of the physical marginal productivity of labour is only possible if perfect competition is assumed to prevail in the market for goods and services. This assumption makes it meaningless to use statistical series expressed in monetary units, unless it is possible to determine the extent of the discrepancy between physical marginal productivity and nominal marginal productivity caused by imperfect competition rather than inflation. However, a far more serious problem is that, for statistical purposes, we can only observe average values; marginal values remain theoretical constructions, often without any empirical basis. Moreover, marginal productivity theory considers factors of production to be homogeneous, which obviously raises formidable statistical problems. The failure to distinguish between the various levels of qualification of labour makes this theory empirically meaningless. Once again there is a gulf between economic theory and practice.

This inability to measure physical marginal productivity in statistical terms is awkward for another reason. In Part I, the Phillips curve was used as an example of the uncertain link between economic theory and observations of economic reality. The various attempts to explain the instability of this curve over time all assume that physical marginal productivity remains constant in the short term. Consequently, changes in the nominal wage rate reflect changes in the rate of inflation. The instability of the Phillips curve is currently considered one of the most puzzling phenomena in macroeconomics. It could perhaps be analysed in a different light if the theoretical content of the concept of productivity differed from that of marginal productivity theory.

Let us assume, for example, that a part of the gains from productivity is used to finance social policy. A broader concept would take account of this "socialized" portion, and variations in the nominal wage rate would thus reflect not only variations in productivity defined in strictly economic terms, but also variations in the financing of social policy, which are influenced by the political balance of power and by the individual and social perception of solidarity.

The difficulties mentioned with regard to labour productivity recur in connection with the marginal productivity of other factors of production. Things are made worse by the particularly abstract nature of physical capital. It is impossible to define units of physical capital or to take account of its heterogeneous nature. Only the financial aspect of capital can be measured, which makes it quite impossible to determine directly the real interest rate as a rate of reward based on the physical marginal productivity of capital. Accordingly, the real interest rate continues to be defined as the difference between the nominal interest rate and the expected rate of inflation. This indirect definition can lead to the absurd situation in which economic models assume a real interest rate which is negative.

If the heterogeneous nature of factors of production is taken into account, this undermines the very basis of marginal productivity theory. One of the advocates of socio-economics, John Hobson, argues as follows (Blaug, 1985). If the quantity of labour increases, the nature of capital will also change. More workers do not necessarily mean more machines, but different ones. In that case, since hiring extra workers causes a change in the production process, how can the increase in production be attributed to a single factor taken in isolation? In other words, the heterogeneous nature of factors of production is a formidable obstacle not only to empirical observation but also to the theoretical construction. Hobson's objection is clearly aimed at the over-abstract content of the theory, but he also argues rather convincingly that such a theoretical approach dodges the issue of motivation, which is an integral part of the concept of productivity.

At the same time, difficulties of interpretation are also raised by the neoclassical hypothesis that factors of production are perfectly substitutable for one another.

The basic idea here is that technologies are interchangeable and that, given the prevailing relative prices of factors of production, a firm will choose the technology that leads to an optimal situation. If, for instance, labour is fairly plentiful in the economy, its relative price will be low and the firm will tend to adopt a relatively labour-intensive technology. In an economy where capital is plentiful, on the other hand, a more capital-intensive technology will be chosen. In other words, economic theory assumes that firms are free to choose from an infinite number of combinations of factors of production in order to achieve the same goal. Although this is once again a theoretical assumption, a number of examples can be found to support this concept of interchangeable technologies. A good example is the textile industry, which in industrialized countries has been entirely automated, whereas in developing countries it still relies on a plentiful labour supply. This example is interesting for three reasons:

1. The difference between the various factors depends on the degree of development. Lack of capital dictates the choice of technology, which thus expresses the country's relative access to productive resources.
2. If the goods produced are homogeneous, some comparison between the various sources of production is possible.
3. Demand for a factor of production is linked to its relative scarcity. A worker in an industrial society is better paid quite simply because the ratio of available machines to the working population is higher than it is in the third world.

As this last argument clearly shows, the concept of rewards to factors based on physical marginal productivity totally bypasses the normative issue of the right to a fair wage. Since the problem of equity is central to the development debate, neoclassical theory may not the most suitable model for analysing third-world countries. Yet if it is restricted to industrialized countries, the distinction it makes between countries and technology choices on the basis of differing access to factors of production becomes much less relevant. The heterogeneous nature of products and factors then becomes important and necessitates a review of the conditions of general equilibrium, something which theory has only been able to achieve by introducing additional hypotheses. This does not help to improve our understanding of productivity.

It must also be acknowledged that infinite combinations of technologies do not provide an acceptable analytical framework. However, once technologies cease to be seen as totally interchangeable, it must be accepted that each type of production requires a specific combination of factors of production which varies not only from industry to industry but from firm to firm. This far more realistic hypothesis no longer allows an allembracing explanation of the link between the reward to a factor of production and its marginal productivity. Whether rewards to factors are expressed in relative or absolute terms, they may remain indeterminate if, for technical reasons, fixed relative proportions of productive resources are necessary. Thus we should cease to refer to production functions which, in the short term, allow continuous substitution of factors of production, and refer instead to manufacturing processes which are designed differently for each product.

However, acknowledgement of the limits to interchangeability has not meant that marginal productivity theory can simply be written off. The following two arguments have come to its aid:

1. First of all, it is unusual for a firm to produce only one good. It mostly includes a whole series of production lines which do not necessarily belong to the same sector. Let us assume that each of these requires fixed proportions of a given quantity of labour and capital. Since these fixed proportions vary from one type of production to another, the overall result will be a certain degree of substitutability of factors within the firm and even more so across the entire industry. Interchangeability is thus provided by the combination of differing fixed resources.
2. Secondly, there is the powerful allocatory mechanism of perfect competition, the operation of which is quite clear. In the long run, it forces a firm to produce at minimum average cost, thus eliminating profit (Ferguson, 1969). The reward to factors of production — which, from the firm's point of view, represents the cost of production — thus equals the marginal productivity of each factor, regardless of how interchangeable technology may be. In the long term, however, fixed proportions of factors of production are much less of a problem and production is influenced by other phenomena, including increases in factors of production, technical progress, introduction of new goods, and increases in demand for new and existing goods and services. This dimension is dealt with by the theory of growth.

Productivity and economic growth

If the reward to factors of production can be defined in terms of their marginal productivity only under conditions of perfect competition, the production function must also be compatible with such perfect market conditions. For theoretical purposes this requirement is met by a homogeneous production function of degree one, which ensures that an increase in factors of production leads to a proportional increase in production. There is thus a constant ratio between the increase in production and the increase in factors of production. Accordingly, economic growth does not alter either the relative reward to factors of production or their marginal productivity in relative terms. In the longer term, returns to scale remain constant. The hypothesis of perfect competition is thus correlated with this technological constraint. However, we know that other kinds of technological development are possible, involving not only a change in the marginal productivity of the factors of production used but also conditions of imperfect competition.

Increasing returns to scale are a common result of mass production. An increase in factors of production leads to an increase in production. The introduction of additional factors of production leads to an increase in their marginal productivity which is not accompanied by an equal change in their reward. The gap between the gain in marginal productivity and the reward to factors of production is taken up by profit. In order to maintain such profit, firms seek to avoid competition by means of either trusts or mergers. Increasing returns to scale thus encourage the development of imperfect competition, which trade unions are only too keen to exploit.

In this connection we clearly need to look more closely at differences in profits from one business to another, the mobility of factors of production, and the role of the state in organizing production:

1. Let us assume that businesses are faced with two different situations in which returns to scale are either constant or increasing. Sooner or later, such businesses will display unequal growth and differentiated profits. This will tend to encourage either trust-forming or mergers, both resulting in imperfect competition. In the case of a trust (i.e. an association of businesses which each remain independent), the policy will be to dictate a price which protects the firm with the lowest profits. This will enable those firms whose average costs have been reduced by increasing returns to scale to enjoy an additional rent of situation. In the case of a merger, the firm with lower profits will be taken over by the one with higher profits. There is thus a close link between the organization of production and the degree of competition. While the exact causal relationship cannot readily be determined, there can be no doubt that the tendency towards trust-forming and mergers influences rewards to factors of production, which as a result no longer reflect changes in marginal productivity. However, differentiated profits as such do not necessary lead to imperfect competition: mobility of factors of production between firms or between different sectors may intervene.

2. Neoclassical theory assumes perfect geographical and occupational mobility of factors of production between industries. If the marginal productivity of a given factor is higher in one industry than in another, perfect mobility between industries should immediately wipe out the difference. However, there are two socio-cultural factors which conflict with this theoretical interpretation, namely rootedness and the development of professional skills.

   The individual's sense of rootedness in a community works against geographical mobility. The influence of this factor varies from person to person, from political system to political system, and from country to country. It is almost certainly a more significant factor in Europe than it is in the United States, but even in Europe it can be overcome; evidence of this can be found in rural depopulation and the resulting urbanization. In the days when workers had tostruggle just to meet their basic needs, mobility was essential to survival. However, as this necessity has receded, non-material needs such as security and rootedness have come to the fore. At the same time, the geographical mobility necessitated by the industrial revolution has generated social costs which are only now being assessed. Time wasted in traffic jams and cancerous urban sprawl are just two examples.

   Such limits to geographical mobility may well be accompanied by the emergence of new, decentralized forms of production made possible by the spread of electronic communications. Such a prospect does, however, raise the question of whether, and if so to what extent, human communication can or should be replaced by electronic devices. Here again, economic theory is inevitably confronted with ethical issues.

   Another obstacle concerns the training and professional skills that such mobility requires. Economic theory dodges this problem by assuming factors of production to be homogeneous. In the current shift towards service activities, and in particular towards office jobs, occupational diversity has a similar role to rootedness. As people's jobs grow increasingly similar in content, such diversity starts to become a cultural necessity rather than an economic factor. At the same time, occupational mobility may be better served by broad, diversified training than by training which only seeks to provide skills specific to a given activity. Here again, change is slow, but the causal relationship may in fact be reversed. Instead of insisting on occupational mobility as a means of facilitating adjustment processes within the economy, the various sectors may come to take more account of occupational diversity. In that case, labour would cease to be a mere factor of production and would come to be seen as a human activity and thus a means of self-realization.

In the case of capital, intersectoral mobility is ensured by depreciation (which also plays a part in fiscal policy) and the maintenance of hidden reserves by firms. The relative importance of the three motives behind depreciation — mobility, taxation and hidden reserves — largely depends on the nature of the capital concerned. For example, depreciation of office buildings — a major factor in the service sector — is almost entirely based on a strategy which seeks to establish hidden reserves and relies on the increasing scarcity of building land. In other words, a link can be established between land use planning, depreciation and mobility of physical capital.

3. Finally, as regards the role of the state in matters of competition, there are those who naïvely call for a strong state to enforce the organization of markets along strictly competitive lines. This is something the competition policies adopted in most industrialized countries patently fail to do. I have endeavoured to show that strict application of the principle of competition will not only run into the technological problem of variable returns to scale, but will also be hampered by limits to geographicaland occupational mobility. The state cannot afford to ignore such limits, which are an integral part of the culture. As with effects that are external to the market, the acknowledgement of such cultural factors necessitates state intervention in the market and thus abandonment of the principle of perfect competition.

When policymakers ask what degree of imperfection can be tolerated without the market becoming uncompetitive, neoclassical economists simply answer that competition must always be as perfect as possible. This rather unhelpful reply means that it is lawyers who eventually have to decide what balance of imperfection and competition is acceptable as they draw up legislation on restrictive trade practices. In other words, lawyers are left to work out the normative criteria which economic theory has failed to provide.

Again and again, the over-abstract nature of economic theory makes it irrelevant when it comes to designing an institutional framework for society. By the same token, it is scarcely acceptable that concept of productivity should continue to be defined in strictly economic terms.

So far we have only assessed the causes of growth in terms of increases in factors of production, which also raises problems of income distribution.

If we examine a second cause of growth, namely technical progress (Rosenberg, 1971), economic analysis becomes particularly problematic. It has resulted either in a multitude of classifications or else in over-abstract theoretical interpretations. Such approaches obscure the origins of technical progress. Clearly, it is not enough to consider only the economic aspect (as is the case in models in which technical progress depends on investment, particularly in human capital), and indeed no-one denies the importance of cultural and institutional factors. Once again, interaction with other disciplines is essential, and is all the more justified by the fact that technical progress alters not only the production function but also the way firms are organized as well as attitudes and motives concerning work. Technical progress engenders a symbolism of its own and becomes part of society's perception of its own destiny. Up to the mid-1960s industrial societies had an optimistic vision of technical progress, which has since been eroded by growing doubts. At the same time there have been major technological changes which, while making work physically less strenuous, have created an additional psychological burden. This would appear to confirm the economic logic that work is by its very nature burdensome. On the other hand, the alleged rationality of human behaviour has not done anything to reduce the constraints of the working environment. Enmeshed in its own rigid structure, economic theory tries to ignore the fact that technical progress implies new attitudes and so new motives. Thus technical progress alters not only the ratio of capital to labour, but the individual's whole perception of the economy.

Neoclassical economic analysis cannot, of course, be blamed for failing to deal with all of these aspects. Economists, on the other hand, *can* be blamed for ignoring the work carried out in other fields and for confining their interest to the refinement of models based on the same old hypotheses. Technical progress continues to be seen in terms of a change in the ratio of capital to labour and its effects on the relative prices of factors of production. It ultimately matters little whether such change is analysed in static or dynamic terms.

For many years theoretical literature referred to technical progress as an increase in the ratio of capital to labour. Technical progress was thus seen in terms of increasing automation of the production process, whereby labour's relative share was reduced. This was supposed to explain the increase in real wages as based on the increase in marginal labour productivity brought about by automation. However, miniaturization of equipment and innovations designed to increase production capacity have also made it possible to view technical progress in terms of capital saved. In that case, technical progress results in a fall rather than a rise in the ratio of capital to labour. An increase in marginal productivity of capital leads to an increase in marginal productivity of labour in relative terms.

This result shows that the relative variation in marginal labour productivity may be either positive or negative, depending on the kind of technical progress involved. Empirical studies having failed to clarify this issue, a pragmatic approach has been adopted in which technical progress is seen as neutral, in the sense that the ratio of capital to labour and thus the relative marginal productivity of each factor both remain constant. Absolute marginal productivity increases, however, since the same level of production can be achieved using less of each factor.

The neoclassical model which explains economic equilibrium in relative terms thus leads to the conclusion that technical progress, being neutral, increases production but does not alter the ratio between the marginal productivities of the two factors of production. Nor does growth affect the relative reward to factors of production. As far as firms are concerned, this means that relative costs remain unchanged, which removes any incentive to economize resources. "Neutral" technical progress thus becomes exogenous to the firm — a product, as it were, of the sociocultural environment.

Another approach involves the time factor in the introduction of technical progress. A firm which is the first to introduce a new technique derives profits from the resulting monopoly position. However, when all firms have adopted the new technique, such profits are eliminated. Perfect competition forces firms to abide by the same relative costs as before. Once again, this shows the high level of interdependence between the degree of competition and technological change.

In the recent period of high unemployment in industrialized countries, another factor has been gaining in significance. The influence of trade unions and of index-linking legislation has resulted in real wages becoming rather inflexible (Carruth and Oswald, 1987) and has helped to disrupt the equilibrium of the labour market, in that supply exceeds demand. This situation signals to firms that labour is relatively plentiful, and technical progress will then tend to be aimed at saving capital, which is scarce by comparison. In that case, production will increase together with underemployment. In the end, technical progress is neutral: the reduction in capital due to economy measures and the reduction in labour due to increasing unemployment leave the ratio of capital to labour unchanged.

It should be noted that this situation only occurs if conditions of imperfect competition prevail in the labour and goods markets simultaneously. Inflexible real wages do indeed go hand in hand with inflexible prices for goods and services, for imperfections in the markets for factors of production are ultimately governed by imperfections in the goods market. This again raises the issue of interaction between degree of competition and organization of production.

The third cause of growth is linked to overall demand for goods and services. Growth in production is not necessarily determined by growth in demand, since international trade may add to domestic production through imports. Growth in foreign demand may likewise include a factor which affects the ratio between the physical marginal productivities of capital and labour. This is the case when changes in international trade flows alter the relative prices of goods and services. This aspect was discussed in Chapter 1 when analysing changes in terms of trade as the classic adjustment mechanism of neoclassical theory. A change in terms of trade will lead to the reorganization of a country's production apparatus and will force changes in the relative prices of factors of producion. If a change in terms of trade causes the relative reward to labour to fall, there will be increased political pressure to introduce protectionist measures. From a strictly neoclassical point of view, such measures can be fairly easily dismissed. In political terms, however, protectionism makes perfect sense, if only because wage-earners also vote.

Empirical measurement of productivity

As with so many issues arising out of the concept of productivity, statistics on the subject are highly conflicting. There are those who maintain that productivity is constantly falling. They base this view on a simple statistic, namely the ratio between a country's domestic product and its working population, or gross average productivity of labour in nominal terms (see Graph 5). Although this statistical definition is the one most commonly used, there are plenty of others (see Schaller, 1975). Such profusion is evidence of the confusion the concept of productivity has created. We will therefore limit our comments to a brief discussion of the definition of average productivity of labour in nominal terms, in the light of the theoretical debate.

Naturally, averages can hardly be compared with the marginal values of theory. Under certain restrictive circumstances, however, it can be shown that the average varies in the same direction as the marginal value. Thus, while the extent of the marginal variation cannot be determined by measuring the average, its general direction can. However, such estimates are bound to be somewhat imprecise, since the observations on which they are based concern two kinds of variation which in practice cannot be separated: the change in marginal and average productivity for a given production function, and the change in the production function itself. In other words, there is no theoretical basis for a definition of productivity in average terms.

Nevertheless, the concept of productivity has continued to be used despite this argument and the two that follow:

1. Firstly, production is always evaluated on the basis of prices. Yet real production series relate to nominal values deflated by a price index. Not only does this practice raise the problem of interpreting

Graph 5: Productivity since 1970

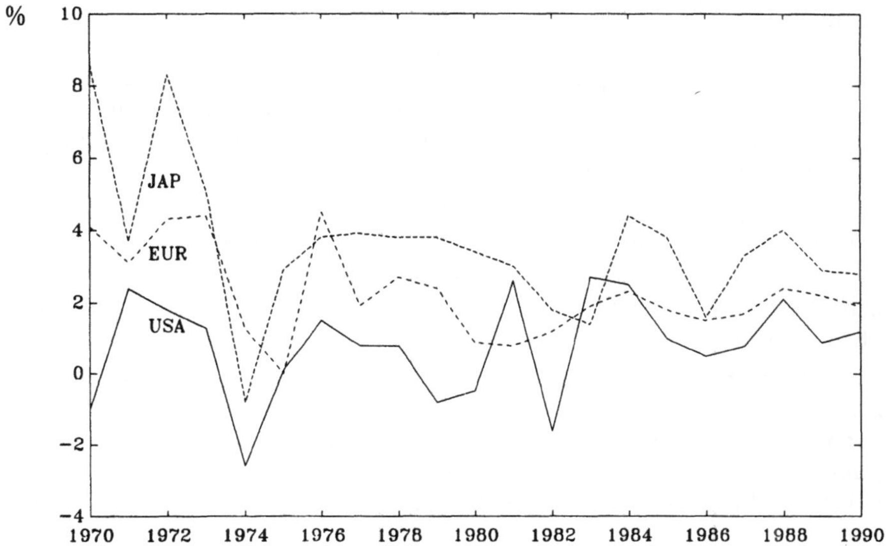

Sources: OECD, "Historical statistics", miscellaneous issues, mimeographed.
OECD, "The OECD economic outlook", December 1988.

NB. 1988-1989 figures are estimates.

the interaction between degree of competition and organization of production, but it also illustrates the problem of aggregation inherent in the compilation of any index. The price series and the type of index chosen directly influence the result, which is also affected by the degree of market imperfection.

2. Secondly, variations in the working population can be interpreted very differently depending on which of the several available series is chosen. Demographic factors, immigration policy, the unemployment rate, the age of commencing an occupation, and the retirement age are all factors which include both economic and institutional aspects. The statistical result thus inevitably depends on how these various factors are weighted.

Explanations for the slower rate of increase in the average productivity of labour in nominal terms cannot therefore be anything other than speculative. Despite this, they are always presented as the result of inexorable economic reasoning "proving" that the statistically perceptible fall in productivity is due to increasing government regulation or else to a slowdown in technical progress.

To what extent is it true that productivity in public enterprises and government departments is lower than in private firms? This question brings us back to the issue of institutional paralysis raised in Chapter 6 when discussing the economic analysis of bureaucracy. The state has become all-pervading, providing extensive public services which in most countries account for a substantial segment of the national product. It is therefore important to know whether public-sector activity has helped to slow down the overall rate of growth in productivity.

The claim that this is due to a slowdown in the rate of innovation is belied by the evident progress in fields such as microelectronics, data processing, telecommunications and genetic engineering. Is it not conceivable that such new technologies have given rise to considerable costs of adaptation which have been underestimated?

My point here is a simple one: not only does the shift to a service economy make it even harder to quantify productivity, it also causes changes of attitude which affect people's motives to work. The issues of public-sector productivity and changing attitudes are closely linked. They will the subject of the closing sections of this chapter.

Private-sector and public-sector productivity

The costs generated by the high level of organization of society relate first of all to the time needed to achieve a consensus and secondly to the increasingly laborious nature of transactions. There is little point in trying to measure such costs empirically. They are reflected in a slower rate of growth in overall productivity within the economy, and their extent is illustrated by the growing number of regulations introduced by collective decision-making mechanisms. We have seen that such regulations are often the result of influence brought to bear on the state by various pressure groups. They therefore also reflect the interface between politics and economics. Increasing regulation is accompanied by expansion of the civil service which, as such, represents an economic activity under state monopoly. This state monopoly on the civil service and on the economy is expressed through legislation, which constitutes another interface, this time between law and the public sector. In short, we are dealing with a service industry.

Like the private economy, the state is becoming increasingly service-oriented. The civil service monopoly is accompanied by other public monopolies in such areas as health care and infrastructure. As these activities account for a major part of each country's added value, the operation of the civil service has become the subject of empirical studies, which can be criticized on exactly the same grounds as the concept of productivity. However, they also raise a more fundamental problem, namely how to evaluate a process for allocating factors of production which is not subject to market forces. Economic theory treats government activities as public goods (whose prices cannot be determined by a market), and sees them as external to the market. As we shall see later on, environmental pollution is treated in exactly the same way.

Criteria for distinguishing between private-sector and public sector productivity

One simple criterion is to take the neoclassical conditions for general equilibrium and ask whether, in clinging as closely as possible to the principle of perfect competition, they enable markets to operate in practice rather than in theory. If not, then we are talking about a public good (Arrow, 1977). In order to assess the external nature of a public good, it must be subjected to cost-benefit analysis in social terms. The purpose of such analysis is to compare the benefits and costs that arise when the state intervenes in a market economy. Formidable problems arise when it comes to assessing and weighting the various components, some of which cannot be quantified (an example being the quality of the service provided to the public by a government employee), while others are only of indirectrelevance.

State intervention is justified not only when there is an externality in the strict sense of the word, but whenever there is a market failure — for instance, when consumers are prevented from expressing the choice which would best serve their interests. To compensate for such market failure, the state intervenes. The same argument has already been encountered with regard to education: the uneducated are clearly unable to appreciate the value of education, so the state declares education a public good. This example typifies an entire range of market failures. More complex kinds of failure occur to an extent which varies according to the amount of the transaction costs that interfere with market forces (the most frequent such cost being lack of transparency). The withholding of information to protect a monopoly on know-how is a further example.

For all of these reasons, state activity, which is analysed as a public good, has grown apace. Average public spending in the OECD countries (including compulsory social security contributions) rose from 28% of gross national product at the beginning of the 1950s to 44% of GNP by the end of the 1970s. Such an increase in public goods raises the issue of how they are to be assessed, since the concept of productivity cannot be used for this purpose.

Neoclassical models propose the following optimal condition: the ratio between the physical marginal productivities of the various factors of production must equal the ratio between their prices, which in turn is determined by the ratio of prices of goods and services. However, since the production of public goods is the consequence of market failure, no competitive prices are available to calculate this ratio. This means that the public sector cannot be assessed in terms of productivity, a concept which, despite all the reservations expressed, remains linked to the private sector. Instead, the public sector must be assessed in political terms, a conclusion which points the way to an immense field of joint economic and political analysis (Frey, 1977).

Despite the fact that the public sector cannot be assessed in terms of productivity, it is often accused of inefficiency and warnings are uttered about stifling bureaucracy. One possible explanation for such shortcomings is that, by their very nature, public goods often require a great deal of labour. Marginal productivity theory indicates that relative scarcity of a factor of production has a positive influence on its marginal productivity. Plentiful labour therefore means low productivity. Yet, as we have just seen, the lack of a market means that a public good is assessed by collective decision-making mechanisms which, among other things, have given government employees a separate legal status. Thus the sole criterion is that generated by the democratic decision-making mechanism. By maintaining the separate status of government employees, public opinion acknowledges the special nature of the civil service, if only on the symbolic grounds that it is there to serve the public interest.

However, the claim that production of a public good can only be judged by democratic means must be qualified. Voting tends to mobilize only the part of the electorate that feels directly concerned by the political decision in question. Furthermore, it can seldom be used to assess the performance of a government department directly. In most cases, penalties are more indirect. While the political authorities have a duty to supervise the civil service, a politician's failure to be re-elected can scarcely be interpreted as punishment for inefficiency.

We must therefore resort to other indicators in order to assess the efficiency of the public sector.

Empirical observations of public-sector productivity

The indicators used are chiefly based on the repetitive aspects of bureaucracy. The number of files dealt with by a particular employee, the number of diplomas awarded by a college, the number of operations performed by a hospital, the number of people using public transport and the number of reports drawn up by the police are all examples of such attempts to measure the efficiency of the public sector. Such series of statistics are then divided by the number of employees working in the sector concerned. This approach is clearly based on the concept of average productivity of labour. The relevant studies, most of which come from the United States, are summarized by Greffe (1981) and have one thing in common: they all indicate that public services are increasingly inefficient. The number of public-sector employees is tending to increase faster than their work as measured in statistical terms. This means that productivity in the sectors concerned is tending to decrease.

Clearly, this result fails to take account of changes in the nature of public services. Increasing consensus costs have made many administrative procedures more involved. It is difficult or impossible to compare a given public service over a period of time or with other public services. On the other hand, it is possible to compare the activity of a public enterprise with that of a private firm. However, the resulting differences in productivity can again be explained by the nature of public services, a good example being the railways. Such private railways as still exist tend to operate one particularly profitable line, whereas nationalized railways seek to provide the broadest possible public service. How, then, can we compare the productivity of nationalized and private railways?

When discussing public-sector efficiency, one regularly hears the allegation that low productivity is caused by a lack of motivation among public service employees. This allegation is based on the idea that office work is more repetitious in the public sector than in the private sector, and also that public service employees lack the stimulus of bonuses and perks, their pay rises usually being linked to seniority rather than performance.

I believe that this interpretation — which is difficult to prove (Brown, Jackson, 1982) — in fact stems from an ingrained hostility to the state based on the classical view that the state is by definition non-productive and merely disrupts the economy. This view was perpetuated by economic models right up to the emergence of public choice theory, which has blurred the boundary between economics and politics. Economic theory is now inescapably confronted with the value judgements inherent in its positivist analysis. Evidence of this can be found in the cultural activities being developed by various private firms in an effort to revive among employees the kind of motivation which office work has evidently ceased to provide.

Externally, there is an increase in sponsoring of cultural events by firms in order to boost their image and at the same time increase their employees' sense of loyalty and thus their motivation to work. Internally, more and more firms are providing extra training in an effort to improve employees' knowledge and skills not only at work but also outside.

This increase in cultural activities indicates that problems of motivation are to be found in the private sector just as much as in the public sector. The money incentive is clearly not enough. The debate on the productivity of public services conceals the real issue, namely the whole purpose of work in a society whose main problem is now choice of production rather than survival. In other words, what are the needs we have to satisfy?

Social change and new motives

The change in the production structure of the industrialized countries has led to new ways of organizing the working environment. The question arises whether this change creates new constraints (such as stress) or whether it satisfies new needs. Whatever the answer, it certainly affects productivity and represents a challenge to purely economic interpretations.

The extreme diversity of service activities makes it particularly hard to devise appropriate indices with which to calculate average productivity of labour in nominal terms. Services appear to be cheaper than industrial activities. The prices prevailing in certain service industries (such as the hotel trade) suggest that service activities require a good deal of labour, which is relatively plentiful and therefore, according to Bhagwati (1984), low in productivity. We have already encountered this argument when discussing the efficiency of the public sector. Moreover, it cannot be over-stressed that the non-material nature of public services makes them unquantifiable, and makes empirical measurement of their productivity an intricate business. A good example is the expansion of financial services, which is only imperfectly reflected in national accounting. The growing importance of the tertiary sector thus necessitates qualitative indicators, which can only be developed in collaboration with other social sciences. Psychological studies on the nature of human motivation and sociological studies of group behaviour can help us to devise ways of organizing work which take account of such factors. Conversely, individual behaviour is shaped by the way in which the economy is organized. This interaction between the institutional framework and the economic workings of society cannot be understood if human behaviour is reduced a single utilitarian dimension. However, it is no easy task to define motivation or identify its components.

The nature of economic motivation

Psychologists are unable to provide a unanimous theory of motivation (Lea *et al.*, 1987), and the empirical studies on which such a theory depends have proved inadequate. It may be that there is no comprehensive theory of motivation, but rather a number of approaches to the subject. Basically, there are two overlapping schools of thought: one holds that people's motives are unchanging, while the other insists that they are manipulated. In the former case, the economy must adapt; in the latter, motives are the result of social constraints or of economic requirements.

Economists avoid this difficulty by maintaining that consumer sovereignty will guide productive effort towards those goods and services which will satisfy consumers' needs. The nature of the latter varies, giving rise to a classification known as Engel's Law. Leaving aside the issue of whether the term "law" can properly be used in economics (since the criterion of falsification is not met), Engel's Law classifies goods according to how an individual's income is allocated. Goods on which expenditure increases at a higher percentage than income are known as "luxury" goods, those on which expenditure increases in proportion to income are known as "normal" goods, and those on which expenditure increases at a lower percentage than income are known as "necessities". Engel's Law thus expresses a hierarchy of needs. However, the classification criterion remains a purely economic one and tells us nothing about the nature of the goods concerned, which depends on the socio-cultural context. Moreover, distinctions between the various categories vary from individual to individual. The theory of utility maximization dodges the issue by assuming that all individuals behave identically.

This tells us little about the various sources of utility. However, the concept of utility includes both biological and social aspects: physiological requirements such as the need for clothing and protection are accompanied by psychological requirements such as the need for security. At the same time, certain goods have a symbolic content, such as the need to display social status or signal one's dominance.

This distinction between biological and social aspects may serve to illustrate the conflicts of motivation which may occur between both individuals and different social groups. The need to increase one's income clashes with the need for more leisure. The need to protect oneself clashes with the need to make new discoveries. Thus merely establishing a hierarchy of needs tells us nothing about their origin, nor does it answer the question of whether individuals' economic motives are constantly manipulated or not.

Consumer protection policies, for example, are indicative of the interest in this debate. The fact that a majority of consumers have opted for state intervention challenges the principle of consumer sovereignty.

However, this does not in itself prove that consumer behaviour is manipulated. First of all, there is no empirical evidence for such a conclusion and, secondly, there may well be other reasons for the rise of the consumer protection movement, such as market imperfections or a wish to create new political pressure groups.

However, consumer organizations' grievances do frequently concern manipulation of needs. From misleading advertisements to sales agreements which curtail consumers' rights, or "hard-sell"methods which take advantage of "weaker" consumer groups such as the elderly, the list of attempts to manipulate economic motives is a long one. This echoes the criticism voiced by Galbraith (1972), who accuses large firms of creating new needs to suit their own technological or administrative requirements. Neither this criticism nor that expressed by the institutionalists, who claim that economic needs are determined by social status, have ever been taken seriously by theoretical economists. However, as was stressed in Part I, such institutional considerations are essential for there to be a workable economic policy. While the consumer protection movement confirms this connection, it does not succeed in proving that motivations are manipulated.

However, doubts must be expressed regarding the alternative claim that economic motives are unchanging. Politically, the classic right-left split is becoming less relevant. New, office-based occupations are creating a new type of employee who no longer identifies with the traditional worker. Organizationally, the old rigid hierarchies are making way for more participatory arrangements. Not only are the boundaries between social strata fading, but rivalries between the different departments or occupations within a firm are expressed differently. Socially, women's claims to economic and political equality point to social changes which are bound to produce new motives. Mainstream economic theory affects to see all of this as reflecting a single, unchanging utilitarian motive. While such an approach may have proved acceptable for purposes of theoretical analysis, we have to recognize that it is based on value judgements.

The following conclusions can therefore be drawn:

1. The nature of economic needs is changing. This will be discussed below with reference to work motivation.
2. The budget constraint on the satisfaction of individual needs is making way for a social constraint. This will be discussed further on with reference to environmental pollution.

Owing to the above changes, the traditional concept of productivity has become irrelevant.

Work motivation

Economic theory maintains that the amount of labour supplied by an individual is determined by a choice between income and leisure. The main source of income is nearly always wages, which thus determine the extent of the budget constraint on purchases of goods and services. For a given level of satisfaction, any combination of income and leisure may be envisaged. Such combinations are deemed to express individual preferences. Work motivation thus derives from two basic needs, the need for income and the need for leisure. For a given level of satisfaction, any combination of these needs may be envisaged. Accordingly, the two needs are measured in relation to one another. This link between income and leisure in relative terms implies that the choice between the two is a matter of indifference. This theoretical assumption can be criticized on three familiar grounds:

1. First of all, the institutional framework is such that the choice between income and leisure is certainly not a matter of indifference. If, for example, labour contracts stipulate an eight-hour working day, only one combination is possible — the individual has no choice.
2. Secondly, both income and leisure may satisfy a number of different needs, so that there is no single link which will serve as a basis for comparison. If, for example, both income and leisure satisfy not only the need to acquire goods but also the need to display social status, on what basis can they be compared?
3. Thirdly, a hierarchy of needs must be established. Neoclassical labour supply theory treats the need for income and the need for leisure as equivalent. However, it takes account of changes in the intensity of needs, in the sense that the worker's preferences will change as his income increases. In that case, the hierarchy of needs will obey the logic expressed in Engel's "Law". Work will have priority as long as necessities must be purchased. As income rises, however, the need for leisure will grow. Leisure is thus a luxury commodity. What causes change in the intensity of needs is still the income level, but also individual preferences. According to the logic of utilitarian theory, work is only considered in instrumental terms.

However, if a hierarchy of human needs is established not only according to economic criteria but also according to psychological or social ones, we will detect different kinds of work motivation which, I believe, are nowadays increasingly important. In the hierarchy proposed by Maslow (1970), four motives are listed in ascending order. Whenever the need underlying one of these motives is satisfied, the following motive becomes more important:

(a) external rewards
(b) intrinsic enjoyment of one's work
(c) social contact
(d) self-realization

Empirical studies show that all four motives play an important part in developed countries (Lea *et al.*, 1987). Economic theory only considers the first motive, and cannot therefore claim to provide a comprehensive explanation. Instead, it must be seen in conjunction with other theories, which would reduce the neoclassical instrumental dimension of labour. Such a shift in approach would also help to tackle the problems raised by current perceptions of the working environment.

If it is accepted that there is a need for a theory of motivation to fill the gaps left by neoclassical economic theory, we must abandon the idea of a general theory and confine ourselves instead to explaining certain specific situations. Work motivation depends on circumstances, which may vary from firm to firm or from occupation to occupation (once again determined by the institutional framework). Observation of social behaviour in various occupations reveals interaction between the various kinds of motivation and the institutional framework. This framework may be modified to take account of new needs, but in that case the purely instrumental interpretation of work must beabandoned.

This narrow interpretation is the reason why the feminist movement has so far proved unable to change the way in which work is organized. This interpretation, as embodied in economic theory, simply reflects our traditional way of thinking. Attempts to adapt the institutional framework to new motivations must therefore overcome both a theoretical and a practical obstacle: general economic theory must make way for an approach with less all-embracing pretentions, and purely economic thinking must cease to dominate the organization of production.

The utilitarian position remains theoretically a very strong one, since it is based on a one-dimensional view of man which has become familiar to the whole of society through its value symbolism. This view is reflected in our education, and continues to be found in the relationship between working and private life. It is also a convenient excuse for making social organization subordinate to economic organization. Nevertheless, there are now signs of a shift in attitudes, with large numbers of individuals apparently unwilling to accept such a one dimensional explanation (Volcker, 1987).

This growing malaise is not expressed in such theoretically powerful terms as the neoclassical approach. There is as yet no alternative theory. In the field of psychology, the theory of motivation is fragmentary. Maslow's hierarchy of needs is subject to criticism. Steady, patient research is therefore needed to construct a theoretical mosaic which will eventually influence attitudes as profoundly as traditional economic theory has done. The ultimate pattern of this mosaic is as yet hard to predict, but one thing is certain: purely economic explanations for social phenomena are bound to prove increasingly unsatisfactory as society succeeds in meeting its basic needs. Even though such needs are now more broadly defined, there can be no doubt that Maslow's analysis is the first stage in a process whereby social motives will gain in significance at the expense of purely economic ones.

Such a transformation will, of course, trigger off a mechanism which links satisfaction and deprivation. As long as a need remains unsatisfied, the individual will do everything to satisfy it, but once it has been met, it is no longer so important. Higher-level needs then come to the fore. An attempt has been made to show that original motives to work are nowadays losing importance and making way for motives such as social esteem, social acceptance of professional skills, selfexploration and self-knowledge. What is it, then, that determines productivity? We can no longer make do with a single explanation, but must consider a number of different explanations which vary from individual from individual, from group to group and from country to country. Similarly, variations in average productivity of labour in nominal terms have become meaningless, for it is no longer clear what we are measuring.

Economic constraints versus social constraints

The change in work motivation (as indicated by the fashion for education and further training) is accompanied by a slackening of budget constraints and an increase in social constraints. This shift in the constraints on human behaviour when maximizing a utility function is of relevance to the environmental debate. It shows that the motivation to work in order to obtain the highest possible income and so purchase goods is bound to result in increasing frustration owing to the fact that many goods are socially constrained. Let us take the car as an example. At the beginning of this century, the car satisfied a number of needs but was subject to a severe budget constraint. As mass production reduced manufacturing costs and national per capita income rose, this constraint grew considerably less and the motor age began. Yet individual satisfaction was soon to be limited by social constraints such as traffic jams and pollution.

The same phenomenon can be observed in the field of leisure, where mass production has again helped to limit individual satisfaction. The growing burden imposed by the economy upon the environment means that an ever-increasing number of goods are socially constrained (Leiss, 1976). For example, in their efforts to escape the inconveniences of mass tourism, individuals are attracted by new goods or services which then become socially constrained in turn. The more pressing environmental problems become, the less the need to purchase goods and services will be satisfied.

It is not certain whether this chain of causality actually exists. All that we have are data indicating that the problem of the environment is likely to get worse whatever policy is adopted. The prospect of an ever-increasing number of goods becoming socially constrained may lead to a change of motivation such as a collective wish to move further up the hierarchy of needs. This conclusion may be over-pessimistic as regards the possibility of substituting new goods for goods which have become too constricting. Nevertheless, the question remains whether, in changing our behaviour, we are acting as liberal individuals who are the best judges of their own interests, or simply bending to force of circumstances. This debate, which concerns the origins of our motives, cannot be settled, but should provide a stimulus for collaboration between economics and the social sciences. Our discussion of the concept of productivity has suggested a number of possible pathways.

The fact that the concept of productivity is so frequently used reveals the predominance of economic thinking in social matters and the degree to which it has shaped our way of thinking. Productivity can serve as a yardstick with which to assess almost every human activity — including pollution.

CHAPTER 9

THE ENVIRONMENTAL DEBATE

Although the environmental debate has been going on for more than thirty years, it is only now beginning to bear fruit. The flood of conflicting opinions it has generated makes the literature extremely difficult to summarize. It includes the full range of arguments which are brought to bear on social issues of any kind. A middle way needs to be found between the views of those who dismiss the problem as insignificant and those who see it as our sole legitimate concern. An initial framework for this debate can be provided by economic theory, which will also draw our attention to the very aspects it glosses over. This brings us back to the reservations expressed earlier with regard to methodology, basic assumptions and instruments. However, our discussion of the concept of productivity has raised another, more fundamental doubt regarding the whole purpose of economics as expressed by neoclassical theory. However, neoclassical theory remains an irreplaceable yardstick and will therefore serve to guide our approach in this chapter.

The first section discusses the problem of the environment from the point of view of economic theory, and enables us to specify the nature of public goods. The second section seeks to demonstrate the shortcomings of this approach. If economic theory is to produce usable recommendations on social affairs, there is no alternative to interdisciplinary collaboration. The environmental debate has been chosen because it illustrates perfectly the growing malaise caused by a purely economic interpretation of social issues. It brings together all the elements discussed so far in this book, two of which are especially significant: rising consensus costs, and the emergence of as yet unclear new motives. Attitudes to the problem of pollution can be divided into two basic camps. There are those who see it as simply one more problem to be solved by economic theory; others see it as a consequence of our way of thinking, and reject a purely economic analysis. The current state of knowledge does not allow us to give an opinion as to the accuracy of either interpretation. Only a combined effort by the various social sciences can produce a coherent analysis of the problem.

Economic theory of the environment

Economic theory considers the environment as external to the market. It is only seen as "economic", and taken into account for theoretical purposes, when one or other of its components becomes scarce. Thus the air is of no interest to economists unless it generates production costs. Pollution controls are what make it a commodity. In other words, the environment is of no concern to the economy unless its constituent parts give rise to explicit costs. They are thus external to the market. However, such externality is hard to define. If considered as a public good — a good whose price cannot be determined by a market — it becomes linked to other instances of market failure. The main categories of failure discussed earlier in connection with productivity include increasing returns to scale. These are not necessarily directly linked with the environment. They may be responsible for a certain amount of environmental damage by allowing mass production, but ultimately they only represent one way oforganizing production. This leads to a situation of imperfect competition such as the natural monopoly, necessitating state intervention. Accordingly, not every market failure can be considered an externality. I would suggest the following narrower definition, which is the first condition proposed by Baumol and Oates (1975, p. 17):

"An externality is present whenever some individual's (say A's) utility or production relationships include real (that is, nonmonetary) variables whose values are chosen by others (persons, corporations, governments) without particular attention to the effects on A's welfare."

Thus the notion of an externality covers an entire range of positive or negative effects which are not reflected in market prices. It may, of course, be imagined that these effects are accompanied by a price paid by anyone who involuntarily alters someone else's utility or production function, but this assumes the existence of an agreement arising out of a decision-making process other than the market. An externality thus clearly concerns effects produced outside the market. It is in the context of microeconomics that theory considers the various alternative ways of integrating such effects into its analysis of the market.

The macroeconomic approach recalls that the economy is not as closed a system as the economic circuit which serves as the basis for national accounting. The running of the economy requires resources which, in turn, do not only generate goods and services but also waste. Input-output analysis attempts to take account of both resources and waste by means of models that show the interaction between the economy and the environment. This approach also raises the basic problem of resource depletion and accumulation of waste, which can only be solved in one of the following three ways:

1. Stabilization of overall production and consumption. This alternative was popularized in the 1960s by the Club of Rome with its call for zero growth.
2. More efficient transformation of resources into goods and services. Optimal allocation of resources will, it is claimed, lead to less waste. However, this requires systematic use of technological knowledge and thus increasing links between economics and technology.
3. More efficient transformation of waste into either productive resources or else substances which can be reabsorbed into the environment (i.e. recycling or regeneration).

The above three alternatives also serve to classify the various recommendations put forward in this area, which will be discussed below.

The changes these recommendations imply indirectly affect production and consumption. Consumption of goods is not total: it produces waste which returns to the environment in some other form. It may give rise to noise or to air and water pollution. Since the nature of the environment is changing, economic externalities must be seen as permanent. The individual's economic strategy must therefore be reversed: instead of maximizing his utility function by consuming as many goods as possible, he must satisfy his needs with the minimum possible consumption of goods. This conclusion brings us back to the issues of social change and new motives discussed in the previous chapter.

The microeconomic approach: externality theory

This approach attempts to subject environmental problems to the price mechanism, with explicit reference to the market economy. However, the concept of externalities is not confined to allocative systems, but is equally applicable to planned economies.

The market succeeds in producing agreement on a single price at which both producers' profits and consumers' utility are maximized. Such maximization strategies are subject to the same budget constraint, namely production costs in the case of producers and disposable income in the case of consumers. The market is thus an optimizing mechanism which, under conditions of perfect competition, results in an allocation of resources whereby expressed needs are satisfied as perfectly as possible. The resulting single price provides a link between producers and consumers and sends a signal to all market agents. Thus a high price signals that supply is relatively low compared with demand, inducing producers to increase their supply and consumers to reduce their demand. Price flexibility is thus the perfect mechanism for adjusting the behaviour of economic agents. However, such adjustment only concerns quantities supplied and demanded, and does not necessitate a real change in behaviour. Behaviour is assumed to be unchanging and also selfish.

The above summary of how the market works recalls the discussion of basic assumptions in Part I, only this time it is no longer a matter of eliminating state intervention but of determining the form it is to take when externalities prevent supply and demand from reaching equilibrium. Equilibrium as determined by market forces is based on individual strategies, whereas the inclusion of externalities involves determining a social optimum. The difference between the individual optimum and the social optimum provides a measure of the external effects, including both social costs and social benefits. Economic activity may have both positive and negative external effects; if the negative effects outweigh the positive ones, microeconomic analysis will result in internalization techniques which increase the price of the good responsible for the pollution and reduce the volume of transactions involving it.

Reference to the market mechanism thus leads to an important conclusion, namely that the purpose is not to eliminate pollution altogether, but to find a social optimum which improves environmental quality in relation to an individual optimum. The cost of eliminating pollution altogether would be socially unacceptable. Reference to market forces also enables us to draw up an inventory of possible government intervention; however, being purely formal, it ignores the factors that cause pollution and accordingly sees government intervention in purely instrumental terms.

The following instruments may be used to subject the problem of the environment to the market mechanism (Frey, 1972):

1. ***Taxation***, which raises the problem of the tax base. Taxes can be either levied on the polluting activity or based on an assessment of the social cost. In the former case, it is hard to decide on the level of tax without first deciding what level of production is environmentally acceptable, which presupposes the existence of socially acceptable pollution standards. In the latter case, the social cost is difficult to quantify, bringing us back to the problem of cost-benefit analysis.

In both cases, taxation increases the cost of producing the good responsible for the pollution and thus brings the external cost of pollution within the firm's accounting structure; as a result, the firm bases its profit-maximizing strategy on a higher price and a lower volume of transactions.

2. ***Subsidies*** to encourage the installation of pollution control equipment. Such subsidies may likewise be granted according to the degree of pollution, which again raises the problem of appropriate standards. At the same time, it is not immediately clear how such subsidies are to be financed; some of the possible arrangements violate the "polluter pays" principle.
3. ***A system of certificates***, entitling holders to cause a limited amount of pollution for a limited period. This is comparable to the system prevailing in international trade. In order to eliminate importers' surplus in the case of goods subject to a quota, the state auctions import licences, which raises their price until the surplus is eliminated. Similarly, in the case of the environment, the number of certificates auctioned diminishes in proportion to the damage attributed to a particular economic activity, which increases the cost to be borne by the polluter. Here again, the social cost must be measurable, and a suitable administrative procedure must be established. The same applies to the following instrument.
4. ***A system of deposits*** on the use of non-renewable resources. Such deposits are refundable once the producer has proved that his use of the resource does not pollute the environment. The difficulties involved in implementing this system are so great that it has so far only been used as a means of recycling packaging (in particular, glass bottles).
5. ***Assigning individual rights of ownership*** over environmental commodities. Such rights have never existed. However, just as rights of land ownership were made inevitable by increasing population, one can conceive of rights of ownership over commodities such as seclusion, peace and quiet, flora and fauna. If such rights were introduced, externalities could be eliminated. Under certain conditions, an improvement in the economic welfare of both polluter and pollutee could be achieved by a process of negotiation. Thus an individual exposed to a negative external effect — say, noise — could "bribe" its originator to turn down the volume. The polluter would then retain the right to produce noise, and would only agree to reduce it if the costs involved did not exceed the sum offered. Similarly, the sum paid by the pollutee could not exceed the additional utility derived from the noise reduction.

Although this last solution could theoretically be achieved through private negotiation and assignment of rights of ownership by the state, such a policy is not workable in practice. The key point, however, is that the assignment of rights of ownership introduces a price-operated exclusion mechanism — exactly as with the other instruments mentioned. Their common feature is thus quite simply the use of market economy principles as means of protecting the environment.

By means of an internalization technique, individual freedom of choice becomes a means of controlling pollution. However, this approach remains a microeconomic one, since the process of internalization relates to a specific market. Overall, such partial solutions may result in less than optimal situations. Since the purpose is not to eliminate pollution altogether but to determine its optimal level in microeconomic terms, interaction between the various pollutants may occur at the macroeconomic level. Measures taken within specific markets may therefore prove inadequate, particularly since they do not necessarily take account of permanent external effects. Classical economic theory overcomes the problem of market aggregation by assuming that the behaviour of a typical economic agent is universal and that the efficient market model applicable at the microeconomic level is equally applicable at the macroeconomic level. However, this theoretical extension of the microeconomic approach does not do justice to the full complexity of the interaction between the economy and the environment. Instead of simply applying microeconomic instruments to macroeconomic problems, we need a broader analytical framework.

The macroeconomic approach: input-output analysis

The problem of the environment is integrated into the economic circuit which forms the basis for traditional national accounting.

The idea of the circuit is a simple one. The economy as a whole is seen as a market which regulates the relationships between overal supply and demand. Such relationships may be expressed in physical terms. The productive input of private households is measured by means of a flow from consumption to production, while the amount of goods and services demanded by such households is measured by means of a contrary flow. Such real flows have a monetary counterpart, namely incomes paid by firms to households, and households' spending on consumption. National accounting only measures monetary flows, and technological production choices thus only appear in terms of the income they generate and the expenditure they make possible. Conceptually, production is perceived as a function in which factors of production are combined. Yet industrial organization theory has shown us that it is really much more than this. It is in fact a network of relationships which gives rise to transaction and consensus costs, as well as strategic coalition-forming and confrontations within individual firms. This influences the manner of production, and must be taken into account when examining the interface between the economy and the environment. A second criticism concerns the production function itself: its oversimplified combination of capital and labour fails to take account of non-renewable resources. Capital formation plays a decisive part in the process of economic growth. This sector records both the savings flows generated by households which decide not to allocate all their income to current expenditure and the investment flows generated by firms which seek to increase their production capacity. Since national accounting records these flows in monetary terms, only the financial aspect of capital is taken into account, neglecting the fact of physical diversity. Yet the interface between the economy and the environment specifically concerns this physical aspect, which is not recorded anywhere.

The foreign sector records import and export flows of goods and services which are included in the definition of a country's domestic product. This sector thus makes it possible to distinguish between the domestic and foreign components of overall supply and demand, which again emphasizes the international dimension of environmental problems.

The public sector is sustained by income transfers in the form of the various taxes levied by the state. Such transfers make it possible to finance the output flows represented by government spending. This view of the state conforms to economic theory, which considers the state exogenous to the relationship between production and consumption. The state has no economic activity of its own, is only indirectly involved in the process of economic growth, and is therefore ignored in the production approach to national accounting. From this point of view, state activities appear non-productive, which — as we shall see — raises formidable conceptual problems when it comes to adopting an environmental policy.

Despite the above reservations, the above pattern of monetary flows between five sectors is currently used to define domestic product, which is commonly accepted as measuring the final value of a country's production and demand over a given year. It thus provides a quantitative expression of the economic sphere in relation to the environment. This traditional definition includes the interactions between the various production units, while total demand also includes demand for the intermediate goods used in the production process.

Traditional input-output analysis brings out these relationships by distinguishing between the various sectors of activity within overall production. Accordingly, trade is no longer confined to the relationship between production and consumption, but also includes the relationship between producers. Such analysis makes it possible to record the flows that lead to total production, which is accordingly defined by adding the values of final production and intermediate production.

This analytical framework can to some extent be adapted to the relationships between the economy and the environment. For example, flows from the environment to the economy are illustrated by raw materials whose only monetary cost is entailed by their extraction, the actual material being free. It may be objected that rights of land ownership also extend to the subsoil. Ore-rich land commands a higher price than land with an unexploitable subsoil. Changes in land rent thus take account of the depletion of non-renewable productive resources. However, this argument cannot be extended to all environmental commodities. The use of air and water in production processes does not generate a monetary flow. Instead, prices for public environmental commodities such as these must be set by society's collective decision-making mechanisms. Since there is no market for such goods, the result is a fictitious price determined by an instrument which takes account of both the scarcity of the good and the potential environmental damage caused by its extraction and use in a production process. Inevitably, setting such fictitious prices involves considerable measurement problems which cannot be solved simply by resorting to quantitative techniques; account must also be taken of the community's perception of environmental damage, yet this is subjective and frequently impossible to quantify. Ample evidence of this is provided by the debate on airport noise.

Flows from the economy to the environment involve waste which is re-absorbed by the environment. In order to express this kind of flow in monetary terms, it is again conceptually possible for society to determine costs for the dumping of waste. The purpose here is clear: monetary equilibrium must be established between the environmental inputs and outputs generated by the economic sphere.

Such equilibrium exists in real terms, based on a law of physics which states that total energy remains unchanged, and that energy cannot be either created or destroyed. All that production processes do is alter its nature, for example by converting potential into kinetic energy. However, although the total mass remains constant, the quality of energy does deteriorate (Georgescu-Roegen, 1979).

This natural equilibrium whereby environmental inputs and outputs are integrated into the traditional economic circuit forms the basis for a model of general equilibrium, the conditions for which can only be determined theoretically.

Extended to the environment, input-output analysis attempts to determine the monetary impact of pollution on inter-industry trade and on the structure of final production and demand. This approach, which requires a knowledge of the pollution coefficients for each industry, is only seldom practicable. Examples are provided by studies of the impact of population growth on the future of the American economy or of water use and waste disposal in Canada (Victor, 1972). Although the use of such input-output models is essentially limited (for lack of appropriate statistics), they do enable the following conclusions to be drawn:

1. Total pollution may be broken down between the various products intended for final consumption. It is thus possible to determine, for example, the proportion of air pollution caused by cars and heating respectively. Such a distinction makes it easier to identify which goods cause proportionally more environmental damage. Such goods can then be made the target of instruments which internalize their external effects.
2. Total pollution may be broken down between intermediate and final production. This is a useful guide for economic policy, which can be directed either at industries or at consumers, according to whether an intermediate or a final product is involved.
3. Allowance for coefficients of pollution entails a change in demand structure owing to the shift in relative prices, which results in environmentally more hazardous goods being abandoned in favour of other goods.
4. Domestic product in which account is taken of the interface between the economy and the environment will be smaller in real terms than traditional domestic product, since monetary input and output flows from the environment to the economy will increase the costs of productive resources and will include expenditure on waste disposal.

National accounting therefore needs to be supplemented by what we may term "environmental accounting". Once a country's economic welfare begins to be directly affected by the level of pollution, it can no longer be seen purely in terms of real per capita domestic product. Numerous statistical attempts have been made to find a way of measuring economic welfare which takes the environment into account. In particular, social indicators have been developed for just this purpose. However, perhaps owing to their excessively descriptive and fragmentary nature, they have failed to break the habit of national accounting which has so profoundly influenced our way of thinking ever since the United Nations first introduced it as a standardized system back in 1953.

Of course, input-output analysis is merely an imperfect attempt to build a macroeconomic model which includes the interface between the environment and the economy. Such analysis is especially restricted by its own hypotheses, which stipulate fixed technical coefficients among the various industries. Similarly, it assumes fixed coefficients of pollution, thereby excluding the possibility of chain reactions as various pollutants interact. Nor do fixed coefficients allow for technological change or innovation — yet such change causes shifts in the quantities of resources used and waste produced.

However, such limitations are trifling when compared with the following:

1. Input-output analysis violates the fundamental law of constant mass, since it omits certain elements which link the economy to the environment. The inevitable result is disequilibrium between inputs and outputs of matter.
2. Such analysis fails to take account of the changes in the environment resulting from the complex process whereby waste is re-absorbed into the environment.

Thus the economic approach, be it microeconomic or macroeconomic, is incapable of providing a monetary assessment of all the interactions triggered off by production processes. Yet, when we turn to environmental policy, even these criticisms fade into the background.

Environmental policy

One of the snags with an economic approach to the environment is that, even from an all-embracing macroeconomic point of view, the environment continues to be considered exogenous to the economy. We have seen that economic theory runs into the same difficulty when dealing with the expansion of the public sector, which is likewise viewed as exogenous to the market. Since both of these externalities — the state and the environment — are a factor in the environmental debate, environmental policy becomes a particularly thorny problem. The central issue — the protection of individual freedoms — risks being obscured by the clash between the following disparate criteria, one of which is economic and the other political:

1. environmental measures must obey the principles of a market economy.
2. collective welfare is based on indicators of the feasilibity and political acceptability of a given measure.

The second of these criteria has resulted in what is the most widespread approach, namely direct controls on the level of pollution. Most governments, included the American administration (Baumol, Oates, 1979), have introduced such controls in the form of regulations that limit pollutant emissions or require the use of techniques designed to protect the environment. Examples of the first type of control are the regulation of fuel-burning systems and the suspension of production if a given threshold for harmful emissions is exceeded. An example of the second type of control is the requirement that cars be fitted with catalytic converters. Market instruments and direct controls are thus in conflict.

This brings us back to the familiar argument about state intervention and to the concept of productivity discussed in the previous chapter. There it was concluded that the productivity of a public good cannot be assessed simply according to economic criteria. Since we are typically dealing with instances of market failure, the efficiency of government measures must also be assessed using criteria arrived at by collective decision-making processes. Accordingly, the question of state intervention in environmental affairs cannot be answered simply by contrasting market instruments with direct controls. Ultimately, such a contrast is only conceivable in an ideological context.

Before showing that environmental policy is not simply a matter of which instrument to choose, let us examine the main advantages and disadvantages of both kinds of instrument.

Taking the advantages first, it must be acknowledged that market-based instruments have an incentive effect (Andersen *et al.*, 1977) in that they allow economic agents to respond to signals resulting from price flexibility. Such instruments thus give economic agents freedom of choice, and the internalization technique leads to a reduction in pollutant emissions. It would be hard to find an economist who does not favour this approach. Indeed, economic literature is fairly unanimous that market instruments are more efficient than direct controls. Since we generally lack practical experience of this type of instrument, the argument is essentially based on a theoretical demonstration of how the market operates when exposed to an internalization technique such as taxation. The result of this reasoning is then compared with the first concrete results of a direct-control approach, and the conclusion is drawn that the price-incentive system is superior. This comparison between incentives and direct controls is evidently biased. It is further distorted by the fact that environmental policy is still very much in its infancy. So far, it has been principally directed at repairing or containing *existing* environmental damage, an example of this approach being the massive public investment in water treatment installations. The somewhat disappointing results of such state intervention will undoubtedly influence the future choice of environmental policy instruments.

Water treatment schemes clearly show one of the advantages of direct controls. Such schemes readily obtain a political consensus. They tackle an environmental problem uniformly, and scarcely differentiate between the various polluters. This avoids the need to identify individual responsibility for pollution, a condition which underlies the "polluter pays" principle in a market economy context.

This comparison between incentives and direct controls shows that market-based instruments are supported by the logic of economic theory, whereas regulations are more in keeping with political practice. The latter are often the only methods that can be used. In theoretical terms, direct controls are comparable to quotas: they attempt to influence quantities rather than prices. There is thus some similarity to the more fundamental theoretical debate between the neoclassical and Keynesian views of how the market operates. This brings us back once again to the discussion in Part I, only this time in the context of second-best solutions, which must be resorted to whenever imperfections prevent the market from functioning optimally. Thus, in the event of market failure, direct controls may prove more efficient than incentives. Another argument concerns the normative issue of equitable income distribution. The problem of equity is ignored in a market designed to allocate the main resources efficiently. However, each situation requires separate assessment; an comprehensive assessment of direct controls is in my opinion not very helpful.

The main advantages of incentives and direct controls are interconnected. The advantages of the former necessarily derive from the disadvantages of the latter and vice versa, and both have intrinsic disadvantages. We will now therefore examine the main disadvantages of the two approaches to pollution control policy.

The disadvantages of incentives should by now be familiar to us, since our general criticism of neoclassical theory specifically applies to externality theory. It should be remembered that such criticism concerns not only the conditions that govern the running of the economy, but also the initial assumption of economic rationality as the sole explanation of human behaviour.

It should also be remembered that the shift from an individual optimum to a social one is necessarily accompanied by income redistribution effects. Increases in the prices of goods and reductions in quantities traded raise the familiar issue of efficiency versus equity. The effect of price increases caused by environmental taxes is to force out of the market those individuals who are subject to the tightest budget constraints. Here the positive aspect of economic theory cannot be dissociated from its normative aspect. We know that the impact of taxes on prices depends on the sensitivity of supply and demand to price changes. The impact of taxation is greater in situations where price elasticity of demand is relatively low, as is typically the case with necessities. On the other hand, where demand is relatively price-elastic, the brunt of the tax will be borne by producers, causing a far greater reduction in quantities traded than when the main burden of taxation is borne by consumers. It is therefore essential to determine the various degrees of elasticity — which may vary from market to market — not only in order to ascertain the effects of taxation on both consumers and producers, but also to evaluate the reduction in trade in the polluting commodity concerned. Unfortunately, empirical studies are too incomplete to provide adequate information on this issue.

Another disadvantage of incentives concerns their empirical assessment. Costs and benefits are seldom quantifiable. In some cases, there are a number of interlocking external effects whose relative influence must be determined. This largely determines the final cost-benefit result, leading to either a tax or a subsidy according to whether the result is positive or negative. In other cases, the external effects cannot be quantified, making it impossible to determine the extent of the measures to be taken. Ultimately, then, only taxes with a clearly defined and easily verifiable tax base can be used to internalize external effects.

A final disadvantage of incentives concerns the exceptional nature of certain instances of pollution. In the event of a disaster, incentives are of no avail — only direct intervention will help.

The disadvantages of direct controls are of a different order, relating to neoclassical economic thinking. One of the main criticisms of direct controls concerns the fact that they have no effect upon relative prices, particularly those of polluting as opposed to non-polluting goods. Accordingly, they do not help to change the composition of final demand, nor do they encourage the emergence of new, non-polluting goods. Furthermore, since there is no adjustment resulting from a change in relative prices, economic agents do not alter their behaviour with regard to the environment. Direct controls (such as compulsory standards) apply indiscriminately; some find them too strict, others too lax. The uniform behaviour which they impose reinforces the belief that the state is essentially repressive.

The second main disadvantage of direct controls is that they require an extensive bureaucracy to supervise their implementation. This undoubtedly raises a problem of administrative organization, since strategies aimed at minimizing transaction costs within public bodies conflict with strategies aimed at maximizing individual utility functions.

Finally, direct controls are often arbitrary, in that they tend to be applied after the event.

This summary of the pros and cons of incentives and direct controls shows that attempts to limit environment policy to either of these two approaches are misguided. Ultimately, the two can only be compared by resorting to normative judgements. However, the following points need to be noted. Firstly, instruments based on economic models tackle the symptoms rather than the causes of pollution. Secondly, the prohibitions resulting from direct controls may lead to phenomena such as black markets, so that the problem of pollution is not eliminated but merely shifted elsewhere (a good example being the illegal international trade in toxic waste). In any case, both incentives and direct controls are evidence of a trend towards ever increasing state intervention in economic affairs. Although the form of such intervention varies according to the instruments chosen, the essential departure from the neoclassical model cannot be disputed. In both cases the goal may be to give concrete expression to the individual desire for freedom. As this book has attempted to show, the real threat to such freedom is not the involvement of the state in all economic decisions, but delays to decisions on the environment because of rising consensus costs. The longer such delays, the greater the eventual constriction of individual freedom of choice. As the available options grow fewer, individuals will increasingly have to adapt to force of circumstances, making direct controls inevitable.

The classical economists who believed that a self-regulating market mechanism would protect individual freedom could probably never have foreseen that part of the current threat to individual freedom stems from purely economic thinking:

1. By defining human behaviour in utilitarian terms, economic theory provides an image of man which has profoundly shaped our way of thinking. Other motives for human activity have been either dismissed or else interpreted as just one more manifestation of selfishness. Economic theory represents a materialistic interpretation of human existence. At the same time, it has eliminated the political and ethical dimensions of man, leaving the economic sphere entirely autonomous. Economic theory has consistently disregarded the environmental context, and has seriously neglected the study of the social environment. Institutional criticisms have failed to reverse the trend towards increasingly abstract models. Study of the natural environment has been left to the natural sciences, and the implicit pact between scientists and economists has aggravated the problem of pollution.

2. Economic theories which assign a passive role to the state fail to grasp the importance of collective decisionmaking mechanisms and the problem of keeping them under democratic supervision. Discussions on the choice of instruments generated by purely economic models fail to consider whether they are workable in practice. In the case of the environment, however, a comprehensive strategy is essential. The sooner such a strategy can be adopted, the easier it will be to apply incentives. Yet there can be no doubt that the strategy must also include direct controls. If individual freedom is to be protected, a proper strategy must be devised quickly — one which will put an end to the age-old feud between market forces and state intervention, allow new motives to emerge, and stimulate public investment in education and research into new non-polluting products. This means that our view of the pollution problem can no longer be limited to the purely economic dimension.

Beyond the economic dimension

Our discussion of environmental policy instruments leads to a clear conclusion, which is that the only possible answer to the problem of environmental pollution is a socio-economic approach. This view is hardly shared by economists, who stress that, here again, what we are faced with is the eminently economic problem of how to determine the optimal level of pollution. This decision is of course subject not only to economic cost constraints, but also to social and political constraints as well as those imposed by the biosphere and by current technology.

However, what is politically and socially possible is determined by collective decision-making mechanisms, and what is technically and biologically possible is determined by the current state of knowledge. Both aspects are thus ultimately matters of individual choice, which is expressed, *inter alia*, by intertemporal preference for immediate consumption or future investment, especially in human capital. In order for opportunity cost to be properly calculated with regard to the environment, not only must it be expressed in well-known terms, but the time-scale applicable to economic decisions must be considerably extended. In theory, such an extension enables the utility of keeping the environment intact for future generations to be compared with the costs of pollution, taking permanent and cumulative effects into account. In practice, all it does is increase the uncertainty surrounding economic decisions.

The problem of evaluating major risks is very apparent in a case such as nuclear energy. Does rational economic calculus come out for or against nuclear energy? It is still commonly claimed that those in favour of nuclear energy are supported by rational arguments while those who reject it are swayed by irrational feelings, yet such a claim fails to take explicit account of the time factor.

To quote A. O. Hirschman (1989, p. 82):

"One of the major ideas in the social sciences — an idea found as far back as Vico and Mandeville, and brilliantly refined during the Scottish enlightenment — is that, because of the limits to forecasting, human actions tend to have unexpected and far reaching consequences."

It is surely therefore better not to cling to a single kind of logic, and to try and move beyond the economic dimension. From here on, our discussion will be limited to the following three aspects of the interaction between the economy and the environment:

1. The links between economics and the natural sciences demonstrate the crucial role of energy in the environmental debate.
2. The political aspect reveals the coalitions and conflicts between different pressure groups.
3. The study of human behaviour emphasizes the importance of the symbolic values which have determined the institutional framework of our society.

The links between economics and environmental science

This approach extends the macroeconomic model to flows between the economic and environmental spheres. Instead of resulting in an input-output analysis, it attempts, in a scientific context, to study the environmental changes caused by permanent externalities. Changes in the atmosphere, in water quality, in fauna and flora, assimilation of waste by the environment, and the degradation process all cause interactions in nature, some of which are as yet unknown. This approach considers the environment as a closed system, in accordance with the law which states that total energy remains unchanged. The consequence of this law is that the volume of resources absorbed by a static economy equals the volume of energy and waste that it produces. However, part of the waste is enriched by atmospheric oxygen and alters the composition of various components of the environment, leading to changes in climate, in the soil and in the subsoil. Two striking examples of such changes are acid rain and the holes in the ozone layer, whose causes and effects are not yet properly understood.

However, it is essential to understand these highly complex interactions if we are to express such changes in monetary terms and determine the scale of the instruments needed to internalize the externalities. Such an evaluation is necessary if individual costs are to be brought into line with social costs. If we fail to understand such interactions, direct controls may again become the only alternative.

The study of interactions caused within the environment by the economy is only one aspect of environmental science. Another, equally important, is the study of energy resources. The global system, including both economic and environmental flows, manifestly has an external source of energy. Through plant photosynthesis, the sun determines production, either directly in the form of agricultural produce, or indirectly in the form of fossil fuels and organic resources. The interaction between the economy and the environment is thus essentially a problem of energy modification. There is no doubt that a technical solution can be found for many kinds of pollution. All such solutions require energy, which thus becomes the crucial link between the economy and the environment. Its role can be formally expressed in terms of energy ecology (Pillet, Odum, 1987), but more specifically raises the problem of non-renewable productive resources. We need to know the rate at which they are becoming depleted, and the extent to which substitutes can be found.

Economic theory provides a rule which, subject to certain hypotheses, links the rate of increase in the price of a non-renewable resource to the rate of interest. In the long term these rates will be equal (Hotelling, 1931). The important consequence of this rule is that non-renewable resources are exploited at a socially optimal rate. Their increasing cost eventually triggers off efforts to find substitutes. However, reassuring though this may seem, in practice it seems to mean very little. While it provides a neat theoretical answer to various complications such as allowance for non-linear costs of extraction, monopoly situations and differences in private and public rates for discounting future profits, the depletion of non-renewable resources remains a normative issue. Society may choose to be either optimistic or pessimistic about the future, but there can be no evading certain facts. Numerous studies have predicted that the coming decades will see a considerable fall in the production of oil, a source which in the 1980s accounted for almost 45% of world primary energy consumption (Stewart, 1983). The very real problem of finding alternative energy sources to oil thus confronts scientists with a clear challenge made worse by two factors.

The first of these is that economic growth contributes to environmental pollution. Reducing the level of pollution increases energy requirements. Water treatment, for example, requires amounts of energy that increase in proportion to the burden the economy places on the environment.

The second factor is that there are well-known alternatives to oil which allow virtually unlimited energy production. The only problem is that they all make pollution worse.

There is thus considerable scope for research in areas ranging from improvement of the current yields from energy sources to their replacement by non-polluting alternatives. Such research, which is starting to get under way, must be accompanied by measures which both internalize the external effects of economic growth and intervene directly in human behaviour in order to control pollution by individuals. Of course, such research can lead to concrete action only if the political will exists and if the implicit pact between the economy and technology has been fully recognized as ideologically biased (Habermas, 1968).

The political dimension

This dimension brings us back to Part II of this book, which showed that the state has a hand in virtually all economic decisions. Despite this, the state is relatively weak, trapped as it is in a web of alliances and conflicts among various pressure groups. In the field of environmental policy, the various interests are affected differently. Moreover, environmental policy does not have a single goal, but several which diverge. Politics, increasingly filtered through the media, likewise lends itself to expressing the value system of the majority of individuals in the country concerned. There are therefore attempts at manipulation in order to give particular pressure groups the external support they seek. Their specific interests must appear to coincide with the interests of most, if not all, citizens. Finally, the policy adopted must fit in with the collective memory as it has evolved through history. It must also be in keeping with both the domestic and the international institutional framework.

For all of these reasons, politics sheds a quite different light on the many recommendations resulting from purely economic models. Not surprisingly, the policies adopted are not those recommended by economists. In the case of the environment, this difference in interpretation is well illustrated by the debate concerning incentives versus direct controls. Economic theory geared to concrete action cannot avoid analysing the feasibility of its policy recommendations. It is therefore merely stating the obvious to suggest that economists and politicians should take a closer look at the links between their respective fields of endeavour.

There have in fact already been attempts to do so (Alt, Chrystal, 1983). However, they merely extend the hypotheses and analytical framework of economic theory to the field of politics. The various pressure groups are assumed to act rationally by maximizing their utility functions. This approach leads to a redefinition of the optimal political decision-making process. Once again, economic reasoning applied to politics emphasizes the fundamental nature of its hypotheses regarding human behaviour.

It is important to realize that politics consists of a network of relationships confronted with transaction costs that increase with the degree of consensus. In an institutional framework governed by democratic rules, the degree of consensus required is that of a majority of voters. The more interests diverge, the greater the cost of achieving this degree of consensus. This approach is necessarily normative, since it attaches far more importance to the distributive aspects of a given policy than economic theory is willing to admit. It also remains subject to society's symbolic view of power. This last factor may serve to demonstrate the full extent of the lip-service paid to the market-economy system when compared with the way in which our economies are actually run.

The divergence between the economic and political interpretations of decision-making mechanisms can be seen in the impact studies performed to camouflage the increase in consensus costs. Let us take a look at some of the special interest groups which clash on matters of environmental policy.

Consumers are divided among themselves. Some call for a restrictive energy policy but continue to consume energy unabated, while others are simply indifferent. The former fail to understand the link between energy production and consumption, while the latter are influenced by publicity in favour of such things as nuclear energy.

Both types of behaviour indicate market failure: consumer sovereignty does not prevail, owing to a lack of information and transparency in the collective decision-making process. Such ignorance may turn into hostility towards environmental measures that entail costs of any kind. An example of such a response is provided by recent legislation in some countries requiring cars to be fitted with catalytic converters.

Producers can be subdivided into three basic categories:

1. Producers who cause pollution are naturally opposed to environment policies of any kind, and disseminate information which plays down the external effects.
2. Producers of services whose activities do not directly cause pollution are not opposed to environment policies, but insist on energy sources, communications and infrastructure remaining available at a cost which does not affect their international competitive position.

3. Producers of environmental commodities (filters, treatment plants, etc.) have an obvious interest in the adoption of measures which will increase demand for such goods.

Each category calls in experts, politicians and government representatives to help assert its own particular viewpoint.

Governments are in no hurry to act as long as no clear majority emerges from efforts to form alliances. Instead, they prefer to wait passively until a particular line of action crystallizes out of the debate. Naturally, the civil service produces documents which supposedly assist the decision-making process. However, in the absence of any clear political will, the civil service may end up concentrating its efforts on forming alliances. Furthermore, it may well be tempted to favour measures which it can easily supervise and which are likely to increase its influence. In other words, the civil service will itself function as a pressure group unless the government takes specific steps to prevent it from doing so.

This summary of the probable attitudes of various special interest groups leads to the following conclusions:

1. The longer decisions are delayed, the more the authorities will have to resort to blanket prohibition, which is hardly conducive to either creativity or innovation. Instead of changes occurring in relative prices and thus, according to economic theory, triggering off a substitution process, investment in research and development will have to be organized by the state. Nor is selective prohibition likely to work, since it encourages alliances among the various minority groups which, each for different reasons, consider such direct intervention as specifically unfair to them.
2. Economic analysis fails to take account of specific political factors. In the case of the environment, economic analysis favours the only two instruments that can really work, namely taxes and subsidies. Both of these are classic political instruments which reflect the sovereignty of the state. Recommendations based on purely economic models cannot therefore help impinging on broader issues. The economy is merely a sub-set of the social whole.
3. Our description of a number of special interest groups indicates the problems involved in organizing a network of relationships. Accordingly, the notion of bounded rationality of human behaviour needs to replace the notion of strict rationality assumed by economic theory. While politicians may believe they act rationally, in actual fact they pursue less laudable aims and their behaviour is influenced by the institutional dimension. What we are therefore dealing with is the sociological concept of organization theory rather than the economic concept of trade theory.

Perceiving new motives

The stated aim of all economic activity is clearly to increase welfare. Historical experience (White, 1967) teaches us that this aim is best served by a growth strategy. The link between economic growth and consumption of goods and services has become so familiar that we immediately associate growth in the consumption of goods with growth in economic welfare. However — as this book has attempted to show in advocating a socio-economic approach — this link needs to be re-examined. Our endless accumulation of goods is harming the environment, and work is now governed by new motives which are located higher in the hierarchy of human needs than the purely instrumental role implicit in the link between economic growth and welfare.

Our discussion of productivity has shown that environmental damage can be attributed to economic growth and population changes.

Much has been written on the theme "to grow or not to grow" (Pringle, 1980). The first of these alternatives is represented by economic theory, in which productive resources are considered as factors exogenous to the production function and no account is taken of the links between the economy and the environment. The second alternative has given rise to an environmental theory of growth based on the work of Forrester (1971). This theory, which misguidedly prescribes drastic limits to all growth, distracts attention from the essential point, which is that economic growth should not be an end in itself, but an instrument of economic welfare.

Moreover, it is impossible for developing countries to see the problem of the environment in terms of such an alternative; there the purpose of growth is to satisfy essential needs, whereas in developed countries it serves more non-material purposes.

The problem of pollution should not, therefore, be seen as solely the concern of rich countries. International coordination must, however, face the problem of inequality in the distribution of basic commodities between developed countries and the third world. Value judgements will become increasingly important. Analysis of the symbols adopted by society could then make it easier to understand the normative content of distribution.

The emergence of new goods and services in the fields of education and culture may lead to a kind of growth that is compatible with environmental protection. The organization of production may be entirely reexamined in order to take fuller account of new motives. Psychologists and sociologists have devised indicators which allow a more complex interpretation of human behaviour than that suggested by the purely utilitarian dimension.

The problem of inequality is increasing together with the population. It is unlikely that population growth will find a self-regulating solution in an approach which attempts to encompass both the economy and the environment. Moral considerations will put economic theory increasingly on the defensive, and it will no longer be possible to avoid ethical issues simply by referring to the supposedly rational behaviour of man.

CONCLUSION

Pure economic theory tends to be self-perpetuating. It has given rise to an entire industry in the fields of education and publication. It develops in order to strengthen established ideological or academic positions. As a result, university economists have grown more and more remote from social issues. Economic theory is pursued as an end in itself rather than as an instrument of economic policy. This retreat into abstraction has been accompanied by the fragmentation of economics into numerous specialist fields whose failure to communicate is an increasingly acute problem. All they have in common is the requirement that their practitioners be versed in the analytical skills of mathematics, statistics and data processing. Far from encouraging interdisciplinary enquiry, such techniques have in turn become ends in themselves; their crucial role in the selection of professional economists may well continue to influence the way society perceives the problems that face it.

This book has shown that a way can be found out of this deadlock if purely economic approaches to social issues make way for new approaches.

First of all, the criticism first uttered by the institutional school is used to warn against a purely reductionist theory which risks perpetuating a value system — exactly what theoretical analysis was supposed to avoid. Ultimately, attempts to reduce the influence of value judgements are every bit as ideological as the construction of theoretical models.

Particular criticism is levelled at the purely deductive method that lies behind such models. The need to compare theory and practice has been rejected by two conflicting schools of thought whose unanimity on this point has made them temporary allies. Theoretical economists, of course, favour deductive reasoning. Practical economists, on the other hand, assert that inductive reasoning is more helpful. In fact, it is clear that only economic research based on both theory and empirical verification can get the methodological debate out of its current tangle. Once again, such research will only be useful if empirical verification is based on something more than mere quantitative methods.

The principle of economic rationality conflicts with the results of sociological and psychological research into human behaviour. In the field of politics, mere reference to the abstract concept of rational human behaviour is not enough. Non-economic insights into human behaviour will encourage cross-fertilization from which economics can only benefit.

This conclusion is confirmed when we examine the role of mathematics and quantitative methods. While their importance and their contribution to the progress of economics cannot be denied, they have just as undeniably led to an excessively one-sided approach. They have also encouraged economists to concentrate on accumulating purely instrumental knowledge in preference to tackling problems of economic policy. This is doubtless the main reason for the frustration felt by economists. Their economic policy recommendations, which are based on a single model, are seldom implemented. However, rather than blame politicians, economists would do well to look more closely at what has been happening in their own back yard.

What has been happening is a revival of the classical model of the economy. Inspired by orthodox liberal thinking, this model emphasizes individual freedom and portrays the economy and the state as implacable foes. It thus helps to sustain two myths which tend to reinforce one another: the myth that the state is a threat to individual freedom, and the myth that the selfregulating market mechanism is superior to all others.

The undeniable reduction in scope for individual manoeuvre has been caused not only by the state but by the very nature of the economic sphere. The state is often merely a scapegoat. Firstly, it is increasingly doubtful whether the economic rationality attributed to individuals actually prevails in today's working environment; secondly, the production of many goods and services does not appear to accord with the principle of consumer sovereignty. The public feels increasingly helpless in the face of economic imperatives, as it witnesses frequent attempts to manipulate the economy, the lack of transparency in the transmission of information, and the lack of vertical and horizontal social mobility which is dictated by current production requirements. Economic theory defends the autonomy of the economic sphere and utterly rejects state intervention. In doing so, it fails to examine the sources of individual sovereignty. It therefore encourages the predominance of economic thinking in social affairs, and at the same time it perpetuates an ideology which ultimately prevents economics from adapting to the dramatic institutional changes that are now taking place. First the industrial revolution and later the emergence of office jobs have left individuals isolated in their occupations. Many are directly threatened by future requirements with regard to data processing. The lack of motivation and creativity which employers so frequently complain of are in fact simply an attempt at self-defence by individuals who feel threatened by changes in their working environment. Efforts to compensate for the reduction in scope for individual manoeuvre dictated by production constraints can be seen in such phenomena as the minimum wage and the consumption ethos.

The introduction of a minimum wage violates the basic principles of the market economy. It reflects a reversal of the hierarchy of values in a specific area. For once, the normative aspects of equity take priority over the usual criteria of efficiency. There are therefore economists who denounce this practice, even claiming that it causes unemployment. However, similar measures are likely to be adopted in other areas such as housing and education, which have been established as basic rights. Suspension of market forces in the fields of labour, housing and education would then be the price to be paid for maintaining social cohesion. A utopian solution would be to draw up a new social contract explicitly based on greater solidarity, both domestically and internationally.

Often the only compensation available to individuals for the economic constraints to which they are subjected is consumption. The marketing of an endless variety of goods caters to this need for sublimation, justifying such marketing strategies as the maintenance of several "competing" brands whose producers are infact competitors in name only, having long since become subsidiaries of a single parent company. The growing feeling that consumer sovereignty is an illusion is reflected in the current use of the word "economy" in public debate to mean businesses rather than the market. This error indicates the importance attributed to the production sector, and this in turn is used to justify the autonomy of the economic sphere. Accordingly, the standard cry of firms accused of lacking a social conscience is that an affordable social policy depends on a healthy business sector.

Unfortunately, consumption as a compensation for individual and social economic constraints is causing more and more environmental problems. The aim of the economy — greater welfare — must be achieved other than by producing more goods. There are ways of doing this which remain compatible with the requirements of the economic sphere:

1. A shift towards production of environmentally safer goods which use fewer non-renewable resources or yield less waste. This represents an immense challenge for research into environmental technology.

2. Reorganization of the working environment in a less hierarchical and more participatory manner, in which labour would be rewarded by means other than greater consumption of goods and services. Motives such as the sense of belonging to a group or the need for self-realization are as yet scarcely acknowledged, but environmental constraints will make them more apparent.

There are those who maintain that these changes can be brought about by the self-regulating market mechanism. However, I believe that this is merely another of the myths kept alive by the revived classical model.

The essential problem of the economy is no longer competition but organization. The imminent development of cognitive data- processing systems can help us to tackle the growing communication problems raised by the highly organized networks our societies have become. However, mere technical elimination of the obstacles to public and private decision-making mechanisms will not be enough to ensure proper supervision of public and private bureaucracies. Individual and collective power strategies are other essential features of highly organized networks such as these. The crucial issue of individual freedom must therefore be resolved, not by ritual appeals to market forces, but by effective supervision of the means of communication by the individuals who make up society. Such supervision requires a more effective democratic mechanism, and can only be achieved by a true state in the political sense of the term. Only thus can the power that exists within the production sphere be used to benefit society in accordance with the democratic ideal. The fact that the environmental debate is really a question of power is what makes it so controversial. For the same reason, it cannot be approached simply with the tools of the market economy. Economic models which ignore this political dimension assume the existence of a self-regulating mechanism which ensures that "the market is always right". In practice, however, all this mechanism does is impose production constraints on the whole of society. Appeals for "a return to market forces" are ultimately no more than calls for the economy to remain independent of the social and political spheres.

If we are to avoid throwing out the baby with the bath-water, economics must open the door to other disciplines. Not only must we stop simply applying market-economy instruments to political and social issues, but new areas of interdisciplinary research must be built up patiently, step by step. While there is nothing spectacular about this approach, it is not the way in which academic research is currently organized. Yet it does not reject the basic premises of the market economy, and indeed it explicitly acknowledges the strengths of economics. Properly used, the market could become a powerful collective decisionmaking mechanism. The strategies of consumers and producers in maximizing their utility and profits respectively remain important motives for human behaviour. However, our understanding of social issues will not be advanced by using increasingly sophisticated models to repeat the same message *ad infinitum.* Just as economic rationality is not the only type of human behaviour, so the market is not the only collective decisionmaking mechanism. This is something which the problem of the environment has forced us to recognize. If we are to avoid ever greater restrictions on individual freedom, we must mobilize our intellectual resources for the following tasks:

1. we must recognize the economy as simply a sub-set of the social whole and analyse it in its overall context; linear cause-and-effect reasoning must make way for multidimensional thinking.
2. we must explicitly acknowledge the ideological content of all economic and social theories.
3. we must develop humanistic concepts which can influence our way of thinking as profoundly as the traditional concepts of utility, profit and labour viewed as a factor of production.

BIBLIOGRAPHY

Alt, J. E., and K. E. Chrystal. (1983). *Political Economics*, Brighton: Harvester Wheatsheaf.

Anderson, F. A., *et al.* (1977). *Environmental Improvement through Economic Incentives.* Baltimore and London: The Johns Hopkins University Press.

Arrow, K. J. (1977). "The Organization of Economic Activity Issues Pertinent to the Choice of Market versus Nonmarket Allocation." In R. H. Haveman and J. Margolis (eds.), *Public Expenditure and Policy Analysis.* Chicago: Rand McNally College Publishing Company.

Atkinson, B., and J. E. Stiglitz. (1980). *Lectures on Public Economics.* New York: McGraw Hill Book Company.

Bank for International Settlements (BIS). (1987). *Annual Report.* Basle: Bank for International Settlements.

Baumol, W. J., and W. E. Oates. (1975). *The Theory of Environmental Policy.* Englewood Cliffs, N. J.: Prentice Hall.

Baumol, W. J., and W. E. Oates. (1979). *Economic Environmental Policy and the Quality of Live.* Englewood Cliffs, N. J.: Prentice Hall Inc.

Becker, G. S. (1981). *A Treatise on the Family.* Cambridge (Mass.): Harvard University Press.

Bell, D. (1981). "Models and Reality in Economic Discourse". In D. Bell and I. Kristol (eds.), *The Crisis in Economic Theory*, New York, Borsic Boots, Inc.

Ben-Porath, Y. (1982). "Economics and the Family — Match or Mismatch?" *Journal of Economic Literature*, 20, 52-64.

Bentley, A. F. (1908). *The Process of Government.* Edited by P. H. Odegard, 1967. Cambridge (Mass.): The Belknap Press of Harvard University.

Berg, M. (1982). *The Machinery Question and the Making of Political Economy.* Cambridge: Cambridge University Press.

Bergier, J. F. (1983). *Histoire économique de la Suisse.* Lausanne: Payot.

Bhagwati, J. N. (1984). "Why are services cheaper in the poor countries?" *The Economic Journal*, 94, 279-286.

Blumenberg, H. (1987). *Das Lachen der Thrakerin, eine Urgeschichte der Theorie.* Frankfurt: Suhrkamp Verlag.

Bössmann, E. (1966). *Die ökonomische Analyse von Kommunikationsbeziehungen in Organisationen.* Berlin: SpringerVerlag.

Boulding, K. E. (1966). "The Economics of Knowledge and the Knowledge of Economics," *American Economic Review, Papers and Proceedings*, 56, 1-13.

Boulding, K. E. (1968). *The Organizational Revolution.* Chicago: Quadrangle Books.

Bridel, P. (1988). "Quelques réflexions sur l'idée de "main invisible," *Revue européenne des sciences sociales*, 26, 81-98.

Brown, C. V., and P. M. Jackson. (1986). *Public Sector Economics* (3rd edition). Oxford: Basil Blackwell.

Bürgenmeier, B. (1977). *Analyse théorique des termes de l'échange: le cas de la Suisse.* Berne and Frankfurt: P. Lang.

Bürgenmeier, B. (1985). "Instruments de la promotion industrielle — Ordre juridique et aspects économiques", *Revue économique et sociale*, 43, 23-34.

Burtt, E. J. (1972). *Social Perspective in the History of Economic Thought.* London: St. James Press.

Canterbery, E. R. (1980). *The Making of Economics.* Belmont: Wadsworth Publishing Company.

Carruth, A., and A. Oswald. (1987). "Wage Inflexibility in Britain," Discussion Paper No. 258, Centre for Labour Economics, London School of Economics.

Chamberlin, E. H. (1933). *The Theory of Monopolistic Competition.* Cambridge, (Mass.): Harvard University Press.

Denis, H. (1967). *Histoire de la pensée économique.* Paris: Presses Universitaires de France.

Dumez, H. (1985). *L'économiste, la science et le pouvoir: le cas Walras.* Paris: Presses Universitaires de France.

Dupuit, J. (1933). *De l'utilité et sa mesure.* Writings selected and re-published by M. de Bernardi, Collection d'écrits inédits ou rares d'économistes, La Riforma Sociale, Turin.

Durkheim, E. (1960). *De la division du travail social.* Paris: Presses Universitaires de France.

Etzioni, A. (1988). *The Moral Dimension: Toward a New Economics.* New York: The Free Press.

Evans, G. (1987). "The Fragility of Sunspots and Bubbles," Technical Report No. 514 of the Institute of Mathematical Studies in the Social Sciences, Stanford University.

Ferguson, C. E. (1969). *The Neoclassical Theory of Production and Distribution.* Cambridge: Cambridge University Press.

Forrester, J. W. (1971). *World Dynamics.* Cambridge (Mass.): Wright-Allen Press.

Frey, B. S. (1972). *Umweltökonomie.* Göttingen: Vandenhoeck & Ruprecht.

Frey, B. S. (1977). *"On the Political Economy of Public Services". In M. S. Feldstein and R. P. Inman (eds.), The Economics of Public Services.* London, etc.: Macmillan.

Frey, B. S. (1981). *Theorie demokratischer Wirtschaftspolitik.* Munich: Verlag Franz Vahlen.

Frey, R. L. (1972). "Umweltschutz als wirtschaftspolitische Aufgabe," *Revue suisse d'économie politique et de statistique,* 108, 453-477.

Friedman, M. (1956). "The Quantity Theory of Money — A Restatement". In M. Friedman (ed.), *Studies in the Quantity Theory of Money.* Chicago: The University of Chicago Press.

Galbraith, J. K. (1982). *The New Industrial State* (2nd edition). London: André Deutsch.

Georgescu-Roegen, N. (1979). *Demain la décroissance.* Lausanne and Paris: P. M. Favre.

Gide, C., and C. Rist. (1944). *Histoire des doctrines économiques depuis les physiocrates jusqu'à nos jours* (6th edition). Paris: Sirey.

Gordon, R. J. (1987). "Postwar Developments in Business Cycle Theory: an unabashedly New-Keynesian Perspective," *Konjunktur,* 174, special report.

Granger, G. G. (1960). *Pensée formelle et sciences de l'homme.* Paris: Aubier.

Greffe, X. (1981). *Analyse économique de la bureaucratie.* Paris: Economica.

Habermas, J. (1969). *Technik und Wissenschaft als Ideologie.* Frankfurt: Suhrkamp Verlag.

Hannan, M. T. (1982). "Families Market and Social Structures," *Journal of Economic Literature,* 20, 65-72.

Hausman, D. (1984). *The Philosophy of Economics: An Anthology.* Cambridge: Cambridge University Press.

Hayek, F. A. von. (1944). *The Road to Serfdom.* London and Henley: Routledge & Kegan Paul.

Hayek, F. A. von. (1958). *Scientism and the study of Society.* Clencoe, ill. The Free Press.

Hirschman, A. O. (1989). "Deux cents ans de rhétorique réactionnaire: le cas de l'effet pervers," *Annales ESC,* 1, 67-86.

Hobson, J. A. (1926). *The Evolution of Modern Capitalism.* New York: George Allen & Unwin Ltd.

Hotelling, H. (1931). "The Economics of Exhaustible Resources", *Journal of Political Economy,* 39, 137-175.

Jacquemin, A. (1987). *The New Industrial Organization, Market Forces and Strategic Behavior.* Oxford: Clarendon Press.

Kellerhals, J., et al. (1982). *Mariages au Quotidien: inégalités sociales, tensions culturelles et organisation familiale.* Lausanne: P. M. Favre.

Keynes, J. M. (1936). *The General Theory of Employment, Interest and Money.* London: Macmillan.

Lea, S. E. G., R. M. Tarpy, and P. Webley. (1987). *The Individual in the Economy, a Survey of Economic Psychology.* Cambridge, etc.: Cambridge University Press.

Le Grand, J., and R. Robinson. (1976). *The Economics of Social Problems.* London, etc.: Macmillan.

Leibenstein, H. (1979). "The Missing Link — Micro-micro Theory?" *Journal of Economic Literature*, 17, 477-502.

Leiss, W. (1976). *The Limits to Satisfaction, an Essay on the Problem of Needs and Commodities.* Toronto and Buffalo: University of Toronto Press.

Lewis, W. A. (1955). *The Theory of Economic Growth.* London, George Allen & Unwin Ltd.

Lucas, R. L. (1976). "Econometric Policy Evaluation: A Critique." In K. Brunner and A. Metzler (eds.), *The Phillips Curve and Labor Market.* Amsterdam: North-Holland.

Lutz, M. A., and K. Lux. (1979). *The Challenge of Humanistic Economics.* Menlo Park, etc.: The Benjamin, Cummings Publishing Company, Inc.

Machlup, F. (1979). *Methodology of Economics and Other Social Sciences.* New York: Academic Press.

Marshall, A. (1890). *Principles of Economics* (8th edition, 1930). London: Macmillan.

Maslow, A. (1970). *Motivation and Personality.* New York: Harper and Row.

McCallum, B. T. (1987). "Postwar Developments in Business Cycle Theory: A Moderately Classical Perspective", *Konjunktur*, 174, special report.

Meehan, E. J. (1982). "Economics and Policy-making, the Tragic Illusion," Contributions in Economics and Economic History, No. 47. London: Greenwood Press.

Mill, J. S. (1940). *Principles of Political Economy.* Edited by W. J. Ashley. London, etc.: Longman, Green & Co.

Myrdal, G. (1957). *Economic Theory and Under-Developed Regions.* London: G. Duckworth & Co.

Nelson, R. H. (1987). "The Economic Profession and the Making of Public Policy," *Journal of Economic Literature*, 25, 49-91.

Olievenstein, C. (1988). *Le non-dit des émotions.* Paris: éditions Odile Jacob.

Olson, M. (1982). *Rise and Decline of Nations*, New Haven, Yale University Press.

Organization for Economic Co-operation and Development (OECD). (1981). *The Welfare State in Crisis*. Paris: Organization for Economic Co-operation and Development.

Parkin, M. (1984). *Macroeconomics*. Englewood Cliffs, N. J.: Prentice Hall Inc.

Pillet, G., and H. T. Odum. (1987). *Energie, écologie, économie*. Geneva: Georg.

Poole, M. (1986). *Towards a New Industrial Democracy: Workers Participation in Industry*. London and New York: Routledge & Kegan Paul.

Pringle, L. (1978). *The Economic Growth Debate*. New York and London: F. Watts.

Pugh, D. S, ed. (1980). *Organization Theory*. Harmondsworth: Penguin Modern Management Texts.

Radner, R. (1986). "The Internal Economy of Large Firms," *The Economic Journal*, Conference Papers, Supplement, 96, 1-22.

Raffestin, C., and M. Bresso. (1979). *Travail, espace, pouvoir*. Lausanne: L'Age d'Homme.

Rawls, J. (1972). *A Theory of Justice*. Oxford: Clarendon Press.

Roig, C., *et al.* (1986). *Le syndicalisme au futur*. Lausanne: L.E.P. Loisirs et pédagogie.

Roll, E. (1973). *A History of Economic Thought*. London: Faber and Faber Ltd.

Rosenberg, N. (1971). *The Economics of Technical Change*. Harmondsworth: Penguin Modern Economic Readings.

Ruskin, J. (1970). *Unto This Last*. Edited by P. M. Parker. London and Glasgow: Collins Publisher.

Sawyer, M. (1987). "Merger: A Case of Market Failure?" *British Review of Economic Issues*, 9.

Schaller, F. (1975). *La Notion de Productivité*. Geneva: Librairie Droz.

Scherer, F. M. (1980). *Industrial Market Structure and Economic Performance* (2nd edition). Chicago: Rand McNally College Publishing Company.

Sen, A. K. (1973). *On Economic Equality*. Oxford: Clarendon Press.

Simon, H. A. (1947). *Administrative Behavior*. New York: Macmillan.

Sombart, W. (1919-21, 4 vols.). *Der moderne Kapitalismus* (4th edition). Munich and Leipzig: Duncker & Humblot.

Stewart, M. (1983). *Controlling the Economic Future: Policy Dilemmas in a Shrinking World*. Brighton: Harvester Wheatsheaf.

Thurow, L. C. (1983). *Dangerous Currents, The State of Economics*. Oxford: Oxford University Press.

Tullock, G. (1986). *The Economics of Wealth and Poverty*. Brighton: Harvester Wheatsheaf.

Veblen, T. (1925). *The Theory of the Leisure Class: An Economic Study of Institutions*. London: George Allen & Unwin Ltd.

Victor, P. A. (1971). *Pollution: Economy and Environment.* London: George Allen & Unwin Ltd.

Volcker, P. A. (1987). "Education and Economic Development," The Inaugural Frederick H. Schultz Distinguished Lecture, Florida Institute of Education, Jacksonville.

Walras, L. (1896). *Etudes d'Economie Sociale.* Lausanne: F. Rouge.

Weber, M. (1967). *L'Ethique protestante et l'esprit du capitalisme* (2nd edition). Paris: Plon.

West, E. G. (1964). "Private versus Public Education, A Classical Economic Dispute," *Journal of Political Economy,* 72, 465-475.

White, L., Jr. (1967). "The Historical Roots of our Ecological Crisis," *Science,* 155, 1203-1207.

Williamson, E. O. (1985). *The Economic Institutions of Capitalism.* New York: The Free Press.

Wolfelsperger, A. (1980). *Economie des inégalités de revenus.* Paris: Presses Universitaires de France.

Zand, D. E. (1981). *Information, Organization and Power.* New York, etc.: McGraw Hill Book Company.

SUBJECT INDEX

189 Current Topics in Microbiology and Immunology

Michael B.A. Oldstone

Department of Neuropharmacology
Division of Virology

The Scripps Research Institute
10666 North Torrey Pines Road
La Jolla, California 92037
USA

Cover illustration: See page 4, Fig. 1a.

Cover design: Harald Lopka, Ilvesheim

ISSN 0070-217X
ISBN-13: 978-3-642-78532-0 e-ISBN-13: 978-3-642-78530-6
DOI: 10.1007/978-3-642-78530-6

Library of Congress Catalog Card Number 15-12910
Softcover reprint of the hardcover 1st edition 1994

SPIN 10096435 27/3020-5 4 3 2 1 0 – Printed on acid-free paper.

Cytotoxic T-Lymphocytes in Human Viral and Malaria Infections

Edited by M. B. A. Oldstone

With 13 Figures and 21 Tables

Springer-Verlag
Berlin Heidelberg New York
London Paris Tokyo
Hong Kong Barcelona
Budapest

Contents

List of Contributors

(Their addresses can be found at the beginning of their respective chapters.)

The Role of Cytotoxic T Lymphocytes in Infectious Disease: History, Criteria, and State of the Art

M. B. A. OLDSTONE

Observations made on children with genetic deficiencies of their immune system reveal that those lacking the capacity to make antibodies nevertheless handle most viral infections as well as normal individuals do. Such a- or hypogammaglobulinemic children are often susceptible to bacterial infections. Conversely, children with genetic deficiencies in their ability to mount cell-mediated immune responses or those who acquire diseases of lymphoid tissues later in life are often susceptible to a range of viral infections (reviewed in GOOD 1991; RICHES 1992).

The immune system consists of humoral (antibody) and cellular (lymphocyte, monocyte, macrophage) responses that most often function synergistically to offer the host protection from invading microbes. Immunization, primarily developed and used most successfully against agents causing acute infection in humans and domestic animals, has been focused toward raising and enhancing antibody responses to glycoprotein or structural protein antigens present on surface virions, although cytotoxic T lymphocytes (CTL) also play major roles in the control of acute infection. Protection from persistent infection is more complex. The viruses are cell associated and often viral surface glycoprotein expression is downregulated (BUCHMEIER and WELSH 1979; OLDSTONE and BUCHMEIER 1982; LIPKIN et al. 1989). In this scenario, to act against virus infected cells, antibodies are not efficient for lysing infected cells. Several million antibody molecules are needed, along with effector molecules of the complement system, to destroy virally infected cells—an ineffective system (SISSONS et al. 1979, 1980).

To better handle persistent infection, the organism's preference is towards the other effector arm of the immune response, consisting of lymphocytes, which detect very low levels of viral antigen on surfaces of infected cells. These lymphocytes are cytotoxic for virally infected cells. Indeed, T cells and CTL by inference are believed to require no more than 100 viral protein (peptide) molecules (DEMOTZ et al. 1990) for activation. CTL can recognize viral sequences expressed on cells that antiviral antibodies are unable to detect. CTL are effective against nonglycosylated immediate–early or early proteins of a virus that are transcribed many hours before structural viral

Viral Immunobiology Laboratory, Division of Virology, Department of Neuropharmacology, The Scripps Research Institute, La Jolla, CA 92037, USA

Current Topics in Microbiology and Immunology, Vol. 189

proteins are made and, most importantly, prior to assembly of the virus into an infectious unit (reviewed in OLDSTONE 1991). Further, CTL recognize infected cells as foreign and destroy them during the latent period of virus infection when the late-acting genes (that encode structural viral proteins) are blocked. CTL can effectively and efficiently recognize and lyse a virally infected cell expressing regulatory proteins (i.e., Nef of human immunodeficiency virus, HIV, immediate–early gene product of cytomegalovirus, CMV) and proteins of the replicative complex (i.e., nonstructural, nuclear protein of influenza virus, Pol and Gag of HIV), all usually made early in the infectious cycle. The strategic advantage to the host in its battle with viruses is that the CTL effector arm can eliminate potential factories (cells) before they produce a finished infectious product (ZINKERNAGEL and ALTHAGE 1977; OLDSTONE 1991).

Now, in 1993, it is abundantly clear that virus-specific CTL are generated in most, if not all, infections by human RNA and DNA viruses. This volume is dedicated towards collecting and disseminating this information. However, the role played in controlling human infection is often circumstantial unless it occurs in genetically deficient or lymphoid-depleted individuals. Yet a plethora of experimental animal studies in which CTL are chemically or genetically deleted combined with reconstitution studies with CTL clones attest to their commanding role in the control of several viral infections, including those with lymphocytic choriomeningitis virus (LCMV), influenza virus, respiratory syncytial virus, CMV infections as well as an important role in rabies and herpes simplex virus infections. Even in the LCMV model, which is acknowledged to be controlled by CTL activity, antibodies can be shown to play a role. For example, CTL reduce viral titers by 4–5 logs (BYRNE and OLDSTONE 1984) and antibodies by 1–2 logs (BALDRIDGE and BUCHMEIER 1992). Interestingly, the murine model of CMV and human CMV point not only to effectiveness of CTL, but a role for NK cells and antibody (BIRON et al. 1989; KOSZINOWSKI et al. 1990). While focusing on CTL, it is nevertheless important to remember the synergistic role of other participants in the immune response.

How do CTL work? CTL recognize proteolytic fragments of viral proteins that are presented at the cell surface by major histocompatibility complex (MHC) glycoprotein molecules (ZINKERNAGEL and DOHERTY 1974; TOWNSEND et al. 1986). MHC molecules are divided into class I and class II, with class I molecules recognized by a CTL subset that bears the CD8 surface marker and class II molecules recognized by CTL or T-helper cells that bear the CD4 surface marker. MHC class I utilizes primarily a cytosolic pathway. MHC class I is found on nearly all cells in the body, an exception being neurons (JOLY et al. 1991; JOLY and OLDSTONE 1992). CTL recognize viral peptides bound to the MHC glycoprotein. The bound peptide sequence is linear and occurs as a consequence of proteolytic fragmentation of a viral protein usually synthesized within the cell. The number of peptides per viral protein able to complex with a MHC glycoprotein in a manner that allows CTL recognition is limited and ranges from one to generally no more than three peptides per viral protein, although recent observations with HIV suggest a larger number of epitopes per viral proteins for this infection (WALKER and PLATA 1990). The size of the peptide has been mapped experimentally and consists optimally of nine to 12 amino acids (reviewed in OLDSTONE 1991), although lower affinity recognition with as few as five amino acids has been noted (WHITTON et al. 1989). Mapping of epitopes utilized recombinant technology, overlapping peptides, and single amino acid truncations from the amino or carboxy termini to initially decode the minimal and optimal peptide size required for CTL recognition as well as recording functional lysis of target cells. Recently the MHC–peptide complex has been directly isolated and chemically identified from virally infected cells (ROTZSCHKE et al. 1990; VAN BLEEK and NATHANSON 1990).

There are a number of milestones in the tale of deciphering CTL activity and structure. The first occurred in 1968, when Brunner and Cerottini, working in Lausanne, Switzerland, reported the use of the quantitative chromium-51 release assay as a marker of membrane injury after cell–cell interaction (BRUNNER et al. 1968). The utility of the assay to study lymphocyte–target cell interactions was appreciated by Cerottini and his colleagues (reviewed in CEROTTINI 1993). Shortly thereafter, Cerottini came as a postdoctoral fellow to Scripps in La Jolla, and on his urging I tested and observed that lymphocytes from mice primed with LCMV lysed (^{51}Cr release) syngeneic LCMV-infected murine targets, but not targets infected either with an indifferent virus or target cells of monkey origin infected with LCMV (OLDSTONE et al. 1969; OLDSTONE and DIXON 1971). Concurrently, Lundstedt in Morgens Volkert's laboratory in Copenhagen, also working with LCMV, found roughly equivalent results (LUNDSTEDT 1969). At this time Martin Raff in Avrion Mitchinson's laboratory in London began utilizing antibody to Th1.2 to segregate T (thymus)-derived from B (bone marrow)-derived lymphocytes, and this reagent was then utilized by Cole, Nathanson, and Pendergast in Baltimore to document that the killer lymphocytes in LCMV mediating cell injury bore the Th1.2 marker (COLE et al. 1972). Next, the seminal observation by ZINKERNAGEL and DOHERTY (1974) in Canberra, Australia, opened wide this field by documenting the requirement for MHC restriction in CTL recognition of the target cell. This contribution also pointed to a role for MHC transplantation antigens and suggested a selective advantage to the host for MHC diversity. Thereafter, many laboratories documented and continue to show CTL killing with MHC restriction and virus specificity for many viruses. In the late 1970s and early 1980s, Askonas (LIN and ASKONAS 1981) in London and Braciale (LUKACHER et al. 1984) in St. Louis, by obtaining and using CTL clones, allowed a more rigorous analysis of CTL recognition and activity. Alain Townsend, Andrew McMichael, and their colleagues provided the next advance when they reported that a peptide from the protein and not the whole viral protein was bound to the MHC for CTL recognition (TOWNSEND et al. 1986). Thereafter, Bevan in La Jolla showed that microinjected cytoplasmic peptide was presented to MHC (MOORE

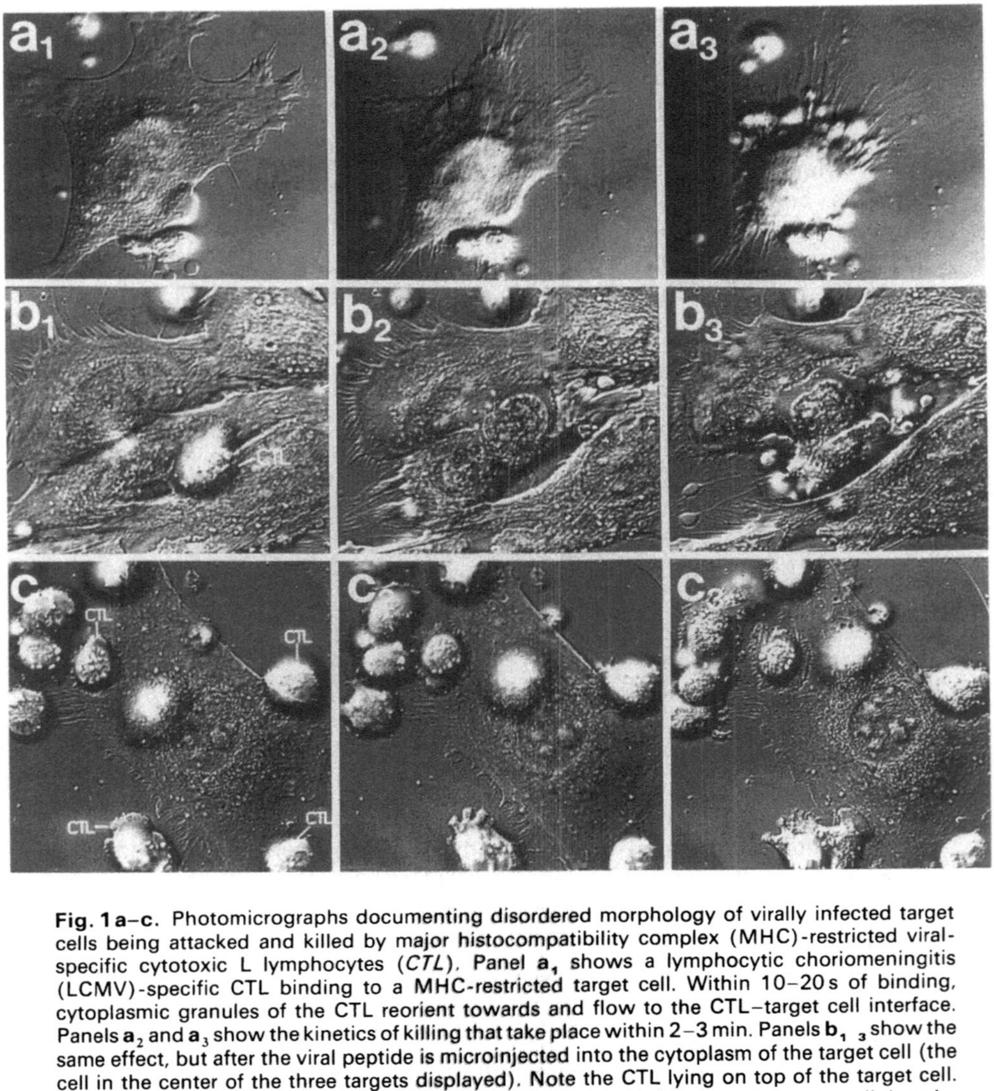

Fig. 1a–c. Photomicrographs documenting disordered morphology of virally infected target cells being attacked and killed by major histocompatibility complex (MHC)-restricted viral-specific cytotoxic L lymphocytes (*CTL*). Panel $\mathbf{a}_1$ shows a lymphocytic choriomeningitis (LCMV)-specific CTL binding to a MHC-restricted target cell. Within 10–20 s of binding, cytoplasmic granules of the CTL reorient towards and flow to the CTL–target cell interface. Panels $\mathbf{a}_2$ and $\mathbf{a}_3$ show the kinetics of killing that take place within 2–3 min. Panels $\mathbf{b}_{1-3}$ show the same effect, but after the viral peptide is microinjected into the cytoplasm of the target cell (the cell in the center of the three targets displayed). Note the CTL lying on top of the target cell. Panels $\mathbf{c}_{1-3}$ by contrast display the interactions of syngeneic CTL and the target cell, but the target cell is expressing an incorrect viral peptide. CTL attach but their cytoplasmic granules fail to reorient towards the target, and the target cell is not killed even after 30 min of observation. Similar findings are seen when the correct peptide is presented by the target cell but to an allogeneic virus-specific CTL. (Unpublished data from K. Hahn, R. DeBiasio, D. Lansing Taylor, and M.B.A. Oldstone, manuscript in preparation, 1993)

et al. 1988), while Whitton, also in La Jolla (WHITTON and OLDSTONE 1989), showed similar results for endogenous processing of a viral minigene encoding the CTL peptide. The conclusion of the first act in this grand theater was the solving of the three-dimensional structure of the MHC class I molecule by Bjorkman, Wiley, Strominger, and colleagues at Harvard (BJORKMAN et al. 1987), revealing two alpha helices bordered by a floor of beta sheaths, the peptide residing in the helices. In concert, Mak and colleagues in Toronto and Davis at Stanford (YANAGI et al. 1985; DAVIS et al. 1986) defined the molecular structure of the T cell receptor that recognizes the peptide–MHC complex. From this brief review, the contributions made by an international group of scientists are evident. Recently, direct isolation of viral peptide, processed by MHC glycoprotein from the infected cell by Nathanson's (VAN BLEEK and NATHANSON 1990) and Rammensee's (ROTZSCHKE et al. 1990) laboratories has been accomplished. Use of this and other data by FALK et al. (1991) provided insights into motifs of peptides bound to MHC molecules. Crystallographic study of different peptides restricted by the same MHC molecule by Wilson's and Peterson's laboratories (FREMONT et al. 1992; MATSUMURA et al. 1992) have enhanced our understanding of structure–function relationships of MHC–peptide interactions.

Once the MHC glycoprotein–peptide complex is on the cell surface, it is recognized by a CTL according to the latter's receptor, composed of alpha and beta chains. If not recognized, the MHC complex likely dissociates, MHC glycoproteins recycle, and the peptide is degraded. The molecular and cellular biology of the molecules involved in CTL attraction to the target, flow and penetration of CTL granules, mechanism of target cell disorder, and death are all current topics of investigation, and several of these points are revealed in photographs from the study of Klaus Hahn and colleagues (Fig. 1).

The MHC heavy chain and its associated light chain (β_2-microglobulin) are encoded by different genes. Their synthesis and assembly occur at the endoplasmic reticulum (ER), and it is currently believed that the assembled MHC molecule does not migrate to the cell surface until a specific peptide binds within the MHC α_1 and α_2 domains (Fig. 2). During this scenario, the β_2-microglobulin is thought to assist in locking the peptide within the MHC groove, causing a change in conformation that allows the complexed molecule to leave the ER. With the exception of neurons (JOLY et al. 1991), other cells studied so far transcribe β_2-microglobulin and the heavy (h) chain of MHC coordinately. Neurons transcribe β_2 normally, but are believed to be deficient in transcription of the MHC h-chain.

This volume presents data from those who have made significant contributions to defining CTL activity to a variety of human viruses and to the protozoa that cause malaria. Further, this volume establishes a foundation for considering CTL activity in several human infections. Research interest in several laboratories for the future is being focused on (a) the correlation of CTL activity in humans with protection and disease and (b) the generation

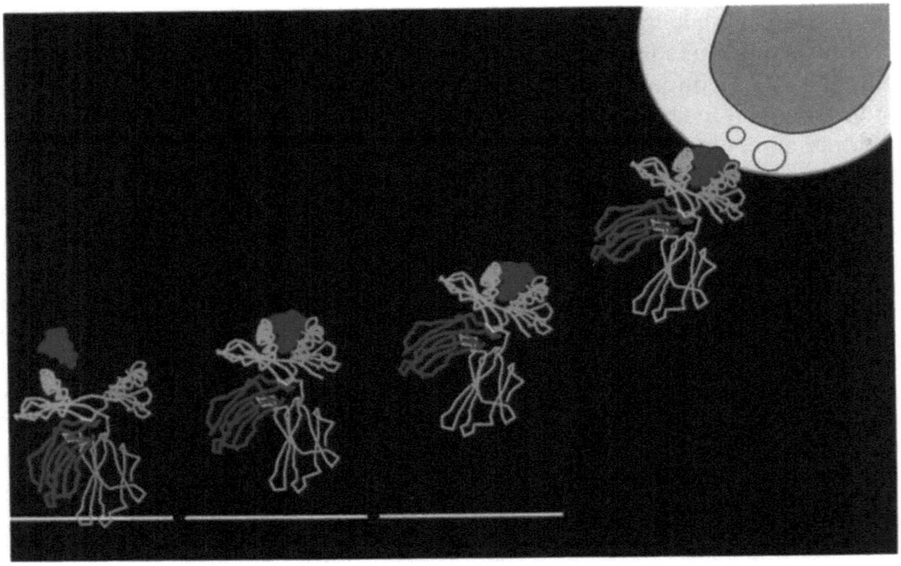

Fig. 2. A cartoon showing sequentially a peptide derived from a viral protein binding within the $\alpha_1-\alpha_2$ helices of the major histocompatibility complex (MHC) glycoprotein, the peptide being locked into place by the β_2-microglobulin and the MHC–peptide complex traveling to the cell surface, where it is to be surveyed by a cytotoxic T lymphocyte (CTL)

and possible use of adoptive therapy of CTL to modulate and treat human infections and cancers.

Acknowledgments. This is Publication Number 8056-NP from the Division of Virology, Department of Neuropharmacology, The Scripps Research Institute, La Jolla, CA. This work was supported in part by USPHS grants AI-09484, NS-12428, AG-04342, and MH-47680.

References

Baldridge JR, Buchmeier MJ (1992) Mechanisms of antibody-mediated protection against lymphocytic choriomeningitis virus infection: mother-to-baby transfer of humoral protection. J Virol 66: 4252–4257

Biron CA, Byron KS, Sullivan JL (1989) Severe herpesvirus infections in an adolescent without natural killer cells. N Engl J Med 320: 1731–1735

Bjorkman PJ, Saper MA, Samraoui B, Bennett WS, Strominger JL, Wiley DC (1987) Structure of the human class I histocompatibility antigen, HLA-A2. Nature 329: 506–511

Brunner KT, Mauel J, Cerottini JC, Chapuis B (1968) Quantitative assay of the lytic action of immune lymphoid cells on ^{51}Cr-labelled allogeneic target cells in vitro: inhibition by isoantibody and by drugs. Immunology 14: 181–196

Buchmeier MJ, Welsh RM (1979) Protein analysis of defecting interfering lymphocytic choriomeningitis virus and persistently infected cells. Virology 96: 503–515

Byrne JA, Oldstone MBA (1984) Biology of cloned cytotoxic T lymphocytes specific for lymphocytic choriomeningitis virus: clearance of virus in vivo. J Virol 51: 682–686

Cerottini J-C (1993) T-cell-mediated cytotoxicity: a historical note. In: Sitkovsky MV, Henkart PA (eds) Cytotoxic cells: recognition, effector function, generation, and methods (in press)
Cole GA, Nathanson N, Prendergast RA (1972) Requirement for theta-bearing cells in lymphocytic choriomeningitis virus-induced central nervous system disease. Nature 238: 335–337
Davis MM, Lindsten T, Gascoigne NR, Goodnew C, Chien YH (1986) T cell receptor gene structure and function. Cell Immunol 99: 24–28
Demotz S, Grey HM, Sette A (1990) The minimal number of class II MHC-antigen complexes needed for T cell activation. Science 249: 1028–1030
Falk K, Rotzschke O, Stevanovic S, Jung G, Rammensee HG (1991) Allele-specific motifs revealed by sequencing of self-peptides eluted from MHC molecules. Nature 351: 290–296
Fremont DH, Matsumura M, Stura EA, Peterson PA, Wilson IA (1992) Crystal structures of two viral peptides in complex with murine MHC class I H-2K^b. Science 257: 919–927
Good RA (1991) Experiments of nature in the development of modern immunology. Immunol Today 12: 283–286
Joly E, Oldstone MBA (1992) Neuronal cells are deficient in loading peptides onto MHC class I molecules. Neuron 8: 1185–1190
Joly E, Mucke L, Oldstone MBA (1991) Viral persistence in neurons explained by lack of major histocompatibility complex class I expression. Science 253: 1283–1285
Koszinowski UH, Val MD, Reddehase MJ (1990) Cellular and molecular basis of protective immune response to cytomegalovirus infection In: McDougall JK (ed) Cytomegaloviruses. Springer, Berlin Heidelberg New York, pp 189–220 (Current topics in microbiology and immunology, vol 154)
Lin Y, Askonas BA (1981) Biological properties of an influenza A virus specific killer T cell clones. Inhibition of virus replication in vivo and induction of delayed hypersensitivity reactions. J Exp Med 154: 225–234
Lipkin WI, Villarreal LP, Oldstone MBA (1989) Whole animal section in situ hybridization and protein blotting: new tools in molecular analysis of animal models for human disease. In: Haase AT, Oldstone MB (eds) In situ hybridization. Springer, Berlin Heidelberg New York, pp 33–54 (Current topics in microbiology and immunology, vol 143)
Lukacher AE, Braciale VL, Braciale TJ (1984) In vivo effector function of influenza virus-specific cytotoxic T lymphocyte clones is highly specific. J Exp Med 160: 814–826
Lundstedt C (1969) Interaction between antigenically different cells: virus-induced cytotoxicity by immune lymphoid cells in vitro. Acta Pathol Microbiol Scand 75: 139–152
Matsumura M, Fremont DH, Peterson PA, Wilson IA (1992) Emerging principles for the recognition of peptide antigens by MHC class I molecules. Science 257: 927–934
Moore MV, Carbone FR, Bevin MJ (1988) Introduction of soluble protein into the class I pathway of antigen processing and presentation. Cell 54: 777–785
Oldstone MBA (1991) Molecular anatomy of viral persistence. J Virol 65: 6381–6386
Oldstone MBA, Buchmeier MJ (1982) Restricted expression of viral glycoprotein in cells of persistently infected mice. Nature 300: 360–362
Oldstone MBA, Dixon FJ (1971) The immune response in lymphocytic choriomeningitis viral infection. In: Miescher P (ed) 6th international symposium of immunopathology. Schwabe, Basel, pp 391–398
Oldstone MBA, Habel K, Dixon FJ (1969) The pathogenesis of cellular injury associated with persistent LCM viral infection. Fed Proc 28: 429
Riches PG (1992) Viral infections complicating immunodeficiencies. Clin Ther 140: 123–129
Rotzschke O, Falk K, Deres K, Schild H, Norda M, Melzger J, Jung G, Rammensee H-G (1990) Isolation and analysis of naturally processed viral peptides as recognized by cytotoxic T cells. Nature 348: 252–254
Sissons JGP, Schreiber RD, Perrin LH, Cooper NR, Muller-Eberhard HJ, Oldstone MBA (1979) Lysis of measles virus-infected cells by the purified cytolytic alternative complement pathway and antibody. J Exp Med 150: 445–454
Sissons JGP, Oldstone MBA, Schreiber RD (1980) Antibody-independent activation of the alternative complement pathway by measles virus-infected cells. Proc Natl Acad Sci USA 77: 559–562
Townsend ARM, Rothbard J, Gotch FM, Bahadur G, Wraith D, McMichael AJ (1986) The epitopes of influenza nucleoprotein recognized by cytotoxic T lymphocytes can be defined with short synthetic peptides. Cell 44: 959–968
van Bleek GM, Nathenson SG (1990) Isolation of an endogenously processed immunodominant viral peptide from the class I H-2K^b molecule. Nature 348: 213–216

Walker RD, Plata F (1990) Cytotoxic lymphocytes against HIV. AIDS 4: 177–184

Whitton JL, Oldstone MBA (1989) Class I MHC can present an endogenous peptide to cytotoxic T lymphocytes. J Exp Med 170: 1033–1038

Whitton JL, Tishon A, Lewicki H, Gebhard J, Cook T, Salvato M, Joly E, Oldstone MBA (1989) Molecular analyses of a five amino acid cytotoxic T lymphocyte (CTL) epitope: an immunodominant region which induces nonreciprocal CTL cross-reactivity. J Virol 63: 4303–4310

Yanagi Y, Chan A, Chin B, Minden M, Mak TW (1985) Analyses of cDNA clones specific for human T cells and the alpha and beta chains, of the T-cell receptor heterodimer from a human T-cell line. Proc Natl Acad Sci USA 82: 3430–3434

Zinkernagel RM, Althage A (1977) Antiviral protection by virus-immune cytotoxic T cells: infected target cells are lysed before infectious virus progeny is assembled. J Exp Med 145: 644–651

Zinkernagel RM, Doherty PC (1974) Restriction of in vitro T cell-mediated cytotoxicity in lymphocytic choriomeningitis within a syngeneic or semiallogeneic system. Nature 248: 701–702

Therapeutic Reconstitution of Human Viral Immunity by Adoptive Transfer of Cytotoxic T Lymphocyte Clones

S. R. RIDDELL and P. D. GREENBERG

1 Introduction

The fundamental role of a competent host T lymphocyte response for promoting the resolution of acute viral infections is supported by the severe and progressive infections observed in individuals with primary or acquired deficiencies of T cell function (ROSEN et al. 1984a, b; REDFIELD et al. 1987;

Fred Hutchinson Cancer Research Center and the Departments of Medicine and Immunology, University of Washington, Seattle, WA 98104-2092, USA

Current Topics in Microbiology and Immunology, Vol. 189

ENGLUND et al. 1988; LJUNGMAN et al. 1989). The critical immune response is comprised of $CD8^+$ cytotoxic T cells (CTL) and $CD4^+$ helper T cells (Th), which recognize degraded fragments of proteins derived from pathogens and presented in association with class I and class II major histocompatibility complex (MHC) molecules, respectively (BRACIALE et al. 1987; YEWDELL and BENNINK 1990). $CD8^+$ CTL function to eradicate viral infection by the direct lysis of infected cells and by the secretion of cytokines such as γ-interferon. The predominant function of $CD4^+$ Th in the host response to infection is the production of cytokines, which in addition to direct antiviral effects facilitate the antiviral activities of macrophages, B cells, and other T cells including $CD8^+$ CTL.

For individuals with viral infections characterized by a latent and/or persistent phase after primary exposure, the maintenance of an MHC-restricted, host virus-specific T cell response is essential for controlling episodes of reactivation. There are striking clinical examples of the consequences of suppressing host immune competence including the fulminant infections that evolve in solid organ and bone marrow transplant (BMT) recipients due to reactivation of cytomegalovirus (CMV), varicella zoster virus (VZV), or herpes simplex virus (HSV), and the occurrence of Epstein Barr virus (EBV)-induced lymphoproliferative syndromes (PURTILO 1980; MEYERS et al. 1987; MARTIN et al. 1984; ZUTTER et al. 1988). The frequency and severity of many of these infections in immunocompromised hosts have been attenuated by the development of antiviral drugs but the requirement for long-term administration in chronically immunosuppressed hosts, the toxicity of the available antiviral agents, and the development of drug-resistant virus isolates has encouraged investigation of novel therapeutic approaches aimed at resolving the underlying immunodeficiency (SARAL et al. 1981; SCHMIDT et al. 1991; GOODRICH et al. 1991). One approach potentially applicable to human diseases and supported by a substantial body of experimental data in murine models is the use of adoptive immunotherapy with antigen-specific T cells to selectively reconstitute or augment deficient T cell responses.

2 Adoptive Immunotherapy of Viral Diseases in Murine Models

The principles for successful adoptive immunotherapy of human diseases have largely been established in experimental models for viral infections and tumors in mice (GREENBERG 1991). Studies in murine models have demonstrated that deficient protective T cell responses to viruses and tumors can be selectively reconstituted by the adoptive transfer of $CD4^+$ and $CD8^+$ antigen-specific T cells (LUKACHER et al. 1984; BYRNE and OLDSTONE 1984; LARSEN et al. 1984; GREENBERG et al. 1985; GREENBERG 1986). The demonstrations in mice that adoptive immunotherapy with $CD8^+$ CTL alone will protect hosts from infections with several viruses including murine CMV, influenza, HSV, and respiratory syncytial virus have provided convincing support for a decisive role of $CD8^+$ CTL responses in antiviral immunity (REDDEHASE et al. 1985; LUKACHER et al. 1984; LARSEN et al. 1984; CANNON et al. 1987). Moreover, the demonstrations that murine antigen-specific T cells isolated and cultured long-term in vitro prior to cell transfer retain efficacy in adoptive immunotherapy has established an important precedent for the treatment of human diseases in which in vitro expansion of effector T cells for therapeutic use is likely to be necessary (LUKACHER et al. 1984; BYRNE and OLDSTONE 1984; CHEEVER et al. 1986).

An extensively studied murine adoptive therapy model is the treatment of murine CMV infection in BALB/c mice. Although murine CMV is species specific and genetically disparate from human CMV, it shares many of the biological properties of the virus, including persistence as a latent infection in healthy hosts and reactivation in immunosuppressed hosts to cause a progressive infection culminating in pneumonitis and hematopoietic failure (GARDNER et al. 1974; JORDAN et al. 1977; SHANLEY et al. 1979; MUTTER et al. 1988).

Experiments in the murine CMV model have investigated the role of individual T cell subsets and T cells of selected antigen specificities in protection from lethal CMV infection. These studies have demonstrated that the adoptive transfer to immunosuppressed mice of T cells obtained from syngeneic animals previously immunized with murine CMV is protective against a lethal virus challenge. The transfer of purified $CD8^+$ T cells alone was sufficient to provide protection, whereas the transfer of purified $CD4^+$ T cells alone was not effective (REDDEHASE et al. 1985). The transfer of $CD8^+$ CTL also provided an antiviral effect in immunosuppressed mice with established murine CMV disease, demonstrating that the antiviral effects of $CD8^+$ CTL are not limited to the prophylactic setting (REDDEHASE et al. 1985).

Reconstitution of a protective response requires transfer of T cells with specificity for the appropriate viral antigens necessary to control and/or eliminate infection. Inoculation of BALB/c mice with murine CMV elicits an immunodominant $CD8^+$ CTL response specific for an epitope of the 89-kD a major immediate–early (IE) viral protein presented in association with single MHC allele, L^d (KOSZINOWSKI et al. 1987; REDDEHASE et al. 1989). Mice can be immunized with a recombinant vaccinia virus expressing the major IE protein, and the adoptive transfer of the $CD8^+$ T cells derived from such mice was found to be effective in protecting naive mice from challenge with a lethal inoculum of CMV, demonstrating that even a very limited repertoire of $CD8^+$ CTL can be sufficient for protective immunity (REDDEHASE et al. 1987a).

3 Cytomegalovirus Infection in Allogeneic Bone Marrow Transplant Recipients—A Model for Specific Adoptive Immunotherapy in Humans

The extension of adoptive immunotherapy from animal models to human diseases is predicated on the isolation and propagation of human antigen-specific T cells and on the ability of such T cells to persist and function in vivo following cell transfer. The first attempts at T cell transfer in humans evolved in the field of cancer immunotherapy (ROSENBERG et al. 1985). These studies have not specifically evaluated the use of MHC-restricted, antigen-specific T cells, but rather have utilized in therapy autologous polyclonal lymphocytes, derived from the peripheral blood or from a tumor biopsy, and activated in vitro with high concentrations of interleukin 2 (IL-2) (ROSENBERG et al. 1986, 1988). Up to 40% of patients with malignant melanoma have demonstrated antitumor responses, but only a small fraction of patients with tumors of other histologies have had measurable responses (ROSENBERG et al. 1988). Efforts to improve the response rate have been difficult, in part because the nature and specificity of the effector cells responsible for the observed antitumor effects have not been defined.

Infections that develop in immunodeficient allogeneic BMT recipients provide unique clinical situations in which the therapeutic and biologic effects of adoptive immunotherapy with T cells of defined specificity and function might be more readily evaluated. In this setting, T cells with the desired antigen specificity can potentially be isolated from the immunocompetent MHC-identical bone marrow donor, and the contribution of transferred effector T cells to host immunity can be readily evaluated in hosts deficient in the respective T cell response after ablative chemoradiotherapy. Our initial efforts in BMT recipients have been directed at developing adoptive immunotherapy as prophylaxis for human CMV infection. Reactivation of CMV occurs in 70%–80% of CMV-seropositive BMT recipients, and in the absence of antiviral therapy up to 50% of patients excreting virus will develop CMV pneumonia or enteritis (MEYERS et al. 1986, 1990). Combination antiviral therapy with ganciclovir and immunoglobulin has improved the survival for these patients. However, even with such therapy, 50% of patients developing CMV pneumonia still have a fatal outcome (REED et al. 1988; EMMANUEL et al. 1988). The median time after transplant to the development of clinically overt CMV disease is 50–60 days, presumably due to the slow replicative cycle of CMV, which allows adequate time to generate CMV-specific T cells in vitro from the bone marrow donor for adoptive transfer to the transplant recipient.

3.1 Contribution of CD8$^+$ and CD4$^+$ Major Histocompatibility Complex-Restricted T Cell Responses to Protection from Cytomegalovirus Disease

The development of effective adoptive immunotherapy for CMV infection after BMT would be facilitated by an understanding of the relative contributions of the CD4$^+$ and CD8$^+$ CMV-specific T cell responses to the control of viral reactivation. BMT recipients transplanted with bone marrow that has not intentionally been depleted of T cells receive with the marrow inoculum a small number of contaminating donor T lymphocytes of both the CD4 and CD8 phenotype. However, the absolute number of memory T cells specific for an individual pathogen is so low that recipients display a profound deficiency of antigen-specific T cell responses in the early post-transplant period. The tempo of immunologic recovery is variable in individual patients and influenced by several factors, including the preexisting immunity of the donor, the intensity of postgrafting immunosuppressive therapy, and the development of graft versus host disease (GVHD; WITHERSPOON et al. 1984; LUM 1987). Thus, the hypothesis that defects of CMV-specific T cell responses may contribute to the development of CMV disease can be directly tested by analyzing the temporal recovery of CMV-specific CD4$^+$ Th and CD8$^+$ CTL responses in individual BMT patients and correlating these responses with the occurrence of CMV disease.

Two studies have assessed CD4$^+$ CMV-specific Th responses of peripheral blood lymphocytes (PBL) obtained from BMT recipients and have demonstrated no correlation between the presence of CD4$^+$ CMV-specific Th and the clinical outcome of CMV infection (MEYERS et al. 1980; QUINNAN et al. 1982). In one of these studies, the ability of fresh PBL to directly lyse CMV-infected target cells in an in vitro assay over an extended duration was evaluated (QUINNAN et al. 1982). This analysis demonstrated that individuals with detectable cytotoxic responses to CMV-infected target cells were more likely to resolve a CMV infection. However, the cytolytic activity measured in this assay reflected both NK cell- and T cell-mediated lysis (QUINNAN et al. 1981). If NK cells were depleted prior to the assay, this method of directly examining T cells from PBL for cytolytic reactivity permitted detection of CD8$^+$ CTL responses only in patients with clinically overt CMV infection and was not sensitive enough to detect CD8$^+$ CTL in individuals without active infection (QUINNAN et al. 1982). Therefore, the specific contribution of endogenous reconstitution of CD8$^+$ CTL responses in preventing CMV infection or progression of subclinical reactivation to disease could only be inferentially determined.

The development of in vitro culture methods with greater sensitivity for detecting CD8$^+$ CMV-specific CTL responses in individuals without active infection has provided the opportunity for a more detailed examination of the role of CD8$^+$ CTL in the pathogenesis of CMV disease after BMT. Stimulation of PBL in vitro with autologous CMV-infected fibroblasts results in the selective expansion of CD8$^+$ CMV-specific CTL precursors which can be detected in a 4- to 6-h cytotoxicity assay (BORYSIEWICZ et al. 1983; SCHRIER and OLDSTONE 1986). The exposure of target cells to γ-interferon prior to infection with CMV upregulates class I MHC gene expression and further increases the sensitivity of short-term cytolytic assays for detecting CD8$^+$ CMV-specific CTL (LAUBSCHER et al. 1988).

Using such in vitro methods, the temporal recovery after allogeneic BMT of CD8$^+$ CMV-specific CTL responses was examined in samples of PBL obtained at 30, 60, and 90 days after transplant and the correlation between presence of these responses and occurrence of CMV disease determined. The initial analysis of 20 patients demonstrated that by day 90 after BMT, 50% of patients had recovered detectable CD8$^+$ CMV-specific CTL responses. Six of the ten patients without recovery of CTL had developed CMV pneumonia, whereas no cases of CMV pneumonia were observed in the ten patients with recovery of CTL responses (REUSSER et al. 1991). This analysis of endogenous reconstitution of CD8$^+$ CMV-specific CTL responses has now been extended to include 58 patients, and the results confirm the initial observations—15 of the 58 patients developed CMV pneumonia, with none of the 15 having evidence of CD8$^+$ CMV-specific CTL responses in the assay prior to or concurrent with the onset of CMV disease (Table 1). Moreover, patients demonstrating recovery of CD8$^+$ CTL responses were protected from the subsequent development of CMV disease.

A simultaneous analysis of the recovery of CD4$^+$ CMV-specific Th responses in the 58 patients demonstrated that all patients with recovery of CD8$^+$ CMV-specific CTL had prior or concurrent recovery of CD4$^+$ CMV-specific Th responses. This would be expected, since recovery of CD4$^+$ Th is likely to be obligatory for the development of detectable CD8$^+$ CTL responses. Althouth a significant correlation between the recovery of CD4$^+$ Th

Table 1. The recovery of cytomegalovirus (CMV)-specific T cell responses after allogeneic bone marrow transplantation (BMT) correlates with protection from CMV pneumonia

	Occurrence of CMV pneumonia (*n*)	Total no. of patients
No recovery of CD4 or CD8	13*	26
Recovery of CD4 and CD8	0*	25
Recovery of CD4 alone	2	7
Recovery of CD8 alone	0	0

CD8$^+$ cytotoxic T lymphocyte and CD4$^+$ T-helper responses were evaluated in samples of peripheral blood lymphocytes obtained at days 30–40, 60–70, and 90–120 after BMT. The responses were assayed and scored as previously described (REUSSER et al. 1991). The diagnosis of CMV pneumonia required the presence of CMV in tissue sections or bronchoalveolar lavage with compatible clinical signs and symtoms. Statistical analysis was performed using Fischer's exact test.
* $p < 0.01$

and protection from CMV disease was observed, two of seven patients with isolated recovery of weak but detectable $CD4^+$ Th responses developed CMV pneumonia, suggesting that this response alone is not sufficient to provide protection (Table 1). Thus, in this temporal analysis of endogenous immune reconstitution in allogeneic BMT recipients, the absence of $CD8^+$ CMV-specific CTL was found to be a major contributing factor to the development of CMV disease, suggesting that early immunologic reconstitution of this response by adoptive immunotherapy might be of significant therapeutic benefit.

3.2 In Vitro Isolation and Expansion of $CD8^+$ Cytomegalovirus Specific CTL Clones

The results from the analysis of endogenous reconstitution of CMV-specific T cell responses in BMT recipients focused our initial efforts on the development of in vitro techniques to isolate and expand $CD8^+$ class I MHC-restricted, CMV-specific CTL for potential use in adoptive immunotherapy. Although polyclonal T cell cultures enriched for $CD8^+$ CMV-specific CTL by several cycles of stimulation with autologous CMV-infected fibroblasts could be readily derived from CMV-seropositive bone marrow donors for use in therapy, this method would not likely provide a population of T cells with sole specificity for CMV antigens, and the adoptive transfer of such polyclonal CTL would carry the risk of inducing GVHD. This concern was reaffirmed by the observation that in some cultures of PBL stimulated with autologous CMV-infected fibroblasts, the CTL lines exhibited specificity for both CMV-infected autologous targets and uninfected allogeneic targets (RIDDELL et al. 1991a). To circumvent this problem, limiting dilution culture methods were developed to isolate individual $CD8^+$ CMV-specific CTL from cultures enriched for $CD8^+$ CMV-specific CTL activity (RIDDELL and GRENBERG 1990; RIDDELL et al. 1991b). The cloning efficiency of $CD8^+$ T cells plated with autologous CMV-infected fibroblasts as stimulator cells, γ-irradiated PBL, and EBV-transformed lymphoblastoid cell lines (LCL) as feeder cells, and recombinant IL-2 varied in different individuals from 2%–10% of plated T cells, with 30%–80% of clones isolated displaying class I MHC-restricted, CMV-specific cytolytic reactivity (RIDDELL et al. 1991b). The clonal origin of the T cells obtained in these cultures was confirmed by restriction endonuclease digestion of genomic DNA and analysis of T cell receptor gene rearrangements.

The number of T cells necessary to mediate a therapeutic effect following adoptive transfer in humans is not known, but estimates derived by extrapolation from animal models would suggest that between 10^8 and 10^{10} cells may be required for efficacy. As described above, $CD8^+$ CMV-specific CTL clones can be induced to proliferate in vitro with retention of MHC-restricted cytolytic function by intermittent stimulation with autologous CMV-infected

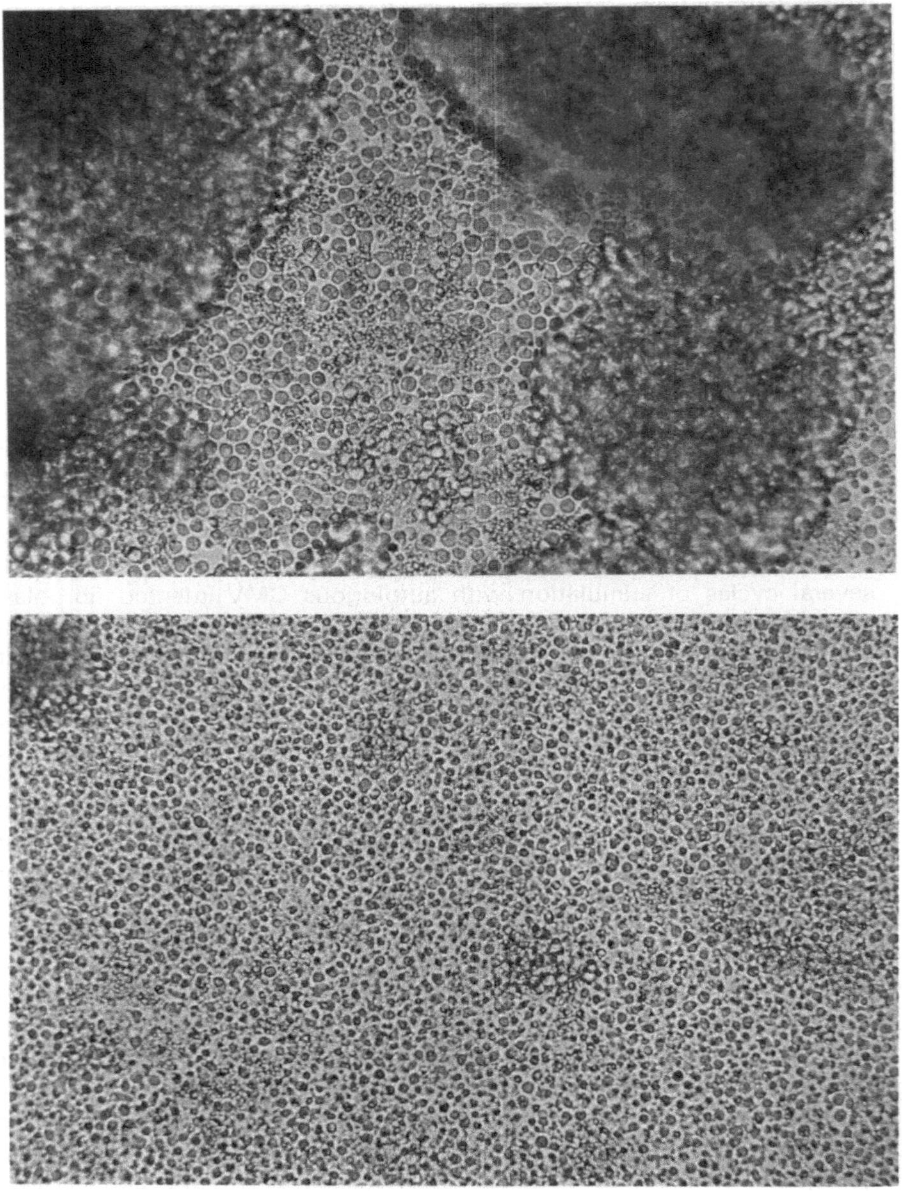

a

b

Fig. 1a, b. Morphology of a CD8⁺ cytomegalovirus (CMV)-specific T cell clone during growth and resting phases after antigen stimulation. A CD8⁺ CMV-specific T cell clone was stimulated with autologous CMV-infected fibroblasts at a responder to stimulator ratio of 20 and interleukin 2 (50 U/ml) was added to the culture at 2 and 4 days after stimulation. Panel a shows the T cells on day 5 after stimulation and illustrates the large, irregular morphology and clusters indicative and proliferating cells. Panel **b**, shows T cells of the same clone entering the resting phase 10 days after antigen stimulation, at which time the cells are small, round, and nonclustered fibroblasts and addition to the cultures of irradiated feeder cells and IL-2. After antigen stimulation and the addition of exogenous IL-2, T cells become large, form clusters, and undergo several days of proliferation before assuming a small, round morphology typical of resting lymphocytes prior to the next cycle of stimulation (Fig. 1). T cell clones grown in this fashion can be plated with irradiated feeder cells in the absence of antigen or IL-2 stimulation and will remain viable in vitro for long periods of time ($>$ 21 days; RIDDELL et al. 1991a). In contrast, T cells cultured in continously high concentrations of IL-2 without cyclical stimulation die rapidly when IL-2 is withdrawn (LENARDO 1991). Moreover, cycles of growth and rest, rather than continuous IL-2-driven expansion, may be important for retention of antigen specificity. The majority of $CD8^+$ CMV-specific T cell clones generated can be grown to 10^8 cells over 8 weeks and some can be expanded to more than 10^{10} cells 12–16 weeks after initial plating (RIDDELL et al. 1991a). To maintain large T cell numbers in these cultures, fibroblasts are grown in large flasks or roller bottles for use as stimulators, and donor PBL are obtained by leukapheresis and cryopreserved for use as feeder cells. Thus, these culture methods are adequate to provide the numerical expansion of human $CD8^+$ CMV-specific CTL clones predicted to be necessary for successful adoptive immunotherapy.

4 Evaluation of the Antigen Specificity of Protective $CD8^+$ Cytomegalovirus-Specific CTL

Despite the apparent importance of $CD8^+$ CTL responses in controlling infection with CMV, the role of specific viral proteins as target antigens for CTL has only recently been evaluated. In murine studies, the specificity of CTL responses to viruses is frequently biased towards a limited number of octa or nonapeptide epitopes derived from a relatively few immunodominant viral proteins and conforming to a binding motif specific for individual MHC molecules (VAN BLEEK and NATHENSON 1990). It is presumed that the immunodominant response detected in healthy individuals resistant to disease reflects the response most effective for preventing disease, although viral factors may also contribute to this limitation of the T cell repertoire (WOLD and GOODING 1991; GOODING 1992; POSAVAD and ROSENTHAL 1992). The use in adoptive immunotherapy of a small number of T cells clones, each specific for a single peptide, may impose a significant constraint on efficacy if the target epitopes are not representative of the immunodominant response or are subject to mutational variation in the pathogen. Thus, it became essential to elucidate whether particular CMV antigens were immunodominant in individuals with protective immunity and to determine the potential for variability of target antigens in different CMV strains.

4.1 Immunodominant Cytomegalovirus-Specific CD8$^+$ CTL Responses Recognize Structural Virion Proteins

The standard method to identify target antigens for CTL employs recombinant vectors to selectively express individual viral genes; however, this could not be efficiently applied to human CMV, as approximately 200 viral proteins may be encoded by the 230-kb CMV genome. Studies with influenza virus had suggested that antigens presented by class I MHC to CD8$^+$ CTL were predominately derived from the processing of newly synthesized viral proteins (BRACIALE et al. 1987). Since the transcription and translation of CMV genes after viral infection occurs sequentially (WALTHEN and STINSKI 1982), metabolic inhibitors could be used to selectively limit viral gene expression at distinct phases of the viral replicative cycle to identify the sets of genes encoding potential target antigens for CMV-specific CTL.

The first viral proteins synthesized after CMV infection are the products of the IE genes, which are required for the activation and subsequent expression of the early (E) genes (STINSKI et al. 1983). The late (L) genes are expressed following the onset of viral replication and encode the majority of the proteins comprising the virion structure (LANDINI and MICHELSON 1988). A sequential metabolic blockade of cells infected with CMV using cycloheximide, an inhibitor of protein synthesis, followed by actinomycin D, and inhibitor of RNA synthesis, will resı it in limiting the expression of viral proteins in infected cells to those encoded by the IE genes (REDDEHASE and KOSZINOWSKI 1984). Similarly, target cells will selectively express only IE and E proteins if infected with CMV in the presence of phosphonoformic acid (GRIFFITHS and GRUNDY 1987). Initial experiments using these approaches suggested that a high frequency of CD8$^+$ CTL from latently infected individuals recognized target cells expressing only IE, or IE and E gene products (BORYSIEWICZ et al. 1988; RIDDELL et al. 1991b). CD8$^+$ CMV-specific CTL clones were isolated to further define the specificity of these responses. Although the majority of CTL clones lysed target cells blocked with cycloheximide and actinomycin D, none of these clones lysed target cells infected with a vaccinia recombinant virus encoding the 72-kDa major IE protein (RIDDELL et al. 1991b). These results suggested that either minor IE proteins were the dominant target antigens for CTL or that structural virion proteins entering the cytoplasm after viral penetration were being processed and presented by the class I pathway prior to de novo endogenous synthesis.

To determine the potential role of structural CMV proteins entering with the virion as target antigens for CD8$^+$ CTL, autologous fibroblasts were pretreated with actinomycin D, infected with CMV, and assayed as targets for CTL in the continued presence of actinomycin D. Under these conditions, no transcription or translation products of the IE genes were detectable in infected cells, and thus the only viral antigens available for class I processing were those proteins entering with the virus (RIDDELL et al. 1991b). Remarkably, actinomycin D-blocked target cells were efficiently lysed in an MHC-

Table 2. Polyclonal CD8⁺ cytomegalovirus (CMV)-specific cytotoxic T lymphocytes (CTL) recognize autologous CMV-infected cells in the absence of endogenous viral gene expression

Donor CTL	Target cell (% lysis)					
	Autologous			MHC mismatched		
	CMV	CMV/ActD	Mock	CMV	CMV/ActD	Mock
SS	46	37	1	8	6	2
CG	23	19	1	4	1	0
MR	64	57	1	12	3	8
BH	48	40	1	6	4	3
KD	66	64	2	4	1	1
DH	48	46	1	7	3	3
TM	45	48	6	5	2	2
CM	39	37	1	2	2	3
5937	42	43	3	2	3	3
6213	35	39	0	3	1	1

Polyclonal CD8⁺ CTL lines were generated from peripheral blood lymphocytes obtained from CMV-seropositive individuals (designated by initials or a unique donor number as shown under the column "Donor CTL"). The CTL cultures were assayed 12–14 days after initiation for cytolytic reactivity against Cr^{51}-labeled autologous and major histocompatibility complex (MHC)-mismatched fibroblasts either mock infected (Mock), infected with CMV for 16 h (CMV), or infected with CMV for 4 h in the presence of the transcriptional inhibitor actinomycin D (CMV/ActD). Data is shown for an effector to target ratio of 10 or 20:1.

restricted manner by polyclonal CTL lines generated from ten consecutive CMV-seropositive individuals (Table 2). Moreover, the overwhelming majority of CD8⁺ CMV-specific CTL clones isolated from these cultures also efficiently lysed target cells infected with CMV in the presence of actinomycin D. Conversely, the rare CTL clones we have isolated that are specific for the 72-kDa IE protein lyse autologous cells infected with the Vac/IE recombinant or with CMV, but as predicted do not lyse cells infected with CMV in the presence of actinomycin D (RIDDELL et al. 1991b). These results, which demonstrate an immunodominant role for introduced structural virion proteins as target antigens for the CD8⁺ CMV-specific CTL response present in individuals with protective immunity, are consistent with recent results in experimental models of antigen processing demonstrating that only cytosolic location and not endogenous synthesis is required for proteins to be processed and presented by the class I pathway (MOORE et al. 1988; YEWDELL et al. 1988).

To gain insight into the variability in the epitopes recognized by CMV-specific CTL, we have analyzed the ability of polyclonal CTL lines and T cell clones to lyse target cells sharing only a single MHC allele with the donor. In the CMV-seropositive donors studied, the CTL response is predominantly restricted by one or at most two of the class I MHC molecules expressed by the individuals' cells with minor responses restricted by the other alleles

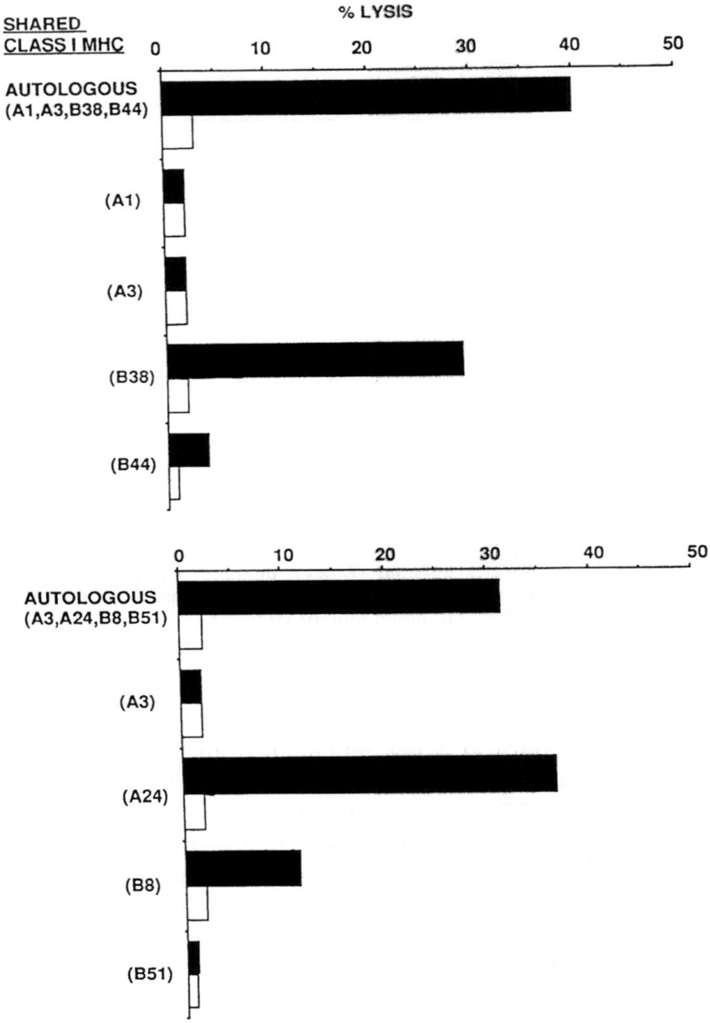

Fig. 2. Polyclonal CD8⁺ cytomegalovirus (CMV)-specific cytotoxic T lymphocyte (CTL) responses in CMV-seropositive individuals are predominantly restricted by a single major histocompatibility complex (MHC) allele. Polyclonal CMV-specific CTL lines were generated by stimulation of peripheral blood lymphocytes with autologous CMV-infected fibroblasts as previously described (RIDDELL et al. 1991b). Cultures were restimulated once and assayed 12–14 days after initiation for recognition of autologous CMV-infected fibroblasts (■), autologous mock-infected fibroblasts (□), and allogeneic fibroblasts sharing only a single class I MHC molecule with the donor and either infected with CMV (■) or mock infected (□). The data is presented at an effector-to-target ratio of 10:1. The class I MHC phenotype of the donor target cell is given in *parentheses* under *Autologous* and the single class I MHC allele shared by allogeneic target cells is indicated in *parentheses*

(Fig. 2). Thus, despite the large number of potential target antigens encoded by CMV, the experimental evidence suggests that the host $CD8^+$ CTL response to CMV is predominantly focused on a small number of epitopes derived from proteins comprising the virion structure. This immunodominant CTL response, capable of recognizing infected cells prior to the onset of viral replication, may be particularly beneficial to the host by controlling viral spread after episodes of reactivation.

4.2 $CD8^+$ CTL Recognition of Cytomegalovirus Proteins in the Absence of Viral Gene Expression Is Selective

At least 20 proteins comprise the virion structure and represent candidate target antigens for the immunodominant CTL response to CMV. The most abundant of these include the envelope proteins GB and GH, the matrix proteins pp 65 and pp 150, and the 150-kDa major capsid protein (LANDINI and MICHELSON 1988; RASMUSSEN 1990; JAHN et al. 1987). The contribution of the envelope proteins GB and GH as target antigens for $CD8^+$ CMV-specific CTL clones representative of the immunodominant response has been evaluated using vaccinia GB and GH recombinant viruses to infect target cells and selectively express the GB or GH proteins. In these experiments, CTL clones that recognize GB- or GH-expressing target cells were not identified. Although GB was not the target antigen of the immunodominant CTL response, $CD8^+$ CTL clones specific for GB could be isolated from seropositive individuals by infection of autologous stimulator cells with Vac/GB to achieve selective expression of the GB protein (RIDDELL et al. 1991b). This was consistent with the results of a limiting dilution analysis in two CMV-seropositive individuals demonstrating a low precursor frequency of GB-specific CTL (BORYSIEWICZ et al. 1988).

The relative absence of CTL specific for GB or GH may reflect the propensity with which these proteins are accessable to the class I antigen processing and presentation pathway early after CMV infection. To determine how efficiently GB was processed for class I presentation compared with proteins recognized by the immunodominant CTL response, we examined the ability of $CD8^+$ GB-specific CTL to lyse cells infected with CMV at various stages of the replicative cycle. GB-specific CTL do not lyse cells infected with CMV in the presence of an actinomycin D blockade, but will lyse cells infected with CMV for longer than 24 h with no metabolic inhibitors (RIDDELL et al. 1991b). By contrast, cells infected with CMV are recognized by CTL representative of the immunodominant response at all stages of the replicative cycle. The failure to present GB envelope protein immediately after viral infection may be due in part to the intimate involvement of the viral envelope in fusion at the plasma membrane, resulting in limited amounts entering the cytosol and being available for presentation with class I MHC molecules. Consistent with CMV envelope proteins serving only a minor role as target antigens for CTL responses, efforts have been unsuccessful to isolate from several individuals CTL specific for a second envelope glycoprotein, GH, despite the use of a vac/GH recombinant virus to selectively express GH in stimulator cells.

The structural proteins comprising the matrix and capsid of CMV are not bound to the cell membrane, but rather enter the cytoplasm following viral fusion. The most abundant protein component of the matrix of CMV is a 65-kDa phosphoprotein (pp65; JAHN et al. 1987). CTL specific for pp65 were identified in the polyclonal CTL response elicited by in vitro stimulation with CMV-infected fibroblasts in the majority of individuals studied, and approximately 50% of the CMV-specific CTL clones isolated from one individual recognized autologous targets infected with Vac/pp65. Moreover, the pp65-specific CTL clones lysed cells infected with CMV in the presence of an actinomycin D blockade, demonstrating that pp65 can be directly processed and presented to $CD8^+$ CTL without the need for endogenous synthesis. The remainder of the $CD8^+$ CMV-specific CTL clones isolated from this individual recognized one or more structural proteins distinct from pp65 that could also be presented by cells infected in the presence of actinomycin D. Construction of recombinant vectors to express additional matrix or capsid proteins should elucidate the relative contributions of these proteins as target antigens for CTL responses to CMV.

4.3 Epitopes Recognized by $CD8^+$ CTL Are Conserved in Clinical Isolates of Cytomegalovirus

The majority of clinical isolates of CMV exhibit substantial genetic heterogeneity by restriction endonuclease digestion (HUANG et al. 1980; CHANDLER and MCDOUGALL 1986). It is unknown whether this genetic variability confers differences in the pathogenesis of CMV infection. However, the recent identification of subgroups of CMV based on heterogeneity in the envelope glycoprotein B gene demonstrates that significant variation may occur in viral genes that encode target antigens for CTL (CHOU and DENNISON 1991). Individuals undergoing allogeneic BMT are potentially at risk for exposure to several genetically different strains of CMV, including the virus transferred with the donor bone marrow inoculum, the endogenous latent CMV strain, and CMV strains transmitted by blood products administered as supportive care after the BMT (CHOU 1986). Thus, it would be advantageous if the T cell clones used in adoptive therapy recognized highly conserved epitopes present in otherwise genetically distinct clinical isolates. Experiments were performed in five individuals in whom the immunodominant response was restricted by different class I MHC molecules to analyze the recognition by CTL of target cells infected either with laboratory strains AD169 or Towne, or with five genetically distinct CMV isolates recently derived from BMT recipients. The epitopes recognized by the $CD8^+$ CTL clones representative of the immunodominant response in these individuals were conserved in all the CMV strains tested, suggesting that the genetic heterogeneity of the virus is unlikely to present a significant obstacle to successful adoptive immunotherapy (GREENBERG et al. 1991).

5 Restoration of $CD8^+$ CTL Responses in Bone Marrow Transplant Recipients by Adoptive Transfer of CTL Clones

The results of our studies investigating the immunobiology of CMV infection after allogeneic BMT supported a crucial role for $CD8^+$ CTL responses in preventing CMV disease and suggested that the adoptive transfer of T cell clones to reconstitute immunity warranted investigation as a prophylactic or therapeutic strategy for CMV infection in BMT recipients. The objectives of our initial adoptive therapy experiments in allogeneic BMT recipients were to determine whether the adoptive transfer of $CD8^+$ CMV-specific CTL clones could be accomplished safely and if transferred T cells could persist and function in vivo. T cell infusions were administered to the patients beginning 28–35 days after BMT. This time point was selected for several reasons. First, differentiation of complications due to the transplant-conditioning regimen, which predominantly occur in the first 21 days after BMT, could be more easily distinguished from toxicities that might occur as a consequence of T cell therapy. Second, our prior studies demonstrated that only 25%–35% of patients have endogenous recovery of $CD8^+$ CMV-specific CTL responses at days 30–40 after transplant (REUSSER et al. 1991; LI and RIDDELL, unpublished data); thus, it should be possible to measure a contribution of transferred CTL in the majority of patients. Third, reconstitution of protective responses would begin before the highest period of infectious risk, since less than 2% of CMV-seropositive BMT patients will develop CMV disease prior to day 35.

Seven CMV-seropositive patients receiving a BMT from CMV-seropositive, HLA-identical related donors have been entered into this study. $CD8^+$ CMV-specific T cell clones were successfully generated from each of the seven bone marrow donors and propagated to cell numbers sufficient for therapy in all patients. Two patients did not receive T cell infusions—one died of bacterial sepsis prior to day 35 and one patient developed severe pulmonary toxicity related to the BMT-conditioning regimen and did not meet the eligibility criteria for T cell therapy at day 35 after BMT. Five patients have received all of the four scheduled T cell infusions.

5.1 Generation and Characterization of CTL Clones for Immunotherapy

Fibroblast lines for use as stimulator and target cells were established from skin biopsies obtained from the MHC-identical bone marrow donors approximately 4 weeks prior to the scheduled BMT. Polyclonal $CD8^+$ CMV-specific CTL were generated by stimulating PBL obtained from the bone marrow donor with autologous CMV-infected fibrolasts, and T cell clones were isolated from the polyclonal CTL cultures by limiting dilution cloning. Screening assays were used to identify $CD3^+$ $CD8^+$ $CD4^-$ T cell clones which lysed autologous CMV-infected fibroblasts in a class I MHC-restricted manner, but failed to lyse uninfected fibroblasts. Clones were also assayed for lysis of fibroblasts and EBV-transformed B cells derived from the BMT recipient to identify and exclude from use in therapy any CTL with cross-reactivity for recipient minor histocompatibility antigens. CTL clones meeting these selection criteria were propagated to large numbers over 5–12 weeks. Prior to administration to the BMT recipient, all clones were assessed for sterility and mycoplasma contamination.

5.2 Clinical Monitoring of Patients Receiving Adoptive Immunotherapy with $CD8^+$ CTL

Significant toxicities including fevers, fluid retention, renal failure, and pulmonary edema have been observed in cancer patients receiving infusions of lymphokine-activated killer (LAK) cells or tumor-infiltrating lymphocytes (TIL) in conjunction with IL-2 (Rosenberg et al. 1986, 1988). The toxicities observed are identical to those seen when IL-2 is administered alone, making assessment of the contribution of the cellular component of this therapy difficult. IL-2-activated killer cells localize in the lungs immediately after infusion, due in part to activation-induced adherence to endothelium, and therefore might contribute to the pulmonary compromise observed in these patients (Fisher et al. 1989). Since, in the adoptive transfer studies in CMV, IL-2 is not administered with or following the transfer of $CD8^+$ CMV-specific CTL, the magnitude of the toxicities observed in the LAK and TIL trials would not be expected.

To minimize any potential side effects of T cell therapy and to provide insight into the number of T cells required to reconstitute detectable responses, one infusion of $CD8^+$ CTL was administered each week for 4 consecutive weeks. Providing no toxicity was encountered, the dose of T cells administered was escalated according to the following schedule: first infusion—3.3×10^7 T cells/m^2; second infusion—1×10^8 cells/m^2; third infusion—3.3×10^8 T cells/m^2; and fourth infusion—1×10^9 T cells/m^2. Although up to ten individual T cell clones were administered with each infusion to achieve the desired cell dose, many doses, including the highest dose, could be achieved with one or a composite of two clones.

All patients were monitored for alterations in vital signs and oxygen saturation during, and for 2 h after completion of, the T cell infusions. There were no significant changes in vital signs or oximetry recordings during this monitoring period with any of the 20 T cell infusions. One patient developed a fever 3 h following the third infusion, but defervesced without antimicrobial therapy. Given that fevers are relatively common after BMT, it was not evident that this temperature elevation was related to T cell therapy. After the initial three patients had completed therapy, subsequent T cell infusions were administered to them in the outpatient department. In these initial patients, no significant immediate toxicities due to T cell transfer were apparent.

Although the T cells used in adoptive transfer are of donor origin, the selection of clones with class I MHC-restricted, CMV-specific cytolytic reactivity should preclude a significant risk of inducing or worsening GVHD. All patients on this study were evaluated for changes in GVHD status on a daily basis while inpatients and twice weekly as outpatients. None of the five patients had any evidence of progression of GVHD during the course of T cell therapy.

5.3 Immunologic Monitoring of Cytomegalovirus-Specific T Cell Responses After Adoptive Transfer of $CD8^+$ CTL

The reconstitution of T cell immunity to CMV in treated patients was evaluated by assaying PBL obtained before initiating T cell therapy and 48 h after each infusion for CMV-specific $CD8^+$ CTL and $CD4^+$ Th responses. Consistent with the severe immunodeficiency observed at this time after allogeneic BMT, three of the five patients had no detectable $CD8^+$ CMV-specific CTL or $CD4^+$ Th responses before T cell transfer, and two patients had weak but detectable responses. In each of the three deficient patients, weak $CD8^+$ class I MHC-restricted CTL responses were detected 48 h after the first T cell infusion and the responses were augmented after each subsequent infusion (RIDDELL et al. 1992a). The CTL responses persisted between infusions, as reflected by assaying samples obtained just prior to the third infusion, implying that the increasing responses observed after each infusion reflected both persistent and recently infused CTL (Table 3). In these three patients, $CD8^+$ CTL responses were achieved by the third infusion that were equivalent in magnitude to those present in the healthy bone marrow donor, despite no evidence of recovery of $CD4^+$ CMV-specific Th responses during the 4 weeks of therapy. It must be emphasized that in 58 patients studied for endogenous reconstitution of CMV-specific T cell responses after allogeneic BMT, the recovery of $CD4^+$ Th responses was

Table 3. Reconstitution of CD8$^+$ cytomegalovirus (CMV)-specific cytotoxic T lymphocyte (CTL) responses in allogeneic bone marrow transplant (BMT) recipients by the adoptive transfer of T cell clones

T cell infusion	Patient no. 6032				Patient no. 6131 Target cell (% lysis)				Patient no. 6025			
	Autologous		Allogeneic		Autologous		Allogeneic		Autologous		Allogeneic	
	CMV	Mock	CMV	Mock	CMV	Mock	CMV	Mock	CMV	Mock	CMV	Mock
Pre #1	2	1	ND	ND	7	6	1	0	4	0	0	1
Post #1	17	4	ND	ND	23	2	1	0	14	0	1	0
Post #2	43	5	6	12	48	3	6	3	12	1	1	1
Pre #3	37	5	3	6	20	2	0	1	12	1	1	1
Post #3	53	8	9	11	33	3	0	1	48	6	2	2
Post #4	83	10	4	5	38	2	2	4	55	6	0	0
Bone marrow donor	53	1	2	2	37	5	4	1	29	1	1	3

CD8$^+$ CMV-specific CTL responses in BMT recipients and their respective bone marrow donors were evaluated in peripheral blood lymphocytes by a CTL generation assay (Riddell et al. 1991b). Peripheral blood lymphocytes were obtained from the recipients immediately before initiating T cell therapy (pre #1), 2 days after each T cell infusion (post #1 to post #4), and just before the third infusion (pre #3). CTL generation cultures were assayed in a 5-h chromium-release assay for class I major histocompatibility complex (MHC)-restricted, CMV-specific cytolytic reactivity 14 days after initiation. Target cells were autologous and allogeneic class I MHC-mismatched fibroblasts either infected with CMV or mock infected. The data are shown for an effector-to-target ratio (E/T) of 20:1 for patient 6032 and the respective bone marrow donor, and at an E/T of 10:1 for patients 6131, 6025, and their respective donors.

obligatory for the endogenous recovery of $CD8^+$ CTL (Table 1). Thus, these functional studies provide compelling evidence for the efficacy of adoptive transfer of CTL clones in restoring $CD8^+$ CMV-specific CTL responses in immunodeficient hosts. Two of the five patients had weak but detectable $CD8^+$ CMV-specific CTL responses and readily detectable $CD4^+$ Th responses at the onset of therapy. Substantial augmentation of $CD8^+$ CTL responses was observed 48 h after the T cell infusions, consistent with the successful transfer of additional effector T cells, although the possibility of endogenous recovery of $CD8^+$ CTL responses could not be excluded in these two patients.

All patients in this study received as prophylaxis for GVHD immunosuppressive therapy consisting of methotrexate and cyclosporine (three patients), methotrexate alone (two patients), or cyclosporine and prednisone (two patients). Since post-transplant immunosuppressive therapy contributes to the prolonged period of impaired immune competence observed after allogeneic BMT, the therapeutic success of adoptive T cell transfer is in part dependent on the ability of transferred T cells to persist in vivo. Observation of the three patients who were deficient in $CD8^+$ CTL and $CD4^+$ Th responses prior to adoptive immunotherapy proved to be particularly informative in the evaluation of long-term persistence of transferred CTL. PBL were obtained at 2 and 4 weeks after the completion of T cell therapy and assayed for CMV-specific $CD8^+$ CTL and $CD4^+$ Th responses. After 2 weeks, the magnitude of the $CD8^+$ CTL responses in the three patients had declined, but was still evident, despite the continued absence of a $CD4^+$ Th response, consistent with a limited survival of a component of the transferred CTL and/or with migration of the infused CTL from the peripheral blood to tissue sites. At 4 weeks, $CD8^+$ CMV-specific CTL responses remained easily detectable in the three patients, but one of the three patients had weak endogenous recovery of a $CD4^+$ CMV-specific Th response, making it possible that endogenous recovery of $CD8^+$ CTL was also contributing to the responses detected (Tables 4, 5). In the other two patients, no recovery of $CD4^+$ CMW-specific Th responses was detected, demonstrating that adoptively transferred CTL clones persist in vivo for at least 1 month after transfer (RIDDELL et al. 1992a). One of the five patients received only a small number of distinct T cell clones, and the unique rearrangements of the T cell antigen receptor genes are being used to identify transferred T cells persisting in the host at later times after T cell therapy. Determining the survival of individual clones in larger numbers of patients would be facilitated by the introduction of a marker gene by gene transfer techniques as has been applied to studies of adoptive immunotherapy in cancer patients (ROSENBERG et al. 1990). Such studies to determine the duration of in vivo survival of adoptively transferred T cell clones and the potential survival advantage of individual clones should be helpful in determining the optimal cell doses and infusion intervals for future studies in CMV and other diseases.

Table 4. Persistence of adoptively transferred CD8$^+$ cytomegalovirus (CMV)-specific cytotoxic T lymphocyte (CTL) responses after adoptive immunotherapy with CD8$^+$ T cell clones

	Patient no. 6032				Patient no. 6131 Target cell (% lysis)				Patient no. 6025			
	Autologous		Allogeneic		Autologous		Allogeneic		Autologous		Allogeneic	
	CMV	Mock	CMV	Mock	CMV	Mock	CMV	Mock	CMV	Mock	CMV	Mock
Post #4	83	10	4	5	38	2	2	4	55	6	0	0
2 weeks post #4	31	2	1	1	30	3	3	2	31	3	2	2
4 weeks post #4	39	5	4	5	31	4	5	4	41	7	2	1

CD8$^+$ CMV-specific CTL responses of PBL obtained from recipients 0, 2, and 4 weeks after completion of the fourth (#4) T cell infusion were evaluated using the CTL generation assay. Target cells include autologous fibroblasts either infected with CMV or mock infected, and HLA-mismatched (allogeneic) fibroblasts either infected with CMV or mock infected. Data are shown for an effector-to-target ratio (E/T) of 20:1 for patient 6032 and an E/T of 10:1 for patients 6131 and 6025.

Table 5. CD4$^+$ cytomegalovirus (CMV)-specific T-helper (Th) responses in recipients of adoptive immunotherapy with CD8$^+$ CMV-specific cytotoxic T lymphocyte

	Patient no. 6032			Patient no. 6131			Patient no. 6025		
	Control	CMV Ag	PHA	Control	CMV Ag	PHA	Control	CMV Ag	PHA
Post #4	1412	560	9951	179	143	22882	466	721	4964
2 weeks post #4	639	861	11255	142	493	41976	121	141	4511
4 weeks post #4	1409	1413	12376	408	1005	56590	201	292	5499
Bone marrow donor	2099	42664	145801	1319	20796	445524	1502	9624	160964

CD4$^+$ CMV-specific Th responses of peripheral blood lymphocytes (PBL) obtained from recipients 0, 2, and 4 weeks after completion of the fourth (#4) T cell infusion were evaluated in a 96-h proliferation assay. Triplicate cultures of 2×10^5 PBL per well were plated in 96 round-bottomed plates with a control antigen preparation derived by glycine extraction of mock-infected fibroblasts, a CMV antigen (CMV Ag) preparation derived by glycine extraction of CMV-infected fibroblasts, and with phytohemagglutinin (PHA, 10 μg/ml). Wells were pulsed with 2 μCi of tritiated thymidine for the final 18 h of the 96-h incubation. The results are shown as the mean counts per minute (cpm) of triplicate wells.

5.4 Virologic Monitoring of Patients Receiving Adoptive Immunotherapy with CD8$^+$ CTL

Reactivation of CMV as defined by a positive shell vial or conventional culture from throat, urine, or blood occurs in 70%–80% of CMV-seropositive individuals receiving an allogeneic BMT from a CMV-seropositive bone marrow donor (MEYERS et al. 1986). CMV viremia, which occurs in 40%–50% of patients, is highly predictive of the subsequent development of CMV disease and is thought to indicate substantial viral replication at sites of reactivation (MEYERS et al. 1990). All patients entered into this study had weekly monitoring of throat, urine, and blood by shell vial assays and culture for CMV to determine the potential antiviral effects of T cell transfer. The initial results of these virologic studies in the five patients are encouraging, although the number of patients treated with adoptive immunotherapy thus far is insufficient for definitive evaluation of the efficacy of reconstituting CD8$^+$ CTL responses in providing protection from CMV disease. None of the five patients treated with T cell infusions have developed CMV viremia or disease. One patient excreted CMV from the throat prior to receiving T cell therapy, and the cultures became negative in the week after the first T cell infusion and remained negative throughout the remainder of the post-BMT course. Three patients had isolated urinary excretion of CMV on a single occasion, as detected by shell vial assay in two and both shell vial assay and culture in one patient. Since normal immunocompetent individuals may excrete virus in the urine for prolonged periods of time after primary CMV infection despite clearance of viremia, the significance of isolated urinary excretion of CMV in these BMT patients is unclear, but may imply that additional host defense mechanisms other than CD8$^+$ CTL are necessary to maintain virus reactivation below a detectable level. The follow-up of a larger cohort of patients receiving adoptive immunotherapy to reconstitute CD8$^+$ CMV-specific CTL responses will assist in precisely defining the antiviral effects. However, the lack of toxicity and the absence of CMV disease observed in the first five patients suggests further investigation of this approach is warranted.

6 Conclusions

The use of adoptive immunotherapy to reconstitute or augment deficient antigen-specific T cell responses as treatment for pathogens and tumors in humans has long been an appealing concept. Results in animal models have established the principles of T cell transfer and validated the therapeutic promise of this approach for both malignant and infectious diseases. The initial investigations of adoptive immunotherapy in human malignant disease have been dissappointing and hindered by the difficulties in reliably isolating and propagating human T cells with MHC-restricted specificity for human tumors. Studies of the adoptive transfer of $CD8^+$ CMV-specific CTL in immunodeficient allogeneic BMT recipients now provide the first evidence in humans that adoptive transfer of T cell clones of defined specificity can be used successfully to restore antigen-specific T cell responses.

Adoptive immunotherapy with $CD8^+$ CMV-specific CTL resulted in no evident toxicities with single infusions of up to 2.2×10^9 T cells and total cell doses of 3.2×10^9. The successful transfer of CMV-specific CTL responses can be detected in the recipients' PBL with small cell doses ($3.3 \times 10^7/m^2$), and the responses measured after the transfer of 3.3×10^8 T cells/m^2 are equivalent in magnitude to those observed in healthy immunocompetent CMV-seropositive individuals. It is possible that the coadministration of $CD4^+$ CMV-specific Th or the administration of exogenous IL-2 would result in the amplification in vivo of lower doses of $CD8^+$ CTL, as has been demonstrated in murine adoptive transfer models (CHEEVER et al. 1982; REDDEHASE et al. 1987b). However, even in the absence of $CD4^+$ Th or IL-2, the data in these patients demonstrated that transferred $CD8^+$ CTL responses capable of functioning as memory T cells persist in the peripheral blood in vivo for at least 1 month. The precise duration of in vivo persistence will require analysis in patients receiving a small number of individual clones in order to facilitate the use of molecular analysis to determine the presence of CTL in PBL obtained at long intervals after therapy.

Allogeneic BMT recipients who recover endogenous $CD8^+$ CMV-specific CTL responses are protected from the development of CMV disease (REUSSER et al. 1991; LI and RIDDELL, unpublished data). Consistent with this, none of the patients who had $CD8^+$ CTL responses reconstituted by adoptive transfer developed CMV disease. However, additional studies of this approach for CMV are required to fully elucidate the biologic and therapeutic consequences of restoring immunity by the adoptive transfer of antigen-specific T cells. Our initial studies of the transfer of $CD8^+$ CTL clones were restricted to patients undergoing allogeneic BMT, but have implications for the use of T cell transfer as a means of diminishing the frequency and severity of CMV disease in solid organ transplant recipients and in patients with acquired immunodeficiency syndrome (AIDS). The infusion of autologous expanded CMV-specific CTL may be particularly useful for AIDS patients with CMV infections, because antiviral drug therapy is often poorly tolerated in this patient population (JACOBSEN and MILLS 1988). The treatment of AIDS patients with active CMV viremia or tissue infection should provide additional insights into the therapeutic potential of $CD8^+$ CTL. Moreover, the use of CTL clones specific for HIV gene products might also be of therapeutic value for HIV infection, particularly if gene transfer approaches to modify the potential for CTL clones to survive and function in vivo prove to be successful (RIDDELL et al. 1992b).

The studies of adoptive T cell transfer for human viral infections also have implications for the treatment of human malignancies. The identification of antigens expressed by human melanoma and recognized by CD8$^+$ CTL suggest that application of specific immunotherapy for this human tumor may soon be possible (VAN DER BRUGGEN et al. 1991). Moreover, the provocative experiments in murine models demonstrating that immunization of mice with syngeneic tumor cells genetically modified to express selected cytokine genes will elicit host CD4$^+$ and CD8$^+$ tumor-specific T cell responses suggests a novel strategy for inducing T cells reactive with tumor antigens expressed by tumors of diverse histologies (FEARON et al. 1990; GOLUMBEK et al. 1991). If such an approach is effective in humans, the feasibility of isolating T cells in vitro with MHC-restricted tumor specificity for use in adoptive immunotherapy will be greatly improved.

Acknowledgements. Supported by grant CA18029 from the National Cancer Institute and a grant from the Cancer Research Institute (SRR). Stanley R. Riddell is a Special Fellow of the Leukemia Society of America. We wish to thank William Britt, University of Alabama (Birmingham), for providing the vaccinia/CMV recombinant viruses.

References

Borysiewicz LK, Morris S, Page J, Sissons JGP (1983) Human cytomegalovirus-specific cytotoxic T lymphocytes: requirements for in vitro generation and specificity. Eur J Immunol 13: 804–809

Borysiewicz LK, Graham S, Hickling JK, Sissons JGP (1988a) Precursor frequency and stage specificity of human cytomegalovirus-specific cytotoxic T cells. Eur J Immunol 18: 269–275

Borysiewicz LK, Hickling JK, Graham S, Sinclair J, Cranage MP, Smith GL, Sissons JGP (1988b) Human cytomegalovirus-specific cytotoxic T cells: relative frequency of stage-specific CTL recognizing the 72 KD immediate early protein and glycoprotein B expressed by recombinant vaccina viruses. J Exp Med 168: 919–932

Braciale TJ, Morrison LA, Sweetser MJ, Sambrook J, Gething MJ, Braciale VL (1987) Antigen presentation pathways to class I and class II MHC restricted T lymphocytes. Immunol Rev 98: 94–114

Byrne JA, Oldstone MBA (1984) Biology of cloned cytotoxic T lymphocytes specific for lymphocytic choriomeningitis virus: clearance of virus in vivo. J Virol 51: 682–686

Cannon MD, Stott EJ, Taylor G, Askonsas BA (1987) Clearance of persistent respiratory syncytial virus infections in immunodeficient mice following transfer of primed T cells. Immunology 62: 133–139

Chandler SH, McDougall JK (1986) Comparison of restriction site polymorphisms among clinical isolates and laboratory strains of human cytomegalovirus. J Gen Virol 67: 2179–2192

Cheever MA, Greenberg PD, Fefer A, Gillis S (1982) Augmentation of the antitumor therapeutic efficacy of long-term cultured T lymphocytes by in vivo administration of purified interleukin 2. J Exp Med 155: 968–980

Cheever MA, Thompson DB, Klarnet JP, Greenberg PD (1986) Antigen-driven long-term cultured T cells proliferate in vivo, distribute widely, mediate specific tumor therapy and persist long term as functional memory T cells. J Exp Med 163: 1100–1112

Chou SW (1986) Acquisition of donor strains of CMV by renal transplant patients. N Engl J Med 314: 1418–1423

Chou SW, Dennison DM (1991) Analysis of interstrain variation in cytomegalovirus glycoprotein B sequences encoding neutralization-related epitopes. J Infect Dis 163: 1229–1234

Emmanuel D, Cunningham I, Joles-Elysec K, Brochstein JA, Kernan NA, Laver J, Stover D, White DA, Fels A, Polsky G, Castro-Malaspina H, Peppard JR, Bartus P, Hammerling U, O'Reilly RJ (1988) Cytomegalovirus pneumonia after bone marrow transplantation successfully treated with the combination of ganciclovir and high dose intravenous immune globulin. Ann Intern Med 109: 777–782

Englund JA, Sullivan CJ, Jordan MC (1988) Respiratory syncytical virus infection in immunocompromised adults. Ann Intern Med 109: 203–208
Erice A, Chou SW, Biron K, Stanat SC, Balfour HH, Jordan MC (1989) Progressive disease due to ganciclovir—resistant cytomegalovirus in immunocompromised patients. N Engl J Med 320: 289–293
Fearon ER, Pardoll DM, Itaya T, Golumbek P, Levitsky HI, Simons JW, Karasuyama H, Vogelstein B, Frost P (1990) Interleukin 2 production by tumor cells bypasses T helper function in the generation of an antitumor response. Cell 60: 397–403
Fisher B, Packard BS, Reed EF, Caraquillo JA, Carter CS, Topalian SL, Yang SC, Yolles P, Larson JM, Rosenberg SA (1989) Tumor localization of adoptively transferred indium-111 labeled tumor infiltrating lymphocytes in patients with metastatic melanoma. J Clin Oncol 7: 250–261
Gardner MB, Officer JE, Parker J, Estes JD, Rongey RW (1974) Induction of disseminated virulent cytomegalovirus infection by immunosuppression of naturally chronically infected wild mice. Infect Immun 10: 966–969
Golumbek PT, Lazenby AJ, Levitsky HI, Jaffee LM, Karasuyama H, Baker M, Pardoll DM (1991) Treatment of established renal cancer by tumor cells engineered to secrete interleukin-4. Science 254: 713–716
Gooding LR (1992) Virus proteins that counteract host immune defenses. Cell 71: 5–7
Goodrich JM, Mori M, Gleaves CA, DuMond C, Cays M, Ebeling DF, Buhles WC, deArmond B, Meyers JD (1991) Early treatment with ganciclovir to prevent cytomegalovirus disease after allogeneic bone marrow transplantation. N Engl J Med 325: 1601–1607
Greenberg PD (1986) Therapy of murine leukemia with cyclophosphamide and immune Lyt 2^+ cells: cytolytic T cells can mediate eradication of disseminated leukemia. J Immunol 136: 1917–1922
Greenberg PD (1991) Adoptive T cell therapy of tumors: mechanisms operative in the recognition and elimination of tumor cells. Adv Immunol 49: 281–335
Greenberg PD, Kern DE, Cheever MA (1985) Therapy of disseminated murine leukemia with cyclophosphamide and immune Lyt-1^+2^- T cells: tumor eradication does not require participation of cytotoxic T cells. J Exp Med 161: 1122–1135
Greenberg PD, Reusser P, Goodrich JM, Riddell SR (1991) Development of a treatment regimen for human cytomegalovirus (CMV) infection in bone marrow transplantation recipients by adoptive transfer of donor-derived CMV-specific T cell clones expanded *in vitro*. Ann NY Acad Sci 636: 184–195
Guillaume JC, Sasaz P, Wechsler J, Lescs MD, Rouzeau JC (1991) Vaccinia from recombinant virus expressing HIV genes. Lancet 337: 1034–1035
Griffiths PD, Grundy JC (1987) Molecular biology and immunology of cytomegalovirus. Biochem J 241: 313–324
Huang E-S, Alford CA, Reynolds DW, Stagno S, Pass RF (1980) Molecular epidemiology of cytomegalovirus infections in women and their infants. N Engl J Med 303: 958–962
Jacobson MA, Mills J (1988) Serious cytomegalovirus disease in the acquired immunodeficiency syndrome (AIDS). Ann Intern Med 108: 585–594
Jahn G, Scholl B-C, Traupe B, Fleckenstein B (1987) The two major structural phosphoproteins (pp65 and pp150) of human cytomegalovirus and their antigenic properties. J Gen Virol 68: 1327–1337
Jordan MC, Shanley JD, Stevens JG (1977) Immunosuppression reactivates and disseminates latent murine cytomegalovirus. J Gen Virol 37: 419–423
Koszinowski UH, Keil GM, Schwarz H, Schickedanz J, Reddehase MJ (1987) A nonstructural polypeptide encoded by immediate early transcription unit I of murine cytomegalovirus is recognized by cytolytic T lymphocytes. J Exp Med 166: 289–294
Landini M-P, Michelson S (1988) Human cytomegalovirus proteins. Prog Med Virol 35: 152–185
Larsen HS, Feng MF, Horohov DW, Moore RN, Rouse BT (1984) Role of T lymphocyte subsets in recovery from herpes simplex virus infection. J Virol 51: 682–686
Laubscher A, Bluestein HG, Spector SA, Zvaifler NJ (1988) Generation of human cytomegalovirus-specific cytotoxic T lymphocytes in a short-term culture. J Immunol Methods 110: 69–77
Lenardo M (1991) Interleukin-2 programs mouse $\alpha\beta$ T lymphocytes for apoptosis. Nature 353: 858–861
Ljungman P, Gleaves CA, Meyers JD (1989) Respiratory virus infection in immunocompromised patients. Bone Marrow Transplant 4: 35–40

Lukacher AE, Braciale VL, Braciale TF (1984) In vivo effector function of influenza virus-specific T lymphocyte clones is highly specific. J Exp Med 160: 814–823
Lum LG (1987) The kinetics of immune reconstitution after human bone marrow transplantation. Blood 69: 369–380
Martin PJ, Shulman HM, Schubach WH, Hansen JA, Fefer A, Miller G, Thomas ED (1984) Fatal Epstein-Barr virus-associated proliferation of donor B cells after treatment of graft versus host disease with a murine anti T cell antibody. Ann Intern Med 101: 310–315
Meyers JD, Flournoy N, Thomas ED (1980) Cytomegalovirus infection and specific cell-mediated immunity after marrow transplant. J Infect Dis 142: 816–824
Meyers JD, Flournoy N, Thomas ED (1986) Risk factors for cytomegalovirus infection after human marrow transplantation. J Infect Dis 153: 478–488
Meyers JD, Bowden RA, Counts GW (1987) Infections after bone marrow transplantation. In: Lode H, Huhn D, Melzahn M (eds) Infections in transplant patients. Thieme, Stuttgart, pp 17–32
Meyers JD, Ljungmann P, Fisher LD (1990) Cytomegalovirus excretion as a predictor of cytomegalovirus disease after marrow transplantation: importance of cytomegalovirus viremia. J Infect Dis 162: 373–380
Moore MW, Carbone FR, Bevan MJ (1988) Introduction of soluble protein into the class I pathway of antigen processing and presentation. Cell 54: 777–785
Mutter W, Reddehase MJ, Busch FW, Behring HJ, Koszinowski UH (1988) Failure in generating hemopoietic stem cells is the primary cause of death from cytomegalovorus disease in the immunocompromised host. J Exp Med 167: 1645–1658
Posavad CM, Rosenthal KL (1992) Herpes simplex virus-infected human fibroblasts are resistant to and inhibit cytotoxic T lymphocyte activity. J Virol 66: 6264–6272
Purtilo DT (1980) Epstein Barr virus induced oncogenesis in immunodeficient individuals. Lancet 1: 300–303
Quinnan GV, Kirmani N, Esber E, Saral R, Manischewitz JF, Rogers JL, Rook AH, Santos GW, Burns WH (1981) HLA-restricted cytotoxic T lymphocytes and non thymic cytotoxic lymphocyte responses to cytomegalovirus infection in bone marrow transplant recipients. J Immunol 126: 2031–2041
Quinnan GV, Kirmani N, Rook AH, Manischewitz JF, Jackson L, Moreschi G, Santos GW, Saral R, Burns WH (1982) HLA-restricted cytotoxic T lymphocytes and non thymic cytotoxic lymphocyte responses to cytomegalovirus infection. N Engl J Med 307: 6–13
Rasmussen L (1990) Immune responses to human cytomegalovirus infection. In: McDougall JK (ed) Cytomegaloviruses. Springer, Berlin Heidelberg New York, pp 221–254 (Current topics in microbiology and immunology, vol 154)
Reddehase MJ, Koszinowski UH (1984) Significance of herpse virus immediate early gene expression in cellular immunity to cytomegalovirus infection. Nature 312: 369–371
Reddehase MJ, Weiland F, Munch K, Jonjic S, Luske A, Koszinowski UH (1985) Interstitial murine CMV pneumonia after irradiation: characterization of cells that limit viral replication during established infection of the lungs. J Virol 55: 264–273
Reddehase MJ, Mutter W, Munch K, Buhring H-J, Koszinowski UH (1987a) CD8-positive T lymphocytes specific for murine cytomegalovirus immediate early antigens mediate protective immunity. J Virol 61: 3102–3108
Reddehase MJ, Mutter W, Koszinowski UH (1987b) In vivo application of recombinant interleukin-2 in the immunotherapy of established cytomegalovirus infection. J Exp Med 165: 650–656
Reddehase MJ, Rothbard JB, Koszinowski UH (1989) A pentapeptide as minimal antigenic determinant for MHC class I restricted lymphocytes. Nature 337: 651–653
Redfield RR, Wright DC, James WD, Jones TS, Brown C, Burke DJ (1987) Disseminated vaccinia in a military recruit with human immunodeficiency virus (HIV) disease. N Engl J Med 316: 673–676
Reed EC, Bowden RA, Dandliker PS, Lilleby KE, Meyers JD (1988) Treatment of cytomegalovirus pneumonia with ganciclovir and intravenous immunoglobulin in patients with bone marrow transplants. Ann Intern Med 109: 783–788
Reusser P, Riddell SR, Meyers JD, Greenberg PD (1991) Cytotoxic T lymphocyte response to cytomegalovirus following allogeneic bone marrow transplantation: pattern of recovery and correlation with cytomegalovirus infection and disease. Blood 78: 1373–1380
Riddell SR, Greenberg PD (1990) The use of anti CD3 and anti CD28 monoclonal antibodies to clone and expand antigen-specific T cells. J Immunol Methods 128: 189–197

Riddell SR, Reusser P, Greenberg PD (1991a) Cytotoxic T cells specific for cytomegalovirus: a potential therapy for immunocompromised hosts. Rev Infect Dis 13: 966–973
Riddell SR, Rabin M, Geballe AP, Britt WJ, Greenberg PD (1991b) Class I MHC-restricted cytotoxic T lymphocyte recognition of cells infected with human cytomegalovirus does not require endogenous viral gene expression. J Immunol 146: 2795–2804
Riddell SR, Watanabe KS, Goodrich JM, Li CR, Agha ME, Greenberg PD (1992a) Restoration of viral immunity in immunodeficient humans by the adoptive transfer of T cell clones. Science 257: 238–241
Riddell SR, Greenberg PD, Overell RW, Loughran TP, Gilbert MJ, Lupton SD, Agosti J, Scheeler S, Coombs RW, Corey L (1992b) Phase I study of cellular adoptive immunotherapy using genetically modified $CD8^+$ HIV-specific T cells for HIV seropositive patients undergoing allogeneic bone marrow transplant. Human Gene Ther 3: 319–338
Rosen FS, Cooper MD, Wedgewood RJP (1984a) The primary immunodeficiencies (part 1). N Engl J Med 311: 235–242
Rosen FS, Cooper MD, Wedgewood RJP (1984b) The primary immunodeficiencies (part 2). N Engl J Med 311: 300–310
Rosenberg SA, Lotze MT, Muul LM et al. (1985) Observations on the systemic administration of autologous lymphokine-activated killer cells and recombinant IL2 for patients with metastasic cancer. N Engl J Med 313: 1485–1492
Rosenberg SA, Lotze MT, Muul LM et al. (1986) A progress report on the treatment of 157 patients with advanced cancer using lymphokine-activated killer cells and interleukin-2 or high dose interleukin-2 alone. N Engl J Med 316: 1310–1321
Rosenberg SA, Packard BS, Aebersold PM, Solomon D et al. (1988) Use of tumor-infiltrating lymphocytes and IL-2 in the immunotherapy of patients with metastatic melanoma: a preliminary report. N Engl J Med 319: 1676–1680
Rosenberg SA, Aebersold P, Cornetta K, Kasid A, Morgan RA, Moen R, Karson EM, Lotze MT, Yang JC, Topalian SL, Merino MJ, Culver K, Miller AD, Blaese MR, Anderson WF (1990) Gene transfer into humans: immunotherapy of patients with advanced melanoma using tumor infiltrating lymphocytes modified by retroviral gene transduction. N Engl J Med 323: 570–578
Saral R, Burns WH, Laskin OL, Santos GW, Lietman PS (1981) Acyclovir prophylaxis of herpes simplex virus infections: a randomized, double blind controlled trial in bone marrow transplant recipients. N Engl J Med 305: 63–67
Schmidt GM, Horak DA, Niland JC, Dancan SR, Forman SJ, Zaia JA (1991) A randomized controlled trial of prophylactic ganciclovir for cytomegalovirus pulmonary infection in recipients of allogeneic bone marrow transplants. N Engl J Med 324: 1005–1011
Schrier RD, Oldstone MBA (1986). Recent clinical isolation of CMV suppress human CMV-specific human leukocyte antigen-restricted cytotoxic T lymphocyte activity. J Virol 59: 127–132
Shanley JD, Jordan MC, Cook ML, Stevens JG (1979) Pathogenesis of reactivated latent murine cytomegalovirus infection. Am J Pathol 95: 67–77
Stinski MF, Thornsen DR, Stenberg RM, Goldstein LC (1983) Organization and expression of the immediate early genes on human cytomegalovirus. J Virol 46: 1–14
Van Bleek GM, Nathenson SG (1990) Isolation of an endogenously processed immunodominant viral peptide from the class I H-2Kb molecule. Nature 348: 213–216
Van der Bruggen P, Traversari C, Chomez P, Lurquin C, De Plaen E, Van den Eynde B, Knuth A, Boon T (1991) A gene encoding an antigen recognized by cytolytic T lymphocytes on a human melanoma. Science 254: 1643–1647
Walthen M, Stinski M (1982) Temporal patterns of human cytomegalovirus transcription: mapping the viral RNAs synthesized at immediate early, early, and late times after infection. J Virol 42: 462–467
Witherspoon RP, Lum LG, Storb R (1984) Immunologic reconstitution after human marrow grafting. Semin Hematol 21: 2–10
Wold WSM, Gooding LR (1991) Region E3 of adenovirus: a cassette of genes involved in host immunosurveillance and virus-cell interactions. Virology 184: 1–8
Yewdell JW, Bennick JR (1990) The binary logic of antigen processing and presentation to T cells. Cell 62: 203–206
Yewdell JW, Bennick JR, Hosaka Y (1988) Cells process exogenous proteins for recognition by cytotoxic T lymphocytes. Science 239: 637–640
Zutter MM, Martin P, Sale GE, Shulman HM, Fisher L, Thomas ED, Durnam D (1988) Epstein Barr virus lymphoproliferation after bone marrow transplantation. Blood 72: 520–529

Cytotoxic T Lymphocytes in Human Immunodeficiency Virus Infection: Responses to Structural Proteins

R. P. JOHNSON and B. D. WALKER

1 Introduction

Following the identification of the human immunodeficiency virus type 1 (HIV-1) as the etiologic agent of acquired immunodeficiency syndrome (AIDS; BARRE-SINOUSSI et al. 1983; GALLO et al. 1984), an intensive effort has been undertaken to characterize humoral and cellular immune responses to this retrovirus. Although the immunologic correlates of protective immunity are yet to be precisely identified, accumulating evidence suggests that cytotoxic T lymphocytes (CTL) may play a central role in containing viral replication during the typically prolonged asymptomatic phase of this illness. The first reports of CTL specific for HIV appeared in 1987 (PLATA et al. 1987; WALKER et al. 1987) and documented a vigorous cellular immune response to this virus in the setting of an illness characterized by immunosuppression. Numerous studies since that time have provided detailed insight into the CTL response to HIV. Investigators have described CTL responses to multiple HIV

Infectious Disease Unit, Massachusetts General Hospital and Harvard Medical School, Boston, MA 02114, USA

Current Topics in Microbiology and Immunology, Vol. 189

proteins, identified over 40 specific epitopes, and begun to illustrate some of the functional roles of these cells.

Although HIV-specific CTL share many characteristics with CTL specific for other viruses, a number of unique features have emerged. These distinguishing features include the remarkably high frequency of activated circulating CTL, the recognition of multiple HIV epitopes, and the paradoxical persistence of viremia in the face of a vigorous virus-specific response. In this review, we will provide an overview of several aspects of HIV-1-specific CTL, including methods of detection, characterization of CTL responses to the HIV structural proteins gag, pol, and env, and a discussion of the functional role of CTL in this infection. Although our focus will be on human HIV-1-specific CTL responses, we will also discuss related findings obtained using immunized mice and rhesus monkeys infected with simian immunodeficiency virus (SIV).

2 Detection of CTL

2.1 Sources of Effector Cells

The initial demonstration of a CTL response to HIV-1 revealed a unique feature of the immune response to this infection, in that virus-specific CTL could be detected using freshly isolated lymphocytes from seropositive subjects (PLATA et al. 1987; WALKER et al. 1987). Both peripheral blood mononuclear cells (PBMC) as well as lymphocytes obtained by bronchoalveolar lavage were shown to mediate lysis of target cells bearing HIV-1 antigens, without the need for an initial period of in vitro stimulation typically required for detection of CTL responses in other viral infections studied up until that time. The vigor of the HIV-1-specific CTL response was not anticipated, particularly in light of the fact that HIV-1 infection was known to be associated with progressive and ultimately profound immunosuppression. Phenotypic studies demonstrated that lysis by these effector cells was mediated predominantly by $CD8^+$ lymphocytes and restricted by HLA class I molecules (PLATA et al. 1987; KOENIG et al. 1988; WALKER et al. 1988; KOUP et al. 1989; RIVIÈRE et al. 1989a; JOHNSON et al. 1991). An exception to this restriction pattern is the circulating envelope-specific CTL response, which is mediated by both HLA class I-restricted and nonrestricted effector mechanisms (MCCHESNEY et al. 1990; see below).The non-major histocompatibility complex (MHC)-restricted lysis of envelope-expressing targets is largely mediated by CD16-bearing lymphocytes (WEINHOLD et al. 1988; RIVIERE et al. 1989a). Although a recent report suggests the presence of CTL activity within freshly isolated CD4 lymphocytes as well as CD8 lymphocytes from infected subjects (KUNDU et al. 1992), this finding remains to be confirmed by other laboratories and appears to be in contrast with the findings of numerous other investigators.

The ability to use fresh PBMC as effector cells and thereby circumvent the usual need for in vitro, antigen-specific stimulation has greatly facilitated the characterization of human CTL responses to this virus. Not only has this characteristic permitted the identification of the major viral proteins recognized by CTL using bulk PBMC (KOENIG et al. 1988; NIXON et al. 1988; WALKER et al. 1988; KOUP et al. 1989; RIVIÈRE et al. 1989a), but in some instances the responses detected using fresh PBMC have been of sufficient magnitude to directly identify specific CTL epitopes using synthetic HIV-1 peptides to sensitize target cells (KOENIG et al. 1990b; JOHNSON et al. 1991). One can detect HIV-1-specific CTL activity using fresh PBMC in the majority of infected adults (RIVIÈRE et al. 1989b; BUSEYNE et al. 1993b). However, detection of CTL activity in unstimulated lymphocytes is relatively infrequent in children infected by vertical transmission (LUZURIAGA et al. 1991; BUSEYNE et al. 1993a).

In vitro stimulation strategies have also been utilized to detect HIV-1 specific CTL in infected subjects. Phytohemagglutinin (PHA)-stimulated lymphoblasts infected in vitro with HIV-1 have been utilized to provide antigen-specific stimulation for expansion of HIV-1-specific CTL from blood, lymph node, and lung (AUTRAN et al. 1988; HOFFENBACH et al. 1989; HADIDA et al. 1992). Stimulation of PBMC from seropositive subjects with autologous PHA-stimulated lymphoblasts without exogenous HIV infection has also resulted in boosting the in vitro measurements of HIV-1-specific CTL activity (NIXON et al. 1988, 1990). This enhancement of CTL activity has been hypothesized to occur because stimulation with PHA induces active HIV-1 replication, thereby providing an antigen-specific stimulus for expanding a memory cell population (NIXON and MCMICHAEL 1991). Others have used modifications of this approach (LIEBERMAN et al. 1992), and the resultant cell lines have provided a source of effector cells that may be used not only for functional studies, but also for pilot studies of adoptive CTL transfer in vivo (LIEBERMAN 1993; HO et al. 1993).

Specific and nonspecific cloning strategies have also been successfully employed to generate HIV-specific CTL clones from seropositive subjects, which have in turn provided the most comprehensive information regarding the spectrum of epitopes recognized of any virus studied to date. Specific stimuli have included HIV-1-infected cells (SETHI et al. 1988; HOFFENBACH et al. 1989), cells exposed to purified recombinant HIV-1 envelope protein (SETHI et al. 1988), UV-inactivated whole virus (SETHI et al. 1988), and autologous lymphocytes sensitized with peptides containing CTL epitopes (JOHNSON et al. 1992). The ability to clone HIV-1-specific CTL using polyclonal stimuli such as PHA and anti-CD3 monoclonal antibodies has greatly facilitated the precise identification of CTL epitopes recognized in natural infection and underscores the relatively high frequency of these cells in the circulating lymphocyte pool. Using monoclonal antibodies directed at the CD3 cell surface molecule, long-term cultures of virus-specific CTL have been generated in a number of studies (WALKER et al. 1989; LITTAUA et al. 1991; DAI et al. 1992; JASSOY et al. 1992; JOHNSON et al. 1991, 1992, 1993). The majority of CTL clones reported to date have been of the same phenotype and restriction pattern as the predominant CTL response observed using freshly isolated cells, namely CD8-positive, class I-restricted lymphocytes. However, at least two reports indicate the identification of CTL clones of the CD4 phenotype (LITTAUA et al. 1992; CURIEL et al. 1993), which were shown in one of these studies to be class II restricted (LITTAUA et al. 1992).

CTL responses to HIV-1 have also been identified following the in vitro stimulation of PBMC obtained from seronegative subjects (SILICIANO et al. 1988; HOFFENBACH et al. 1989) and from seronegative HIV-1 vaccine recipients (ORENTAS et al. 1990; HAMMOND et al. 1991, 1992; COONEY et al. 1993). The phenotype of cells obtained following in vitro stimulation of seronegative persons has been exclusively the CD4 phenotype and class II restricted. Both CD8-positive class I-restricted and CD4-positive class II-restricted CTL have been recovered following in vitro stimulation of PBMC from uninfected vaccine recipients (HAMMOND et al. 1992; SILICIANO et al. 1992; COONEY et al. 1993). Cellular immune responses to HIV-1 have also been studied in murine models of infection (TAKAHASHI et al. 1988) and in the SIV-infected rhesus macaque model (TSUBOTA et al. 1989; MILLER et al. 1990, 1991; SHEN et al. 1991; BOURGAULT et al. 1992; VENET et al. 1992), providing additional sources of retrovirus-specific CTL.

2.2 Sources of Target Cells

Cytotoxic T cells recognize processed viral peptides presented in association with MHC molecules (TOWNSEND et al. 1986; TOWNSEND and BODMER 1989; YEWDELL and BENNINK 1992). For $CD8^+$ CTL, these antigens consist of peptides eight to 11 amino acids in length that are presented in the cleft of a class I MHC molecule (ROTZSCHKE et al. 1990; FALK et al. 1991a; JARDETZKY et al. 1991). For $CD4^+$ CTL, antigens consist of peptides 13–17 amino acids in length that are presented by a class II MHC molecule (RUDENSKY et al. 1991; CHICZ et al. 1992). Although exceptions exist, in general, peptides presented to $CD8^+$ CTL are derived from proteins synthesized within the presenting cell (endogenous pathway), whereas peptides presented to $CD4^+$ CTL are derived from endocytosed proteins not necessarily synthesized in the presenting cell (exogenous pathway; TOWNSEND and BODMER 1989; YEWDELL and BENNINK 1992).

The requirement for the endogenous synthesis of viral antigens in target cells used to detect $CD8^+$ CTL has resulted in the use of various expression systems that express recombinant viral antigens in cells of appropriate MHC types. An additional feature that has prompted the use of recombinant expression systems is the fact that HIV-1 is a cytopathic retrovirus and therefore results in a lytic infection of CD4-bearing cells. B lymphoblastoid cell lines (B-LCL) infected with recombinant vaccinia viruses have been used in the majority of reported studies (reviewed in VENET and WALKER 1993) and have facilitated the identification of CTL responses to both structural and regulatory proteins. Tumor cell lines which have been stably transfected with plasmids expressing HIV-1 gene products have also served as a stable source of antigen-expressing target cells (PLATA et al. 1987). Autologous cell lines such as fibroblasts that have been transduced using a defective retroviral vector for the stable expression of HIV-1 genes have been used for this purpose as well (WARNER et al. 1991). Infected cells such as pulmonary alveolar macrophages (PLATA et al. 1987; HOFFENBACH et al. 1989; AUTRAN et al. 1990, 1991) and lymphocytes (HOFFENBACH et al. 1989; ORENTAS et al. 1990; TAKAHASHI et al. 1991) have served as target cells in studies that have provided evidence that HIV-1 proteins are recognized in the context of natural infection. In addition, incubation of autologous cells with purified envelope protein (SETHI et al. 1988; SILICIANO et al. 1988, 1989) or whole virus (SETHI et al. 1988) has been used to identify HIV-1-specific CTL, particularly of the CD4 phenotype.

3 CTL Specific for Human Immunodeficiency Virus Structural Proteins

3.1 Gag-Specific CTL

CTL directed at internal viral proteins such as gag are an important component of the cellular immune response to many viral infections, including HIV. Studies of murine influenza-specific CTL demonstrated that CTL were able to recognize the highly conserved internal nucleoprotein (TOWNSEND et al. 1984), and subsequent studies have shown that the nucleoprotein is the major target for cross-reactive CTL in this infection (YEWDELL et al. 1985). Although the observation that viral proteins such as the influenza nucleoprotein that are not expressed on the cell may serve as targets for immune responses was initially surprising, an improved understanding of the pathway of antigen presentation to class I-restricted CTL provided the conceptual basis for the recognition of internal viral proteins (YEWDELL and BENNINK 1992).

CTL specific for the relatively conserved HIV-1 gag protein make up a major portion of the cell-mediated responses directed against this virus. Following the initial report by WALKER et al. (1987), gag-specific CTL have been detected in PBMC of over 80% of subjects tested (NIXON et al. 1988; KOUP et al. 1989; RIVIÈRE et al. 1989a). In some subjects, remarkably high rates of lysis may be found using unstimulated PBMC as effector cells, ranging up to 80% specific lysis of gag-expressing targets using an effector-to-target ratio of 100:1 (JOHNSON et al. 1991). Cell depletion studies and analysis of inhibition by monoclonal antibodies established that the effector cells in PBMC which mediate the gag-specific CTL activity are $CD3^+$ $CD8^+$ and restricted by HLA class I molecules (NIXON et al. 1988; KOUP et al. 1989; RIVIERE et al. 1989a; JOHNSON et al. 1991). A single report suggests that $CD4^+$ CTL specific for gag may be detectable in PBMC (KUNDU and MERIGAN 1992), although this observation awaits confirmation.

These initial reports analyzed CTL activity against target cells expressing the full-length 55-kDa gag protein. However, in naturally infected cells, the 55-kDa protein is subsequently cleaved by the HIV-1 protease into smaller subunits: p24, p17, p7, and p6. Examination of CTL activity against recombinant vaccinia viruses expressing the p24 and p17 subunits has demonstrated that majority of this activity in circulating PBMC is directed against p24 (JOHNSON et al. 1991; KOUP et al. 1991b; BUSEYNE et al. 1993b). Limiting dilution analysis has also demonstrated that most of the gag-specific activity in fresh, unstimulated PBMC is directed against epitopes in p24, although increased recognition of p17 was noted in CTL precursors (KOUP et al. 1991b).

Since the initial report of a gag CTL epitope in 1988, at least 25 different peptides containing gag epitopes have been identified; they are summarized in Table 1 and Fig. 1. For a smaller number of these peptides, the minimal amino acids necessary for target cell sensitization have been defined. These epitope-mapping studies have been performed using a number of different effector cell approaches, including bulk unstimulated PBMC, PHA-stimulated PBMC, CTL clones obtained by limiting dilution, and in vitro stimulation with autologous cells superinfected with laboratory strains of virus as outlined above. The first HIV-1 CTL epitope was defined by Nixon et al., who examined the ability of PBMC cultured with autologous PHA-stimulated lymphocytes to lyse B-LCL-incubated synthetic peptides corresponding to p24 (NIXON et al. 1988). This approach has been used to identify a number of epitopes in both p24 and p17 (GOTCH et al. 1990; NIXON et al. 1988, 1990; PHILLIPS et al. 1991).

CTL epitopes in gag have also been identified using CTL clones and unstimulated PBMC. CTL clones developed by the limiting dilution culture of lymphocytes stimulated with a CD3-specific monoclonal antibody, recombinant IL-2, and irradiated allogeneic PBMC from seronegative donors (WALKER et al. 1989) have proved very useful for the identification and detailed characterization of CTL epitopes. These CTL clones can be maintained in long-term tissue culture and frozen and thawed without loss of CTL activity and have made possible the fine mapping of the specificity of CTL clones and analysis of the effects of sequence variation (JOHNSON et al. 1991, 1993). A total of eight CTL epitopes in p17 and p24 were defined in this fashion. A particularly notable feature was the recognition of multiple gag epitopes (up to four) by the same individual and the presentation of more than one gag epitope by the same HLA molecule. Reports by other investigators have described additional epitopes using this technique as well. In selected patients, vigorous gag-specific responses in unstimulated PBMC have also allowed the epitopes to be identified without in vitro stimulation or culture (JOHNSON et al. 1991). Although the vast majority of the gag-specific CTL clones have been $CD8^+$ and restricted by HLA class I antigens, a single report exists of a $CD4^+$, HLA class II-restricted CTL clone which recognizes an epitope in p24 (LITTAUA et al. 1992). The relative rarity of such clones and the fact that most investigators have found that bulk PBMC responses have been shown to be restricted by class I antigens (NIXON et al. 1988; KOUP et al. 1989; RIVIERE et al. 1989a; JOHNSON et al. 1991) suggest that the overall contribution of $CD4^+$ CTL to the detectable gag-specific response is relatively small.

Alternative approaches to the identification of CTL epitopes include the use of peptide binding assays and of CTL prediction algorithms. Peptide binding assays have been derived in which synthetic HIV peptides have been tested for their ability to bind to purified HLA molecules attached to a solid support. This approach has been used by several groups to identify viral peptides that bind to MHC molecules (CHOPPIN et al. 1990, 1991a, b; FRELINGER et al. 1990). However, only a subset of peptides identified in this fashion are known to contain CTL epitopes. The application of an algorithm which predicts the existence of CTL epitopes based on the relative rarity of tetrapeptide sequences in comparison to sequenced human proteins has been described by CLAVERIE et al. (1988). Four epitopes were identified in this fashion, two lying in p24 and one each in p7 and p6. Lines from HIV-1-seropositive subjects were prepared by in vitro stimulation of PBMC with autologous HIV-infected cells and tested for lysis of autologous cells incubated with peptides predicted by the algorithm. The four epitopes predicted in this fashion were shown to sensitize targets for lysis by effector cells prepared using this technique, and lysis appeared to be restricted by HLA-A2. However, none of these epitopes has yet been confirmed by other investigators and most of the peptides do not clearly exhibit the characteristics of a recently proposed HLA-A2 binding motif (FALK et al. 1991b).

The gag-specific CTL response has also been investigated in the SIV macaque model of infection (VOWELS et al. 1989; MILLER et al. 1990; YAMAMOTO et al. 1990b; VENET et al. 1992). Detection of SIV-specific CTL has generally required in vitro expansion in the presence of a stimulus such as Con A and has not been detectable in freshly isolated PBMC. Cytolytic activity has been identified in lymphocytes derived from PBMC as well as lymph nodes (REIMANN et al. 1991) and skin lesions (YAMAMOTO et al. 1992). A dominant nine-amino acid gag epitope (aa 182–190 of SIV mac251) recognized by MHC class I-restricted CTL has been characterized, and the restricting antigen has been sequenced and termed Mamu-A*01

Table 1. Human immunodeficiency virus type 1 gag peptides recognized by human cytotoxic T lymphocytes

Figure number	HLA	Amino acids	Sequence	Reference
1	A2	71–85	GSEELRSLYNTVATL	NIXON and MCMICHAEL 1991
1	A2	77–85	SLYNTVATL	JOHNSON et al. 1991 and unpublished data
2	A2	88–115	VHQRIEIKDTKEALDKIEEEQNKSKKKA	ACHOUR et al. 1990
3	A2	193–203	GHQAAMQMLKE	CLAVERIE et al. 1988
4	A2	219–233	HAGPIAPGQMREPRG	CLAVERIE et al. 1988
5	A2	418–433	KEGHQMKDCTERQANF	CLAVERIE et al. 1988
6	A2	446–460	GNFLQSRPEPTAPPF	CLAVERIE et al. 1988
7	A3	18–31	KIRLRPGGKKKYKL	JASSOY et al. 1992
8	A11	84–92	TLYCVHQRI	T. Harrer, E. Harrer, B.D.W., unpublished data
9	A11	343–363	LEEMMTACQGVGGPGHKARVL	R.P.J. and B.D.W, unpublished data
10	A33	263–277	KRWIILGLNKIVRMY	BUSEYNE et al. 1993b
11	B8	25–35	GKKKYKLHIV	PHILLIPS et al. 1991
12	B8	253–267	NPPIPVGEIYKRWII	GOTCH et al. 1990
12	B8	253–274	NPPIPVGEIYKRWIILGLNKIV	JOHNSON et al. 1991
12	B8	256–270	IPVGEIYKRWIILGL	BUSEYNE et al. 1993b
13	B8	313–334	VKNWMTETLLVQNANPDCKTIL	JOHNSON et al. 1991
13	B8	323–339	VQNANPDCKYILKAL	NIXON and MCMICHAEL 1991
14	B12(44)	169–184	IPMFSALSEGATPQDL	BUSEYNE et al. 1993b
15	B14	173–194	SALSEGATPQDLNTMLNTVGGH	JOHNSON et al. 1991
15	B14	181–191	PQDLNTMLNTV	KOENIG et al. 1990a
15	B14	183–189	DLNTMLNTVGGHQAA	NIXON and MCMICHAEL 1991
16	B14	305–313	RAEQASQEV	JOHNSON et al. 1991
17	B27	263–277	KRWIILGLNKIVRMY	NIXON et al. 1988
17	B27	263–272	KRWIILGLNK	BUSEYNE et al. 1993b
18	Bw52	193–214	GHQAAMQMLKETINEEAAEWDR	JOHNSON et al. 1991
19	Bw57	143–164	VHQAISPRTLNAWVKVVEEKAF	JOHNSON et al. 1991
20	Bw57	153–174	NAWVKVVEEKAFSPEVIPMFSA	JOHNSON et al. 1991
21	Bw62	18–31	KIRLRPGGKKKYKL	JOHNSON et al. 1991 and unpublished data
22	Bw62	268–278	LGLNKIVRMYS	JOHNSON et al. 1991 and unpublished data
23	Cw3	145–150	QAISPR	LITTAUA et al. 1991
24	DQw1	140–148	GQMVHQAIS	LITTAUA et al. 1992
25	DQw3	140–148	GQMVHQAIS	LITTAUA et al. 1992

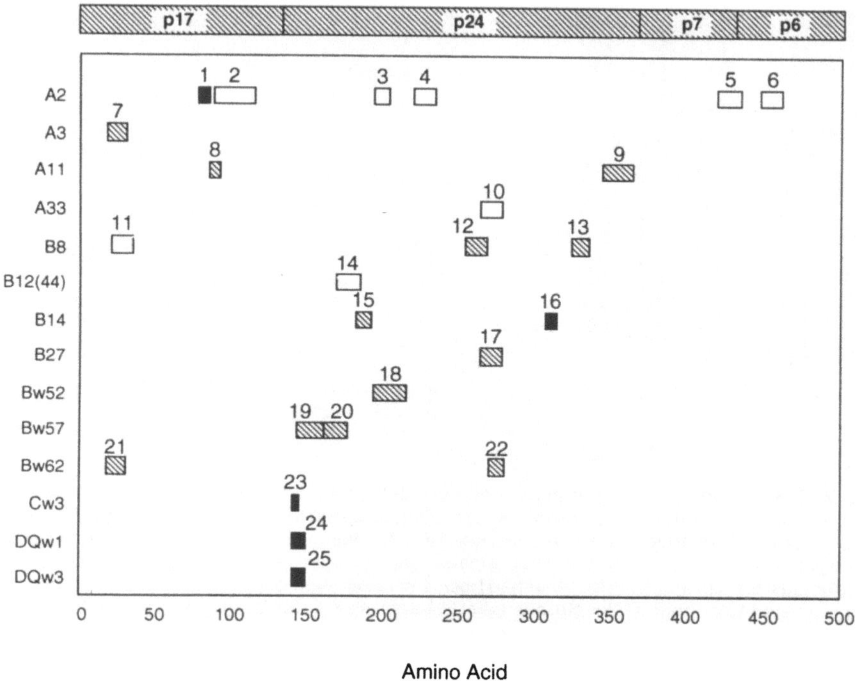

Fig. 1. Human immunodeficiency virus type 1 (HIV-1) gag peptides recognized by human cytotoxic T lymphocytes (CTL). Only epitopes with defined major histocompatibility complex restriction have been included. *Open bars* indicate epitopes that have been defined using polyclonal effector cells and not yet confirmed by other investigators. *Hatched bars* indicate epitopes that have been defined using polyclonal effectors and confirmed by other investigators or epitopes defined using CTL clones. *Black bars* indicate epitopes that have been finely mapped to minimal epitopes. *Numbers* refer to epitope sequences listed in Table 1. Numbering of amino acids corresponds to the HXB2R molecular clone (MYERS et al. 1991)

(YAMAMOTO et al. 1990a). Because all Mamu-A*01-positive animals appear to generate a CTL response to this epitope, a variety of immunization strategies are presently being evaluated in Mamu-A*01 animals.

Although the identification of HIV-1 gag CTL epitopes is likely to be incomplete, several general themes have emerged. The gag-specific response in HIV-1 infected humans appears to be remarkably heterogeneous. Multiple epitopes have been identified, and as many as five gag CTL epitopes have been shown to be recognized by a single individual (JOHNSON et al. 1991 and unpublished data). Multiple HLA types may be utilized to present gag epitopes, even in the same individual, and the same HLA type may in turn present more than one gag epitope. Similar findings have also been noted for other HIV-1 proteins such as reverse transcriptase (RT) and nef (see below and accompanying article by Rivière). An example of the breadth and vigor of

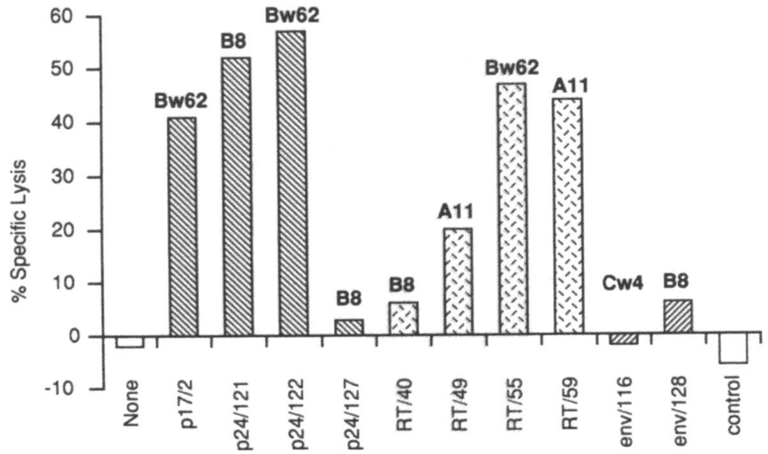

Fig. 2. Recognition of multiple human immunodeficiency virus type 1 (HIV-1) cytotoxic T lymphocyte (CTL) epitopes by unstimulated peripheral blood mononuclear cells (PBMC) from a HIV-1-seropositive donor. Fresh, unstimulated PBMC were used as effector cells at an effector-to-target ratio of 100:1 in a 6-h ^{51}Cr-release assay. Target cells consisted of autologous B lymphoblastoid cell line (B-LCL) that had been sensitized with peptides (100 μg/ml) previously demonstrated to contain CTL epitopes (WALKER et al. 1988; JOHNSON et al. 1991, 1992, 1993). The HLA restriction element for each peptide is indicated above the *bar*

the HIV-1-specific CTL response is shown in Fig. 2, in which unstimulated PBMC from an HIV-1-seropositive subject were shown to recognize at least six CTL epitopes. A total of 14 distinct HIV-1 CTL epitopes have been identified in this subject (WALKER et al. 1988; JOHNSON et al. 1991, 1992 and unpublished data). These results stand in marked contrast to the observations obtained regarding virus-specific CTL responses in inbred mouse strains. In these systems, CTL responses to viruses are dominated by one or two immunodominant epitopes (BRACIALE et al. 1989), and the absence of the appropriate MHC type may result in a failure to mount a CTL response to a particular virus (BENNINK and YEWDELL 1988). It remains to be seen whether these differences are related to the genetic heterogeneity of humans as opposed to the inbred mice or whether this is related to the chronic antigenic stimulation observed with HIV-1 infection. Another intriguing observation is the presence of overlapping CTL epitopes. Although epitopes are distributed throughout gag, several "hot spots" exist, where a series of overlapping CTL epitopes have been observed, each presented by a different HLA type. These regions can be identified in Fig. 1. In several cases, the epitopes have been finely mapped and shown to consist of distinct overlapping epitopes, as has been observed for nef (CULMANN et al. 1989, 1991) and gp41 (JOHNSON et al. 1992). The basis for such overlapping epitopes remains unclear. Possibilities include common pathways of antigen processing of peptides or chance association.

3.2 Reverse Transcriptase-Specific CTL

The HIV-1 polymerase gene encodes the viral RT protein, which is essential for replicative function. Because this protein exhibits the least variation among sequenced isolates, CTL responses to this protein might be expected to be highly cross-reactive with a number of different isolates and therefore important in vaccination strategies designed to elicit cross-protective immunity. As has previously been shown for the influenza virus polymerase (BENNINK et al. 1982), the HIV-1 polymerase is a major target of virus-specific CTL (WALKER et al. 1988). Freshly isolated PBMC from infected persons in various stages of HIV-1 infection were found to lyse autologous B-LCL infected with recombinant vaccinia viruses expressing the RT protein, and this lysis is restricted by class I antigens (WALKER et al. 1988).

Specific epitopes recognized by RT-specific CTL have been identified using cloned CTL from infected subjects, and these studies demonstrate that the CTL response to this protein is directed at a number of different epitopes (Table 2, Fig. 3). In one study, PBMC from two subjects with high levels of RT-specific lysis were stimulated in vitro with a CD3-specific monoclonal antibody in the presence of irradiated allogeneic feeder cells and interleukin 2 and cloned at limiting dilution (WALKER et al. 1989). Using recombinant HIV-1 vaccinia viruses expressing truncated portions of the RT protein, regions containing CTL epitopes were identified, and fine mapping of these epitopes was achieved using synthetic HIV-1 RT peptides. Five different peptides containing RT CTL epitopes were identified throughout the protein and found to be restricted by multiple different HLA class I antigens. In one of these subjects, two different epitopes restricted by the same class I antigen were identified. No epitopes were recognized by both individuals. Examination of the peptides containing these CTL epitopes revealed a high degree of homology among sequenced isolates, suggesting that CTL responses to the RT might be cross-reactive with multiple strains. This initial study indicated that the CTL response to a conserved retroviral protein is highly heterogeneous in infected persons and suggested that the immunogenic viral epitopes are different in different individuals. Similar heterogeneity was observed in another report on RT-specific CTL, in which multiple regions of the RT protein were found to contain CTL epitopes recognized using in vitro expanded lymphocytes from four seropositive subjects (LIEBERMAN et al. 1992).

Other studies investigating the CTL response to HIV-1 RT have utilized a murine system in which mice were immunized with a recombinant vaccinia-RT virus (HOSMALIN et al. 1990). In contrast to the heterogeneous response to HIV-1 RT which had been observed in humans (WALKER et al. 1988; LIEBERMAN et al. 1992), a single immunodominant epitope distinct from previously reported epitopes was identified in the immunized mice, located in the N-terminal region of the RT. When autologous target cells sensitized with the peptide containing this epitope were tested in a small cohort of infected

Table 2. Human immunodeficiency virus type 1 pol cytotoxic T lymphocyte epitopes recognized by human CTL

Figure number	HLA	Amino acids	Sequence	Reference
1	A2	464–472	I L K E P V H G V	Walker et al. 1988; Tsomides et al. 1991
2	A11	313–321	A I F Q S S M T K	Walker et al. 1988 and unpublished data
3	A11	496–507	Q I Y Q E P F K N L K T G	Walker et al. 1988 and unpublished data
4	A28	585–609	E K E P I V G A E T F Y V D G A A N R E T R L G K	R.P.J., B.D.W., unpublished data
5	B8	160–184	I E T V P V K L K P G M D G P K V K Q W P L T E E	Walker et al. 1988
6	B14	636–660	A I Y L A L Q D S G L E V N I V T D S Q Y A L G I	R.P.J., B.D.W., unpublished data
7	Bw60	355–366	T K I E E L R Q H L L R	Walker et al. 1988 and unpublished data
8	Bw62	415–426	L V G K L N W A S Q I Y	Walker et al. 1988 and unpublished data
9	Bw62	464–473	I L K E P V H G V Y	R.P.J., B.D.W., unpublished data

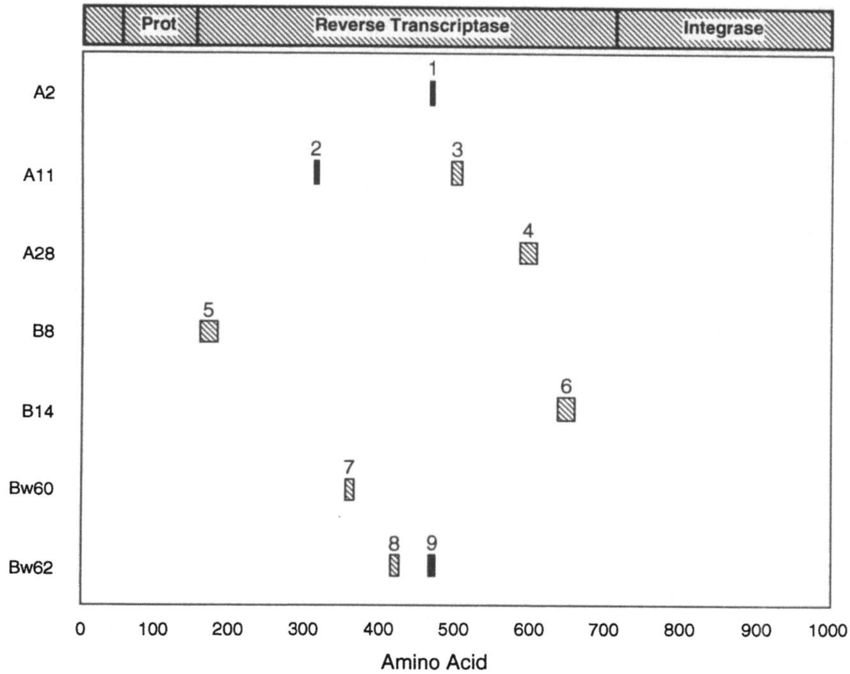

Fig. 3. Human immunodeficiency virus type 1 (HIV-1) reverse transcriptase peptides recognized by human cytotoxic T lymphocytes (CTL). *Prot,* protease. *Numbers* refer to epitope sequences listed in Table 2. See also legend to Fig. 1

subjects using freshly isolated lymphocytes as effector cells, consistent lysis was observed in three of 12 patients. Although lysis could be inhibited by anti-CD3 and anti-CD8 monoclonal antibodies, there did not appear to be any correlation between any HLA antigen and responsiveness to this epitope.

3.3 Envelope-Specific CTL

The HIV-1 envelope protein is also a target for CTL in infected subjects, although characterization of this response has proved complicated for a number of reasons. Analysis of CTL activity directed against the HIV-1 envelop glycoprotein gp160 has revealed the presence of both HLA-restricted and MHC-unrestricted lysis of env-expressing targets in PBMC. The initial report by WALKER et al. (1987), demonstrating inhibition of envelope-specific lysis with an anti-CD3 monoclonal antibody, suggested that the effector cells in PBMC were T lymphocytes, although data on restriction of lysis by HLA antigens were not definitive. Subsequent reports from other groups also demonstrated difficulties in precisely characterizing the effector cells of the envelope-specific response. KOENIG et al. (1988) noted that lysis of env-expressing target cells by PBMC was not MHC restricted, although it could be completely inhibited by anti-CD3 monoclonal antibody and partially inhibited by anti-CD8 monoclonal antibody. Similarly, RIVIÈRE and colleagues (1989a) were unable to demonstrate MHC-restricted lysis of env-expressing targets using PBMC and suggested that envelope-specific, antibody-dependent cellular cytotoxicity (ADCC) might be a second effector mechanism. Using PBMC depleted of NK cells, KOUP et al. (1989) demonstrated lysis of env-expressing targets in an HLA class I-restricted fashion, consistent with the identity of effector cells as CTL. Additional early evidence supporting the existence of MHC-restricted CTL mediating lysis of env-expressing targets was also provided by KOENIG et al. (1988), who derived CTL clones by limiting dilution, which were shown to be $CD8^+$ and HLA class I restricted.

These reports suggested the possibility that killing against envelope-expressing targets was being mediated by two different effector cell populations, one HLA-restricted and the other non-HLA-restricted. In order to distinguish killing of env-expressing target cells by the two populations of effector cells, MCCHESNEY et al. (1990) utilized recombinant vaccinia viruses which expressed gp160 in either an unmodified form or in a form which had a deletion in the signal peptide. The mutant envelope construct lacking the signal peptide was not expressed on the cell surface and could therefore not serve as a target for ADCC. Using these constructs to assess CTL activity and total envelope-specific cytolytic activity, the authors noted that fresh PBMC from only about one third of subjects tested were able to lyse autologous targets infected with the signal deletion construct, although 92% of subjects were able to recognize the unmodified gp160-expressing targets. Confirmatory data have been obtained in studies performed on rhesus monkeys infected with SIV (YAMAMOTO et al. 1990a) that support the existence of both ADCC mediating MHC-unrestricted killing and CTL mediating MHC-restricted killing. A detailed characterization of the HLA-unrestricted lysis of envelope-expressing targets has been provided by TYLER et al. (1989), who described a $CD3^-$ and $CD16^+$ cell population which was able to lyse target cells expressing gp160 in an MHC-unrestricted fashion. Cytophilic antibody specific for gp 120 could be dissociated from these cells. These data suggest that the HLA-unrestricted lysis against envelope-expressing cells consist predominantly of natural killer and killer cells which are armed in vivo with antibodies against gp160. Thus, the cytolytic response in PBMC appears to consists primarily of two populations of cells: classical CTL, which are $CD3^+$ $CD8^+$ and restricted by HLA class I antigens, and armed killer cells, which are $CD3^-$ $CD16^+$.

The existence of both HLA-restricted and -unrestricted killing against the HIV envelope has complicated the identification of CTL epitopes in this protein. Owing in part to this difficulty, the initial descriptions of envelope CTL epitopes occurred using experimental systems not employing CTL from

HIV-1-seropositive subjects. TAKAHASHI et al. (1988) analyzed CTL derived from BALB/c mice that had been immunized with recombinant vaccinia virus containing gp160 derived from the IIIB strain. CTL derived from these mice following antigenic stimulation in vitro were $CD8^+$ and MHC restricted. Epitope mapping demonstrated that the dominant response was directed against a single epitope in a highly variable portion of gp160, the V3 loop, which also contains one of the major epitopes recognized by neutralizing antibodies. This initial response demonstrating an immunodominant CTL response in mice directed against a highly variable portion of the envelope raised the disturbing possibility that HIV-1 envelope-specific CTL would be largely type specific. Using a different technique, SILICIANO et al. (1988) derived $CD4^+$ envelope-specific CTL from PBMC from HIV-1-seronegative donors using in vitro stimulation with gp120 and a soft agar gel cloning technique. The specificity of one of these clones was mapped to a relatively conserved region of gp120. However, a single conservative amino acid substitution was able to abrogate recognition of the variant peptide (SILICIANO et al. 1988; CALLAHAN et al. 1990).

In recent years, a number of CTL epitopes have been derived using CTL clones and PBMC from HIV-1-infected humans (Table 3, Fig. 4). Epitopes identified using $CD8^+$ CTL clones have been largely in gp41 (TAKAHASHI et al. 1991; DAI et al. 1992; JOHNSON et al. 1992), although epitopes also have been identified in gp120 (JOHNSON et al. 1993 and R.P.J., S. Hammond, R. Siliciano and B.D.W., manuscript in preparation). A particularly interesting region lies in the extracellular domain of gp41 immediately adjacent to the immunodominant B cell epitope. This region contains a ten-amino acid stretch which contains CTL epitopes recognized by HLA-A28-, B8-, and B14-restricted CTL (DAI et al. 1992; JOHNSON et al. 1992) and overlaps with a CTL epitope recognized by $CD4^+$ CTL obtained from HIV-1-seronegative volunteers who had been immunized with rgp160 (HAMMOND et al. 1991). Reports using unstimulated PBMC or PBMC stimulated with HIV-infected lymphoblasts have suggested the existence of multiple CTL epitopes distributed throughout gp120 and gp41, lying both in conserved and variable regions of gp160 (CLERICI et al. 1991; DADAGLIO et al. 1991).

These results from the studies described above suggest that there are a number of potential CTL epitopes in gp160 and that these epitopes lie in both conserved and variable regions. However, interpretation of the data obtained from HIV-1-seropositive subjects is complicated by the fact that detection of CTL activity is assessed using target cells expressing HIV-1 envelope derived from laboratory strains of HIV-1. Because of the sequence variation observed in HIV-1 envelope, which may approach 30% at the amino acid level, CTL assays conducted using HIV-1 proteins derived from laboratory strains are likely to underestimate the total CTL response. Recent data from our laboratory using CTL obtained from a laboratory worker who was accidentally infected with HIV-1 IIIB help to address this issue (R. P. Johnson, W. A.

Table 3. Human immunodeficiency virus (HIV) type 1 envelope peptides recognized by human cytotoxic T lymphocytes

Figure number	HLA	Amino acids	Sequence	Reference
1	A2	034–055	LWVTVYYGVPVWKEATTTLFCA	Dadaglio et al. 1991
2	A2	112–124	WDQSLKPCVKLTP	Clerici et al. 1991
3	A2	188–207	TTSYTLTSCNTSVITQACPK	Dadaglio et al. 1991
4	A2	291–307	SVEINCTRPNNNTRKSI	Dadaglio et al. 1991
5	A2	308–322	RIQRGPGRAFVTIGK	Clerici et al. 1991; Dadaglio et al. 1991
6	A2	369–375	PEIVTHS	Dadaglio et al. 1991
7	A2	377–387	(K)NGGEFFYCNS	Dadaglio et al. 1991
8	A2	416–435	LPCRIKQFINMWQEVGKAMY	Dadaglio et al. 1991
8	A2	421–436	KQIINMWQEVGKAMYA	Clerici et al. 1991
9	A2	489–508	VKIEPLGVAPTKAKRRVVQR	Dadaglio et al. 1991
10	A2	827–841	DRVIEVVQGAYRAIR	Clerici et al. 1991
11	A3	37–46	TVYYGVPVWK	R.P.J, S. Hammond, R. Siliciano, B.D.W., manuscript in preparation
12	A3	770–780	RLRDLLLIVTR	Takahashi et al. 1991
13	A24	770–780	RLRDLLLIVTR	R. Koup, personal communication
14	A24	586–593	YLKDQQLL	Dai et al. 1992
15	A30	837–856	YRAIRHIPRRIRQGLERILL	Lieberman et al. 1992
16	B8	586–593	YLKDQQLL	Johnson et al. 1992
17	B8	837–856	YRAIRHIPRRIRQGLERILL	Lieberman et al. 1992
18	B14	584–592	ERYLKDQQL	Johnson et al. 1992
19	B27	781–802	IVELLGRRGWEALKYWWNLLQY	Lieberman et al. 1992
20	B35	592–616	LLGIWGCSGKLICTTAVPWNASWSN	R.P.J, S. Hammond, R. Siliciano, B.D.W., manuscript in preparation
21	Cw4	376–383	FNCGGEFF	Johnson et al. 1993
22	DR4	410–429	GSDTITLPCRIKQFINMWQE	Siliciano et al. 1988
23	DPw4.2	579–590	RILAVERYLKDQ	Hammond et al. 1991

Pepide amino acids enclosed in parentheses do not correspond to sequenced HIV isolates.

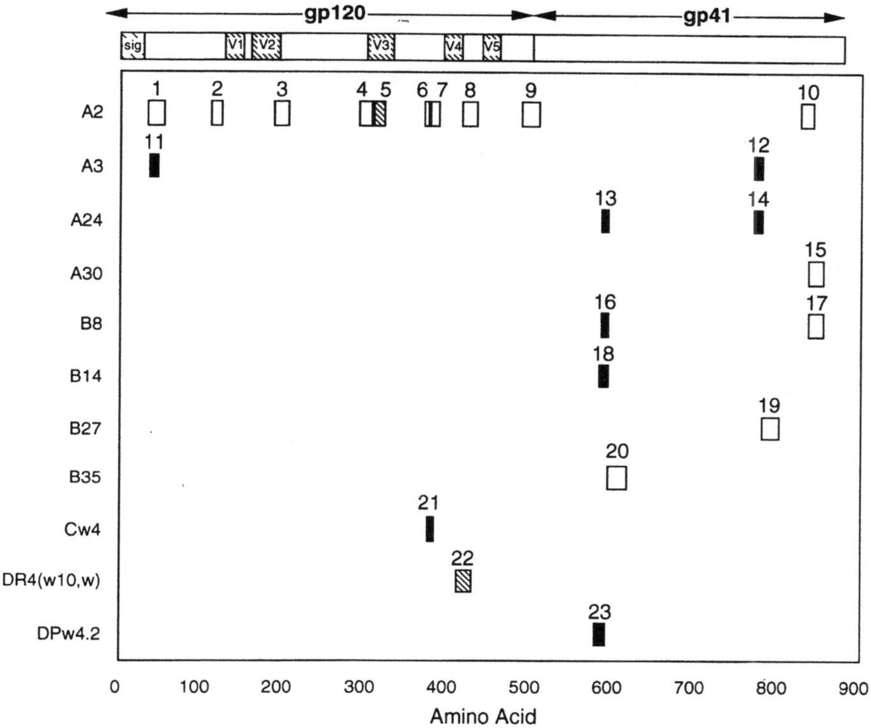

Fig. 4. Human immunodeficiency virus type 1 (HIV-1) envelope peptides recognized by human cytotoxic T lymphocytes (CTL). *Sig*, signal peptide; *gp*, glycoprotein. The five hypervariable regions of gp120 are indicated *V1–V5*. *Numbers* refer to epitope sequences listed in Table 3. See also legend to Fig. 1

Blattner, manuscript in preparation). CTL clones derived from this subject and screened for CTL activity against target cells expressing HIV-1 IIIB proteins suggest that the CTL response is directed against both relatively conserved and variable regions of gp160. In the only subject studied so far, CTL activity would have been underestimated by approximately half, had target cells not expressed autologous viral proteins.

4 Functional Aspects of CTL

Although HIV-1 infection is associated with a vigorous CTL response, this response is clearly insufficient to eliminate the virus from the infected host. A number of functional studies have now begun to more specifically address the functional role of CTL in HIV-1 infection.

4.1 Production of Cytokines by CTL

HIV-1-specific CTL not only lyse infected cells, but are also induced to release a number of inflammatory cytokines upon recognition of their specific target epitopes. Both cerebrospinal fluid (CSF)-derived as well as PBMC-derived CTL clones have been shown to release γ-interferon (IFN-γ), tumor necrosis factor alpha (TNF-α), and TNF-β in an epitope-specific and HLA class I-restricted fashion, paralleling the HIV-1-specific cytolytic activity of these cells (JASSOY et al. 1993). These studies suggest that the elevated levels of these inflammatory cytokines that are found in the serum and CSF of patients with HIV-1 infection may be due at least in part to the vigorous HIV-1-specific CTL response and may have important implications for understanding HIV-1 disease pathogenesis, providing a physiologic link between the virus-specific immune response and some of the neuropathologic sequelae of HIV-1 infection. For example, TNF-α may contribute as a local host defense by directly inhibiting HIV-1 replication (HARTSHORN et al. 1987) or by upregulating class I expression, leading to augmented recognition of infected target cells (VIDOVIC et al. 1990; JOLY et al. 1991; SETHNA and LAMPSON 1991). Alternatively, IFN-γ, TNF-α, and TNF-β have been shown to be capable of inducing HIV-1 expression in promonocyte and T cell lines in vitro (MATSUYAMA et al. 1991; BISWAS et al. 1992), and TNF-α release by HIV-1-specific CTL has been shown to be sufficient to upregulate HIV-1 replication in chronically infected bystander cells (HARRER et al. 1993). In addition, release of cytokines by CTL may contribute to the pathogenesis of HIV-1-related neurologic disorders such as AIDS dementia complex (ADC). A vigorous CTL response has been detected in the CSF of persons with ADC, and these cells release IFN-γ, TNF-α, and TNF-β upon recognition of their respective target cells (JASSOY et al. 1992). IFN-γ has been shown to induce metabolic changes in macrophages and microglial cells, leading to altered metabolic pathways for kynurinine and tryptophan, which may lead to elevated levels of neopterin and quinolonic acid, which have been associated with HIV-1 infection (WERNER et al. 1987; HEYES et al. 1991). TNF-α and TNF-β stimulate astrocytes to proliferate and may result in reactive gliosis (SELMAJ and RAINE 1988), and TNF-α has also been linked to demyelination in the central nervous system (CNS; SELMAJ et al. 1990). These histopathologic changes are typically seen in HIV-1-related neurologic disorders and suggest that the state of immune activation may be related to ultimately deleterious effects.

4.2 CTL and Immune Escape

The paradox of ongoing HIV replication in the face of a vigorous virus-specific CTL has prompted investigation into potential mechanisms used by HIV to avoid suppression by, and to eventually escape from, the host immune response. One leading hypothesis to explain the escape of HIV from immune control postulates that sequence variation in HIV results in the evolution of viruses that are not recognized by the host immune response. HIV isolates exhibit extensive variation, as do other lentiviruses. Variation occurs even in a single subject, leading to the concept that HIV-1-seropositive patients are infected with a mixture of related viruses, referred to as quasispecies. According to this hypothesis, viruses that have developed mutations in CTL epitopes that decrease recognition by CTL would fail to be recognized and have a selective advantage in vivo. Some evidence to support sequence variation as a mechanism for escape already exists with regard to humoral immunity (REITZ et al. 1988; ALBERT et al. 1990; NARA et al. 1990). However, available data have not yet definitively established a link between sequence variation and escape from antibodies directed against HIV-1.

Several reports have addressed the relationship between sequence variation in vivo and recognition by CTL. PHILLIPS et al. (1991) examined CTL responses and sequence variation in a cohort of HIV-1-seropositive hemophiliacs. HIV-1 gag CTL epitopes were identified which were presented by either HLA-B8 or HLA-B27, and CTL responses to these epitopes were evaluated longitudinally. In addition, segments of HIV-1 DNA coding for these CTL epitopes were amplified using the polymerase chain reaction (PCR), sequenced, and variant peptides corresponding to the deduced amino acid sequences tested for recognition by CTL. Examination of sequence variation occurring in HLA-B8-restricted CTL epitopes in p17 and p24 revealed the appearance of mutations which resulted in either a loss of recognition by CTL or, in one instance, a shift in recognition of CTL from one peptide to a variant peptide. The relative frequency of viruses containing the variant sequence varied over time, but there was no clear selection over time of viruses containing mutant sequences which were not recognized. Sequence variation was also observed in an HLA-B27-restricted CTL epitope in p24, but in contrast to the HLA-B8-restricted CTL epitopes, this variant did not result in a loss of sequence variation. Using a similar approach, MEYERHANS et al. (1991) observed the appearance of sequence variation in the same HLA-B27-restricted CTL epitope, but did not observe that any of these changes resulted in a loss of recognition by CTL. The relationship of sequence variation and recognition by CTL has also been addressed in the SIV model (CHEN et al. 1992). As noted above, the SIV-gag-specific CTL response in infected rhesus macaques expressing the Mamu-A*01 MHC type is directed against a single immunodominant epitope (amino acids 182–190 in the SIV p28 gap protein; MILLER et al. 1991). CHEN et al. (1992) examined sequence variation in this epitope in three SIV-infected monkeys expressing the Mamu-A*01 haplotype. Sequence variation occurred within the CTL epitope, but did not appear to occur more frequently within the CTL epitope than in surrounding areas. Furthermore, there did not appear to be a significantly increased frequency of nonsynonymous nucleotide substitutions (i.e., nucleotide changes which result in amino acid substitutions) compared with synonymous substitutions. None of the observed amino acid substitutions resulted in a loss of recognition by CTL, although the CTL utilized in these assays of variant peptides were not derived from the monkeys from whom the sequence data were derived.

These conflicting data do not unequivocally support the hypothesis that sequence variation is a major mechanism of escape from CTL. The data obtained by PHILLIPS et al. (1991) as well as unpublished data obtained from our laboratory suggest that variant viruses may appear which are not recognized by CTL and that in some cases, a shift in CTL specificity may occur. However, this does not always appear to be the case, as evidenced by the data from other groups (MEYERHANS et al. 1991; CHEN et al. 1992). It is possible that the failure to observe sequence variants arising which escape CTL recognition for certain CTL epitopes may reflect structural constraints on the virus that limit its ability to mutate in a specified region. Critical evidence that is lacking thus far is a clear demonstration that viruses with mutations in CTL epitopes have a selective advantage in vivo.

Mechanisms other than sequence variation which may allow HIV to escape CTL responses have been proposed, but specific data in favor of these hypotheses is lacking at this time. HIV-1 infection of lymphocytes has been observed to produce a transient decrease in the expression of MHC class I molecules in transformed cell lines and PHA-stimulated lymphocytes (KERKAU et al. 1989; SCHEPPLER et al. 1989). This downregulation of HLA class I expression was shown to decrease killing by allogeneic CTL, but no specific data have been published regarding the effects on killing by HIV-1-specific CTL. Decreased expression of lymphocyte function associated antigen-1 (LFA-1) on PBMC obtained from HIV-1 seropositive subjects has also been reported (AMIEL et al. 1988). However, the ability of HIV-1-specific $CD8^+$ CTL to kill HIV-infected lymphocytes (HOFFENBACH et al. 1989; ORENTAS et al. 1990; TAKAHASHI et al. 1991 and RPJ, BDW, unpublished data) suggests that this downregulation of selected cell surface markers does not prevent recognition of infected cell lines by HIV-1-specific CTL, and further experiments are necessary to define the role that downregulation of cell surface molecules on infected lymphocytes may play. Other potential mechanisms of immune escape from CTL that have been observed in other viral infections, such as selective blocks in antigen presentation to the class I pathway (DEL VAL et al. 1989), may also be operative in HIV-infected cells, but there is no specific evidence for this possibility at the present time.

4.3 Inhibition of Human Immunodeficiency Virus Type 1 Replication by CTL

The ability of CTL to lyse cells expressing viral antigens in in vitro assays suggests that these cells are likely to be active in vivo in inhibiting viral replication. Evidence for the protective role of CTL against viral infection in general arises from the observations that adoptive transfer of virus-specific CTL, including influenza, lymphocytic choriomeningitis virus, and murine cytomegalovirus, is effective in preventing viral infection in naive mice. However, only preliminary evidence has appeared to date which addresses the ability of HIV-1-specific CTL to inhibit viral replication. Preliminary data from other investigators (KOENIG et al. 1991) and unpublished data from our group (R.P.J., V. Johnson and B.D.W.) have demonstrated that HIV-1-specific CTL clones are able to inhibit viral replication in vitro. This inhibition of viral replication is largely HLA restricted, but there is also a component which is not HLA restricted. The non-HLA-restricted inhibition of viral replication is mediated, in part, by the release of soluble factors which may be related to the soluble inhibitory factors produced by $CD8^+$ lymphocytes identified in previous studies by C. WALKER and colleagues (1986; WALKER and LEVY 1989). The ability of these CTL clones to inhibit viral replication has also been studied in adoptive transfer experiments carried out in the severe combined immunodeficiency (SCID)-hu-PBMC model. In this system, mice with SCID are reconstituted with PBMC and then subsequently infected with HIV-1. Preliminary results utilizing the transfer of nef-specific CTL clones (KOENIG et al. 1991, 1992) and RT-specific CTL clones (KOUP et al. 1991a) into HIV-1-infected SCID-hu-PBMC mice suggests that these clones are also effective in inhibiting viral replication in this animal model, although both HLA-restricted and non-HLA-restricted inhibition of viral replication has been observed. Clearly, further research is needed in order to more precisely characterize the relative contributions of cytolytic and noncytolytic pathways in inhibiting viral replication.

4.4 Vaccine-Related Issues

At least 14 different HIV-1 vaccine candidates are presently in various stages of clinical trials, both as prophylactic vaccines for subjects not yet exposed to the virus and as therapeutic vaccines in an attempt to alter the disease course in patients already infected. The cellular immune response to these vaccine candidates has begun to be investigated in a number of these trials. The majority of these vaccine candidates are based on recombinant HIV-1 proteins and would not be expected to generate significant class I-restricted CTL responses, but have induced class II-restricted, $CD4^+$, envelope-specific CTL. Following repeated immunization with the MicroGeneSys gp160 immunogen in an alum, adjuvant CD4-positive, class II-restricted CTL were identified in three of eight recipients (ORENTAS et al. 1990), and an epitope in a highly conserved region of gp41 (aa 584–595) was identified as major target for this response (HAMMOND et al. 1991). Recently class II-restricted CTL clones specific for gp120 which are able to lyse infected cells have also been identified in recipients of this vaccine (SILICIANO et al. 1992).

Recent studies using a primary immunization with a recombinant HIV-1 envelope-vaccinia virus followed by boosting with recombinant gp160 vaccine have yielded evidence that vaccination can also induce class I-restricted CTL, which can be detected following in vitro stimulation with viral antigen (HAMMOND et al. 1992; SILICIANO et al. 1992; COONEY et al. 1993). The CTL generated by this vaccination regimen consist of strain-specific CTL directed at a gp120 epitope as well as more broadly reactive CTL specific for a relatively conserved region of gp41 (R.P.J., S. Hammond, R. Siliciano, and B.D.W., manuscript in preparation). A similar prime-boost regimen in a separate cohort of subjects also demonstrated striking induction of HIV-1-specific CTL activity, including both $CD4^+$ and $CD8^+$ CTL responses (COONEY et al. 1993).

Relatively few data are available regarding the CTL response induced by therapeutic vaccination of seropositive subjects. CTL responses to HIV-1 envelope protein have been investigated in recipients of the MicroGeneSys soluble gp160 vaccine, which was associated with variable increases in both $CD4^+$, class II-restricted as well as $CD8^+$, class I-restricted CTL (KUNDU et al. 1992). Confirmation of therapeutic vaccine-induced CTL responses as well as correlation of immunization with improved clinical and virologic parameters are still needed.

5 Conclusions

Data from numerous investigators have now confirmed that HIV-1 infection is associated with an extremely vigorous CTL response, which is broadly directed at multiple epitopes. Multiple restricting class I antigens have been identified, and the functional activities of the HIV-1-specific CTL have begun to be defined. Nevertheless, the precise role of the CTL response as it relates to the pathogenesis of AIDS remains unclear.

By analogy to other animal models of viral disease, it is likely that CTL directed against HIV-1 play a significant role as a host defense in this infection. Further definition of the importance of the HIV-specific CTL response is likely to come from a number of different avenues of research. A protective immune response to a primate retrovirus appears to have been achieved in the rhesus macaque model, in which protection against high dose challenge has been demonstrated using a live attenuated SIV which is deleted of the nef protein (DANIEL et al. 1992). This model offers the opportunity to define the contribution of virus-specific CTL to the observed protection. The role of CTL in containing virus replication and disease progression in long-term seropositive persons who maintain normal CD4 counts is also likely to contribute to our understanding of the protective role of the cellular immune response in this infection. In this regard, more data are needed to determine whether relative protective effects are conferred by recognition of specific CTL epitopes, whether the CTL response can be broadened by specific immunization strategies, and how immune escape contributes to pathogenesis. Although target cells expressing recombinant viral antigens are readily lysed, more data are needed regarding the ability of these CTL to lyse infected target cells, including infected cells other than $CD4^+$ lymphocytes. Additional studies are needed to clarify the mechanism of declining CTL responses with disease progression and to clarify the potential pathogenic role of a persistent and vigorous CTL response, such as by direct tissue injury or through release of inflammatory cytokines. Further studies are also needed to clarify the potential role of $CD4^+$, class II-restricted CTL in this infection. Answers to these and other questions posed by the continuing and expanding HIV epidemic should facilitate the development of both therapeutic and preventive interventions and should greatly enhance understanding of the role of cellular immunity in human viral diseases in general.

References

Achour A, Picard O, Zagury D, Sarin PS, Gallo RC, Naylor PH, Goldstein AL (1990) HGP-30, a synthetic analogue of human immunodeficiency virus (HIV) p17, is a target for cytotoxic lymphocytes in HIV-infected individuals. Proc Natl Acad Sci USA 87: 7045–7049

Albert JB, Abrahamsson E, Nagy E, Aurelius H, Grines G, Mystrom G, Fenyo EM (1990) Rapid development of isolate-specific neutralizing antibodies after primary HIV-1 infection and consequent emergence of virus variants which resist neutralization by autologous sera. AIDS 4:107–112

Amiel C, Béné MC, May T, Canton P, Faure GC (1988) LFA-1 expression in HIV infection. AIDS 2:211–214

Autran B, Mayaud CM, Raphael M, Plata F, Denis M, Bourguin A, Guillon JM, Debre P, Akoun G (1988) Evidence for a cytotoxic T-lymphocyte alveolitis in human immunodeficiency virus-infected patients. AIDS 2: 179–183

Autran B, Plata F, Guillon JM, Joly P, Mayaud C, Debre P (1990) HIV-specific cytotoxic T lymphocytes directed against alveolar macrophages in HIV-infected patients. Res Virol 141:131–136

Autran B, Sadat SB, Hadida F, Parrot A, Guillon JM, Plata F, Mayaud C, Debre P (1991) HIV-specific cytotoxic T lymphocytes against alveolar macrophages: specificities and down-regulation. Res Virol 142:113–118

Barre-Sinoussi F, Chermann JC, Rey R, Nugeyre MT, Chamaret S, Gruest J, Daguet C, Axler-Blin C, Vezinet-Brun F, Rouziousx C, Rozenbaum W, Montagnier L (1983) Isolation of a T-lymphotrophic retrovirus from a patient at risk for acquired immunodeficiency syndrome (AIDS). Science 220:868–871

Bennink JR, Yewdell JW (1988) Murine cytotoxic T lymphocyte recognition of individual influenza virus proteins: high frequency of nonresponder MHC class I alleles. J Exp Med 168:1935–1939

Bennink JR, Yewdell JW, Gerhard W (1982) A viral polymerase involved in recognition of influenza virus-infected cells by a cytotoxic T-cell clone. Nature 296: 75–76

Biswas P, Poli G, Kinter AL, Justement JS, Stanley SK, Maury WJ, Bressler P, Orenstein JM, Fauci AS (1992) Interferon gamma induces the expression of human immunodeficiency virus in persistently infected promonocytic cells (U1) and redirects the production of virions

to intracytoplasmic vacuoles in phorbol myristate acetate-diferentiated U1 cells. J Exp Med 176: 739–750
Bourgault I, Venet A, Levy JP (1992) Three epitopic peptides of the simian immunodeficiency virus Nef protein recognized by macaque cytolytic T lymphocytes. J Virol 66: 750–756
Braciale TJ, Sweetser MT, Morrison LA, Kittlesen DJ, Braciale VL (1989). Class I major histocompatibility complex-restricted cytolytic T lymphocytes recognize a limited number of sites on the influenza hemagglutinin. Proc Natl Acad Sci USA 86: 277–281
Buseyne F, Griscilli C, Blanche S, Schmitt D, Rivière Y (1993a) Detection of HIV-specific cell-mediated cytotoxicity in the peripheral blood from infected children. J Immunol 150: 3569–3581
Buseyne F, McChesney M, Porrot F, Kovarik S, Guy B, Rivière Y (1993b) Gag-specific cytotoxic T lymphocytes from HIV-1 infected individuals: gag epitopes are clustered in three regions of the p24 gag protein. J Virol 67: 694–702
Callahan KM, Fort MM, Obah EA, Reinherz EL, Siliciano RF (1990) Genetic variability in HIV-1 gp120 affects interactions with HLA molecules and T cell receptor. J Immunol 144: 3341–3346
Chen WC, Shen L, Miller MD, Ghim SH, Hughes AL, Letvin NL (1992) Cytotoxic T lymphocytes do not appear to select for mutations in an immunodominant epitope of simian immunodeficiency virus gag. J Immunol 149: 4060–4066
Chicz RM, Urban RG, Lane WS, Gorga JC, Stern LJ, Vignali DA, Strominger JL (1992) Predominant naturally processed peptides bound to HLA-DR1 are derived from MHC-related molecules and are heterogeneous in size. Nature 358: 764–768
Choppin J, Martinon F, Gomard E, Bahraoui E, Connan F, Bouillot M, Levy JP (1990) Analysis of physical interactions between peptides and HLA molecules and application to the detection of human immunodeficiency virus 1 antigenic peptides. J Exp Med 172: 889–899
Choppin J, Martinon F, Connan F, Gomard E, Levy J-P (1991a) HLA-binding regions of HIV-1 proteins. I. Detection of seven HLA binding regions in the HIV-1 nef protein. J Immunol 147: 569–574
Choppin J, Martinon F, Connan F, Pauchard M, Gomard E, Levy JP (1991b) HLA-binding regions of HIV-1 proteins. II. A systematic study of viral proteins. J Immunol 147: 575–583
Claverie JM, Kourilsky P, Langlade DP, Chalufour PA, Dadaglio G, Tekaia F, Plata F, Bougueleret L (1988) T-immunogenic peptides are constituted of rare sequence patterns. Use in the identification of T epitopes in the human immunodeficiency virus gag protein. Eur J Immunol 18: 1547–1553
Clerici M, Lucey DR, Zajac RA, Boswell RN, Gebel HM, Takahashi H, Berzofsky JA, Shearer GM (1991) Detection of cytotoxic T lymphocytes specific for synthetic peptides of gp160 in HIV-seropositive individuals. J Immunol 146: 2214–2219
Cooney EL, McElrath MJ, Corey L, Hu SL, Collier AC, Arditti D, Hoffman M, Coombs RW, Smith GE, Greenberg PD (1993) Enhanced immunity to human immunodeficiency virus (HIV) envelope elicited by a combined vaccine regimen consisting of priming with a vaccinia recombinant expressing HIV envelope and boosting with gp160 protein. Proc Natl Acad Sci USA 90: 1882–1886
Culmann B, Gomard E, Kieny MP, Guy B, Dreyfus F, Saimot AG, Sereni D, Levy JP (1989) An antigenic peptide of the HIV-1 NEF protein recognized by cytotoxic T lymphocytes of seropositive individuals in association with different HLA-B molecules. Eur J Immunol 19: 2383–2386
Culmann B, Gomard E, Kieny MP, Guy B, Dreyfus F, Saimot AG, Sereni D, Sicard D, Levy JP (1991) Six epitopes reacting with human cytotoxic $CD8^+$ T cells in the central region of the HIV-1 NEF protein. J Immunol 146: 1560–1565
Curiel TC, Wong JW, Gorcyzka P, Schooley RT, Walker BD (1993) $CD4^+$ HIV-1 envelope-specific cytotoxic T-lymphocytes derived from the peripheral blood cells of an HIV-1 infected individual. AIDS Res Hum Retroviruses 9: 61–68
Dadaglio G, Leroux A, Langlade DP, Bahraoui EM, Traincard F, Fisher R, Plata F (1991) Epitope recognition of conserved HIV envelope sequences by human cytotoxic T lymphocytes. J Immunol 147: 2302–2309
Dai LC, West K, Littaua R, Takahashi K, Ennis FA (1992) Mutation of human immunodeficiency virus type 1 at amino acid 585 on gp41 results in loss of killing by $CD8^+$ A24-restricted cytotoxic T lymphocytes. J Virol 66: 3151–3154
Daniel M, Kirchoff F, Czajak SC, Sehgal PK, Desrosiers RC (1992) Protective effects of a live attenuated vaccine with a deletion in the nef gene. Science 258: 1938–1941
Del Val M, Münch K, Reddehase MJ, Koszinowski UH (1989) Presentation of CMV immediate-

early antigen to cytolytic T lymphocytes is selectively prevented by viral genes expressed in the early phase. Cell 58: 305–313

Falk K, Rotzschke O, Deres K, Metzger J, Jung G, Rammensee HG (1991a). Identification of naturally processed viral nonapeptides allows their quantification in infected cells and suggests an allele-specific T cell epitope forecast. J Exp Med 174: 425–434

Falk K, Rotzschke O, Stevanovic S, Jung G, Rammensee HG (1991b) Allele-specific motifs revealed by sequencing of self-peptides eluted from MHC molecules. Nature 351: 290–296

Frelinger JA, Gotch FM, Zweerink H, Wain E, McMichael AJ (1990) Evidence of widespread binding of HLA class I molecules to peptides. J Exp Med 172: 827–834

Gallo RC, Salahuddin SZ, Popovic M, Shearer GM, Kaplan M, Haynes BF, Palker TJ, Redfield R, Oleske J, Safai B, White G, Foster P, Markham PD (1984) Frequent detection and isolation of cytopathic retroviruses (HTLV-III) from patients with AIDS and at risk for AIDS. Science 224: 500–502

Gotch FM, Nixon DF, Alp N, McMichael AJ, Borysiewicz LK (1990) High frequency of memory and effector gag specific cytotoxic T lymphocytes in HIV seropositive individuals. Int Immunol 2: 707–712

Hadida F, Parrot A, Kieny MP, Sadat SB, Mayaud C, Debre P, Autran B (1992) Carboxyl-terminal and central regions of human immunodeficiency virus-1 NEF recognized by cytotoxic T lymphocytes from lymphoid organs. An in vitro limiting dilution analysis. J Clin Invest 89: 53–60

Hammond SA, Obah E, Stanhope P, Monell CR, Strand M, Robbins FM, Bias WB, Karr RW, Koenig S, Siliciano RF (1991) Characterization of a conserved T cell epitope in HIV-1gp41 recognized by vaccine-induced human cytolytic T cells. J Immunol 146: 1470–1477

Hammond SA, Bollinger RC, Stanhope PE, Quinn TC, Schwartz D, Clements ML, Siliciano RF (1992) Comparative clonal analysis of human immunodeficiency type 1 (HIV-1)-specific $CD4^+$ and $CD8^+$ cytotoxic T lymphocytes isolated from seronegative humans immunized with candidate HIV-1 vaccines. J Exp Med 176: 1531–1543

Harrer T, Harrer E, Jassoy T, Johnson R, Walker B (1993) Induction of HIV-1 replication in a chronically infected T cell line by cytotoxic T lymphocytes. J Acquir Immune Defic Syndr 6: 865–871

Hartshorn KL, Neumeyer D, Vogt MW, Schooley RT, Hirsch MS (1987) Activity of interferons alpha, beta, and gamma against human immunodeficiency virus replication in vitro. AIDS Res Hum Retroviruses 3: 125–133

Heyes M, Brew B, Martin A, Price R, Salazar A, Sidtis J, Yergey J, Mouradian M, Sadler A, Keilp J, Rubinow D, Markey S (1991) Quinolonic acid in cerebrospinal fluid and serum in HIV-1 infection: relationship to clinical and neurological status. Ann Neurol 29: 202–209

Ho M, Armstrong J, Mc Mahon D, Pazin G, Huang XL, Rinaldo C, White-side T, Tripoli C, Levine G, Moody D et al. (1993) A phase 1 study of adoptive transfer of autologous $CD8^+$ T lymphocytes in patients with acquired immunodeficiency syndrome (AIDS)-related complex or AIDS. Blood 81: 2093–2101

Hoffenbach A, Langlade DP, Dadaglio G, Vilmer E, Michel F, Mayaud C, Autran B, Plata F (1989) Unusually high frequencies of HIV-specific cytotoxic T lymphocytes in humans. J Immunol 142: 452–462

Hosmalin A, Clerici M, Houghten R, Pendleton CD, Flexner C, Lucey DR, Moss B, Germain RN, Shearer GM, Berzofsky JA (1990) An epitope in human immunodeficiency virus 1 reverse transcriptase recognized by both mouse and human cytotoxic T lymphocytes. Proc Natl Acad Sci USA 87: 2344–2348

Jardetzky TS, Lane WS, Robinson RA, Madden DR, Wiley DC (1991) Identification of self peptides bound to purified HLA-B27. Nature 353: 326–329

Jassoy C, Johnson RP, Navia BA, Worth J, Walker BD (1992) Detection of a vigorous HIV-1-specific cytotoxic T lymphocyte response in cerebrospinal fluid from infected persons with AIDS dementia complex. J Immunol 149: 3113–3119

Jassoy CJ, Harrer T, Rosenthal T, Navia BA, Worth J, Johnson RP, Walker BD (1993) HIV-1-specific cytotoxic T cells release interferon gamma, tumor necrosis factor (TNF)-alpha and TNF-beta when they encounter their target antigens. J Virol 67: 2844–2852

Johnson RP, Trocha A, Yang L, Mazzara GP, Panicali DL, Buchanan TM, Walker BD (1991) HIV-1 gag-specific cytotoxic T lymphocytes recognize multiple highly conserved epitopes. Fine specificity of the gag-specific response defined by using unstimulated peripheral blood mononuclear cells and cloned effector cells. J Immunol 147: 1512–1521

Johnson RP, Trocha A, Buchanan TM, Walker BD (1992) Identification of overlapping HLA

class I-restricted cytotoxic T cell epitopes in a conserved region of the human immunodeficiency virus type 1 envelope glycoprotein: definition of minimum epitopes and analysis of the effects of sequence variation. J Exp Med 175: 961–971
Johnson RP, Trocha A, Buchanan T, Walker BD (1993) Recognition of a highly conserved region of human immunodeficiency virus type I gp120 by a HLA-Cw4-restricted cytotoxic T lymphocyte clone. J Virol 67: 438–445
Joly E, Mucke L, Oldstone MB (1991) Viral persistence in neurons explained by lack of major histocompatibility class I expression. Science 253: 1283–1285
Kerkau T, Schmitt LR, Schimpl A, Wecker E (1989) Downregulation of HLA class I antigens in HIV-1-infected cells. AIDS Res Hum Retroviruses 5: 613–620
Koenig S, Earl P, Powell D, Pantaleo G, Merli S, Moss B, Fauci AS (1988) Group-specific, major histocompatibility complex class I-restricted cytotoxic responses to human immunodeficiency virus 1 (HIV-1) envelope proteins by cloned peripheral blood T cells from an HIV-1-infected individual. Proc Natl Acad Sci USA 85: 8638–8642
Koenig S, Fuerst S, Wood LV, Woods R, Jones G, Fauci AS (1990a) Structural and functional characteristics of HIV-specific CTL. 6th international conference on AIDS, San Francisco, CA
Koenig S, Fuerst TR, Wood LV, Woods RM, Suzich JA, Jones GM, de ICVF, Davey RTJ, Venkatesan S, Moss B et al. (1990b) Mapping the fine specificity of a cytolytic T cell response to HIV-1 nef protein. J Immunol 145: 127–135
Koenig S, Jones G, Boone E, Brewah A, Newell A, Torbett B, Mosier D, Fauci AS (1991) Inhibition of HIV replication by HIV-specific CTL. 7th international conference on AIDS, Florence, Italy
Koenig S, van Kuyk R, Jones G, Torbett B, Mosier D, Brewah Y, Leath S, Davey V, Yannelli J, Rosenberg S, Fauci A, Lane H (1992) Adoptive transfer of a nef-specific CTL clone into hu-PBL-SCID mice and an HIV-infected patient. 8th international conference on AIDS/III STD World Congress, Amsterdam, The Netherlands, ThA1573
Koup RA, Sullivan JL, Levine PH, Brettler D, Mahr A, Mazzara G, McKenzie S, Panicali D (1989) Detection of major histocompatibility complex class I-restricted, HIV-specific cytotoxic T lymphocytes in the blood of infected hemophiliacs. Blood 73: 1909–1914
Koup R, Hesselton R, Johnson RP, Walker BD, Sullivan J (1991a) Effect of adoptively transferred CTL on HIV replication in the Hu-PBL-SCID mouse model. National Cooperative Vaccine Development Conference, Marco Island, FL
Koup RA, Pikora CA, Luzuriaga K, Brettler DB, Day ES, Mazzara GP, Sullivan JL (1991b) Limiting dilution analysis of cytotoxic T lymphocytes to human immunodeficiency virus gag antigens in infected persons: in vitro quantitation of effector cell populations with p17 and p24 specificities. J Exp Med 174: 1593–1600
Kundu S, Katzenstein D, Moses L, Merigan T (1992) Enhancement of human immunodeficiency virus (HIV) specific $CD4^+$ and $CD8^+$ cytotoxic T-lymphocyte activities in HIV infected asymptomatic patients given recombinant gp160 vaccine. Proc Natl Acad Sci USA 89: 11204–11208
Kundu SK, Merigan TC (1992) Equivalent recognition of HIV proteins, Env, Gag and Pol, by $CD4^+$ and $CD8^+$ cytotoxic T-lymphocytes. AIDS 6: 643–649
Lieberman J (1993) ACTG, Washington, D.C.
Lieberman J, Fabry JA, Kuo MC, Earl P, Moss B, Skolnik PR (1992) Cytotoxic T lymphocytes from HIV-1 seropositive individuals recognize immunodominant epitopes in gp160 and reverse transcriptase. J Immunol 148: 2738–2747
Littaua RA, Oldstone MB, Takeda A, Debouck C, Wong JT, Tuazon CU, Moss B, Kievits F, Ennis FA (1991) An HLA-C-restricted $CD8^+$ cytotoxic T-lymphocyte clone recognizes a highly conserved epitope on human immunodeficiency virus type 1 gag. J Virol 65: 4051–4056
Littaua RA, Oldstone MB, Takeda A, Ennis FA (1992) A $CD4^+$ cytotoxic T-lymphocyte clone to a conserved epitope on human immunodeficiency virus type 1 p24: cytotoxic activity and secretion of interleukin-2 and interleukin-6. J Virol 66: 608–611
Luzuriaga K, Koup RA, Pikora CA, Brettler DB, Sullivan JL (1991) Deficient human immunodeficiency virus type 1-specific cytotoxic T cell responses in vertically infected children. J Pediatr 119: 230–236.
Matsuyama T, Kobayashi N, Yamamoto N (1991) Cytokines and HIV infection: is AIDS a tumor necrosis factor disease? AIDS 5: 1405–1417
McChesney M, Tanneau F, Regnault A, Sansonetti P, Montagnier L, Kieny MP, Rivière Y (1990) Detection of primary cytotoxic T lymphocytes specific for the envelope glycoprotein of HIV-1 by deletion of the env amino-terminal signal sequence. Eur J Immunol 20: 215–220

Meyerhans A, Dadaglio G, Vartanian JP, Langlade DP, Frank R, Asjo B, Plata F,S. W-H (1991) In vivo persistence of a HIV-1-encoded HLA-B-27-restricted cytotoxic T lymphocyte epitope despite specific in vitro reactivity. Eur J Immunol 21: 2637–2640
Miller MD, Lord CI, Stallard V, Mazzara GP, Letvin NL (1990) The gag-specific cytotoxic T lymphocytes in rhesus monkeys infected with the simian immunodeficiency virus of macaques. J Immunol 144: 122–128
Miller MD, Yamamoto H, Hughes AL, Watkins DI, Letvin NL (1991) Definition of an epitope and MHC class I molecule recognized by gag-specific cytotoxic T lymphocytes in SIVmac-infected rhesus monkeys. J Immunol 147: 320–329
Myers G, Berzofsky JA, Rabson AB, Smith TF, Wong-Staal F (eds) (1991) Human retroviruses and AIDS 1991: a compilation and analysis of nucleic acid and amino acid sequences. Los Alamos, N.M., Los Alamos National Laboratory
Nara PL, Smit L, Dunlop N, Hatch W, Merges M, Waters D, Kelliher J, Gallo RC, Fischinger PJ, Goudsmit J (1990) Emergence of viruses resistant to neutralization by V3-specific antibodies in experimental human immunodeficiency virus type 1 IIIB infection of chimpanzees. J Virol 64: 3779–3791
Nixon DF, McMichael AJ (1991) Cytotoxic T-cell recognition of HIV proteins and peptides [editorial]. AIDS 5: 1049–1059
Nixon DF, Townsend AR, Elvin JG, Rizza CR, Gallwey J, McMichael AJ (1988) HIV-1 gag-specific cytotoxic T lymphocytes defined with recombinant vaccinia virus and synthetic peptides. Nature 336: 484–487
Nixon DF, Huet S, Rothbard J, Kieny MP, Delchambre M, Thiriart C, Rizza CR, Gotch FM, McMichael AJ (1990) An HIV-1 and HIV-2 cross-reactive cytotoxic T-cell epitope. AIDS 4: 841–845
Orentas RJ, Hildreth JE, Obah E, Polydefkis M, Smith GE, Clements ML, Siliciano RF (1990). Induction of $CD4^+$ human cytolytic T cells specific for HIV-infected cells by a gp160 subunit vaccine. Science 248: 1234–1237
Phillips RE, Rowland JS, Nixon DF, Gotch FM, Edwards JP, Ogunlesi AO, Elvin JG, Rothbard JA, Bangham CR, Rizza CR et al. (1991) Human immunodeficiency virus genetic variation that can escape cytotoxic T cell recognition. Nature 354: 453–459
Plata F, Autran B, Martins LP, Wain HS, Raphael M, Mayaud C, Denis M, Guillon JM, Debre P (1987) AIDS virus-specific cytotoxic T lymphocytes in lung disorders. Nature 328: 348–351
Reimann KA, Snyder GB, Chalifoux LV, Waite BC, Miller MD, Yamamoto H, Spertini O, Letvin NL (1991) An activated $CD8^+$ lymphocyte appears in lymph nodes of rhesus monkeys early after infection with simian immunodeficiency virus. J Clin Invest 88: 1113–1120
Reitz MS Jr., Wilson C, Naugle C, Gallo RC, Robert-Guroff M (1988) Generation of a neutralization-resistant variant of HIV-1 is due to selection for a point mutation in the envelope gene. Cell 54: 57–63
Rivière Y, Tanneau SF, Regnault A, Lopez O, Sansonetti P, Guy B, Kieny MP, Fournel JJ, Montagnier L (1989a) Human immunnodeficiency virus-specific cytotoxic responses of seropositive individuals: distinct types of effector cells mediate killing of targets expressing gag and env proteins. J Virol 63: 2270–2277
Rivière Y, Tanneau SF, Regnault A, Lopez O, Sansonetti P, Guy B, Kieny MP, Fournel JJ, Montagnier L (1989b) Multiple cytotoxic effector cells are induced by infection with the human immunodeficiency virus. Res Immunol 140: 110–115
Rotzschke O, Falk K, Deres K, Schild H, Norda M, Metzger J, Jung G, Rammensee HG (1990) Isolation and analysis of naturally processed viral peptides as recognized by cytotoxic T cells. Nature 348: 252–254
Rudensky A, Preston HP, Hong SC, Barlow A, Janeway CAJ (1991) Sequence analysis of peptides bound to MHC class II molecules. Nature 353: 622–627
Scheppler JA, Nicholson JK, Swan DC, Ahmed AA, McDougal JS (1989) Down-modulation of MHC-I in a $CD4^+$ T cell line, CEM-E5, after HIV-1 infection. J Immunol 143: 2858–2866
Selmaj KW, Raine CS (1988) Tumor necrosis factor mediates myelin and oligodendrocyte damage in vitro. Ann Neurol 23: 339–346
Selmaj KW, Farooq M, Norton WT, Raine CS, Brosnan CF (1990) Proliferation of astrocytes in vitro in response to cytokines. A primary role for tumor necrosis factor. J Immunol 144: 129–135
Sethi KK, Naher H, Stroehmann I (1988) Phenotypic heterogeneity of cerebrospinal fluid-derived HIV-specific and HLA-restricted cytotoxic T-cell clones. Nature 335: 171–181

Sethna M, Lampson L (1991) Immune modulation within the brain: recruitment of inflammatory cells and increased major histocompatibility antigen expressing following intracerebral injection of interferon-gamma. J Neuroimmunol 34: 121–132
Shen L, Chen ZW, Miller MD, Stallard V, Mazzara GP, Panicali DL, Letvin NL (1991) Recombinant virus vaccine-induced SIV-specific $CD8^+$ cytotoxic T lymphocytes. Science 252: 440–443
Siliciano RF, Lawton T, Knall C, Karr RW, Berman P, Gregory T, Reinherz EL (1988) Analysis of host-virus interactions in AIDS with anti-gp 120 T cell clones: effect of HIV sequence variation and a mechanism for $CD4^+$ cell depletion. Cell 54: 561–575
Siliciano RF, Knall C, Lawton T, Berman P, Gregory T, Reinherz EL (1989) Recognition of HIV glycoprotein gp120 by T cells. Role of monocyte CD4 in the presentation of gp120. J Immunol 142: 1506–1511
Siliciano RF, Bollinger RC, Callahan KC, Hammond SA, Liu AY, Miskovsky EP, Rowell JF, Stanhope PE (1992) Clonal analysis of T-cell responses to the HIV-1 envelope proteins in AIDS vaccine recipients. AIDS Res Human Retroviruses 8: 1349–1352
Takahashi H, Cohen J, Hosmalin A, Cease KB, Houghten R, Cornette JL, DeLisi C, Moss B, Germain RN, Berzofsky JA (1988) An immunodominant epitope of the human immunodeficiency virus envelope glycoprotein gp160 recognized by class I major histocompatibility complex molecule-restricted murine cytotoxic T lymphocytes. Proc Natl Acad Sci USA 85: 3105–3109
Takahashi K, Dai LC, Fuerst TR, Biddison WE, Earl PL, Moss B, Ennis FA (1991) Specific lysis of human immunodeficiency virus type 1-infected cells by a HLA-A3.1-restricted $CD8^+$ cytotoxic T-lymphocyte clone that recognizes a conserved peptide sequence within the gp41 subunit of the envelope protein. Proc Natl Acad Sci USA 88: 10277–10281
Townsend A, Bodmer H (1989) Antigen recognition by class I-restricted T lymphocytes. Annu Rev Immunol 7: 601–624
Townsend AR, McMichael AJ, Carter NP, Huddleston JA, Brownlee GG (1984) Cytotoxic T-cell recognition of the influenza nucleoprotein and hemagglutinin expressed in transfected mouse L cells. Cell 39: 13–25
Townsend AR, Bastin J, Gould K, Brownlee GG (1986). Cytotoxic T lymphocytes recognize influenza haemagglutinin that lacks a signal sequence. Nature 324: 575–577
Tsomides TJ, Walker BD, Eisen HN (1991) An optimal peptide recognized by $CD8^+$ T cells binds very tightly to the restricting class I major histocompatibility complex protein on intact cells but not to the purified class I protein. Proc Natl Acad Sci USA 88: 11276–11280
Tsubota H, Lord CI, Watkins DI, Morimoto C, Letvin NL (1989) A cytotoxic T lymphocyte inhibits acquired immunodeficiency syndrome virus replication in peripheral blood lymphocytes. J Exp Med 169: 1421–1434
Tyler DS, Nastala CL, Stanley SD, Matthews TJ, Lyerly HK, Bolognesi DP, Weinhold KJ (1989) GP120 specific cellular cytotoxicity in HIV-1 seropositive individuals. Evidence for circulating $CD16^+$ effector cells armed in vivo with cytophilic antibody. J Immunol 142: 1177–1182
Venet A, Walker BD (1993) Epitopes in HIV/SIV infection. AIDS 7 (Suppl 1): S117–S126
Venet A, Bourgault I, Aubertin AM, Kieny MP, Levy JP (1992) Cytotoxic T lymphocyte response against multiple simian immunodeficiency virus A (SIV) proteins in SIV-infected macaques. J Immunol 148: 2899–2908
Vidovic M, Sparacio S, Elovitz M, Benveniste E (1990) Induction and regulation of class II major histocompatibility complex mRNA expression in astrocytes by interferon-gamma and tumor necrosis factor-alpha. J Neuroimmunol 30: 189–200
Vowels BR, Gershwin ME, Gardner MB, Ahmed AA, McGraw TP (1989) Characterization of simian immunodeficiency virus-specific T-cell-mediated cytotoxic response of infected rhesus macaques. AIDS 3: 785–792
Walker BD, Chakrabarti S, Moss B, Paradis TJ, Flynn T, Durno AG, Blumberg RS, Kaplan JC, Hirsch MS, Schooley RT (1987). HIV-specific cytotoxic T lymphocytes in seropositive individuals. Nature 328: 345–348
Walker BD, Flexner C, Paradis TJ, Fuller TC, Hirsch MS, Schooley RT, Moss B (1988) HIV-1 reverse transcriptase is a target for cytotoxic T lymphocytes in infected individuals. Science 240: 64–66
Walker BD, Flexner C, Birch LK, Fisher L, Paradis TJ, Aldovini A, Young R, Moss B, Schooley RT (1989) Long-term culture and fine specificity of human cytotoxic T-lymphocyte clones reactive with human immunodeficiency virus type 1. Proc Natl Acad Sci USA 86: 9514–9518

Walker CM, Levy JA (1989) A diffusible lymphokine produced by $CD8^+$ T lymphocytes suppresses HIV replication. Immunology 66: 628–630
Walker CM, Moody DJ, Stites DP, Levy JA (1986) $CD8^+$ lymphocytes can control HIV infection in vitro by suppressing virus replication. Science 234: 1563–1566
Warner JF, Anderson CG, Laube L, Jolly DJ, Townsend K, Chada S, St Louis D (1991) Induction of HIV-specific CTL and antibody responses in mice using retroviral vector-transduced cells. Aids Res Hum Retroviruses 7: 645–655
Weinhold KJ, Lyerly HK, Matthews TJ, Tyler DS, Ahearne PM, Stine KC, Langlois AJ, Durack DT, Bolognesi DP (1988) Cellular anti-GP120 cytolytic reactivities in HIV-1 seropositive individuals. Lancet 1: 902–905
Werner E, Bitterlich G, Fuchs D, Hausen A, Reibnegger G, Szabo G, Dierich M, Wachter H (1987) Human macrophages degrade tryptophan upon induction by interferon-gamma. Life Sci 41: 273–280
Yamamoto H, Miller MD, Tsubota H, Watkins DI, Mazzara GP, Stallard V, Panicali DL, Aldovini A, Young RA, Letvin NL (1990a) Studies of cloned simian immunodeficiency virus-specific T lymphocytes. Gag-specific cytotoxic T lymphocytes exhibit a restricted epitope specificity. J Immunol 144: 3385–3391
Yamamoto H, Miller MD, Watkins DI, Snyder GB, Chase NE, Mazzara GP, Gritz L, Panicali DL, Letvin NL (1990b) Two distinct lymphocyte populations mediate simian immunodeficiency virus envelope-specific target cell lysis. J Immunol 145: 3740–3746
Yamamoto H, Ringler DJ, Miller MD, Yasutomi Y, Hasunuma T, Letvin NL (1992) Simian immunodeficiency virus-specific cytotoxic T lymphocytes are present in the AIDS-associated skin rash in rhesus monkeys. J Immunol 149: 728–734
Yewdell JW, Bennink JR (1992) Cell biology of antigen processing and presentation to major histocompatibility complex class I molecule-restricted T lymphocytes. Adv Immunol 52: 1–123
Yewdell JW, Bennink JR, Smith GL, Moss B (1985) Influenza A virus nucleoprotein is a major target antigen for cross-reactive anti-influenza A virus cytotoxic T lymphocytes. Proc Natl Acad Sci USA 82: 1785–1789

Cytotoxic T Lymphocytes in Human Immunodeficiency Virus Infection: Regulator Genes

Y. RIVIERE, M. N. ROBERTSON, and F. BUSEYNE

1 Introduction

Like all retroviruses, the human immunodeficiency virus (HIV) provirus contains two long terminal repeat elements (LTR) along with the three structural genes—*gag, pol,* and *env*—that are essential for virus replication. In addition to these genetics elements, HIV contains at least six additional genes: *tat, rev, nef, vif, vpr,* and *vpu,* whose functions impart both positive and negative effects on the HIV life cycle (for review see CULLEN 1991; GREENE 1991; HASELTINE 1991; STEFFIE and WONG STAAL 1991; FEINBERG and GREENE 1992).

After attachment of the virion to its cellular receptor—the CD4 molecule—and penetration of the virion core into the cell, reverse transcription of the RNA genome into double-stranded DNA occurs. Following DNA synthesis, the viral DNA transits to the nucleus, and integration of the viral DNA into cellular DNA occurs to form the provirus. Once the provirus has been incorporated into the cellular DNA, both cellular and viral factors are required to initiate expression of viral genes. After activation of the provirus, the HIV life cycle can be divided into early and late stages by a transition in the character of viral transcripts produced following infection: early viral transcripts are the 2-kb RNA encoding the early regulatory nonstructural proteins with regulatory functions, the Tat, Rev and Nef proteins. The Tat protein is a powerful transactivator of HIV gene expression, and the Rev protein's main

Unité de Virologie et Immunologie Cellulaire, Institut Pasteur, 75724 Paris Cedex 15, France

Current Topics in Microbiology and Immunology, Vol. 189

function is to effect the transport of unspliced and singly spliced mRNA from the nucleus to the cytoplasm. Both Tat and Rev proteins are essential for HIV replication: loss of Tat function results in the absence of viral RNA and protein expression, and in the absence of Rev, viral structural proteins are not synthesized (in contrast to the Tat and Nef regulatory proteins). The transition from the early to the late stage in the virus cycle is dependent on the Rev protein; the Rev protein may act at a post-transcriptional level by activating cytoplasmic expression of unspliced and singly spliced mRNA encoding the products of the *gag*, *pol*, and *env* genes.

In contrast to the essential role of Tat and Rev in HIV replication, the four other additional proteins, Nef, Vif, Vpr, and Vpu have been called nonessential, because they can be deleted without completely abrogating the ability of the virus to replicate.

The p27-kDa Nef is a myristylated protein produced early in infection, since its mRNA is detectable along with the two regulatory nuclear proteins, Tat and Rev. The Nef protein is cytoplasmic and partly associated with membranes; it is not required for virus replication in vitro, but in vivo experiments with Simian immunodeficiency virus (SIV)-infected macaques indicate that in vivo Nef is important for virus expression and pathogenicity (KESTLER et al. 1991). On the cellular level, CD4 and interleukin 2 (IL-2) are downregulated by Nef expression. While the function of Nef still remains controversial, the Nef protein can possibly be classified among the regulatory proteins of HIV.

The precise functional role of the three other additional genes, *vpu*, *vpr*, and *vif*, in the viral cycle is not clear. The p15-kDa Vpu protein seems to interact with gp160–CD4 complexes in the late Golgi apparatus and to be involved in viral release. The p23-kDa Vif protein presumably plays a role in the late step of the replication cycle (infectious virion assembly) or in the early step (virus attachment and entry). The p18-kDa Vpr protein function is not well defined; the Vpr protein is made late in infection and because this protein is present in the virion, it could be considered as a structural protein.

2 Specificity of the Cellular Immune Response in Human Immunodeficiency Virus Type 1-Infected Donors to Non-structural Viral Proteins

HIV-specific cytotoxic lymphocytes which can specifically lyse target cells expressing HIV antigen have been described by a number of investigators (for review see MILLS et al. 1989; NIXON and MCMICHAEL 1991). In HIV-1-infected individuals, two forms of anti-HIV-specific cytotoxic activities can be detected: lysis mediated by major histocompatibility complex (MHC)-restricted cytotoxic T lymphocytes (CTL) and lysis mediated by antibody-dependent cellular cytotoxicity (ADCC), the latter involving non-MHC-restricted cytolytic activities of effector cell populations bearing HIV-specific cytophilic antibodies that direct their lytic activities. In HIV-1-infected individuals, ADCC has been shown to be mainly directed at the envelope glycoprotein (McCHESNEY et al. 1990; TANNEAU et al. 1990), but any other viral protein shown to be expressed at the surface of infected cells may be a target for ADCC.

A characteristic of HIV infection is the long-lasting detection of HIV-specific cytotoxic activities from fresh peripheral blood mononuclear cells (PBMC) without in vitro stimulation; this is likely to be due to a persistent antigenic stimulation in vivo. CTL activity derived from PBMC is vigorous and directed at most viral structural (Gag, Pol, Env) and nonstructural (Tat, Rev, Nef, Vpu, Vif) proteins (for review see AUTRAN and LETVIN 1991; NIXON and McMICHAEL 1991; VENET et al. 1993).

We and other investigators have been able to detect cytotoxic effector cells in the PBMC of HIV-1-infected individuals directed at most viral proteins, including structural and nonstructural proteins. In this paper, we will review cytotoxic activities specific for the nonstructural proteins. Using recombinant vaccinia viruses that express specific HIV proteins and Epstein-Barr virus (EBV)-transformed B lymphocytes as target cells, we have found that a variable percentage of HIV-1-infected donors have cytotoxic effector cells directed at Nef, Vif, and Rev (Table 1 and BUSEYNE et al. 1992). These virus-specific cytotoxic activities were detected in PBMC isolated from the blood immediately after lymphocyte separation and without in vitro stimulation (RIVIÈRE et al. 1989). We and others have found that nef-specific activities are MHC restricted and linked to $CD8^+$ $CD3^+$ T lymphocytes (KOENIG et al. 1990; BUSEYNE et al. 1992). It is likely that the Rev- and Vif-specific activities are also MHC restricted.

Table 1. Specificity and frequency of the cytotoxic activities from human immunodeficiency type 1 (HIV-1)-seropositive donor peripheral blood mononuclear cells

	Circulating[a]		In vitro restimulated			
			I[c]		II[d]	
	n	%	*n*	%	*n*	%
p27Nef	10/25	40	10/20	50	18/28	64
p23Vif	4/18	22	3/6	50	11/27	41
p14Tat	–[b]		2/6	33	1/26	4
p20Rev	3/13	23	7/16	44	8/22	36
p15Vpu	–[b]		–[b]		–[b]	
p18Vpr	–[b]		–[b]		–[b]	
p55Gag	35/54	65	25/29	86	26/28	93

[a] From BUSEYNE et al. 1992.
[b] There are no published data on circulating cytotoxic activities specific for p14Tat nor for any cytotoxic activities specific for p15 Vpu or p18 Vpr.
[c] From BUSEYNE et al. 1993a and unpublished results.
[d] From LAMHAMEDI-CHERADI et al. 1992.

In HIV-infected subjects, in vitro mitogen stimulation of T lymphocytes from PBMC or other lymphoid organs has been used to establish HIV-specific CTL lines or clones. These mitogen-induced effector cells have been used by a number of investigators to define CTL epitopes located in structural as well as nonstructural HIV proteins. Table 1 summarizes the frequency of recognition of the different nonstructural HIV proteins that have been reported (BUSEYNE et al. 1992; LAMHAMEDI-CHERADI et al. 1992). The p27Nef, p23Vif, and p20Rev proteins were recognized by CTL derived from stimulated PBMC with a similar frequency in the two different studies (range, 50%–64% for p27Nef, 41%–50% for p23Vif, and 36%–44% for p20Rev). The difference in the results for the Tat-specific CTL likely reflects the small number of individuals tested (six) in one study. Nothing has been reported concerning p15Vpu- or p18Vpr-specific CTL activity. Taken together, these results show that it has been possible to generate CTL specific to the nonstructural proteins of HIV (p27Nef, p23Vif, and p20Rev) from about 50% of the donors, although the same CTL lines react against p55Gag for 86% or more of the donors studied. This could be due to the fact that non-structural proteins are smaller and less conserved than the p55Gag.

3 Epitope Mapping of p27Nef: Two Regions of the Protein are Targets for Most of the CTL Activities

The p27nef protein CTL recognition has been extensively studied during recent years by several investigators (CHENCINER et al. 1989; CULMAN et al. 1989, 1991; RIVIÈRE et al. 1989; KOENIG et al. 1990; CHEYNIER et al. 1992; LAMHAMEDI-CHERADI et al. 1992; HADIDA et al. 1992a; BUSEYNE et al. 1993b). In particular, CTL lines or clones were derived by in vitro stimulation with mitogen such as phytohemagglutinin A or by anti-CD3 antibody and subsequent expansion with exogenous IL-2. These cell lines or clones were $CD3^+$ $CD8^+$ T cells. After characterization of the p27Nef CTL activity using autologous B-EBV targets infected with specific recombinant vaccinia viruses, epitope mapping of the protein was performed by using as targets B-EBV autologous cells coated with different peptides spanning the Nef amino acid sequence. Twenty-four different peptides have been shown to define epitopic regions within the p27Nef protein. Eighteen are clustered into two adjacent regions of the central portion of Nef (aa 66–106 for 11 peptides, aa 113–147 for seven) and four are clustered into the C-terminal end of the protein (aa 176–206; BOURGAULT et al. 1992; BUSEYNE et al. 1993b; CULMANN et al. 1989, 1991 and unpublished data; HADIDA et al. 1992a; JASSOY et al. 1992; KOENIG et al. 1990; MICHEL et al. 1992; and Table 2). For 23 of the T cell lines or clones, the MHC-restrictive element has been identified.

Table 2. Published epitopic regions within the p27 Nef protein

Species/Virus	Amino acid number	Amino acid sequence	MHC restriction	Reference
Human/HIV	66–80	VGFPVTPQVPLRPMT	A1	Hadida et al. 1992a
Human/HIV	73–82	QVPLRPMTYK	A3.1	Koenig et al. 1990
Human/HIV	73–82	QVPLRPMTYK	A3, B35, A11	Culmann et al. 1991
Human/HIV	73–82	QVPLRPMTYK	B35 or C4	Buseyne et al. 1993b
Human/HIV	73–82	QVPLRPMTYK	A2	Robertson and Rivière, unpublished
Human/HIV	74–81	VPLRPMTY	B35	Culmann et al. unpublished
Human/HIV	74–85	VPLRPMTYKAAV	B35 or C4, B17	Buseyne et al. unpublished
Macaque/SIV	108–123	LRAMTYKLAIDMSHFI	nd	Bourgault et al. 1992
Human/HIV	78–93	MTYKAAVDLSHFLKEK	nd	Culmann et al. 1989
Human/HIV	83–94	AAVDLSHFLKEK	A11	Culmann et al. 1991
Human/HIV	84–91	AVDLSHFL	Bw62	Culmann et al., unpublished
Human/HIV	84–92	AVDLSHFLE	A11	Culmann et al., unpublished
Human/HIV	86–100	DLSHFLKEKGGLEGL	B35 or C4	Buseyne et al. 1993b
Human/HIV	89–97	HFLKEKGGL	B8	Culmann et al., unpublished
Human/HIV	93–106	EKGGLEGLIHSQRR	A1	Hadida et al. 1992a
Human/HIV	113–128	WIYHTQGYFPDWQNYT	B17 & B37	Culmann et al. 1989
Human/HIV	113–128	WIYHTQGYFPDWQNYT	A1	Hadida et al. 1992a
Human/HIV	115–125	YHTQGYFPDW	B17	Culmann et al. 1991
Human/HIV	116–125	HTQGYFPDW	B17	Culmann et al., unpublished
Human/HIV	117–128	TQGYFPDWQNYT	B17 & B37	Culmann et al. 1991
Human/HIV	117–124	TQGYFPDW	Bw62	Culmann et al., unpublished
Human/HIV	120–128	YFPDWQNYT	B17 & B37	Culmann et al., unpublished
Human/HIV	120–144	YFPDWQ—TFGWCYK	A24	Jassoy et al. 1992
Macaque/SIV	155–169	DWQDYTSGPGIRYPK	nd	Bourgault et al. 1992
Human/HIV	126–138	NYTPGPGVRYPLT	B7	Culmann et al. 1991
Human/HIV	132–147	GVRYPLTFGWCYKLVP	A1	Hadida et al. 1992a
Human/HIV	132–147	GVRYPLTFGWCYKLVP	B18	Culmann et al. 1991
Macaque/SIV	164–178	GIRYPKTFGWLWKLV	nd	Bourgault et al. 1992
Human/HIV	134–144	GVRYPLTFGWCYKLVP	B18 et B49	Culmann et al., unpublished
Human/HIV	155–168	EANKGENTSLLHPV	nd	Rivière et al., unpublished
Human/HIV	176–185	PEREVLEWRF	nd	Rivière et al., unpublished
Mouse/RVV nef	175–190	DPEREVLEWRFDSRLA	H2d (IA, IE)	Michel et al. 1992
Mouse/RVV nef	182–198	EWRFDSRLAFHHVAREL	H2d (IA, IE)	Michel et al. 1992
Human/HIV	182–198	EWRFDSRLAFHHVAREL	A1 & B8	Hadida et al. 1992a
Human/HIV	188–201	RLAFHHVARELHPE	B35 or C4	Buseyne et al. 1993b
Human/HIV	192–206	HHVARELHPEYFKNC	A1	Hadida et al. 1992a

HIV, human immunodeficiency virus; SIV, simian immunodeficiency virus; RVV, recombinant vaccinia virus; MHC, major histocompatibility complex; nd, not determined.

Altogether, 15 distinct HLA molecules were shown to present 19 different peptides.

Four independent laboratories have reported that six different HLA molecules present peptides within the aa 66–85 region and four different HLA molecules have been reported to present peptides within the aa 84–97 region (Table 2). However, because the synthetic peptides that were used were 10–15 amino acids long, which is longer than the 8- to 9-mer expected length for naturally processed viral peptides (RÖTZCHKE et al. 1990; VAN BLEEK and NATHENSON 1990), it is likely that they included more than one unique T cell epitope; accordingly, a recent study performed by Culmann-Penciolelli et al., shows that peptide 73–82 was presented by the A3 and A11 molecules, peptide 74–81 by B35, and peptide 84–92 by A11 (Culmann-Penciolelli et al., personal communication). Within the aa 176–206 sequence of the C-terminal region, HADIDA et al. (1992b) recently reported that several HLA class I molecules (A1, A2, A24, B5, B8, and B31) efficiently present either identical or distinct peptides.

All these results show that the p27Nef protein is a very common target for CTL recognition in HIV-infected persons. Analysis of the various amino acid sequences published for the p27Nef protein revealed that the central region (aa 62–166) is rather conserved within HIV-1, HIV-2, and SIV isolates (MYERS et al. 1992). In experimentally infected macaques, three peptides from the homologous central region of SIV/nef (aa 108–123, aa 155–169, and aa 164–178) have been shown to include a T cell epitope (BOURGAULT et al. 1992; Table 2); these results could be explained by structural similarities between the nonhuman and the human primate MHC molecules. On the other hand, in splenocytes from mice immunized with recombinant vaccinia virus (RVV) encoding the HIV-1/Lai *nef* gene and stimulated in vitro with the homologous recombinant Nef protein, $CD4^+$ cytotoxic T cell activities restricted by MHC class II molecules of the H-2d haplotype were found directed to two peptides within the C-terminal region (MICHEL et al. 1992).

Both the great diversity of Nef peptides recognized by CTL and their HLA restricting elements show that the p27Nef protein is a widely recognized target for CTL in HIV-1-infected subjects, as is the case for the p24gag protein (BUSEYNE et al. 1993a). Because the *nef* gene is expressed early in the viral cycle through a Rev-independent RNA (ROBERT-GUROFF et al. 1990), it is likely that induction of HIV Nef-specific CTL activity will be beneficial to the infected host, allowing elimination of target cells expressing the Nef protein before release of the progeny virus, as has been shown for target cells acutely infected with vaccinia virus (ZINKERNAGEL and ALTHAGE 1977).

A recent report shows that infection with a live, attenuated SIV with a deletion in the Nef gene protects rhesus macaques against challenge by intravenous inoculation of the homologous live pathogenic SIV (DANIEL et al. 1992). The mechanisms responsible for the protective immunity observed in these experiments are not known. A possible role of CTL has been advanced;

surprisingly, the Nef deletion was in the central region of SIV nef (aa 58 to 118), which is very similar to the central region of HIV-1/Nef, where most Nef-specific CTL epitopes in HIV-infected humans are clustered. Another possibility would be protection by viral interference, but this seems unlikely because Nef is required for maintaining high virus loads during the course of persistent infection in vivo and a very small proportion of cells are thought to be infected by the Nef-deleted SIV (KESTLER et al. 1991).

4 Discussion

Analysis of the antigenic specificity of the CTL response directed to non-structural proteins in HIV infection reveals that almost all proteins could be targets for CTL- mediated lysis. A similar observation could be made for the viral structural proteins. In most viral infections, the functions of antigen-specific T lymphocyte are required for recovery from viral infection, for clearance of virus, and for control of persistent infection. In the case of HIV infection, little information is known about the biological role of the CTL in the course of this long infectious process, in which the disease usually appears after a long incubation period.

The control of HIV replication in $CD4^+$ T cells by autologous $CD8^+$ T cells from the PBMC of HIV-infected donors is a well-established phenomenon (WALKER et al. 1986). The precise mechanism of this antiviral activity, as well as the identification of the CD8 subsets responsible for this activity, needs further investigation. The antiviral activity has been shown to be mediated by a soluble $CD8^+$ T cell-derived factor that has not yet been identified, but the most efficient inhibition of virus replication further requires contact between the infected $CD4^+$ T cells and effector $CD8^+$ T cells (for review see RIVIÈRE 1990). Interestingly, $CD8^+$ T cells from patients with acquired immunodeficiency syndrome (AIDS) showed reduced or no such inhibitory activity (BRINCHMANN et al. 1990). Although the killing process per se may or may not be involved in the mechanism by which $CD8^+$ T cells control HIV replication (WALKER et al. 1991), this does not rule out the possibility that the same subset of $CD8^+$ T cells, i.e., HIV-specific CTL, are responsible for this activity. In fact, the treatment of severe combined immunodeficient (SCID) mice reconstituted with human T cells and infected with HIV by the injection of MHC-compatible HIV Nef-specific CTL clones leads to the control of HIV replication (KOENIG et al. 1992). In experimentally SIV-infected macaques, the presence of SIV-specific CTL activity correlates with both a reduced efficiency in isolating virus from the blood of these monkeys and with their extended survival (MILLER et al. 1990). In HIV-infected subjects, we have shown a link between the rate of evolution to AIDS-related complex (ARC) and AIDS and the absence of Gag-specific

CTL activity (RIVIÈRE et al. 1991). All these reports support the concept that a candidate AIDS vaccine should also induce a HIV-specific CTL activity.

Acknowledgements. We are grateful to B. Culmann for providing unpublished results and for helpful discussions. We thank L. Chakrabarti and M.L Michel for critical review of the manuscript.

References

Autran B, Letvin NL (1991) HIV epitopes recognized by cytotoxic T-lymphocytes. AIDS 5:S145–S150

Bourgault I, Venet A, Levy JP (1992) Three epitopic peptides of the simian immunodeficiency virus nef protein recognized by macaque cytolytic T lymphocytes. J Virol 66:750–756

Brinchmann JE, Gaudernack G, Vartdal F (1990) $CD8^+$ T cells inhibit HIV replication in naturally infected $CD4^+$ T cells. J Immunol 144:2961–2966

Buseyne F, McChesney M, Tanneau F, Montagnier L, Rivière Y (1992) Characterization of the cytotoxic immune responses to HIV-1. In: P Racz, N Letvin, J Gluckman (eds) Cytotoxic T cells in HIV and other retroviral infections. Basel, Karger, pp 81–85

Buseyne F, McChesney M, Porrot F, Kovarik S, Guy B, Rivière Y (1993a) Gag-specific cytotoxic T lymphocytes from human immunodeficiency virus type 1-infected individuals: gag epitopes are clustered in three regions of the $p24^{gag}$ protein. J Virol 67:694–702

Buseyne F, Blanche S, Schmitt D, Griscelli C, Rivière Y (1993b) Detection of HIV-specific cell mediated cytotoxicity in the peripheral blood from infected children. J Immunol 150: 3569–3581

Chenciner N, Michel F, Dadaglio G, Langlade-Demoyen P, Hoffenbach A, Leroux A, Garcia-Pons F, Rautmann G, Guy B, Guillon JM, Mayaud C, Girard M, Autran B, Kieny MP, Plata F (1989) Multiple subsets of HIV-specific cytotoxic T lymphocytes in humans and in mice. Eur J Immunol 19:1537–1544

Cheynier R, Langlade-Demoyen P, Marescot M-R, Blanche S, Blondin G, Wain-Hobson S, Griscelli C, Vilmer E, Plata F (1992) Cytotoxic T lymphocytes responses in the pheripheral blood of children born to human immunodeficiency virus-1-infected mothers. Eur J Immunol 22:2211–2217

Cullen BR (1991) Regulation of HIV-1 gene expression. FASEB J 5:2361–2368

Culmann B, Gomard E, Kieny MP, Guy B, Dreyfus F, Saimot A-G, Sereni D, Levy JP (1989) An antigenic peptide of the HIV-1 nef protein recognized by cytotoxic T lymphocytes of seropositive individuals in association with different HLA-B molecules. Eur J Immunol 19:2383–2386

Culmann B, Gomard E, Kieny M-P, Guy B, Dreyfus F, Saimot A-G, Sereni D, Sicard D, Levy JP (1991) Six epitopes reacting with human cytotoxic $CD8^+$ T cells in the central region of the HIV-1 nef protein. J Immunol 146:1560–1565

Daniel MD, Kirchhoff F, Czajak SC, Sehgal PK, Desrosiers RC (1992) Protective effects of a live attenuated SIV vaccine with a deletion in the *nef* gene. Science 258:1938–1941

Feinberg MB, Greene WC (1992) Molecular insights into human immunodeficiency virus type 1 pathogenesis. Curr Opin Immunol 4:466–474

Greene WC (1991) The molecular biology of human immunodeficiency virus type 1 infection. N Engl J Med 324:308–317

Hadida F, Parrot F, Kieny MP, Sadat-Sowti B, Mayaud C, Debrè P, Autran B (1992a) Carboxyl-terminal and central regions of human immunodeficiency virus-1 *nef* recognized by cytotoxic T lymphocytes from lymphoid organs. J Clin Invest 89:53–60

Hadida F, Samri A, Hosmalin A, Spohn R, Jung G, Debrè P, Autran B (1992b). Characterization of several promiscuous CTL epitopes in the C-terminal region of Nef. 8th international conference on AIDS, Amsterdam, ThA 1576

Haseltine WA (1991) Molecular biology of the human immunodeficiency virus type 1. FASEB J 5:2349–2360

Jassoy C, Johnson RP, Navia BA, Worth J, Walker BD (1992) Detection of a vigorous HIV-1 specific cytotoxic T lymphocyte response in cerebrospinal fluid from infected persons with AIDS dementia complex. J Immunol 149: 3113–3119
Kestler III HW, Ringler DJ, Mori K, Panicalli DL, Sehgal PK, Daniel MD, Desrosiers RC (1991) Importance of the *nef* gene for maintenance of high virus loads and for development of AIDS. Cell 65: 651–662
Koenig S, Fuerst TR, Wood LV, Woods RM, Suzich JA, Jones GM, De La Cruz VF, Davey RT, Venkatesan S, Moss B, Biddison WE, Fauci AS (1990) Mapping the fine specificity of a cytolytic T cell response to HIV-1 *nef* protein. J Immunol 145: 127–135
Koenig S, Van Kuyk R, Jones G, Torbett B, Mosier D, Brewah YA, Leath S, Davey VJ, Yannelli J, Rosenberg S, Fauci AS, Lane HC (1992) Adoptive transfer of a nef-specific CTL clone into hu-PBL-SCID mice and an HIV-infected patient. 8th international conference on AIDS, Amsterdam, ThA 1573
Lamhamedi-Cherradi S, Culmann-Penciolelli B, Guy B, Kieny M-P, Dreyfus F, Saimot A-G, Sereni D, Sicard D, Levy JP, Gomard E (1992) Qualitative and quantitative analysis of human cytotoxic T-lymphocyte responses to HIV-1 proteins. AIDS 6: 1249–1258
McChesney M, Tanneau F, Regnault A, Sansonetti P, Montagnier L, Kieny M-P, Rivière Y (1990) Detection of primary cytotoxic T lymphocytes specific for the envelope glycoprotein of HIV-1 by deletion of the env amino-terminal signal sequence. Eur J Immunol 20: 215–220
Michel F, Hoffenbach A, Froussard P, Langlade-Demoyen P, Kaczorek M, Kieny MP, Plata F (1992) HIV-1 *env, nef* and *gag*-specific T-cell immunity in mice: conserved epitopes in *nef* p27 and *gag* p25 proteins. AIDS Res Hum Retrovirus 8: 469–478
Miller MD, Lord CI, Stallard V, Mazzara G, Letvin NL (1990) The gag specific cytotoxic T lymphocytes in rhesus monkeys infected with the simian immunodeficiency virus of macaques. J Immunol 144: 122–128
Mills KHG, Nixon DF, McMichael AJ (1989) T-cell strategies in AIDS vaccines: MHC-restricted T-cell responses to HIV proteins. AIDS 3: S101-S110
Myers G, Berzofsky JA, Korber RF, Smith T, Pavlakis GN (1992) A compilation and analysis of nucleic acid and amino-acid sequences. Los Alamos National Laboratory, Los Alamos, N Mex
Nixon DF, McMichael AJ (1991) Cytotoxic T-cell recognition of HIV proteins and peptides. AIDS 5: 1049–1059
Riviere Y (1990) The cellular immune response to the human immunodeficiency virus. Curr Opin Immunol 2: 424–427
Rivière Y, Tanneau-Salvadori F, Regnault A, Lopez O, Sansonetti P, Guy B, Kieny MP, Fournel JJ, Montagnier L (1989) Human immunodeficiency virus-specific cytotoxic responses of seropositive individuals: distinct types of effector cells mediate killing of targets expressing gag and env proteins. J Virol 63: 2270–2277
Rivière Y, McChesney M, Porrot F, Tanneau F, Buseyne F, Regnault A, Kovarik S, Sansonetti P, Lopez O, Mollereau M, Pialoux G, Marie C, Chamaret S, Kieny MP, Tekaia F, Montagnier L (1991) Relation between HIV disease stages and the activities of HIV specific cytotoxic effector cells. In: Girard M, Valette L (eds) 6è Colloque des Cent Gardes. Mèrieux, Lyon
Robert-Guroff M, Popovic M, Gartner S, Markham P, Gallo RC, Reitz M (1990) Structure and expression of tat, rev and nef specific transcripts of human immunodeficiency virus type 1 in infected lymphocytes and macrophages. J Virol 64: 3391–3398
Robertson MN, Buseyne F, Schwartz O, Rivière Y (1993) Expression of the HIV-1 nef protein by a retroviral vector in an efficient way to present antigen to specific cytotoxic lymphocytes. AIDS Research and human retroviruses 9(12): 1211–1217
Rötzchke O, Falk K, Deres H, Schild H, Norda N, Metzger J, Jüng G, Rammensee HG (1990) Isolation and analysis of naturally processed viral peptides as recognized by cytotoxic T cells. Nature 348: 252–254
Steffy K, Wong-Staal F (1991) Genetic regulation of human immunodeficiency virus. Microbiol Rev 55: 193–205
Tanneau F, McChesney M, Lopez O, Sansonetti P, Montagnier L, and Rivière Y (1990) Primary cytotoxicity against the envelope glycoprotein of human immunodeficiency virus-I: evidence for antibody-dependent cellular cytotoxicity in vivo. J Infect Dis 162: 837–843
Van Bleck GM, and Nathenson SG (1990) Isolation of an endogenously processed immuno-dominant viral peptide from the class I H-2kb molecule. Nature 348: 213–216
Venet A, Gomard E, Levy J (1993) Human T cell responses to HIV. In: Thomas DB (ed) Viruses and the cellular immune responses. Marcel Dekker. New York, pp 165–200

Walker CM, Moody DJ, Shites DP, and Levy JA (1986) CD8⁺ lymphocytes can control HIV infection in vitro by suppressing virus replication. Science 234: 1563–1566
Walker CM, Erickson AL, Hsueh FC, Levy JA (1991) Inhibition of human immunodeficiency virus replication in acutely infected CD4⁺ cells by CD8⁺ cells involves a noncytotoxic mechanism. J Virol 65: 5921–5927
Zinkernagel RM, Althage A (1977) Antiviral protection by virus-immune cytotoxic T cells: infected target cells are lysed before infectious virus progeny is assembled. J Exp Med 145: 644–651

Cytotoxic T Lymphocytes Specific for Influenza Virus

A. McMichael

1 Introduction

Influenza virus has proved an excellent model for the study of the specificity of cytotoxic T lymphocytes (CTL) and of the processing of viral antigens. Fundamental information about these processes has been gained in both mice and humans. At the same time, a considerable amount has been learned about the role of CTL in influenza viral infections, particularly in mice. The virus has proved to be a malleable tool because it can be readily grown, the full nucleotide structure has been determined (in the 1970s; reviewed in Lamb 1983), there are multiple antigenic variants, many of which have been sequenced, the three-dimensional structures of haemagglutinin and neuraminidase are known (Varghese et al. 1983; Wiley et al. 1981) and, for human studies, it has the advantage that it has infected a very high percentage of the population. All of these features combine to make this a safe and invaluable model for the study of theoretical aspects of T cell function as well as investigating the practical issues of how T cells control virus infections. Studies with influenza virus answered long-standing questions about the interaction between viral antigens and class I molecules of the major histocompatibility complex (MHC). Along the way came information about mutant and variant MHC molecules and the demonstration that peptide

Institute of Molecular Medicine, John Radcliffe Hospital, Oxford, UK

Current Topics in Microbiology and Immunology, Vol. 189

epitopes presented by class I MHC molecules are recognised by CTL. More recently, the virus has been invaluable for the elucidation of the antigen-processing pathways.

2 Influenza as a Model for the Study of Antigen Presentation

2.1 Identification of Peptide Epitopes

Influenza virus is a negative strand RNA virus, whose genome is segmented into eight subunits which can be reassorted in dually infected cells (reviewed in PALESE and YOUNG 1983). The eight RNA segments code for ten proteins, seven of which are present in the virus (LAMB 1983). These are two surface glycoproteins, haemagglutinin and neuraminidase, the viral matrix protein, three RNA polymerases, PB1, PB2 and PA and the nucleoprotein NP. In infected cells three other proteins are expressed, the non-structural proteins NS1 and NS2 and a surface protein encoded by the matrix segment M2. The haemagglutinin and the neuraminidase are highly variable, much of the variation being selected by the humoral immune response (WILEY et al. 1981). Human infections are caused by type A and type B viruses, which, although similar, are structurally quite distantly related. Antigenic differences in the surface glycoproteins of type A virus are the basis of the division of the virus into the major subtypes H1N1, H2N2 and H3N2. When these subtypes first appeared, they caused pandemic influenza because of poor or absent pre-existing humoral immunity in humans; H1N1 virus is thought to have caused the 1919 pandemic, H2N2 caused the Asian influenza of 1957 and H3N2 the Hong Kong influenza of 1968. In subsequent years there was antigenic drift in both haemaglutinin and neuraminidase of each subtype, selected by the humoral immune response in human populations. Such strains are normally identified by their year and place of isolation, e.g. A/Puerto Rico/1934 (A/PR/8/34, an H1N1 virus). The virus can infect most mammalian cell types, but the infection is productive in only a few. This appears to relate to the cleavage of the haemagglutinin into subunits HA1 and HA2, which is essential for virus infectivity and function (GARTEN et al. 1989).

CTL specific for influenza virus were first demonstrated in mice in 1977 (ZWEERINK et al. 1977) and shortly after in humans (MCMICHAEL et al. 1977). Similar strategies were used, lymphocytes were removed from previously infected individuals, restimulated with autologous virus infected cells for 7–14 days and then tested for lytic activity on virus-infected target cells. MHC class I restriction, the hallmark of CTL-mediated lysis of target cells (ZINKERNAGEL and DOHERTY 1979), was demonstrated in both mice and humans. An early finding was that CTL did not discriminate between major virus subtypes; for instance, H3N2-specific CTL-lysed H1N1 infected cells equally well even when human donors were used who had never been infected with the latter virus (McMichael and Askonas 1978). At first it was thought that CTL recognized shared epitopes in the surface glycoproteins, such as haemagglutinin, even though these were in some cases only 30% homologous; later experiments showed that the CTL were largely recognising conserved internal virus proteins (see below). Influenza-specific CTL proved to be exquisitely sensitive to small changes in MHC structure. CTL failed to recognise viral antigen presented by serologically defined HLA A2 molecules (McMichael 1978), which were then shown to differ in amino acid sequence (Biddison et al. 1980; Krangel et al. 1982); subsequently, similar findings were made for other HLA antigens such as HLA B27 (Breuning et al. 1982; Parham et al. 1988). In each case, the variant HLA class I molecules differ in only one to four amino acids. These variants are therefore very like the mutants of H-2 K^b, both structurally and functionally (Nathenson et al. 1986).

In 1981 the first CTL clones specific for influenza virus were derived (Lin and Askonas 1981). Like the polyclonal cultures, most of these were fully cross-reactive when tested with different influenza virus strains. Of the strain-specific clones, some recognised HA (Lukacher et al. 1984), but two clones were identified that distinguished between 1934 and 1968 viruses (Bennink et al. 1982; Townsend and Skehel 1982). Using reassorted viruses, in which RNA segments had been mixed, both Bennink et al. and Townsend et al. mapped the specificity of their CTL clones. The former mapped to PB2 polymerase and the latter to NP, both of which differed in a few amino acids between the 1934 and 1968 virus strains. These results were followed up by testing CTL against target cells transfected with cDNA corresponding to single virus products. Braciale et al. (1984) had demonstrated HA-specific CTL, but Townsend et al. demonstrated that his clone was NP specific and, in the same study, that the majority of polyclonal CTL in H-2^b mice were specific for NP (Townsend et al. 1984). Subsequently, the majority of murine and human CTL were shown to react with NP, PB2, HA and M (Bennink et al. 1986; Yewdell et al. 1985; Gotch et al. 1987a); it is of interest that the anti-M response, which is prominant in humans (Gotch et al. 1987), is barely found in mice, although the murine cell line P815 transfected with HLA A2 can readily present virus to human matrix protein-specific CTL (Rowland-Jones and McMichael, unpublished).

These findings raised the question of how an internal protein was presented to CTL when it could not be detected intact on the surface of infected cells. Arguing that the internal virus proteins might be processed in a similar way to protein antigens presented by class II MHC, Townsend et al. transfected fragments of NP into target cells and demonstrated that fragments were recognized by CTL, but that different fragments appeared to be presented by different MHC class I antigens (Townsend et al. 1985).

GOODING and O'CONNELL (1983) had previously carried out a similar experiment with CTL specific for the T antigen of SV40. It was later demonstrated that cells transfected with cDNA for haemaglutinin with the signal sequence deleted lysed those targets very efficiently, even though HA was absent from the cell surface (TOWNSEND et al. 1986a). From all of these results it was argued that CTL might recognize cytoplasmic proteins degraded to peptide fragments. Therefore, peptides were added to uninfected cells and it was found that CTL lysed the targets (TOWNSEND et al. 1986b). Furthermore, in the initial experiments it was clear that H-2Db and HLA B37 presented different peptides from NP. These results implied that the class I MHC molecules bound antigenic peptides in a specific fashion and presented them to CTL.

Shortly after these findings were made, the crystal structure of HLA A2 was solved and unidentified electron density, thought (and now known) to be a mixture of peptides, was present in a cleft on the membrane-distal surface of the molecule (BJORKMAN et al. 1987a, b). Most of the polymorphism in the MHC class I molecules was in residues whose side chains contributed to this groove, and as further class I molecules, HLA A68, B27 and H-2K^b, have been solved (FREMONT et al. 1992; GARRETT et al. 1989; MADDEN et al. 1992; ZHANG et al. 1992), it has become clear that there are fine differences in the grooves of different class I molecules, explaining why they bind different peptide epitopes.

Several epitopes have been identified in the various proteins of influenza virus that are presented by different MHC class I molecules; these are summarised in Table 1. It is clear that different class I MHC molecules select different peptide epitopes. Peptides have been eluted from different class I MHC molecules (FALK et al. 1991b; HUNT et al. 1992; JARDETZKY et al. 1991), and it is clear that peptides binding to each are short and have different sequence motifs. Thus, peptides binding to HLA A2 have leucine or isoleucine at position 2 and leucine, isoleucine or valine at position 9 (HUNT et al. 1992) and often an aromatic residue at position 3 (PARKER et al. 1992); peptides binding to HLA B27 have arginine at position 2, often an aromatic residue at position 3 and usually an arginine or lysine at position 9 (JARDETZKY et al. 1991). Peptides are most commonly nine amino acids in length, but the range is from eight to 12. Experiments on presentation of influenza virus by site-directed mutant MHC molecules orientated peptides with the amino terminus on the left and the carboxyl terminus on the right (LATRON et al. 1991). For instance, the introduction of an arginine at position 116 in the floor of the groove in HLA A2 impaired presentation of the influenza matrix peptide 58–66, but normal titration could be restored by changing position 9 to arginine. More recently, exchange of six amino acids which form the B pocket in the groove from HLA B27 sequence to HLA A2 sequence changed the specificity of the second anchor residue in the peptide from arginine to leucine (COLBERT et al. 1993). Fine structural analysis has revealed that the amino terminus binds into the A pocket at the left-hand end of the groove, where there are four conserved tyrosines (MADDEN et al. 1992).

Table 1. Cytotoxic T lymphocyte epitopes in influenza A virus

Virus Protein	First residue	Amino acid sequence	MHC restriction	References
Nucleoprotein (NP)	50-	SDYEGRLI	H-2K^k	Bastin et al. 1987; Cossins et al. 1993
	91-	KTGGPIYKR	HLA Aw68	Cerundolo et al. 1991; Guo et al. 1992
	147-	TYQRTRALV	H-2K^d	Bodmer et al. 1988; Falk et al. 1991a
	342-	FEDLRVLSFI	HLA B37	McMichael et al. 1986
	366-	ASNENMETL	H-2D^b	Falk et al. 1991a; Townsend et al. 1986b
	380-	ELRSRYWAI	HLA 38	Sutton et al. 1993
	383-	SRYWAIRTR	HLA B2705	Huet et al. 1990
Matrix protein (M1)	58-	GILGFVFTL	HLA A2	Gammon et al. 1992; Gotch et al. 1987b; Morrison et al. 1992
Haemagglutinin (HA)	204-	LYQNVGTYV	H-2 K^d	Hahn et al. 1992
	210-	TYVSVGTSTL	H-2 K^d	Hahn et al. 1992
	259-	FEANGNLI	H-2 K^k	Gould et al. 1991
(HA2)	10-	IEGGWTGMI	H-2 K^k	Gould et al. 1991
		IYSTVASSL	H-2 K^d	Milligan et al. 1990
Non-structural protein-1	152-	EEGAIVGEI	H-2 K^k	Cossins et al. 1993

These form a hydrogen bond network with the amino terminus; disruption of this network by changing one of these tyrosines to phenylalanine greatly peptide presentation (LATRON et al. 1992). Similarly at the C terminus, hydrogen bonds are formed in the F pocket with Thr-84 and Tyr-143 (MADDEN et al. 1992). The most detail is known about how the HLA A68 presents peptide NP101–109. HLA A68 has been crystallised with this peptide in the groove and the three-dimensional structure determined (GUO et al. 1992; SILVER et al. 1992). Again, the amino terminus fits in the A pocket and the carboxyl terminus in the F pocket, the interactions being very similar to those described for HLA B27. Because of the conservation of the A and F pockets in classical class I molecules, it is likely that they all bind peptides in the same way.

Experiments on influenza virus have also revealed details of antigen processing. As more epitopes are determined, there appears to be some clustering of epitopes in influenza NP (Table 1). This may indicate sites of preferential cleavage, perhaps related to the three-dimensional structure of NP. Similar clustering has been found in HIV gag and HIV nef (CULMANN et al. 1991), two other proteins in which multiple epitopes are known (McMichael et al., unpublished). Clustered epitopes in restricted regions mean that many overlap, with possible consequences in terms of competition for processing pathways or binding to class I molecules.

2.2 Processing of Influenza Virus Proteins

TOWNSEND and colleagues argued that peptides generated in the cytoplasm need to be transported into the endoplasmic reticulum (ER), where they would meet the MHC molecules (TOWNSEND and BODMER 1988). Because epitopes were found in many different places in given proteins, they could not have common signal sequences. This implied a role for transporters to take peptides across the ER membrane. A mutant cell line, RMA-S, was found where class I MHC was not expressed on the cell surface but unfolded heavy chains were present in the ER (TOWNSEND et al. 1989b). Addition of influenza NP epitope peptides to these cells stabilised expression of class I molecules on the surface, probably by binding to unstable empty molecules (TOWNSEND et al. 1989a). Thus, these cells could present added peptide, but when infected with influenza virus, CTL did not react. Added peptide is thought to bind to empty class I molecules on the surface of cells because they can still bind and present in the presence of brefeldin A, which inhibits passage of proteins through the Golgi network (NUCHTERN et al. 1989; YEWDELL and BENNINK 1989). In the RMA-s cell line, empty class I molecules come out to the surface in an unstable form that can be stabilised by cooling, addition of anti-MHC antibody or binding a (influenza NP) peptide epitope (LJUNGGREN et al. 1990). All of these data implied that there was a fault in the antigen-processing pathway in RMA-S. A human mutant cell line, 721.174, and its derivative T2, showed a similar phenotype (CERUNDOLO et al. 1990). This fault could be corrected by transfecting with a minigene for a peptide, influenza matrix 57–68, encompassing the epitope presented by HLA A2 (58–66), provided it had a signal sequence to take it into the ER (ANDERSON et al. 1991); this again supported the assumption that the fault was in the delivery of peptide into the ER. The T2/721.174 cell lines have a large deletion in the class II region of the MHC and this region was therefore targeted in the search for possible transporter genes. Two, *TAP-1* and *TAP-2*, which encode the two chains of an adenosine triphosphate (ATP)-binding cassette transporter protein (SPIES et al. 1992), were found in this region in HLA and the equivalent region of H-2 (DEVERSON et al. 1990; MONACO et al. 1990; SPIES et al. 1990; TROWSDALE et al. 1990), and transfection of these genes into mutant cell lines corrected the defect (SPIES et al. 1992). It is clear, therefore, that the transporters are important in the processing of cytoplasmic antigens. However, it is still not absolutely certain that they actually transport peptides; LEVY et al. (1991) using a microsome preparation found that added peptides could enter the microsomes without the need for ATP. Despite this finding, it is widely held that the *TAP* gene products actually transport peptides.

It is very clear that the antigen-processing pathway for peptides presented by class I and II MHC is very different. MORRISON et al. (1986) first showed differential susceptibility of the processing of HA epitopes to class I- and II-restricted T cell clones to chloroquine and fixation of antigen-presenting cells. Later, it was shown that T2 cells retained the ability to present to class II-restricted T cells, while presentation through class I was lost (ZWEERINK et al. 1993).

Once in the ER, peptides bind to MHC class I molecules. TOWNSEND has demonstrated that they stabilise newly folded class I molecules (ELLIOTT et al. 1991; TOWNSEND et al. 1990). Binding affinities are greatest for optimum length peptides (ELLIOTT et al. 1991), which can bind to free heavy chain in the absence of β_2-microglobulin. It is not clear, however, where the optimum length peptide is generated. A likely candidate for mediating the proteolytic cleavage is the multi-catalytic protease complex (GLYNNE et al. 1991; KELLY et al. 1991; MARTINEZ and MONACO 1991; ORTIZ-NAVARETTE et al. 1991). Two components of the 20–30 that make up the particle are encoded within the MHC, although in experimental systems, the T2 cell line with the transporters transfected back, but still deficient in these two genes, present antigen perfectly well (MOMBURG et al. 1992). If this complex generates peptides which are transported into the ER, it is likely they are cleaved to the optimum length within the ER. The known specificity of proteases is to clip on the C-terminal side of hydrophobic or charged residues (DJABALLAH and RIVETT 1992). In an analysis of more than 50 peptide epitopes that have been carefully defined, we have noted that the C terminus is highly preserved ELLIOTT et al. (1983). Isoleucine and leucine are the commonest residues, followed by arginine and lysine and, in some cases, tyrosine and phenylalanine.

Occasionally, phenylalanine and valine have been found; the majority of amino acids have never been observed. The three types of C terminus correlate with the pocket close to the F pocket in the peptide-binding groove, with position 116 playing a key role. If this is tyrosine (as in HLA A2), the C terminus tends to be isoleucine, leucine or valine (in descending order of frequency). If residue 116 is aspartic acid (as in HLA B27), arginine or lysine are preferred, although isoleucine is sometimes found. If 116 is serine, tyrosine is preferred, possibly forming a hydrogen bond. These requirements are not absolute and there are exceptions, but these are still within this limited range of amino acids. Therefore, it has been suggested that the C terminus is largely determined by the proteases (ROTZSCHKE and FALK 1991; ELLIOTT et al. 1993). Peptides would then be delivered into the ER, by the transporters, with hydrophobic or positively charged termini. Further modification of the peptides would occur at the N terminus, either before or after peptide has bound. It has been suggested that the MHC-encoded protease components divert the protease activity away from cleaving after acidic residues; acidic C termini have not yet been found in epitope peptides (Gaczynska et al. 1993). There is some evidence that the amino acid sequences flanking the epitope may affect processing (CERUNDOLO et al. 1991; EISENLOHR et al. 1992), but other evidence implies that the position of the epitope in the protein has little effect (HAHN et al. 1992). Overall, there is still much to learn about the generation of the epitope peptides and it should be emphasised that there is still no firm evidence that the proteasome is responsible for proteolytic cleavage of viral proteins in the cytoplasm of infected cells.

2.3 T Cell Receptors Used by Anti-Influenza CTL

T cell receptors used by influenza-specific CTL have been analysed by determining the receptors of cloned CTL (BOWNESS et al. 1993; MOSS et al. 1991). MOSS et al. found that for CTL recognising influenza matrix protein and presented by HLA A2, there was a very large predominance of T cell clones with $V_\alpha 10$ and $V_\beta 17$. More recent results have confirmed that $V_\beta 17$ occurs in about 70% of all T cell clones that recognise this particular peptide epitope (Lehner and Borysiewicz, personal communication). Very similar receptors, differing in only one or two conservative amino acids, have been found in receptors generated from different individuals. This is a remarkable result considering the enormous diversity of the total T cell receptor repertoire, with over 10^{14} possibilities (DAVIS and BJORKMAN 1989). Similar results were obtained by Bowness et al. for HLA B27-restricted CTL recognising an NP peptide. Here, $V_\beta 7$ and 8 and $V_\alpha 12, 14$ and 22 were preferred with, again, very similar receptors in clones derived from different individuals. Furthermore, in both the HLA A2- and B27-restricted responses there was marked conservation of J_α and conservation of the junctional region in the

β-chain, normally the most variable part of the receptor because of the contributions of V_β, D_β, J_β plus random N-diversity. These results imply that T cell receptor usage of HLA class I virus-specific CTL is highly restricted, although even in very similar receptors, fine specificity differences can be identified (Bowness et al. and Haurum et al., unpublished). These results have at least one important implication, namely that in HLA-associated disease, different individuals may use very similar receptors and have similar fine specificities and cross-reactions. In the context of influenza, the findings also suggest at new explanation for the lethal combination of staphylococcal and influenza virus infecion (ROBERTSON et al. 1958), namely that superantigens may subvert the reacting, clonally restricted, T cells.

3 Influenza-Specific CTL in Recovery from Infection

YAP et al. (YAP and ADA 1978b) were the first to transfer CTL-enriched cultures to mice with influenza pneumonitis. CD8-positive cells were found to reduce lung virus titres, while CD8-depleted cells did not. These experiments were repeated and extended later with influenza-specific CTL clones with similar results (LIN and ASKONAS 1981; LUKACHER et al. 1984). Both NP-specific and HA-specific clones mediate the effect. Nude mice are vulnerable to influenza infection; they have a higher mortality and survivors secrete virus chronically (WELLS et al. 1981a). Nude mice recovered when CTL were transferred. In these experiments passive antibody failed to clear virus (WELLS et al. 1981b). All of these experiments point to a role for CTL in the recovery phase of influenza virus infection, a conclusion supported by histological inspection of recovering lungs (MACKENZIE et al. 1989). It is obvious that CTL cannot neutralise free virus, but by killing infected cells before the generation of new virus particles CTL could terminate virus replication. It is also possible that CTL release γ-interferon with direct effects on virus replication in infected cells as well as activating natural killer cells and causing up-regulation of class I MHC antigens to enhance presentation (MORRIS et al. 1982). Recently, there has been a discrepant result; Tite et al. immunised mice with a recombinant NP preparation and found good protection from infection with live virus in the absence of a CTL response, but in the presence of a $CD4^+$ T cell response (TITE et al. 1990a). Now that it is known that CD4 T cells can be divided into Th1 and Th2 subsets according to the pattern of cytokines secreted, it will be important to reassess the roles of these subsets protection. It is likely that in real life several types of immune response will combine to give protective immunity.

YAP et al. (YAP and ADA 1978a) measured the CTL response in mouse spleens early in influenza virus infection. They found that CTL were measurable before the primary IgM antibody response. Thus, CTL could be largely responsible for the initial clearance of virus early in an infection. In some infections, this phase is associated with briefly enhanced symptoms, for instance a fever and rash. It should also be pointed out that although in other infections CTL may contribute to immunopathology (BUCHMEIER et al. 1980; CANNON et al. 1988; KRETH et al. 1982; PLATA et al. 1987; SETHI et al. 1988), this does not appear to be the case in influenza infection.

In humans, CTL activity was measured in volunteers who were challenged intranasally with influenza virus (MCMICHAEL et al. 1983b). There was a correlation between the levels of CTL activity and clearance of intranasal virus, measured 3 and 4 days later. Anti-haemagglutinin antibody also protected, but there were individuals who appeared to be protected by CTL in the absence of any neutralising antibody. Similarly, patients with hypogammaglobulinaemia appear to have handled pandemic influenza normally, despite any protection from administered γ-globulin (MACCALLUM 1971).

How does this fit in to the epidemiology of influenza virus infection in humans, particularly the observation that humans are repeatedly infected with the virus throughout life? Neutralising antibody is primarily directed against the HA and selects HA variants in the population (WEBSTER et al. 1982; WILEY et al. 1981). Thus, protection by antibody becomes progressively less efficient as the years go by. In contrast, human CTL recognise the less variable internal virus proteins particularly NP and M1 (GOTCH et al. 1987a). In vitro, CTL cross-react between viruses of different subtypes. Thus, a good CTL memory response might protect against most strains of virus. Although CTL cannot protect against infection, they should clear virus more rapidly resulting in less severe disease, as in the volunteer studies (MCMICHAEL et al. 1983b). However, clinical experience is that humans are susceptible to several moderate to severe attacks of influenza in a lifetime. The probable explanation is that in the absence of persisting viral antigen, CTL memory declines after acute infection. When CTL responses in naturally infected humans were observed over time such a decline was observed, giving an approximate half-life of 4 years for influenza-specific CTL (MCMICHAEL et al. 1983a). Recently, more evidence has been obtained in mice to suggest that CTL memory requires persisting viral antigen (OEHEN et al. 1992).

The real test of CTL immunity in humans comes when a new pandemic virus strain appears, as occurred in 1919, 1957 and 1968. A very high proportion of humans are susceptible at these times because of a complete absence of protective antibody (except in the elderly) and the mortality is high. Yet, at the same time many individuals have subclinical infections (FOY et al. 1976); perhaps many of these individuals are protected by cross-reactive CTL and clear virus rapidly (ASKONAS et al. 1982). This hypothesis can be tested when a new pandemic strain emerges.

4 Influenza Vaccine Design

This knowledge of cellular immunity to influenza virus infection has implications for vaccine design. Most of the influenza vaccines in use are killed virus preparations or subunit vaccines. These cannot be expected to deliver cytoplasmic antigens efficiently to the class I antigen-processing system. Studies on vaccines in mice and humans showed that they are poor at stimulating CTL responses (McMichael et al. 1981; Webster and Askonas 1980). Influenza vaccines are not entirely satisfactory. At least one study has shown that over several years, annual vaccination is slightly less effective than no vaccination followed by natural infection (Hoskins et al. 1979).

Knowledge of antigen processing and peptide epitope presentation to CTL suggests new ways of vaccinating to maximise the CTL response. Recombinant virus vaccines such as vaccinia are effective in inducing CTL responses in animals and humans (Bennink et al. 1984; Gotch et al. 1991); however, their use for influenza vaccination is unlikely, except possibly in the face of a very severe pandemic. Recombinant bacteria such as oral salmonella have been shown to induce CTL responses to influenza NP, but rather inefficiently (Gao et al. 1991, 1992). Recombinant proteins and killed virus preparations are not efficient in generating CTL responses (Tite et al. 1990b; Webster and Askonas 1980), probably because the injected materials fail to find their way into the class I MHC-processing pathway. An alternative approach would be to use peptides to induce a pure CTL response, although multiple peptides would have to be used to cover the common HLA types and hence the majority of the population. Immunisation with peptides alone can induce CTL responses, but not at a very high level (Gao et al. 1991). Modification of the injected peptide by addition of a lipid tail (Deres et al. 1989) or mixing with immune-stimulating complexes (ISCOM; Berzofsky 1991; Takahashi et al. 1990) appears to make the immunisation more efficient. An interesting new approach has been the injection of cDNA for NP intramuscularly, which primes for CTL responses in mice (Ulmer et al. 1993). These issues are being addressed in a number of virus infections where vaccines are urgently needed such as HIV, hepatitis C and malaria; much of the knowledge gained on priming CTL responses with recombinant material will be common to all of these infections.

5 Conclusions

Influenza virus has proved to be an invaluable tool for unravelling the mechanisms by which internal antigens are processed and presented to CTL. Studies on infection in vivo have led to a better understanding of the role of

CTL in acute virus infections in general, as well as influenza. These insights should lead to better vaccines in the near future.

References

Anderson K, Cresswell P, Gammon M, Hermes J, Williamson A, Zweerink H (1991) Endogenously synthesized peptide with an endoplasmic reticulum signal sequence sensitizes antigen processing mutant cells to class I-restricted cell-mediated lysis. J Exp Med 174 (2): 489–492

Askonas BA, McMichael AJ, Webster, RG (1982) The immune response to influenza virus and the problem of protection against infection. In: Beare AS (eds) Basic and applied influenza research CRC Press, Boca Raton, pp 157–188

Bastin J, Rothbard J, Davey J, Jones I, Townsend, A (1987) Use of synthetic peptides of influenza nucleoprotein to define epitopes recognized by class I restricted cytotoxic T lymphocytes. J Exp Med 165: 1508

Bennink JR, Yewdell JW, Gerhard W (1982) A viral polymerase involved in recognition of influenza virus-infected cells by a cytotoxic T cell clone. Nature 296: 75–76

Bennink JR, Yewdell JW, Smith GL, Moller C, Moss B (1984) Recombinant vaccinia virus primes and stimulates influenza haemagglutinin-specific cytotoxic T cells. Nature 311 (5986): 578–579

Bennink JR, Yewdell JW, Smith GL, Moss B (1986) Anti-influenza cytotoxic T lymphocytes recognise the three viral polymerases and a non-structural protein: reponsiveness to individual viral antigens is MHC controlled. J Virol 61: 1098–1102

Berzofsky JA (1991) Mechanisms of T cell recognition with application to vaccine design. Mol Immunol 28(3): 217–223

Biddison WE, Ward FE, Shearer GM, Shaw S (1980) The self determinants recognised by human virus immune T cells can be distinguished from the serologically defined HLA antigens. J Immunol 124: 548–552

Bjorkman P, Saper M, Samraoui B, Bennett W, Strominger J, Wiley D (1987a) Structure of human class I histocompatibility antigen, HLA-A2 Nature 329: 506–511

Bjorkman PJ, Saper MA, Samraoui B, Bennett WS, Strominger JL, Wiley DC (1987b) The foreign antigen binding site and T cell recognition regions of class I histocompatibility antigens. Nature 329: 512–518

Bodmer HC, Pemberton RM, Rothbard JB, Askonas BA (1988) Enhanced recognition of a modified peptide antigen by cytotoxic T lymphocytes specific for influenza nucleoprotein. Cell 52: 253–258

Bowness PA, Moss PAH, Rowland-Jones SL, Bell JI, McMichael AJ (1993) Conservation of T cell receptor usage by HLA B27-restricted influenza specific cytotoxic T lymphocytes suggests a general pattern for antigen-specific MHC class-I restricted responses. Eur J Immunol (in press)

Braciale TJ, Braciale VL, Henkel TJ, Sambrook J, Gething M-J (1984) Cytotoxic T lymphocyte recognition of the influenza haemagglutinin gene product expressed by DNA mediated gene transfer. J Exp Med 159: 341–349

Breuning MH, Lucas CJ, Breur BJ, Engelsma MY, DeLange GG, Dekker AJ, Biddison WE, Ivanyi P (1982) Subtypes of HLA B27 detected by cytotoxic T lymphocytes and their role in self recognition. Hum Immunol 5: 259–268

Buchmeier MJ, Welsh RM, Dutko FJ, Oldstone MBA (1980) The virology and immunology of lymphocytic choriomeningitis virus infection. Adv Immunol 30: 275–331

Cannon MJ, Openshaw PJM, Askonas B (1988) Cytotoxic cells clear virus but augment lung pathology in mice infected with respiratory syncytial virus. J Exp Med 168: 1163–1168

Cerundolo V, Alexander J, Anderson K, Lamb C, Cresswell P, McMichael A, Gotch F, Townsend A (1990) Presentation of viral antigen controlled by a gene in the major histocompatibility complex. Nature 345 (6274): 449–452

Cerundolo V, Tse AGD, Salter RD, Parham P, Townsend A (1991) CD8 independence and specificity of cytotoxic T lymphocytes restricted by HLA Aw68.1. Proc R Soc Lond [B] 244:169–177

Colbert R, Rowland-Jones S, McMichael AJ, Frelinger J (1993) Proc Natl Acad Sci USA (in press)

Cossins J, Gould KG, Smith M, Driscoll P, Brownlee, GG (1993) Precise prediction of a Kk-restricted cytotoxic T cell epitope in the NS1 protein of influenza virus using an MHC allele-specific motif. Virology 193 (1):289–295

Culmann B, Gomard E, Kieny M-P, Guy B, Dreyfus F, Saimot A-G, Sereni D, Sicar D, Levy J-P (1991) Six epitopes reacting with human cytotoxic CD8$^+$ T cells in the central region of the HIV nef protein. J Immunol 146: 1560–1565

Davis MM, Bjorkman PJ (1989) T-cell receptor genes and T-cell recognition. Nature 334:395–402

Deres K, Schild H, Weissmuller K-H, Jung G, Rammensee H-G (1989) In vivo priming of virus specific cytotoxic T lymphocytes with synthetic lipopeptide vaccine. Nature 342: 561–564

Deverson EV, Gow JR, Coadwell WJ, Monaco JJ, Butcher GW, Howard JC (1990) MHC class II region encoding proteins related to the multidrug resistance family of transmembrane transporters. Nature 348: 738–741

Djaballah H, Rivett AJ (1992) Peptidylglutamyl-peptide hydrolase activity of the multicatalytic proteinase complex: evidence for a new high-affinity site, analysis of cooperative kinetics, and the effect of manganese ions. Biochemistry 31 (16): 4133–4141

Eisenlohr LC, Yewdell JW, Bennink JR (1992) Flanking sequences influence the presentation of an endogenously synthesized peptide to cytotoxic T lymphocytes. J Exp Med 175: 481–487

Elliott T, Cerundolo V, Elvin J, Townsend A (1991) Peptide induced conformational change of a class I heavy chain. Nature 351:402

Elliott T, Smith M, Driscoll P, McMichael A (1993) Peptide selection by class I molecules of the major histocompatibility complex. Current Biol (in press)

Falk K, Rötzchke O, Deres K, Metzger J, Jung G, Rammensee H-G (1991a) Identification of naturally processed viral nonapeptides allows their quantification in infected cells and suggests an allele-specific T cell epitope forecast. J Exp Med 174: 425–434

Falk K, Rotzschke O, Stevanovic S, Jung G, Rammensee, H-G (1991b) Allele specific motifs revealed by sequencing of self peptides eluted from MHC molecules. Nature 351: 290–296

Foy HM, Cooney MK, Allan I (1976) Longitudinal studies of types A and B influenza among Seattle schoolchildren and their families, 1968–1974. J Infect Dis 134: 362–369

Fremont DH, Matsumura M, Stura EA, Peterson PA, Wilson IA (1992) Crystal structures of two viral peptides in complex with murine MHC class I H-2Kb. Science 257(5072): 919–927

Gaczynska M, Rock KL, Goldberg AL (1993) γ-interferon and expression of MHC genes regulate peptide hydrolysis by proteasomes. Nature 365: 264–267

Gammon MC, Bednarek MA, Biddison WE, Bondy SS, Hermes JD, Mark GE, Williamson AR, Zweerink HJ (1992) Endogenous loading of HLA-A2 molecules with an analog of the influenza virus matrix protein-derived peptide and its inhibition by an exogenous peptide antagonist. J Immunol 148(1): 7–12

Gao XM, Zheng B, Liew FY, Brett S, Tite J (1991) Priming of influenza virus-specific cytotoxic T lymphocytes vivo by short synthetic peptides. J Immunol 147(10): 3268–3273

Gao X-M, Tite JP, Lipscombe M, Rowland-Jones S, Ferguson DJP, McMichael AJ (1992) Recombinant Salmonella typhimurium invading nonphagocytic cells are resistant to recognition by antigen specific cytotoxic T lymphocytes. Infect Immun 60: 3780–3789

Garrett TPJ, Saper MA, Bjorkman PJ, Strominger JL, Wiley DC (1989) Specificity pockets for the side chains of peptide antigens in HLA-Aw68. Nature 342: 692

Garten W, Stieneke A, Shaw E, Wikstrom P, Klenk H-D (1989) Inhibition of proteolytic activation of influenza virus hemagglutinin by specific peptidyl chloralkyl ketones. Virology 172: 25–31

Glynne R, Powis SH, Beck S, Kelly A, Kerr L-A, Trowsdale J (1991) A proteasome-related gene between the two ABC transporter loci in the class II region of the human MHC. Nature 353: 357–359

Gooding LR, O'Connell KA (1983) Recognition by cytotoxic T lymphocytes of cells expressing fragments of the SV40 tumour antigen. J Immunol 131: 2580–2586

Gotch FM, McMichael AJ, Smith GL, Moss B (1987a) Identification of the virus molecules recognised by influenza specific cytotoxic T lymphocytes. J Exp Med 165: 408–416

Gotch F, Rothbard J, Howland K, Townsend A, McMichael A (1987b) Cytotoxic T lymphocytes recognise a fragment of influenza virus matrix protein in association with HLA-A2. Nature 326: 881–882

Gotch FM, Hovell R, Delchambre M, Silvera P, McMichael AJ (1991) Cytotoxic T lymphocyte response simian immunodeficiency virus by cynomolgus macaque monkeys immunized with recombinant vaccinia virus. AIDS 5: 317–320
Gould KG, Scotney H, Brownlee GG (1991) Characterization of two distinct major histocompatibility complex class I Kk-restricted T-cell epitopes within the influenza A/PR/8/34 virus hemagglutinin. J Virol 65(10): 5401–5409
Gould KJ, Scotney H, Townsend ARM, Bastin J, Brownlee GG (1987) Mouse H-2k-restricted cytotoxic T cells recognize antigenic determinants in both the HA1 and HA2 subunits of the influenza A/PR/34 hemagglutinin. J Exp Med 166: 693
Guo H-C, Jardetzky TS, Garrett TP, Lane WS, Strominger JL, Wiley DC (1992) Different length peptides dind to HLA Aw68 similarly at their ends but bulge out in the middle. Nature 360: 364–366
Hahn YS, Hahn CS, Braciale VL, Braciale TJ, Rice CM (1992) CD8$^+$ T cell recognition of an endogenously processed epitope is regulated primarily by residues within the epitope. J Exp Med 176(5): 1335–1341
Hoskins TW, Davies JR, Smith AJ, Miller CL, Allchin A (1979) Assessment of inactivated influenza A vaccine after three outbreaks of influenza A at Christ's Hospital. Lancet i: 33–35
Huet S, Nixon DF, Rothbard J, Townsend ARM, Ellis SA, McMichael AJ (1990) Structural homologies between two HLA B27 restricted peptides suggest residues important for interaction with HLA B27. Int Immunol 2: 311–316
Hunt DF, Henderson RA, Shabanowitz J, Sakaguchi K, Michel H, Sevilir N, Cox AL, Appella E, Engelhard VH (1992) Characterization of peptides bound to the class I MHC molecule HLA A2.1 by mass spectometry. Science 255: 1261–1263
Jardetzky TS, Lane WS, Robinson RA, Madden DR, Wiley DC (1991) Identification of self peptides bound to purified HLA-B27. Nature 353: 326–329
Kelly A, Powis SH, Glynne R, Radley E, Beck S, Trowsdale J (1991) Second proteasome-related gene in the human MHC class II region. Nature 353: 667–668
Krangel MS, Taketani S, Biddison WE, Strong DM, Strominger JL (1982) Comparative structural analysis of HLA-A2 antigens distinguishable by cytoxic T lymphocytes: variants M7 and DR1. Biochemistry 21: 6313–6321
Kreth HW, Kress L, Kress HG, Ott HF, Eckert G (1982) Demonstration of primary cytotoxic T cells in venous blood and cerebrospinal fluid in children with mumps meningitis. J Immunol 128: 2411–2415
Lamb RA (1983) The influenza virus RNA segments and their encoded proteins. In: Palese P, Kingsbury D (eds) Genetics of influenza virus. Springer, Vienna New York, pp 21–69
Latron F, Moots R, Rothbard J, Garrett T, Strominger JL, McMichael AJ (1991) Positioning of a peptide in the cleft of HLA A2 by complementing amino acid changes. Proc Natl Acad Sci USA 88: 11325–11329
Latron F, Pazmany L, Morrison JRM, Saper M, McMichael AJ, Strominger JL (1992) A critical role for conserved residues in the cleft of HLA-A2 in presentation of a nonapeptide to T cells. Science 257: 964–967
Levy F, Gabathuler R, Larsson R, Kvist S (1991) ATP is required for in vitro assembly of MHC class I antigens but not for transfer of paptides across the ER membrane. Cell (in press)
Lin Y, Askonas BA (1981) Biological properties of an influenza A virus specific killer T cell clone. J Exp Med 154: 225–234
Ljunggren HG, Stam NJ, Ohlen C, Neefjes JJ, Hoglund P, Heemels MT, Bastin J, Schumacher TN, Townsend A, Karre K et al. (1990) Empty MHC class I molecules come out in the cold. Nature 346(6283): 476–480
Lukacher AE, Braciale VL, Braciale TJ (1984) In vivo effector function of influenza virus specific cytotoxic T lymphocyte clones is highly specific. J Exp Med 160: 814–826
MacCallum FO (1971) Hypogammaglobulinaemia in the United Kingdom. 7. The role of humoral antibodies in protection against and recovery from bacterial and viral infections in hypogammaglobulinaemia. Med Res Engl 310: 72–85
Mackenzie CD, Taylor PM, Askonas BA (1989) Rapid recovery of lung histology correlates with clearance of influenza virus by specific CD8$^+$ cytotoxic T cells. Immunology 67: 375–381
Madden DR, Gorga JC, Strominger JL, Wiley DC (1992) The three dimensional structure of HLA-B27 at 2.1 Å resolution suggests a general mechanism for tight peptide binding to MHC. Cell 70: 1035–1048
Martinez CK, Monaco JJ (1991) Homology of the proteasome subunits to a major histocompatibility complex-linked LMP gene. Nature 353: 664–667

McMichael AJ (1978) HLA restriction of human cytotoxic T lymphocytes specific for influenza virus: poor recognition of virus associated with HLA A2. J Exp Med 148: 1458
McMichael AJ, Askonas BA (1978) Influenza virus specific cytotoxic T cells in man; induction and properties of the cytotoxic T cell. Eur J Immunol 8: 705–710
McMichael AJ, Ting A, Zweerink HJ, Askonas BA (1977) HLA restriction of cell mediated lysis of influenza virus infected human cells. Nature 270: 524–526
McMichael AJ, Gotch FM, Cullen P, Askonas BA, Webster RG (1981). The human cytotoxic T cell response to influenza A vaccination. Clin Exp Immunol 43: 276–285
McMichael AJ, Gotch FM, Dongworth DW, Clark A, Potter CW (1938a) Declining T cell immunity to influenza 1977–1982. Lancet ii: 762–764
McMichael AJ, Gotch FM, Noble GR, Beare PAS (1983b) Cytotoxic T-cell immunity to influenza. N Engl J Med 309: 13–17
McMichael A, Gotch F, Rothbard J (1986) HLA B37 determines an influenza A virus nucleoprotein epitope recognized by cytotoxic T lymphocytes. J Exp Med 164(1397): 1397–1406
Milligan GN, Morrison LA, Gorka J, Braciale VL, Braciale TJ (1990) The recognition of a viral antigenic moiety by class I MHC-restricted cytolytic T lymphocytes is limited by the availability of the endogenously processed antigen. J Immunol 145(10): 3188–3193
Momburg F, Ortiz-Navarrete V, Neefjes J, Goulmy E, van de Wal Y, Spits H, Powis SJ, Butcher GW, Howard JC, Walden P, Hammerling GJ (1992) Proteasome subunits encoded by the major histocompatibility complex are not essential for antigen presentation. Nature 360: 174–177
Monaco J, Cho S, Attaya M (1990) Transport protein genes in the murine MHC: possible implications for antigen processing. Science 250: 1723–1726
Morris AG, Lin Y-L, Askonas BA (1982) Immune interferon release when a cloned cytotoxic T cell meets its correct influenza-infected target cell. Nature 295: 150–152
Morrison J, Elvin J, Latron F, Gotch F, Moots R, Strominger JL, McMichael AJ (1992) Identification of the nonamer peptide from influenza A matrix protein and the role of pockets of HLA A2 in its recognition by cytotoxic T lymphocytes. Eur J Immunol 22: 903–907
Morrison LA, Lukacher AE, Braciale VL, Fan D, Braciale TJ (1986) Differences in antigen presentation to MHC class I- and class II-restricted influenza virus-specific cytolytic T lymphocyte clones. J Exp Med 163: 903
Moss PAH, Moots RJ, Rosenberg WMC, Rowland-Jones SJ, McMichael AJ, and Bell JI (1991) Extensive conservation of alpha and beta chains of the human T cell antigen receptor recognizing HLA-A2 and influenza matrix peptide. Proc Natl Acad Sci USA 88: 8987–8991
Nathenson SG, Geliebter J, Pfaffenbach GM, Zeff RA (1986) Murine major histocompability complex class I mutants: molecular analysis and structure function implications. Annu Rev Immunol 4: 471–521
Nuchtern JG, Bonifacino JS, Biddison WE, Klausner RD (1989) Brefeldin A implicates egress from the endoplasmic reticulum in class I restricted antigen presentation. Nature 339: 223–226
Oehen S, Waldner H, Kundig TM, Hengartner H, Zinkernagel RM (1992) Antivirally protective cytotoxic T cell memory to lymphocytic choriomeningitis virus is governed by persisting antigen. J Exp Med 176(5): 1273–1281
Ortiz-Navarette V, Seelig A, Gernold M, Frentzel S, Kloetzel PM, Hammerling GJ (1991) Subunit of the 20S proteasome (multicatalytic proteinase) encoded by the major histocompatibility complex. Nature 353: 6662–6664
Palese P, Young JK (1983) Molecular epidemiology of influenza virus. In: Palese P, Kingsbury D (eds) Genetics of influenza virus. Springer, Vienna New York, pp 321–326
Parham P, Lomen CE, Lawlor DA, Ways JP, Holmes N, Coppin HL, Salter RD, Wan AM, Ennis PD (1988) Nature of polymorphism in HLA-A, -B and -C molecules. Proc Natl Acad Sci USA 85: 4005–4009
Parker KC, Bednarek MA, Hull LK, Utz U, Cunningham B, Zweerink HJ, Biddison WE, Coligan JE (1992) Sequence motifs important for peptide binding to the human MHC class I molecule, HLA-A2. J Immunol 149(11): 3580–3587
Plata F, Autran B, Martins LP, Wain-Hobson S, Raphael M, Mayaud C, Denis M, Guillon JM, Debre P (1987) AIDS virus specific cytotoxic T lymphocytes in lung disorders. Nature 328: 348–351
Robertson L, Caley JP, Moore J (1958) Importance of staphylococcus aureus in pneumonia in the 1957 epidemic of influenza A. Lancet ii: 233–236

Rotzschke O, Falk K (1991) Naturally-occurring peptide antigens derived from the MHC class-I-restricted processing pathway. Immunol Today 12(12): 447–455
Sethi KK, Naher H, & Stroehmann I (1988) Phenotypic heterogeneity of cerebrospinal fluid-derived cytotoxic T cell clones. Nature 335: 178–180
Silver ML, Guo H-C, Stominger JL, Wiley DC (1992) Atomic structure of a human MHC molecule presenting an influenza virus peptide. Nature 360: 367–369
Spies T, Bresnahan M, Bahram S, Arnold D, Blanck GEM, Pious D, DeMars R (1990) A gene in the major histocompatibility complex class II region controlling the class I antigen presentation pathway. Nature 348: 744–747
Spies T, Cerundolo V, Colonna M, Cresswell P, Townsend A, De Mars R (1992) Presentation of endogenous viral antigen dependent on putative peptide transporter heterodimer. Nature 355: 644–646
Sutton J, Rowland-Jones S, Rosenberg W, Nixon D, Gotch F, Gao M, Murray N, Spoonas A, Driscoll P, Smith M, Willis A, McMichael AJ (1993) A sequence pattern for peptides presented to cytotoxic T lymphocytes by HLA B8 revealed by analysis of epitopes and eluted peptides. Eur J Immunol 23: 447–453
Takahashi H, Takeshita T, Morein B, Putney S, Germain RN, Berzofsky JA (1990) Induction of $CD8^+$ cytotoxic T cells by immunization with purified HIV-1 envelope protein in ISCOMs [see comments]. Nature 344 (6269): 873–875
Tite JP, Hughes JC, O'Callaghan D, Dougan G, Russell SM, Gao XM, Liew FY (1990) Anti-viral immunity induced by recombinant nucleoprotein of influenza A virus. II. Protection from influenza infection and mechanism of protection. Immunology 71 (2): 202–207
Townsend A, Bodmer H (1989) Antigen recognition by class I-restricted cytotoxic T lymphocytes. Annu Rev Immunol 7: 601–624
Townsend ARM, Skehel JJ (1982) Influenza A specific cytotoxic T cell clones that do not recognise viral glycoproteins. Nature 300: 655
Townsend ARM, McMichael AJ, Carter NP, Huddlestone JA, Brownlee GG (1984) Cytotoxic T cell recognition of the influenza nucleoprotein and haemagglutinin expressed in transfected mouse L cells. Cell 39: 13–25
Townsend ARM, Gotch FM, Davey J (1985) Cytotoxic T cells recognize fragments of the influenza nucleoprotein. Cell 42: 457–467
Townsend ARM, Bastin J, Gould K, Brownlee GG (1986a) Cytotoxic T lymphocytes recognise influenza haemagglutinin that lacks a signal sequence. Nature 234: 575
Townsend ARM, Rothbard J, Gotch FM, Bahadur G, Wraith D, McMichael AJ, (1986b) The epitopes of influenza nucleoprotein recognized by cytotoxic T lymphocytes can be defined with short synthetic peptides. Cell 44: 959–968
Townsend A, Ohlen C, Bastin J, Ljunggren HG, Foster L, Karre K (1989a) Association of class I major histocompatibility heavy and light chains induced by viral peptides. Nature 340 (6233): 443–448
Townsend A, Ohlen C, Foster L, Bastin J, Ljunggren HG, Karre K (1989b) A mutant cell in which association of class I heavy and light chains is induced by viral peptides. Cold Spring Harb Symp Quant Biol 1: 299–308
Townsend A, Elliott T, Cerundolo V, Foster L, Barber B, Tse A (1990) Assembly of MHC class I molecules analyzed in vitro. Cell 62 (2): 285–295
Trowsdale J, Hanson I, Mockridge I, Beck S, Townsend ARM, Kelly A (1990) Sequences encoded in the class II region of the MHC related to the ABC superfamily of transporters. Nature 348: 741–744
Ulmer J, Donnelly JJ, Parker SE, Rhodes GH, Felgner PL, Dwarki VJ, Gromkowski SH, Deck RR, DeWitt CM, Friedman A, Hawe LA, Leander KR, Martinez D, Perry HC, Shiver JW, Montgomery DL, Liu MA (1993) Heterologous protection against influenza by injection of DNA encoding a viral protein. Science 259: 1749–1749
Varghese JN, Laver WG, Colman PM, (1983) Structure of the influenza glycoprotein antigen neuraminidase at 2.9Å resolution. Nature 305: 35–40
Webster RG, Askonas BA (1980) Cross-protection and cross-reactive cytotoxic T-cells induced by influenza virus vaccines in mice. Eur J Immunol 10: 396–402
Webster RG, Laver WG, Air GM, Schild GC (1982) Molecular mechanisms of variation in influenza viruses. Nature 296: 115–121
Wells MA, Ennis FA, Albrecht P (1981a) Recovery from a viral repsiratory tract infection. 1. Influenza pneumonia in normal and T deficient mice. J Immunol 126: 1036–1041

Wells MA, Ennis FA, Albrecht P (1981b) Recovery from a viral respiratory infection. II. Passive transfer of immune spleen cells to mice with influenza pneumonia. J Immunol 126: 1042–1046

Wiley DC, Wilson IA, Skehel JJ (1981) Structural identification of the antibody-binding sites of Hong Kong influenza haemagglutinin and their involvement in antigenic variation. Nature 289: 373–378

Yap KL, Ada GL (1978a) Cytotoxic T cells in the lungs of mice infected with influenza A virus. Scand J Immunol 7: 73–80

Yap KL, Ada GL (1978b) Transfer of specific cytotoxic T lymphocytes protects mice inoculated with influenza virus. Nature 273: 238–240

Yewdell JW, Bennink JR, Smith GL, Moss B (1985) Influenza A virus nucleoprotein is a major target for cross-reactive anti-influenza A virus specific cytotoxic T lymphocytes. Proc Natl Acad Sci USA 82: 1785–1789

Yewdell YW, Bennink JR (1989) Brefeldin A specifically inhibits presentation of protein antigens to cytotoxic T lymphocytes. Science 244: 1072

Zhang W, Young AC, Imarai M, Nathenson SG, Sacchettini JC (1992) Crystal structure of the major histocompatibility complex class I H-2Kb molecule containing a single viral peptide: implications for peptide binding and T-cell receptor recognition. Proc Natl Acad Sci USA 89(17): 8403–8407

Zinkernagel RM, Doherty PC (1979). MHC-restricted cytotoxic T cells: studies on the biological role of polymorphic major transplantation antigens determining T cell restriction-specificity, function and responsiveness. Adv Immunol 27: 51

Zweerink HJ, Gammon MC, Utz U, Sauma SY, Harrer T, Hawkins JC, Johnson RP, Sirotina A, Hermes JD, Walker BD, et al. (1993) Presentation of endogenous peptides to MHC class I-restricted cytotoxic T lymphocytes in transport deletion mutant T2 cells. J Immunol 150(5): 1763–1771

Zweerink HT, Askonas BA, MIlican D, Courtneidge SA, Skehel JJ (1977) Cytotoxic T cells to type A influenza virus; viral haemagglutinin induces A-strain specificity while infected cells confer cross-reactive cytotoxicity. Eur J Immunol 7: 630–635

Cytotoxic T Lymphocytes in Dengue Virus Infection

I. Kurane and F. A. Ennis

1 Introduction

1.1 Dengue Viruses

Dengue viruses are members of the family Flaviviridae and there are four serotypes, dengue virus types 1, 2, 3, and 4. The genome of dengue viruses consists of a single-stranded RNA nearly 11 kb in length which is plus-

Division of Infectious Diseases and Immunology, Department of Medicine, University of Massachusetts Medical Center, Worcester, MA 01655, USA

Current Topics in Microbiology and Immunology, Vol. 189

stranded and infectious (RICE et al. 1986). Dengue virus genome codes for three structural proteins, capsid (C), PreM, which is a precursor to membrane (M), and envelope (E), and seven nonstructural proteins, NS1, NS2a, NS2b, NS3, NS4a, NS4b, and NS5 (ZHAO et al. 1986; MACKOW et al. 1987; HENCHAL and PUTNAK 1990). The functions of these proteins are not clearly understood. NS3 protein has been reported to have protease activity (PREUGSHAT et al. 1990) and also contains conserved epitopes characteristic of helicases (GOLBALENYA et al. 1989). The virion consists of RNA genome surrounded by a lipid bilayer containing E and M proteins. Dengue viruses infect monocytes and other macrophages (HALSTEAD et al. 1977), B lymphoblastoid cells (SUNG et al. 1975; THEOFILOPOULOS et al. 1976), T cell tumor lines (KURANE et al. 1990), epithelial cells (SMITH and WRIGHT 1985), fibroblasts (KURANE et al. 1992), and endothelial cells (ANDREWS et al. 1978) in vitro. However, it is believed that in vivo monocytes and other macrophages are the important source of dengue virus replication (HALSTEAD et al. 1977; BOONPUCKNAVIG et al. 1976, 1979).

1.2 Illness Caused by Dengue Virus Infection

Dengue virus infection can be asymptomatic or cause two forms of illness, dengue fever (DF) and dengue hemorrhagic fever (DHF; HALSTEAD 1980, 1992; HAYES and GUBLER 1992). DF is a self-limited febrile disease. After an incubation period of 2–7 days, a sudden onset of fever occurs and body temperature rapidly rises to 39.4°C–41.1°C. The fever is usually accompanied by frontal or retroorbital headache. Back pain occasionally precedes fever. Myalgia or bone pain occurs soon after onset. A transient, macular, generalized rash which blanches under pressure as well as nausea, vomiting, lymphadenopathy and taste aberrations may develop. One to two days after defervescence a generalized morbilliform maculopapular rash appears, which spares the palms and soles and disappears in 1–5 days. Patients usually recover from these symptoms within 10 days after onset without complications.

On the other hand, some patients infected with dengue virus leak plasma into interstitial spaces, resulting in hypovolemia and possibly circulatory collapse. This severe and life-threatening syndrome, which is always accompanied by thrombocytopenia and sometimes frank hemorrhage, is termed DHF. The incubation period of DHF is presumed to be similar to that of DF. In the first phase, illness starts with relatively mild symptoms: a fever, malaise, vomiting, headache, anorexia, and cough. Rapid clinical deterioration and collapse follows after 2–5 days. In the second phase, the patients have cold clammy extremities, warm trunk, flushed face, restlessness, irritability, and midepigastric pain. This crisis lasts for 24–36 hours, and children recover rapidly once convalescene starts. The common hematologic abnormalities are an increase in hematocrit, thrombocytopenia, mild leukocytosis, prolonged bleeding time, and decreased prothrombin time. The World Health Organization categorizes DHF cases into four grades, from less severe (grade 1) to severe (grade 4; TECHNICAL ADVISORY COMMITTEE ON DENGUE HEMORRHAGIC FEVER FOR SOUTHEAST ASIAN AND WESTERN PACIFIC REGIONS 1980). Grades 3 and 4, in which plasma leakage is so profound that shock occurs, are also referred to as dengue shock syndrome (DSS).

1.3 Epidemiology of Dengue Virus Infection

Dengue viruses are transmitted to humans by mosquitoes, principally *Aedes aegypti.* Forest cycles of dengue virus transmission between monkeys and mosquitoes have also been reported (GUBLER 1988). Dengue virus infections are a serious cause of morbidity and mortality in many areas of the world: Southeast and South Asia, Australia, Central and South America, and the Caribbean (HALSTEAD 1981, 1988, 1992). Dengue virus infections can be estimated to occur in up to 100 million individuals yearly (HALSTEAD 1988). A total of 250 000–500 000 cases of DHF/DSS occur throughout the world annually, and case fatality rate is 1%–5% (HALSTEAD 1992). Since DHF/DSS was first recognized in the 1950s, 1.5 million cases have been hospitalized and 33 000 infected individuals have died as a result of this syndrome (HALSTEAD 1988). These facts indicate that dengue virus infection is one of the most important human infectious diseases.

It has been reported that in Thailand as many as 99% of cases of DHF/DSS occur in children who have antibody to dengue virus before dengue virus infection that causes DHF/DSS (SANGKAWIBHA et al. 1984; HALSTEAD 1980, 1988). These patients can be divided into two groups: (1) children who are over 1 year of age and show secondary antibody responses and (2) children who are less than 1 year of age and show primary immune responses. Children who are over 1 year of age comprise about 90% of all DHF/DSS cases. These cases are observed in secondary infections by a dengue virus of a different serotype from that which caused the primary infections. On the other hand, children who are less than 1 year of age and who develop DHF/DSS during primary infections are those born to dengue virus antibody-positive mothers. These observations have been supported by other epidemiological studies in Thailand and in Cuba (BURKE et al. 1988; GUZMAN et al. 1984, 1990). It has been reported that antibodies to dengue viruses at subneutralizing concentrations augment dengue virus infection of Fcγ receptor-positive cells such as monocytes (HALSTEAD and O'ROURKE 1977). Dengue virions and immunoglobulin G (IgG) antibody to dengue virus form virus-antibody complexes, and binding of these virus–antibody complexes to FcγR via the Fc portion of IgG results in augmentation of dengue virus infections (KURANE et al. 1991a). Based on the epidemiological and laboratory studies it has been hypothesized that antibodies to dengue viruses and other serotype cross-reactive-immune responses contribute to the pathogenesis of DHF/DSS. However, the pathogensis of DHF/DSS is not clearly understood.

2 Dengue Virus-Specific Human Cytotoxic T Lymphocytes

It is generally accepted that cytotoxic T lymphocytes (CTL) play a critical role during viral infections. Adoptive transfer of virus-specific (CTL) can protect mice from disease caused by lymphocytic choriomeningitis virus (LCMV) or influenza virus (BYRNE and OLDSTONE 1984; MOSKOPHIDIS et al. 1987; KUWANO et al. 1988). On the other hand, depending on timing and number of cells, the adoptive transfer of virus-specific CTL has resulted in development of significantly severe symptoms during infection with LCMV or respiratory syncytial virus (BAENZIGER et al. 1986; CANNON et al. 1988). These observations suggest that virus-specific CTL contribute to recovery from virus infections, but can also induce immunopathology in certain situations.

Analysis of CTL responses in dengue virus infections is important for understanding the mechanisms of recovery from dengue virus infections and the pathogenesis of DHF/DSS. This knowledge would be useful for the development of dengue vaccines which induce protective immune responses but do not induce immune responses that may lead to immunopathology. There is no good animal model to analyze DHF/DSS; therefore, analysis of dengue virus-specific human T lymphocytes is necessary to understand the role of T lymphocytes in dengue virus infections. In this review, we will focus on human cytotoxic T cell responses to dengue viruses and discuss possible roles of these CTL in the pathogenesis of DHF/DSS.

2.1 Dengue Virus-Specific Human $CD4^+$ $CD8^-$ CTL

2.1.1 Detection of $CD4^+$ CTL in Bulk Cultures

Dengue virus-specific human memory $CD4^+$ $CD8^-$ T lymphocytes were first demonstrated by KURANE et al. (1989 a) using peripheral blood mononuclear cells (PMBC) from healthy individuals who had been naturally infected with dengue viruses or immunized with a live, attenuated experimental vaccine. Dengue antigen-specific proliferation of these $CD4^+$ $CD8^-$ T memory cells was induced by noninfectious dengue antigens (Ag) prepared from infected green monkey kidney cells. $CD4^+$ memory T cells induced by primary dengue virus infection were mainly serotype-specific, but serotype-cross-reactive responses were noted at lower, but significant, levels (KURANE et al. 1989b). In some individuals, however, $CD4^+$ memory T cells after primary infections were solely serotype-specific (unpublished observation). Dengue virus-specific CD4$^+$ CD8$^-$ memory T lymphocytes stimulated by noninfectious dengue virus Ag for 7 days in bulk cultures lysed dengue Ag-pulsed autologous target cells in HLA class II-restricted fashion (unpublished observation). These cells did not lyse dengue Ag-pulsed autologous target cells without in vitro incubation. These observations suggest that dengue virus infections induce dengue virus-specific CD4$^+$ CTL.

2.1.2 Dengue Virus-Specific CD4$^+$ CTL Clones

Dengue virus-specific CD4$^+$ CTL clones were established and analyzed for virus and dengue serotype specificities (KURANE et al. 1991b). These CTL clones lysed dengue virus-infected or dengue Ag-pulsed autologous target cells. Thirteen dengue virus-specific CD4$^+$ CTL clones were established from an individual who had been immunized with yellow fever vaccine 2 years earlier and had been infected with dengue 3 virus 1 year before. In bulk culture proliferation assays, the PBMC from this donor responded to dengue 3 antigen, and they also responded to dengue 1, 2, and 4 antigens to lower, but significant, levels. Six patterns of virus and dengue serotype specificities were observed (Table 1). All of these CD4$^+$ CTL clones were HLA class II restricted, and HLA DP, HLA DQ, and HLA DR were all used as restriction elements by various clones (KURANE et al. 1991b). Dengue virus-specific CD4$^+$ CTL clones were also established from the PBMC of four other individuals (Table 1). CD4$^+$ CTL clones from each individual have at least

Table 1 Virus and dengue serotype specificity of dengue virus-specific cytotoxic T lymphocyte (CTL) clones

Donor (Type of infection)	Type of clone	Virus and dengue serotype specificity of clones
CD4$^+$ CD8$^-$ CTL		
#1 (D3)	Serotype-specific	D3
	Subcomplex-specific	D1, D2, D3; D2, D3, D4
	Serotype-cross-reactive	D1, D2, D3, D4
	Flavi-cross-reactive	D1, D2, D3, D4, WNV
		D1, D2, D3, D4, WNV, YFV
#2 (D4)	Serotype-specific	D4
	Subcomplex-specific	D2, D4
#3 (D4)	Serotype-specific	D4
	Subcomplex-specific	D1, D3, D4
#4 (D4)	Serotype-specific	D4
	Subcomplex-specific	D2, D4
#5 (D1)	Serotype-specific	D1
	Subcomplex-specific	D1, D3
CD8$^+$ CD4$^-$ CTL		
#2 (D4)	Serotype-specific	D4
	Subcomplex-specific	D2, D4
	Serotype-cross-reactive	D1, D2, D3, D4

D1 –4, dengue virus types 1–4; WNV, West Nile virus; YFV, yellow fever virus.

two patterns of virus and dengue serotype specificities. These results indicate that serotype specificities of dengue virus-specific $CD4^+$ CTL are heterogeneous in each individual and that infection with one serotype of dengue virus induces both serotype-specific and serotype-cross-reactive $CD4^+$ memory CTL in most individuals.

2.2 Dengue Virus-Specific $CD8^+$ $CD4^-$ CTL

Dengue virus-specific $CD8^+$ $CD4^-$ CTL were reported by BUKOWSKI et al. (1989), using PBMC from an individual who had been infected with dengue 4 virus. They incubated this donor's PBMC with infectious dengue viruses for 7–9 days and demonstrated that these PBMC lysed dengue virus-infected autologous fibroblasts. The effector cells were determined to be $CD8^+$ $CD4^-$ T cells and the lysis was HLA class I restricted. The $CD8^+$ CTL generated in bulk cultures were serotype cross-reactive. Dengue virus-specific $CD8^+$ CTL clones were established from the PBMC of the same individual. These clones had three patterns of serotype specificities: (1) specific for dengue virus type 4, (2) cross-reactive for dengue virus types 2 and 4, and (3) cross-reactive for dengue virus types 1, 2, 3, and 4 (Table 1). Although dengue virus-specific $CD8^+$ CTL have been analyzed using the PBMC from one individual so far, the results suggest that the dengue virus-specific $CD8^+$ memory CTL of an individual who was infected with one serotype of dengue virus are also heterogeneous, and both serotype-specific and serotype-cross-reactive $CD8^+$ memory CTL are induced after primary infection.

2.3 Proteins Recognized by Dengue Virus-Specific CTL

2.3.1 Proteins Recognized by $CD4^+$ CTL

As described above, dengue virus genes code for three structural proteins, C, PrM, E, and seven nonstructural proteins, NS1, NS2a, NS2b, NS3, NS4a, NS4b, and NS5. Proteins recognized by dengue virus-specific $CD4^+$ CTL have been determined mainly using dengue virus-specific clones. KURANE et al. (1991b) reported that seven of 12 dengue virus-specific $CD4^+$ clones recognized NS3 protein (Table 2). These included a dengue 3-specific clone, two dengue subcomplex-specific clones, three dengue serotype-cross-reactive clones, and a flavivirus cross-reactive clone. These results suggest that the NS3 protein has at least four epitopes recognized by the dengue virus-specific $CD4^+$ CTL of this donor. NS3 was also recognized by a $CD4^+$ T cell clone specific for dengue virus types 1, 3, and 4, established from a dengue 4-immune donor, and by a dengue 4-specific clone and a clone cross-reactive for dengue virus types 2 and 4 established from another dengue 4-immune donor (Table 2).

Table 2. Dengue virus proteins recognized by dengue virus-specific cytotoxic T lymphocytes (CTL)

Donor (Type of infection)	Protein recognized	Types of clones
$CD4^+$ $CD8^-$ CTL		
# 1 (D3)	NS3	Serotype-specific
		Subcomplex-specific
		Serotype-cross-reactive
		Flavi-cross-reactive
# 2 (D4)	NS3	Serotype-specific
		Subcomplex-specific
	E	Serotype-specific
# 3 (D4)	NS3	Subcomplex-specific
	E	Serotype-specific
	C or PrM	(Undetermined)
$CD8^+$ $CD4^-$ CTL		
# 2 (D4)	NS3	Serotype-specific
		Subcomplex-specific
		Serotype-cross-reactive
	E	(Bulk culture)

E protein was recognized by a dengue 4-specific clone from a dengue 4-immune donor, and by four dengue 4-specific clones from another dengue 4-immune donor (Table 2). Recently, we have established dengue virus-specific $CD4^+$ CTL clones from two individuals which recognize either C or PrM protein. These results indicate that NS3 and E proteins are the two major proteins recognized by dengue virus-specific $CD4^+$ CTL, and C or preM protein is also recognized by some $CD4^+$ CTL. These results suggest that multiple epitopes on NS3 protein are recognized by distinct $CD4^+$ CTL clones with a variety of virus and dengue serotype specificities and that epitope (s) on E protein are recognized by serotype-specific clones. However, more studies are needed to confirm these observations.

2.3.2 Proteins Recognized by $CD8^+$ CTL

Bukowski et al. (1989) have reported that $CD8^+$ CTL generated in bulk cultures from PBMC of a dengue 4 virus-immune donor recognized nonstructural proteins and E proteins, but did not identify which nonstructural proteins were recognized (Table 2). Recently, we established dengue virus-specific $CD8^+$ CTL clones from this individual and found that all of the $CD8^+$ CTL clones examined to date recognize epitopes on NS3 protein (Table 2). These clones include a dengue 4-specific clone, three clones cross-reactive for dengue virus types 2 and 4, and one clone cross-reactive for dengue virus types 1, 2, 3, and 4. These results indicate that NS3 and E proteins are recognized by the $CD8^+$ CTL of this donor and suggest that NS3 contains major $CD8^+$ CTL epitopes.

2.4 Epitopes Recognized by Dengue Virus-Specific CTL

The epitopes recognized by dengue virus-specific CTL have not been defined in detail; however, the epitopes have been localized using recombinant vaccinia viruses to some degree. The epitopes recognized by $CD4^+$ CTL clones established from a dengue 3 virus-immune donor were localized within amino acids (aa) 1–452 on the NS3 protein. There seems to be at least four $CD4^+$ CTL epitopes in this region, because $CD4^+$ CTL clones with four different serotype cross-reactivities recognize epitopes on aa 1–452.

Epitopes recognized by $CD8^+$ CTL clones have been localized within aa 453–618 on NS3 protein. These $CD8^+$ CTL clones have three different serotype cross-reactivities; therefore, there seems to be at least three $CD8^+$ CTL epitopes within aa 453–618 of NS3.

2.5 Activation of Dengue Virus-Specific CTL In Vivo

Dengue virus-specific $CD4^+$ $CD8^-$ and $CD4^-$ $CD8^+$ memory T cells are present in individuals who have been infected and recovered from dengue virus infections (KURANE et al. 1989a; BUKOWSKI et al. 1989). These T lymphocytes acquire CTL activity upon stimulation with dengue virus antigens in vitro, suggesting that these memory CTL are also activated and become cytotoxic in vivo. It is important to determine whether these dengue virus-specific CTL are activated and mediate cytotoxic T cell functions in vivo during dengue virus infections. It is known that activated T lymphocytes produce interleukin 2 (IL-2; SMITH 1980; BALKWILL and BURKE 1989) and interferon gamma (IFN-γ; GRANELLI-PIPERNO et al. 1986; BALKWILL and BURKE 1989) and release soluble IL-2 receptor (sIL-2R; RUBIN et al. 1985). $CD4^+$ T cells and $CD8^+$ T cells release soluble CD4 molecule (sCD4) and soluble CD8 molecule (sCD8) upon activation, respectively (FUJIMOTO et al. 1983; TOMKINSON et al. 1989). Therefore, levels of these markers in the sera should reflect the activation of T cells in vivo, although these markers do not reflect the cytotoxic functions of these T cells.

We recently reported that levels of IL-2, IFN-γ, sIL-2R, and sCD4 are elevated in the sera of patients with DHF/DSS or DF compared to the levels of these markers in the sera of healthy Thai children (KURANE et al. 1991c). The level of sCD8 was highly elevated in patients with DHF/DSS, but not in patients with DF. The levels of sIL-2R, sCD4, and sCD8 in the patients with DHF/DSS were significantly higher than the levels in patients with DF. These results strongly suggest that T lymphocytes are activated in vivo during dengue virus infection, and activation of $CD4^+$ and $CD8^+$ T cells is much greater in patients with DHF/DSS than in patients with DF. These results suggest that high levels of T cell activation may be associated with the pathogenesis of DHF/DSS. However, the possibility that the higher levels of $CD4^+$ and $CD8^+$ T cell activation in DHF/DSS may reflect a high level of inflammatory responses rather than actually causing the symptoms of DHF/DSS cannot be ruled out yet.

3 Analyses of Dengue Virus-Specific CTL Using Animal Models

Animal models are not available to analyze the complications of severe dengue virus infections, DHF/DSS, although development of animal models for dengue virus research has been attempted. However, mice have been successfully used to analyze dengue virus-specific CTL. Dengue virus-specific $CD8^+$ CTL were demonstrated by PANG et al. (1988) using dengue virus-infected mice. ROTHMAN et al. demonstrated dengue virus-specific $CD8^+$ CTL using mice with H-2^b, H-2^d, or H-2^k haplotypes, and dengue virus proteins recognized by CTL generated in bulk cultures were determined. Interestingly, CTL from mice with these three haplotypes show different patterns of protein recognition. $CD8^+$ CTL from H-2^k mice predominantly recognize NS3 protein, and those from H-2^b mice recognize NS2b, NS4a, or NS4b protein. $CD8^+$ CTL from H-2^d mice recognize NS3, structural proteins, and NS1 or NS2a protein (A. L. Rothman, unpublished observations). This heterogeneity of protein recognition depending on major histocompatibility complex (MHC) is consistent with observations of dengue virus-specific human CTL. However, it is of interest that NS3 protein is recognized by murine CTL from two of the three H-2 haplotypes. Analyses of dengue virus-specific $CD4^+$ CTL using mouse models have not been reported yet.

4 Possible Role of Dengue Virus-Specific CTL in Dengue Virus Infections

The role of T lymphocytes in dengue virus infections is not well understood. Based on the analysis of CTL in other virus systems, such as influenza virus and LCMV, and on the observation that dengue virus-specific $CD4^+$ and $CD8^+$ CTL lyse dengue virus-infected autologous cells, it is reasonable to consider that dengue virus-specific CTL eliminate dengue virus-infected monocytes, thereby controlling dengue virus infections.

Possible immunopathological roles for serotype-cross-reactive immune responses in dengue virus infections have been suggested based on epidemiological observations. Most patients with DHF/DSS recover quickly after receiving intravenous fluids, and little pathologic changes have been observed compared to the severity of disease in patients with DHF/DSS. Perivascular edema was observed, but destruction of vascular endothelial cells was not apparent (BAHMARAPRAVATI et al. 1968). These clinical and pathological studies suggest that plasma leakage observed in DHF/DSS is due to malfunction of vascular endothelial cells rather than structural destruction. It is not known how dengue virus-specific CD4$^+$ and CD8$^+$ CTL contribute to the pathogenesis of DHF/DSS. However, the high levels of activation of CD4$^+$ and CD8$^+$ T cells in DHF/DSS, as demonstrated by the high sCD4 and sCD8 levels in the sera of patients with DHF/DSS, suggest possible roles for CTL in this immunopathology (KURANE and ENNIS 1992).

Antibodies to dengue virus enhance dengue virus infection of monocytes and other macrophages by forming dengue virus-antibody complexes during secondary infections with a serotype different from that which caused primary infection. Dengue virus-specific CD4$^+$ CTL are stimulated and produce IFN-γ, IL-2, and other lymphokines. IFN-γ upregulates the expression of FcγR on monocytes (GUYRE et al. 1983; PERUSSIA et al. 1983) and further augments antibody-dependent enhancement of infection (KONTNY et al. 1988). IFN-γ also upregulates the expression of HLA class I and class II molecules (Kelley et al. 1983). An increased number of dengue virus-infected cells and upregulation of HLA molecules facilitates recognition of dengue virus antigens by CD4$^+$ and CD8$^+$ T lymphocytes and results in much higher levels of T cell activation. Higher levels of T cell activation results in higher levels of lymphokines. IFN-γ-activated monocytes secrete higher levels of monokines and chemical mediators. Lysis of activated, dengue virus-infected monocytes may result in release of intracellular contents. These monocytes may release monokines and chemical mediators as the result of interaction with CTL. These interactions between CTL and infected monocytes could result in high levels of lymphokines, monokines, chemical mediators, and anaphylatoxins during a short period of time. A rapid increase in the levels of these mediators generated by interactions of dengue virus-infected monocytes and dengue virus-specific CD4$^+$ and CD8$^+$ CTL would lead to plasma leakage, shock, derangement of coagulation, and hemorrhagic manifestations of DHF/DSS. However, these possible mechanisms are not proven and future studies are necessary.

5 Future Research

As reviewed above, dengue virus-specific human CTL have been detected and analyzed to some degree. There are, however, many questions that remain to be answered. In this section we will discuss some of these important questions.

5.1 Determination of the Epitopes Recognized by Dengue Virus-Specific CTL

Recognition of proteins by dengue virus-specific CTL has been analyzed, and NS3 and E proteins seem to be two major proteins which contain multiple epitopes for $CD4^+$and $CD8^+$ CTL. However, the epitopes have not been defined at amino acid levels yet. Epitopes will be mapped by using overlapping synthetic peptides or by isolation and analysis of natural peptides from antigen-presenting cells (FALK et al. 1991; RUDENSKY et al. 1991). Determination of predominant CTL epitopes in conjunction with the definition of HLA alleles which present these epitopes will provide useful information for the development of effective subunit vaccines.

5.2 T Cell Receptor Usages of Dengue Virus-Specific CTL

It is understood that T cells recognize a peptide which bound to an HLA molecules via T cell antigen receptors (TcR). Past studies have suggested that T cells which express restricted sets of TcR-variable region genes are involved in the pathogenesis of certain inflammatory diseases (ACHA-ORBEA et al. 1988; WACHERPFENNIG et al. 1990). Selective clonal expansion of T cells with certain TcR may lead to pathologic conditions in DHF/DSS. It has been reported that suppression of T cells expressing certain TcR-variable region genes prevents T cell-mediated diseases (ACHA-ORBEA et al. 1988; URBAN et al. 1988). If dengue virus-specific CTL contribute to the pathogenesis of DHF/DSS, and these CTL express restricted sets of TcR genes, prevention and control of DHF/DSS may be possible. If dengue virus-specific CTL mainly contribute to recovery from infection, stimulation of T cells expressing certain sets of TcR may enhance protective immunity against dengue virus infection. Thus, analysis of T cell receptor usage of dengue virus-specific CTL will expand our understanding of human T cell responses to dengue viruses.

5.3 Lymphokine Production by Dengue Virus-Specific CTL

Recently, it has been reported that human $CD4^+$ T cells can be divided into two functionally distinct subsets similar to murine $CD4^+$ T cells (PELTZ 1991; ROMAGNANI 1991). Th1 cells produce IL-2, IFN-γ, and lymphotoxin upon stimulation, whereas Th2 cells produce IL-4, IL-5, IL-6, and IL-10. In inflammatory and allergic diseases, one subset becomes dominant, and it is assumed that the dominant subset of $CD4^+$ T cells contribute to the pathogenesis by producing a unique set of lymphokines (DEL PRETE et al. 1991). It is also known that $CD8^+$ T cells have the ability to produce certain lymphokines as well as $CD4^+$ T cells (SALGAME et al. 1991). Although dengue virus-specific $CD4^+$ and $CD8^+$ CTL are mainly selected based on their cytotoxic activities, it is possible that these CTL contribute to the pathogenesis and recovery by their other functions such as lymphokine production. Analysis of lymphokine production by these dengue virus-specific CTL is important for our understanding of the roles of these CTL in vivo.

5.4 Animal Models to Analyze Dengue Virus Infection

The development of animal models to analyze the pathogenesis of systemic dengue virus infections has not been successful, although dengue virus-specific murine CTL were detected. Lethal intracerebral infection of mice with neuroadapted dengue virus has been used as a model to examine protective immunity against dengue virus infection (KAUFMAN et al. 1987; SCHLESINGER et al. 1987). One highly neuroadapted strain of dengue 1 virus induces clinical disease after intraperitoneal inoculation; however, disease manifests as encephalitis (HOTTA et al. 1981). These models are not sufficient, because encephalitis is not commonly seen in human dengue virus infections. The protective and immunopathological roles of dengue virus-specific CTL should be determined in vivo using reliable animal models. Successful development of animal models suitable for analyzing systemic dengue virus infections is needed.

5.5 Analyses of Dengue Virus-Specific CTL Activated In Vivo During Dengue Virus Infections

So far, dengue virus-specific human CTL have been analyzed using lymphocytes of individuals who had been infected with dengue virus and recovered from infection. Thus, analysis has been done by in vitro expansion and activation of memory CTL. It is important to understand the CTL responses in vivo during acute dengue virus infection. It has been reported that activated T lymphocytes are present in the PBMC of patients with DHF/DSS (KURANE et al. 1991c). Analysis of dengue virus-specific CTL using lymphocytes from patients with DF or DHF/DSS will be needed to further understand the role of these CTL in vivo.

6 Conclusions

Dengue virus infections are a major public health problem in tropical and subtropical areas of the world. The world Health Organization has stressed the importance of developing dengue virus vaccines (BRANDT 1988); however, safe and effective vaccines have not been developed. Dengue vaccines should develop protective immunity, but should not induce immune responses which may lead to DHF/DSS during future dengue virus infections. Although dengue virus-specific $CD4^+$ $CD8^-$ and $CD4^-$ $CD8^+$ CTL have been demonstrated and analyzed to some degree, there are many questions that should be addressed. The dengue virus proteins which contain CTL epitopes should be determined, and major CTL epitopes should be mapped. Furthermore, the role of these CTL in vivo needs to be clearly understood. Understanding human CTL response to dengue virus will provide useful information not only for the development of safe and effective vaccines, but also for more effective treatment of dengue virus infections.

Acknowledgements. This work was supported by grants from the U.S. Army Medical Research and Development Command (DAMA 17-86-C-6208) and from the National Institutes of Health (NIH-RO1-AI30624, NIH-T32-A107272). The opinions contained herein are those of the authors and should not be construed as representing the official policies of the Department of Army or the Department of Defense of the USA.

References

Acha-Orbea H, Mitchell DJ, Timmermann L, Wraith D, Tausch G, Waldor M, Zamvil S, McDevitt H, Steinman L (1988) Limited heterogeneity of T cell receptors from lymphocytes mediating autoimmune encephalomyelitis allows specific immune intervention. Cell 54: 263–273

Andrews BS, Theofilopoulos AN, Peters CJ, Loskutoff DJ, Brandt WE, Dixon FJ (1978) Replication of dengue and junin viruses in cultured rabbit and human endothelial cells. Infect Immun 20: 776–781

Baenziger J, Hengartner H, Zinkernagel RM, Cole GA (1986) Induction or prevention of immunopathological disease by cloned cytotoxic T cell lines specific for lymphocytic choriomeningitis virus. Eur J Immunol 16: 387–393

Balkwill FR, Burke F (1989) The cytokine network. Immunol Today 10: 299–304

Bhamarapravati N, Tuchinda P, Boonyapaknavik V (1968) Pathology of Thailand haemorrhagic fever: a study of 100 autopsy cases. Ann Trop Med Parasitol 61: 500–510

Boonpucknavig V, Bhamarapravati N, Boonpucknavig S, Futrakul P, Tanpaichitr P (1976) Glomerular changes in dengue hemorrhagic fever. Arch Pathol Lab Med 100: 206–212

Boonpucknavig S, Boonpucknavig V, Bhamarapravati S, Nimmanitya S (1979) Immunofluorescence study of skin rash in patients with dengue hemorrhagic fever. Arch Pathol Lab Med 103:463–466

Brandt WE (1988) Current approaches to the development of dengue vaccines and related aspects of the molecular biology of flaviviruses. J Infect Dis 157: 1105–1111

Bukowski JF, Kurane I, Lai C-J, Bray M, Falgout B, Ennis FA (1989) Dengue virus-specific cross-reactive $CD8^+$ human cytotoxic T lymphocytes. J Virol 63: 5086–5091

Burke DS, Nisalak A, Johnson D, Scott RM (1988) A prospective study of dengue infections in Bangkok. Am J Trop Med Hyg 38: 172–180

Byrne JA, Oldstone MBA (1984) Biology of cloned cytotoxic T lymphocytes specific for lymphocytic choriomeningitis virus: clearance of virus in vivo. Virology 53: 682–686

Cannon MJ, Openshaw PJM, Askonas BA (1988) Cytotoxic T cells clear virus but augment lung pathology in mice infected with respiratory syncytial virus. J Exp Med 168: 1163–1168

Del Prete GF, De Carli M, Mastromauro C, Biagiotti R, Macchia D, Falagiani P, Ricci M, Romagnani S (1991) Purified protein derivative of mycoplasm tuberculosis and excretory-secretory antigen(s) of Toxocara canis expand in vitro human T cells with stable and opposite (type 1 T helper of type 2 T helper) profile of cytokine production. J Clin Invest 88: 346–350

Falk K, Rotzschke O, Stevanovic S, Jung G, Rammensee HG (1991) Allele-specific motifs revealed by sequencing of self-peptides eluted from MHC molecules. Nature 351: 290–296
Fujimoto J, Levy S, Levy R (1983) Spontaneous release of the Leu-2 (T8) molecule from human T cells. J Exp Med 159: 752–766
Golbalenya AE, Donchenko AP, Koonin EV, Blinov VM (1989) N-terminal domains of putative helicases of flavi- and pestiviruses may be serine proteases. Nucleic Acids Res 17: 3889–3897
Granelli-Piperno A, Andrus L, Steinman RM (1986) Lymphokine and nonlymphokine mRNA levels in stimulated human T cells. J Exp Med 163: 922–937
Gubler DJ (1988) Dengue PP223–260. In: Monath TP (ed) The arboviruses: epidemiology and ecology. CRC Press, Boca Raton
Guzman MG, Kouri GP, Bravo J, Soler M, Vazquez S, Santos M, Villaescusa R, Basanta P, Indan G, Ballester JM (1984) Dengue haemorrhagic fever in Cuba. II. Clinical investigations. Trans R Soc Trop Med Hyg 78: 239–241
Guzman MG, Kouri GP, Bravo J, Soler M, Vazquez S, Morier L (1990) Dengue hemorrhagic fever in Cuba, 1981: a prospective seroepidemiologic study. Am J Trop Med Hyg 42: 279–284
Guyre PM, Morganerli P, Miller R (1983) Recombinant immune interferon increases immunoglobulin G Fc receptors on cultured human mononuclear phagocytes. J Clin Invest 72: 393–397
Halstead SB (1980) Immunological parameters of togavirus diesease syndromes. Schlesinger RW (ed) The togaviruses: biology, structure, replication. Academic, New York, pp 107–173
Halstead SB (1981) Dengue hemorrhagic fever—a public health problem and a field for research. Bull WHO 58: 1–21
Halstead SB (1988) Pathogenesis of dengue. Challenges to molecular biology. Science 239: 476–481
Halstead SB (1992) Dengue viruses. In: Gorbach SL, Bartlett JG, Blacklow NR (eds) Infectious diseases. Saunders, Philadelphia, PP 1830–1835
Halstead SB, O'Rourke EJ (1977) Dengue viruses and mononuclear phagocytes. I. Infection enhancement by non-neutralizing antibody. J Exp Med 146: 210–217
Halstead SB, O' Rourke EJ, Allison AC (1977) Dengue virus and mononuclear phagocytes. II. Identity of blood and tissue leukocytes supporting in vitro infection. J Exp Med 146: 218–219
Hayes EB, Gubler DJ (1992) Dengue an dengue hemorrhagic fever. Pediatr Infect Dis J 11: 311–317
Henchal EA, Putnak R (1990) The dengue viruses. Clin Microbiol Rev. 3: 376–396
Hotta H, Murakami I, Miyasaki K, Takeda Y, Shirane H, Hotta S (1981) Inoculation of dengue virus into nude mice. J Gen Virol 52: 71–76
Kaufman BM, Summers PL, Dubois DR, Eckels KH (1987) Monoclonal antibodies against dengue 2 virus E-glycoprotein protect mice against lethal dengue infection. Am J Trop Med Hyg 36: 427–434
Kelley VE, Fiers W, Strom TB (1983) Cloned human interferon-γ, but not interferon-β or -α, induces expression of HLA-DR determinants by fetal monocytes and myeloid leukemic cell lines. J Immunol 132: 240–245
Kontny U, Kurane I, Ennis FA (1988) Gamma interferon augments Fc receptor-mediated dengue virus infection of human monocytic cells. J Virol 62: 3928–3933
Kurane I, Ennis FA (1992) Immunity and immunopathology in dengue virus infections. Semin Immunol 4: 121–127
Kurane I, Innis B, Nisalak A, Hoke C, Nimmanritya S, Meager A, Ennis FA (1989a) Human T cell responses to dengue virus antigens. Proliferative responses and interferon gamma production . J Clin Invest 83: 506–513
Kurane I, Meager A, Ennis FA (1989b) Dengue virus-specific human T cell clones: serotype cross-reactive proliferation, interferon gamma production, and cytotoxic activity. J Exp Med 170: 763–775
Kurane I, Kontny U, Janus J, Ennis FA (1990) Dengue-2 virus infection of human mononuclear cell lines and establishment of persistent infections. Arch Virol 110: 91–101
Kurane I, Mady BJ, Ennis FA (1991a) Antibody-dependent enhancement of dengue virus infection. Rev Med Virol 1: 211–221
Kurane I, Brinton MA, Samson AL, Ennis FA (1991b) Dengue virus-specific, human $CD4^+$

CD8⁻ cytotoxic T cell clones: multiple patterns of virus crossreactivity recognized by NS3-specific T cell clones. J Virol 65: 1823–1828
Kurane I, Innis BL, Nimmannitya S, Nisalak A, Meager A, Janus J, Ennis FA (1991c) Activation of T lymphocytes in dengue virus infections: high levels of soluble interleukin 2 receptor, soluble CD4, soluble CD8, interleukin 2 and interferon gamma in sera of children with dengue. J Clin Invest 88: 1473–1480
Kurane I, Janus J, Ennis FA (1992) Dengue virus infection of human spin fibroblasts in vitro: production of IFN-β, IL-6 and GM-CSF. Arch Virol 124: 21–30
Kuwano K, Scott M, Young JF, Ennis FA (1988) HA2 subunit of influenza A H1 and H2 subtype viruses induces a protective cross-reactive cytotoxic T lymphocyte response. J Immunol 140: 1264–1268
Mackow E, Makino Y, Zhao B, Zhang Y-M, Markoff L, Buckler-White A, Guiler M, Chanock R, Lai C-J (1987) The nucleotide sequence of dengue type 4 virus. Analysis of genes coding for nonstructural proteins. Virology 159: 217–228
Moskophidis D, Cobbold SP, Waldmann H, Lehmann-Grube F (1987) Mechanism of recovery from acute virus infection: treatment of lymphocytic choriomeningitis virus-infected mice with monoclonal antibodies reveals that Lyt-2+ T lymphocytes mediate clearance of virus and regulate the antiviral antibody response. J Virol 61: 1867–1874
Pang T, Devi S, Blanden RV, Lam SK (1988) T cell-mediated cytotoxicity against dengue-infected target cells. Microbiol Immunol 32: 511–518
Peltz G (1991) A role for CD4⁺ T-cell subsets producing a selective pattern of lymphokines in the pathogenesis of human chronic inflammatory and allergic diseases. Immunol Rev 123: 23–35
Perussia B, Dayton ET, Lazarus R, Fanning V, Trinchieri G (1983) Immune interferon induces the receptor for monomeric IgG1 on human monocytic and myeloid cells. J Exp med 158: 1092–1113
Preugschat F, Yao C-W, Strauss JH (1990) In vitro processing of dengue virus type 2 nonstructural proteins NS2A, NS2B and NS3. J Virol 64: 4364–4374
Rice CM, Strauss EG, Strauss JH (1986) Structure of the flavivirus genome. In: Schlesinger S, Schlesinger MJ (eds) The togaviridae and flaviviridae. Plenum, New York, pp 279–326
Romagnani S (1991) Human Th1 and Th2 subsets: doubt no more. Immunol Today 12: 256–257
Rubin LA, Kurman CC, Fritz ME, Biddison WE, Boutin B, Yarchoan B, Nelson DL (1985) Soluble interleukin 2 receptors are released from activated human lymphoid cells in vitro. J Immunol 135: 3172–3177
Rudensky AY, Preston-Hurlburt P, Hong S-C, Barlow A, Janeway CA (1991) Sequence analysis of peptides bound to MHC class II molecues. Nature 353: 622–627
Salgame P, Abrams JS, Clayberger C, Goldstein H, Convit J, Modlin RL, Bloom BR (1991) Differing lymphokine profiles of functional subsets of human CD4 and CD8 T cell clones. Science 254: 279–282
Sangkawibha N, Rojanasuphot S, Ahandrink S, Viriyapongse S, Jatanasen S, Salitul V, Phanthumachinda B, Halstead SB (1984) Risk factors in dengue shock syndrome: a prospective epidemiologic study in Rayong, Thailand. Am J Epidemiol 120: 653–669
Schlesinger JJ, Brandriss MW, Walsh EE (1987) Protection of mice against dengue 2 virus encephalitis by immunization with the dengue 2 virus non-structural glycoprotein NS1. J Gen Virol 68: 853–857
Smith KA (1980) T cell growth factor. Immunol Rev 31: 337–352
Smith GW, Wright PJ (1985) Synthesis of proteins and glycoproteins in dengue type 2 virus-infected Vero and Aedes albopictus cells. J Gen Virol 66: 559–571
Sung JS, Diwan AR, Falkler WA Jr, Yang H-Y, Halstead SB (1975) Dengue carrier culture and antigen production in human lymphoblastoid lines. Intervirology 5: 137–149
Technical Advisory Committee on dengue hemorrhagic fever for Southeast Asian and Western Pacific regions (1980) Guide for diagnosis, treatment and control of dengue hemorrhagic fever. World Health Organization, Geneva
Theofilopoulos AN, Brandt WE, Russell PK, Dixon FT (1976) Replication of dengue-2 virus in cultured human lymphoblastoid cells and subpopulations of human peripheral leukocytes. J Immunol 117: 953–961
Tomkinson BE, Brown MC, Ip SH, Carrabis S, Sullivan JL (1989) Soluble CD8 during T cell activation. J Immunol 142: 2230–2236

Urban JL, Kuman V, Kono DH, Gomez C, Horvath S, Clayton J, Ando D, Sercarz E, Hood L (1988) Restricted use of T cell receptor V genes in murine autoimmune encephalomyelitis raises possibilities for antibody therapy. Cell 54: 577–592

Wacherpfennig KW, Ota K, Endo N, Seidman J, Rosenzweig A, Weiner H, Hafler D (1990) Shared human T cell receptor Vβ usage to immunodominant regions of myelin basic protein. Science 248: 1016–1017

Zhao B, Mackow E, Buckler-White A, Markoff L, Chanock R, Lai C-J, Makino Y (1986) Cloning full-length dengue type 4 viral DNA sequences: analysis of genes coding for structural proteins. Virology 155: 77–88

Cytotoxic T Cells in Paramyxovirus Infection of Humans

S. DHIB-JALBUT[1] and S. JACOBSON[2]

1 Introduction

Paramyxoviruses include a number of human and animal pathogens that enter the host and spread through the respiratory tract. In humans, paramyxoviruses include measles virus (MV), mumps virus (MPS), parainfluenza virus (the causative agent of croup), and respiratory syncytial virus (RSV), which causes bronchitis and pneumonitis in infants. In animals, important pathogens include canine distemper, rinderpest, Newcastle disease, and parainfluenza viruses.

Paramyxoviruses are enveloped viruses with a diameter ranging from 150–250 nm. The envelope is a spherical lipoprotein that consists of the hemagglutinin (HA)–neuraminidase (HN) and the fusion (F) proteins. The core is a helical ribonucleoprotein which contains nonsegmented single-stranded RNA genome with a negative polarity. MV, which is the focus of this review, contains a 16-kb genome that codes for six structural proteins—nucleocapsid (NC), phosphoprotein (P), matrix (M), F, HA, large (L) protein—and at least two nonstructural viral proteins (C and V). The first five structural

[1] Neurology and Pathology Departments, University of Maryland at Baltimore, Baltimore, MD 21201, USA
[2] Neuroimmunology Branch, National Institutes of Neurological Disorders and Stroke, National Institutes of Health, Bethesda, MD, USA

Current Topics in Microbiology and Immunology, Vol. 189

proteins have been purified from an MV-infected Daudi cell line by affinity chromatography and from recombinant vaccinia viruses and have been used to study the cellular immune response to the individual viral proteins. The virus attaches to the host cell surface by binding of the HA protein to cell surface receptors followed by fusion of the virion envelope with the cell membrane. The role of neuraminidase and cleavage of the F protein in virus–cell interaction varies among the different members of the paramyxovirus family. Once in the cell cytoplasm, the viral transcriptase carried in the virion is used to synthesize viral mRNA complementary to the viral-negative stranded RNA. Viral proteins are then translated and assembled into virion that bud out from the host cell surface (KINGSBURY 1985).

This chapter reviews the cytotoxic T lymphocyte (CTL) response to three human paramyxoviruses, namely, MV, MPS, and RSV. The CTL response to measles virus has been more extensively studied than other paramyxoviruses and, therefore, it will be discussed in detail.

2 The CTL Response to Measles Virus

Measles virus is a contagious human pathogen that causes an acute exanthematous febrile illness which is self-limiting. In rare cases, serious complications involving the central nervous system (CNS) can take place. These include post-measles encephalomyelitis (PME), subacute sclerosing panencephalitis (SSPE), and subacute measles encephalitis (SME) in the immunocompromised host. Vaccination with the live-attenuated virus has resulted in near eradication of measles in the developed world and has reduced drastically the incidence of complications (NORRBY 1985).

A cellular immune response to MV develops during acute infection which is believed to be responsible for the exanthematous rash (SURINGA et al. 1970). Because of its lymphotropism, transient immunosuppression can occur during acute measles (NORRBY 1985). However, during convalescence a cytotoxic T cell response develops which is usually maintained over the life of the individual (KRETH et al. 1979; JACOBSON et al. 1985). Abnormalities in the CTL to MV have been found in multiple sclerosis (MS; JACOBSON et al. 1985), SSPE (DHIB-JALBUT et al. 1989a), and healthy individuals who had acquired immunity to MV through vaccination rather than natural infection (WU et al. 1993). Thus, we will discuss the MV CTL in relation to acute infection, immunity following natural infection, vaccination, and in disease states such as PME, SSPE, and MS.

2.1 Measles Virus CTL in Healthy Individuals

Measles infection produces a lifelong immunity, and neutralizing antibodies remain detectable throughout the life of the individual (NORRBY 1985). MV

CTL is not detectable in freshly isolated peripheral blood lymphocytes (PBL) from healthy individuals, but can be generated following in vitro stimulation with the virus (LUCAS et al. 1983; JACOBSON et al. 1985). PBL stimulated with the Edmonston strain of MV and cultured for 1 week generate CTL that lyse MV-infected Epstein-Barr virus (EBV)-transformed B cell targets. This response is measles specific, primarily $CD4^+$, and restricted by MHC class II molecules (JACOBSON et al. 1984, 1985, 1987). The magnitude of the MV CTL response in healthy individuals ranges between 18% and 50% with a mean of $26.0 \pm 10.4\%$ (n, 22) specific lysis (JACOBSON et al. 1985). MV-reactive CTL clones of either the $CD4^+$ or $CD8^+$ phenotype have been generated from healthy individuals with a remote history of measles infection (JACOBSON et al. 1984; VAN BINNENDIJK et al. 1989). The phenotype of the CTL clones generated appears to have a relationship to the antigen-presenting cell. Measles antigen presented by macrophages predominantly produces $CD4^+$ class II-restricted CTL clones, whereas measles antigen presented by EBV-transformed B cell predominantly stimulates the production of $CD8^+$ class I-restricted CTL clones (VAN BINNENDIJK et al. 1989).

In vitro stimulation of PBL with the MV polypeptides HA, F, NC, or M results in the generation of MV CTL responses (Fig. 1; JACOBSON et al. 1987; DHIB-JALBUT et al. 1989b), indicating that an exogenous endocytic pathway, in addition to an endogenous intracytoplasmic pathway, are used in processing MV antigen. In addition, CTL clones generated from cultures stimulated with the whole virus show diverse reactivity to different MV polypeptides including HA, F, and NC (VAN BINNENDIJK et al. 1989). The frequency of $CD4^+$ clones specific for F and NC seems to be higher than that for the HA protein. Vaccinia virus recombinants expressing HA, F, or NC have been shown to generate cellular immune responses and to be protective against

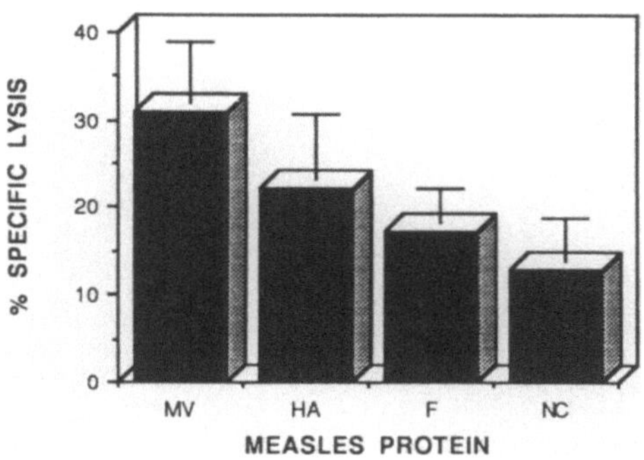

Fig. 1. Cytotoxic T lymphocyte response to measles virus (*MV*) and the MV proteins hemagglutinin (*HA*), fusion protein (*F*), and nucleocapsid (*NC*). Peripheral blood lymphocytes (PBL) were stimulated with MV or purified MV polypeptide and tested for lysis of MV-infected autologous Epstein-Barr virus-transformed B cells at an effector-to-target ratio of 20:1. The graph shows the mean ($\pm$ standard deviation) percentage of specific lysis from three healthy individuals (DHIB-JALBUT et al. 1989a)

measles infection in mice and rats, which suggests a potential for MV subunit vaccine in humans (BRINKMANN et al. 1991).

The significance of MV CTL precursors in the production of long-term immunity to measles is not understood. However, recent studies in our laboratory of in vitro MV CTL response (which is predominantly $CD4^+$) in patients with vaccine failure and healthy vaccinated peer controls suggest a role for MV CTL in protection (WU et al. 1993). While the majority of patients with measles vaccine failure showed a high MV CTL response during convalesccence, vaccinated healthy peer controls had very low MV CTL compared to healthy individuals with a remote history of measles infection, but their influenza CTL was not different from the other groups (Fig. 2). This would seem to indicate that natural infection results in a higher and sustained MV CTL response compared to a low and perhaps unsustained MV CTL response in vaccinees, which puts the latter group at a risk for infection. This would suggest that $CD4^+$ MV CTL may be involved in the maintenance of long-term immunity. Support for a $CD4^+$ T cell role in protection against MV can be derived indirectly from knowledge of measles infection in children with human immunodeficiency virus (HIV) and experimental measles infection in Lewis Rats: children with HIV and low $CD4^+$ T cell counts develop fulminating measles pneumonitis, but survive acute measles if they have been vaccinated (KAPLAN et al. 1992). This would suggest that while $CD4^+$ T cells may not be required for disease production, they assist in reducing complications and enhancing recovery. Since measles antibody levels do not correlate with $CD4^+$ cell counts in asymptomatic HIV patients (SHA et al. 1991), it is possible that $CD4^+$ T-helper cells are sufficient to maintain measles antibodies, but reduction in $CD4^+$ MV CTL may increase the risk of complications

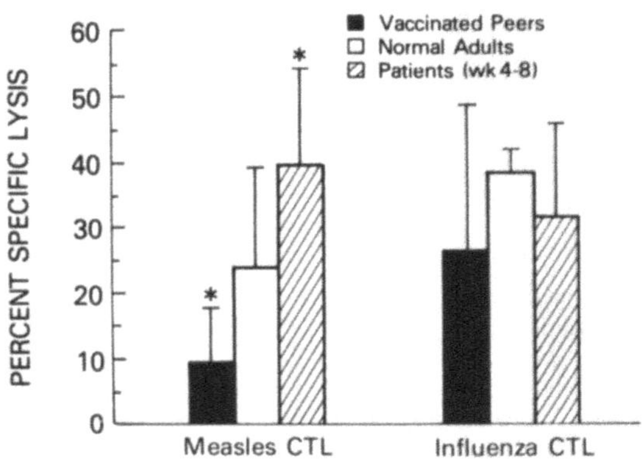

Fig. 2. Measles virus- and influenza virus-specific cytotoxic T lymphocyte responses in healthy, previously vaccinated individuals (vaccinated peers; $n = 7$), healthy adults with a history of natural infection ($n = 5$), and in patients 4–8 weeks after acute measles ($n = 18$). The graph shows the mean percentage of specific lysis ($\pm$ SD) of autologous virus-infected Epstein-Barr virus-transformed B cell targets at an effector-to-target ratio of 40:1. The *asterisk* indicates a statistically significant difference compared to healthy adults

and delay recovery from acute measles. Furthermore, CD4$^+$ T cells in the absence of CD8$^+$ T cells and neutralizing antibody are sufficient to protect Lewis rats from measles encephalitis when immunized with recombinant vaccinia virus expressing MV proteins (BRINKMANN et al. 1991).

2.2 Measles Virus CTL in Acute Infection

Cytotoxic T cells against MV-infected targets can be demonstrated in PBL from the majority of patients with acute measles infection. A number of studies suggest that MV cytotoxicity during acute infection consists of three components: (1) natural killer cells, (2) major histocompatibility complex (MHC) class I-restricted CTL, and (3) MHC class II-restricted CTL. PBL obtained from patients with acute measles can lyse MV-infected phytohemagglutinin (PHA)-stimulated blast cells. A significant component of this cytotoxicity is not MHC restricted and can be eliminated by depleting the PBL of FC-bearing cells, suggesting that NK cells represent a major component of cytotoxicity during acute measles. Class I-restricted MV-specific CTL could still be demonstrated in PBL after depletion of FC-bearing cells, though in small magnitude (KRETH et al. 1979; SISSONS et al. 1985; VAN BINNENDIJK et al. 1990).

Recently, we have examined the MV CTL response in PBL from 18 patients with acute measles 1 week–2 months after rash. Cytotoxicity against uninfected and MV-infected autologous EBV-transformed B cell targets was measured in unstimulated PBL and in PBL stimulated with MV in vitro. While MV CTL was low in unstimulated PBL (< 5% specific lysis), 15 of the 18 patients had significant elevation in MV CTL when MV-stimulated PBL were used as effectors, with a mean specific lysis of 40 ± 14.4% (Fig. 2). The CTL response was MV specific, as MV-stimulated PBL produced much lower lysis of influenza virus-infected targets, as shown in Table 1. Analysis of the MHC

Table 1. Virus specificity of the measles virus (MV) cytotoxic T lymphocyte (CTL) response during acute measles shown as percent lysis of autologous virus-infected Epstein-Barr virus (EBV)-transformed B cell targets at effector-to-target ratio of 40:1

Case	Effectors	Targets		
		Measles-infected	Infuenza-infected	Uninfected
1	Unstimulated	1	10	2
	Measles	60	19	17
	Influenza	4	61	2
2	Unstimulated	12	5	1
	Measles	59	12	2
	Influenza	8	12	3
3	Unstimulated	3	3	0
	Measles	26	5	1
	Influenza	25	38	3

restriction of the CTL response from three patients with acute infection against class I- or class II-matched targets suggested that both class I- and class II-restricted CTL exist in the PBL from those patients when tested within 3 weeks after infection (E. Hurwitz, S. Dhib-Jalbut, and H. F. Mc Farland, unpublished data). In a recent study, stimulation of PBL from children 3–4 weeks after contracting acute measles, with MV-infected EBV-transformed B cells as antigen-presenting cells resulted in the generation of MV-specific clones. These clones were predominantly $CD8^+$ class I-restricted CTL, though $CD4^+$ class II-restricted CTL were also generated, but in smaller frequency (VAN BINNENDIJK et al. 1989). Collectively, these studies indicate that both class I-restricted and class II-restricted MV-specific CTL are generated during acute measles. While cell-mediated immunity is important for recovery from acute measles infection, the relative significance of class I- and class II-restricted CTL in recovery from the acute infection and in establishing lifelong immunity to MV is not understood. Three of the 18 patients with acute measles that we studied had low MV CTL at two time points following rash. These three patients recovered without complications, suggesting that MV CTL in low frequency may be sufficient for recovery or that MV CTL is not critical for recovery.

2.3 Measles Virus CTL in Post-Measles Encephalomyelitis

PME is a serious complication of measles that occurs within 3 weeks after the infection and has a 10%–20% fatality rate. Pathologically, the CNS shows a striking resemblance to post-rabies vaccine encephalomyelitis and experimental allergic encephalomyelitis (EAE) in animals, thus suggesting a T cell-mediated attack against the CNS. MV proteins and RNA are usually undetectable in the CNS and there is little evidence for intrathecal anti-measles antibody synthesis (JOHNSON et al. 1984). One hypothesis for the pathogenesis of PME is that MV invades the CNS and induces an autoimmune T cell response directed against a component of the CNS. This is supported by the presence of T cell reactivity to myelin basic protein (MBP) in the peripheral blood of patients with PME (JOHNSON et al. 1984) and the development of MBP-reactive T cells in the course of measles encephalitis in the rat. These MBP-reactive T cells can transfer a disease similar to EAE into naive syngeneic animals (LIEBERT et al. 1987), suggesting that PME might be a T cell-mediated disease.

A second hypothesis is that MV-specific CTL are generated in the course of PME and attack virus-infected CNS cells. In fact, FLEISCHER and KRETH (1983) have demonstrated the presence of CTL clones in the CSF of a patient with PME. More than half of the clones showed MV-specific cytotoxicity and appeared to be HLA class I-restricted (KRETH et al. 1979). Thus, it can be postulated that CTL could recognize MV antigen or a cross-reacting antigen on cerebral endothelial cells and other CNS cells, thus leading to tissue damage. However, the lack of demonstrable MV antigen in the CNS and lack of evidence for T cell cross-reactivity between MV and MBP weaken, but do not exclude, this hypothesis (RICHERT et al. 1988).

2.4 Measles Virus CTL in Subacute Sclerosing Panencephalitis

SSPE is a rare complication of measles which is characterized by a slowly progressive, persistent CNS infection with MV that eventually results in death. The neurons and oligodendrocytes contain MV genome with partially restricted MV protein synthesis, associated with parenchymatous inflammation, gliosis, and variable degrees of demyelination. The serum and CSF contain highly elevated levels of measles antibodies. The pathogenesis of SSPE is not well understood, but a number of hypotheses exist, including (a) defective virus, (b) mutation affecting the M protein, which restricts packaging and budding of the virus, (c) antibody modulation, and (d) infection with MV at a critical differentiation and maturational stage of the CNS and immune system. Another aspect of the pathogenesis of SSPE addresses the failure of the immune system to contain and eliminate the infection. In this regard, a number of hypotheses are plausible: (a) since neurons do not express MHC molecules, this could favor viral persistence, as the infected cells cannot be recognized by CTL, (b) mutations affecting viral epitopes that are critical for CTL recognition of infected cells, or (c) defective MV-specific CTL response (DHIB-JALBUT et al. 1989a).

We have examined the in vitro generation of MV CTL in PBL from patients with SSPE. PBL stimulated with the Edmonston strain of MV for 7 days were tested for lysis of MV-infected autologous EBV-transformed B cells. Since B cells express both MHC class I and class II molecules, this assay measures both MHC class I- and class II-restricted CTL. Two of the four patients had markedly reduced MV CTL compared to healthy donors. One had a moderately low MV CTL response and the fourth had a response comparable to the healthy controls. The response from the later two patients was surprisingly low in the face of an overwhelming persistent infection. Further analysis of the CTL response indicated that the bulk of the killing was mediated by NK cells. Thus, it appears that patients with SSPE may have a defect in the generation of HLA-restricted MV-specific CTL, since the CTL responses to influenza virus and MPS were intact (Fig. 3; DHIB-JALBUT et al. 1989a). As virus-specific CTL plays a role in the recovery from virus infection, a defective MV CTL response in SSPE could contribute to the lack of MV clearance from the CNS. In fact, experimental MV infection of Lewis rat brain supports a role for $CD4^+$ in protection and for $CD8^+$ T cells in recovery. Immunization of Lewis rats with vaccinia recombinants expressing the HA, F, or NC protein protected rats from MV encephalitis. This protection was not affected by $CD8^+$ T Cell depletion and appeared to be CD4 dependent

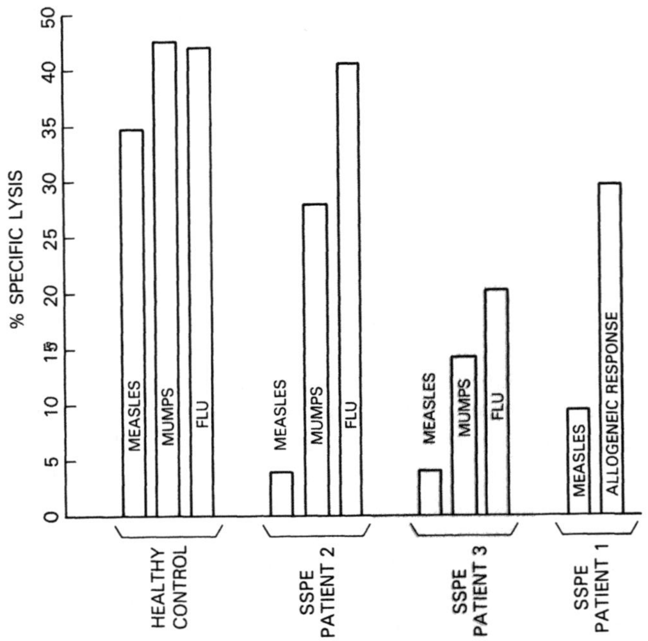

Fig. 3. Virus-specific lysis of autologous targets by measles virus (MV), mumps virus, influenza virus (*flu*), or allogeneic effectors at an effector-to-target ratio of 40: 1 in one healthy control and three subacute sclerosing panencephalitis (*SSPE*) patients. Note the specific reduction in MV cytotoxic T lymphocytes compared to other responses. (Reproduced with permission from DHIB-JALBUT et al. 1989a)

(BRINKMANN et al. 1991). However, in a different study, depletion of $CD8^+$ T cells resulted in prolonged recovery from measles encephalitis and persistence of MV antigen in neurons for a longer period (MAEHLEM et al. 1989).

2.5 Measles Virus CTL in Multiple Sclerosis

MS is an inflammatory demyelinating disease of the CNS of unknown etiology. A heightened antibody response to MV in the serum and CSF has been confirmed in a number of laboratories, but the mechanism for this increased response and its relationship to the pathogenesis of MS remain unclear (DHIB-JALBUT and MCFARLIN 1990). More recently, a defect in the generation of MHC class II-restricted MV-specific CTL has been found in PBL in the majority of MS patients, but not in healthy controls or patients with other neurologic disease of nonviral etiology (JACOBSON et al. 1985). This defect was not predominantly directed against a single MV polypeptide (Fig. 4) and

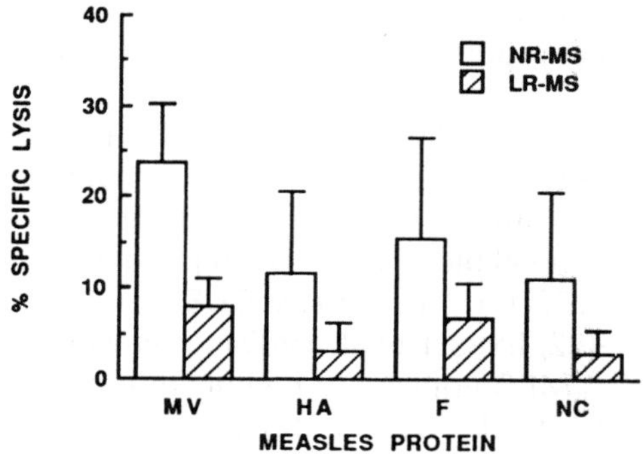

Fig. 4. Cytotoxic T lymphocyte (CTL) responses to measles virus (MV) and its polypeptides hemagglutinin (*HA*), fusion protein (F), and nucleocapsid (*NC*) in six multiple sclerosis (MS) patients with normal MV-CTL response (*NR-MS*) and eight MS patients with low MV CTL (*LR-MS*). Note that the reduction in MV CTL is not due to a defect predominantly involving a single MV polypeptide

did not appear to be due to sequestration of MV CTL in the CNS (DHIB-JALBUT et al. 1989b). The majority of MS patients with reduced MV CTL were subsequently shown to have reduced herpes simplex type I CTL, which is predominantly class II restricted (DESILVA et al. 1991). CTL responses to influenza virus and MPS, which are primarily class I restricted, were intact (JACOBSON et al. 1985; GOODMAN et al. 1989). The defect in generation of an MV CTL response is not MS specific, since it has been found in patients with SSPE (DHIB-JALBUT et al. 1989a) and in patients with human T cell leukemia/lymphoma virus type 1 (HTLV-I)-associated myelopathy (HAM/TSP; JACOBSON et al. 1990). Thus, it appears that the reduction of MHC class II-restricted CTL may be associated with viruses that establish persistence or alternatively may reflect a generalized defect in HLA class II-restricted CTL in MS. Whether the reduced MV CTL in MS is due to reduction in T-helper cell function or differentiation into effector CTL remains unclear.

3 The CTL Response to Mumps Virus

MPS is primarily a childhood infection of the salivary glands causing parotitis, and in rare cases the virus spreads to the kidneys, testicles, and CNS (WOLINSKY and SERVER 1985). Most cases of MPS complications are self-limiting and resolve without sequelae. Patients are left with lifelong immunity and antibodies are detectable in the serum of healthy individuals for many years after the infection. Like MV, MPS is a lymphotropic virus, and lymphoproliferative and virus-specific CTL responses can be generated in vitro from healthy individuals (ENSSLE et al. 1987; KRESS and KRETH 1982; GOODMAN et al. 1989). A cellular immune response to MPS probably develops early during infection and inflammation is readily present in affected tissue. This is further supported by the demonstration of CTL during acute infection and in the spinal fluid of patients with MPS meningitis (KRETH et al. 1982; FLEISHER and KRETH 1983).

The precursor frequency of MPS-specific CTL in PBL of healthy individuals with previous exposure of MPS has been estimated to range between 1/500 and 1/8000 (ENSSLE et al. 1987). Studies of the phenotype and HLA restriction of MPS-specific CTL in peripheral blood and CSF of patients with MPS meningitis demonstrated that MPS CTL are largely $CD8^+$ and HLA class I restricted (KRESS and KRETH 1982; ENSSLE et al. 1987). Interestingly, the magnitude of the CTL response to MPS appears to be linked to certain HLA class I antigens, specifically HLA B7, B13, B27, and Bw52, which may in turn influence the clinical expression of MPS infection.

Recently, GOODMAN et al. (1989) demonstrated that PBL from healthy individuals cultured with MPS for 7 days generated MPS CTL that contained both $CD4^+$ class II-restricted and $CD8^+$ class I-restricted CTL, when EBV-transformed class I and class II expressing B cells were used as targets. The magnitude of this MPS-specific CTL response in healthy individuals ranged between 20% and 65% with a mean of 44.5%. Approximately 40%–60% of the MPS CTL response appeared to be $CD4^+$ class II restricted.

The significance of MPS CTL in recovery from MPS infection and maintenance of long-term immunity is not clear. It appears that MPS CTL are not that critical for recovery from acute infection, as the course of mumps in the hamster is not altered by cyclophosphamide treatment and persistent MPS infection has not developed in immunocompromised patients (WOLINSKY et al. 1985).

4 The CTL Response to Respiratory Syncytial Virus

RSV was initially classified among the paramyxoviruses based on its morphological features. However, because the helical NC of RSV was found to be smaller than that of other paramyxoviruses, it is currently classified in a separate genus, the pneumoviruses. RSV consists of six major structural proteins: a nucleoprotein (N), surface protein (SP), fusion protein (F), matrix protein (M), glycoprotein (G), and phosphoprotein (P; MCINTOSH and CHANOCK 1985).

RSV is a common cause of respiratory tract infection and pneumonia in infants and children. Children lacking cellular immunity are unable to clear the infection effectively and continue to shed virus for several months. In contrast to other paramyxoviruses, immunity to RSV is not permanent and reinfection is common. While serum antibodies to RSV are believed to play a role in protection, cell-mediated immunity is considered important for recovery (MCINTOSH and CHANOCK 1985).

Cell-mediated cytotoxicity has been examined in infants following naturally acquired RSV infection. PBL from these infants showed a peak cytotoxicity against autologous RSV-infected mononuclear cells at 1 week postinfection. Cytotoxicity against allogeneic targets was also present but lower in magnitude, suggesting that RCV cytotoxicity is mediated at least in part by virus-specific CTL (CHIBA et al. 1989).

In healthy adults, RSV-specific memory CTL can be stimulated in vitro by culturing PBL with virus. These PBL manifest class I-restricted CTL response against B lymphoblastoid cell targets infected with recombinant vaccinia viruses expressing the different RSV individual proteins. While N, M, SH, F, and a 22 K were recognized by RSV CTL, most of the response was directed against the N. Fewer individuals developed CTL to G or P (CHERRIE et al. 1992). Similar studies in the mouse identified 22 K protein as the major target for CTL followed by the F and N, but little recognition of P and no recognition of G, SH, or M was observed (NICHOLAS et al. 1990). Interestingly, repeated stimulation of murine CTL with RSV resulted in selective growth of $CD4^+$ CTL which recognized virus-infected but not vaccinia recombinant-infected targets. This is consistent with the concept that different antigen-processing pathways are used by $CD4^+$ and $CD8^+$ CTL. The same group of investigators examined RSV CTL in healthy adults. CTL could be generated after two repeated stimulations of PBL with RSV, and as with MV the CTL was primarily $CD4^+$class II restricted (NICHOLAS et al. 1990).

Collectively, these studies seem to indicate that RSV-specific $CD8^+$ CTL develops during acute infection and probably plays a role in recovery. $CD4^+$ CTL, on the other hand, which can be generated from healthy adults, may play a role in protection. It would be significant to determine whether $CD4^+$ CTL can be generated from infants and children after recovery from RSV infection. If not, this would suggest a role for $CD4^+$ CTL in protection, as infants and children are at higher risk than adults for reinfection.

5 Conclusions

The CTL response to the three human paramyxoviruses, MV, MPS, and RSV, share a number of characteristics. All three viruses can generate both $CD8^+$ class I-restricted and $CD4^+$ class II-restricted CTL. The $CD8^+$ response seems to play a role in the pathogenesis of and recovery from acute infection. The $CD4^+$ response is demonstrable after recovery and may play a role in long-term immunity. With MV and RSV, a CTL response to the individual viral polypeptides has been demonstrated, and further analysis of the fine specificity of CTL epitopes should provide useful information for the development of effective subunit vaccines.

Acknowledgement. We would like to thank Ms. Berñadette Pasko for preparing the typescript for the manuscript.

References

Brinckmann UG, Bankamp B, Reich A, Ter Meulen V, Liebert UG (1991) Efficacy of individual measles virus structural proteins in the protection of rats from measles encephalitis. J Gen Virol 72: 2491–2500

Cherrie AH, Anderson K, Wertz GW, Openshaw PJ (1992) Human cytotoxic T cells stimulated by antigen in dendritic cells recognize the N, SH, F, M, 22 K, and 1 b proteins of respiratory syncytial virus. J Virol 66: 2102–2110

Chiba Y, Higashidate Y, Suga K, Honjo K, Tsutsumi H, Ogra PL (1989) Development of cell-mediated cytotoxic immunity to respiratory syncytial virus in human infants following naturally acquired infection. J Med Virol 28: 133–139

DeSilva SM, McFarland HF (1991) Multiple sclerosis patients have reduced HLA class II-restricted cytotoxic responses specific for both measles and herpes virus. J Neuroimmunol 35: 219–226

Dhib-Jalbut S, McFarlin DE (1990) Immunology of multiple sclerosis. Ann Allergy 64: 433–444

Dhib-Jalbut S, Jacobson S, McFarlin DE, McFarland HF (1989a) Impaired human leukocyte antigen-restricted measles virus-specific cytotoxic T-cell response in subacute sclerosing panencephalitis. Ann Neurol 25: 272–280

Dhib-Jalbut S, McFarlin DE, McFarland HF (1989b) Measles virus polypeptide specificity of the cytotoxic T-lymphocyte response in multiple sclerosis. J Neuroimmunol 21: 205–212

Enssle KH, Wagner H, Fleischer B (1987) Human mumps virus-specific cytotoxic T lymphocytes. Quantitative analysis of HLA restriction. Hum Immunol 18: 135–149

Fleischer B, Kreth HW (1983) Clonal expansion and functional analysis of virus-specific T-lymphocytes from cerebrospinal fluid in measles encephalitis. Hum Immunol 7: 239–248

Fleisher B, Kreth HW (1983) Clonal analysis of HLA-restricted virus-specific cytotoxic T-lymphocytes from cerebrospinal fluid in mumps meningitis. J Immunol 150: 2187

Goodman AD, Jacobson S, McFarland HF (1989) Virus-specific cytotoxic T lymphocytes in multiple sclerosis: a normal mumps virus response adds support for a distinct improvement in the measles virus response. J Neuroimmunol 22: 201–209

Jacobson S, Richert JR, Biddison WE, Satinsky A, Hartzman RJ, McFarland HF (1984) Measles virus-specific $T4^+$ human cytotoxic cell clones are restricted by class II HLA antigens. J Immunol 133: 754–757

Jacobson S, Flerlage ML, McFarland HF (1985) Impaired measles virus-specific cytotoxic T cell responses in multiple sclerosis. J Exp Med 162: 839–850

Jacobson S, Rose JW, Flerlage ML, Mingioli EE, McFarlin DE, McFarland HF (1987) Measles virus-specific human cytotoxic T-cells generated in bulk culture. Analysis of measles virus antigenic specificity. In: Mahy B, Kolakofsky D (eds) The biology of negative strand virus, chap 37. Elsevier Science, New York, pp 283–289

Jacobson S, Gupta A, Matson D, Mingioli E, McFarlin DE (1990) Immunological studies in tropic spastic paraparesis. Anal Neurol 27: 149–156

Johnson RT, Griffin DE, Hirsch RL, Wolinsky JS, Roedenbeck S, Lindo de Suriano I, Vaisberg A (1984) Measles encephalomyelitis—clinical and immunologic studies. N Engl J Med 330: 137–145

Kaplan LJ, Daum RS, Smaron M, McCarthy LA (1992) Severe measles in immunocompromised patients. JAMA 267: 1237–1241

Kingsbury DW (1985) Orthomyxo- and paramyxoviruses and their replications. In: Fields BN et al. (eds) Virology, chap 50. Raven, New York, pp 1157–1178

Kress HG, Kreth HW (1982) HLA-restriction of secondary mumps—specific cytotoxic T lymphocytes. J Immunol 129: 844

Kreth HW, Ter Meulen V, Eckert G (1979) Demonstration of HLA restricted killer cells in patients with acute measles. Med Microbiol Immunol 165: 203–214

Kreth HW, Kress L, Kress HG, Oh HF, Eckert G (1982) Demonstration of primary cytotoxic T-cells in venous blood and cerebrospinal fluid of children with mumps meningitis. J Immunol 128: 2411

Liebert UG, Linington C, ter Meulen V (1987) Induction of autoimmune reactions to myelin basic protein in measles virus encephalomyelitis in Lewis rats. J Neuroimmunol 17: 103

Lucas CJ, Biddison WE, Nelson DL, Shaw S (1983) Killing of measles virus-infected cells by human cytotoxic T-cells. Infect Immunol 38: 226–232

Maehem J, Olsson T, Love A, Klareskog L, Norrby E, Kristensson K (1989) Persistence of measles virus in rat brain neurons is promoted by depletion of CD8⁺ T-cells. J Neuroimmunol 21:149–155

McIntosh K, Chanock RM (1985) Respiratory syncytial virus. In: Fields BN et al. (eds) Virology, chap 54. Raven, New York, pp 1285–1304

Nicholas JA, Rubino KL, Levely ME, Adams EG, Collins PL (1990) Cytolytic T-lymphocyte responses to respiratory syncytial virus: effector cell phenotype and target proteins. J Virol 64:4232–4241

Norrby E (1985) Measles. In: Fields BN et al. (eds) Virology, chap 55. Raven, New York, pp 1305–1321

Richert JR, Robinson ED, Reuben-Bornsidl CA, Johnson AH, McFarland HF, McFarlin DE, Hartzman RT (1988) Measles virus-specific T-cell clones. Studies of alloreactivity and antigenic cross reactivity. J Neuroimmunol 19:59–68

Sha BE, Harris AA, Benson CA, Atkinson WL, Urbanski PA, Stewart JA, Williams WW, Murphy RL, Phair JP, Levin SA, Kessler HA (1991) Prevalence of measles antibodies in asymptomatic human immunodeficiency in virus-infected adults. J Infect Dis 164:473–475

Sissons Patrick JG, Colby SD, Harrison WO, Oldstone MB (1985) Cytotoxic lymphocytes generated in vivo with acute measles virus infection. Clin Immunol Immunopathol 34:60–68

Suringa DWR, Bank LJ, Ackerman AB (1970) Role of measles virus in skin lesions and Koplik's spots. N Engl J Med 283:1139–1142

Van Binnendijk RS, Poelen MCM, DeVries P, Voorma HO, Osterhaus ADME, Uytdehaag FGCM (1989) Measles virus-specific human T cell clones. Characterization of specificity and function of $CD4^+$ helper/cytotoxic and $CD8^+$ cytotoxic T-cell clones. J Immunol 142: 2897–2854

Van Binnendijk RS, Poelen MCM, Kuijpers KC, Osterhaus ADME, Uytdehaag FGCM (1990) The predominance of $CD8^+$ T cells after infection with measles virus suggests a role for $CD8^+$ class I MHC-restricted cytotoxic T lymphocytes (CTL) in recovery from measles. Clonal analysis of human $CD8^+$ class I MHC-restricted CTL. J Immunol 144: 2394–2399

Wolinsky JS, Server AC (1985) Mumps virus. In: Fields BN et al. (eds) Virology, chap 53. Raven, New York, pp 1255–1284

Wu VH, McFarland HF, Mayo K, Hanger L, Griffin DE, Dhib-Jalbut S (1993) Measles virus-specific cellular immunity in patients with vaccine failure. J Clin Microbiol 31:118–122

Cytotoxic T Cells and Human Herpes Virus Infections

L. K. BORYSIEWICZ[1] and J. G. P. SISSONS[2]

[1] Department of Medicine, University of Wales College of Medicine, Heath Park, Cardiff CF4 4XN, UK

[2] Department of Medicine, University of Cambridge Clinical School, Hills Road, Cambridge CB2 2QQ, UK

Current Topics in Microbiology and Immunology, Vol. 189

1 Introduction

This chapter reviews what is currently known about the role of cytotoxic T lymphocytes (CTL) in human herpesvirus infections.

1.1 Importance of Human Herpesviruses

Herpesviruses are large, double-stranded DNA viruses which infect a wide range of vertebrate hosts. They all establish persistent or latent infection and are widely prevalent in their host population. Members of the family cause a range of diseases, distinct syndromes often being associated with primary infection and with reactivation of the virus from latency—some members have in addition been associated with certain tumours. The tendency of all these viruses to reactivate and produce disease in the context of immunosuppression has long suggested that the immune response—particularly the T cell response—plays an important role in controlling infection in the normal host. It is important to emphasise that although this review is restricted to CTL, they are only one component of the immune response: T cells mediating help and delayed hypersensitivity and antibody may also play a role in the control of infection.

1.2 Methods and Problems in the Study of Human Virus-Specific CTL

Although we cannot deal in any detail with the methodology of CTL assays, there are some points worth emphasising and which are important to bear in mind when interpreting published work in this area. In murine experimental models, CTL can be directly sampled from lymph nodes and spleen at any chosen time point during an experimentally induced virus infection. The contribution of CTL to the overall immune response can be analysed by depletion and adoptive transfer experiments and the role of immunogenetic factors clearly defined using inbred strains. In humans by contrast, peripheral blood is usually the only compartment that can be sampled, and it is often difficult to obtain samples during a natural virus infection. These two factors in particular mean that in order to obtain activated effector T cells, memory cells present in peripheral blood have to be subjected to secondary restimulation in vitro and, depending on the protocol adopted, this can lead to a selection bias. It is in addition obviously more difficult to examine the influence of immunogenetic factors and very difficult to do clinical experiments to establish an unequivocal protective role for CTL.

The method adopted for assaying human virus specific CTL varies, although almost all culminate in an assay of chromium release from appropriately major histocompatibility complex (MHC)-matched target cells infected with virus or expressing a particular virus gene product; the extent to which MHC restriction and natural killer cell activity are controlled varies considerably between reported studies. Secondary in vitro restimulation of CTL precursors is usually achieved by culturing peripheral blood mononuclear cells (PBMC) with virus or virus-infected cells for 1–2 weeks, with addition of exogenous interleukin-2 (IL-2); alternatively, a recombinant protein or peptide epitope may be used. Usually during this period the cells are kept as a bulk culture, but they may be set up in limiting dilution culture, which allows CTL precursors to be quantitated. The T cells may also be cloned following restimulation and before being assayed, which potentially introduces a major selection step, although it has proved particularly difficult to maintain human $CD8^+$ CTL clones. A better understanding of the factors involved in T cell activation should lead to improvement in the efficiency with which T cells can be activated in vitro: as an example, the recent recognition of the interaction between the B7 molecule on the antigen-presenting cell and CD28 on the T cell, as a major co-stimulatory signal inducing IL-2 production even in $CD8^+$ CTL, is likely to be important in this context (see SCHWARTZ 1992).

2 Virology and Biology of Herpesvirus Infections

This topic is dealt with in depth in recent reviews and texts (ROIZMAN 1990). Here we only deal briefly with aspects relevant to the immunolgy of the infection.

2.1 Human Herpesviruses

There are currently six recognized human herpesviruses, whose nomenclature is shown in Table 1.

2.2 Genome Structure

Herpesviruses have large, double-stranded DNA genomes coding for 150–200 proteins. All have now been completely sequenced at the DNA level, revealing blocks of conserved genes but with others distinctive for a particular virus (BAER et al. 1984; DAVISON and SCOTT 1986; CHEE et al. 1990). These homologies justify the grouping of vricella zoster virus (VZV) and herpes simplex virus types 1 and 2 (HSV-1 and -2) as alpha herpesviruses and show that the relatively recently isolated human herpesvirus 6 is closer to

Table 1. The human herpesviruses

Common name	Designation	Subfamily	Genome size (kilobase pairs)	Site of persistence
Herpes simplex virus 1	Human herpesvirus 1	α	152	Neurons (sensory ganglia)
Herpes simplex virus 2	Human herpesvirus 2	α	152	Neurons (sensory ganglia)
Varicella zoster virus	Human herpesvirus 3	α	125	Neurons (sensory ganglia)
Epstein-Barr virus	Human herpesvirus 4	γ	172	B cells, oropharyngeal epithelium
Cytomegalovirus	Human herpesvirus 5	β	235	Monocytes, epithelial cells
	Human herpesvirus 6	β	170	Monocytes, T cells

cytomegalovirus (CMV) than to the other herpesviruses. The sequencing has also revealed genes with homology to cellular genes: in the case of human CMV (HCMV), which has the largest genome of the human herpesviruses, its extra size is accounted for by many extra open reading frames coding for glycoproteins; some of these show homology to human cellular proteins including the class I MHC heavy chain (BECK and BARRELL 1988) and G protein-coupled receptors (CHEE et al. 1990). Homologies to cellular genes exist in other herpesviruses, for instance to the C3b receptor in HSV and to IL-10 in Epstein-Barr virus (EBV).

2.3 Regulation of Gene Expression

Herpesvirus genes are expressed in a temporally regulated sequence designated immediate–early (IE), early and late (this nomenclature is not used in the case of EBV, although there are broadly analogous genes expressed in its latent and lytic cycles). The control of transcription of these genes is critical to initiating the infection; it is also important to emphasise that gene expression may be restricted in some tissues, particularly those in which the virus persists or is latent. In addition expression of viral genes may be linked to the state of activation or differentiation of the cell; for instance, HCMV is not expressed in monocytes, but is when these cells differentiate into tissue macrophages (IBANEZ et al. 1991; TAYLOR-WIEDEMAN et al. 1991), and the extent of EBV gene expression varies in different B cell and Burkitt lymphoma lines (MURRAY 1992; ROWE et al. 1992). These differences in viral gene expression dependent on cell type probably result from the presence or absence of specific cellular transcription factors which bind to the promoter regulatory region of viral genes. Such cellular factors are particularly important in controlling transcription of IE genes (GARCIA-BLANCO and CULLEN 1991). Viral proteins may have transactivating functions; for instance, the HSV vMW65 virion protein transactivates the IE genes of the virus (ROIZMAN and SEARS 1990), and the IE proteins themselves transactivate expression of the early viral genes and may autoregulate their own expression (STAMMINGER and FLECKENSTEIN 1990). In addition, certain viral IE genes may also be capable of transactivating cellular genes (HAGEMEIER et al. 1992). These considerations are all important in determining which gene products are available for recognition by the immune response.

2.4 Latency and Persistence

The alpha herpesviruses establish latent infection in neuronal cells in sensory ganglia, whence they periodically reactivate and are transported down the axon to infect cells at the nerve ending. There is little or no viral transcription occurring for most of the time, the only consistent transcript detected in HSV latency in neurons being the latency-associated transcript (LAT), which is not expressed as protein and whose function is uncertain (see ROIZMAN and SEARS 1990). Whether the infected neuron is susceptible to attack by CTL or other immunological mechanisms is again uncertain, but seems unlikely.

EBV persists in a small fraction of B cells. In lymphoblastoid B cell lines in vitro, the EBV DNA exists as an episome which is maintained at constant copy number as the cells divide; EBV also persists in epithelial cells in the oropharynx. There is probably restricted EBV gene expression in the B cell, whereas viral replication occurs in the oropharyngeal epithelium. The extent to which these two sites of persistence are accessible to the immune response in vivo is uncertain, although it is assumed that the potential of EBV to induce B cell transformation is somehow restrained in vivo by the T cell response (ROWE et al. 1992).

There is less certainty concerning the sites at which HCMV persists, but HCMV DNA is present in monocytes in normal virus carriers and probably also persists at epithelial sites such as the salivary gland. There appears to be little or no transcription in monocytes, and the extent to which either site of persistence is accessible to the immune response is again unknown (TAYLOR-WIEDEMAN et al. 1991; IBANEZ et al. 1991). Human herpesvirus 6 replicates in activated T cells in vitro and is detectable in PBMC, probably in T cells and monocytes in vivo (see THOMSON et al. 1991).

The mechanisms by which latency is maintained are in general relatively poorly understood, but are a major area of current study in herpes virology.

3 CTL in Experimental Herpes Virus Infections

Although this review deals with human CTL, there is a great deal of work on experimental herpesvirus infections in animals, especially the mouse. This is reviewed elsewhere (MESTER and ROUSE 1991; KOSZINOWSKI et al. 1990), but we refer briefly to those aspects which seem particularly pertinent to the role of CTL in human herpesvirus infections.

3.1 Herpes Simplex Virus in the Mouse

Although a number of animal models of HSV infection have been described, how representative they are of the human disease, and thus how well the recorded immune responses accord with man, is arguable (MESTER and ROUSE 1991). The mouse has been particularly used to study challenge inoculation by a number of routes—the most representative probably being the ear clearance model, particularly when used to study local protection. The zosteriform spread model has been used to examine factors that may be important in recrudescent disease, although no reproducible model of latency and reactivation is established in the mouse (MESTER and ROUSE 1991). $CD4^+$ delayed-type hypersensitivity (DTH) cells were of particular importance in the clearance of low-dose virus such as with local ear inoculation, whereas $CD8^+$ CTL protect against high-dose infection. Murine $CD8^+$ CTL clear HSV-infected cells in vivo in immunodepletion studies (NASH et al. 1987). In addition, shedding of virus at the site of infection may be reduced by $CD8^+$ T cells (BONNEAU and JENNINGS 1988). These murine $CD8^+$ CTL recognise both viral glycoproteins, and in limiting dilution studies approximately 30% of the CTL response is directed against IE antigens (MARTIN et al. 1988). In order to study recurrent disease, the guinea pig vaginal model has been used: genital infection can be produced and reactivation induced by similar mechanisms to those which reactivate human infection. For these reasons it is used as a model in which to test candidate HSV vaccines. The obvious disadvantage is that there is less scope for manipulating the immune system: the absence of specific T cell markers in this animal makes detailed examination of the CTL response difficult, although CTL have been described (STANBERRY 1991).

3.2 Murine Cytomegalovirus Infection

The cytomegaloviruses are species specific and HCMV does not infect the mouse. However, murine CMV (MCMV), although not able to productively infect human cells, has somewhat similar biology to HCMV and has been used as a model of HCMV infection.

Koszinowski, Reddehase and colleagues have reported extensive studies of the role of CTL in MCMV infection using the Balb/c strain of mice and have recently reviewed these in detail (KOSZINOWSKI et al. 1990). Following infection via the footpad, MCMV-specific CTL are recoverable from the draining lymph node. In acute infection there is a dominant population (about 50% of the MCMV-specific $CD8^+$ CTL) detectable showing specificity for determinants expressed at IE times (principally the major IE protein of MCMV). Other CTL are specific for unidentified structural proteins of the virion, detected by their ability to lyse target cells infected with UV-inactivated virus (REDDEHASE et al. 1984); during persistent infection, the former population predominate. In adoptive transfer experiments into irradiated MCMV-infected mice, $CD8^+$ CTL specific for the 89-kDa IE protein transfer protection from lethal MCMV infection (REDDEHASE et al. 1987). The clearance of MCMV from the lungs of infected mice has also been shown to be mediated by the same $CD8^+$ population (M. Reddehase, personal communication). This protective CTL response has been mapped to a pentapeptide from the IE protein which binds to H2-L^d. Mice vaccinated with a recombinant vaccinia virus expressing the 89-kDa protein are also protected from subsequent lethal challenge (JONJIC et al. 1988). In CD8-depleted mice, $CD4^+$ cells can transfer a degree of protection from lethal challenge, but require an accessory cell for the effect. However, the clearance of MCMV from the salivary gland has been shown to depend completely on $CD4^+$ cells and to be mediated by γ-interferon produced by these cells (JONJIC et al. 1989; LUCIN et al. 1992).

Whilst this elegant work clearly demonstrates a role for IE-specific CTL in this model, it has to be remembered that the work does all apply to a single inbred mouse strain, and the extent to which the results are generalisable to HCMV infection remains to be determined.

It is worth mentioning that MCMV is also one of the few experimental virus infections in which a protective role for NK cells has been convincingly shown (BUKOWSKI et al. 1985).

3.3 Other Experimental Infections

A recently described herpesvirus isolated from wild mice seems to have the characteristics of a murine equivalent of EBV (SUNIL-CHANDRA et al. 1992a, b). If initial studies are borne out, this could become an extremely valuable model, as the only other experimental model of EBV is EBV infection of cottontop tamarinds. This latter model has been used to study candidate EBV vaccines, particularly that based on gp340; studies to date have provided evidence of protection against EBV - induced lymphomagenesis in this model (MORGAN 1991).

4 CTL in Herpes Simplex Virus Infection

4.1 Asymptomatic Persistent Infection

As described above, HSV-specific CTL responses have been extensively investigated in a variety of murine models. In these experimental systems, such cells have been shown to mediate a variety of protective responses, but a major difficulty in their interpretation is knowing how representative they are of human HSV infection, particularly in considering episodes of reactivation in man (MESTER and ROUSE 1991). Initial attempts to demonstrate the presence of CTL activity against HSV in man frequently resulted in generation of $CD4^+$ CTL in vitro (TORPEY and LINDSLEY 1989; MESTER and ROUSE 1991; SCHMID 1988) at a relatively high precursor frequency of 1/4000–1/20 000 PBMC. These experiments predominantly used a secondary in vitro stimulation protocol where UV-inactivated virus was added to PBMC. It may therefore not be surprising that as with other human herpesviruses when this protocol is used, e.g. HCMV (BORYSIEWICZ et al. 1983), T cells with this phenotype predominated. ZARLING et al. (1986, 1988; YASUKAWA and ZARLING

1985) investigated the specificity of this CD4 CTL response in a series of human CD4$^+$ CTL clones. They showed that such isolated clones recognised HSV glycoproteins gB and gD (ZARLING et al. 1986). In addition, these CD4$^+$ CTL clones secreted IL-2 (ZARLING et al. 1988).

However, YASUKAWA et al. (1989) found that by altering the in vitro stimulation protocol to co-culture PBMC with HSV-infected cells, they were able to establish CD8$^+$ CTL lines. These studies have been extended by TIGGES et al. (1992), who used HSV-2-infected irradiated stimulator cells with PBMC from a subject with recurrent genital herpes. They then cloned the responding cells by limiting dilution, using phytohemagglutinin (PHA) and allogeneic irradiated feeder cells, to generate seven HSV-specific CD8$^+$ CTL clones. Six of these were HSV-2 specific, one cross-reacting with HSV-1. One clone recognised IE viral antigens, whereas five recognised virion proteins that did not require de novo viral protein synthesis in the infected target cells. Only one of the clones was further defined using HSV-2 vaccinia recombinants as being gD-2 specific.

4.2 Disease and Immunosuppression

The cutaneous location of HSV-1 lesions makes them ideally suited to examine infiltration by T cells. CUNNINGHAM et al. (1985) found that CD4$^+$ T cells are the first cells to infiltrate a cutaneous lesion, together with macrophages, although whether these cells mediate direct cytotoxicity or are the counterpart of the murine CD4$^+$ DTH cells is unknown. By day 3, CD8$^+$ T cells are present in the lesion. Similarly, in the cornea affected by herpetic keratitis, both CD4$^+$ and CD8$^+$ T cells were present, together with increased MHC class II expression on surrounding epithelium (CUNNINGHAM and NOBLE 1989).

5 CTL in Varicella Zoster Virus Infection

There have been a relatively limited number of studies of VZV-specific CTL, and there is no specific animal model. However, one interesting clinical aspect of VZV infection is that a live vaccine has been used for some time and offers a chance to assess the induction of effector T cells in vivo.

5.1 Asymptomatic Persistent Infection

VZV-specific CTL can be generated from the peripheral blood of most normal seropositive patients. The generation of both CD4$^+$ and CD8$^+$ CTL has been reported, with more concentration on CD4$^+$ CTL in published work. It seems probable that the phenotype of the responding cell to a considerable extent reflects the method of secondary in vitro stimulation: most studies have used inactivated VZV antigen, whereas few have used VZV-infected cells. The target cells used are usually VZV-infected lymphoblastoid cell lines, but expression of VZV may not be complete in such cells. Infected fibroblasts have also been used. VZV is characteristically strongly cell associated, which leads to difficulty in achieving synchronous infection of target cells. It is presumably this difficulty in using a system which allows endogenous expression of VZV that has led to the use of inactivated VZV antigen for in vitro restimulation.

HAYWARD et al. (1986a) first reported the generation of CD4$^+$ VZV-specific CTL clones. Arvin and colleagues (see ARVIN 1992) have also reported the generation of VZV-specific CTL using inactivated VZV antigen. They also reported that if CD4$^+$ cells were removed from these experiments at the beginning of the period of in vitro restimulation, then CD8$^+$ CTL could be generated (ARVIN et al. 1991). This lack of requirement for CD4$^+$ cells to generate a CD8$^+$ response and the ability of inactivated antigen to generate a CD4 or CD8 CTL response with equal facility are both noteable. HICKLING et al. (1987) used VZV-infected autologous B cell lines to restimulate, and fibroblasts (which do not express class II MHC molecules) as the target cells, and found that class I-restricted CTL could be demonstrated in four subjects. The frequency of VZV-specific T cells generated by this latter protocol was also estimated by limiting dilution analysis (LDA): the reported frequencies varied from 11 to 30 per 10^6 T cells (HICKLING et al. 1987). Direct VZV-specific cytotoxicity for infected fibroblasts in unstimulated PBMC had been detected by BOWDEN et al. (1985) and reported to be partially HLA restricted; however, such direct class I-restricted cytotoxicity was not detectable by HICKLING et al. (and is in general unusual in normal individuals in any persistent infection). Particular care must be taken to exclude induced NK cytotoxicity in this system (HAYWARD et al. 1986b).

It has been suggested that the frequency of VZV-specific CTL is maintained by subclinical reactivation. There are reports of VZV DNA being detected in the PBMC of immunosuppressed individuals after bone marrow transplantation and of this correlating with return of proliferative T cell responses (WILSON et al. 1992). Whether VZV DNA is intermittently detectable in normal individuals is not reported.

5.2 Disease and Immunosuppression

In one report of studies on subjects with varicella, direct CTL cytotoxicity could not be demonstrated using fresh PBMC, although it was present after restimulation as in normal VZV carriers (DIAZ et al. 1989).

There are several reports of subjects who have been studied after an episode of herpes zoster. The frequency of T cells responding to VZV antigen in proliferation assays is increased for up to 2 years following zoster, compared to age-matched controls (HAYWARD et al. 1991). Conversely, the frequency of proliferating T cells declines with increasing age in subjects who have *not* had clinical zoster, as assessed by LDA and crude proliferation assays (HAYWARD and HERBERGER 1987).

The frequency of $CD8^+$ class I-restricted VZV-specific CTL assessed by LDA has also been reported to be increased following zoster in a few subjects (HICKLING et al. 1987).

5.3 Specificity for Viral Gene Products

Using recombinant vaccinia viruses expressing the IE62 protein and glycoprotein I of VZV, precursor frequencies of $CD4^+$ and $CD8^+$ CTL specific for these two proteins, assessed by LDA, have been reported to be similar in normal virus carriers—of the order of 1/100 000, although the range was very wide (ARVIN et al. 1991). The same authors also found that CTL with the same specificity could be induced by vaccination of VZV-uninfected volunteers with the Oka VZV vaccine (SHARP et al. 1992). CTL specific for gpIV and gpV of VZV have also been reported with similar frequencies to those cited above (SHARP et al. 1992). There are no reports of specificity for other VZV proteins, the above appearing to be the only ones reported in the literature.

6 CTL in Epstein-Barr Virus Infection

Unlike the generation of most human virus-specific CTL, which requires secondary in vitro stimulation with autologous virus-infected cells, EBV CTL activity was identified by MOSS et al. (1978) after observing regression of EBV-transformed B cells in vitro. In vitro infection of PBMC from seronegative subjects with EBV resulted in the outgrowth of EBV nuclear antigen (EBNA)-positive B cell lines; however, in seropositive subjects, initial outgrowth of colonies was halted. This regression was T cell dependent and could be diluted out such that a quantitative estimate of the relative number of T cells mediating this effect could be made. Further studies allowed the establishment of classical $CD8^+$, MHC class I-restricted CTL lines and clones (RICKINSON et al. 1981; MOSS et al. 1988). Although most further studies have focused on the nature, specificity and role of these $CD8^+$ cells, as with the other herpesviruses, $CD4^+$, MHC class II-restricted CTL have also been described (MOSS et al. 1988).

6.1 Asymptomatic Persistent Infection, Disease and Immunosuppression

The role of EBV-specific cytotoxic T cells in protecting the host against the range of clinical disease associated with the virus remains an important issue, but one that is difficult to approach directly, particularly in the absence of a good animal model of disease. No specific $CD8^+$ CTL activity can be found in seronegative subjects, but shortly after symptomatic primary infection with infectious mononucleosis CTL are present in PBMC (ENSSLE and FLEISCHER 1990), and this response persists at a high precursor frequency throughout life (RICKINSON et al. 1981; ENSSLE and FLEISCHER 1990; ALP et al. 1990).

Clinically, EBV has been associated with a number of diseases which are particularly apparent in immunosuppressed subjects, namely monoclonal and polyclonal B cell lymphoma (NALESNIK 1991), oral hairy leukoplakia and interstitial pneumonitis. In addition, Burkitt's lymphoma and nasopharyngeal carcinoma are strongly associated with EBV, although association with immunosuppression in this context is less well established. Indeed, the tumour cells of Burkitt's lymphoma may have a phenotype which expresses only EBNA-1, together with reduced expression of adhesin molecules, thereby precluding lysis by CTL (GREGORY et al. 1988). Following immunosuppression with a range of pharmacological agents, there is increased shedding of EBV, but although it was initially suggested that this was associated with reduced specific CTL in PBMC, later studies by YAO et al. (1985) failed to define a direct association. The increased incidence of EBV-associated lymphoproliferative disease with prolonged use of agents such as cyclosporin A and FK506, which suppress T cell activation, does, however, implicate mechanisms based on cellular immune responses. However, tumour regression often occurs within 1–2 weeks of stopping such medication, suggesting that CTL may not be directly involved in this process (NALESNIK 1991).

Another condition associated with outgrowth of EBV-transformed B cells is the X-linked lymphoproliferative syndrome (XLP) (PURTILLO 1991). This disease is characterised by a seemingly unique susceptibility of male members of affected families to EBV. This results in often fatal infectious mononucleosis, hypogammaglobulinaemia or malignant lymphoma, with 60% of males dying by 10 years of age. A defect has been identified located at Xq25–26 (WYANDT et al. 1989). A number of EBV-specific defects have been identified in these individuals, including a failure of NK and $CD8^+$ CTL responses to EBV-transformed B cells. However, the nature of the disease phenotype is still unclear, as a number of other defects are reported, including an early susceptibility to a variety of other viruses (for example, 5% had measles pneumonitis), as well as a failure to mount an efficient IgM response with immunoglobulin class switching to experimental challenge with ϕX174 (PURTILLO et al. 1989). Thus, although the failure to generate an effective $CD8^+$ CTL response may be associated with the development of EBV-associated lymphoproliferation, this does not occur in isolation, even in this genetically defined disorder.

Defining the precise role of $CD8^+$ CTL in γ-herpesvirus infections has been hampered by the absence of an animal model. The cottontop tamarind colony established in Bristol, UK, is a unique resource: the animals develop widespread lymphoma on exposure to EBV (SHOPE et al. 1973), but they are a protected species, precluding their widespread use as an experimental model. Recently, a murine herpesvirus with many of the features of EBV infection has been described by Nash and colleagues (SUNIL-CHANDRA et al. 1992a, b) and this may provide a model system where pathogenesis can be investigated in more detail.

6.2 Specificity for Viral Gene Products

Initial characterisation of the virus products recognised by these CTL was hampered by the failure to serologically define which virus product was involved. The concentration on membrane-associated proteins led to the circular definition of the target structure as LYDMA (lymphocyte-determined membrane antigen) that was present on autologous EBV-transformed cell lines (RICKINSON et al. 1981). However, as firstly influenza-specific CTL and then other virus-specific CTL were shown to recognise nuclear antigens, and then peptide fragments of these antigens associated with MHC class I, attention focused on the range of viral proteins expressed in EBV-transformed B cells in vitro. Less than 5% of EBV-transformed B cells express viral proteins associated with the lytic cycle of replication, and yet BCL are killed by EBV-specific $CD8^+$ CTL. Thus, a detailed examination of latency-associated proteins as targets for CTL has been pursued.

EBV-transformed B cells are known to express six viral nuclear proteins (EBNA), three membrane proteins (latent membrane proteins, LMP) and two small EBV-encoded RNAs (EBER; SAMPLE and KIEFF 1991). These proteins subserve a number of functions involved with maintenance of episomal replication and transmission of the genome (EBNA-1), immortalisation of B cells and alteration of host cell gene expression (EBNA-2), and inhibition of terminal differentiation of epithelial cells (LMP-1).

The mechanisms involved in immortalisation of B cells have not been fully elucidated. After binding of virus to the C3d (CD21) receptor, there is increased expression of CD23 (a B cell-derived B cell growth factor) with partial activation of the infected B cells (GORDON et al. 1986). EBNA-2 and EBNA-leader protein (EBNA-LP) are expressed after 8–12 h, with the other EBNAs and LMP after 32 h (ALFIERI et al. 1991). These latter changes are coincident with increased CD21 and CD23, together with increased c-*myc* expression. The EBER are not maximally expressed until 70 h post-infection. EBNA-2 is crucial for transformation; EBNA-2-deleted virus does not immortalise B cells, but this capacity is restored by replacing the gene

(HAMMERSCHMIDT and SUGDEN 1989). EBNA–LP, whilst not essential for immortalisation, augments the capacity of EBNA-2^{+} virus to mediate this function (ROONEY et al. 1989). These observations based on studies with a mutant virus are consistent with the view that the other latency-associated viral proteins may also have an important role, and the function of EBNA-2 may be to activate expression of these and host cell genes to favour continued growth. This may be achieved by EBNA-2, which with LMP-1 protects infected cells from natural apoptosis (GREGORY et al. 1991).

Whilst attention focused on possible membrane-associated antigens that may induce a CTL response, the first suggestion was that LMP-1 may act as a CTL target (THORLEY-LAWSON and ISRAELSOHN 1987). In this study, a sequence of the LMP protein was able to activate a CTL response, but was not recognised as a peptide fragment in the conventional manner. Killing of double-transfected P815 murine tumour cells expressing HLA A11 and LMP was observed (MURRAY et al. 1988); however, the same group subsequently found that the determinant recognised was associated with the murine H-2 K^{d}, and not the transfected HLA gene (MURRAY et al. 1990). Recently, MOSS et al. (1991) have reported an epitope for CTL in LMP using vaccinia-infected target cells.

The definition of target EBV latent gene proteins for specific CTL has been aided by the identification of two distinct types of EBV: A and B. They are separated on the basis of their differences in the *Bam* H1 WYH and *Hind*III E regions—corresponding to sequence divergence in EBNA 2, 3, 4 and 6. The EBV type B proteins are both antigenically distinct and are less efficient in B cell immortalisation (RICKINSON et al. 1987). When EBV regression assays were performed using type A- or B-EBV, most donors had equivalent responses, but two subjects were identified in whom the response to type A virus was stronger than to type B, suggesting that epitopes specific to type A predominated in these individuals (BURROWS et al. 1990). A series of experiments using type A-specific CTL and type B-transformed autologous target cells, infected with vaccinia recombinants, demonstrated EBNA-2 (epitope located in the N-terminal 100 amino acids) and EBNA-3a (MURRAY et al. 1990) specificity. Peptides within EBNA-2 (DTPLIPLTIF—HLA A2; APOLLANI et al. 1992), EBNA-3 (FLRGRAYGI—HLA B8; BURROWS et al. 1990, 1992; MISKO et al. 1991) and EBNA-6 (EENLLDFVRF—HLA B44; APOLLANI et al. 1992; KEHVIQNAFRK—HLA A11), defined on the basis of sequence divergence between type A and B virus, but also by conformation with predictive algorithms (DELISI and BERZOFSKY 1985; ROTHBARD and TAYLOR 1988), are recognised by appropriately restricted specific CTL lines and clones (MOSS et al. 1991). Anti-IgM-activated B cell blasts infected with vaccinia recombinants expressing the EBV latent genes were also used as target cells, with CTL clones generated from autologous B cell lines (B95.8 transformed) to define B-type epitopes (MOSS et al. 1991). It is of particular interest that to date no CTL epitopes have been identified in EBNA-1, especially as Burkitt's lymphoma cells, which express only this EBNA protein

(ROWE et al. 1986), are relatively resistant to CTL lysis. Whether this is due to lack of appropriate virus antigen and/or reduced MHC class I, intercellular adhesion molecule (ICAM) and LFA-3 expression (GREGORY et al. 1988) is unknown (see below).

An important question in relation to the possible role of CTL in surveillance against persistent virus infection is whether selection of variant virus in vivo may occur by mutation in the CTL epitope. Such escape mutants are well described with antibody responses in lentivirus infection, and such a CTL escape mechanism has been proposed in HIV infection (PHILLIPS et al. 1991). APOLLONI et al. (1992) examined the sequence variation in the type A EBNA-3 (FLRGRAYGI) and EBNA-6 (EENLLDFVRF) epitopes in a number of clinical isolates (nasopharyngeal carcinoma, infectious mononucleosis, healthy donors) and laboratory strains. The EBNA-6 epitope was conserved in all viruses studied, but there was considerable variation in the EBNA-3 epitope. This epitope was not found in type B virus, but is conserved between even geographically distant type A viruses. B95.8 virus (maintained in vitro in marmoset cells) has an intermediate type (C-terminal isoleucine—leucine). This single change resulted in a 15-fold reduction in efficiency of the peptide as a CTL target. Systematic replacement of each amino acid in the FLRGRAYGL peptide resulted in only five peptides having a greater capacity to sensitize target cells for CTL lysis. From these observations it has been calculated that the CTL clone LC13 has a specificity for its target peptide of 1 in 4.7×10^{10}—a specificity greater than that for antibody–antigen interaction (BURROWS et al. 1992).

The question remains as to whether CTL recognise the structural and lytic pathway gene products of EBV. By analogy with CTL responses to other herpesviruses, it is probable that such a population of CTL precursors (CTLp) is present in PBMC. Various attempts have been made with individual proteins; POTHEN et al. (1991) induced T cell proliferation in vitro with the p17 and p50 components of the early antigen complex, but only $CD4^+$ T cell lines were established. As with all such studies, the difficulty may well lie with the inability to present the appropriate antigen in an autologous stimulator cell to induce specific $CD8^+$ CTL in vitro.

$CD4^+$ CTL restricted through MHC class II have been identified against EBV (MOSS et al. 1988; MISKO et al. 1984), including some with specificity for a number of structural proteins such as gp340. However, the role of such cells in vivo in the case of EBV, as with the other herpesviruses, is unknown. In seven seropositive subjects, the CTL frequency and MHC restriction was estimated, but no direct CD4 frequency could be estimated (BOURGAULT et al. 1991). Furthermore, during primary EBV mononucleosis, $CD8^+$ CTL were present but no $CD4^+$ CTL were detected in antibody-blocking experiments (ENSSLE and FLEISCHER 1990). However, the observations that long-term lines and clones may be detected raises the question as to whether the in vitro conditions used to generate class II-restricted responses in these studies might prejudice the outgrowth of such CTL. In both these studies EBV-transformed B cell lines were used to stimulate the cultures; thus, only a minority of the stimulator cells would have expressed structural proteins that may predominantly active $CD4^+$ responses. The assay protocol may therefore favour the detection of latency associated protein-specific CTL.

It is possible that $CD4^+$ CTL may be important in the very early response to EBV. When naive cells from EBV-seronegative donors were co-cultured with EBV-transformed B cell lines, surprisingly $CD4^+$ CTL, including type A- and B-EBV-specific CTL, were generated (MISKO et al. 1991), whereas in most such attempts with other herpesviruses no response is observed (TORPEY and LINDSLEY 1989; BORYSIEWICZ et al. 1983; HICKLING et al. 1987; YASUKAWA et al. 1989).

The nature of the restricting element in some EBV responses has also been difficult to determine. CHEN et al. (1989), using HLA-loss variants of the EBV-transformed cell line 721, which has lost HLA A and B determinants, yet retains HLA C molecules, have shown that this class I determinant may also serve as a restriction element. SVEDMYR and JONDAL (1975) described a population of EBV-specific, yet not MHC-restricted, CTL in PBMC of patients with EBV mononucleosis, which have not been detected in other herpesvirus infections. STRANG and RICKINSON (1987) re-examined this response and suggested that in the polyclonal activation of T and B cells that ensues following primary EBV infection, CTL with multiple MHC specificities are generated, which could explain the original 1975 findings.

7 CTL in Human Cytomegalovirus Infection

7.1 Asymptomatic Persistent Infection

As for detection of CTL in other human persistent virus infections, BORYSIEWICZ et al. (1983), used a secondary in vitro stimulation protocol which co-cultured PBMC with autologous HCMV-infected fibroblasts in the presence of exogenous IL-2. Using this approach, HCMV-specific CTL were detected in bulk cultures of PBMC, the requirement of cell-associated virus rather than free virus for generation of CD8+ CTL was confirmed, and a predilection of effector CTL for non-structural HCMV proteins identified (BORYSIEWICZ et al. 1983, 1988). Subsequently, this approach has been used by others to confirm these observations, and it was reported that recent clinical isolates of HCMV may suppress such CTL (SCHRIER and OLDSTONE 1986). A modification of this in vitro protocol, which enables the detection of HCMV-specific CTL after 6 days culture, has been described (LAUBSCHER et al. 1988).

Bulk culture of CTL has major limitations. Although it allows the detection of a response, this is in essence a qualitative measure, as in vitro amplification does not allow the magnitude of ^{51}Cr release to be directly related to the number of CTLp initiating a culture. Thus, BORYSIEWICZ et al. (1988) used limiting dilution culture with split-well analysis to estimate the frequency and stage specificity of HCMV CTL. In PBMC of normal HCMV-seropositive subjects, such CTL are present at 1/5000 to 1/50000 PBMC. This frequency is comparable to that described for EBV CTL (see above), but much greater than that for VZV (1/60000), even in subjects with recent clinical reactivation (HICKLING et al. 1987).

These studies initially confirmed the preferential lysis of HCMV-infected cells treated with phosphonoformate to inhibit de novo production of HCMV structural proteins (BORYSIEWICZ et al. 1988). However, the limiting dilution technique was also adapted to estimate the relative number of CTL against individual HCMV gene products (BORYSIEWICZ et al. 1988), as discussed below.

HCMV-specific $CD4^+$, MHC class II-restricted CTL have also been described (LINDSLEY et al. 1986). Such CTL were shown to kill autologous HCMV-infected monocytes, suggesting that they may have a role in controlling the infection in monocytes, which can be infected by the virus and which may indeed be an important site of virus persistence in vivo (TAYLOR-WIEDEMAN et al. 1991). However, it is difficult to pursue these studies in the detail that has proved possible for MHC class I-restricted CTL responses, as the only readily available target cell that supports a full lytic cycle of HCMV replication is the human diploid fibroblast, which does not constitutively express MHC class II determinants, even when HCMV infected.

7.2 Disease and Immunosuppression

Initial studies of the CTL response against HCMV focused on direct detection of these effector cells in PBMC without requirement for in vitro stimulation. QUINNAN et al. (1982) detected MHC class I-restricted responses in PBMC of transplant recipients in a direct CTL assay using HCMV-infected frozen target cells of known MHC type. They found that the absence of this response, in the presence of clinical HCMV infection, was associated with a poor prognosis and recommended the assay for direct clinical use. However, BRENING et al. (1984) found that the assay was difficult to interpret in clinical use, and no CTL could be detected by this approach in asymptomatic persistently HCMV-infected subjects (QUINNAN et al. 1982, 1984). However, this approach was used to detect the presence of HCMV CTL in renal transplant recipients and in patients with acquired immunodeficiency syndrome (AIDS) (ROOK et al. 1985).

HCMV may infect a number of different cell types in vivo, in contrast to the restriction of in vitro replication to human diploid fibroblasts. In normal subjects such cells probably include epithelial cells, monocytes/macrophages, and bone marrow precursor cells (MINTON et al. 1993); in HCMV disease, other cells including polymorphonuclear leukocytes may also be infected. In addition, the state of cell differentiation and division may itself determine whether virus replication can proceed; monocytes cultured in vivo with T cell supernatant medium or in the presence of corticosteroids permit full virus replication in vitro with detection of released infectious particles (LATHEY and SPECTOR 1991). Thus, the potential range of infected target cells in vivo may well be greater than that so far studied in vitro.

To date, studies with MCMV in Balb/c mice have suggested that CTL are important in protection against primary infection and in recovery from established infection after adoptive transfer (REDDEHASE et al. 1987). In man, such studies are necessarily correlative. QUINNAN'S original observations suggest that these cells may be directly protective in bone marrow transplant recipients. We have performed quantitative studies to determine the CTLp frequency in renal and heart lung transplant recipients. With administration of immunosuppression, CTLp were low, but in survivors of HCMV pneumonitis the CTLp frequency increased (ALP et al., manuscript submitted). In the convalescent phase of HCMV pneumonitis, we have to date been unable to recover HCMV-specific CTL in bronchoalveolar lavage lymphocytes (R. Smyth, unpublished observations). Furthermore, where cytotoxicity of HCMV-infected cells by bronchoalveolar lymphocytes from bone marrow transplant recipients with HCMV pneumonitis has been observed, this cytotoxicity was abrogated by anti-Leu-11b, indicating that NK cells rather than specific CTL were involved (BOWDEN et al. 1988).

Such observations bear on the question of the possible role of CTL in the pathogenesis of organ-specific HCMV-induced injury. On the basis of studies in MCMV and the low frequency of HCMV pneumonitis (as compared with HCMV retinitis) in HIV-infected patients, who may have difficulty in mounting an effective $CD8^+$ CTL response, Grundy et al. (1987) suggested that HCMV-induced lung injury was immunopathogenically mediated. However, in a recent study CARMICHAEL et al. (1993) have found that although the HIV-1-specific CTL response in PBMC is reduced with the development of stage IV disease and a low CD4 count, the CTL response to EBV is preserved with normal numbers of CTLp until very late in the disease. Were the same to apply for HCMV-specific CTL, then lack of $CD8^+$ CTL might not be the explanation for the difference in HCMV disease observed in AIDS patients.

The temporal relationship between the development of HCMV-specific CTL responses following bone marrow transplantation and HCMV-related complications has been re-examined by REUSSER et al. (1991). A total of 20 bone marrow transplant recipients were studied for the presence of HCMV-specific CTL in bulk culture after in vitro stimulation with HCMV-infected fibroblasts. Of the 20 donors providing the transplant to the recipients, 17 generated such responses; of the 20 recipients, ten developed a HCMV-specific CTL response within 2 months of transplantation and only one developed significant HCMV disease. Six of the ten who failed to generate such CTL developed fatal HCMV pneumonitis. Again, this study suggests that the $CD8^+$ CTL response is protective against pneumonitis and not harmful to the host. Furthermore, it provides a rationale for considering adoptive transfer therapy against this disease in the transplant recipient; such studies are in progress in Seattle (RIDDELL et al. 1992).

7.3 Specificity for Viral Gene Products

Using vaccinia recombinants encoding the HCMV 72-kDa IE-1 protein and a structural protein, glycoprotein B, it was found that a high proportion of CTL clones recognised the IE product (20%–60%) as compared with glycoprotein B (<4%; BORYSIEWICZ et al. 1988). The fine specificity of the 72-kDa IE-1 protein-specific CTL restricted by HLA B13 has been determined and the peptide located in exon 4 of IE-1 (ALP et al., manuscript submitted). Interestingly, this region has no overlap peptides inducing CD4 T cell proliferation (ALP et al. 1991). CTL epitopes have also been identified in glycoprotein B (613-PSLKIFIAGNSAYEY-V-628) in association with HLA A2 (PARKER et al. 1992). Recently, using a range of vaccinia recombinants expressing truncates of glycoprotein B, we have found multiple CTL epitopes dependent on the MHC type of the subject tested, thereby suggesting that no immunodominant CTL region in this protein can be identified (unpublished observation).

RIDDELL et al. (1991) have identified an MHC class I-restricted CTL response against a HCMV structural protein, although the precise specificity remains to be identified. They employed polyclonal activation of PBMC (RIDDELL and GREENBERG 1990) with limiting dilution cloning to isolate HCMV-specific CTL. They have also identified CTL specific for HCMV 72-kDa IE-1 response in bulk culture and individual clones (RIDDELL et al. 1991). However, they also found that HCMV-infected actinomycin D-treated target cells were killed, implying that there was no requirement for de novo viral protein synthesis to sensitize the cell (as would be the case with IE-1-specific CTL) and suggesting that a structural protein entering with the input virus could sensitize the infected cell to MHC class I-restricted CTL lysis (RIDDELL et al. 1991).

8 Conclusions on the Role of Herpes Virus-Specific CTL In Vivo

8.1 Relationship Between CTL Activity and Virus Reactivation

No definite conclusion can be reached on the role that CTL play in reactivation of latent infection. It seems intrinsically unlikely that they play any role in inhibiting the actual induction of IE gene expression from hitherto latent virus and more likely that they may control reactivation episodes once they have occurred, perhaps preventing reactivation from achieving clinical significance by containing it at local sites. Indeed, it can be argued that the maintenance of the relatively high CTL frequencies observed in asymptomatic herpes-virus carriers may be secondary to continual or frequent restimulation in vivo, consequent on expression of viral genes due to reactivation.

There is a need for more studies of CTL using the cell types naturally carrying virus in vivo as targets.

8.2 Evidence for Protective Role of CTL

It is similarly difficult to draw firm conclusions on the protective role of CTL in human herpesvirus infections. Their protective role is inferred from the increased morbidity from herpesvirus infections in subjects with impairment of T cell responses, although other effector T cell functions are almost invariably concomitantly impaired. Any more definite conclusions are only likely to result from the selective induction of CTL by immunisation or possibly by the human adoptive transfer experiments referred to below in the context of HCMV.

8.3 Possible Role in Immunopathology

There are experimental models in which CTL appear to play a pathogenic role, the best known being the lymphocytic choriomeningitis virus model, in which CTL produce cerebral damage following intracerebral inoculation of virus in immunocompetent adult mice (BUCHMEIER et al. 1980). Is there any immunopathogenic role for CTL in herpesvirus infections? As noted above, it has been suggested that HCMV-specific CTL may be responsible for the pathogenesis of HCMV pneumonitis (GRUNDY et al. 1987). However, this is speculative, based on the relative rarity of this condition in AIDS patients and its peak incidence in bone marrow transplant recipients at the time of reconstitution. There is as yet no direct evidence in man to support this interesting suggestion.

8.4 Role Relative to Other Immune Responses

The concentration on CTL in this review does not imply that other immunological mechanisms are of little importance in resistance to herpesvirus infections. Antibody is likely to play a major role in resistance to primary infection. There is evidence that the administration of CMV-immune globulin to seronegative transplant recipients does reduce the incidence of severe HCMV disease (SNYDMAN 1991). However, given that reactivation and disseminated infection may occur in the face of circulating antibody, it seems less likely that it is of primary importance in controlling reactivation.

There is increasing evidence for some redundancy in the immune system. In experimental models, the depletion of $CD8^+$ cells can lead to $CD4^+$ T cells controlling MCMV infection (JONJIC et al. 1989). Congenital absence of $CD8^+$ T cells, as in "knockout" mice for β_2-microglobulin which have no class I MHC, appears to increase the likelihood of compensatory antiviral $CD4^+$ CTL responses developing in the case of LCMV (MULLER et al. 1992).

9 The Induction of CTL In Vivo by Immunisation

There are currently candidate vaccines in development for each of the human herpesviruses (except HHV-6). Two of these, which are live attenuated vaccines, have been administered to human subjects quite extensively (for VZV and CMV); there are also a number of subunit vaccines in development for each of the viruses, and some of these have been used in experimental models. All of these candidate vaccines have been developed with the primary purpose of inducing neutralising antibody to envelope proteins; however, given the recognition of the importance of CTL in controlling persistent infections, there is interest in whether these vaccines can induce virus-specific CTL. There have also been attempts to adoptively transfer human herpesvirus specific CTL.

9.1 Induction of CTL by Vaccines

HSV vaccines are in development, based on recombinant glycoproteins such as gB, and two such vaccines are now entering trials for the prevention of reactivation episodes in people with recurrent genital herpes. However, as yet there have not been any reported studies of the immune responses they induce in humans (ALLEN and HITCHCOCK 1991).

VZV vaccines based on recombinant glycoproteins are also in development, but a live attenuated candidate vaccine—the Oka strain vaccine—has been quite extensively used for some time. The vaccine has been shown to provide a degree of immunity from primary VZV infection in previously seronegative subjects who are immunosuppressed and in normal individuals at particular risk of VZV infection (GERSHON and STEINBERG 1989, 1990). This vaccine is reported to induce VZV-specific CTL of both $CD4^+$ and $CD8^+$ phenotype; such CTL show specificity for the IE-62 protein and for gpI, with frequencies comparable to those induced by natural infection (ARVIN 1992).

The vaccine enhances proliferative T cell frequencies in seropositive elderly subjects (from 1/68000 before vaccination to 1/40000) as effectively as it does in younger subjects (LEVIN et al. 1992).

EBV, a candidate vaccine based on gp340, has been used in cottontop tamarins to prevent EBV-induced lymphomas (FINERTY et al. 1992; MORGAN 1991). Its ability to induce CTL in this experimental model is not known and it has not so far been given to humans, although at the time of writing it seems that clinical trials may start soon. A particular target population for an EBV vaccine would probably be those in the Far East and China at risk of nasopharyngeal carcinoma.

CMV vaccines have attracted interest because of the severity of the clinical disease which HCMV produces in transplant populations and in the infected neonate. Potential target populations for a vaccine are seronegative pregnant mothers and transplant recipients. The only CMV vaccine which has been used to any extent in humans is a live Towne strain virus, which is presumed to be attenuated, although there is no marker for attenuation. This vaccine is reported to give a level of protection to seronegative transplant recipients comparable to that given by previous infection with CMV, the risk of CMV disease in vaccinated subjects approximating to that in unvaccinated CMV seropositive subjects (reviewed in GONCZOL and PLOTKIN 1990). The immune response this vaccine induces in recipients includes induction of proliferative T cell responses, but there is no description of the induction of CTL by the vaccine. Subunit CMV vaccines based on CMV glycoproteins are now in development, although none have yet been subjected to human trials.

9.2 Adoptive Transfer of Human CTL

Although it might be thought impracticable to apply on any scale, adoptive transfer of human virus-specific CTL is being seriously explored by at least one group. HCMV-specific CTL $CD8^+$ clones were grown in vitro from seropositive bone marrow donors by the system described above and then administered to the recipients of bone marrow transplants from the same donors during the period when they are at maximum risk of CMV infection. The Seattle group have reported that after transfer of increasing numbers of these CTL (from 10^8 to 10^9 cells in four doses over 4 weeks), CMV-specific cytotoxicity could be detected in the PBMC of recipients for up to 1 month (RIDDELL et al. 1992). It will be of great interest to see whether this adoptive transfer confers protection from clinically significant CMV disease in the recipients. However, such protection may be difficult to demonstrate, as a large number of subjects might well be needed to show a benefit if all receive the current CMV prophylaxis regimes which have already been shown to diminish the incidence of CMV disease very significantly (GOODRICH et al. 1991). It would seem unlikely that this approach will be pursued for herpes-virus infections other than CMV.

9.3 Other Approaches

Other approaches to the induction or boosting of CTL immunity might be feasible, but are largely speculative. There are no reports of the effect of LAK cells, as used in the therapy of cancers, for treating virus infections in immunosuppressed individuals, although these could in some respects be regarded as a necessary control for the effects of the adoptive immunotherapy approach described above. The use of "post-infective" immunisation by administering vaccines to seropositive subjects at risk, in order to boost their immunity including CTL, might also be worth considering. A trial of this approach has already been reported in HIV infection, although there is no convincing evidence of clinical benefit as yet (REDFIELD et al. 1991).

10 Conclusions

The evidence for the role of CTL in animal models of virus infections, coupled with the availability of an in vitro functional assay, has led to numerous studies of their possible role in human herpesvirus infection. CTL can be demonstrated in all human herpesvirus infections, but so far evidence for their protective role is, perhaps inevitably, indirect at best. Given the current level of interest in both the mechanisms of induction of CTL and the immunological control of persistent virus infections (additionally driven by work on HIV infection), we should learn considerably more about the role of CTL in herpesvirus infections over the next few years.

References

Alfieri C et al. (1991) Early events in Epstein-Barr virus infection of human B lymphocytes. Virology 181: 595

Allen WP, Hitchcock PJ (eds) (1991) Herpes simplex virus vaccine workshop 1989. Rev Infect Dis 13 [Suppl 11]: S891–S979

Alp N et al. (1990) Automation of limiting dilution cytotoxicity assays. J Immunol Methods 129: 269–276

Alp N et al. (1991) The fine specificity of cellular immune responses in man to human cytomegalovirus immediate early 1 protein. J Virol 65: 4812–4820

Apollani A et al. (1992) Sequence variation of cytotoxic T cell epitopes in different isolates of Epstein-Barr virus. Eur J Immunol 22: 183–189

Arvin AM (1992) Cell-mediated immunity to varicella-zoster virus. J Infect Dis 166 [Suppl 1]: S35–S41

Arvin AM et al. (1991) Equivalent recognition of a varicella-zoster virus immediate early protein (IE62) and glycoprotein 1 by cytotoxic T lymphocytes of either CD^4 or $CD8^+$ phenotype. J Immunol 146: 257–264

Baer R et al. (1984) DNA sequence and expression of the B95-8 Epstein-Barr virus genome. Nature 310: 207–211

Beck S, Barrell BG (1988) HCMV encodes a glycoprotein homologous to MHC class-1 antigen. Nature 331: 269–272
Bergen RE et al. (1991) Human T cells recognize multiple epitopes of an immediate early/tegument protein (IE62) and glycoprotein I of varicella-zoster virus. Viral Immunol 4:151–166
Bonneau RH, Jennings SR (1988) Modulation of acute and latent herpes simplex virus infection in C57BL/6 mice by adoptive transfer of immune lymphocytes with cytolytic activity. J Virol 63:1480–1484
Borysiewicz LK et al. (1983) Requirements for in vitro generation of human cytomegalovirus specific cytotoxic T cell lines. Eur J Immunol 13:804–809
Borysiewicz LK et al. (1988a) Human cytomegalovirus-specific cytotoxic-T-cells: their precursor frequency and stage specificity. Eur J Immunol 18: 269–275
Borysiewicz LK et al. (1988b) Human cytomegalovirus specific cytotoxic T cells recognise the 72kD immediate early protein and glycoprotein B in recombinant vaccinia viruses. J Exp Med 168:919–931
Bourgault I et al. (1991) Limiting dilution analysis of the HLA restriction of EBV-specific cytolytic T lymphocytes. Clin Exp Immunol 84:501–507
Bowden RA et al. (1985) Lysis of varicella zoster virus infected cells by lymphocytes from normal humans and immunosuppressed pediatric leukaemia patients. Clin Exp Immunol 60: 387–395
Bowden RA et al. (1988) Increased cytotoxicity against cytomegalovirus-infected target cells by bronchoalveolar lavage cells from bone marrow transplant recipients with cytomegalovirus pneumonitis. J Immunol Methods 158:773–779
Brening MK et al. (1984) Human and murine MHC-restricted cytotoxic lymphocyte responses to CMV infection. Birth Defects 20:375–379
Buchmeier MJ et al. (1980) The virology and immunobiology of lymphocytic choriomeningitis virus infection. Adv Immunol 30:275–331
Bukowski JF et al. (1985) Adoptive transfer studies demonstrating the antiviral effect of natural killer cells in vivo. J Exp Med 161:40–52
Burrows SR et al. (1990a) An Epstein-Barr virus-specific cytotoxic T cell epitope in EBV nuclear antigen 3 (EBNA3). J Exp Med 171:345–349
Burrows SR et al. (1990b) Patterns of reactivity of Epstein-Barr virus specific T cells in type A donor cultures after reactivation with A- or B-transformants. Cell Immunol 127:47
Burrows SR et al. (1992) The specificity of recognition of a cytotoxic T lymphocyte epitope. Eur J Immunol 22:191–195
Carmichael A et al. (1993) Quantitative analysis of the human immunodeficiency virus type 1 (HIV-1)-specific cytotoxic T lymphocyte (CTL) response at different stages of HIV-1 infection: differential CTL responses to HIV-1 and Epstein-Barr virus in late disease. J Exp Med 177:249–256
Chee MS et al. (1990) Analysis of the protein-coding content of the sequence of human cytomegalovirus strain AD169. In: McDougall JK (ed) Cytomegaloviruses. Springer, Berlin Heidelberg New York, pp125–170 (Current topics in microbiology and immunology, vol154)
Chen BP et al. (1989) Restriction of Epstein-Barr virus specific cytotoxic T cells by HLA-A, -B and -C molecules. Hum Immunol 26(2):137–147
Cunningham AL, Noble JR (1989) Role of keratinocytes in recurrent herpetic lesions. Ability to present herpes simplex virus antigen and act as targets for T lymphocytotoxicity in vitro. J Clin Invest 83:490–496
Cunningham AL et al. (1985) Evolution of recurrent herpes simplex lesions: an immunohistologic study. J Clin Invest 75:226–233
Davison AJ, Scott JE (1986) The complete DNA sequence of varicella-zoster virus. J Gen Virol 67:1759–1816
DeLisi C, Berzofsky JA (1985) T cell antigen sites tend to be amphipathic structures. Proc Natl Acad Sci USA 81:7632
Diaz PS et al. (1989) T lymphocyte cytotoxicity with natural varicella-zoster virus infection and after immunization with live attenuated varicella vaccine. J Immunol 142:636–641
Enssle KH, Fleischer B (1990) Absence of EBV specific, HLA class II-restricted CD4$^+$ cytotoxic T cells in infectious mononucleosis. Clin Exp Immunol 79:409–415
Finerty S et al. (1992) Protective immunization against Epstein-Barr virus-induced disease in cottontop tamarins using the virus envelope glycoprotein gp340 produced from a bovine papillomavirus expression vector. J Gen Virol 73:449–453

Garcia-Blanco MA, Cullen BR (1991) Molecular basis of latency in pathogenic human viruses. Science 254: 815–820
Gershon AA, Steinberg SP (1989) Varicella vaccine collaborative study group of the National Institute of Allergy and Infectious Diseases. Persistence of immunity to varicella in children with leukemia immunized with live attenuated varicella vaccine. N Engl J Med 320: 892–897
Gershon AA, Steinberg S (1990) Live attenuated varicella vaccine: protection in healthy adults in comparison to leukemic children. J Infect Dis 161: 661–666
Gonczol E, Plotkin S (1990) Progress in vaccine development for prevention of human CMV infection. In: McDougall JK (ed) Cytomegaloviruses. Springer, Berlin Heidelberg New York, p 255 (Current topics in microbiology and immunology, vol 154)
Goodrich JM et al. (1991) Early treatment with ganciclovir to prevent CMV disease after bone marrow transplantation. N Engl J Med 325: 1601–1607
Gordon J et al. (1986) Control of human B-lymphocyte replication: transforming Epstein-Barr virus exploits three distinct viral signals to undermine three separate control points in B-cell growth. Immunology 58: 591
Gregory CD et al. (1988) Down-regulation of cell adhesion molecules LFA-3 and ICAM-1 in Epstein-Barr virus positive Burkitt's lymphoma underlies tumour cell escape from virus-specific T cell surveillance. J Exp Med 167: 1811–1824
Gregory CD et al. (1991) Activation of Epstein-Barr virus latent genes protects human B cells from death by apoptosis. Nature 349: 612–614
Grundy JE et al. (1987) Is cytomegalovirus interstitial pneumonitis in transplant recipients an immunopathological condition? Lancet 2: 996–999
Hagemeier C et al. (1992) The 72K IE1 and 80K IE2 proteins of human cytomegalovirus independently transactivate the c-fos, c-myc and hsp70 promoters via basal promoter elements. J Virol 73: 2385–2393
Hammerschmidt W, Sugden B (1989) Genetic analysis of the immortalising functions of Epstein-Barr virus in human B lymphocytes. Nature 340: 393–395
Hardy I et al. and the Varicella Vaccine Collaborative Study Group (1991) The incidence of Zoster after immunization with live attenuated varicella vaccine—a study in children with leukemia. N Engl J Med 325: 1545–1550
Hayward AR, Herberger M (1987) Lymphocyte responses to varicella zoster virus in the elderly. J Clin Immunol 7: 174–178
Hayward AR et al. (1986a) Cellular interactions in the lysis of varicella zoster virus infected human fibroblasts. Clin Exp Immunol 63: 141–146
Hayward AR et al. (1986b) Specific lysis of varicella zoster virus-infected B lymphoblasts by human T cells. J Virol 58: 179–184
Hayward A et al. (1991) Varicella-Zoster virus-specific immunity after herpes zoster. J Infect Dis 163: 873–875
Hickling J et al. (1987) Varicella zoster virus specific cytotoxic T lymphocytes (Tc): detection and frequency analysis of HLA class I restricted Tc in human peripheral blood. J Virol 61: 3463–3469
Ibanez CE et al. (1991) Human cytomegalovirus productively infects primary differentiated macrophages. J Virol 65: 6581–6588
Jonjic S et al. (1988) A non-structural viral protein expressed by a recombinant vaccinia virus protects against lethal cytomegalovirus infection. J Virol 62: 1653–1658
Jonjic S et al. (1989) Site-restricted persistent cytomegalovirus infection after selective long-term depletion of CD4+ T lymphocytes. J Exp Med 169: 1199–1212
Koszinowski UH et al. (1990) Cellular and molecular basis of the protective immune response to cytomegalovirus infection. In: McDougall JK (ed) Cytomegaloviruses. Springer, Berlin Heidelberg New York, pp 189–220 (Current topics in microbiology and immunology, vol-154)
Lathey JL, Spector SA (1991) Unrestricted replication of human cytomegalovirus in hydrocortisone-treated macrophages. J Virol 65: 6371–6375
Laubscher A et al. (1988) Generation of human cytomegalovirus-specific cytotoxic T lymphocytes in a short term culture. J Immunol Methods 110: 69–77
Levin MJ et al. (1992) Immune response of elderly individuals to a live attenuated varicella vaccine. J Infect Dis 166: 253–259
Lindsley MD et al. (1986) HLA-DR-restricted cytotoxicity of cytomegalovirus-infected monocytes mediated by Leu-3-positive T cells. J Immunol 136: 3045–3051
Lucin P et al. (1992) Gamma interferon dependent clearance of CMV infection in the salivary gland. J Virol 66: 1977–1984

Martin S et al. (1988) Herpes simplex type-1 specific cytotoxic T cells recognise virus nonstructural proteins. J Virol 62: 2265–2273
Mester JC, Rouse BT (1991) The mouse model and understanding immunity to herpes simplex virus. Rev Infect Dis 13 [Suppl 11]: S935–945
Minton EJ et al. (1993) Human cytomegalovirus infection of the monocyte/macrophage lineage: bone marrow progenitors may act as a reservoir for the virus, but monocyte differentiation is required for viral gene expression (in press)
Misko IS et al. (1984) HLA DR-antigen associated restriction of EBV specific T-cell colonies. Int J Cancer 33: 239
Misko IS et al. (1991a) Cytotoxic T lymphocyte discrimination between type A Epstein-Barr virus transformants is mapped to an immunodominant epitope in EBNA3. J Gen Virol 72: 405–409
Misko IS et al. (1991b) Composite response of naive T cells to stimulation with the autologous lymphoblastoid cell line is mediated by CD4 cytotoxic T cell clones and includes an Epstein-Barr virus-specific component. Cell Immunol 132: 295–307
Morgan AJ (1991) Control of viral disease: the development of EBV vaccines. Springer Semin Immunopathol 13: 249–262
Moss DJ et al. (1978) Long-term T-cell mediated immunity to Epstein-Barr virus in man. I. Complete regression of virus-induced transformation in cultures of seropositive donor leukocytes. Int J Cancer 22: 662
Moss DJ et al. (1988) Cytotoxic T cell clones discriminate between A- and B-type Epstein-Barr virus transformants. Nature 331: 719–721
Moss DJ et al. (1991) Immune regulation of Epstein-Barr virus; EBV nuclear antigen as a target for EBV-specific T cell lysis. Springer Semin Immunopathol 13: 147–156
Muller D et al. (1992) LCMV-specific, class II-restricted cytotoxic T cells in B2-microglobulin-deficient mice. Science 255: 1576–1578
Murray RJ (1992) Identification of target antigens for the human cytotoxic T cell response to Epstein-Barr virus (EBV): implications for the immune control of EBV-positive malignancies. J Exp Med 176: 157–168
Murray RJ et al. (1988) Epstein-Barr virus-specific cytotoxic T cell recognition of transfectants expressing the virus-coded latent membrane protein LMP. J Virol 62: 3747–3755
Murray RJ et al. (1990a) Cross recognition of a mouse H2-peptide complex by human HLA-restricted cytotoxic T cells. Eur J Immunol 20: 659–664
Murray RJ et al. (1990b) Human cytotoxic T-cell responses against Epstein-Barr virus nuclear antigens demonstrated by using recombinant vaccinia viruses. Proc Natl Acad Sci USA 87: 2906–2910
Nalesnik MA (1991) Lymphoproliferative disease in organ transplant recipients. Springer Semin Immunopathol 13: 199–216
Nash AA et al. (1987) Different roles for the L3T4$^+$ and Lyt2$^+$ T cell subsets in the control of an acute herpes simplex virus infection of the skin and nervous system. J Gen Virol 68: 825–833
Parker KC et al. (1992) Sequence motifs important for peptide binding to the human MHC class molecule HLA A2. J Immunol 149: 3580–3587
Petersen CM et al. (1989) Immunosuppressive properties of electrophoretically "slow" and "fast" form alpha2-macroglobulin. Effects on cell-mediated cytotoxicity and (allo-) antigen-induced T cell proliferation. J Immunol 142: 629–635
Phillips RE et al. (1991) Human immunodeficiency virus genetic variation that can escape cytotoxic T cell recognition. Nature 354: 453–459
Pothen S et al. (1991) Human T-cell recognition of Epstein-Barr virus-associated replication antigen complexes. Int J Cancer 49: 656–660
Purtillo DT (1991) X-linked lymphoproliferative disease (XLP) as a model of Epstein-Barr virus-induced immunopathology. Springer Semin Immunopathol 13: 181–197
Purtillo DT et al. (1989) Detection of X-linked lymphoproliferative disease (XLP) using molecular and immunovirological markers. Am J Med 87: 421
Quinnan GV et al. (1982) Cytotoxic T cells in CMV infection. N Engl J Med 307: 7–13
Quinnan GV et al. (1984) HLA-restricted cytotoxic T lymphocytes are an early immune response and important defense mechanism in cytomegalovirus infections. Rev Infect Dis 6: 156–163
Reddehase MJ et al. (1984) The cytolytic T lymphocyte response to the murine cytomegalovirus. II. Detection of virus stage-specific antigens by separate populations of in vivo active cytolytic T lymphocyte precursors. Eur J Immunol 14: 56–61
Reddehase MJ et al. (1987) CD8-positive T lymphocytes specific for murine cytomegalovirus immediate early antigens mediate protective immunity. J Virol 61: 3102–3108

Redfield RR et al. (1991) A phase 1 evaluation of the safety and immunogenicity of vaccination with recombinant gp160 in patients with early HIV infection. N Eng J Med 324: 1677–1684
Reusser P et al. (1991) Cytotoxic T-lymphocyte response to cytomegalovirus after human allogeneic bone marrow transplantation: pattern of recovery and correlation with cytomegalovirus infection and disease. Blood 78: 1373–1380
Rickinson AB et al. (1981) Long-term cell-mediated immunity to Epstein-Barr virus. Cancer Res 41: 4216
Rickinson AB et al. (1987) Influence of the Epstein-Barr virus nuclear antigen EBNA2 on the growth phenotype of virus-transformed B cells. J Virol 61: 1310
Riddell SR, Greenberg PD (1990) The use of anti-CD3 and anti-CD28 monoclonal antibodies to clone and expand human antigen specific T cells. J Immunol Methods 128: 189–201
Riddell SR et al. (1991a) Class I MHC-restricted cytotoxic T lymphocyte recognition of cells infected with human cytomegalovirus does not require endogenous viral gene expression. J Immunol 146: 2795–2804
Riddell SR et al. (1991b) Cytotoxic T cells specific for cytomegalovirus: a potential therapy for immunocompromised patients. Rev Infect Dis 13 [Suppl 11]: S966–973
Riddell SR et al. (1992) Restoration of viral immunity in immunodeficient humans by the adoptive transfer of T cell clones. Science 257: 238–241
Roizman B (1990) Herpesviridae. In: Fields BN, Knipe DM (eds) Virology, Raven, New York, pp 1787–1794
Roizman B, Sears AE (1990) Herpes simplex viruses and their replication. In: Fields BN, Knipe DM (eds) Virology, Raven, New York, pp 1795–1841
Rook AH et al. (1985) Deficient HLA-restricted, cytomegalovirus specific cytotoxic T cells and natural killer cells in patients with the acquired deficiency syndrome. J Infect Dis 152: 627–630
Rooney C et al. (1989) Influences of Burkitt's lymphoma and primary B cells on latent gene expression by the non-imortalising P3J-HR-1 strain of Epstein-Barr virus. J Virol 63: 1531
Rothbard JB, Taylor WR (1988) A sequence pattern common to T cell epitopes. EMBO J 7: 93–100
Rowe DT et al. (1986) Restricted expression of EBV latent genes and T-lymphocyte detected membrane antigen in Burkitt's lymphoma cells. EMBO J 5: 2599
Rowe M et al. (1992) Three pathways of Epstein-Barr virus gene activation from EBNA1-positive latency in B lymphocytes. J Virol 66: 122–131
Sample C, Kieff E (1991) Molecular basis for Epstein-Barr virus induced pathogenesis and disease. Springer Semin Immunopathol 13: 133–146
Schmid DS (1988) The human MHC-restricted cellular response to herpes simplex virus is mediated by $CD4^+$, $CD8^-$ T cells and is restricted to the DR region of the MHC complex. J Immunol 140: 3610–3616
Schrier RD, Oldstone MBA (1986) Recent isolates of CMV suppress CMV-specific human leukocyte antigen-restricted cytotoxic T lymphocyte activity. J Virol 69: 127–132
Schwartz RH (1992) Costimulation of T lymphocytes: the role of CD28, CTLA-4, and B7/BB1 in interleukin-2 production and immunotherapy. Cell 71: 1065–1068
Sharp M et al. (1992) Kinetics and viral protein specificity of the cytotoxic T lymphocyte response in healthy adults immunized with live attenuated varicella vaccine. J Infect Dis 165: 852–858
Shope T et al. (1973) Malignant lymphoma in cotton topped marmosets after innoculation with Epstein-Barr virus. Proc Natl Acad Sci USA 70: 2487–2491
Snydman DR (1991) Prevention of cytomegalovirus-associated diseases with immunoglobulin. Transplant Proc XXIII: [3, Suppl 3]: 131–135
Stamminger T, Fleckenstein B (1990) Immediate-early transcription regulation of human cytomegalovirus. In: McDougall JK (ed) Cytomegaloviruses. Springer, Berlin Heidelberg New York, p 154 (Current topics in microbiology and immunology, vol 154)
Stanberry LR (1991) Evaluation of herpes simplex virus vaccines in animals: the guinea pig vaginal model. Rev Infect Dis 13 [Suppl 11]: S920–923
Strang G, Rickinson AB (1987) Multiple HLA class I-dependent cytotoxicities constitute the "non-HLA-restricted" response in infectious mononucleosis. Eur J Immunol 17: 1007–1013
Sunil-Chandra NP et al. (1992a) Virological and pathological features of mice infected with murine gammaherpesvirus 68. J Gen Virol 73: 2347–2356
Sunil-Chandra NP et al. (1992b) Murine gammaherpesvirus 68 establishes a latent infection in mouse B lymphocytes in vivo. J Gen Virol 73: 3275–3279

Svedmyr E, Jondal M (1975) Cytotoxic effector cells specific for B cell lines transformed by Epstein-Barr virus are present in patients with infectious mononucleosis. Proc Natl Acad Sci USA 72:1622

Taylor-Wiedeman J et al. (1991) Monocytes as a major site of persistence of human cytomegalovirus in peripheral blood mononuclear cells. J Gen Virol 72:2059–2064

Thomson BJ et al. (1991) The molecular and cellular biology of human herpesvirus-6. Rev Med Virol 1:89–99

Thorley-Lawson DA, Israelsohn ES (1987) Generation of specific cytotoxic T cells with a fragment of the Epstein-Barr virus-encoded p63/latent membrane protein. Proc Natl Acad Sci USA 84: 5484

Tigges MA et al. (1992) Human $CD8^+$ herpes simplex virus-specific cytotoxic T-lymphocyte clones recognize diverse virion protein antigens. J Virol 66:1622–1634

Torpey DJ, Lindsley MD (1989) HLA-restricted lysis of herpes simplex virus-infected monocytes and macrophages is mediated by $CD4^+$ and $CD8^+$ T lymphocytes. J Immunol 142: 1325–1332

Wilson A et al. (1992) Subclinical VZV viraemia, herpes zoster and T lymphocyte immunity to VZV antigens after bone marrow transplantation. J Infect Dis 165:119–126

Wyandt HE et al. (1989) Chromosomal deletion of Xq25 in an individual with X-linked lymphoproliferative disease. Am J Hum Genet 33:426

Yao QY et al. (1985) In vitro analysis of the Epstein-Barr virus: host balance in long-term renal allograft recipients. Int J Cancer 35:43

Yasukawa M, Zarling JM (1985) Human cytotoxic T cell clones directed against herpes simplex virus infected cells. III. Analysis of viral glycoproteins recognised by CTL clones by using recombinant herpes simplex viruses. J Immunol 134:2679–2682

Yasukawa M et al. (1989) Differential in vitro activation of $CD4^+CD8^-$ and $CD8^+CD4^-$ herpes simplex virus-specific human cytotoxic T cells. J Immunol 143:2051–2057

Zarling JM et al. (1986) Human cytotoxic T cell clones directed against herpes simplex virus-infected cells. IV. Recognition and activation by cloned glycoproteins gB and gD. J Immunol 136:4669–4673

Zarling JM et al. (1988) Herpes simplex virus (HSV)-specific proliferative and cytotoxic T cell responses in humans immunised with an HSV type 2 glycoprotein subunit vaccine. J Virol 62:4481–4485.

Cytotoxic T Lymphocyte Responses Against Measles Virus

F. G. C. M. UYTDEHAAG, R. S. VAN BINNENDIJK, M. J. H. KENTER, and A. D. M. E. OSTERHAUS

1 Introduction

In a great number of viral diseases, an important function has been attributed to cytotoxic T cells (CTL) in recovery from infection, by clearing virus-infected cells and in the induction of protective immunity against these diseases by vaccination (YAP et al. 1978; ASKONAS et al. 1988; LEHMANN-GRUBE et al. 1988; KLAVINSKIS et al. 1990; KAST et al. 1986; REDDEHASE et al. 1987; CANNON et al. 1987; DOHERTY et al. 1992). A host of questions still remains concerning the role of CTL in protection against and pathogenesis of measles. Are CTL with different phenotypes equally involved in the clearance of measles virus (MV) from infected tissue? Which MV poly- peptides and, more specifically, which epitopes of these proteins are presented by the different major histocompatibility complex (MHC) allomorphs and are recognized by major populations of CTL? Do memory CTL play a role in preventing disease upon reinfection with measles virus? Are CTL in any way

Department of Virology, Erasmus University Rotterdam, P.O. Box 1738, 3000 DR Rotterdam, The Netherlands

Current Topics in Microbiology and Immunology, Vol. 189

involved in the abnormalities which may accompany acute and chronic MV infection?

Analysis of the immune response in natural MV infections and following immunization using modern tools of immunology is required to increase our understanding of the role of CTL in measles and thereby optimize the development of new generations of measles vaccines. In this chapter, we will review the present knowledge of the functions and specificities of CTL against MV.

2 Major Histocompatibility Complex Class I- and Class II-Restricted Cytotoxic T Cells

T cells recognize antigen on the surface of an antigen-presenting cell by means of a specific T cell antigen receptor (TCR). Two types of TCR exist: the $TCR_{\alpha\beta}$ and the $TCR_{\gamma\delta}$ (CLEVERS et al. 1988). T cells expressing $TCR_{\alpha\beta}$ recognize antigens (peptides) bound in the groove of MHC molecules: in humans HLA and in mice H-2 (TOWNSEND et al. 1986; BJORKMAN et al. 1987; VAN BLEEK and NATHENSON 1990; RUDENSKY et al. 1991; MONACO et al. 1992; RÖTZSCHKE et al. 1990; JORGENSEN et al. 1992). Two phenotypes of $TCR_{\alpha\beta}$-expressing T cells are distinguished, each expressing a unique cell surface glycoprotein, termed CD8 and CD4, that function as coreceptors binding to nonpolymorphic portions of the MHC antigen-presenting molecules (DOYLE and STROMINGER 1987; CONNOLLY et al. 1990). T cells expressing CD8 (T CD8) recognize antigen presented by MHC class I molecules, whereas T cells expressing CD4 (T CD4) recognize antigen presented by MHC class II molecules. Cross-linking of either CD8 or CD4 with the $TCR_{\alpha\beta}$ by the same MHC molecule is essential for T cells to become functional: T CD8 as cytotoxic T cells and T CD4 as T-helper cells (EMMRICH et al. 1986; GABERT et al. 1987; JANEWAY 1992). However, activated T CD4 can also have cytotoxic potential. In relation to possible differences between the roles that T CD8 and T CD4 play as CTLs in measles-associated immunity and pathology, it is noteworthy that class I molecules are expressed on almost all cells, while class II molecules are only expressed on cells of the immune system, notably B cells, dendritic cells, and macrophages.

The MHC class I antigen-presenting molecule is a heterodimer consisting of a polymorphic α-chain and a nonpolymorphic β_2m protein. In an exocytic vesicle, possibly the endoplasmic reticulum (ER), peptides of intracellular proteins (e.g., structural proteins of MV) may form stable complexes with the MHC class I α- and β_2m-chains, which can then be transported via the constitutive secretory pathway to the cell surface for recognition by T CD8 (YEWDELL and BENNINK 1992). MHC class II antigen-presenting molecules also exist of two polypeptide chains α and β, which become associated in ER with a third protein, the invariant chain, thereby preventing peptide binding to class II molecules in ER (NEEFJES et al. 1991). In contrast to class I, class II molecules sample peptides from degraded extracellular proteins internalized by endocytosis in an endosomal compartment (NEEFJES and PLOEGH 1992). Stable peptide–class II complexes are then transported to the cell surface for recognition by T CD4. Analysis of peptides isolated from cell lysates and from immunoaffinity purified MHC class I and class II molecules, as well as the identification of the three-dimensional structures of both types of molecules, has provided compelling evidence for an antigen-binding groove on MHC molecules that can accommodate peptides of restricted length: eight to 11 residues for class I molecules and of variable size—12–24 residues— for class II molecules (VAN BLEEK and NATHENSON 1991; FALK et al. 1991; FREMONT et al. 1992; ZHANG et al. 1992; MADDEN et al. 1991; JARDETZKY et al. 1991; HUNT et al. 1992; STERN and WILEY 1992; BJORKMAN et al. 1987; CHICZ et al. 1992; BROWN et al. 1993). In addition, these studies have initiated the analysis of peptides from a large number of antigenic proteins for residues that are critical in binding to MHC molecules or the recognition by TCR. Although many of the details of antigen processing remain to be clarified, it is clear that different MHC class I and class II molecules acquire antigenic peptides from different sources and present them to phenotypically distinct CTL. Current knowledge of antigen processing and presentation and the controversial issues linked to this subject are outlined in several excellent recent reviews (YEWDELL and BENNINK 1992; MONACO 1992; LONG 1992; BRACIALE and BRACIALE 1991; BIJLMAKERS and PLOEGH 1993).

3 Measles Virus Morphogenesis and Structure

MV, a member of the genus *Morbillivirus* of the family Paramyxoviridae, has a single negative-strand RNA genome which encodes the six structural proteins. The nucleoprotein (N), which is part of the transcription complex, forms together with the phosphoprotein (P) and the large (L) protein, which are components of the viral replication complex, the nucleocapsid containing the virus genome. The matrix (M) protein and two transmembrane glycoproteins, the hemagglutinin (H) protein and the fusion (F) protein, incorporated into a lipid bilayer contribute to the formation of the virus envelope surrounding the nucleocapsid (NORRBY and OXMAN 1990; NORRBY 1992). The H and the F transmembrane glycoproteins are cotranslationally inserted in ER of a virus-infected cell. Following glycosylation, both glycoproteins are transported via the constitutive secretory pathway to the cell surface, where they anchor in the cell membrane. The mature form of the H protein is composed of two copies of the protein forming a peplomer protruding from the virus envelope. The mature F protein consists of a nonglycosylated F1 subunit complexed to a glycosylated F2 subunit via disulphide bounds. At the cell surface, both proteins associate to form multimers before incorporation into virus particles (MORRISON and PORTNER 1992; NORRBY 1992; SATO et al. 1988; SCHEID and CHOPPIN 1977). MV is an antigenically rather stable virus, as are all paramyxoviruses. However, epitope variations do occur in the envelope glycoproteins (in the H protein more frequently than in the F protein) and in the internal proteins (in the N and P proteins less frequently than in the M protein; BARRETT 1991).

In principle, all of the viral proteins produced in a MV-infected cell can become target antigens for T CD8 and T CD4. However, with respect to the T CD4 response, it is far from clear how the cytosolic proteins, e.g., the M protein, get access to a lysosomal (MHC class II) compartment. Likewise, it is still debated where in the cell the transmembrane glycoproteins H and F, once cotranslationally inserted into ER, are degraded into MHC class I-presentable peptides. The antigen processing of MV proteins will be discussed in Sect. 6.

4 Cytotoxic T Cells in the Immune Response to Measles Virus

Recovery from many virus infections may depend on cell-mediated and antibody-mediated immunity. The importance of cell-mediated immunity in measles became first apparent from studies in immunodeficient children. Agammaglobulinemic patients who produce no detectable virus-specific antibodies showed the normal sequence of clinical symptoms and developed resistance to reinfection after contracting measles, whereas children with functional T cell deficiencies often suffered from fatal giant cell pneumonia (OLDING-STENKVIST and BJORNVATN 1976; BURNET 1968; MITUS et al. 1959; GOOD and ZAK 1956). The transient immunosuppression associated with measles (reviewed by MCCHESNEY and OLDSTONE 1989) has initially hampered investigation of cellular immunity against MV. Cytotoxic cells able to destroy MV infected target cells in vitro were demonstrated in peripheral blood leukocytes from patients with subacute sclerosing panencephalitis (SSPE), from MV-immune adults, and from children after live measles vaccination or during natural measles infection. This cellular cytotoxicity appeared to be antibody dependent (ADCC; PERRIN et al. 1977; KRETH and WIEGAND 1977; KRETH et al. 1979; WHITTLE et al. 1980). The first indications for the involvement of MHC-restricted CTL in measles came from a study by KRETH and coworkers (1979), showing that peripheral blood lymphocytes from children with acute measles killed virus-infected target cells with which they shared HLA antigens. At the same time, WRIGHT and LEVY (1979) described the generation of HLA class I-restricted CTL specific for MV from peripheral blood using MV-infected fibroblasts. MV-specific T CD8 were subsequently demonstrated in peripheral blood lymphocytes of healthy adult MV-seropositive individuals, predominantly in a high responder (LUCAS et al. 1982) or in expanded T cell cultures during secondary immune response in vitro (SETHI et al. 1982). Thus, these early studies already suggested that T CD8 may play a role in the immune response against measles and may persist as memory cells in immune individuals. The technology for establishing antigen-specific T cell lines and clones has permitted a more detailed analysis of immune responses to MV. T cell clones specific for MV were first generated in vitro from a patient with multiple sclerosis who was previously shown to be a high responder to MV. These clones had cytotoxic activity, bore the CD4 antigen, and recognized MV in association with HLA class II antigens (RICHERT et al. 1983, 1985, 1986; JACOBSON et al. 1984, 1985a, b). In addition to HLA class II-restricted T cells, HLA class I-restricted CTL could be clonally expanded in vitro from cerebrospinal fluid of a child with measles encephalitis (FLEISCHER and KRETH 1983). Subsequently, it was reported that T CD4 can be detected upon in vitro stimulation of peripheral blood lymphocytes in the majority of MV-immune subjects (JACOBSON et al. 1985b). The authors speculated that in vivo MV-specific CTL are predominantly T CD4 (JACOBSON et al. 1987/1988). This was, however, not fully in agreement with the earlier findings on T CD8 in MV-immune individuals. At present, it is clear that the antigen presentation form (infectious virus versus noninfectious particles or soluble viral proteins) influences in vitro induction and frequency of T CD4 and T CD8 in different viral systems (MORRISON et al. 1988; VAN BINNENDIJK et al. 1989, 1992a). Thus, in contrast to earlier reports (McFARLAND et al. 1980; GREENSTEIN and McFARLAND 1983), it was shown that peripheral blood mononuclear cells respond upon in vitro stimulation with MV antigen in the majority (75%) of measles immune adults. Depending on the form of antigen presentation—Epstein-Barr virus-transformed B cell lines (B-LCL) either infected with live virus or pulsed with UV-inactivated virus—we could isolate T CD8 and T CD4 clones from such cultures, suggesting the existence of MV-specific memory at both the T CD4 and T CD8 level (VAN BINNENDIJK et al. 1989). Recently, using synthetic nonamer peptides representing HLA-A2.1-presentable epitopes of MV, which do not require additional processing by antigen-presenting cells, KRETH and coworkers showed the generation of MV-specific T CD8 from peripheral blood of MV-immune individuals (NANAN et al. 1992). In addition, we identified and cloned T CD8 as effector cells predominating in MV-specific immune responses in three children with acute measles (VAN BINNENDIJK et al. 1990, 1991). Substantiating this finding, in 31 out of 48 vaccinated schoolchildren involved in a measles outbreak, T CD8 could be expanded from peripheral blood lymphocyte cultures upon specific stimulation with live MV (VAN BINNENDIJK et al. 1992b). Investigating the pathogenesis of MV-induced encephalitis in a mouse model, NIEWIESK and associates (1993) found that T CD8 are an important component of the immune response to MV. Finally, WILD and colleagues demonstrated the induction of T CD8 in mice following immunization with vaccinia virus recombinants coding for MV proteins (BEAUVERGER et al. 1993). A number of studies have demonstrated a role for T CD4 as well as T CD8 in protection against MV-induced encephalitis (BANKAMP et al. 1991; BRINCKMANN et al. 1991; NIEWIESK et al. 1993; DE VRIES et al. 1988). It is unsolved whether in these models T CD4 participate in conferring protection by functioning as CTL. The absence of MHC class II expression in cells of the brain would render them unsusceptible for lysis by T CD4, though virus infection may induce γ-interferon production leading to expression of MHC class II molecules on the potential targets. In the study by NIEWIESK et al. (1993), T CD4 were generally only weakly lytic, and susceptibility to MV-induced encephalitis clearly correlated with inefficient induction of T CD8. Also, in rats depleted of T CD8, persistence of MV in brain neurons is promoted (MAEHLEN et al. 1989). It has been suggested that T CD4 with cytolytic potential may terminate ongoing immune responses by killing antigen-presenting cells rather than eliminate infected target cells early in infection (BRAAKMAN et al. 1987). Clearly, additional studies are necessary to determine the relative roles of both T CD4 and T CD8 in protection against measles in vivo, the outcome of which will aid to optimize the design of new measles vaccines (see Sect. 7).

Collectively, the recent data indicate that, as is the case in other virus infections (ASKONAS et al. 1988; LEHMANN-GRUGE et al. 1988), T CD8 are involved in recovery from measles and may function as memory cells in maintaining lifelong immunity against measles.

5 Epitopes of Measles Virus Proteins for T CD4 and T CD8

Further analysis of antigenic structures and of the role of different structural proteins and epitopes thereof in the induction of protective immunity is likely to be important in the development of new generations of vaccines against measles. It may be speculated that the induction of specific CTL is an important aspect of this immunity. It has been shown that in principle all the structural proteins of MV can elicit specific T cell reactivity in human individuals, as assayed by proliferative responses of lymphocytes in bulk cultures or of T cell lines or clones to purified proteins of MV (BELLINI et al. 1981; ROSE et al. 1984; RICHERT et al. 1986; JACOBSON et al. 1987/1988, 1989; DHIB-JALBUT et al. 1988; VAN BINNENDIJK et al. 1989; ILONEN et al. 1990). Here we discuss the reported T cell epitopes of MV proteins as found in man, mice, and rats.

5.1 Fusion Protein

Identification of MHC class I- and class II-restricted T cell epitopes of the F protein of MV has been subject of extensive studies. Using genetically engineered F protein, nested sets of synthetic peptides spanning the F protein and T cell clones, a number of antigenic regions for T CD4 and T CD8 were identified. The core sequences required for HLA binding and T cell recognition were determined by using combined N- and C-terminal deleted peptides (VAN BINNENDIJK et al. 1993; see Fig. 1). Three T CD4 epitopes, an HLA DR2- (aa 379–390), an HLA DQ 5, 6- (aa 427–435), and an HLA DRw53- (aa 454–463) restricted epitope were identified that cluster between aa 379–466. One peptide recognized by T CD4 in association with HLA DQw1 also

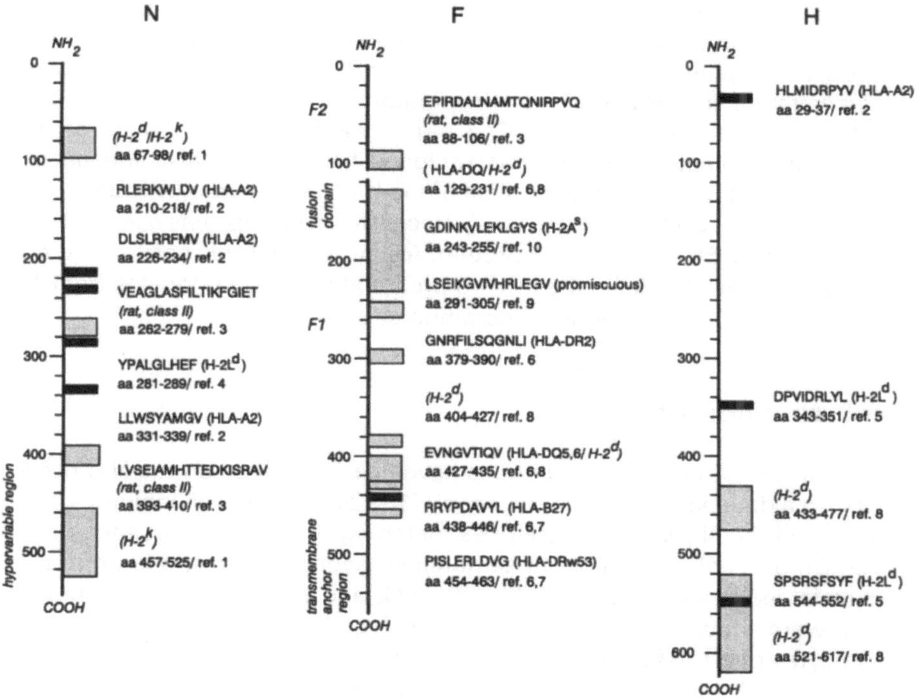

Fig. 1. T cell epitopes identified on the nucleoprotein (*N*), fusion protein (*F*), and hemagglutinin protein (H) of measles virus. Sequence of the N protein according to BUCKLAND et al. (1988); the H protein according to ALKHATIB and BRIEDIS (1986); and the F protein according to RICHARDSON et al. (1986), with the numbering of amino acid sequences starting at the first methionine residue. *ref. 1,* GIRAUDON et al. (1991); *ref. 2,* NANAN et al. (1992); *ref. 3,* Liebert (personal communication); *ref. 4,* BEAUVERGER et al. (1993); *ref. 5,* Beauverger (personal communication); *ref. 6,* VAN BINNENDIJK et al. (1993); *ref. 7,* VAN BINNENDIJK et al. (1992a); *ref. 8,* Versteeg (personal communication); *ref. 9,* PARTIDOS and STEWARD (1990); PARTIDOS et al. (1991); *ref. 10,* PARTIDOS and STEWARD (1992). *Dark bars* represent epitopes recognized by T CD8; *light bars* represent epitopes recognized by T CD4

represents a T cell epitope for mice of the H-2^d haplotype (VAN BINNENDIJK et al. 1993; Versteeg, personal communication). An additional mouse (H-2^d) class II-restricted epitope, from which the minimal sequence has not yet been determined, is located between aa 404–427 of the F protein (Versteeg, personal communication). In the same region of the F protein, a nonamer sequence (aa 438–446) was found that matches the HLA B27 binding motif. The synthetic peptide corresponding to aa 438–446 indeed sensitized target cells for recognition by the HLA B27-restricted T CD8 clone. The presently known T CD4 epitopes of the F protein all have the common features of MHC class II binders (VAN BINNENDIJK et al. 1993). Using several criteria that predict sequence motifs binding to MHC class II molecules, PARTIDOS et al. (1991; PARTIDOS and STEWARD 1990, 1992) identified two sequences on the F protein that indeed appeared to represent T cell epitopes (Fig. 1). The region aa 291–305 contains an immunodominant epitope of promiscuous nature, since the corresponding peptide induced MV-specific proliferative T cell responses in different haplotype strains of mice and proliferative responses in peripheral blood lymphocytes of apparently HLA- disparate MV-immune individuals. The other region, aa 243–255, contains an H-$2A^s$-restricted T cell epitope. The region aa 129–231 contains an HLA DQ-restricted epitope recognized by cloned T CD4 which also appears to be a class II-restricted epitope for mice of the H-2^d haplotype (VAN BINNENDIJK et al. 1993 and unpublished results). Recently, an epitope has been identified at position aa 86–106 of the F protein. A synthetic peptide corresponding to this sequence stimulates the in vitro proliferation of lymphocytes from MV-immune rats (Liebert, personal communication).

5.2 Nucleoprotein

Several T CD4 and T CD8 epitopes have been identified on the N protein of MV. In a data base search NANAN et al. (1992 and personal communication) screened the N protein for epitopes matching the anchor sequence of HLA A2. On basis of this search, three nonamer peptides corresponding to the N protein sequences aa 210–218, 226–234, and 331–339 were synthesized that were shown to induce MV-specific T CD8 from peripheral blood lymphocytes of HLA A2-positive MV-immune individuals (Fig. 1). An epitope recognized by mouse T CD8 in association with H-$2L^d$ has been identified on the N protein (aa 281–289) by scanning the sequence of the protein for H-$2L^d$ motifs and testing the corresponding peptides for their capacity to sensitize target cells for killing by MV-specific T CD8 (BEAUVERGER et al. 1993; Fig. 1). This epitope appeared also to be conserved in the N protein of canine distemper virus, a morbillivirus closely related to MV. Two regions on the N protein, possibly containing H-2 class II-restricted antigenic epitopes for T-helper cells, were reported (GIRAUDON et al. 1991). An immunodominant epitope is located in a highly conserved region near the N terminus (aa 67–98), whereas a second epitope which is antigenic in mice of the H-2^k haplotype is located in the hypervariable region near the C terminus of the N protein (Fig. 1). Finally, two class II-restricted epitopes for rat T cells have been identified recently, using synthetic peptides corresponding to the aa 262–279 and aa 393–410 sequences of the N protein (Liebert, personal communication).

5.3 Hemagglutinin Protein

The mapping of T cell epitopes on the H protein has started only recently. Thus, an HLA A2-restricted epitope has been identified near the N terminus on the H protein (aa 29–37) which is recognized by T CD8 (NANAN et al. 1992 and personal communication). Using polyclonal H protein-reactive CTL generated in Balb/c (H-2^d) mice and nonamer peptides corresponding to different H-$2L^d$ motifs present in the primary sequence of the H protein, two T cell epitopes on the H protein were identified. With two peptides corresponding to aa 343–351 and aa 544–552, respectively, similar levels of target cell lysis were found as with targets that constitutively expressed the H protein (Beauverger, personal communication; Fig. 1). Finally, using genetically engineered H proteins and class II-restricted cloned T cells we have identified two regions (aa 433–477 and aa 521–617) containing putative T cell epitopes for mice of the H-2^d haplotype (Versteeg, personal communication; Fig. 1). It is expected that in the near future more epitopes will be identified on these important structural proteins of MV.

5.4 Large and Matrix Proteins

Thus far only one, HLA A2-restricted, epitope for T CD8 has been identified on the L protein (NANAN et al. 1992). Based on recently determined HLA DQw2 binding motif, a putative epitope can be identified on the M protein of MV, and a peptide corresponding to this sequence is at presently being tested for binding to HLA DQW2 (Koning, personal communication).

In conclusion, it appears that T cell epitopes of the F, H, and N proteins of MV are scattered along the entire sequence of these structural proteins and that different MHC class I and class II molecules bind different sets of peptides. Size of peptides and conservation of "anchor" residues in peptide sequences are shown to be critical for allele-specific binding. Due to these allele-specific peptide motifs, it has been possible to predict allele-specific binding motifs in the protein sequences of the structural proteins of MV. Testing of the corresponding peptides for binding to the respective alleles and for their capacity to elicit T cell responses in vitro using lymphocytes of MV-immune individuals has identified T cell epitopes on MV proteins. The binding affinity of a MV peptide for an MHC molecule and subsequently the affinity of the TCR for the peptide–MHC complex largely determines the immunogenicity of an epitope. Thus, the MHC class I and class II haplotype differences among individuals in the human outbred population may be responsible for variations in the immune response of different individuals to the same antigens. The identification of MV peptide sequences which correspond with binding motifs of the most frequent MHC allomorphs may lead to the characterization of immunodominant T cell epitopes of MV proteins and is therefore important for the development of new generations of MV vaccines.

6 Processing of Cytosolic and Transmembrane Proteins of Measles Virus

As briefly mentioned in Sect. 2, it is now widely appreciated that MHC class I and class II molecules travel along different biosynthetic routes to the cell surface and sample different cellular compartments for antigenic peptides (YEWDELL and BENNINK 1992; NEEFJES and PLOEGH 1992). All data thus far available are consistent with the notion that MHC class I molecules are loaded with peptides in ER or *cis*-Golgi complex and with a role for the TAP1–TAP2 peptide transporter complex in the import of peptides from the cytosol to these compartments (BRACIALE and BRACIALE 1991; MONACO 1992; BIJLMAKERS and PLOEGH 1993). In addition, the generation of antigenic peptides for presentation by MHC class I molecules is believed to take place in the cytosol. While appealing for presentation of peptides originating from proteins biosynthesized in the cytosol, this general view of antigen presentation seems difficult to reconcile with presentation of transmembrane proteins by MHC class I molecules. Thus, in MV-infected cells the H and F transmembrane proteins are cotranslationally imported in ER and yet MHC class I molecules present peptides of these proteins at the cell surface (VAN BINNENDIJK et al. 1992a). Are these peptides generated in ER? Proteolytic degradation can indeed occur in ER, but is rather selective (BONIFACINO et al. 1990), and apart from generation of signal sequence-derived peptides, there is no evidence supporting generation of MHC class I-presentable peptides of transmembrane proteins in ER. Is it possible that peptides for MHC class I presentation originate from cytosolic processing of transmembrane proteins and, if so, how do these proteins reach the cytosol? We have recently addressed these questions using antigen presentation-defective mutant cell lines and a cloned T CD8 recognizing the nonamer peptide sequence RRYP-DAVYL of the F protein of MV in association with HLA B27 (Fig. 1). The mutant T2 cell line transfected with the HLA B27 gene but lacking high expression of HLA B2705 molecules at the cell surface, when infected with MV, did not function as a target cell for lysis by the T CD8 clone (VAN BINNENDIJK et al. 1992a). As T2 cells lack multiple genes that may be involved in antigen presentation, including *TAP1* and *TAP2* genes and the *LMP-2* and *LMP-7* genes encoding the proteasome components (DE MARS et al. 1984; SALTER and CRESSWELL 1986; KELLY et al. 1991; GLYNNE et al. 1991; YANG et al. 1992), these results suggest that at least one gene, which is absent in T2, plays a role in presentation of this epitope of the F protein by MHC class I molecules. Using the TAP2 peptide transporter deficient EBV transformed B cell line BM 36.1 expressing HLA B2705, we recently obtained evidence that the presentation of the HLA B27-restricted epitope of the F protein of MV by an EBV transformed B cell line requires a functional TAP1–TAP2 peptide transporter (Kenter et al. submitted). Thus, it appears that the cytosol is a processing compartment yielding MHC class I-presentable peptides of ER luminal domains of transmembrane proteins. How these transmembrane proteins get access to the cytosol is as yet unknown.

In contrast to MHC class I molecules, MHC class II molecules sample endocytic compartments for antigenic peptides (NEEFJES et al. 1991). However, there is evidence from several studies employing different experimental systems, that epitopes of endogenous cytosolic proteins are presented by MHC class II molecules (see LONG 1992 for review). In principal, several mechanisms could explain presentation of cytosolic proteins by MHC class II molecules. Most unlikely, cytosolic processing may yield peptides loading MHC class II molecules in ER even in the presence of the invariant chain (NEWCOMB and CRESSWELL 1993). Secondly, autophagy, sequestration of cytosolic material by ER derived membranes, may result in the delivery of cytosolic proteins to autophagic lysosomes. This mechanism could perhaps also explain those examples of MHC class II-mediated presentation of transmembrane proteins that are resistant to acidotropic agents such as chloroquine, primaquine, and ammonium chloride (VAN BINNENDIJK et al. 1992a). Finally, chaperoning molecules may be involved in the transport of cytosolic proteins or peptides thereof to compartments that are sampled by class MHC II molecules (see also review by LONG 1992).

With the rapid progress in understanding antigen presentation by MHC class I molecules to T CD8, development of new vaccination strategies has coevolved. In particular the design of vehicles to import exogenous protein antigens into the class I antigen presentation route has received considerable attention.

7 Alternative Strategies for Vaccination Against Measles: A Focus on Cytotoxic T Cells

Only a few years after MV had been adapted to in vitro cell cultures systems, the first live attenuated measles vaccines based on the Edmonston B strain of MV were prepared (KATZ 1965). Although live measles vaccines have been highly successful, there are still considerable disadvantages associated with their use. Perhaps the most important of these is that they cannot be used in the presence of maternally derived MV-specific antibodies, which is a major drawback for their use in developing countries. Almost simultaneously with the introduction of live attenuated measles vaccines, Tween-ether- and formaldehyde-inactivated whole virus preparations were introduced as measles vaccines. Although the majority of these preparations were shown to induce MV-neutralizing and hemagglutination-inhibiting serum antibodies, these antibodies were shown to persist only for relatively short periodes, compared to antibodies induced by natural MV infection or vaccination with live attenuated measles vaccines. More important was the observation that individuals vaccinated with the inactivated vaccines were often not protected against MV infection and that their symptoms were often more severe than those observed in nonvaccinated children. This manifestation of measles became known as atypical measles syndrome (FULGINITI and HELFER 1980). NORRBY and coworkers (1975) suggested that an inappropriate immune response to the F protein of the virus, which resulted in the absence of biologically active fusion-inhibiting antibodies, was at the basis of this failure. As we and others have shown, MV-specific T CD8 may play an important role in recovery from measles (see Sect. 4) and it may not be expected that the inactivated measles vaccines used would have specifically stimulated this population of T lymphocytes; the absence of this T cell response may, therefore, be another or additional explanation for the failure of this type of vaccines. Consequently, an important requirement for novel generations of measles vaccines should be that they elicit a MV-specific T CD8 response and memory and this preferably in the presence of MV-specific maternally derived antibodies. Evaluating the present candidates for novel generations of measles vaccines in this light, the two most promising approaches seem the use of live recombinant viruses or bacteria and immune-stimulating complex the (ISCOM) matrix for the presentation of the MV glycoproteins (for review see OSTERHAUS and DE VRIES 1992). It may be expected that live recombinant vaccinia and avipox viruses, expressing the F and the H protein of MV, which are considered serious candidates for measles vaccines, will indeed induce the required T CD8 response and memory, since de novo synthesis of the respective proteins is established after immunization. If administered along the proper routes, they may also be effective in the presence of maternally derived MV-specific serum antibodies. Although nonreplicating subunit vaccines are generally not capable of inducing a specific T CD8 response, we and others have recently shown that when incorporated in the ISCOM matrix, viral and other proteins may elicit a specific T CD8 response in vivo and in vitro (for review see CLAASSEN and OSTERHAUS 1992). As mentioned in Sect. 6, this is probably related to the observation that proteins presented by the ISCOM matrix, are processed for HLA class I-restricted CTL recognition in a way similar to de novo synthesized proteins. We showed that live MV and MV-F ISCOM allow presentation by MHC class I molecules, while other nonreplicating presentations of the F protein only permitted MHC class II-restricted presentation (VAN BINNENDIJK et al. 1992a). This observation, together with the demonstration that F-ISCOM are potent inducers of long-lasting specific serum antibodies (even in the presence of specific serum antibodies), which include biologically active F-specific antibodies and of solid protection against morbillivirus infections (for review see OSTERHAUS and DE VRIES 1992), indicates that the ISCOM presentation form is a serious candidate for the development of a new generation of measles vaccines.

Acknowledgements. The authors wish to thank Dr. W. Kreth, Dr. R. Nanan, Dr. U. Liebert, Dr. F. Wild, Dr. P. Beauverger, Dr. J. Versteeg, Dr. F. Koning, and Dr. J. H. Brown for kindly sharing their unpublished data and Conny Kruyssen for help preparing this manuscript.

References

Alkhatib G, Briedis DJ (1986) The predicted primary structure of the measles virus hemagglutinin. Virology 150: 479–484

Askonas BA, Taylor PM, Esquivel F (1988) Cytotoxic T cells in influenza infection. Ann N Y Acad Sci 532: 230–237

Bankamp B, Brinckmann UG, Reich A, Niewiesk S, ter Meulen V, Liebert UG (1991) Measles virus nucleocapsid protein protects rats from encephalitis. J Virol 65: 1695–1700

Barrett T, Subbaroa SM, Belsham GJ, Mahy BW (1991) The molecular biology of morbilliviruses. In: Kingsbury DW (ed) The paramyxoviruses. Plenum, New York, pp 83–102

Beauverger P, Buckland R, Wild TF (1993) Measles virus antigen induces both type specific and canine distemper cross reactive CTLs in mice: localisation of a common NP L^d-restricted epitope. J Gen Virol (in press)

Bellini WJ, McFarlin DE, Silver GD, Mingioli ES, McFarland HF (1981) Immune reactivity of the purified hemagglutinin of measles virus. Infect Immun 32: 1051–1057

Bijlmakers MJ, Ploegh HL (1993) Putting together an MHC class I molecule. Curr Biol 5: 21–26

Bjorkman PJ, Saper MA, Samraoui B, Bennet WS, Strominger JL, Wiley DC (1987) The foreign antigen binding site and T cell recognition regions of class I histocompatibility antigens. Nature 329: 512–518

Bonifacino JS, Cosson P, Klausner RD (1990) Colocalized transmembrane determinants for ER degradation and subunit assembly explain the intracellular fate of TCR chains. Cell 63: 503–513

Braakman E, Rotteveel FTM, van Bleek G, van Seventer GA, Lucas K (1987) Are MHC class II-restricted cytotoxic T lymphocytes important? Immunol Today 8: 265–267

Braciale TJ, Braciale VI (1991) Antigen presentation: structural themes and functional variations. Immunol Today 12: 124–129

Brinckmann UG, Bankamp B, Reich A, ter Meulen V, Liebert AG (1991) Efficacy of individual measles virus structural proteins in the protection of rats from measles encephalitis. J Gen Virol 72: 2491–2500

Brown JH, Jardetzky TS, Gorga JC, Stern LJ, Urban RG, Strominger JL, Wiley DC (1993) The three-dimensional structure of the human class II histocompatibility antigen HLA-DR1. Nature (in press)

Buckland R, Gerald C, Barker D, Wild TF (1988) Cloning and sequencing of the nucleoprotein gene of measles virus (Hallé strain). Nucleic Acids Res 16: 11821–11826

Burnet FM (1968) Measles as an index of immunological function. Lancet 2: 610–613

Cannon J, Scott EJ, Taylor G, Askonas BA (1987) Clearance of persistent respiratory syncytial virus infection in immunodeficient mice following transfer of primed T cells. Virology 62: 133–183

Chicz RM, Urban RG, Lane WS, Gorga JC, Stern LJ, Vignali DAA, Strominger JL (1992) Predominant naturally processed peptides bound to HLA-DR1 are derived from MHC-related molecules and are heterogeneous in size. Nature 358: 764–768
Claassen I, Osterhaus A (1992) The iscom structure as an immune enhancing moiety: experience with viral systems. Res Immunol 143 (5): 531–541
Clevers H, Alarcon B, Wileman T, Terhorst C (1988) The T cell receptor/CD3 complex: a dynamic protein ensemble. Annu Rev Immunol 6: 629–662
Connally JM, Hansen TH, Ingold HL, Potter TA (1990) Recognition by CD8 by cytotoxic T lymphocytes is ablated by several subtitutions in the class I α3 domain: CD8 and the T cell receptor recognize the same class I molecule. Proc Natl Acad Sci USA 87: 2137–2141
DeMars R, Chang CC, Shaw S, Reitnauer PJ, Sondel PM (1984) Homozygous deletion that simultaneously eliminates expression of class I and class II antigens of EBV-transformed B-lymphoblastoid cells. Hum Immunol 11: 77–80
De Vries P, van Binnendijk RS, van der Marel P, van Wezel AL, Voorma HO, Sundquist B, UytdeHaag FGCM, Osterhaus ADME (1988) Measles virus fusion protein presented in immune-stimulating complex (ISCOM) induces haemolysis-inhibiting and fusion-inhibiting antibodies, virus-specific T cells and protection in mice. J Gen Virol 69: 549–559
Dhib-Jalbut S, McFarland HF, Mingioli ES, Sever JL, McFarlin (1988) Humoral and cellular immune responses to matrix protein of measles virus in subacute sclerosing panencephalitis. J Virol 62: 2483–2489
Doherty PC, Allan W, Eichelberg M (1992) Roles of $\alpha\beta$ and $\tau\delta$ T cell subsets in viral immunity. Annu Rev Immunol 10: 123–151
Doyle C, Strominger JL (1987) Interaction between CD4 and class II MHC molecules mediates cell adhesions. Nature 330: 256–258
Emmrich F, Strittmatter U, Eichmann K (1986) Synergism in the activation of human CD8 T cells by crosslinking the T cell receptor complex with CD8 differentiation antigen. Proc Natl Acad Sci USA 83: 8292–8302
Falk K, Rötschke O, Stevanovic S, Jung G, Rammensee H-G (1991) Allele specific motifs revealed by sequencing of self peptides eluted from MHC molecules. Nature 351: 290–296
Fleischer B, Kreth HW (1983) Clonal expansion and functional analysis of virus-specific T lymphocytes from cerebrospinal fluid in measles encephalitis. Hum Immunol 7: 239–248
Fremont DH, Matsummura M, Stura EA, Peterson PA, Wilson IA (1992) Crystal structures of two viral peptides in complex with murine H-$2K^b$. Science 257: 991–927
Fulginiti VA, Helfer RE (1980) Atypical measles in adolescent siblings 16 years after killed measles virus vaccine. J Am Med Assoc 244: 804–806
Gabert J, Langlet C, Zamoyska R, Parnes JR, Schmitt-Verhulst AM, Malissen B (1987) Reconstitution of MHC class I specificity by transfer of the T cell receptor and Lyt-2 genes. Cell 50: 545–554
Giraudon P, Buckland R, Wild TF (1991) The immune response to measles virus in mice. T-helper response to the nucleoprotein and mapping of the T-helper epitopes. Virus Res 22: 41–54
Glynne R, Powis SH, Beck S, Kelly A, Kerr LA, Trowsdale J (1991) A proteasome-related gene between the two ABC transporter loci in the class II region of the human MHC. Nature 353: 357–360
Good RA, Zak SJ (1956) Disturbances in gamma globulin synthesis as 'experiments of nature.' Paediatrics 18: 109–149
Greenstein JI, McFarland HF (1983) Response of human lymphocytes to measles virus after natural infection. Infect Immun 40: 198–204
Hunt DF, Michel H, Dickinson T, Shabanowitz J, Cox AL, Sakaguchi E, Appella A, Grey HM, Sette A (1992) Peptides presented to the immune system by the murine class II MHC molecules I-Ad. Science 256: 1817–1820
Ilonen J, Mäkelä MJ, Ziola B, Salmi A (1990) Cloning of human T cells specific for measles virus haemagglutinin and nucleocapsid. Clin Exp Immunol 81: 212–217
Jacobson S, Richert JR, Biddison WE, Satinsky A, Hartzman RJ, McFarland HF (1984) Measles virus-specific T4 human cytotoxic T cell clones are restricted by class II HLA antigens. J Immunol. 33: 754–757
Jacobson S, Flerlage ML, McFarland HF (1985a) Impaired measles virus-specific cytotoxic T cell responses in multiple sclerosis. J Exp Med 162: 839–850
Jacobson S, Nepom GT, Richert JR, Biddison WE, and McFarland HF (1985b) Identification of a specific HLA DR2 Ia molecule as a restriction element for measles virus-specific HLA class II-restricted cytotoxic T cell recognition. J Exp Med 161: 263–268

Jacobson S, Rose JW, Flerlage ML, McFarlin DE, McFarland HF (1987/1988) Induction of measles virus-specific human cytotoxic T cells by purified measles virus nucleocapsid and hemagglutinin polypeptides. Viral Immunol 1: 153–162

Jacobson S, Sekaly RP, Jacobson CL, McFarland HF, Long EO (1989) HLA class II-restricted presentation of cytoplasmic measles virus antigens to cytotoxic T cells. J Virol 63: 1756–1762

Janeway CA Jr (1992) The T cell receptor as a multicomponent signalling machine: CD4/CD8 coreceptors and CD45 in T cell activation. Annu Rev Immunol 10: 645–674

Jardetzky TS, Lane WS, Robinson RA, Madden DR, Wiley DC (1991) Identification of self peptides bound to purified HLA-B27. Nature 353: 326–329

Jorgensen JL, Reay PA, Ehrich EW, Davis MM (1992) Molecular components of T cell recognition. Annu Rev Immunol 10: 835–873

Kast WM, Bronkhorst AM, De Waal LP, Melief CJM (1986) Cooperation between cytotoxic and helper T lymphocytes in protection against a lethal sendai virus infection. J Exp Med 164: 723–738

Katz SL (1965) Immunization with live attenuated measles virus vaccines: five years experience. Arch Gesamte Virusforsch 16: 222–230

Kelly A, Powis S, Glynee R, Radley E, Beck S, Trowsdale J (1991) Second proteasome-related gene in the human MHC class II region. Nature 353: 667–668

Klavinskis LS, Whitton JL, Joly E, Oldstone MBA (1990) Vaccination and protection from a lethal virus infection: identification, incorporation and use of a cytotoxic T lymphocyte glycoprotein epitope. Virology 178: 393–400

Kreth HW, Wiegand G (1977) Cell-mediated cytotoxicity against measles virus in SSPE II. Analysis of cytotoxic effector cells. J Immunol 118: 296–302

Kreth HW, ter Meulen V, Eckert G (1979) Demonstration of HLA restricted killer cells in patients with acute measles. Med Microbiol Immunol 165: 203–214

Lehmann-Grube FD, Moskophidis D, Lohler J (1988) Recovery from acute virus infection. Ann N Y Acad Sci 532: 238–255

Long EO (1992) Antigen processing for presentation to $CD4^+$ T cells. New Biologist 4: 274–282

Lucas CJ, Biddison WE, Nelson DL, Shaw S (1982) Killing of measles virus-infected cells by human cytotoxic T cells. Infect Immun 38: 226–232

Madden DR, Gorga JC, Strominger JL, Wiley DC (1991) The structure of HLA-B27 reveals nonamer self peptides bound in an extended conformation. Nature 353: 321–325

Maehlen J, Olsson T, Löve A, Klareskog L, Norrby E (1989) Persistence of measles virus in rat brain neurons is promoted by depletion of $CD8^+$ T cells. J Neuroimmunol 21: 149–155

McChesney MB, Oldstone MBA (1989) Virus-induced immunosuppression: infections with measles virus and human immunodeficiency virus. Adv Immunol 45: 355–380

McFarland HF, Pedone CA, Mingioli ES, McFarlin DE (1980) The response of human lymphocyte subpopulations to measles, mumps and vaccinia viral antigens. J Immunol 125: 221–225

Mitus A, Enders JF, Craig JM, Holloway A (1959) Persistence of measles virus and depression of antibody formation in patients with giant cell pneumonia after measles. N Engl J Med 261: 882–889

Monaco JJ (1992) Pathways of antigen processing. A molecular model of MHC class I restricted antigen processing. Immunol Today 13: 173–178

Morrison LA, Braciale VL, Braciale TJ (1988) Antigen form influences induction and frequency of influenza-specific class I and class II MHC-restricted cytolytic T lymphocytes. J Immunol 141: 363–368

Morrison T, Portner A (1992) Structure, function, and intracellular processing of the glycoproteins of paramyxoviridae. In: Kingsbury DW (ed) The paramyxoviruses. Plenum, New York, pp 347–382

Nanan R, Petzold K, Carstens C, Kreth HW (1992) Correct prediction of HLA-A2.1 epitopes of measles virus. Immunobiology 186: 10

Neefjes JJ, Ploegh HI (1992) Intracellular transport of MHC class II molecules. Immunol Today 5: 179–184

Neefjes JJ, Schumacher TNM, Ploegh HL (1991) Assembly and intracellular transport of major histocompatibility complex molecules. Curr Opin Cell Biol 3: 601–609

Newcomb JR, Cresswell P (1993) Characterization of endogenous peptides bound to purified HLA-DR molecules and their absence from invariant chain-associated $\alpha\beta$ dimers. J Immunobiol 150: 499–507

Niewiesk S, Brinckmann U, Bankamp B, Sirak S, Liebert UG, ter Meulen V (1993) Susceptibility to measles virus-induced encephalitis in mice correlates with impaired antigen presentation to cytotoxic T lymphocytes. J Virol 67: 75–81
Norrby E (1992) Immunobiology of paramyxoviruses. In: Kingsbury DW (ed) The paramyxoviruses. Plenum, New York, pp 481–507
Norrby E, Oxman MN (1990) Measles virus. In: Fields BN (ed) Virology, vol 1. Raven, New York, pp 1013–1044
Norrby E, Enders-Ruckle G, ter Meulen V (1975) Differences in the appearance of antibodies to structural components of measles virus after immunization with inactivated and live virus. J Infect Dis 132: 262–269
Olding-Stenkvist E, Bjorvatn B (1976) Rapid detection of measles virus in skin rashes by immunofluorescence. J Infect Dis 134: 463–469
Osterhaus ADME, de Vries P (1992) Vaccination against acute respiratory virus infections and measles in man. Immunobiology 184: 180–192
Partidos CD, Steward MW (1990) Prediction and identification of a T cell epitope in the fusion protein of measles virus immunodominant in mice and humans. J Gen Virology 71: 2099–2105
Partidos CD, Steward MW (1992) The effects of a flanking sequence on the immune response to a B and a T cell epitope from the fusion protein of measles virus. J Gen Virol 73: 1987–1994
Partidos CD, Stanley CM, Steward MW (1991) Immune responses in mice following immunization with chimeric synthetic peptides representing B and T cell epitopes of measles virus proteins. J Gen Virol 72: 1293–1299
Perrin LH, Tishon A, Oldstone MBA (1977) Immunologic injury in measles infection. III. Presence and characterization of human cytotoxic lymphocytes. J Immunol 118: 282–290
Reddehase MJ, Mutter W, Munch K, Buhring HJ, Koszinowski UH (1987) CD8-positive T lymphocytes specific for murine cytomegalovirus immediate-early antigens mediate protective immunity. J Virol 61: 3102–3108
Richardson C, Hull D, Greer P, Hasel K, Berkovich A, Englund G, Bellini W, Rima B, Lazzarini R (1986) The nucleotide sequence of the mRNA encoding the fusion protein of measles virus (edmonston strain): a comparison of fusion proteins from several different paramyxoviruses. Virology 155: 508–523
Richert JR, McFarland HF, McFarlin DE, Bellini WJ, Lake P (1983) Cloned measles virus-specific T lymphocytes from a twin with multiple sclerosis. Proc Natl Acad Sci USA 80: 555–559
Richert JR, McFarland HF, McFarlin DE, Johnson AH, Woody JH, Hartzman RJ (1985) Measles-specific T cell clones derived from a twin with multiple sclerosis: genetic restriction studies. J Immunol 34: 1561–1566
Richert JR, Rose JW, Reuben-Burnside C, Kearns MC, Jacobson S, Mingioli ES, Hartzman RJ, McFarland HF, McFarlin DE (1986) Polypeptide specificities of measles virus-reactive T cell lines and clones derived from a patient with multiple sclerosis. J Immunol 137: 2190–2194
Rose JW, Bellini WJ, McFarlin DE, McFarland HF (1984) Human cellular immune response to measles virus polypeptides. J Virol 49: 988–991
Rötzschke O, Falk F, Deres K, Schild H, Norda M, Metzger J, Jung G, Rammensee HG (1990) Isolation and analysis of naturally processed viral peptides as recognized by cytotoxic T cells. Nature 348: 252–254
Rudensky AY, Preston-Hurlburt P, Hong S-C, Barlow A, Janeway CA Jr (1991) Sequence analysis of peptides bound to MHC class II molecules. Nature 353: 622–626
Salter RD, Cresswell P (1986) Impaired assembly and transport of HLA-A and -B antigens in a mutant TxB cell hybrid. EMBO J 5: 943–949
Sato TA, Kohama T, Sugiura A (1988) Intracellular processing of measles virus fusion protein. Arch Virol 98: 39–50
Scheid A, Choppin PW (1977) Two disulphide-linked chains constitute the active F protein of paramyxoviruses. Virology 80: 54–66
Sethi KK, Stroehmann I, Brandis H (1982) Generation of cytolytic T-cell cultures displaying measles virus specificity and human histocompatibility leukocyte antigen restriction. Infect Immun 36: 657–661
Stern LJ, Wiley DC (1992) The human class II MHC protein HLA-DR1 assembles as empty $\alpha\beta$ heterodimers in the absence of antigenic peptide. Cell 68: 465–477
Townsend ARM, Rothbard J, Gotch FM, Bahadur G, Wraith D, McMichael J (1986) The epitopes of influenza nucleoprotein recognized by cytotoxic T lymphocytes can be defined with short synthetic peptide. Cell 44: 959–968

Van Binnendijk RS, Poelen MCM, de Vries P, Voorma HO, Osterhaus ADME, UytdeHaag FGCM (1989) Measles virus-specific human T cells clones. Characterization of specificity and function of $CD4^+$ helper/cytotoxic and $CD8^+$ cytotoxic T cell clones. J Immunol 142: 2847–2854
Van Binnendijk RS, Poelen MCM, Kuijpers KC, Osterhaus ADME, UytdeHaag FGCM (1990) The predominance of $CD8^+$ T cells after infection with measles virus suggests a role for $CD8^+$ class I MHC-restricted cytotoxic T lymphocytes (CTL) in recovery from measles. Clonal analyses of human $CD8^+$ class I MHC-restricted CTL. J Immunol 144: 2394–2399
Van Binnendijk RS, Poelen MCM, de Vries P, UytdeHaag FGCM, Osterhaus AGCM (1991) A role for $CD8^+$ class I MHC-restricted CTLs in recovery from measles: implications for the development of inactivated measles vaccine. Vaccine 91. Cold Spring Harbor Laboratory Press, Cold Spring Harbor
Van Binnendijk RS, van Baalen CA, Poelen MCM, de Vries P, Boes J, Cerundolo V, Osterhaus ADME, UytdeHaag FGCM (1992a) Measles virus transmembrane fusion protein synthesized de novo or presented in ISCOM is endogenously processed for HLA class I- and II-restricted cytotoxic T cell recognition. J Exp Med 176: 119–128
Van Binnendijk RS, Rumke HC, Van Eijdhoven MJA, Bosman A, Hirsch R, Van Loon AM, Benne CA, Van Dijk WC, Rima BK, Van der Heijden RWJ, UytdeHaag FGCM, Osterhaus ADME (1992b) A measles outbreak in vaccinated schoolaged children in the Netherlands: identification of clinically and subclinically infected children by evaluation of virus-specific antibody and T cell responses. Thesis, University of Utrecht (ISBN 90–393–0244–87)
Van Binnendijk RS, Versteeg-van Oosten JPM, Poelen MCM, Brugghe HF, Hoogerhout P, Osterhaus ADME, UytdeHaag FGCM (1993) Human HLA class I- and class II-restricted cloned cytotoxic T lymphocytes identify a cluster of epitopes on the measles virus fusion protein. J Virol 67: 2276–2284
Van Bleek GM, Natheson SG (1990) Isolation of an endogenous processed immunodominant viral peptide from the H-2Kb molecule. Nature 348: 213–216
Van Bleek GM, Nathenson SG (1991) The structure of the antigen binding groove of major histocompatibility complex class I molecules determines specific selection of self peptides. Proc Natl Acad Sci USA 88: 11032–11036
Whittle HC, Mee J, Werblinska J, Yakuba J, Onuora A, Gomwalk N (1980) Immunity to measles in malnourished children. Clin Exp Immunol 42: 144–151
Wright LL, and Levy NL (1979) Generation on infected fibroblasts of human T and non-T lymphocytes with specific cytotoxicity, influenced by histocompatibility, against measles virus-infected cells. J Immunol 122: 2379–2386
Yang Y, Water JB, Früh K, Petersen PA (1992) Proteasomes are regulated by interferon τ: implications for antigen processing Proc Natl Acad Sci USA 89: 4928–4932
Yap KL, Ada GL, McKenzie ISC (1978) Transfer of specific cytotoxic T cells protects mice inoculated with influenza viruses. Nature 273: 238–239
Yewdell JW, Bennink JR (1992) Cell biology of antigen processing and presentation to major histocompatibility complex class I molecule-restricted T lymphocytes. Adv Immunol 62: 1–123
Zhang W, Young ACM, Imarai M, Nathenson SG, Sacchettini JC (1992) Crystal structure of the major histocompatibility complex class 1 H-2 K^b molecule containing a single viral peptide: implications for peptide binding and T-cell receptor recognition. Proc Natl Acad Sci USA 89: 8403–8407

The Class I-Restricted Cytotoxic T Lymphocyte Response to Predetermined Epitopes in the Hepatitis B and C Viruses

A. CERNY[1], C. FERRARI[1,2], and F. V. CHISARI[1]

1 Introduction

Hepatitis B and C viruses (HBV and HCV) both originally identified as causative agents of transfusion-associated hepatitis share a propensity to induce acute and chronic hepatitis and hepatocellular carcinoma (TIOLLAIS et al. 1981; CHOO et al. 1989). Despite these biological similarities, the two viruses differ considerably. HBV has a partially double-stranded DNA genome of about 3200 nucleotides, infectious particles are 42 nm in size and are enveloped, and the virus belongs to the hepadnavirus family; HCV has a positive-stranded RNA genome of approximately 10000 nucleotides, is less than 80 nm in size, is probably enveloped due to its sensitivity to organic solvents, and it is related to the Togaviridae or Flaviviridae (HOUGHTON et al. 1991).

The mechanisms whereby HBV and HCV cause acute hepatocellular injury and initiate the sequence of events leading to chronic liver disease and ultimately to hepatocellular carcinoma are not well understood. It is possible that both direct, virus-related or indirect, i.e., immunologically mediated, mechanisms may play an important role. Analysis of the direct cytopathic

[1] The Scripps Research Institute, Department of Molecular and Experimental Medicine, 10666 North Torrey Pines Road, La Jolla, CA 92037, USA
[2] Cattedra Malattie Infettive, Universita degli Studi di Parma, Parma, Italy

effects of HBV and HCV for host liver cells has been hampered due to the lack of suitable animal models and tissue culture systems. Several clinical observations underline the contribution of the host immune response to liver cell injury: (a) infection acquired early in life occurring in an immunologically immature host leads to a chronic asymptomatic carrier state; (b) chronic carriers without evidence of liver cell injury are frequent for both viruses; and (c) immunosuppression has a beneficial effect on liver cell injury in chronic hepatitis B or C (HOLLINGER 1990; ALTER 1991).

At its most fundamental level, the cellular immune response involves multimolecular interaction between antigenic peptides, HLA molecules, and T cell receptors (TCR). Unlike antigen recognition by B cell immunoglobulin receptors, the two general classes of T cells do not recognize native antigen in solution; rather they recognize short antigenic peptides that have reached the cell surface via two quite different pathways (reviewed in ROTHBARD and GEFTER 1991).

Human $CD4^+$ T cells recognize short antigenic peptides derived by proteolytic cleavage of exogenous antigen present in the antigen-binding groove of HLA class II molecules at the surface of phagocytic antigen-presenting cells (APC) such a macrophages and B cells. Effector functions of this subset of T lymphocytes include secretion of lymphokines promoting growth and differentiation of antigen specific B cells and cytotoxic T lymphocytes (CTL) as well as activation of inflammatory cells (MOSSMANN et al. 1986). $CD4^+$ T cell-mediated cytotoxicity has been described in other human viral infections such as herpesvirus (YASUKAWA and ZARLING 1984; HAYWARD et al. 1986) and will not be further discussed in this review.

Human $CD8^+$ T cells recognize short antigenic peptides (usually nine to 11 residues) in the antigen-binding groove of HLA class I molecules which are present at the surface of the cells in which their precursor (e.g., virus-derived) proteins were originally synthesized (MONACO 1992). The antigenic peptides are derived by proteolytic cleavage of endogenously synthesized antigen in the cytoplasm. The processed peptides are then bound by a family of transporter proteins (encoded within the HLA locus), which shuttle them into the lumen of the endoplasmic reticulum, where they are scanned for the presence of HLA allele-specific binding motifs by the antigen-binding domain of resident HLA class I proteins. Peptides containing the appropriate motif are bound by the corresponding HLA class I molecule, which then associates with β_2-microglobulin and moves to the cell surface as an integral membrane protein, where it can present the antigenic peptide to the appropriately rearranged TCR on a $CD8^+$ T cell. The T cell subset specificity of this interaction derives from the fact that multimolecular HLA–peptide–TCR complex is stabilized by accessory interactions such as those between the CD8 molecule on the T cell and the HLA class I molecule involved in the complex.

Due to a precedent in other systems, it has been assumed that the HLA class I-restricted, $CD8^+$ CTL response to endogenously synthesized HBV and

HCV antigens is the effector limb in pathogenesis. This was an untestable hypothesis until recently, due to the absence of the necessary reagents and experimental systems—specifically, since both viruses do not infect continuous human cell lines in tissue culture, and the only animal models of HBV (woodchuck, ground squirrel, duck) and HCV (chimpanzee) infection that could be used for such studies involve species for which the immune system is not entirely defined.

2 CTL Response to Hepatitis B Virus

2.1 Analysis of CTL in the Peripheral Blood

To circumvent these problems, we set out several years ago to develop alternative modalities to present class I-bound, processed viral antigen to the CTL repertoire in HBV-infected patients and transgenic mice. In the course of these studies, we drew upon the experience of McMichael and Townsend and colleagues (GOTCH et al. 1987), who showed that murine class I-restricted CTL responses could be induced by stimulation with synthetic peptides derived from the corresponding antigen. Accordingly, in our analysis of HBV-infected patients, we stimulated peripheral blood mononuclear cells (PBMC) with pools of randomly designed, 15- to 20-residue synthetic HBV-derived peptides followed by restimulation with autologous Epstein-Barr virus (EBV)-transformed B cell lines that had been stably transfected with vectors that express the corresponding HBV-encoded protein. Although this process was relatively inefficient, it yielded HBV-specific CTL lines and clones that were assessed for phenotype, HLA restriction, recognition of endogenously synthesized antigen, and antigenic fine specificity. In this manner, we defined two HLA-A2-restricted CTL epitopes in the viral nucleocapsid ($HBcAg_{18-27}$) and envelope ($HBsAg_{335-343}$) proteins (GUILHOT et al. 1992; BERTOLETTI et al. 1991; PENNA et al. 1991; BERTOLETTI et al. 1993; NAYERSINA et al. 1993) and two additional completely overlapping epitopes within $HBcAg_{141-151}$ that, remarkably, are restricted by two independent HLA class I molecules (HLA-A31 and HLA-Aw68) in patients with acute viral hepatitis (MISSALE et al. 1993). In contrast to these results in patients with acute hepatitis, it is extremely interesting and potentially very important that thus far we have not detected a CTL response to any of these epitopes in the peripheral blood of a large number of HLA class I-matched patients with chronic hepatitis (BERTOLETTI et al. 1993; MISSALE et al. 1993).

It is interesting that the CTL epitope located between HBcAg residues 141 and 151 (STLPETTVVRR; MISSALE et al. 1993) completely overlaps a critical domain in the viral nucleocapsid protein that is essential for its nuclear localization and genome packaging functions (ECKHARDT et al. 1991; NASSAL 1992), as well as processing of the precore protein (SCHLICHT and

SCHALLER 1989). Because of this feature, the CTL response to this epitope could be especially effective at viral clearance since viral mutations in this region might be lethal for the virus itself. This study yielded an unexpected bonus for investigators interested in the molecular basis of HLA class I–antigenic peptide interaction, because the CTL response to this epitope was found to be dually restricted by the HLA-A31 and HLA-Aw68 alleles and, even more unexpectedly, both responses are focused on precisely the same 11-residue sequence. Perhaps most importantly, we discovered, by alanine substitution and competition analysis, that both of these class I alleles utilize the same HLA-binding motif, which consists of a threonine in position 2, a leucine in position 3, and an arginine at the carboxy terminus of an 11-residue peptide. Furthermore, one patient yielded two independent CTL clones whose antigenic fine specificity differed according to the HLA allele that restricted the response (i.e., glutamic acid 145 and valine 149 are epitopic residues for the HLA-A31-restricted clone, and the two threonine residues at positions 146 and 147 are seen by the TCR of the clone restricted by HLA-Aw68), once again emphasizing the multispecificity and polyclonality of the CTL response to HBV during acute hepatitis. Finally, the influence of peptide–class I interactions on TCR recognition was demonstrated by the observation that neither clone could recognize its cognate antigenic peptide when presented by the alternate restriction element. In addition to the substantial fundamental implications of this discovery, the identification of broadly presented epitopes such as this could have significant practical value for the development of a peptide-based CTL vaccine for termination of chronic HBV infection.

As we pursued these studies using randomly designed peptides, we discovered that the two HLA-A2-restricted CTL epitopes that were identified in this way were short peptides (9-mer and 10-mer) that displayed the ideal HLA-A2.1 allele-specific binding motif (xLxxxxxxV) that Rammensee and his collaborators (FALK et al. 1991) had independently found by eluting naturally synthesized cellular peptides from the HLA-A2.1-binding groove. Accordingly, a large panel of peptides was designed corresponding to ideal and alternative HLA-A2.1-binding motifs present within the HBV envelope, nucleocapsid, polymerase, and X proteins. We subsequently screened these peptides by stimulation of PBMC from HLA-A2-positive patients with acute hepatitis and identified additional HLA-A2-restricted CTL epitopes. During the course of these studies we learned that CTL lines that recognize endogenously synthesized antigen could be established simply by repeated stimulation with peptide rather than with stable, autologous, HBV transfectants, thereby greatly simplifying the CTL activation procedure.

Some of these peptides have already been used to examine the HBV-specific CTL response in several HLA-A2-positive patients with acute hepatitis. These studies demonstrated that some epitopes are recognized by most of the acutely infected patients, while the others are recognized by only a few, suggesting that factors other than the HLA-binding motif influence immunogenicity. It is also clear that some acutely infected patients respond to many of the epitopes, while the response of others is much more restricted. However, we will need to study an expanded panel of patients with an extended panel of epitopes before a definitive epitope recognition hierarchy is established.

Another very interesting and important observation is that some acutely infected patients studied with this panel of peptides failed to respond to any of them, similar to chronically infected patients and uninfected normal controls. It is possible, therefore, that these actuely infected nonresponders might ultimately fail to clear the virus. Alternatively, it is possible that they actually have chronic hepatitis which presented clinically with a flare that was misdiagnosed as acute hepatitis; or they may produce a perfectly good response to other epitopes, restricted by HLA-A2 or any of their other class I alleles, that we have not yet tested. A less likely possibility is that they are infected by variant viral genomes that do not encode any of these epitopes. To examine these clinically important alternatives, it will be necessary to follow these patients sequentially, to extend the analysis to new epitopes, and to determine the amino acid sequence in the region of these epitopes that is encoded by the viral genomes with which each of these patients is infected. It is exciting to think that we might possibly have identified a marker to distinguish patients who are destined to clear the virus from those who will become chronically infected by HBV. If this proves to be true in our future studies, not only will we have gained an important insight into the biology of viral persistence, but we may have developed a means to select patients who might benefit from early intervention with antiviral or immunomodulatory therapy designed to prevent the establishment of the chronic HBV carrier state.

Perhaps the most important fact to emerge from these studies is that the HBV-specific CTL response is remarkably polyclonal and multispecific within individual patients who succeed in clearing the virus, presumably conferring a high degree of protection against this dangerous viral pathogen. The diversity of the response also minimizes the likelihood that a mutation at any one of these epitopes would confer a selective survival advantage to the mutant virus. However, the possibility that such mutants may be actually selected in a minor proportion of patients who express a weaker and less heterogenous CTL response, such as patients with chronic hepatitis B, cannot be ruled out at present. Escape mutants in this setting would not be the original cause of virus persistence, but only a consequence of a prior defect in the antiviral immune response. The basis for the difference in the immunogenicity of these epitopes and the differential responsiveness of the patients is not clear at present, nor is the clinical significance of a strong response to many epitopes in certain patients versus a weak response to one or a few epitopes in others.

The fact that this sequential stimulation strategy worked so well, whereas many prior attempts failed to detect HBV-specific CTL in freshly isolated peripheral blood lymphocytes PBL without prior stimulation or following stimulation with stably transfected autologous B cell lines (BCL) without preliminary expansion with specific peptides, suggests that the HBV-specific CTL precursors are probably present in the peripheral blood compartment at very low frequency. Despite the effectiveness of this strategy in patients with acute hepatitis, however, we have rarely seen a response to these epitopes in patients with chronic hepatitis using the same stimulation conditions. The reasons for this are unclear. Possible mechanisms include: (a) the CTL response may be absolutely dependent on T cell help derived from a concomitant HBV-specific, $CD4^+$ T cell response, which we have shown is universally present in patients who clear the virus and absent in those who do not (FERRARI et al. 1991); (b) there may be a "hole" in the T cell repertoire for HBV-encoded antigens in patients with chronic hepatitis, due to the induction of immunological tolerance; (c) these patients may have a defect in processing of HBV antigens such that they do not cleave or transport the approriate peptide subunits to the appropriate HLA class I molecule; (d) they may express variant HLA class I alleles that cannot bind the peptides; (e) they may be infected by viral variants that do not contain the epitopes needed for viral clearance; and (f) they may generate a suppressive T cell response to HBV antigenic stimulation. Further studies will be needed to discriminate among these possibilities.

These data also suggest that HBV mutants that result in deletion of a single epitope or even an entire protein should not lead to escape of this antigenically complex virus from immune recognition unless the CTL response in that patient is functionally defective, and thus monoclonal or oligoclonal, or unless the mutation also confers a growth advantage on the mutant virus. Since we have shown that the HBV major, middle, and large envelope proteins are all good targets of the HBsAg-specific CTL response (NAYERSINA et al. 1993), just as the two nucleocapsid proteins are good targets of the HBcAg-specific CTL response (BERTOLETTI et al. 1991; MISSALE et al. 1993), even mutant viruses that lose the ability to synthesize one or more of these proteins in their entirety should not escape CTL recognition in the setting of a normal immune response, because the epitopes would still be generated by processing of the remaining protein(s). If, for some reason, however, a mutant can escape recognition in the original host, it should be irrelevant to subsequent hosts unless they have exactly the same HLA haplotype as the proband, a very rare situation indeed.

The principal strength of this peptide stimulation strategy is that it permits analysis of the CTL response to pathogens whose genome has been cloned and sequenced, but which are not infectious for autologous or surrogate stimulator/target cells in vitro. Indeed, as will be discussed below, we have recently extended the strategy for analysis of the HLA-A2-restricted CTL response to HCV with very encouraging results, and we will explore the CTL response restricted by other class I alleles as their binding motifs become defined.

There are, however, numerous limitations to this strategy which deserve attention. First, it requires knowledge of the amino acid sequence of the viral protein(s) in question; this is not needed for the initial identification of the CTL response to viral pathogens that are infectious in vitro. Second, to be most efficient, the strategy must be limited to epitopes presented by common HLA alleles whose binding motifs have been defined. Third, it has the potential to miss CTL responses to nonconserved epitopes, since the patient's CTL may be primed in vivo to an epitope that differs at one or more positions from the peptide used for in vitro expansion and screening. This problem can be readily overcome by focusing on highly conserved peptides carrying the HLA-binding motif of interest; but, correspondingly, this requires that the amino acid sequences of multiple independently cloned viral isolates must be known. Fourth, for these reasons plus the fact that not all peptides containing a given HLA-binding motif actually bind the restriction element with equal affinity, the process is inefficient and expensive, requiring the synthesis of many peptides, only a small proportion of which will prove to be CTL epitopes. This can be overcome to some extent by prescreening the peptides for HLA-binding affinity and focusing on the conserved peptides with the highest affinity for the corresponding allele. Obviously, this interposes an intermediate step in the strategy. It is worthwhile to do so, however, since in preliminary studies done in collaboration with R. Kubo and A. Sette (Cytel Corp., La Jolla, CA) we have found that only approximately 25% of HBV-derived peptides with the HLA-A2-binding motif actually bind to this molecule with reasonably high affinity. Importantly, slightly more than one third of these high-affinity peptides have proven to be epitopes recognized by CTL in acutely infected patients, while virtually none of the peptides with low binding affinity are reactive in this system. Finally, it is possible that this peptide stimulation strategy could lead to the in vitro induction of a primary CTL response that does not reflect in vivo priming by the pathogen. Indeed, we have recently shown in healthy uninfected donors that this can occur. While this represents a potential, but surmountable problem for the assessment of the pathogenetic significance of a given CTL response in infected individuals, it represents a major opportunity if one is interested in defining the CTL repertoire to any intracellular pathogen.

In vivo- and in vitro-primed CTL can be distinguished firstly on the basis of their precursor frequency in the peripheral blood and secondly according to the surface expression of CD45 isoforms (Alexander et al. 1992). We found a ten to 100-fold higher precursor frequency of HLA-A2-restricted CTL precursor specific for a single HBV epitope in the peripheral blood of patients with chronic hepatitis B than in normal subjects. Depletion of CD45 RO^+ PBMC reduces the CTL precursor frequency of chronically infected patients to the level of normal subjects, suggesting that in vivo-primed CTL precursors are CD45 RO^+ (A. Cerny, M. A. Brothers, and F. V. Chisari, unpublished observation).

Obviously, all of the foregoing comments carry important implications for understanding the role of the CTL response in viral pathogenesis and immunobiology. Additionally, these observations are also relevant for the possible development of peptide-based CTL vaccines. In this context, A. Vitiello and R. Chesnut (Cytel) have recently shown in preliminary studies, that a formulation containing the highly conserved HLA-A2-restricted CTL epitope we identified in the HBV nucleocapsid protein ($HBcAg_{18-27}$) is immunogenic in HLA-A2.1 transgenic mice (A. Vitiello, and R. Chesnut, personal communication). Pilot studies to evaluate the immunogenicity of this formulation in HLA-A2-positive humans and chronic HBV carriers are currently underway.

2.2 Analysis of Intrahepatic CTL

Immunohistochemical studies on the intrahepatic inflammatory infiltrates in chronic hepatitis associated with HBV infection demonstrate an increase in $CD8^+$ mononuclear cells predominantly in the infiltrates of periportal areas (piecemeal necrosis; YANG et al. 1988). This observation was corroborated by studies using different cloning strategies to derive T cell clones from liver biopsies that showed that most of the clones were $CD8^+$ and cytotoxic (HOFFMANN et al. 1986; MEUER et al. 1988). The information derived from these studies remains limited, due to the unavailability of tools to further study antigen specificity at the time when they were performed.

It is very interesting that two groups of investigators have demonstrated the presence of $CD8^+$ CTL in the intrahepatic inflammatory infiltrates in patients with chronic HBV infection using recombinant HBcAg and HBsAg particles for in vitro stimulation. Ferrari and colleagues have demonstrated that hepatitis core antigen is an important target of the intrahepatic TCR (FERRARI et al. 1987) and that $CD4^+$ and $CD8^+$ HBcAg-specific T cells are present in the intrahepatic inflammatory cell infiltrate during chronic HBV infection. While the $CD8^+$ T cells were shown to be cytotoxic in antigen-nonspecific cytotoxicity assays, the systems needed to demonstrate antigen-specific killing were not available when these studies were done.

In contrast, Barnada and colleagues have demonstrated that an epitope within the pre-S2 domain of the viral envelope protein was also recognized by intrahepatic $CD4^+$ and $CD8^+$ T cell clones during chronic HBV infection. With the use of synthetic peptides, an HLA-A3-restricted epitope could be precisely mapped to pre-S2 residues 120–134 (BARNABA et al. 1989). Interestingly, exogenously added HBV envelope antigen was also able to sensitize antigen-specific B cells for CTL-mediated lysis (BARNABA et al. 1990). Both of these observations suggest that class I-restricted, $CD8^+$ CTL reponses can be induced by certain exogenous particulate antigens, presumably by entry into the class I processing pathway of professional APC. While it cannot be proven that this occurred in the aforementioned study of infected patients, it must have occurred in the study by Berkower's group in which class I-restricted T cells specific for pre-S1 residues 21–28 were identified in the peripheral blood of HBsAg subunit vaccine recipients (JIN et al. 1988). It is remarkable that in addition to the classical pathway for induction of class I-restricted CTL by endogenously synthesized antigen, this generally unappreciated alternative pathway appears to be utilized for the CTL response to multiple HBV-derived antigens, perhaps underscoring the importance of elimination of this dangerous viral pathogen by the host.

3 CTL Response to Hepatitis C Virus

3.1 Analysis of CTL in the Peripheral Blood

In an early study performed before the identification of HCV as the major cause of non-A, non-B hepatitis in 1989, IMAWARI et al. (1989) described a human $CD8^+$ T cell clone derived from the peripheral blood of a patient with non-A, non-B hepatitis cytotoxic for autologous and allogeneic hepatocytes from patients with non-A, non-B hepatitis. Due to the lack of information on the agent responsible for non-A, non-B hepatitis, the fine specificity of this CTL clone was undefined.

In an attempt to define the molecular targets of the HCV-specific CTL response in the peripheral blood of chronically infected patients, we adopted an in vitro expansion strategy similar to the one we had previously used for HBV using HCV-derived synthetic peptides (Cerny et al., manuscript in preparation). We focused our analysis on CTL epitopes restricted by HLA-A2 for which the binding motif xLxxxxxxV or xLxxxxxxxV had been previously identified (FALK et al. 1991). The HCV-1 amino acid sequence was then scanned for the presence of the HLA-A2.1-binding motif and 53 peptides were identified for synthesis. Two peptides were derived from the core region, two from E1, six from E2/NS1, nine from NS2, nine from NS3, ten from NS4, and 15 from NS5.

Eight subjects positive for the HLA-A2 allele with hepatitis C infection were identified, PBMC were stimulated individually with the entire panel of 53 peptides, and cultures were tested after initial expansion for peptide-specific CTL activity. Six patients (C-1 to C-6) had biopsy-proven chronic active hepatitis associated with HCV infection, and subjects H-1 and H-2 had no signs of liver disease. Table 1 summarizes our results. Peptide-specific cytotoxic T cell activity was observed against seven out of 53 peptides. Four of the eight subjects showed CTL responses to at least one of the peptides. Subject C-2 responded to five peptides, two of which are derived from HCV core and one from NS3, NS4, and NS5 respectively. Subject C-3 responded to four peptides, including HCV $core_{178-187}$, but not HCV $core_{131-140}$. C-5, in

Table 1. Summary of hepatitic C virus (HCV) peptide specific CTL responses

HCV	Amino acid residues	Patients responding[a]
Core	131–140	C-2, C-5
Core	178–187	C-2, C-3
NS3	1169–1177	C-3
NS3	1406–1415	C-2, C-3, C-5
NS4	1789–1797	C-2, H-1
NS4	1807–1816	C-3
NS5	2252–2260	C-2

[a] Peripheral blood mononuclear cells were stimulated with the panel of 53 peptides and cultures were tested after initial in vitro expansion for peptide-specific CTL activity. A difference in the specific lysis of peptide-pulsed target cells and nonpulsed target cells of 15% at an effector-to-target cell ratio of 40/1-1/80 was considered to represent a positive CTL response and was confirmed by additional rounds of restimulation and subsequent cloning.

contrast, recognized HCV $core_{131-140}$, but not HCV $core_{178-187}$. Subject H-1 responded to only one peptide: $NS4_{1789-1797}$. Several of the peptides were found to be stimulatory for more than one patient, probably reflecting a higher degree of immunogenicity.

Four of the subjects (C-1, C-4, C-6 and H-2) did not show any significant induction of CTL activity with this panel of peptides. Both patients without overt liver disease as well as patients with chronic liver disease belong to this subset.

Further characterization of the CTL effector cells demonstrated that they were $CD8^+$, HLA-A2 restricted, and, in the case of $NS3_{1406-1415}$-specific CTL, capable of recognizing endogenously synthesized antigen (data not shown).

Due to the limited number of observations and the cross-sectional design of this study, it is at this time difficult to correlate the CTL response found with the clinical status or the virological parameters of the subjects studied. It is noteworthy that three patients with biopsy-proven chronic active hepatitis (CAH) did not have detectable CTL in their peripheral blood. Several possible explanations may account for this. First, the CTL precursor frequency specific for the peptides used in peripheral blood may be below our detection limit in these patients. Second, it may be that the CTL precursor frequency fluctuates in a given subject and the cross-sectional format of our pilot study fails to reveal this. Third, the patient may have a variant HLA-A2 allele cross-reacting serologically, but having a different HLA-binding motif. Several variants of HLA-A2 have been described that cross-react serologically, but not at the level of CTL restriction (LOPEZ and CASTRO 1989; RÖTZSCHKE et al. 1992). Fourth, HCV-specific CTL may be sequestered at the site of infection, i.e., the liver, and not detectable in the peripheral blood. Finally, the patient may be infected with a variant HCV isolate containing amino acid substitutions

Table 2. Representation of the hepatitis C virus (HCV) CTL epitope sequences in different HCV subtypes

HCV	Amino acid residues	HCV Subtype				
		I[a]	II	III	IV	ND
Core	131–140	3[b]/3[c]	8/8	1/3	2/2	7/8
Core	178–187	3/3	1/11	0/3	2/2	2/8
NS3	1169–1177	2/3	0/5	0/1	0/1	0/1
NS3	1406–1415	4/5	0/5	0/1	0/1	0/1
NS4	1789–1797	3/3	0/5	0/1	0/1	0/1
NS4	1807–1816	3/3	5/5	0/1	0/1	1/1
NS5	2252–2260	3/3	0/5	0/1	0/1	0/1

ND, not determined.
[a] Subtype of HCV as described (OKAMOTO et al. 1992).
[b] Number of sequences that show no amino acid substitutions within a given epitope.
[c] Total number of sequences deposited in GenEMBL covering a given epitope.

within the CTL epitopes tested that we derived from the HCV-1 sequence. In fact, HCV, a positive-stranded RNA virus, displays considerable sequence variability among reported isolates. The representation of the peptide sequences within the HCV subtypes whose sequence is available through the Gen EMBL data base is shown in Table 2.

The peptide sequence $NS3_{1406-1415}$, which was recognized by CTL from three subjects, is present in four out of five HCV-I subtypes predominant in the US and Europe. The fifth isolate, HCV-H, differs only with respect to one conservative Ileu to Val substitution at position 7. This makes it an interesting epitope for further study and a potential candidate for a peptide-based HCV vaccine as discussed above for HBV.

It is noteworthy that the peptide $NS3_{1169-1177}$ is part of the viral serine proteinase close to residue Ser 1165, which is one of the three catalytic site residues (GRAKOUI et al. 1993). Changes within that sequence may thus affect proteinase activity and compromise viral replication. This sequence is a biologically particularly important molecular target for the host immune system.

The link between HCV infection and the presence of autoantibodies is well established. One set of autoantibodies was originally defined by its reactivity with cryostat sections of rat liver and kidney and called LKM antibodies. A subset of LKM antibodies termed LKM-1 recognize epitopes within the human cytochrome p450IID6 protein and are associated with autoimmune hepatitis type II (MANNS et al. 1991). A significant proportion of patients with the disorder, particularly in southern Europe, are infected with HCV (LENZI et al. 1991). The presence of other microsomal autoantigens has been suggested in these patients (LENZI et al. 1991).

We therefore undertook an amino acid sequence comparison using the SwissProt data base and identified two human cytochrome p450 sequences related to HCV $core_{178-187}$, i.e., p450IIA6 and p450IIA7 (NEBERT and

Table 3. Hepatitis C virus (HCV) core 178–187 and related human cytochrome p450 amino acid and HCV sequences

Origin	Residues	Sequence[b]
HCV-1 core	178–187	L L A L L S C L T V
Cytochrome p450 IIA6	9–18	• V • • • V • • • •
Cytochrome p450 IIA7	9–18	• V • • • A • • • •
HCV subtype II ($n=8$[a])	178–187	• • • • • • • • • I
HCV subtype II ($n=2$[a])	178–187	• • • • • • • • • T
HCV J5 (III)	178–187	• • • • • • • I • •
HCV J6 (III)	178–187	• • • • • • • I • T
HCV KF	178–187	• S • • M • • • • T
HCV 476	178–187	• S • • M • • • • A

[a] Designates the number of isolates containing the amino acid sequence indicated.
[b] Amino acid sequence comparison was performed using the SwissProt and GenEMBL data bases and identified two human cytochrome p450 sequences related to HCV $core_{178-187}$. Identical amino acids are shown as dots. The amino acid single letter code is used.

NELSON 1991; Table 3). They display an eight-amino acid sequence identity, one conservative substitution (Leu to Val), and one nonconservative substitution (Ser to Val and Ser to Ala, respectively). Both cytochrome p450 mono-oxygenase sequences contain the HLA-A2 anchor residues, since both Leu and Val can serve as anchor residues at position 2 (R. Kubo and A. Sette personal communication). HCV sequences deposited in Gen EMBL show a sequence variability in the HCV $core_{178-187}$ sequence as well (Table 3). Given the fact that both HCV and cytochrome p450 sequences are polymorphic, coincidental sequence identity may occur in an HCV-infected individual. This suggests the possibility of molecular cross-reactivity at the level of CTL between HCV and autoantigens expressed on hepatocyte class I molecules, a hypothesis that we are currently addressing experimentally. Such a scenario could also account for geographic differences in the incidence of HCV-associated autoimmunity, assuming sequence identity within a CTL epitope between a prevalent HCV and cytochrome p450 genotype in a give population. Sequence identity was, however, not required for cross-recognition of a D^b-restricted mouse CTL epitope in HCV NS5 (aa 2422–2437). Three peptides derived from variant HCV isolates containing different single amino acid substitutions were also able to sensitize target cells for CTL-mediated lysis (SHIRAI et al. 1992).

The finding that multiple HCV-derived peptides serve as CTL epitopes restricted by a single class I restriction element underlines the multispecificity of the human cellular immune response against HCV. This observation parallels results obtained in a study on the $CD4^+$ proliferative TCR of PBMC to recombinant HCV-derived proteins: all viral proteins were found to be immunogenic in that study, and responsiveness was detectable in more than half of seropositive individuals (BOTARELLI et al. 1993).

The general experimental strategy reviewed here, i.e., selection of candidate CTL epitopes using a HLA-binding motif applied to a known sequence and subsequent screening of peptides for CTL induction, is expected to be a useful approach for the analysis of the CTL response in other systems as well.

3.2 Analysis of Intrahepatic CTL

The analysis of the intrahepatic CTL response has the advantage of reflecting the local immune response at the site of infection more faithfully. The requirement to perform a liver biopsy and the limited amount of tissue obtained with the associated sampling error are inherent problems associated with this approach. The local response may also be diluted due to the local recruitment of antigen-nonspecific inflammatory cells. On the other hand, HCV-spcific CTL may be sequestered at the site of infection, i.e., the liver, and not detectable in the peripheral blood.

Using an in vitro expansion protocol involving the use of a bispecific anti-CD3/anti-CD4 antibody allowing for the selective expansion of $CD8^+$ cells, Koziel and coworkers described class I-restricted $CD8^+$ CTL clones derived from liver biopsies from the two subjects evaluated recognizing epitopes within E1 and E2(NS1)/NS2 (Koziel et al. 1992). One epitope in E1 (aa 235–242) is restricted by HLA-B35 and a second epitope in NS2 (aa 826–837) is restricted by HLA-A29; a third epitope situated within E2(NS1)/NS2 is restricted by HLA-A2. Attempts to detect CTL in the peripheral blood of these same patients using a similar experimental approach were unsuccessful, suggesting a compartmentalization of the antiviral CTL response at the site of infection and tissue damage (B. Walker and M. Koziel, personal communication).

Another study used experimental HCV infection of chimpanzees, which allows for the study of all phases of the natural history of HCV infection. NS3 was found to be the dominant target of intrahepatic CTL-mediated immunity. The two animals studied had NS3-specific CTL restricted by distinct class I restriction elements that in one animal could be detected as long as 28 weeks postinfection (C. M. Walker, personal communication). Important information regarding the protective versus pathogenic potential of CTL can be expected from such studies.

4 Comparison of the CTL Response to Hepatitis B and C Viruses

It is interesting to note that in contrast to chronic HCV infection, this and other laboratories have not been successful in consistently identifying cytotoxic T cell responses in the peripheral blood of patients with chronic

HBV infection (MISSALE et al. 1993). This discrepancy may be due to a more vigorous antiviral CTL response in HCV infection as compared to HBV.

Alternatively, the CTL response to HBV may be more compartmentalized and restricted to the liver. Both HBV and HCV have been found to be detectable in PBMC of chronically infected patients (BOUFFARD et al. 1992; BAGINSKI et al. 1991). Subtle differences in tropism and expression, however, such as an enhanced presence of replicating virus in circulating professional APC (dendritic cells, monocytes, and B cells) could according to this hypothesis be the basis of the more systemic nature of the immune response against HCV.

5 Conclusions

The past several years have seen the definition of the molecular events underlying HLA class I restriction and have allowed a molecular analysis of CTL specificity. This technology applied to HBV and HCV pathobiology has and will yield a wealth of detailed information useful in many areas of heptitis research such as to elucidate pathogenesis, to refine diagnostics, and to develop new therapeutic concepts.

Autoimmunity due to molecular mimicry as suspected by clinical observations and by the finding of highly related amino acid sequences, illustrated by the case of the HCV CTL epitope $core_{178-187}$ and cytochrome p450, provide testable experimental hypotheses that may lead to a molecular definition of CTL-mediated autoimmunity.

The cytotoxic T cell response to both HBV and HCV is surprisingly multispecific, involving epitopes in different structural and nonstructural proteins and also polyclonal, especially considering the fact that the studies done with HLA-A2-binding peptides only reveal a small segment of the class I-restricted CTL response. Similar observations have been made in other human viral diseases such as human immunoreactivity virus (HIV; WALKER et al. 1989), varicella zoster virus (VZV; ARVIN 1992), herpes simplex virus (HSV; TIGGES et al. 1992), and cytomegalovirus (CMV; RIDDELL et al. 1991). Viral escape due to mutation of a CTL epitope as reported in a monoclonal mouse system is not likely to be relevant for viral persistence in the above human viral diseases (PIRCHER et al. 1990), except in individuals whose entire CTL response is focused on a single viral determinant, if such patients can be identified. If this occurs, any mutant virus should be irrelevant for the next host in view of the diversity of human HLA alleles, unless that mutation also confers a positive growth advantage to the virus that is independent of any immune selection pressure. This, indeed, might be the basis for the relative prevalence of an HLA-All-restricted EBNA-4 epitope loss mutant of EBV recently reported to occur in highly HLA-A11-positive populations (De

CAMPOS-LIMA et al. 1993). The issue remains controversial, however, since indirect evidence for a role of viral escape mutants has been reported in a longitudinal study of HIV-infected hemophiliac donors documenting the emergence of mutants with changes in CTL epitopes within HIV gag abolishing recognition by CTL from the same individual (Phillips et al. 1991). However, no selection of mutations in an immunodominant CTL epitope in simian immunodeficiency virus (SIV) gag could be detected when compared to the flanking non-epitope-coding region in a study done in rhesus monkeys (CHEN et al. 1992).

The key question remains unanswered, however: how can a virus persist under a polyclonal, multispecific immune attack? Apart from escape by mutation of epitopes, many different examples of modulation of the immune response in various viral infections have been reported and reviewed recently (GOODING 1992). They include interference with class I antigen translocation, cytokine production and function, and lymphocyte signal transduction.

The experimental strategy reviewed in this paper, i.e., selection of candidate CTL epitopes using an HLA-binding motif applied to a virus sequence and subsequent screening of peptides for CTL induction, may be generally useful for the analysis of the CTL response in other systems where APC that synthesize the target protein of interest are not available.

Acknowledgements. This work was supported by grants RO1 AI 20001, AI26626, and RR 00833 from the National Institutes of Health and funds from Cytel Corporation, La Jolla, CA. Andreas Cerny was supported by a fellowship of the Schweizerische Stiftung für Medizinisch Biologische Stipendien. We thank R. Kubo, A. Sette, A. Vitiello, R. Chestnut, C. M. Walker, and B. Walker for sharing unpublished data, our clinical collaborators A. Redeker, J. Person, and J. McHutchison for referral of patients, L. Wilkes and K. Cox for the processing of blood samples, P. Fowler and M.A. Brothers for technical assistance, and B. Weier for secretarial help. This is manuscript number 8133-MEM from the Scripps Research Institute.

References

Alexander D, Shiroo M, Robinson A, Biffen M, Shivnan E (1992) The role of CD45 in T-cell activation—resolving the paradoxes? Immunol Today 13: 477–481

Alter MJ (1991) Epidemiology of community-acquired hepatitis C. In: Hollinger FB, Lemon SM, Margolis HS (ed) Viral hepatitis and liver disease. Williams and Wilkins, Baltimore, pp 410–413

Arvin AM (1992) Cell-mediated immunity to varicella-zoster virus. J Inf Dis 166 (Suppl 1): S35–41

Baginski I, Chemin I, Bouffard P, Hantz O, Trepo C (1991) Detection of polyadenylated RNA in hepatitis B virus-infected peripheral blood mononuclear cells by polymerase chain reaction. J Inf Dis 163: 996–1000

Barnaba V, Franco A, Alberti A, Balsano C, Benvenuto R, Balsano F (1989) Recognition of hepatitis B virus envelope proteins by liver-infiltrating T lymphocytes in chronic HBV infection. J Imunol 143: 2650–2655

Barnaba V, Franco A, Alberti A, Benvenuto R, Balsano F (1990) Selective killing of hepatitis B envelope antigen-specific B cells by class I-restricted, exogenous antigen-specific T lymphocytes. Nature 345: 258–260

Bertoletti A, Chisari FV, Penna A, Guilhot S, Galati L, Fowler P, Vitiello A, Chesnut RC, Fiaccadori F, Ferrari C (1993) Definition of a minimal optimal cytotoxic T cell epitope within the hepatitis B virus nucleocapsid protein. J Virol 67: 2376–2380

Bertoletti A, Ferrari C, Fiaccadori F, Penna A, Margolskee R, Schlicht JH, Fowler P, Guilhot S, Chisari FV (1991) HLA class I restricted human cytotoxic T cells recognize endogenously syn- thesized hepatitis B virus nucleocapsid antigen. Proc Natl Acad Sci USA 88: 10445–10449

Botarelli P, Brunetto MR, Minutello MA, Calvo P, Unutmaz D, Weiner AJ, Choo Q-L, Shuster JR, Kuo G, Bonino F, Houghton M, Abrignani S (1993) T-lymphocyte response to hepatitis C virus in different clinical courses of infection. Gastroenterology 104: 580–587

Bouffard P, Hayashi PH, Acevedo R, Levy N, Zeldis JB (1992) Hepatitis C virus is detected in a monocyte/macrophage subpopulation of peripheral blood mononuclear cells of infected patients J Inf Dis 166: 1276–1280

Cerny A, McHutchison JG, Pasquinelli C, Brothers MA, Fowler P, Houghton M, Chisari FV (in preparation)

Chen ZW, Shen L, Miller MD, Ghim SH, Hughes AL, Letvin NL (1992) Cytotoxic T lymphocytes do not appear to select for mutations in an immunodominant epitope of simian immunodeficiency virus gag. J Immunol 149: 4060–4066

Choo QL, Kuo G, Weiner AJ, Overby LR, Bradley DW, Houghton M (1989) Isolation of a cDNA clone derived from a blood-borne non-A, non-B viral hepatitis genome. Science 244: 359–362

De Campos-Lima P-O, Gavioli R, Zhang Q-J, Wallace LE, Dolcetti R, Rowe M, Rickinson AB, Masucci MG (1993) HLA-A11 epitope loss of Epstein-Barr virus from a highly A11 + population. Science 260: 98–100

Eckhardt SG, Milich DR, McLachlan A (1991) Hepatitis B virus core antigen has two nuclear localization sequences in the arginine-rich carboxyl terminus. J Virol 65: 575–582

Falk K, Roetzschke O, Stevanovic S, Jung G, Rammensee H-G (1991) Allele-specific motifs revealed by sequencing of self-peptides eluted from MHC molecules. Nature 351: 290–296

Ferrari C, Penna A, Giuberti T, Tong MJ, Ribera E, Fiaccadori F, Chisari FV (1987) Intrahepatic, nucleocapsid antigen specific T cells in chronic active hepatitis. Br J Immunol 139: 2050–2058

Ferrari C, Bertoletti A, Penna A, Cavalli A, Valli A, Missale G, Pilli M, Fowler P, Giuberti T, Chisari FV, Fiaccadori F (1991) Identification of immunodominant T cell epitopes of the hepatitis B virus nucleocapsid antigen. J Clin Invest 88: 214–222

Gooding LR (1992) Virus proteins that counteract host immune defenses. Cell 71: 5–7

Gotch F, Rothbard J, Howland K, Townsend A, McMichael A (1987) Cytotoxic T lymphocytes recognize a fragment of influenza matrix protein in association with HLA-A2 Nature 326: 881–882

Grakoui A, McCourt DW, Wychowski C, Feinstone SM, Rice CM (1993) Characterization of the hepatitis C virus-encoded serine proteinase: determination of proteinase-dependent polyprotein cleavage sites. J Virol 67: 2832–2843

Guilhot S, Fowler P, Portillo G, Margolskee RF, Ferrari C, Bertoletti A, Chisari FV (1992) Hepatitis B virus (HBV)-specific cytotoxic T cell response in humans: production of target cells by stable expression of HBV-encoded proteins in immortalized human B cell lines. J Virol 66: 2670–2678

Hayward AR, Pontesilli O, Herberger M, Laszlo M, Levin M (1986) Specific lysis of varicella zoster virus-infected B lymphoblasts by human T cells. J Virol 58: 179–184

Hoffmann RM, Pape GR, Rieber P, Eisenburg J, Döhrmann J, Zachoval R, Paumgartner G, Riethmüller G (1986) Cytolytic T cell clones derived from liver tissue of patients with chronic hepatitis B Eur J Immunol 16: 1635–1638

Hollinger FB (1990) Hepatitis B virus. In: Fields BN, Knipe DM et al. (eds) Virology. Raven, New York, pp 2171–2236

Houghton M, Richman K, Berger K, Lee C, Dong C, Overby L, Weiner A, Bradley D, Kuo G, Choo Q-L (1991) Hepatitis C virus (HCV), a relative of the pestiviruses and flaviviruses. In: Hollinger FB, Lemon SM, Margolis HS (eds) Viral hepatitis and liver disease. Williams and Wilkins, Baltimore, pp 328–333

Imawari M, Nomura M, Kaieda T, Moriyama T, Oshimi K, Nakamura I, Gunji T, Ohnishi S, Ishikawa T, Nakagama H, Takaku F (1989) Establishment of a human T cell clone cytotoxic for both autologous and allogeneic hepatocytes from chronic hepatitis patients with type non-A, non-B virus. Proc Natl Acad Sci USA 86: 2883–2887

Jin Y, Shih W-K, Berkower I (1988) Human T cell response to the surface antigen of hepatitis B virus (HBsAg). J Exp Med 168: 293–306
Koziel MJ, Dudley D, Wong JT, Dienstag J, Houghton M, Ralston R, Walker BD (1992) Intrahepatic cytotoxic T lymphocytes specific for hepatitis C virus in persons with chronic hepatitis. J Immunol 149: 3339–3344
Lenzi M, Johnson PJ, McFarlane IG, Ballardini G, Smith HM, McFarlane BM, Bridger C, Vergani D, Bianchi FB, Williams R (1991) Antibodies to hepatitis C virus in autoimmune liver disease: evidence for geographical heterogeneity. Lancet 338: 277–280
Lopez de Castro JA (1989) HLA-B27 and HLA-A2 subtypes: structure, evolution and function. Immunol Today 10: 239–246
Manns MP, Griffin KJ, Sullivan KF, Johnson EF (1991) LKM-1 autoantibodies recognize a short linear sequence in p450IID6, a cytochrome p-450 monooxygenase J Clin Invest 88: 1370–1378
Meuer SC, Moebius U, Manns MM, Dienes HP, Ramadori G, Hess G, Hercend T Meyer zum Büschenfelde K-H (1988) Clonal analysis of human lymphocytes infiltrating the liver in chronic hepatitis B and primary biliary cirrhosis. Eur J Immunol 18: 1447–1452
Missale G, Redeker A, Person J, Fowler P, Guilhot S, Schlicht H-J, Ferrari C, Chisari FV (1993) HLA-A31 and Aw68 restricted cytotoxic T cell responses to a single hepatitis B virus nucleocapsid epitope during acute viral hepatitis. J Exp Med 177: 751–762
Monaco, JJ (1992) A molecular model of MHC class I restricted antigen processing. Immunol Today 13: 173–179
Mosmann TR, Cherwinski H, Bond MW, Giedlin MA, Coffman RL(1986) Two types of murine helper T cell clone. I. Definition according to profiles of lymphokine activities and secreted proteins J Immunol 136: 2348–2357
Nassal M (1992) The arginine-rich domain of the hepatitis B virus core protein is required for pregenome encapsidation and productive viral positive-strand DNA synthesis but not for virus assembly. J Virol 66: 4107–4116
Nayersina R, Fowler P, Guilhot S, Missale G, Cerny A, Schlicht H-J, Vitiello A, Chesnut R, Person JL, Redeker AG, Chisari FV (1993) HLA A2 restricted cytotoxic T lymphocyte responses to hepatitis B surface antigen group and subtype specific epitopes during hepatitis B virus infection. J Immunol 150: 4659–4671
Nebert DW, Nelson DR (1991) P450 gene nomenclature based on evolution. Methods Enzymol 206: 3–11
Okamoto H, Sugiyama Y, Okada S, Kurai K, Akahane Y, Sugai Y, Tanaka T, Sato K, Tsuda F, Miyakawa Y, Mayumi M (1992) Typing hepatitis C virus by polymerase chain reaction with type-specific primers: applications to clinical surveys and tracing infectious sources. J Gen Virol 73: 673–679
Penna A, Chisari FV, Bertoletti A, Missale G, Fowler P, Giuberti T, Fiaccadori F, Ferrai C (1991) Cytotoxic T lymphocytes recognize an HLA-A2 restricted epitope within the hepatitis B virus nucleocapsid antigen. J Exp Med 174: 1565–1570
Phillips RE, Rowland-Jones S, Nixon DF, Gotch FM, Edwards JP, Ogunlesi AO, Rothbard JA, Bangham CRM, Rizza CR, McMichael AJ (1991) Human immunodeficiency virus genetic variation that can escape cytotoxic T cell recognition. Nature 354: 453–459
Pircher H, Moskophidis D, Rohrer U, Bürki K, Hengartner H, Zinkernagel RM (1990) Viral escape by selection of cytotixic T-cell-resistant virus variants in vivo. Nature 346: 629–633
Riddell SR, Rabin M, Geballe AP, Britt WJ, Greenberg PD (1991) Class I MHC-restricted cytotoxic T lymphocyte recognition of cells infected with human cytomegalovirus does not require endogenous viral gene expression. J Immunol 146: 2795–2804
Rothbard JB, Gefter ML (1991) Interactions between immunogeneic peptides and MHC proteins. Annu Rev Immunol 9: 527–565
Rötzschke O, Falk K (1991) Naturally occurring peptide antigens derived from the MHC class I restricted processing pathway. Immunol Today 12: 447–455
Rötzschke O, Falk K, Stevanovic S, Jung G, Rammensee H-G (1992) Peptide motifs of closely related HLA class I molecules encompass substantial differences. Eur J Immunol 22: 2453–2456
Schlicht HJ, Schaller H (1989) The secretory core protein of human hepatitis B virus is expressed on the cell surface. J Virol 63: 5399–5404
Shirai M, Akatsuka T, Pendleton CD, Houghten R, Wychowski C, Mihalik K, Feinstone S, Berzofsky JA (1992) Induction of cytotoxic T cells to a cross-reactive epitope in the hepatitis C virus nonstructural RNA polymerase-like protein. J Virol 66: 4098–4106

Tigges MA, Koelle D, Hartog K, Sekulovich RE, Corey L, Burke RL (1992) Human CD8$^+$ herpes simplex specific cytotoxic T lymphocyte clones recognize diverse virion protein antigens. J Virol 66:1622–1634

Tiollais P, Charnay P, Vyas GN (1981) Biology of hepatitis B virus. Science 213:406–411

Walker BD, Flexner C, Birch-Limberger K, Fisher L, Paradis TJ, Aldovini A, Young R, Moss B, Schooley RT (1989) Long-term culture and fine specificity of human cytotoxic T-lymphocyte clones reactive with human immunodeficiency virus type 1. Proc Natl Acad Sci USA 86:9514–9518

Yang P-M, Su I-J, Lai M-Y, Huang G-T, Hsu H-C, Chen D-S, Sung J-L. (1988) Immunohistochemical studies on introhepatic lymphocyte infiltrates in chronic type B hepatitis, with special emphasis on the activation status of the lymphocytes. Am J Gastroenterology 83: 948–953

Yasukawa M, Zarling JM (1984) Human cytotoxic T cell clones directed against herpes simplex virus-infected cells. I. Lysis restricted by HLA class II MB and DR antigens. J Immunol 133: 422–427

Cytotoxic T Lymphocytes in Humans Exposed to *Plasmodium falciparum* by Immunization or Natural Exposure*

S. L. HOFFMAN[1], M. SEDEGAH[1,2], and A. MALIK[1]

1 The Problem of Malaria and Efforts to Control the Disease

Malaria is one of the most important infectious diseases in the world. It is estimated that 2.1 billion people live in areas of the world where malaria is transmitted and that there are 100–300 million new cases of malaria and one

[1] Malaria Program, Naval Medical Research Institute, Bethesda, MD 20889-5607, USA
[2] Pan American Health Organization, Washington DC 20037, USA

* The opinions and assertions herein are the private ones of the authors and are not to be construed as official or as reflecting the views of the U.S. Navy or the Naval Service at large.

Current Topics in Microbiology and Immunology, Vol. 189

to two million deaths caused by malaria every year (WHO 1991). In the past 10–20 years, the severity of the malaria problem has worsened in many areas because of the emergence of drug-resistant strains of the parasite, resistance to insecticides of the *Anopheles* sp. mosquitoes that transmit the disease, socioeconomic problems that have led to a decreased capacity to optimally utilize existing tools to combat the disease, and movement of nonimmune populations into areas where malaria is transmitted. Accordingly, there are now renewed efforts to control this disease. A major focus of research efforts is to develop vaccines against malaria, including vaccines designed to produce protective cytotoxic T lymphocytes (CTL; HOFFMAN et al. 1991). To understand how such vaccines might work, it is important to understand the life cycle of the parasite.

2 Life Cycle of *Plasmodium falciparum*

Plasmodium falciparum is transmitted to humans by the bite of female *Anopheles* sp. mosquitoes. The mosquito injects sporozoites that pass to the liver, where they enter hepatocytes within 30 min (FAIRLEY 1947). It is unknown whether the sporozoites pass through another cell, such as a reticuloendothelial cell, on the way from the circulation to hepatocytes. Most of the uninucleate sporozoites develop in hepatocytes during 6–10 days to mature liver stage schizonts, which have 10000–40000 uninucleate merozoites. After rupturing out of hepatocytes, each merozoite can invade an erythrocyte, where during the next 48 h each uninucleate merozoite can develop to a mature erythrocytic stage schizont with an average of 16 merozoites. These erythrocytic stage schizonts then rupture, thus releasing merozoites, each of which can then reinvade an erythrocyte, initiating the cycle of amplification, rupture, and reinvasion that leads to increasing levels of parasitemia and the clinical manifestations of malaria. Some of the parasites within infected erythrocytes do not develop to erythrocytic stage schizonts, but instead become sexual forms of the parasite called gametocytes. If a mosquito ingests blood infected with gametocytes, the gametocytes develop during an average of 14 days to sporozoites that can be inoculated into other humans. Parasites that cause malaria in rodents such as *P. yoelii* and *P. berghei* have a similar life cycle, but develop much more rapidly in the liver (40–48 h). Since sporozoites and merozoites in circulation are extracellular and mature human erythrocytes are not known to have major histocompatibility antigens on their surface, infected hepatocytes are considered the primary, and perhaps the only, target of CTL against *P. falciparum*.

3 Rationale for Work on CD8$^+$ CTL Against Pre-erythrocytic *Plasmodium* Species Antigens

Immunization of mice (NUSSENZWEIG et al. 1969) and humans (CLYDE et al. 1973; RIECKMANN et al. 1979) with radiation attenuated *Plasmodium* sp. sporozoites protects against challenge with live sporozoites, but does not protect against challenge with infected erythrocytes. The protective immunity induced by the irradiated sporozoite vaccine must therefore be directed against extracellular sporozoites in the circulation (antibodies) or against parasites within hepatocytes (antibodies or cellular immune responses). This is consistent with the observation that irradiated sporozoites develop only partially within hepatocytes and never mature to the late liver schizont stage. Because the sera from mice (VANDERBERG et al. 1969) and humans (CLYDE et al. 1973) immunized with irradiated sporozoites precipitates the surface coat of sporozoites, for many years antibodies against sporozoites were thought to be the major immune effectors responsible for this protection. However, in 1977 it was reported that mu-suppressed mice (mice that could not produce antibodies) immunized with irradiated sporozoites were protected against challenge (CHEN et al. 1977), and several years ago it was shown that adoptive transfer of T cells from mice immunized with irradiated sporozoites protected naive mice against challenge with live sporozoites at a time when the mice had no detectable circulating antisporozoite antibodies (EGAN et al. 1987). Furthermore, in some strains of mice the immunity induced by immunization with irradiated sporozoites was completely reversed by in vivo depletion of CD8$^+$ T lymphocytes (SCHOFIELD et al. 1987; WEISS et al. 1988). The antibodies induced by this form of immunization were not adequate to protect on their own, and it appeared that CD8$^+$ CTL were required for this protective immunity. CTL must recognize their target peptides in combination with major histocompatibility complex (MHC) proteins. These data indicated that the protective CTL could not be directed against extracellular sporozoites in the circulation and must be directed against *Plasmodium* sp. peptides in association with class I MHC molecules on the surface of infected hepatocytes. However, when these discoveries were made, no *Plasmodium* sp. antigen had ever been detected on the surface of infected hepatocytes, inflammatory infiltrates had been shown to be infrequent in the livers of mice infected with malaria (MEIS et al. 1987), and there was considerable debate regarding whether hepatocytes express class I MHC molecules and whether immune CTL could pass from the sinusoids into the space of Disse and attack infected hepatocytes. Within a year it was shown that mice immunized with irradiated *P. berghei* sporozoites and challenged with live sporozoites developed antigen-specific, CD8$^+$ T cell-dependent infiltrates in their livers and that spleen cells from these mice eliminated *P. berghei*-infected hepatocytes from in vitro culture in an MHC-restricted and antigen-specific manner (HOFFMAN et al. 1989a). These studies demonstrated that *Plasmodium* sp. peptides were recognized on infected hepatocytes by T cells and indicated that immune cells could reach, recognize, and destroy infected hepatocytes. They did not indicate which specific *Plasmodium* sp. antigens on hepatocytes were recognized by CTL.

Another intriguing observation supporting the role of CTL in protection against malaria was made several years later. An association was noted between the presence of HLA Bw53 (class I) and protection against severe malaria in Gambians (HILL et al. 1991). HLA Bw53 was found in 16.9% of cases of severe malaria, in 25.4% of controls with mild malaria, and in 25% of adults without malaria. The relative risk of severe malaria among individuals with HLA Bw53 compared with those without this allele was 0.59.

HLA Bw53 is found in 15%–40% of the population of sub-Saharan Africa, but is found in less than 1% of Caucasians and Orientals; like the sickle cell trait, it may have been selected because it protects against severe malaria. The presence of HLA Bw53 is not as protective as the HbS carrier state; only 1.2% of patients with severe malaria in the Gambia study had HbS, while 12.9% of controls with mild malaria carried HbS (relative risk 0.08). Nonetheless, the decreased association of HLA Bw53 with severe malaria suggests that naturally acquired CTL against *Plasmodium* sp. proteins protect against severe malaria. The logical targets for CTL are infected hepatocytes. Most deaths occur in children less than 5 years of age, and these children are not protected against developing malaria infections. Thus, such data raise the possibility that under natural conditions of exposure, CTL against infected hepatocytes reduce mortality by reducing the burden of infection, not by preventing infection. This is consistent with the recent report that use of insecticide-impregnated bednets does not reduce the incidence of parasitemia in Gambian villages, but has a dramatic effect on mortality (ALONSO et al. 1991).

4 CD8$^+$CTL Against the Circumsporozoite Protein

4.1 Rationale for Work

When work began in earnest on CTL in malaria, the only characterized sporozoite or liver (pre-erythrocytic) stage antigen available for study was the circumsporozoite (CS) protein (YOSHIDA et al. 1980). Kumar reported that B10.BR mice immunized with irradiated *P. falciparum* sporozoites and recombinant vaccinia expressing the *P. falciparum* CS protein (PfCSP) produced CTL against a single 23-amino acid region from the carboxy terminus of the CS protein, Pf 7G8 CS368–390 (KPKDELDYENDIEKKICK-MEKCS; KUMAR et al. 1988). It was next reported that BALB/c mice immunized with *P. berghei* (ROMERO et al. 1989) or *P. yoelii* (WEISS et al. 1990) sporozoites produced CTL against 12-amino acid (residues 249–260, NDDSYIPSAEKI) and 16-amino acid (residues 281–296, SYVPSAE-QILEFVKQI) regions of the respective CS proteins. WEISS demonstrated that the CTL eliminated infected hepatocytes from in vitro culture; the CTL recognized this 16-amino acid peptide on the surface of infected hepatocytes with class I MHC. ROMERO reported that adoptive transfer of CTL clones against the analogous epitope on the *P. berghei* CS protein completely protected against challenge in vivo. RODRIGUES (RODRIGUES et al. 1991) subsequently reported that adoptive transfer of CTL clones against the *P. yoelii* CS protein protected even if transferred 3 h after sporozoites were inoculated, at a time when the sporozoites had left the circulation and were within hepatocytes. Infected hepatocytes were clearly the target of these CTL. RODRIGUES also showed that protective clones could be found in the liver in apposition to infected hepatocytes (RODRIGUES et al. 1992), but that only CTL clones expressing the adhesion molecule CD44 were protective. This suggests that in addition to epitope specificity and cytolytic capacity, homing is critical for protection. This view has been supported by studies in the *P. yoelii* and *P. berghei* rodent model system that show that the induction of CTL by active immunization does not indicate that an animal will be protected (FLYNN et al. 1990; SEDEGAH et al. 1992a; SATCHIDANANDAM et al. 1991).

The mechanism by which the CTL eliminate infected hepatocytes has as yet not been established. Schofield showed that treatment of fully immune A/J mice with antibodies to γ-interferon abrogated the irradiated sporozoite-induced protective immunity (SCHOFIELD et al. 1987). This was not the case in BALB/c mice immunized with irradiated *P. berghei* sporozoites (HOFFMAN et al. 1989a). However, Weiss has recently shown that protective immunity conferred by adoptive transfer of a $CD8^+$CTL clone against a 10-amino acid peptide (SYVPSAEQIL) on the *P. yoelii* CS protein is eliminated by in vivo treatment with anti-γ-interferon (WEISS et al. 1992). Weiss has also shown that this $CD8^+$ CTL clone protects against both *P. yoelii* and *P. berghei*, despite the fact that the two CS proteins vary by two amino acids at the site of the CTL epitope (WEISS et al. 1992).

In addition to the adoptive transfer experiments, it has been shown that immunization of BALB/c mice with recombinant *Salmonella typhimurium* expressing the *P. berghei* CS protein induces protective immunity in 50%–75% of mice and that this protection is eliminated by in vivo depletion of $CD8^+$ T cells (AGGARWAL et al. 1991). Likewise, immunization of BALB/c with recombinant P815 mastocytoma cells expressing the *P. yoelii* CS protein also induces $CD8^+$ T cell-dependent protective immunity in 50%–75% of recipient mice (KHUSMITH et al. 1991).

4.2 CD8$^+$ T Cell-Dependent Cytolytic Activity Against the *P. falciparum* Circumsporozoite Protein

4.2.1 Volunteers Immunized with Radiation-Attenuated Sporozoites

The studies in the rodent model systems provided a compelling rationale for developing vaccines for humans that would induce similar CTL against the PfCSP. However, at the time such work was contemplated, no one had shown that humans produced CTL to any *Plasmodium* sp. protein, and in fact, there was only one report in the world's literature demonstrating that humans produced CTL against any parasite protein (YANO et al. 1989). MALIK and collaborators (1991) developed an assay for demonstrating CD8$^+$ CTL against the PfCSP. To provide effector cells, humans were immunized by the bites of previously irradiated *Anopheles stephensi* mosquitoes carrying NF54/3D7 *P. falciparum* sporozoites in their salivary glands (EGAN et al. 1993). Peripheral blood mononuclear cells were harvested and stimulated in vitro with recombinant vaccinia virus expressing the PfCSP (7G8 clone of *P. falciparum*) for 6 days. These effectors were then incubated with autologous Epstein-Barr virus (EBV)-transformed B lymphocytes that had been transiently transfected with the gene encoding the 7G8 PfCSP 48 h previously. Using this method, MALIK and colleagues demonstrated that three of four immunized volunteers produced CTL against the PfCSP and that this cytolytic activity was antigen specific, genetically restricted, and dependent on CD8$^+$ T lymphocytes. They reported that cytolytic activity could not be demonstrated each time an assay was run; six of nine, seven of 11, and two of 12 assays were positive in the three individuals shown to have cytolytic activity. They also reported the presence of cytolytic activity 13 weeks after last immunization in one volunteer.

Stimulating with vaccinia-infected cells in vitro was consumptive of large numbers of human cells. Since a peptide including amino acids 368–390 of the Pf 7G8 CS (Table 1) had previously been shown to include a CTL epitope in B10.BR mice (KUMAR et al. 1988), this peptide was studied in the same system. Three of the four volunteers were shown to have CTL directed at one or more epitopes included within this peptide. In one volunteer, overlapping 20-amino acid peptides representing the entire carboxy terminus of the 7G8 CS protein were studied, and only peptide 368–390 was able to label target cells for killing by CTL. CTL from this volunteer recognized both the 7G8 *P. falciparum* sequence and the sequence based on the immunizing sporozoites (3D7) that differed by one amino acid (Table 1). It has not been established whether the variant amino acid residue is actually included within the CTL epitope. However, this finding is of potential importance because of concerns regarding polymorphism of this epitope and the reasons why polymorphism has developed at this site. If the polymorphism is the result of immune selection and CTL against one sequence do not recognize CTL against variant

Table 1. Variation in the region of the only know human CD8$^+$ CTL epitope on the *P. falciparum* circumsporozoite (CS) protein

Strain or isolate	Amino acid residue										
	367	368	369	370	371	372	373	374	375	376	377
7G8 T9/101;406$_{3-5}$; T4R	**N**	K	**P**	**K**	D	**E**	L	**D**	Y	**E**	**N**
NF54/3D7; XP$_{8,9}$; X$_{10,11}$; T9-98; 406$_{1,7,8}$; 427$_{1-10}$; 419$_{10}$; GAM1										A	
AE7, PNG2						Q					
ItG2: W/L; PNG1, PNG X 22; T9-94; WEL	D					Q					
MCK+; AE28; GAM2; MS2; Palo Alto; 366$_{1,5,8-10}$ 399$_{1-10}$; LE5						Q				A	
HB3; X5; XP$_{12,13}$; PNG4; BRA1	G		S								
PNG3	D					Q		C			S
GAM3; 366$_{2-4,6,7}$; 406$_{10}$; 419$_{1-9}$;						Q		N			
GAM4; 406$_2$				R						A	
GAM5; 406$_{3,9}$										A	D

In mice and humans, a peptide including amino acid residues 368–390 of the 7G8 *P. falciparum* CS protein (Pf 7G8 CS 368–390, KPKDELDYENDIEKKICKMEKCS; DAME et al. 1984) has been shown to include a CD8$^+$ CTL epitope. No variation has been identified from amino acids 378–390. Amino acids 367–377 of the CS protein of the 7G8 clone of *P. falciparum* are shown, and identified variations in this region (LOCKYER et al. 1989; DOOLAN et al. 1992; SHI et al. 1992) are listed. Amino acid 367 is also included, because there are data suggesting that there is a CTL epitope in the region from amino acid 351–370 (DOOLAN et al. 1991), and no variation has been shown from amino acid residues 351–366, but variation has been identified at amino acid residue 367.

sequences, the usefulness of a vaccine designed to produce CTL against only one variant will be limited. The importance of polymorphism at important CD8$^+$ CTL sites remains to be elucidated. However, variation has been identified in isolates from around the world (Table 1; LOCKYER et al. 1989; DOOLAN et al. 1992; SHI et al. 1992), suggesting that the variation is the result of immune selection (GOOD et al. 1988).

Having established that volunteers immunized with irradiated *P. falciparum* sporozoites produced CTL against the PfCSP, the investigators asked whether the demonstration of CTL by their assay indicated that a volunteer would be protected. As predicted by previous murine studies (FLYNN et al. 1990; SEDEGAH et al. 1992a; SATCHIDANANDAM et al. 1991), the presence of CTL against this epitope did not indicate that a volunteer would be protected aginst challenge, and the absence of cytolytic activity did not indicate that a volunteer would not be protected (MALIK et al. 1991).

Table 2. HLA types of the four Kenyans naturally exposed to malaria and three individuals immunized with irradiated *P. falciparum* sporozoites who have been shown to have CD8⁺ T cell dependent cytolytic activity against peptide Pf CS 368–390 (MALIK et al. 1991; SEDEGAH et al. 1992)

Volunteer	Class I				Class II			CTL
	A	B	Bw4/w6	C	DR	DRw52/53	Dq	
6	2, 32	w48, 45	w6, w6	w6	w8, w11	w52	w7,w1	+
9	30, w34	w42, w48	w6, w6	w4	ND	ND	ND	+
10	2, 28	51, 15	w4, w4	w4	w11, 7	w52, w53	w7, w2	+
8	30, 32	w58, -	w4	w6	w11, -	w52	w1, w7	+
1H	11, 24	35, -	ND	w4, -	[a]	[a]	w1	+
3W	1, 3	8, 35	ND	w4,	1, 7	w53, -	w1, w2	+
4R	1, 28	44, w57	ND	w6, -	7, w11	w52, w53	w3	+

[a] Not typeable by conventional methods.

4.2.2 Kenyans Naturally Exposed to Malaria

Knowing that humans immunized with irradiated sporozoites produced $CD8^+$ CTL against the region of PfCSP including amino acids Pf 7G8 CS 368–390, Sedegah and coworkers set out to determine whether humans naturally exposed to malaria produced CTL against this region of the CS protein. This region was of particular interest because it had been previously shown that there was a correlation between lymphocyte proliferation to peptides Pf 7G8 CS 361–380 and 371–390 and resistence to reinfection with malaria among Kenyan adults (HOFFMAN et al. 1989; MASON et al., unpublished). Eleven Kenyans were selected because their lymphocytes had been shown to proliferate after stimulation with one of these peptides and because they were also resistant to reinfection with malaria (nine of the 11 volunteers). They were studied at a single time point at the end of a period of low malaria transmission, and four of the 11 volunteers were shown to have cytolytic activity against autologous EBV-transformed B cells pulsed with the Pf 7G8 CS 368–390 peptide. In three of the four cases, the cytolytic activity was reversed by depletion of $CD8^+$ T cells, but in no case did depletion of $CD4^+$ T cells reduce cytolytic activity (SEDEGAH et al. 1992b). Individuals of various HLA phenotypes have been shown to have $CD8^+$ T cell-dependent cytolytic activity against target cells pulsed with peptide 368–390 (Table 2). Thus far, minimal CTL epitopes have not been identified and T cell clones against this region of the CS protein have not been produced. Thus, restriction elements have not been clearly delineated.

4.2.3 HLA B35-Restricted Activity Among Gambians Naturally Exposed to Malaria

Using the techniques described in Sect. 5.1 below, HILL and colleagues (1992) eluted peptides from HLA B35. In addition to a proline at position 2, they found these peptides generally included a tyrosine at position 9. They found ten peptide sequences from the four pre-erythrocytic stage proteins described below that had prolines at positions 2 and tyrosines at position 8 (six sequences), position 9 (one sequence), or position 10 (three sequences). Six of these sequences were from PfCSP, and four of the six were from variants of the first eight to ten amino acids of Pf CS 7G8 368–390, the previously identified human CTL epitope (see Sects. 4.2.1 and 4.2.2 above). One of eight Gambians tested had cytolytic activity against peptide Pf CS 7G8 368–375 (KPKDELDY). Cells from this volunteer that were stimulated with peptide KPKDELDY did not lyse targets pulsed with peptides KPKD**Q**L**N**Y or K**S**KDELDY, sequences from other known variants (Table 1). Cells from a second volunteer recognized peptide K**S**KDELDY, but did not recognize the variant peptides KPKDELDY, KPKD**Q**LDY, or KPKD**Q**L**N**Y (Table 1). This cytolytic activity was inhibited by an anti-CD8 monoclonal antibody. These data demonstrate for the first time that single amino acid changes at the site of PfCSP CTL epitopes can eliminate recognition by CTL. Identification of a minimal CTL epitope in the region of Pf CS 7G8 368–390 with the greatest polymorphism supports the hypothesis that this polymorphism has arisen secondary to immune pressure (GOOD et al. 1988).

5 $CD8^+$ CTL Against Liver Stage Antigen-1

5.1 HLA Bw53-Restricted, $CD8^+$ T Cell-Dependent Cytolytic Activity Against Liver Stage Antigen-1 in Gambians Naturally Exposed to Malaria

Elegant studies that followed up the demonstration of an association between HLA Bw53 and lack of severe malaria (see Sect. 3 above) have recently been reported (HILL et al. 1992). The investigators sequenced peptides eluted from HLA B53 and found that most peptides had a proline at position 2. They then synthesized 60 8- to 10-amino acid peptides from four *P. falciparum* pre-erythrocytic stage antigens, Pf CSP (DAME et al. 1984), TRAP/Pf SSP2 (ROBSON et al. 1988; ROGERS et al. 1992a), liver stage antigen-1 (LSA-1; GUERIN-MARCHAND et al. 1987; ZHU and HOLLINGDALE 1991), and Pfs16 (MOELANS et al. 1991), that had prolines in position 2. These peptides were studied to determine whether they bound to HLA B53 in an HLA assembly assay. Eight peptides were found to bind, three from PfCSP, two from TRAP/PfSSP2, one from LSA-1, and two from Pfs16. Six individuals in one village and nine individuals in a village with much lower transmission of malaria were tested during a period of low malaria transmission. Using a classical restimulation CTL assay, they showed that none of the individuals had CTL against the PfCSP, PfSSP2/TRAP, and Pfs16 peptides.However, three of six volunteers in the first village and one of nine volunteers in the second village had HLA B53, peptide-specific, $CD8^+$ T cell-dependent cytolytic activity against the LSA-1 peptide referred to as ls6 (KPIVQYDNF). This epitope was shown to be invariant in nine *P. falciparum* isolates that they sequenced. These findings suggest that CTL against this LSA-1 peptide may be involved in the partial protection against severe malaria associated with HLA Bw53.

5.2 HLA B35-Restricted CTL Against Liver Stage Antigen-1

One of eight Gambians was shown to have cytolytic activity against the LSA-1 peptide (ls8, KPNDKSLY) eluted from HLA B35 as described in Sects. 4.2.3 and 5.1 above (HILL et al. 1992). There was no indication as to whether the cytolytic activity was dependent on $CD8^+$ T cells.

6 $CD4^+$ CTL Against the Circumsporozoite Protein

6.1 Rationale for Work

DEL GIUDICE and colleagues immunized mice subcutaneously at the base of the tail with a peptide including amino acids 59–79 of the *P. yoelii* CS protein (YNRNIVNRLLGDALNGKPEEK) and using regional lymph node cells produced a $CD4^+$ T cell clone that recognized this peptide and a shorter peptide (PyCS 61–70 in BALB/c mice and PyCS 59–70 in C57BL/6 mice; DEL GIUDICE et al. 1990). This clone eliminated infected hepatocytes from culture (RENIA et al. 1991) and adoptively transferred protection against *P. yoelii.* The clone was never shown to have cytolytic activity against target cells pulsed with the peptide, but the in vitro activity against infected hepatocytes was not reversed by anticytokine treatment. It is not certain whether these clones are directly cytolytic or whether they mediate protection through another mechanism. Nonetheless, working in the less infective, but uniformly lethal, *P. berghei* system, CORRADIN and colleagues have found that immunization of mice at the base of the tail with the analogous *P. berghei* peptide presented as a branched chain polymer protects mice (unpublished observation). The mechanism of this protection has not been established, but such data identify protective $CD4^+$ T cells against an epitope amino terminal of the repeat region of the *P. yoelii* CS protein.

6.2 $CD4^+$ CTL Against the *P. falciparum* Circumsporozoite Protein in Volunteers Immunized with Irradiated *P. falciparum* Sporozoites

Moreno and colleagues have recently reported the production of a $CD4^+$ T cell clone with cytolytic activity from an individual immunized with radiation

Table 3. Variation in the region of the only known human CD4$^+$ CTL epitope on the *P. falciparum* circumsporozoite (cs) protein

Strain or isolate	*Amino acid residue (7G8 sequence)*													
	329	330	331	332	333	334	335	336	337	338	339	340	341	342
7G8	**K**	H	I	**E**	**Q**	Y	L	**K**	**K**	I	**K**	N	S	**I**
NF54/3D7; $XP_{8,9,}$ $X_{10,11,}$; $427_{1-4,6-10}$				K	E			N			Q			L
T4; T4R; T9-101; WEL; W/L; PNG X 22; T9-94; MCK$^+$; AE28; AE7; HB3; X_5; $XP_{12,13}$; PNG2; BRAI											Q			L
ItG2G1; ItG2					K						Q			L
366_1; 399_{1-10}; 406_{1-9} 419_{10};	Q				K				T					L
T9-98									T					L
427_5								N	T					L
LE5, 366_9	Q				K				T		Q			L
MS2, Palo Alto Brazil X4; BRA2	Q				K				R		Q			L
366_{2-7}	Q				K				Q		R			L
$366_{8,10}$	Q				K				Q		Q			L
406_{10}; 419_{1-9}	Q				K				Q					L
GAM1	Q				K				T		Q			L
GAM2	Q				K				T					L
GAM3	Q				K			Q			Q			L
GAM4	Q				K			Q						L
GAM5								N	T		Q			L
GAM6	Q				K			Q			R			L

In humans, a peptide including amino acid residues 326–345 of the NF54/3D7 *P. falciparum* CS protein (Pf 3D7 CS 326–345, EYLN**KIQNSLSTEW**SPCSVT; Caspers et al. 1989; Campbell 1989) that is analogous to amino acid residues 333–352 of the 7G8 CS protein seqence (Dame et al. 1984) has been shown to include a CD4$^+$ CTL epitope (Moreno et al. 1991). The minimal epitope recognized in the context of HLA DR7 has been shown to be amino acids Pf 3D7 CS 330–339 (KIQNSLSTEW) (= Pf 7G8 337–346). No variation has been identified in amino acids Pf 3D7 CS 336–345 (Pf 7G8 CS 343–352). Amino acids 329–342 of the 7G8 clone of *P. falciparum* are shown, and identified variations among isolates in the region (Lockyer et al. 1989; Doolan et al. 1992; Shi et al. 1992) are listed. Amino acid residues 329–332 are included, since Pf 7G8 326–345 (PSDKHIEQYLKKIKNSISTE) has been shown to include a T-helper epitope, and no variation has been shown in amino acids 326–328 of the 7G8 sequence.

attenuated *P. falciparum* sporozoites (MORENO et al. 1991). They have mapped the epitope to residues 330–339 (KIQNSLSTEW) of the NF54/3D7 sequence of the PfCSP (CASPERS et al. 1989; CAMPBELL 1989) and demonstrated that this peptide is recognized in the context of HLA DR7. This epitope corresponds to amino acids 337–346 of the 7G8 sequence of the PfCSP (DAME et al. 1984) and is found in a polymorphic region of the CS protein (Table 3; LOCKYER et al. 1989; DOOLAN et al. 1992; SHI et al. 1992). It has therefore been suggested that, as for the $CD8^+$ CTL epitope described above, the variation in this region is a result of immune selection.

7 $CD4^+$ CTL Against Other Pre-erythrocytic Antigens in Murine Models

TSUJI and colleagues (1990) immunized mice with irradiated *P. berghei* sporozoites, stimulated spleen cells with an extract of blood stage *P. berghei* parasites, and derived a $CD4^+$ T cell clone that produces interleukin 2 (IL-2) and γ-interferon when stimulated with blood stage parasite extract. The clone also lyses target cells pulsed with blood stage *P. berghei* extract. More importantly, adoptive transfer of this clone protects against sporozoite challenge, but not against blood stage challenge. This strongly suggests that the clone is recognizing a parasite antigen expressed in infected hepatocytes. Neither the *P. berghei* antigen recognized by this clone, nor its *P. falciparum* analog has been identified.

8 CTL Against the *P. falciparum* Circumsprozoite Protein Among Australians Naturally Exposed to Malaria

Doolan and colleagues stimulated peripheral blood mononuclear cells from Australians who had been previously exposed to malaria (DOOLAN et al. 1991) with a mixture of CS protein peptides. Their studies showed that after two cycles of stimulation, cells from three of 42 donors had cytolytic activity against a mixture of overlapping 20-amino acid peptides spanning amino acid residues 341–412 (Pf CSP 7G8). Like the results with volunteers immunized with irradiated sporozoites (MALIK et al. 1991), cytolytic activity could not be demonstrated each time an assay was run, suggesting to the investigators that there is a low frequency of these cells in the peripheral blood. They did not report on whether the activity was dependent on a particular subset of T lymphocytes or genetically restricted, but two of the three positive donors were HLA Bw57. They produced a T cell line from one donor and demonstrated that the line lysed target cells pulsed with peptides Pf 7G8 CS 351–370, 371–390, or 376–395. These data indicate that there is at least one CTL epitope within residues Pf7G8 CS 351–370 and at least one more within residues Pf 7G8 CS 371–390. However, the T cell subset specificity and genetic restriction of this cytolytic activity remains to be established.

9 Rationale for Work on CD8$^+$ CTL Against Sporozoite Surface Protein-2

Immunization with irradiated sporozoites completely protects against malaria, but none of the subunit *P. berghei* or *P. yoelii* CS protein vaccines have given protection comparable to the irradiated sporozoite vaccine. Furthermore, in the human studies the presence of CTL against the PfCSP did not guarantee that the individual would be protected and, likewise, one individual who was not shown to have CTL was protected against challenge (MALIK et al. 1991). Considering the complexity of sporozoites, it was not logical to assume that all protection induced by the whole organism vaccine was mediated by CTL against a single short stretch of amino acids on a single protein. Thus, there has been considerable effort to identify additional targets of irradiated sporozoite-induced protective immunity. Mice were immunized with irradiated *P. yoelii* sporozoites, and a monoclonal antibody directed at a 140-kDa sporozoite protein was produced (CHAROENVIT et al. 1987). The gene encoding this protein was cloned and sequenced (HEDSTROM et al. 1990; ROGERS et al. 1992a), and the protein was named sporozoite surface protein-2 (PySSP2). To determine whether immunization with irradiated sporozoites not only produced antibodies, but also CTL against PySSP2, a 1.5-kb fragment of the gene encoding PySSP2 was transfected into P815 mouse mastocytoma cells. When these transfected cells were used as targets in CTL assays, mice immunized with irradiated sporozoites were shown to produce CTL against PySSP2 (KHUSMITH et al. 1991). KHUSMITH et al. subsequently produced CD8$^+$ CTL clones against PySSP2 and showed that adoptive transfer of one of these clones completely protected against challenge, establishing that CTL against PySSP2 could completely protect against this highly infectious parasite in the absence of any other parasite specific immune responses (S. KHUSMITH, unpublished). Like the anti-CS protein CTL clones, these clones protected when adoptively transferred into mice 3 h after sporozoite inoculation, indicating that they were attacking infected hepatocytes. Mice were also immunized with the P815 cells expressing PySSP2, and approximately 50% were protected against challenge (KHUSMITH et al. 1991). KHUSMITH then went on to show that although immunization with the *P. yoelii* CS protein or PySSP2 vaccines gave only partial protection against malaria (50%–75%), immunization with transfected P815 cells expressing, *P. yoelii* CSP and PySSP2 produced 100% protection (KHUSMITH et al. 1991). Furthermore, as after immunization with irradiated sporozoites, this protective immunity was completely reversed by in vivo depletion of $CD8^+$ T cells.

The gene encoding the *P. falciparum* SSP2 (PfSSP2) has now been identified and characterized (ROGERS et al. 1992b) and shown to be the previously described thrombospondin-related anonymous protein (TRAP; ROBSON et al. 1988). Work is in progress to identify CTL epitopes on PfSSP2 and to produce vaccines that will induce protective CTL in humans against PfSSP2 and PfCSP.

10 Conclusion

The study of human CTL against *Plasmodium* sp. peptides is in its infancy. There is a compelling rationale for work on the identification, characterization, and induction of class I-restricted, $CD8^+$ CTL against pre-erythrocytic stages of *P. falciparum*. The data supporting work on $CD4^+$ CTL is not as complete, but is also solid. Work is now, or will soon be, underway in a number of laboratories to use synthetic peptide, recombinant protein, live vector-delivered antigen and plasmid DNA vaccines to induce CTL in humans against PfCSP, PfSSP2, PfLSA-1, and other *P. falciparum* proteins expressed in infected hepatocytes. In parallel studies, a number of scientists are attempting to characterize further the qualities of CTL associated with protection, to identify and characterize additional CTL epitopes on these proteins, and to optimize vaccine delivery systems in the rodent model systems. Duplicating the non-strain-specific, sterile, consistently protective immunity induced in humans by the irradiated sporozoite vaccine will almost certainly require constructing vaccines that induce a essentially all vaccinees protective CTL against at least one epitope that is present in all strains of parasites. It will probably also require induction of protective antibody responses.

Acknowledgements. This work was supported in part by the Naval Medical Research and ONR grant N00014-89-J-1856 to the Pan American Health Organization.

References

Aggarwal A, Kumar S, Jaffe R, Hone D, Gross M, Sadoff J (1991) Oral Salmonella: malaria circumsporozoite recombinants induce specific $CD8^+$ cytotoxic T cells. J Exp Med 172: 1083–1090

Alonso PL, Lindsay SW, Armstrong JR, Conteh M, Hill AG, David PH, Fegan G (1991) The effect of insecticide-treated bed nets on mortality of Gambian children. Lancet 337: 1499–1502

Campbell JR (1989) DNA sequence of the gene encoding a *Plasmodium falciparum* malaria candidate vaccine antigen. Nucleic Acids Res 17: 5854

Caspers P, Gentz R, Matile H, Pink JR, Sinigaglia F (1989) The circumsporozoite protein gene from NF54, a *Plasmodium falciparum* isolate used in malaria vaccine trial. Mol Biochem Parasitol 35: 185–190

Charoenvit Y, Leef ML, Yuan LF, Sedegah M, Beaudoin RL (1987) Characterization of *Plasmodium yoelii* monoclonal antibodies directed against stage-specific antigens. Infect Immun 55: 604–608

Chen DH, Tigelaar RE, Weinbaum FI (1977) Immunity to sporozoite-induced malaria infection in mice. 1. The effect of immunization of T and B cell-deficient mice. J Immunol 118: 1322–1327

Clyde DF, McCarthy VC, Miller RM, Hornick RB (1973) Specificity of protection of man immunized against sporozoite-induced falciparum malaria. Am J Med Sci 266: 398–401

Dame JB, Williams JL, McCutchan TF, Weber JL, Wirtz RA, Hockmeyer WT, Sanders GS, Reddy EP, Maloy WL, Haynes JD, Schneider I, Roberts D, Diggs CL, Miller LH (1984) Structure of the gene encoding the immunodominant surface antigen on the sporozoite of the human malaria parasite *Plasmodium falciparum*. Science 225: 593–599

Del Giudice G, Grillot D, Renia L, Muller I, Corradin G, Louis JA, Mazier D, Lamberd PH (1990) Peptide-primed CD4$^+$ cells and malaria sporozoites. Immunol Lett 25: 59–64

Doolan DL, Houghten RA, Good MF (1991) Location of human cytotoxic T cell epitopes within a polymorphic domain of the *Plasmodium falciparum* circumsporozoite protein. Int Immunol 3: 511–506

Doolan DL, Saul AJ, Good MF (1992) Geographically restricted heterogeneity of the *Plasmodium falciparum* circumsporozoite protein; relevance for vaccine development. Infect Immun 60: 675–682

Egan JE, Weber JL, Ballou WR, Hollingdale MR, Majarian WR, Gorden DM, Maloy WE, Hoffman SL, Wirtz RA, Schneider I, Woollett GR, Young JF and Hockmeyer WT (1987) Efficacy of murine malaria sporozoite vaccines: implications for human vaccine development. Science 236: 453–456

Egan JE, Hoffman SL, Haynes JD, Sadoff JC, Schneider I, Grau GE, Hollingdale MR, Ballou WR, Gordon DM (1993) Humoral immune response in volunteers immunized with irradiated *Plasmodium falciparum* sporozoites. Am J Trop Med Hyg (in press)

Fairley NH (1947) Sidelights on malaria in man obtained by subinoculation experiments. Trans R Soc Trop Med Hyg 40: 621–676

Flynn JL, Weiss WR, Norris KA, Seifert HS, Kumar S, So M (1990) Generation of a cytotoxic T-lymphocyte response using a Salmonella antigen-delivery system. Mol Microbiol 4: 2111–2118

Good MF, Kumar S, Miller LH (1988) The real difficulties for malaria sporozoite vaccine development: nonresponsiveness and antigenic variation. Immun Today 9: 351–355

Guerin-Marchand C, Druilhe P, Galey B, Londono A, Patarapotikul J, Beaudoin RL, Dubeaux C, Tartar A, Mercereau-Puijalon O, Langsley G (1987) A liver-stage-specific antigen of *Plasmodium falciparum* characterized by gene cloning. Nature 329: 164–167

Hedstrom RC, Campbell JR, Leef ML, Charoenvit Y, Carter M, Sedegah M, Beaudoin RL, Hoffman SL (1990) A malaria sporozoite surface antigen distinct from the circumsporozoite protein. Bull WHO 68: 152–157

Hill AV, Allsopp CE, Kwiatkowski D, Anstey NM, Twumasi P, Rowe PA, Bennett S, Brewster D, McMichael AJ, Greenweed BM (1991) Common west African HLA antigens are associated with protection from severe malaria. Nature 352: 595–600

Hill AV, Elvin J, Willis AC, Aidoo M, Allsopp CE, Gotch FM, Gao XM, Takiguchi M, Greenwood BM, Townsand AR, McMichael AJ, and Whittle HC (1992) Molecular analysis of the association of HLA-B53 and resistance to severe malaria. Nature 360: 434–439

Hoffman SL, Isenbarger D, Long GW, Sedegah M, Szarfman A, Waters L, Hollingdale MR, van der Miede PH, Finbloom DS, Ballou WR (1989a) Sporozoite vaccine induces genetically restricted T cell elimination of malaria from hepatocytes. Science 244: 1078–1081

Hoffman SL, Oster CN, Mason C, Beier JC, Sherwood JA, Ballou WR, Mugambi M, Chulay JD (1989b) Human lymphocyte proliferative response to a sporozoite T cell epitope correlates with resistance to falciparum malaria. J Immunol 142: 1299–1303

Hoffman SL, Nussenzweig V, Sadoff JC, Nussenzweig RS (1991) Progress toward malaria preerythrocytic vaccines. Science 252: 520–521

Khusmith S, Charoenvit Y, Kumar S, Sedegah M, Beaudoin RL, Hoffman SL (1991) Protection against malaria by vaccination with sporozoite surface protein 2 plus CS protein. Science 252: 715–718

Kumar S, Miller LH, Quakyi IA, Keister DB, Houghten RA, Maloy WL, Moss B, Berzofsky JA, Good MF (1988) Cytotoxic T cells specific for the circumsporozoite protein of *Plasmodium falciparum*. Nature 334: 258–260

Lockyer MJ, Marsh K, Newbold CI (1989) Wild isolates of *Plasmodium falciparum* show extensive polymorphism in T cell epitopes of the circumsporozoite protein. Mol Biochem Parasitol 37: 275–280

Malik A, Egan JE, Houghton RA, Sadoff JC, Hoffman SL (1991) Human cytotoxic T lymphocytes against *Plasmodium falciparum* circumsporozoite protein. Proc Natl Acad Sci USA 88: 3300–3304

Meis JFGM, Jap PHK, Verhave JP, Meuwissen JHET (1987) Cellular response against exoerythrocytic forms of *Plasmodium berghei* in rats. Am J Trop Med Hyg 30: 506–510

Moelans IIMD, Meiss JFGM, Kocken C, Konongs RNH, Schoemakers JGG (1991) A novel protein antigen of the malaria parasite *Plasmodium falciparum*, located on the surface of gametes and sporozoites. Mol Biochem Parasitol 45: 193–204

Moreno A, Clavijo P, Edelman R, Davis J, Sztein M, Herrington D, Nardin E (1991) Cytotoxic $CD4^+$ T cells from a sporozoite-immunized volunteer recognize the *Plasmodium falciparum* CS protein. Int Immunol 3: 997–1003

Nussenzweig R, Vanderberg J, Most H (1969) Protective immunity produced by the injection of x-irradiated sporozoites of *Plasmodium berghei*: IV. Dose response, specificity and humoral immunity. Milit Med 134: 1176–1182

Renia L, Marussig MS, Grillot D, Pied S, Corradin G, Miltgen F, Del Giudice G, Mazier D (1991) In vitro activity of $CD4^+$ and $CD8^+$ T lymphocytes from mice immunized with a synthetic malaria peptide. Proc Natl Acad Sci USA 88: 7963–7967

Rieckmann KH, Beaudoin RL, Cassells JS, Sell DW (1979) Use of attenuated sporozoites in the immunization of human volunteers against falciparum malaria. Bull WHO 57: 261–265

Robson KJH, Hall JRS, Jennings MW, Harris TJR, Marsh K, Newbold CI, Tate VE, Weatherall DJ (1988) A highly conserved amino-acid sequence in thrombospondin, properdin and in proteins from sporozoites and blood stages of a human malaria parasite. Nature 335: 79–82

Rodrigues MM, Cordey A-S, Arreaza G, Corradin G, Romero P, Maryanski JL, Nussenzweig RS, Zavala F (1991) $CD8^+$ cytolytic T cell clones derived against the *Plasmodium yoelii* circumsporozoite protein protect against malaria. Int Immunol 3: 579–586

Rodrigues MM, Nussenzweig RS, Romero P, Zavala F (1992) The in vivo cytotoxic activity of $CD8^+$ T cell clones correlates with their levels of expression of adhesion molecules. J Exp Med 175: 895–905

Rogers WO, Malik A, Mellouk S, Nakamura K, Rogers MD, Szarfman A, Gordon DM, Nussler AK, Aikawa M, Hoffman SL (1992a) Characterization of *Plasmodium falciparum* sporozoite surface protein 2. Proc Natl Acad Sci USA 89: 9176–9180

Rogers WO, Rogers MD, Hedstrom RC, Hoffman SL (1992b) Characterization of the gene encoding sporozoite surface protein 2, a protective *Plasmodium yoelii* sporozoite antigen. Mol Biochem Parasitol 53: 45–52

Romero P, Maryanski JL, Corradin G, Nussenzweig RS, Nussenzweig V, Zavala F (1989) Cloned cytotoxic T cells recognize an epitope in the circumsporozoite protein and protect against malaria. Nature 341: 323–325

Satchidanandam V, Zavala F, Moss B (1991) Studies using a recombinant vaccinia virus expressing the circumsporozoite protein of *Plasmodium berghei*. Mol Biochem Parasitol 48: 89–100

Schofield L, Villaquiran J, Ferreira A, Schellekens H, Nussenzweig RS, Nussenzweig V (1987) Gamma-interferon, $CD8^+$ T cells and antibodies required for immunity to malaria sporozoites. Nature 330: 664–666

Sedegah M, Chiang CH, Weiss WR, Mellouk S, Cochran MD, Houghton RA, Beaudoin RL, Smith D, Hoffman SL (1992a) Recombinant pseudorabies virus carrying a plasmodium gene: herpesvirus as a new live viral vector for inducing T- and B-cell immunity. Vaccine 10: 578–584

Sedegah M, Sim BKL, Mason C, Nutman T, Malik A, Roberts C, Johnson A, Ochola J, Koech D, Were B, Hoffman SL (1992b) Naturally acquired $CD8^+$ cytotoxic T lymphocytes against *Plasmodium falciparum* circumsporozoite protein. J Immunol 149: 966–971

Shi Y-P, Alpers MP, Povoa MM, Lal AA (1992) Diversity in the immunodominant determinants of the circumsporozoite protein of *Plasmodium falciparum* parasites from malaria-endemic regions of Papua New Guinea and Brazil. Am J Trop Med Hyg 47: 844–851

Sinigaglia F, Guttinger M, Kilgus J, Doron DM, Matile H, Etlinger H, Trezeciak A, Gillessen D and Pink JRL (1988) A malaria T cell epitope recognized in association with most mouse and human MHC class II molecule. Nature 336: 778–780

Tsuji M, Romero P, Nussenzweig RS, Zavala F (1990) $CD4^+$ cytolytic clone confers protection against murine malaria. J. Exp Med 172: 1353–1357

Vanderberg J, Nussenzweig R, Most H (1969) Protective immunity produced by the injection of X-irradiated sporozoites of *Plasmodium berghei*. V. In vitro effects of immune serum on sporozoites. Milit Med 134: 1183–1190

Verhave JP, Strickland GT, Jaffe HA, Ahmed A (1978) Studies on the transfer of protective immunity with lymphoid cells from mice immune to malaria sporozoites. Immunol 121: 1031–1033

Weiss WR, Sedegah M, Beaudoin RL, Miller LH, Good MF (1988) $CD8^+$ T cells (cytotoxic/suppressors) are required for protection in mice immunized with malaria sporozoites. Proc Natl Acad Sci USA 85: 573–576

Weiss WR, Mellouk S, Houghten RA, Sedegah M, Kumar S, Good MF, Berzofsky JA, Miller LH, Hoffman SL (1990) Cytotoxic T cells recognize a peptide from the circumsporozoite protein on malaria-infected hepatocytes. J Exp Med 171: 763–773

Weiss WR, Berzovsky JA, Houghten R, Sedegah M, Hollingdale M, Hoffman SL (1992) A T cell clone directed at the circumsporozoite protein which protects mice against both *P. yoelii* and *P. berghei*. J Immunol (in press)

WHO (1991) World Health Organization Expert Committee on Biological Standardization. Techn Rep Ser 610: 1977

Yano A, Aosai F, Ohta M, Hasekura H, Sugane K, Hayashi S (1989) Antigen presentation by *Toxoplasma gondii*-infected cells to $CD4^+$ proliferative T cells and $CD8^+$ cytotoxic cells. J Parasitol 75: 411–416

Yoshida N, Nussenzweig RS, Ptocynjak P, Nussenzweig V, Aikawa M (1980) Hybridoma produces protective antibodies directed against the sporozoite stage of malaria parasites. Science 207: 71–73

Zhu J, Hollingdale MR (1991) Structure of *Plasmodium falciparum* liver stage antigen-1. Mol Biochem Parasitol 48: 223–226

Subject Index

Current Topics in Microbiology and Immunology

Volumes published since 1989 (and still available)

Vol. 146: **Mestecky, Jiri; McGhee, Jerry (Ed.):** New Strategies for Oral Immunization. International Symposium at the University of Alabama at Birmingham and Molecular Engineering Associates, Inc. Birmingham, AL, USA, March 21–22, 1988. 1989. 22 figs. IX, 237 pp. ISBN 3-540-50841-4

Vol. 147: **Vogt, Peter K. (Ed.):** Oncogenes. Selected Reviews. 1989. 8 figs. VII, 172 pp. ISBN 3-540-51050-8

Vol. 148: **Vogt, Peter K. (Ed.):** Oncogenes and Retroviruses. Selected Reviews. 1989. XII, 134 pp. ISBN 3-540-51051-6

Vol. 149: **Shen-Ong, Grace L. C.; Potter, Michael; Copeland, Neal G. (Ed.):** Mechanisms in Myeloid Tumorigenesis. Workshop at the National Cancer Institute, National Institutes of Health, Bethesda, MD, USA, March 22, 1988. 1989. 42 figs. X, 172 pp. ISBN 3-540-50968-2

Vol. 150: **Jann, Klaus; Jann, Barbara (Ed.):** Bacterial Capsules. 1989. 33 figs. XII, 176 pp. ISBN 3-540-51049-4

Vol. 151: **Jann, Klaus; Jann, Barbara (Ed.):** Bacterial Adhesins. 1990. 23 figs. XII, 192 pp. ISBN 3-540-51052-4

Vol. 152: **Bosma, Melvin J.; Phillips, Robert A.; Schuler, Walter (Ed.):** The Scid Mouse. Characterization and Potential Uses. EMBO Workshop held at the Basel Institute for Immunology, Basel, Switzerland, February 20–22, 1989. 1989. 72 figs. XII, 263 pp. ISBN 3-540-51512-7

Vol. 153: **Lambris, John D. (Ed.):** The Third Component of Complement. Chemistry and Biology. 1989. 38 figs. X, 251 pp. ISBN 3-540-51513-5

Vol. 154: **McDougall, James K. (Ed.):** Cytomegaloviruses. 1990. 58 figs. IX, 286 pp. ISBN 3-540-51514-3

Vol. 155: **Kaufmann, Stefan H. E. (Ed.):** T-Cell Paradigms in Parasitic and Bacterial Infections. 1990. 24 figs. IX, 162 pp. ISBN 3-540-51515-1

Vol. 156: **Dyrberg, Thomas (Ed.):** The Role of Viruses and the Immune System in Diabetes Mellitus. 1990. 15 figs. XI, 142 pp. ISBN 3-540-51918-1

Vol. 157: **Swanstrom, Ronald; Vogt, Peter K. (Ed.):** Retroviruses. Strategies of Replication. 1990. 40 figs. XII, 260 pp. ISBN 3-540-51895-9

Vol. 158: **Muzyczka, Nicholas (Ed.):** Viral Expression Vectors. 1992. 20 figs. IX, 176 pp. ISBN 3-540-52431-2

Vol. 159: **Gray, David; Sprent, Jonathan (Ed.):** Immunological Memory. 1990. 38 figs. XII, 156 pp. ISBN 3-540-51921-1

Vol. 160: **Oldstone, Michael B. A.; Koprowski, Hilary (Eds.):** Retrovirus Infections of the Nervous System. 1990. 16 figs. XII, 176 pp. ISBN 3-540-51939-4

Vol. 161: **Racaniello, Vincent R. (Ed.):** Picornaviruses. 1990. 12 figs. X, 194 pp. ISBN 3-540-52429-0

Vol. 162: **Roy, Polly; Gorman, Barry M. (Eds.):** Bluetongue Viruses. 1990. 37 figs. X, 200 pp. ISBN 3-540-51922-X

Vol. 163: **Turner, Peter C.; Moyer, Richard W. (Eds.):** Poxviruses. 1990. 23 figs. X, 210 pp. ISBN 3-540-52430-4

Vol. 164: **Bækkeskov, Steinnun; Hansen, Bruno (Eds.):** Human Diabetes. 1990. 9 figs. X, 198 pp. ISBN 3-540-52652-8

Vol. 165: **Bothwell, Mark (Ed.):** Neuronal Growth Factors. 1991. 14 figs. IX, 173 pp. ISBN 3-540-52654-4

Vol. 166: **Potter, Michael; Melchers, Fritz (Eds.):** Mechanisms in B-Cell Neoplasia 1990. 143 figs. XIX, 380 pp.
ISBN 3-540-52886-5

Vol. 167: **Kaufmann, Stefan H. E. (Ed.):** Heat Shock Proteins and Immune Response. 1991. 18 figs. IX, 214 pp.
ISBN 3-540-52857-1

Vol. 168: **Mason, William S.; Seeger, Christoph (Eds.):** Hepadnaviruses. Molecular Biology and Pathogenesis. 1991. 21 figs. X, 206 pp.
ISBN 3-540-53060-6

Vol. 169: **Kolakofsky, Daniel (Ed.):** Bunyaviridae. 1991. 34 figs. X, 256 pp.
ISBN 3-540-53061-4

Vol. 170: **Compans, Richard W. (Ed.):** Protein Traffic in Eukaryotic Cells. Selected Reviews. 1991. 14 figs. X, 186 pp.
ISBN 3-540-53631-0

Vol. 171: **Kung, Hsing-Jien; Vogt, Peter K. (Eds.):** Retroviral Insertion and Oncogene Activation. 1991. 18 figs. X, 179 pp.
ISBN 3-540-53857-7

Vol. 172: **Chesebro, Bruce W. (Ed.):** Transmissible Spongiform Encephalopathies. 1991. 48 figs. X, 288 pp.
ISBN 3-540-53883-6

Vol. 173: **Pfeffer, Klaus; Heeg, Klaus; Wagner, Hermann; Riethmüller, Gert (Eds.):** Function and Specificity of γ/δ T Cells. 1991. 41 figs. XII, 296 pp.
ISBN 3-540-53781-3

Vol. 174: **Fleischer, Bernhard; Sjögren, Hans Olov (Eds.):** Superantigens. 1991. 13 figs. IX, 137 pp.
ISBN 3-540-54205-1

Vol. 175: **Aktories, Klaus (Ed.):** ADP-Ribosylating Toxins. 1992. 23 figs. IX, 148 pp.
ISBN 3-540-54598-0

Vol. 176: **Holland, John J. (Ed.):** Genetic Diversity of RNA Viruses. 1992. 34 figs. IX, 226 pp. ISBN 3-540-54652-9

Vol. 177: **Müller-Sieburg, Christa; Torok-Storb, Beverly; Visser, Jan; Storb, Rainer (Eds.):** Hematopoietic Stem Cells. 1992. 18 figs. XIII, 143 pp. ISBN 3-540-54531-X

Vol. 178: **Parker, Charles J. (Ed.):** Membrane Defenses Against Attack by Complement and Perforins. 1992. 26 figs. VIII, 188 pp. ISBN 3-540-54653-7

Vol. 179: **Rouse, Barry T. (Ed.):** Herpes Simplex Virus. 1992. 9 figs. X, 180 pp.
ISBN 3-540-55066-6

Vol. 180: **Sansonetti, P. J. (Ed.):** Pathogenesis of Shigellosis. 1992. 15 figs. X, 143 pp.
ISBN 3-540-55058-5

Vol. 181: **Russell, Stephen W.; Gordon, Siamon (Eds.):** Macrophage Biology and Activation. 1992. 42 figs. IX, 299 pp.
ISBN 3-540-55293-6

Vol. 182: **Potter, Michael; Melchers, Fritz (Eds.):** Mechanisms in B-Cell Neoplasia. 1992. 188 figs. XX, 499 pp.
ISBN 3-540-55658-3

Vol. 183: **Dimmock, Nigel J.:** Neutralization of Animal Viruses. 1993. 10 figs. VII, 149 pp.
ISBN 3-540-56030-0

Vol. 184: **Dunon, Dominique; Mackay, Charles R.; Imhof, Beat A. (Eds.):** Adhesion in Leukocyte Homing and Differentiation. 1993. 37 figs. IX, 260 pp.
ISBN 3-540-56756-9

Vol. 185: **Ramig, Robert F. (Ed.):** Rotaviruses. 1994. 37 figs. X, 380 pp.
ISBN 3-540-56761-5

Vol. 186: **zur Hausen, Harald (Ed.):** Human Pathogenic Papillomaviruses. 1994. 37 figs. XIII, 274 pp. ISBN 3-540-57193-0

Vol. 187: **Rupprecht, Charles E.; Dietzschold, Bernhard; Koprowski, Hilary (Eds.):** Lyssaviruses. 1994. 50 figs. Approx. 280 pp. ISBN 3-540-57194-9

Vol. 188: **Letvin, Norman L.; Desrosiers, Ronald C. (Eds.):** Simian Immunodeficiency Virus. 1994. 37 figs. X, 240 pp.
ISBN 3-540-57274-0

MIX
Papier aus verantwortungsvollen Quellen
Paper from responsible sources
FSC® C105338

If you have any concerns about our products,
you can contact us on
ProductSafety@springernature.com

In case Publisher is established outside the EU,
the EU authorized representative is:
Springer Nature Customer Service Center GmbH
Europaplatz 3, 69115 Heidelberg, Germany

Printed by Libri Plureos GmbH
in Hamburg, Germany